Cr
THE R

There are more than sixty Rough Guide titles covering
destinations from Amsterdam to Zimbabwe & Botswana

Forthcoming titles include
China • Hawaii • Jamaica • Mallorca
Rhodes • Vietnam

Rough Guides Reference Series
Classical Music • Jazz • World Music

Rough Guide Phrasebooks
Czech • French • German • Greek • Italian • Spanish

Rough Guide Credits

Text editor:	Alison Cowan
Series editor:	Mark Ellingham
Editorial:	Martin Dunford, Jonathan Buckley, Jo Mead, Samantha Cook, Amanda Tomlin, Annie Shaw, Lemisse Al-Hafidh, Catherine McHale, Paul Grey
Production:	Susanne Hillen, Andy Hilliard, Melissa Flack, Alan Spicer, Judy Pang, Link Hall, Nicola Williamson, David Callier
Marketing & Publicity:	Richard Trillo, Simon Carloss (UK), Jean-Marie Kelly, Jeff Kaye, Andrew Rosenberg (US)
Finance:	John Fisher, Celia Crowley
Administration:	Tania Hummel

Acknowledgments

Our special thanks for their help with this new edition to Irene Michaelaki and Athena Petraki at the Municipal Tourist Office in Haniá, Jackie Richardson in Sitía, Sharon Bowen in Mália, Caroline Harber in Paleohóra, Professor Costis Davaras, Ephor of Antiquities for Eastern Crete, and to Diana Mortimer, Nicola Hatton, Alison McDowall, Margaret Maxwell and John Stevens. Valuable assistance was also rendered by Yiorgos Yeorgamlis, Frosso Bora, Apostolis Kimalis, Alexandra Gressman, Roswitha Esslinger, Michaelis Georgiousakis, Emman Milonakis, Yiorgos Sakilakis, Maria Picassi and Manolis Nikolodakis. Thanks also to Kiría Zoe Xirou and the staff of the Greek National Tourist Office in London.

To all involved at Rough Guides the usual humble gratitude: especially to Alison and Jules for painless and sympathetic editing, Jeannie Muchnik, Tania Smith, Andrew Tibber, Link, Nicola, Micromap Ltd for map updates, and to Celia and Simon, who never get a mention.

From previous editions, continued thanks to Chryssa in Haniá, Pandelis Iliakis, Alex in Haniá, Vangeli in Loutró, Kate Berens, Susanne Hillen, Mark Ellingham, Tim Salmon, Marc Dubin, Martin Dunford, Jack Holland, Pavlos Seliniotakis, Manolis Sgouros, Howard Potts, Aliki in Haniá, and Anne Marie Barrett and Bob Defee. And for their specialist input to Gideon Henderson, Pete Raine, Bruce Caughey, Jerry Graham and Carol Phile.

Above all, to Stretch and to J.D. for their support and inspiration; and to Jake for the sleepless nights.

Finally, it couldn't have happened without all the readers who sent in their comments, advice and criticisms: the full roll of honour appears on p.337.

This third edition published 1995 by Rough Guides Ltd, 1 Mercer Street, London WC2H 9QJ.
Reprinted in February 1996.

Distributed by the Penguin Group:

Penguin Books Ltd, 27 Wrights Lane, London W8 5TZ
Penguin Books USA Inc., 375 Hudson Street, New York 10014, USA
Penguin Books Australia Ltd, 487 Maroondah Highway, PO Box 257, Ringwood, Victoria 3134, Australia
Penguin Books Canada Ltd, 10 Alcorn Avenue, Toronto, Ontario, Canada M4V 1E4
Penguin Books (NZ) Ltd, 182–190 Wairau Road, Auckland 10, New Zealand

Previous editions published in the UK by Harrap Columbus (1988 & 1991).
Rough guides were formerly published as Real Guides in the United States and Canada

Typeset in Linotron Univers and Century Old Style to an original design by Andrew Oliver.
Printed in the United Kingdom by Cox and Wyman Ltd (Reading).
Illustrations in Part One and Part Three by Ed Briant.
Illustration on p.1 by Simon Fell; Illustration on p.287 by Henry Iles.

352p. Includes index.

A catalogue record for this book is available from the British Library.
ISBN 1–85828–132–6

Crete

THE ROUGH GUIDE

Written and researched by
John Fisher and Geoff Garvey

Additional research by
Mick Rebane

THE ROUGH GUIDES

MAP LIST

Crete	vi	Áyios Nikólaos	133
		Lató	140
Ferry links	18	Gourniá	143
Iráklion province	54–55	Sitía	151
Iráklion	58–59	Palace of Zákros	161
Palace of Knossós	78	Ierápetra	169
Tílissos	89	Réthimnon province	178–179
Palace of Mália	97	Réthimnon	181
Górtys	105	Haniá province	214–215
Palace of Festós	109	Haniá	218–219
Ayía Triádha	112	Samarian gorge	251
Lasíthi province	124–125	Gávdhos	283

MAP SYMBOLS

REGIONAL MAPS

— Major road

— Minor road

----- Track or path

++++ Railway

– – – Ferry route

----- Chapter division boundary

----- Provincial boundary

✈ Airport

✛ Monastery or convent

◼ Castle

◆ Ancient site

∩ Cave

⋏⋏ Mountain range

⫶⫶⫶ Gorge

▲ Peak

⸸ Lighthouse

▨ Beach

TOWN MAPS

— Railway

▬▬ Fortifications

◼ Building

✚ Church

◧ Mosque

▦ Park

CONTENTS

Introduction vi

| PART ONE | BASICS | 1 |

Getting There from Britain 3
Getting There from Ireland 8
Getting There from North America 9
Getting There from Australasia 14
Getting There from Mainland Greece 15
Surviving Athens 16
Travellers with Disabilities 20
Visas and Red Tape 22
Insurance 23
Costs, Money and Banks 25
Health Matters 27

Information and Maps 28
Getting Around 31
Accommodation 34
Eating and Drinking 37
Communications: Post, Phones and
  Media 41
Police, Trouble and Harassment 43
Opening Hours and Public Holidays 44
Festivals and Entertainment 45
Work 47
Directory 48

| PART TWO | THE GUIDE | 51 |

■ 1   Iráklion 53

■ 2   Lasíthi 123

■ 3   Réthimnon 176

■ 4   Haniá 212

| PART THREE | CONTEXTS | 287 |

The Historical Framework 289
Monumental Chronology 302
The Discovery of Bronze Age Crete 304
Crete in Myth 310
Wildlife 313
Books 322
Language 326
Glossary 331

Index 333

INTRODUCTION

Crete is a great deal more than just another Greek island. Much of the time, especially in the cities or along the developed north coast, it doesn't feel like an island at all, but a substantial land in its own right. Which of course it is – a mountainous, wealthy and at times surprisingly cosmopolitan one with a tremendous and unique history. There are two big cities, **Iráklion** and **Haniá**, a host of sizeable, historic towns, and an island culture which is uniquely Cretan: the Turks were in occupation less than a hundred years ago, and the Greek flag raised for the first time only in 1913.

Long before, Crete was distinguished as the home of Europe's earliest civilization. It was only at the beginning of this century that the legends of King Minos, and of a Cretan society which ruled the Greek world in prehistory, were confirmed by excavations at Knossós and Festós. Yet **the Minoans** had a remarkably advanced and cultured society, at the centre of a substantial maritime trading empire, as early as 2000 BC. The artworks produced on Crete at this time are unsurpassed anywhere in the ancient world, and it seems clear, wandering through the Minoan palaces and towns, that life on Crete in those days was good. The apparently peaceful Minoan culture survived a number of major disasters,

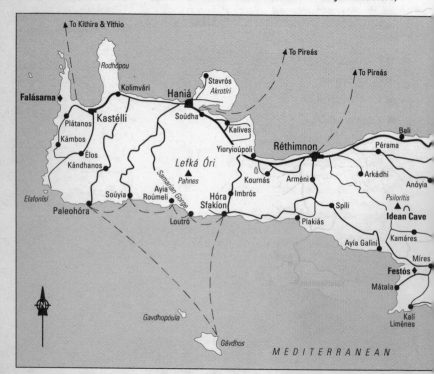

following each of which the palaces were rebuilt on an even grander scale. It is only after a third that significant numbers of weapons start to appear in the ruins, probably because Mycenaean Greeks had taken control of the island. Nevertheless, for nearly 500 years, by far the longest period of peace the island has seen, Crete was home to a civilization well ahead of its time.

The Minoans are believed to have come originally from Anatolia, and the island's position as meeting point – and strategic fulcrum – between east and west has played a crucial role in its **subsequent history**. Control passed from Greeks to Romans to Saracens, through the Byzantine Empire to Venice, and finally to Turkey for 200 years. During World War II Crete was occupied by the Germans, and gained the dubious distinction of being the first place to be successfully invaded by parachute. Each one of these diverse rulers has left some mark, and more importantly they have marked the islanders and forged for the land a personality toughened by endless struggles for independence.

Today, with a flourishing agricultural economy, Crete is one of the few Greek islands which could support itself without tourists. Nevertheless, tourism is heavily promoted, and is rapidly taking over parts of the island altogether. Along the populous **north coast**, Crete can be as sophisticated as you want it, and the northeast, in particular, can be depressingly overdeveloped. In the less known coastal reaches of the **south** it's still possible to find yourself alone, but even here places which have not yet been reached are getting harder and harder to find. By contrast, the high mountains of the interior are barely touched, and one of the best things to do on Crete is to hire a Vespa and head for remoter villages, often only a few kilometres off some heavily beaten track.

The **mountains**, which dominate the view as you approach and make all but the shortest journey an expedition, are perhaps the most rewarding aspect of Crete. In the west, the White Mountains are snowcapped right into June, Psilorítis (Mount Ida) in the centre is higher still, and in the east the heights continue through the Dhíkti and Sitía ranges to form a continuous chain from one end of the island to the other. They make a relatively small place – Crete is about 260km long by 60km at its widest, roughly the size of Jamaica – feel much larger. There are still many places where the roads cannot reach.

Where to go

Every part of Crete has its loyal devotees and it's hard to pick out highlights – but on the whole if you want to get away from it all you should head for the ends of the island – west, towards **Haniá** and the smaller, less well-connected places along the south and west coasts, or east to **Sitía**. Wherever you're staying, though, you don't have to go far inland to escape the crowds.

Whatever you do, the first main incentive is to get away from the urban blight of **Iráklion** (Heraklion) as quickly as possible – having paid the obligatory, and rewarding, visits to the **archeological museum** and nearby **Knossós**. The **Minoan sites** are of course one of the major attractions of Crete: as well as Knossós itself there are many other grand remains scattered around the centre of the island – **Festós** and **Ayía Triádha** in the south (with Roman **Górtys** to provide contrast) and **Mália** on the north coast. Almost wherever you go, though, you'll find some kind of reminder of this history – the town of **Gourniá** near the tourist enticements of **Áyios Nikólaos**, the palace of **Zákros** over in the far east or the lesser sites scattered around the west.

For many people, unexpected highlights also turn out to be Crete's **Venetian forts** – dominant at **Réthimnon**, magnificent at Frangokástello, and found in various stages of ruin around most of the island; the **Byzantine churches** – most famously at **Kritsá** but again to be discovered almost anywhere; and, at Réthimnon and Haniá, cluttered **old towns** full of Venetian and Turkish relics.

The mountains and valleys of the interior also deserve far more attention than they get. Only the **Lasíthi** plateau in the east and the **Samarian gorge** in the west really see large numbers of visitors, but almost anywhere you can turn off the main roads and find agricultural villages going about their daily life, and often astonishingly beautiful scenery. This is especially true in the west, where the Lefká Óri – the **White Mountains** – dramatically dominate every view, and numerous lesser gorges run parallel to the Samarian one down to the Libyan Sea. But there's lovely country behind Iráklion, too, in the foothills of the Psilorítis range, and especially on the other side of these mountains in the **Amári Valley**, easily reached from Réthimnon. The east also has its moments, in the Dhíkti range and in the spectacular cliff drive from Áyios Nikólaos to Sitía.

As for **beaches**, you'll find great ones almost anywhere on the north coast. From Iráklion to Áyios Nikólaos there's very heavy development, and most package tourists are aiming for the resort hotels here. These places can be fun if nightlife and crowds are what you're after – especially the biggest of them, like **Mália** and **Áyios Nikólaos**, which have the added advantage of being large enough to have plenty of cheap food and accommodation, plus good transport links. Mália also has sand as good as any on the island (if you can find it through the crowds), but Áyios Nikólaos really doesn't have much of a beach of its own. Further east things get quieter: **Sitía** is a place of real character, and beyond it on the east coast are a number of beautifully tranquil places – especially **Zákros** – and one which is very busy with day-trippers, **Vái**. To the west there's another tranche of development around **Réthimnon**, but the town itself is relatively unscathed, and a rather lesser cluster of apartments and smaller hotels near **Haniá**, the most attractive of the big towns. Other places at this end of the island tend to be on a smaller scale.

Along the **south coast**, resorts are far more scattered, and the mountains come straight down to the sea much of the way along. Only a handful of places are really developed – **Ierápetra**, **Ayía Galíni**, **Mátala**, **Paleohóra** – and a few more, like **Plakiás** and **Makriyialós**, on their way. But lesser spots in between, not always easy to get to, are some of the most attractive in Crete.

When to go

As the southernmost of all Greek islands, Crete has by far the longest summers: you can get a decent tan here right into October and swim at least from April until early November.

Spring is the prime time to come: in April and May the island is relatively empty of visitors, the weather clear and not overpoweringly hot, and every scene is brightened by a profusion of wild flowers.

By mid-June the rush is beginning. **July and August** are not only the hottest, the most crowded and most expensive months, they are also intermittently blighted by fierce winds and accompanying high seas, which make boat trips very uncomfortable and at their worst can mean staying indoors for a day or more at a time. The south coast is particularly prone to these.

In September the crowds gradually begin to thin out, and **autumn** can again be a great time to visit – but now the landscape looks parched and tired, and there's a feeling of things gradually winding down.

Winters are mild, but also vaguely depressing: many things are shut, it can rain sporadically, sometimes for days, and there's far less life in the streets. In the mountains it snows, even to the extent where villages can be cut off; on the south coast it's generally warmer, soothed by a breeze from Africa. You may get a week or more of really fine weather in the middle of winter; but equally you can have sudden viciously cold snaps right through into March.

CRETE'S WEATHER					
Month	Average daytime temperature		Average water temperature		Average rainy days
	°C	°F	°C	°F	
January	12	52	15	59	14
February	12	52	15	59	11
March	14	57	16	61	8
April	17	62	17	62	6
May	21	70	20	68	3
June	23	74	23	74	1
July	25	77	24	75	0
August	26	79	25	77	0
September	25	77	24	75	2
October	21	70	23	74	6
November	18	64	19	66	8
December	14	57	17	62	12

Readings from Iráklion, roughly in the centre of the island.

Crete's mystery is extremely deep. Whoever sets foot on this island senses a mysterious force branching warmly and beneficently through his veins, senses his soul begin to grow.

Níkos Kazantzakís, *Report to Greco*

THE

BASICS

GETTING THERE FROM BRITAIN

The vast majority of visitors to Crete are on some form of package tour which includes a charter flight direct to the island. This is certainly the simplest way of going about things, and even if you plan to travel independently, a seat on a charter to Iráklion or Haniá is the most straightforward way to start out. But charters – the only way of getting straight to Crete – do have their drawbacks, especially if your plans don't fit neatly into their two-week straitjacket. Anyone planning a longer visit will have to fly to Athens and take the ferry or a domestic flight from there; see pp.15–19 for details of connections.

Overland alternatives take three to four days' of non-stop travel, but if you want to take your time over the journey then driving or taking the train can be enjoyable, while taking the bus remains the cheapest option of all.

BY PLANE

The only way to fly direct to Crete is with a **charter**. Be warned that, on the whole, there is a shortage of flights to Crete, especially to Haniá, and that if you try to book at the last minute you may be forced to fly to Athens instead; **student flights** operate only into Athens.

For details of **agents and operators** dealing in charter and discounted scheduled flights, check the list in the box on p.4. Other good sources of information are the ads in London's *Time Out* magazine, and the travel pages in the *Observer* and other Sunday newspapers. *Teletext* is also worth a look, as is your local travel agent.

CHARTER AND DISCOUNTED FLIGHTS

From **London Gatwick** you can get a charter to Iráklion for about £140 for a low-season night flight, rising to around £230 at peak time; flights to Haniá are around £20 more expensive, and seats are very much harder to come by. From **Manchester**, you can expect to pay around £190–200 (low) to £230 (high) to Iráklion; more like £250 to Haniá. Virtually no flights operate over the winter (Nov–April).

It's worth noting that **non-EU nationals** who buy charter tickets to Greece must buy a return ticket, of no fewer than three days and no more than two weeks, and must accompany it with an accommodation voucher for at least the first few nights of their stay – check that the ticket satisfies these conditions or you could be refused entry. In practice, the "accommodation voucher" is a formality; it has to name an existing hotel but you're not expected to use it (and probably won't be able to if you try). Accommodation vouchers are not neccessary when booking sceduled flights (see over).

Student or **under-26 flights** are available at fairly reasonable rates, starting at just under £100 for a low-season charter, rising to about £180 for special reductions on scheduled flights. Be warned, though, that you must be a legitimate student as you may well be required to prove your credentials on boarding, especially leaving Greece. People have been denied seats for not having valid ISIC cards. *Campus Travel* and *STA* have some of the best deals and also offer one-way tickets – by combining these you can stay much longer than a month.

Travelling **via Athens** may be your only option if you're booking at the last minute, since budget tickets to Athens are available long after all the Crete flights have gone. Prices for charter flights to Athens from London in midsummmer start at around £160 (Manchester £180, Glasgow £200).

Finally, remember that **reconfirmation** of charter flights is vital and should be done at least 72 hours in advance.

SCHEDULED FLIGHTS

The advantages of **scheduled flights** are that they can be pre-booked well in advance and have longer ticket validities. However, many of the cheaper scheduled fares do have an advance-purchase and/or minimum-stay requirement, so check conditions carefully.

There are no direct scheduled flights to Crete from the UK. The best you can do is go with *Olympic*, changing planes in **Athens**: the cheapest official (SuperAPEX) fare is over £400 from London even in the low season, rising to around £450 at peak times. All other airlines into Athens use a separate terminal some distance from the *Olympic* one, so be sure to leave plenty of time for the connection. Night flights on *Olympic* are a bargain possibility, costing between £160 and £390 depending on season; you'll need to get in early for these, however, as they go quickly. Otherwise, *British Airways* and *Virgin* have daily scheduled flights to Athens costing from £160 (low season) to £360 (high).

AGENTS AND OPERATORS

Air Travel Advisory Bureau, Charles House, 28 Charles Square, London N1 6HT (☎0171/836 5000). *Reliable for charter flights.*

Alecos Tours, 3a Camden Road, London NW1 (☎0171/267 2092). Regular *Olympic Airways* consolidator.

Avro, 1 Weir Rd, London SW19 8UX (☎0181/715 0000). *Weekly summer charters to Iráklion from Gatwick and Manchester.*

Campus Travel, 52 Grosvenor Gardens, London SW1 (☎0171/730 3402); 541 Bristol Rd, Selly Oak, Birmingham (☎0121/414 1848); 39 Queen's Rd, Clifton, Bristol (☎0117/929 2494); 5 Emmanuel St, Cambridge (☎0223/324283); 53 Forest Rd, Edinburgh (☎0131/668 3303); 166 Deansgate, Manchester (☎0161/273 1721); 13 High St, Oxford (☎01865/242067). *Student/youth travel specialists, with branches also in YHA shops and on university campuses all over Britain. Campus usually has its own student/youth charter flights to Athens during the summer.*

Council Travel, 28a Poland St, London W1 (☎0171/287 3337). *Flights and student discounts.*

Eclipse Flights, First Choice House, Peel Cross Rd, Salford, Manchester M5 2AN (☎01293/554444). *Charter flights to Iráklion and Haniá from Gatwick and Manchester.*

Flyaway Travel, Unit 4, Perronet House, St George's Rd, London SE1 (☎0171/620 3333). *Budget flights to Athens.*

South Coast Student Travel, 61 Ditchling Rd, Brighton (☎01273/570226). *Student experts but plenty to offer non-students as well.*

Springways Travel, 28 Vauxhall Bridge Rd, London SW1 (☎0171/976 5833). *Reliable discount flight agent.*

STA Travel, 74 Old Brompton Rd, London W7 (☎0171/937 9962); 25 Queen's Rd, Bristol (☎0117/929 4399); 38 Sidney St, Cambridge (☎01223/66966); 75 Deansgate, Manchester (☎0161/834 0668); and personal callers at 117 Euston Rd, London NW1; 28 Vicar Lane, Leeds; 36 George St, Oxford; and offices at the universities of Birmingham, London, Kent and Loughborough. *Discount fares, with particularly good deals for students and young people.*

Travel Bug, 597 Cheetham Hill Rd, Manchester (☎0161/721 4000). *Large range of discounted tickets.*

Travel Cuts, 295 Regent St, London W1 (☎0171/255 1944). *Often has discount flights.*

World Wide Journeys, 243 Euston Rd, London NW11 2BU (☎0171/388 0888). *Travel agent specializing in charters to Crete.*

AIRLINES

Balkan Airlines, 322 Regent St, London W1 (☎0171/637 7637).

British Airways, 156 Regent St, London W1 (☎0181/897 4000 and ☎0345/222111).

ČSA Czechoslovak Airlines, 72 Margaret St, London W1 (☎0171/255 1898).

LOT Polish Airlines, 313 Regent St, London W1R 7PE (☎0171/580 5037).

Malev Hungarian Airlines, 10 Vigo St, London W1X 1AJ (☎0171/439 0577).

Olympic Airways, 11 Conduit St, London W1 (☎0171/409 3400).

Virgin Airways, Virgin Megastore, 14–16 Oxford St, London W1 (☎01293/747747).

East European airways, such as *ČSA*, *Balkan*, *Malev* and *LOT* are often cheaper — around £120 one-way, £240 return for much of the year — but nearly always involve delays, with connections in (respectively) Prague, Sofia, Budapest and Warsaw. These airlines can also be relied on to provide a number of cheap seats to students or those under 26. It is not always possible to book discount fares direct from these airlines, and you'll often pay more by going through an agent (see opposite).

You should always **reconfirm** your return flight — there have been problems with overbooking on flights out of Crete. Because of difficulties encountered getting through to these numbers (which seem to be constantly engaged) many travel agents on the island now offer to confirm flights for a small fee.

PACKAGES AND TOURS

If you intend to do little more than stay in one place soaking up the sun, a **package holiday** can offer exceptional value. Especially if you buy one of these at a last-minute discount price, you may find it costs little more than a flight — and you can use the accommodation offered as much or as little as you want. Any high-street travel agent can sell you a standard package to the major resorts of eastern Crete, but for something a bit less predictable at the west end of the island, try one of the smaller, specialist operators listed below.

There are all kinds of deals available, depending on whether you opt for **hotel or apartment accommodation** and whether or not you include car rental as part of your holiday. *Simply Crete*, for example, offers a three-bedroom villa with pool in Haniá (sleeping 6) for two weeks in high season at around £515 per person, including flights and transfers. Two-person deals in a self-catering one-bedroom apartment cost around £450–520 per person per week in high season. There are considerable reductions on all these prices in low season.

Crete is also a great place for **walking**, especially in spring when lower temperatures combine with a profusion of wild flowers, and a number of companies offer guided rambling holidays. *Ramblers' Holidays* (see below), for example, provides a one-week package in May for around £530 per person, including flights, B&B accommodation and guided walks.

SPECIALIST TOUR OPERATORS

The Best of Greece, 23–24 Margaret St, London W1N 8LE (☎0171/255 2320). Limited number of exclusive villa and hotel arrangements from a long-established operator — offers packages to five-star and deluxe hotels along the whole north coast.

Explore Worldwide (RGC), 7 High St, Aldershot, Hampshire (☎01252/319448). Offers an organized rambling tour round the White Mountains, taking in the Samarian gorge.

Freelance Holidays, 40b Grove Rd, Stratford upon Avon, Warks CV37 6PB (☎01789/297705). A wide variety of villas, apartments and hotel-based packages throughout the island, with some in tranquil, less-visited locations.

Kosmar Holidays, 358 Bowes Rd, Arnos Grove, London N11 1AN (☎0181/368 6833). Self-catering apartments throughout Crete, including Eloúnda and Áyios Nikólaos in the east, Haniá and Paleohóra in the west.

Peregrine Holidays, 40/41 South Parade, Summertown, Oxford OX2 7JP (☎01865/511642). Natural history tours of the island, with the emphasis on wildlife, although some archeological sites are included.

Pure Crete, 79 George St, Croydon, Surrey CR0 1LD (☎0181/760 0879). Specializes in village houses and farms in western Crete.

Ramblers' Holidays, Longcroft House, Fretherne Rd, Welwyn Garden City, Herts AL8 6PQ (☎01707/ 331133). Easy walking tours in western Crete, taking in the Samarian gorge and White Mountains.

Simply Crete, Chiswick Gate, 598–608 Chiswick High Rd, London W4 5RT (☎0181/994 4462 or 5226). Excellent selection of villas, small hotels and special-interest tours.

Sunvil Holidays, Sunvil House, Upper Square, Old Isleworth, Middx TW7 7BJ (☎0181/568 4499). Bigger company, with a good choice of smaller resorts.

Travel Club of Upminster, Station Rd, Upminster, Essex RM14 2TT (☎04022/25000). Better-than-average apartments and hotels.

Waymark Holidays, 44 Windsor Rd, Slough SL1 2EJ (☎01753/516477). Walks in the mountains and gorges of western Crete.

BY TRAIN

Travelling **by train** from Britain to Greece takes around three and a half days and fares are more expensive than flights. Obviously, trains will only take you as far as mainland Greece, from where you'll have to continue your journey by plane or ferry (see "Getting There from Mainland Greece", pp.15–19). However, with a regular ticket stopovers on the way are possible – in France, Switzerland and Italy – while with an *InterRail* (see below) or *Eurail* (p.13) train pass you can take in Greece as part of a wider rail trip around Europe.

The most practical **route** from Britain takes in France, Switzerland and **Italy** before crossing on the ferry from Bari or Brindisi to Pátra (Patras). *British Rail* does not currently sell any through ticket to Greece which routes via the states of former Yugoslavia. This has meant an increased demand for tickets on the Italian route which has put an extra burden on trains and ferries. Book seats on both well in advance, especially in summer (for further ferry information, see "By Car: Le Shuttle and the Ferries" below).

TICKETS AND PASSES

Regular **train tickets** from Britain to Greece are not good value. A standard second-class London to Athens return costs at least £380, though if you are **under 26**, you can get a *BIJ* ticket, discounting these fares by around 25 percent; these are available through *Eurotrain* and *Wasteels* (see box above for addresses). Both regular and *BIJ* tickets have two months' return validity, or can be purchased as one-ways, and the Italy routes include the ferry crossing. The tickets also allow for stopovers, so long as you stick to the route prescribed.

Better value by far is to buy an **InterRail pass**, available to anyone resident in Europe for six months. You can buy it from *British Rail* (or any travel agent), and the pass offers unlimited travel on a zonal basis on up to 25 European rail networks. The only extras you pay are supplements on certain express trains, plus half-price fares in Britain (or the country of issue) and on the cross-Channel ferries. The pass includes the ferry from Brindisi in southern Italy to Pátra in Greece, but *not* travel on the Pireás–Crete ferries. To reach Greece from the UK you'll need a pass valid for at least two zones; Greece is zoned with Italy, Turkey and Slovenia. Once you reach Crete there are no

RAIL TICKET OFFICES

Eurotrain, 52 Grosvenor Gardens, London SW1 (☎0171/730 3402).

International Rail Centre, Victoria Station, London SW1 (☎0171/834 2345).

Wasteels, Victoria Station, London SW1 (☎0171/834 7066).

BUS TICKET OFFICES

National Express Eurolines, 52 Grosvenor Gardens, London SW1 (☎0171/730 0202).

Olympic Bus, 70 Brunswick Centre, London WC1 (☎0171/837 9141).

trains at all, of course. Prices are currently £209 for a one-month pass if you're under 26, £269 for the over-26 version which, due to restrictions, is only valid beyond the Belgian frontier; a £69 return fare from London gets you to the starting point.

Finally, anyone over sixty and holding a British Rail Senior Citizen Railcard, can buy a **Rail Europe Senior Card** (£21 for 1 year). This gives up to fifty-percent reductions on rail fares throughout Europe and thirty percent off sea crossings.

BY BUS

With charter flights at such competitive rates, it's hard to find good reasons for wanting to spend three or four days on a **bus** to Greece – particularly if your final destination is Crete. Just for the record, the main operators to Athens are *Olympic Bus* (£100–120 return) and the more reliable *National Express Eurolines* (£200–220 return) – see the box above for booking numbers. The route is via France and Italy with a ferry across to Greece. Stops of about twenty minutes are made every five or six hours, with the odd longer break for roadside café meals.

BY CAR: LE SHUTTLE AND THE FERRIES

If you have the time and inclination, **driving to Greece** can be a pleasant proposition. Realistically, though, it's really only worth considering if you have at least a month to spare, are going to travel in Greece for an extended period, or want to take advantage of various stopovers en route. If Crete is your main goal, you'd be better off flying, and renting a car once you're on the island.

It's important to plan ahead. The **Automobile Association** (AA) provides a comprehensive service offering general advice on all facets of driving to Greece; their European Route Service (contact AA on ☎01256/20123) can arrange a detailed printout of a route to follow. Driving licence, vehicle registration documents and insurance are essential; a Green Card is recommended. The most popular **route** is down through France and Italy to catch one of the Adriatic ferries. A much longer alternative through eastern Europe (Hungary, Romania and Bulgaria) is just about feasible, but driving through former Yugoslavia is unsafe; in any case, these eastern routes are less than convenient for ferries to Crete.

CROSSING THE CHANNEL

The **Le Shuttle** service through the Channel Tunnel doesn't significantly affect travel times for drivers to Greece, though it does of course speed up the cross-Channel section of the journey. *Le Shuttle* operates trains 24 hours a day, carrying cars, motorcycles, buses and their passengers, and taking 35 minutes between Folkestone and Calais. At peak times, services operate every fifteen minutes, making advance bookings unnecessary; during the night, services still run hourly. Full return fares from May to August cost around £300 per vehicle (passengers included), but look out for special offers which can halve this, and for big discounts in the low season.

The alternative **cross-Channel** options for most travellers are the conventional **ferry** or **hovercraft** links between **Dover** and Calais or Boulogne (the quickest and cheapest routes), **Ramsgate** and Dunkerque, or Newhaven and Dieppe.

CROSS-CHANNEL INFORMATION

Hoverspeed, Dover (☎01304/240101); London (☎0181/5547061). *To Boulogne and Calais.*

Le Shuttle, Customer Services Centre (☎01303/271100). *Information and ticket sales.*

P&O European Ferries, Dover (☎01304/203388); Portsmouth (☎01705/772244); London (☎0181/575 8555). *To Calais.*

Sally Line, Ramsgate (☎01843/595522); London (☎0181/858 1127). *To Dunkerque.*

Stena Sealink Line, Ashford (☎01233/647047). *To Calais and Dieppe.*

Ferry **prices** vary according to the time of year and, for motorists, the size of your car. The Dover–Calais/Boulogne runs, for example, start at about £180 return low season, £220 return high season for a car with up to five passengers. **Foot passengers** should be able to cross for about £50 return year round; taking a **motorbike** costs from £80 to 90 return.

ITALY–GREECE FERRIES

On the Italian run, there are regular **ferries** from Ancona, Bari, Brindisi and Otranto to **Pátra** (at the tip of the Peloponnese) or **Igoumenítsa** (the port for Epirus in northwestern Greece); both sail via the island of **Corfu**, on which you can stop over at no extra charge if you get this specified on your ticket. It takes about nine hours from Brindisi – much the most common port of departure – to Corfu and from there it's two more hours to Igoumenítsa, ten to Pátra. The passenger fare in peak season is around £28–35/$45–55 to Corfu/Igoumenítsa, £31–38/$50–60 to Pátra, with a twenty-percent reduction for students on most of the lines. These figures normally include a small port tax and off-season should be at least thirty percent lower. Small cars are charged about £35–55/$55–90; motorbikes around £25/$40. If you're taking a car over in mid-season it's essential to book in advance, otherwise you may face a two- or three-day wait.

Brindisi is in many ways the best place to leave from – if only because there are far more ferries from here – and it's a reasonably interesting place to wait around. On the other hand embarkation is a chaotic nightmare. Less stressful departure points include Ancona, much further north hence less driving but a longer, more expensive ferry trip, and Bari. The cheapest ferry is run by *R-Lines* from Otranto, 70km south of Brindisi, to Corfu/Igoumenítsa; there are currently four sailings weekly (Mon, Wed, Thurs and Sat) throughout the year departing Otranto at 10.30pm and arriving at Igoumenítsa eleven hours later. The passenger fare is £21–28/$35–45 depending which type of seat you choose, and cabins are available from £30/$48 per person; the charge for taking a small car is £19/$30, but again booking ahead is advisable during high season.

Heading for Crete, Pátra is the obvious destination: from there you can avoid Athens altogether and continue down through the Peloponnese to **Yíthio** (or less conveniently to Monemvassía or Neápoli) where you can pick up the twice-weekly ferry to Kastélli Kisámou in western Crete (see

"Getting There from Mainland Greece", p.18). On the train, it's an easy run from Pátra to Athens. The ferry companies *Marlines* and *Minoan* operate a service from Ancona to Pátra and Iráklion (48hr): about £150/$225 for a small car, plus £75/$112 per person deck class, or over £150/$225 per person in a cabin. *Marlines* currently sails on Fridays and *Minoan* on Saturdays.

For advance UK bookings for the Italy–Greece ferries, see the list of **British agents** below.

THE ITALY–GREECE ROUTES

Note: all timings are approximate.

From Ancona *Marlines, Strintzis, ANEK* and *Minoan* to Igoumenítsa (24hr) and Pátra (34hr); daily or nearly so year round. *Minoan* sails via Corfu, with separate lines for Pátra, Kefalloniá,and Cesme (Turkey) half the year; *Strintzis* and *ANEK* via Corfu; *Marlines* has a summer extension from Pátra to Iráklion (Crete). Most sailings between 8pm and 10pm, but there are a number of afternoon departures.

From Bari *Ventouris* to Pátra direct (20hr), nearly daily; to Corfu, Igoumenítsa (12hr) and Pátra (20hr); daily departures year round between 8pm and 9pm. To Pátra via Corfu and/or Igoumenítsa on *Poseidon Lines, Arkadia Lines.*

From Brindisi *Fragline* and *Adriatica* to Corfu, Igoumenítsa (11hr) and Pátra (20hr). *Hellenic Mediterranean Lines* to Corfu and Pátra, three to seven a week depending on season; Igoumenítsa , Kefalloniá, Ithaki, Paxí and Zákinthos, served on separate sailings during summer. *European Seaways* to Corfu, Igoumenítsa and Pátra. *Marlines* to Igoumenítsa and Brindisi. Several ferries leave every day in season, most between 8pm and 10.30pm; at least one daily in winter.

From Otranto *R-Lines* to Corfu and Igoumenítsa (9hr); five weekly, May–Oct only.

From Trieste *ANEK* to Igoumenítsa , Corfu and Pátra (43hr). One weekly in summer, tagged onto Ancona service.

SAMPLE FARES

*Prices below are one-way high/low-season fares; **port taxes** (£3–5 per person in each direction) are not included. Note that substantial reductions apply on most lines for both **InterRail** or **Eurail** pass-holders, and those **under 26**. Slight discounts are usually available on **return fares***.

Igoumenítsa from Bari or Brindisi: deck class £28–35 ($42–52)/£15–25 ($22–37); car £36–55 ($55–85)/£20–45 ($30–70).

Pátra from Bari or Brindisi: deck class £31–£38 ($45–60)/£20–30 ($30–45); car £36–54 ($54–80)/£25–45 ($35–70).

Igoumenítsa from Ancona: deck class £40/50 ($60/75); car £65/£95 ($100/145).

UK AGENTS

For details of local agents in Greece, see the respective listings for Pátra and Igoumenítsa. The following are UK agents for advance bookings:

Amathis Travel, 51 Tottenham Court Rd, London W1 (☎0171/636 6158). *Agents for Hellenic Mediterranean.*

Serena Holidays, 40 Kenway Rd, London SW5 (☎0171/244 8422). *For Adriatica Lines.*

Viamare Travel Ltd, Graphic House, 2 Sumatra Rd, London NW6 (☎0171/431 4560). *For ANEK, Arkadia, Fragline, Marlines, R-Lines, Strintzis, Ventouris. Also for Salamis and Poseidon Lines, which route Pireás–Rhodes or Crete–Limassol–Haifa.*

GETTING THERE FROM IRELAND

Summer charter flights to Crete are easy to pick up from either Dublin or Belfast (around £200 return and upwards), while year-round scheduled flights operate daily to Athens with connections on to Iráklion.

Fares on **scheduled flights** with *British Airways* (routed via Heathrow) work out at around £490 from Belfast to Athens, with an add-on fare of around £100 to Iráklion. *Aer Lingus* don't have a direct scheduled service to Greece from Dublin, but for a comparable price will book you to Iráklion via Heathrow, where you change to another carrier. For youth and student discount fares, the best first stop is *USIT* (see below for address).

For a typical two-week **package** in a self-catering apartment (based on 2 people sharing), you can expect to pay from £200 per person low season to £500 high season (Belfast); from IR£230 to IR450 (Dublin). For larger groups sharing, things can work out significantly cheaper. See the box below for travel agents' addresses.

Travelling to London in the first place to pick up a cheap charter from there may save you a little money, but on the whole it's rarely worth the time and effort. For the record, budget flights to London are offered by *British Midland*, *BA*, *Aer Lingus* and *Ryan Air*. Buying a *Eurotrain* boat and train ticket to London from *USIT* will slightly undercut plane fares but by this time you're starting to talk about a journey of days not hours to Greece, with the trip to Crete itself still to come.

FLIGHTS, PACKAGES AND TOURS

Aspro Holidays, 19 Donegal Place, Belfast BT1 5AB (☎01232/322550). *Self-catering apartments and studios and flight-only charters.*

Balkan Tours, 37 Ann St, Belfast BT1 4EB (☎01232/246795). *Direct charter flights, as well as self-catering apartments along the central north coast.*

Budget Travel, 134 Lower Baggot St, Dublin 2 (☎01/661 1866). *Self-catering apartments and studios; also sells flight-only charters.*

Joe Walsh Tours, 8–11 Baggot St, Dublin (☎01/676 0991). *General budget fares agent, selling*

charters and self-catering apartments on the north coast (May–Oct).

Thomas Cook, 118 Grafton St, Dublin (☎01/677 1721). *Mainstream package-holiday and flight agent, with occasional discount offers.*

Unijet, Unit 3, Lyndon Court, Queen St, Belfast BT1 5EF (☎01232/314656). *Self-catering studio packages based around the north coast.*

USIT. Branches at: Aston Quay, O'Connell Bridge, Dublin 2 (☎01/679 8833); 10–11 Market Parade, Cork (☎021/270 900); Fountain Centre, College St, Belfast (☎01232/324073). *Student and youth specialist.*

AIRLINES

Aer Lingus, 41 Upper O'Connell St, Dublin (☎01/844 4777); 46–48 Castle St, Belfast (☎01232/245151); 2 Academy St, Cork (☎021/274331).

British Airways, 9 Fountain Centre, College St, Belfast (☎0345/222111); in Dublin, contact *Aer Lingus*.

GETTING THERE FROM NORTH AMERICA

Only a few carriers fly directly to Greece from North America, so most North Americans travel to a gateway European city, and pick up a connecting flight on from there with an associated airline. If you have time, you may well discover that it's cheaper to arrange the final Crete-bound leg of the journey yourself, in which case your only criterion will be finding a suitable and good value North America–Europe flight; for details of onward flights from the UK, see "Getting There from Britain", pp.3–8.

In general there just isn't enough traffic on the US–Greece routes to make for very cheap fares. The **Greek national airline**, *Olympic*

AIRLINES IN NORTH AMERICA

Air Canada (in Canada, call directory inquiries, ☎1-800/555-1212, for local toll-free number; US toll-free number is ☎1-800/776-3000).

Air France (☎1-800/237-2747; in Canada, ☎1-800/667-2747).

Alitalia (☎1-800/223-5730).

British Airways (in US, ☎1-800/247-9297; in Canada ☎1-800/668-1059).

Canadian Airlines (in Canada, ☎1-800/665-1177; in US, ☎1-800/426-7000).

ČSA Czechoslovak Airlines (☎1-800/223-2365).

Delta Airlines (☎1-800/241-4141).

Iberia (in US, ☎1-800/772-4642; in Canada, ☎1-800/423-7421).

KLM (in US, ☎1-800/374-7747; in Canada, ☎1-800/361-5073).

LOT Polish Airlines (☎1-800/223-0593).

Lufthansa (☎1-800/645-3880).

Olympic Airways (☎1-800/223-1226).

Sabena (☎1-800/955-2000).

Swissair (☎1-800/221-4750).

TAP Air Portugal (☎1-800/221-7370).

TWA (☎1-800/892-4141).

United Airlines (☎1-800/538-2929).

Airways, is the only carrier to fly "direct" to Crete from North America, landing briefly in Athens; these flights serve New York (JFK) only. From Boston, Montréal and Toronto, *Olympic* fly to Athens, offering reasonably priced add-on flights to Crete (either Iráklion or Haniá), leaving from the same Athens terminal that you will fly into.

SHOPPING FOR TICKETS

Discount ticket outlets – advertised in the Sunday travel sections of major newspapers – come in several forms. **Consolidators** buy up blocks of tickets that airlines don't think they'll be able to sell at their published fares, and unload them at a discount. Many advertise fares on a one-way basis, enabling you to fly into one city and out from another without penalty. Consolidators normally don't impose advance purchase requirements (although in busy times you should book ahead just to be sure of getting a ticket), but they do often charge very stiff fees for date changes. **Discount agents** also deal in blocks of tickets offloaded by the airlines, but they typically offer a range of other travel-related services like insurance, rail passes, youth and student ID cards, car rentals and tours. These agencies tend to be most worthwhile for students and under-26s, who can benefit from special fares and deals. **Travel clubs** are another option – most charge an annual membership fee, which may be worth it for their discounts on air tickets and car rental. Some agencies specialize in **charter flights**, which may be even cheaper than anything available on a scheduled flight, but again there's a trade-off:

departure dates are fixed, and withdrawal penalties are high (check the refund policy). Student/youth fares can sometimes save you money, though again the best deals are usually those offered by seat consolidators advertising in Sunday newspaper travel sections.

Don't automatically assume that tickets purchased through a travel specialist will be cheapest – once you get a quote, check with the airlines and you may turn up an even better deal. In addition, exercise caution and *never* deal with a company that demands cash up front or refuses to accept payment by credit card.

For destinations not handled by discounters – which applies to most regional airports – you'll have to deal with airlines' published fares. The cheapest way to go is with an **APEX** (Advance Purchase Excursion) ticket. This carries certain restrictions: you have to book – and pay – at least 21 days before departure and spend at least seven days abroad (maximum stay 3 months), and you're liable to penalties if you change your schedule. On transatlantic routes there are also winter **Super APEX** tickets, sometimes known as "Eurosavers" – slightly cheaper than an ordinary Apex, but limiting your stay to between 7 and 21 days. Some airlines also issue **Special APEX** tickets to those under 24, often extending the maximum stay to a year.

EUROPEAN CONNECTIONS

There are direct flights to:
Iráklion from Amsterdam, Rome and Vienna.

DISCOUNT TRAVEL COMPANIES

Air Brokers International

323 Geary St, Suite 411, San Francisco, CA 94102 (☎1-800/883-3273).
Consolidator.

Air Courier Association

191 University Blvd, Suite 300, Denver, CO 80206 (☎303/278-8810).
Courier flight broker.

Airhitch

2472 Broadway, Suite 200, New York, NY 10025 (☎212/864-2000).
Standby-seat broker: for a set price, they guarantee to get you on a flight as close to your preferred destination as possible, within a week.

Council Travel

Head Office: 205 E 42nd St, New York, NY 10017 (☎1-800/743-1823).
Student travel organization with branches in many US cities. A sister company, Council Charter (☎1-800/223-7402), specializes in charter flights.

Discount Travel International

Ives Building, 114 Forrest Ave, Suite 205, Narberth, PA 19072 (☎1-800/334-9294).
Discount travel club.

Educational Travel Center

438 N Frances St, Madison, WI 53703 (☎1-800/747-5551).
Student/youth discount agent.

Encore Travel Club

4501 Forbes Blvd, Lanham, MD 20706 (☎1-800/444-9800).
Discount travel club.

Interworld Travel

800 Douglass Rd, Miami, FL 33134 (☎305/443-4929).
Consolidator.

Last Minute Travel Club

132 Brookline Ave, Boston, MA 02215 (☎1-800/LAST MIN).
Travel club specializing in standby deals.

Moment's Notice

425 Madison Ave, New York, NY 10017 (☎212/486-0503).
Discount travel club.

New Frontiers/Nouvelles Frontières

Head offices: 12 E 33rd St, New York, NY 10016 (☎1-800/366-6387); 1001 Sherbrook E, Suite 720, Montréal, H2L 1L3 (☎514/526-8444).

French discount travel firm. Other branches in LA, San Francisco and Québec City.

Now Voyager

74 Varick St, Suite 307, New York, NY 10013 (☎212/431-1616).
Courier flight broker.

STA Travel

Head office: 48 E 11th St, New York, NY 10003 (☎1-800/777-0112; nationwide).
Worldwide specialist in independent travel with branches in the Los Angeles, San Francisco and Boston areas.

TFI Tours International

Head office: 34 W 32nd St, New York, NY 10001 (☎1-800/745-8000).
Consolidator; other offices in Las Vegas, San Francisco, Los Angeles.

Travac

Head office: 989 Sixth Ave, New York NY 10018 (☎1-800/872-8800).
Consolidator and charter broker; has another branch in Orlando.

Travel Avenue

10 S Riverside, Suite 1404, Chicago, IL 60606 (☎1-800/333-3335).
Discount travel agent.

Travel Cuts

Head office: 187 College St, Toronto, ON M5T 1P7 (☎416/979-2406).
Canadian student travel organization with branches all over the country.

Travelers Advantage

3033 S Parker Rd, Suite 900, Aurora, CO 80014 (☎1-800/548-1116).
Discount travel club.

UniTravel

1177 N Warson Rd, St Louis, MO 63132 (☎1-800/325-2222).
Consolidator.

Worldtek Travel

111 Water St, New Haven, CT 06511 (☎1-800/243-1723).
Discount travel agency.

Worldwide Discount Travel Club

1674 Meridian Ave, Miami Beach, FL 33139 (☎305/534-2082).
Discount travel club.

Note that fares are heavily dependent on **season**, and are highest from June to September; they drop either side of this, and you'll get the best deals during the low season, November–February (excluding Christmas). Note that flying on weekends ordinarily adds US$50 or so to the return fare; **price ranges quoted in the sections below assume midweek travel**.

FROM THE USA

New York–Crete prices with *Olympic* range from about US$870 return in winter, rising to US$1110 for a maximum thirty-day stay with seven-day advance purchase; there's a small saving of around US$18 in taxes to be had by booking right through from the States. Otherwise, **charter** flights will probably be the best and

cheapest way of getting direct to Crete – check with your travel agent and scan the Sunday papers to see what's on offer.

Non-stop *Olympic* flights to **Athens** from New York are similarly priced, ranging from US$700 to US$1100, with **add-on flights** to Iráklion or Haniá available for around US$59 each way. *Olympic* also flies out of **Boston** once a week in winter, twice a week in summer, at much the same rates. *Delta* and *TWA* have daily services from New York to Athens via Frankfurt and while fares cost around US$300 more than with *Olympic*, a consolidator or agent might be able to get you a flight for around half the cost the airlines themselves quote: return trips run from around US$600 in winter, US$900 in summer. *United* flights to Athens are via Paris, and there's a good service from **Washington**

SPECIALIST TOUR OPERATORS

USA

Archeological Tours, 271 Madison Ave, New York, NY 10016 (☎212/986-3054). *Specialist archeological tours.*

Astro Tours, 216 Fourth Ave S, Seattle, WA 98104 (☎206/467-7777). *Cruise packages to the Greek islands.*

Classic Adventures, PO Box 153, Hamlin, NY 14464-0153 (☎1-800/777-8090). *Hiking, biking and walking tours in June and September, covering archeological sites and coastal trips.*

Cloud Tours Inc., 645 Fifth Ave, New York, NY 10022 (☎1-800/223-7880 or 212/753-6104). *Six- or nine-day tours combining Crete with other islands, such as Santoríni, Míkonos, Kos and Rhodes.*

Crown Peters, 33–36 Broadway, Astoria, NY 11106 (☎718/932-7800). *Cruises and independent packages to Crete and other islands.*

Educational Tours and Cruises, 14 (R) Wyman St, Medford, MA 02155 (☎1-800/275-4109). *Custom-designed tours to Greece and the islands, specializing in art, history, food and wine, ancient drama, painting, birdwatching, etc.*

Epirotiki Lines, 551 Fifth Ave, New York, NY 10176 (☎212/949-7273). *Greek cruise specialist.*

Globus Gateway, 92–25 Queens Blvd, Rego Park, NY 11374 (☎1-800/221-0090). *Offers a variety of city and island packages, including a cruise that calls at Santoríni, Crete (tour of Knossós), Rhodes, Patmos and Míkonos .*

Grecian Travel Inc., 29–11 Ditmard Blvds, Astoria, NY 11105 (☎1-800/368-6262). *For years, a leader in travel to Greece.*

Guaranteed Travel, 83 S St, Box 269, Morristown, NJ 07963 (☎201/540-1770). *Specializes in "Greece-Your-Way" independent travel.*

Homeric Tours, 55 E 59th St, New York, NY 10017 (☎1-800/223-5570). *All-inclusive tours from 9 to 23 days, as well as cruises and charter flights.*

Odyssey Travel Center, 7735 Old Georgetown Rd, Bethseda, MD 20814 (☎401/657-4647). *Specialists to Greece and the Greek islands.*

Tourlite International, 551 Fifth Ave, New York, NY 10176 (☎212/5991-1624). *Selection of tours to various Greek islands, with extensions to Egypt, Israel and Turkey*

CANADA

Adventures Abroad, 1027 W Broadway, Suite 310, Vancouver, BC, VGH 1E3 (☎604/732-9922). *General operator, offering group and individual tours and cruises.*

Auratours, 1470 Peel St, Suite 252, Montréal, Québec H3A 1TL (☎1-800/363-0323). *General operator, offering group and individual tours and cruises.*

Trianena Poseidon Tours International, 72 Hutchison St, Montréal, Québec H3N 1ZL (☎1-800/361-0374). *Custom-made tours, yacht charters and cruises, and apartment and villa vacations.*

DC and **Chicago** – the lowest return winter fare from DC starts at around US$800. One particularly good deal is on *LOT Polish Airlines*, which flies out of New York and Chicago to Athens several times a week via Warsaw. Fares run from around US$700 return.

Since all scheduled flights to Athens from the **West Coast** go via New York or another eastern city, you basically end up paying for a transcontinental flight on top of the transatlantic fare: return APEX tickets from Seattle, San Francisco or Los Angeles on *TWA* or *Delta* start at US$920 in winter, rising to over US$1200 in summer. Most European airlines (including *Air France*, *British Airways*, *Iberia*, *KLM* and *Lufthansa*) also connect the West Coast with Greece via their "homeports" in Europe, but these stopovers can often mean a wait of a few hours, sometimes even an overnight stop – be sure to ask your ticket agent.

FROM CANADA

As with the US, air fares **from Canada** to Athens vary tremendously depending upon where you start your journey. The best-value scheduled fare is on *Olympic*, who fly non-stop out of Montréal and Toronto once a week in winter for CDN$1100 return, twice a week in summer for CDN$1500.

KLM operates several flights a week to Athens via Amsterdam, from Toronto, Montréal, Vancouver and Edmonton – from Toronto, expect to pay around CDN$1150 in winter, CDN$1500 in high season. Travellers from Montréal can also try the European carriers *Air France*, *Alitalia*, *British Airways*, *Iberia*, *Lufthansa*, *Sabena*, *Swissair* and *TAP Air Portugal*, all of which operate several flights a week to Athens via major European cities. One unlikely source for good deals is *Czechoslovak Airlines* (*ČSA*), which flies out of Montréal to Athens via Prague for a fare of around CDN$1100.

Finally, *Air Canada* flies to Vienna with connections to Athens on *Olympic*, with flights from Vancouver costing CDN$1600 in winter, CDN$1800 in summer.

RAIL PASSES

A **Eurail pass** is not likely to pay for itself if you're planning to stick to Greece and will only take you as far as the mainland, so it's only worth considering if you plan to travel to Greece from elsewhere in Europe. The pass, which must be purchased before arrival in Europe, allows unlimited free train travel in Greece and sixteen other countries. The **Eurail Youthpass** (for under-26s) costs US$398 for 15 days, US$578 for one month or US$768 for two months; if you're 26 or over you'll have to buy a **first-class pass**, available in 15-day (US$498), 21-day (US$648), one-month (US$798), two-month (US$1098) and three-month (US$1398) increments.

You stand a better chance of getting your money's worth out of a **Eurail Flexipass**, which is good for a certain number of travel days in a two-month period. This, too, comes in under-26/first-class versions: five days cost US$255/US$348; 10 days, US$398/US$560; and fifteen days, US$540/US$740. A further alternative is to attempt to buy an *InterRail* pass in Europe (see "Getting There From Britain") – most agents don't check residential qualifications, but once you're in Europe it'll be too late to buy a *Eurail* pass if you have problems. You can purchase *Eurail* passes from one of the agents listed below.

RAIL CONTACTS IN NORTH AMERICA

CIT Tours, 342 Madison Ave, Suite 207, New York, NY 10173 (☎1-800/223-7987).

DER Tours/GermanRail, 9501 W Divon Ave, Suite 400, Rosemont, IL 60018 (☎1-800/421-2929).

Rail Europe, 226 Westchester Ave, White Plains, NY 10604 (☎1-800/438 7245).

ScanTours, 1535 6th St, Suite 205, Santa Monica, CA 90401 (☎1-800/223-7226).

GETTING THERE FROM AUSTRALASIA

Thanks to the number of Greeks who've adopted the country, connections between Australia and Greece are good, though from New Zealand things are less promising. Given the prices and most people's travel plans, you'll probably do better looking for some kind of Round-the-World ticket that includes Greece. If London is your first destination in Europe, and you've picked up a reasonably good deal on a flight there, it's probably best to wait until you reach the UK before arranging your onward travel to Greece; see "Getting There from Britain" for all the details.

Note that the **prices** given on the facing page are in Australian/New Zealand dollars for published mid-season return fares; the specialist travel agents listed below should be able to get at least ten percent off these. **Students** and anyone **under 26** should try *STA Travel* in the first instance which has a wide range of discounted fares on offer.

AGENTS AND AIRLINES

TRAVEL AGENTS

Adventure World, 73 Walker St, N Sydney (☎02/956 7766); 8 Victoria Ave, Perth (☎09/221 2300).

Flight Centres, *Australia*: Circular Quay, Sydney (☎02/241 2422); Bourke St, Melbourne (☎03/650 2899); plus other branches nationwide. *New Zealand*: National Bank Towers, 205–225 Queen St, Auckland (☎09/309 6171); Shop 1M, National Mutual Arcade, 152 Hereford St, Christchurch (☎09/379 7145); 50–52 Willis St, Wellington (☎04/472 8101); other branches countrywide.

Grecian Holidays, 115 Pitt St, Sydney (☎02/231 1277); 71 Grey St, Brisbane (☎07/846 4006).

Grecian Mediterranean Holidays, 49 Ventnor Ave, West Perth (☎09/321 3930).

Grecian Tours Travel, 237a Lonsdale St, Melbourne (☎03/663 3711).

Greek Tours, Floor 2, 243 Edward St, Brisbane (☎07/221 9700).

House of Holidays, 298 Clayton Rd, Clayton, Victoria (☎03/543 5800).

STA Travel, *Australia*: 732 Harris St, Ultimo, Sydney (☎02/212 1255); 256 Flinders St, Melbourne (☎03/347 4711); other offices in Townsville, Cairns and state capitals. *New Zealand*: Traveller's Centre, 10 High St, Auckland (☎09/309 9995); 233 Cuba St, Wellington (☎04/385 0561); 223 High St, Christchurch (☎03/379 9098); other offices in Dunedin, Palmerston North and Hamilton.

AIRLINES

☎008 numbers are toll free, but only apply if dialled outside the city in the address.

Aeroflot, 388 George St, Sydney (☎02/233 7148). No NZ office.

Alitalia, Orient Overseas Building, 32 Bridge St, Sydney (☎02/247 1308); Floor 6, Trust Bank Building, 229 Queen St, Auckland (☎09/379 4457).

British Airways, 64 Castlereagh St, Sydney (☎02/258 3300); Dilworth Building, cnr. Queen and Customs streets, Auckland (☎09/367 7500).

Garuda, 175 Clarence St, Sydney (☎02/334 9900); 120 Albert St, Auckland (☎09/366 1855).

KLM 5 Elizabeth St, Sydney (☎02/231 6333/008 222 747). No NZ office.

Lufthansa/Air Lauda, 143 Macquarie St, Sydney (☎02/367 3800); 109 Queen St, Auckland (☎09/303 1529).

Olympic Airways, *S.A.* Floor 3, 37–49 Pitt St, Sydney (☎02/251 2044). No NZ office.

Qantas, International Square, Jamison St, Sydney (☎02/957 0111/236 3636); Qantas House, 154 Queen St, Auckland (☎09/303 2506).

Singapore Airlines, 17 Bridge St, Sydney (☎02/236 0111); Lower Ground Floor, West Plaza Building, cnr. Customs and Albert streets, Auckland (☎09/379 3209).

Thai 75–77 Pitt St, Sydney (☎02/844 0999/008 221 320); Kensington Swan Building, 22 Fanshawe St, Auckland (☎09377 3886).

United 10 Barrack St, Sydney (☎02/237 8888); 7 City Rd, Auckland (☎09/307 9500).

Note: all Australian phone numbers are due to have extra digits added over the next two years.

FROM AUSTRALIA

Cheapest fares to Athens **from Australia** are with *Aeroflot* ($1650), flying weekly out of Sydney via Moscow, and *Thai* ($2242), which flies from Sydney, Melbourne, Perth or Brisbane via Bangkok. Otherwise, you can fly daily from Perth or Sydney, and several times a week from Melbourne or Brisbane, for $2399 with one of the following: *Olympic* (via Bangkok), *Alitalia* (Bangkok, Rome), *Singapore* (Singapore), *KLM* (Singapore, Amsterdam), *Lufthansa* (Frankfurt), and *United* (Los Angeles, Washington, Paris). **Add-on fares to Iráklion or Haniá** from Athens with *Olympic* run to around another $160–180.

British Airways and Qantas can get you to London via Singapore or Bangkok for the same price as other airlines, but charge an extra $430 to Athens, while giving you a free return flight within Europe. You can undercut this with their *Global Explorer Pass* ($2499), a **Round-the-World** fare that allows six stopovers worldwide wherever these two airlines fly to (except South America). Also worth considering is *Garuda*'s $1685 fare from Sydney, Townsville or Cairns via Jakarta to Europe, from where you could pick up a cheap onward flight or continue **overland** to Athens. **Departure tax** from Athens, sometimes added to the ticket at the time of purchase, is $33.

FROM NEW ZEALAND

From New Zealand, best deals to Athens are with *Thai* ($2399 via Bangkok) or *Singapore* ($2499 via Singapore), and a very versatile offer with *Lufthansa* ($2899), who can route you through anywhere that Air New Zealand or Qantas fly – including Los Angeles, Singapore, Sydney, Hong Kong or Tokyo – for a stopover. British Airways/Qantas can get you to Europe, but not Athens, for $2699, so again you're better off with their *Global Explorer Pass* (see above) at $3099. Surprisingly expensive at $3974 are *Alitalia* (via Rome) and *United* (Los Angeles, Washington, Paris). **Departure tax** from Athens is $42.

GETTING THERE FROM MAINLAND GREECE

Not everyone flies direct to Crete. Cheap charter flights to Athens abound, while many people choose to see more of Greece on the way – either travelling by train, using *InterRail* and *Eurail* tickets, or even driving across Europe. For how to reach Athens and the mainland in the first place, see the relevant "Getting There" sections above; and read on for details of how to move on to Crete.

BY PLANE

Olympic operates at least five flights a day from **Athens to Iráklion** in peak season – less through the winter – and three or four daily to **Haniá**; journey time is less than an hour. This may seem a lot, but in summer they are all booked well in advance. The flights are probably good value when weighed against a twelve-hour ferry trip: one-way prices are around £47/US$70 to Haniá, £52/US$78 to Iráklion. There's also a twice-weekly service (Tues and Sat) to **Sitía** for a one-way price of £57/US$86. Flights leave from the West terminal, for details of which see "Surviving Athens" overleaf.

Fully booked or not, it can be worth trying for a **stand-by** ticket, especially if you arrive at the airport in the middle of the night and can be first in the queue next morning. You have to purchase

TRAVELLING VIA ATHENS AND PIREÁS

You may well find yourself travelling to Crete via **Athens**. This is not necessarily a hardship. The Greek capital is, admittedly, not much of a holiday resort, with its concrete architecture, dire traffic, and air pollution, but it has modern excitements of its own, as well as its superlative ancient sites. A couple of nights' stopover will allow you to take in the Acropolis, Ancient Agora and major museums, wander around the old quarter of Plaka and the bazaar area, and sample some of the country's best restaurants and clubs. Even a morning flight into Athens allows you enough time to take a look at the Acropolis and Plaka, before heading down to the port of **Pireás** (Piraeus) to catch one of the early evening ferries on to Crete.

What follows is a brief guide to getting in and out of the city, and some pointers on what to do while you're there. For a full treatment of the city, check the *Rough Guide to Greece*.

ARRIVING
Athens airport – Ellinikón – has two separate terminals: **West** (Dhitikó) which is used by *Olympic Airways* (both national and international), and **East** (Anatolkó) which is used by all the other airlines. The terminals are on opposite sides of the runway, so you have to drive halfway round the perimeter fence to get from one to the other. *Olympic* buses connect the two regularly from around 6am to midnight; taxis are available, too, and should cost no more than 200dr.

Both terminals have money exchange facilities, open 24 hours at the east terminal, 7am to 11pm at the west one; the west terminal also has automatic teller machines that accept *Visa, Mastercard, Cirrus* and *Plus* cards. Insist on some small denomination notes to pay for your bus ticket or taxi ride.

It's about 9km **to central Athens** or to the ferry port of **Pireás** (Piraeus). The easiest way to travel is by **taxi**, which should cost around 1000–1500dr, depending on traffic. Make sure that the meter is switched on, as new arrivals are often charged over the odds. You may find that you have fellow passengers in the cab: this is permitted, and each drop-off will pay the full fare.

If you're happy to carry your bags around, you could also travel in by **bus**. The blue and yellow #091 Express Bus connects both terminals with the centre of Athens (Omónia and Síndagma squares). It runs every half-hour 6am–9pm, every 40 minutes from 9pm to 12.20am, and every hour (on the half hour) 1.30–5.30am. Tickets cost 160dr; 200dr between 1.30 and 5.30am.

Bus #19 runs from both airport terminals to **Pireás**, allowing you to get straight to the ferry. It has 12 departures daily between 6am and 9.20pm. Tickets again cost 160dr. Take the bus to the end of the route, Platía Karaïskáki, which fronts the main harbour, with the Crete ferry agencies.

All international **trains** arrive at the Stathmós Laríssis, just to the northwest of the city centre. There are hotels in this area or you can take yellow trolley bus (#1) immediately outside to reach Síntagma square.

Baggage
If you are just spending the day in Athens, and want to **store your baggage**, you can do so for 200dr per piece at *Pacific Ltd*, Nikis 26 – just off Síndagma (Mon–Sat 7am–8pm, Sun 7am–2pm).

ACCOMMODATION
Finding **somewhere to stay** in Athens is unlikely to be a major problem except at the very height of summer – though it's best to phone ahead. A small selection of places are listed below – you can book more upmarket rooms through the hotel reservations desk inside the National Bank of Greece on Síndagma square. There is also a **Tourist Office** inside the National Bank, which can supply you with maps of the city.

If you're only in town for a quick stay, **Pláka**, the oldest quarter of the city, is the best area. It spreads south of Síndagma square, is in easy walking range of the Acropolis, and has lots of outdoor restaurants and cafés. It's possible to **stay** in the port of Pireás, too, though since most Crete ferries leave late in the evening, and arrive at Pireás early morning, there's no real need, and you might as well make the most of your time in Athens.

All the listings below are in the Pláka; price categories are for a double room in high season:

4000–6000dr
George's Guest House, Níkis 46 (**☎**32 26 474).
John's Place, Patróou 5 (**☎**32 29 719).
Solonion, Spírou Tsangari 11 (**☎**32 20 008).

6000–8000dr
Dioskouri, Pittákou 6 (**☎**32 48 165).
Kouros, Kódhrou 11 (**☎**32 27 431).
Phaedra, Herefóndos 16 (**☎**32 27 795).

8000–16000dr
Acropolis House, Kódhrou 6 (**☎**32 22 344).
Adonis, Kódhrou 3 (**☎**32 49 737).
Myrto, Níkis 40 (**☎**32 27 237).
Nefeli, Iperídhou 16 (**☎**32 28 044).

EATING AND DRINKING

Pláka is bursting with touristy restaurants, most very pleasantly situated but poor value. Three with nice sites and good food are *Kouklis* (Tripíodhon 14), *O Platanos* (Dhioyénous 4) and *ly Klimataria* (Klepsídhras 5). *Eden* (liossíou 12) is a decent vegetarian restaurant.

THE CITY AND SIGHTS

Central Athens is a compact, easily walkable area. Its hub is **Síndagma Square** (Platía Sintágmatos), flanked by the Parliament, banks and airline offices, and, as mentioned, the National Bank with the Tourist Office. Pretty much everything you'll want to see in a fleeting visit – the Acropolis, Pláka, the major museums – is within 20–30 minutes' walk of here. Just east of the square, too, are the **National Gardens** – the nicest spot in town for a siesta.

Pláka and the Bazaar

Walk south from Síndagma, along Níkis or Filellínon streets, and you'll find yourself in Pláka, the surviving area of the nineteenth-century, pre-Independence, village. Largely pedestrianized, it is a delightful area just to wander around – and it is the approach to the Acropolis.

For a bit of focus to your walk, take in the fourth-century BC **Monument of Lysikrates**, used as a study by Byron, to the east, and the Roman-era **Tower of the Winds** (Aéridhes), to the west. The latter adjoins the Roman forum. Climb north from the Tower of the Winds and you reach **Anafiótika**, with its whitewashed Cycladic-style cottages (built by workers from the island of Anáfi) and the eclectic **Kanellópoulos Museum** (Tues–Sun 8.30am–2.45pm; 400dr).

Head north from the Roman Forum, along Athinás or Eólou streets, and you come to an equally characterful part of the city – the **bazaar** area. This shows Athens in its Near Eastern lights. The best bit is the old Central Market Building, on the corner of Athinás and Evripídhou. **Monastiráki square** is worth a look, too, with its Turkish mosque. On Sundays a genuine **Flea Market** sprawls to its west, out beyond the tourist shops promoted as the "Athens Flea Market".

The Acropolis and Ancient Agora

Even with a few hours to spare between flight and ferry, you can take in a visit to the **Acropolis** (Mon–Fri 8am–6.45pm/5pm summer/winter, Sat & Sun 8.30am–2.45pm; 1500dr/students 800dr). The complex of temples, rebuilt by Pericles in the Golden Age of the Fifth Century BC, is focused on the famed Parthenon. This, and the smaller Athena Nike and Erechtheion temples are given context by a small museum housing some of the original statuary left behind by Lord Elgin.

If you have more time, make your way down to the **Theatre of Dionysos**, on the south slope (Mon–Sat 9am–2.45pm, Sun 9am–1.45pm; 400dr), and/or the Ancient (Classical Greek-era) **Agora**, northwest of the Acropolis hill (Tues–Sun 8.30am–2.45pm; 800dr), presided over by the Doric **Thiseion**, or Temple of Hephaestus.

Museums

As a preparation for Crete's ancient sites, two of Athens's museums are especially worth visiting. Most importantly, the **National Archeological Museum** (Patissíon 28; Mon 12.30–6.45pm, Tues–Fri 8am–6.45pm; Sat & Sun 8.30am–12.45pm; 1500dr, students 750dr) contains, upstairs, the brilliant Minoan frescoes from Thíra (Santoríni). Even more spectacular than anything surviving on Crete itself, these were also important evidence in the earthquake theory of the Minoan destruction. The Mycenaean treasures downstairs are also relevant to Crete, besides being great in their own right.

The **Benáki Museum** (Koumbári 1; 8.30am–2pm; closed Tues) is wonderful on a much smaller scale and has some fascinating material on Venizélos and the rebellions against the Turks.

ON TO CRETE: PIREÁS

Pireás (Piraeus), the port of Athens, is the last stop on the single-line **metro**, which you can board at Omónia or Monastiráki squares. The journey takes about 25 minutes – trains run from 5.30am to midnight – and there's a flat fare of 75dr. If you're travelling by rail from Pátra, the train continues through Athens down to Pireás. **Taxis** cost around 100dr from the city centre or the airport.

You can buy **ferry tickets** from agencies at the harbour in Pireás, or in central Athens (there are several outlets on Lefóros Amalías, which runs south of Síndagma square). Wherever you buy from, make sure you get a ticket on one of the main lines (*ANEK*, *Minoan* or *Rethymnakí*), which are fast, efficient and direct.

The **ferries for Crete** leave from the main harbour, just south of the metro station (see p.18). You can get a meal, or buy **provisions for the trip**, all around the port; prices tend to be lower if you head inland a block or two.

a ticket (credit card will do) in order to get on the stand-by list: if, in the end, you don't manage to fly they should give you a full refund. Once you're on the list, despite appearances, the system works pretty well – just make sure you are by the departure gate when they call out the names of the lucky few for each flight.

There are four flights a week from **Rhodes to Iráklion**, and three a week **from Thessaloníki**, as well as regular flights from some of the smaller islands. All of these, again, tend to be heavily booked, and the short hops are relatively expensive.

BY FERRY

The vast majority of ferry traffic to Crete goes **from Pireás** (the port of Athens), though there are also services from the Peloponnese and from many of the Cycladic and Dodecanese islands.

The cheapest class of ticket is **deck class**, variously called *tríti* or *gámma*. This gives you the run of most boats except for the upper-class restaurant and bar. Seats and cabins (see facing page) are also available on all lines sailing between Pireás and Iráklion. The service to Crete is daily throughout the year, with additional sailings in summer; most leave in the evening (see below) but you can check current schedules with the ferry agents in Pireás, listed in the box opposite.

FROM PIREÁS

The **ferries for Crete** leave from the heart of the port, not far to the south of the metro station – simply turn left and follow the harbour round. If you've arrived by bus get someone to point you in the right direction, basically down the hill from Platía Koraí.

Two major lines operate on this route, *ANEK* and *Minoan*, each with a daily ferry to Iráklion and to Haniá (though *Minoan* sometimes runs only one ferry to Haniá, in which case services are on Mon, Wed, Fri and Sat). In theory the *Minoan* ferries leave at 6.30pm and the *ANEK* ones half an hour later, but in practice they race to be first out of the harbour and continue jostling for position all the way to Crete, where they arrive around twelve

FERRY LINKS

---

hours later (sooner in good weather). There's virtually nothing to choose between the two: both charge around £15/US$23 for a deck-class passenger, £30–50/US$45–75 for a small car. *Rethymniaki* also offers a service from Pireás to Réthimnon, with departures Monday, Wednesday and Friday at 7.15pm, Sunday at 8am. Beware of tickets offered on any other line – these will almost certainly involve a roundabout route through the Cyclades and take twice as long.

It's a matter of opinion whether it's worth paying extra for a berth or cabin on the overnight journey. The older ferries' sleeping quarters tend to be airless and thoroughly unpleasant on an Aegean summer night, while the newer ones are efficiently air-conditioned and far more comfortable. Travelling on deck (or in the seats available to deck-class passengers) can be fine – even idyllic in the right conditions – but it can also be crowded, noisy and cold. If you do go this way, embark early to claim some space. The Aegean is usually calm and comfortable, but high winds (especially in Aug) sometimes make for a very queasy crossing.

FROM THE PELOPONNESE

Much the most useful of the other services is that from the **Peloponnese to Kastélli Kisámou**, on

the *Theseus*, a boat operated by *Miras Ferries* (see box above). On its basic summer schedule this runs twice a week from Kalamáta, on Wednesday and Saturday nights (from mid-July to end Aug thrice weekly, Wed noon, Thurs morning and Sat night); from Yíthio on Tuesday afternoon and Saturday morning; from Neápoli Tuesday and Saturday around 1am; and from Monemvassía Monday and Friday nights. Some of these services go via the island of Kíthira, and most operate just once a week in winter.

OTHER ROUTES

You can also get to Iráklion from the larger of the **Cycladic** islands (daily from Thíra) and from **Rhodes**; and to Sitía and Áyios Nikólaos from Rhodes and the Dodecanese. There's also a weekly service to Iráklion from **Israel and Cyprus**. All of these ferries are included in the "Travel Details" at the end of each regional chapter.

It's worth knowing that boats to Crete from or via the Greek islands are invariably behind schedule (4hr late is normal), as Crete is the last stop. For up-to-date sailing times, check with the shipping agents or port police in Pireás. The EOT office in Síndagma Square in Athens publishes a regularly updated schedule of sailings from Pireás.

TRAVELLERS WITH DISABILITIES

It is all too easy to wax lyrical over the attractions of Crete: the stepped, narrow alleys, the thrill of clambering around the great archeological sites. It is almost impossible, on the other hand, for the able-bodied travel writer to see these attractions as potential hazards for anyone who has some difficulty in walking or is wheelchair-bound or suffers from some other disability.

However, don't be discouraged. It is possible to enjoy an inexpensive and trauma-free holiday on the island if some time is devoted to gathering **information** before arrival. However, much existing or readily available information is out of date – you should always try to double-check. A number of addresses of contact organizations are published opposite. The *National Tourist Organization of Greece* is a good first step as long as you have specific questions to put to them; they publish a useful questionnaire which you could send to hotels or owners of apartment/villa accommodation.

PLANNING A HOLIDAY

There are **organized tours and holidays** specifically for people with disabilities – both *Thomsons* and *Horizon* in Britain will advise on the suitability of holidays advertised in their brochures. If you want to be more independent, it's perfectly possible, provided that you do not leave home with the vague hope that things will turn out all right, and that "people will help out" when you need assistance. This cannot be relied on. You must either be completely confident that you can manage alone, or travel with an able-bodied friend (or two).

It's important to become an authority on where you must be self-reliant and where you may expect help, especially regarding transport and accommodation. For example, to get between the terminals at Athens airport, you will have to fight for a taxi; it is not the duty of the airline staff to find you one, and there is no trace of an organized queue.

It is also vital to **be honest** – with travel agencies, insurance companies, companions, and, above all, with yourself. Know your limitations and make sure others know them. If you do not use a wheelchair all the time but your walking capabilities are limited, remember that you are likely to need to cover greater distances while travelling (often over tougher terrain and in hotter weather than you are used to). If you use one, take a wheelchair with you, have it serviced before you go, and carry a repair kit.

Read your travel **insurance** small print carefully to make sure that people with a pre-existing medical condition are not excluded. And use your travel agent to make your journey simpler: **airlines** or bus companies can cope better if they are expecting you, with a wheelchair provided at airports and staff primed to help. A **medical certificate** of your fitness to travel, provided by your doctor, is also extremely useful; some airlines or insurance companies may insist on it.

Make a **list** of all the facilities that will make your life easier while you are away. You may want a ground-floor room, or access to a large elevator; you may have special dietary requirements, or need level ground to enable you to reach stores, beaches, bars, and places of interest. You should also keep track of all your other special needs, making sure, for example, that you have extra supplies of drugs – carried with you if you fly – and a prescription including the generic name in case of emergency. Carry spares of any kind of drug, clothing or equipment that might be hard to find in Crete; if there's an association representing people with your disability, contact them early in the planning process.

USEFUL CONTACTS

National Tourist Organization of Greece : See p.29 for addresses.
Offers general advice on terrain and climate. They have nothing specific for disabled visitors except a brief list of hotels which may be suitable.

GREECE

Association Hermes, Patriarchou 13, Grigouiou E, 16542, Argyroupolis (☎01/99-61-887). *Can advise disabled visitors to Greece.*

Evyenia Stravropoulou, Lavinia Tours: Egnatía 101, 541 10 Thessaloníki (☎031/240-041). *Will advise disabled visitors and has tested many parts of Greece in her wheelchair. She also organizes tours within Greece.*

UK

Holiday Care Service, 2 Old Bank Chambers, Station Rd, Horley, Surrey RH6 9HW (☎01293/774535).
Publishes a fact sheet, and also runs a useful "Holiday Helpers" service for disabled travellers.

Mobility International, 228 Borough High St, London SE1 1JX (☎0171/403 5688)
Issues a quarterly newsletter on developments in disabled travel.

Opus 23, Sourdock Hill, Barkisland, Halifax, West Yorkshire HX4 0AG (☎01422/375999).
Part of Grecofile; will advise on and arrange independent holidays, or for those with carers.

RADAR: 25 Mortimer St, London W1N 8AB (☎0171/250 3222).
Publishes fact sheets and an annual guide to international travel for the disabled.

Tripscope, Evelyn Rd, London W4 5JL (☎0181/994 9294).
Transport advice to most countries for all disabilities.

NORTH AMERICA

Directions Unlimited, 720 N Bedford Rd, Bedford Hills, NY 10507 (☎1-800/533-5343).
Tour operator specializing in custom tours for people with disabilities.

Information Center for People with Disabilities, Fort Point Place, 27-43 Wormwood St, Boston, MA 02210 (☎617/727-5540; TDD ☎617/345-9743).
Clearing house for information, including travel, primarily in Massachusetts.

Jewish Rehabilitation Hospital, 3205 Place Alton Goldbloom, Montréal, PQ H7V 1R2 (☎514/688-9550, ext 226).
Guidebooks and travel information.

Kéroul, 4545 Ave Pierre de Coubertin, CP 1000, Station M, Montréal, PQ H1V 3R2 (☎514/252-3104).
Organization promoting and facilitating travel for mobility-impaired people, primarily in Québec.

Mobility International USA, PO Box 10767, Eugene, OR 97440 (Voice and TDD: ☎503/343-1284).
Information and referral services, access guides, tours and exchange programmes.

Society for the Advancement of Travel for the Handicapped (SATH), 347 Fifth Ave, New York, NY 10016 (☎212/447-7284).
Non-profit travel-industry referral service that passes queries on to its members as appropriate; allow plenty of time for a response.

Travel Information Service, Moss Rehabilitation Hospital, 1200 West Tabor Rd, Philadelphia, PA 19141 (☎215/456-9600).
Telephone information and referral service.

Twin Peaks Press, Box 129, Vancouver, WA 98666; ☎206/694-2462 or 1-800/637-2256).
Publisher of the Directory of Travel Agencies for the Disabled, listing more than 370 agencies worldwide; Travel for the Disabled; the Directory of Accessible Van Rentals and Wheelchair Vagabond, loaded with personal tips.

AUSTRALIA

ACROD, PO Box 60, Curtain, ACT 2605 (☎06/682 4333).

Barrier Free Travel, 36 Wheatley St, North Bellingen, NSW 2454 (☎066/551733).

NEW ZEALAND

Disabled Persons Assembly, PO Box 10–138, The Terrace, Wellington (☎04/472 2626).

VISAS AND RED TAPE

UK and all other EU nationals need only a valid passport for entry to Greece; you are no longer stamped in on arrival or out upon departure, and in theory at least enjoy uniform civil rights with Greek citizens. US, Australian, New Zealand and Canadian citizens, and most other Europeans, receive entry and exit stamps in their passports and can stay, as tourists, for ninety days.

If you are planning to **travel overland**, you should check current visa requirements for France and Italy, or Hungary, Romania and Bulgaria; transit visas for most of these territories are at present issued at the borders, though at a higher price than if obtained in advance at a local consulate.

GREEK EMBASSIES ABROAD

Australia 9 Turrana St, Yarralumla, Canberra, ACT 2600 (☎062/273-3011).

Britain 1a Holland Park, London W11 (☎0171/221 6467).

Canada 80 Maclaren St, Ottawa, ON K2P 0K6 (☎613/238-6271).

Ireland 1 Upper Pembroke St, Dublin 2 (☎01/767254).

New Zealand Cumberland House, 237 Willis St, PO Box 27157, Wellington (☎04/847-556).

USA 2221 Massachusetts Ave NW, Washington, DC 20008 (☎202/667-3168).

VISA EXTENSIONS

If you wish to stay in Crete (or elsewhere in Greece) for longer than three months, you should officially apply for an **extension**. This can be done through the *Ipiresía Allodhapón* (Aliens' Bureau) in Iráklion; prepare yourself for concerted bureaucracy. Elsewhere you visit the local police station, where staff are apt to be more cooperative.

Visitors from **non-EU countries**, unless of Greek descent, are currently allowed only one six-month extension to a tourist visa, which costs 11,000dr. In theory, **EU nationals** are allowed to stay indefinitely but, at the time of writing, must still present themselves every six months or year, according to whether they have a non-employment resident visa or a work permit; the first extension is free, but you will be charged for subsequent extensions.

In all cases, the procedure should be set in motion a couple of weeks before your time runs out – and, if you don't have a work permit, you will be required to present pink, personalized bank **exchange receipts** (see "Costs, Money and Banks", p.25) totalling at least 45,000dr for the preceding three months, as proof that you have sufficient funds to support yourself without working.

Some individuals get around the law by leaving Greece every three months and re-entering a few days later for a new tourist stamp. However, security and immigration personnel don't always look very kindly on this practice.

If you **overstay** your time and then leave voluntarily, you'll be given a 22,000dr spot fine upon departure, effectively a double-priced retroactive visa extension – no excuses will be entertained.

CUSTOMS REGULATIONS

For anyone travelling between EU countries, limits on goods which have been already taxed

Several countries maintain **foreign consulates in Iráklion** – British at Papalexándrou 16 (☎224-012), Dutch at 25 Avgoústou 23 (☎246-202), German at Zografóu 7 (☎226-288), Norwegian at Platía Ay. Dimítriou 24 (☎220-536) – for other nationalities, refer to the embassy in Athens.

have been relaxed enormously. However, **duty-free allowances** are as follows: two hundred cigarettes or fifty cigars, two litres of still table wine, one litre of spirits and 60ml of perfume. When leaving Greece for your home country, your normal domestic Customs and Excise regulations apply.

Exporting **antiquities** without a permit is a serious offence; **drug smuggling**, it goes without saying, incurs severe penalties.

INSURANCE

British and other EU nationals are officially entitled to free medical care in Greece upon presentation of an E111 form (see "Health Matters" pp.27–8). "Free", however, means admittance only to the lowest grade of state hospital and does not include nursing care or the cost of medications. If you need prolonged medical care, you'll prefer to make use of private treatment, which is expensive.

Some form of **travel insurance**, therefore, is advisable – and essential for **North Americans and Australasians**, whose countries have no formal health-care agreements with Greece (other than allowing for free emergency trauma treatment).

For **medical claims**, keep receipts, including those from pharmacies. You will have to pay for all private medical care on the spot (insurance claims can be processed if you have hospital treatment) but it can all be (eventually) claimed back. Travel insurance usually provides cover for the **loss of baggage, money and tickets**, too. If you're thinking of **renting a moped** or motorbike in Greece, make sure the policy covers motorbike accidents.

In all cases of loss or theft of goods, you will have to contact the local police to have a **report** made out so that your insurer can process the claim. This can occasionally be a tricky business in Greece, since many officials simply won't accept that anything could be stolen on their turf, or at least don't want to take responsibility for it. Be persistent and if necessary enlist the support of the local tourist police or tourist office.

EUROPEAN COVER

In Britain, there are a number of low-cost specialist insurance companies including *Endsleigh*, 97–107 Southampton Row, London WC1 (☎0171/436 4451), *Campus Travel*, 52 Grosvenor Gardens, London SW1 (☎0171/730 3402), and *Columbus*, 17 Devonshire Square, London EC2 (☎0171/375 0111). At all of these you can buy two weeks' basic cover in Greece for around £15, £22 for a month.

Most **banks** and **credit card** issuers also offer some sort of vacation insurance, often automatic if you pay for the holiday with a card. In these circumstances, it's vital to check what the policy actually covers.

NORTH AMERICAN COVER

Before buying an insurance policy, check that you're not already covered. **Canadians** are usually covered for medical mishaps overseas by their provincial health plans. Holders of official student/teacher/youth cards are entitled to accident coverage and hospital in-patient benefits. **Students** will often find that their student health coverage extends during the vacations and for one term beyond the date of last enrolment. Bank and credit cards (particularly *American Express*) often have levels of medical or other insurance included, and travel insurance may also be included if you use a major credit or charge card to pay for your trip. **Homeowners' or renters'** insurance often covers theft or loss of documents, money and valuables while overseas, though conditions and maximum amounts vary from company to company.

After exhausting the possibilities above, you might want to contact a specialist **travel insurance** company; your travel agent can usually recommend one, or see the box below. Policies are comprehensive (accidents, illnesses, delayed or lost luggage, cancelled flights, etc), but maximum payouts tend to be meagre. Premiums vary, so shop around. The best deals are usually to be had through student/youth travel agencies – *ISIS* policies, for example, cost US$48–69 for fifteen days (depending on coverage), US$80–105 for a month, US$149–207 for two months, and up to US$510–700 for a year.

Most North American travel policies apply only to items lost, stolen or damaged while in the custody of an identifiable, responsible third party – hotel porter, airline, left luggage, etc. Even in these cases you will have to contact the local police within a certain time limit to have a complete report made out so that your insurer can process the claim. Note also that very few insurers will arrange on-the-spot payments in the event of a major expense or loss; you will usually be reimbursed only after going home.

AUSTRALIAN COVER

In **Australia**, *CIC Insurance*, offered by *Cover-More Insurance Services* (Level 9, 32 Walker St, North Sydney; ☎02/202 8000; branches in Victoria and Queensland), has some of the widest cover available and can be arranged through most travel agents. It costs from AUS$140 for 31 days.

TRAVEL INSURANCE COMPANIES IN NORTH AMERICA

Access America, PO Box 90310, Richmond, VA 23230 (☎1-800/284-8300).

Carefree Travel Insurance, PO Box 310, 120 Mineola Blvd, Mineola, NY 11501 (☎1-800/323-3149).

International Student Insurance Service (ISIS) – sold by *STA Travel*, see "Getting There from North America" for addresses.

Travel Assistance International, 1133 15th St NW, Suite 400, Washington, DC 20005 (☎1-800/ 821-2828).

Travel Guard, 1145 Clark St, Stevens Point, WI 54481 (☎1-800/826-1300).

Travel Insurance Services, 2930 Camino Diablo, Suite 300, Walnut Creek, CA 94596 (☎1-800/937-1387).

COSTS, MONEY AND BANKS

Although Crete is no longer *really* cheap, it remains inexpensive in comparison with anywhere in northern Europe and, if you're willing to cut a few corners and avoid the more overtly developed areas, you can get by on relatively little.

Prices depend on where and when you go. The cities and tourist resorts are usually more expensive and costs increase in July, August and at Easter. **Solo travellers** invariably spend more than if they were sharing food and rooms. An additional frustration is the relative lack of single rooms. **Students** with an *International Student Identity Card* (*ISIC*) can get free – or fifty-percent discount off – admission fees at most archeological sites and museums. These, and other occasional discounts, tend to be more readily available to EU students. A *FIYTO* card (available to non-students under 26) has fewer benefits, though is still worth having – both cards are available from student/youth travel agencies.

SOME BASIC COSTS

In most places, it should be possible to manage on around £12–15/US$18–22 a day, assuming you're prepared to camp and rough it a little; whilst on £15–20/US$22–30 a day you can start to enjoy some comfort. With a budget of £25/US$38 you won't have to worry too much about watching the pennies.

Buses on Crete are efficient and still fairly cheap, although fares are rising. Travelling the length of the island, from Haniá to Sitía, costs around £12/US$18 one way. You should always be able to find a basic **room** for two for around £10/US$15 a night, although popular tourist venues like Áyios Nikólaos are more expensive in high season, and the coast is generally pricier than the inland areas and the mountains. **Single accommodation**, too, is rare and much poorer value (you'll often have to pay the full double price). **Campsites** cost about £2/US$3 a person or less and, with discretion, you can camp on your own near the beaches for free, although you should be sensitive to increasing local concerns about squalor and rubbish. A solid **taverna meal**, even with considerable quantities of local wine, should rarely work out much above £6/US$9 a head, though if you're eating seafood in a touristy place you can pay more than double that.

CURRENCY AND EXCHANGE

Greek currency is the **drachma** (*Dhrahmí*), with the **exchange rate** at present around 380 to the pound, 240 to the US dollar.

The most common **notes** in circulation are those of 50, 100, 500, 1000 and 5000 drachmas (*dhrahmés*) with a 10,000 note due shortly; while **coins** come in denominations of 5, 10, 20, 50, and 100; you might come across 1dr and 2dr coins, though they're rarely used these days. The airports at Haniá and Iráklion should always have an exchange booth operating for passengers on incoming international flights, but it's well worth taking some local currency to tide you over the first few hours.

Restrictions on taking currency in and out of Greece have in theory been lifted, at least within the EU, but if you plan to bring in large quantities of cash it's best to declare it so that there are no problems taking it back out again. If you have any reason to believe that you'll be acquiring large quantities of drachmas – from work or sale of goods – declare everything on arrival, then request, and keep, the pink, personalized **receipts** for each exchange transaction. Otherwise you may find that you can only re-exchange a limited sum of drachmas on departure. These pink receipts are also essential for obtaining a visa extension (see "Visas and Red Tape", p.22).

CHANGING MONEY

Travellers cheques are accepted at all banks and, when they're closed, at quite a number of hotels, agencies and tourist stores. If you intend to spend much time away from the bigger centres, though, you should plan to have a fair amount of currency to hand. **Eurocheques** supported by a Eurocheque card are also honoured at Greek banks and post offices – and are probably the easiest way of all to carry your money – but they're not widely accepted by stores.

Banks on Crete are normally open Mon–Thurs 8am–2pm, Fri 8am–1.30pm. Certain branches in the tourist centres open extra hours in the evenings and Saturday mornings to change money. Always take your passport with you as proof of identity and be prepared for at least one long queue – often you have to line up once to have the transaction approved and again to pick up the cash. **Commissions** can vary considerably (400–800dr per transaction is typical), even between branches of the same bank, so ask first. Remember, though, that both commission and rate will be worse if you change money at a hotel or travel agent.

Two alternatives to banks are **travel agents** and **official tourist offices**. The former often serve as general purpose information centres in smaller resorts and will change travellers cheques and banknotes. Although they're likely to be trustworthy it's a good idea to have a rough idea in your mind of what the official exchange rate is. The government tourist offices are to be found in most of the major centres and usually stay open until quite late in the evening; they offer exchange facilities at a rate similar to (and sometimes better than) the banks.

Exchanging money at the **post office** also has considerable advantages in Greece. You miss out on the queues at banks and have access to exchange almost anywhere you go. Many out-of-the-way places will have a post office but no bank. Commissions levied for both travellers cheques and cash tend, at about 300dr per transaction, to be lower than at the banks. If you have a post office **giro account** you will be able to draw money out at almost any post office in Crete.

CREDIT CARDS, ATMS AND EMERGENCY MONEY

Major **credit cards** are widely accepted, but only by the more expensive stores, hotels and restaurants: they're useful for renting cars, for example, but no good in the cheaper tavernas or rooms places. If you run short of money, you can also get a **cash advance on a credit card**, though there's a minimum limit of around 15,000drs (about £40/US$60): the *Emborikí Trápeza* (Commercial Bank), *Trápeza Pisteos* (Credit Bank) and *Ioniki Trápeza* (Ionic Bank) handle *Visa/American Express*; whilst the *Ethnikí Trápeza* (National Bank) acts for *Mastercard*. Some private exchange places will also give advances on credit cards, with a lower minimum, but they may charge more.

It's much easier to use the network of 24-hour **ATMs**, although these are presently confined to the major towns along the north coast; and, due to the frequency of power and computer failures, you'd be wise not to rely solely on this means of getting hold of cash. Check with your bank whether your card offers this facility before relying on it, too.

Failing this, you'll have to arrange to have **money wired** from home in an emergency. Though this is theoretically very quick, you should in practice count on delays of three to six days for receipt of telexed funds. You can pick up the sum in foreign currency, or even travellers cheques, but there tend to be heavy commissions.

HEALTH MATTERS

There are no required inoculations for Greece, though it's wise to have a typhoid-cholera booster, and to ensure that you are up to date on tetanus and polio. Don't forget to take out travel insurance (see "Insurance", pp.23–4), so that you're covered in case of serious illness or accidents.

The **water** is safe pretty much everywhere, despite the fact that everyone drinks the bottled stuff instead. Crete has few of the **water shortages** which bedevil smaller islands – it's only in isolated villages or resorts that have grown faster than the plumbing can cope with that you're likely to come across any problem.

SPECIFIC HEALTH PROBLEMS

The main **health problems** experienced by most visitors have to do with overexposure to the sun, and the odd nasty creature from the sea. To combat the former, wear a hat and drink plenty of fluids in the hot months to avoid any danger of **sunstroke**, and don't underestimate the power of even a hazy sun to burn. **Hayfever** sufferers should be prepared for an earlier season than at home. For protection against perils at sea, a pair of goggles for swimming and footwear for walking over wet rocks are useful.

HAZARDS OF THE DEEP

You may just have the bad luck to meet an armada of **jellyfish**, especially in late summer; they come in various colours and sizes including

invisible and minute. Various over-the-counter remedies are sold in resort pharmacies; baking soda or ammonia also help to lessen the sting.

Less vicious but more common are **sea urchins**, which infest rocky shorelines year round; if you are unlucky enough to step on, or graze one, a sterilized needle and olive oil are effective for removing spines from your anatomy. The worst maritime danger – fortunately very rare – seems to be the **weever fish**, which buries itself in tidal zone sand with just its poisonous dorsal and gill spines protruding. If you tread on one the sudden pain is unmistakably excruciating, and the venom is exceptionally potent. Consequences can range up to permanent paralysis of the affected area, so the imperative first aid is to immerse your foot in as hot water as you can stand. This degrades the toxin and relieves the swelling of joints and attendant pain.

MOSQUITOS

While **mosquitos** (*kounóupia*) don't carry anything worse than a vicious bite, they can be infuriating in places. The best solution is to burn pyrethrum incense coils (*spíres* or *fidhákia* in Greek), widely and cheaply available on Crete. If you're going to be staying in hotels you can also use an electrical device, called a *Vape-Nat* in Greece, which activates a chemical tablet. These are widely available from pharmacies, for much less than they cost at home. A recently developed refinement of this contraption uses a 40-day fluid cartridge rather than tablets; it sells on the island under the name *Baygon*. Whilst eating or drinking outdoors, a rub-on stick such as *Autan*, is equally effective.

MEDICAL ATTENTION

For **minor complaints** it's enough to go to the local *farmakío*. Greek **pharmacists** are highly trained and dispense a number of medicines which in other countries can only be prescribed by a doctor. In the larger towns there'll usually be one who speaks good English. If you regularly use any **prescription drug** you should bring along a copy of the prescription together with the generic name of the drug – this will help should you need to replace it and also avoid possible problems with Customs officials.* **Homeopathic and herbal** remedies are also widely available: there are homeopathic pharmacies in Iráklion and Haniá, and probably elsewhere too.

DOCTORS AND HOSPITALS

For serious medical attention you'll find English-speaking **doctors** in any of the bigger towns or resorts: the tourist police or your consulate should be able to come up with some names if you have any difficulty.

British and other EU nationals are officially entitled to **free medical care** in Greece, by

---

*A warning needs to be sounded about codeine, which is illegal in Greece. If you import any – and it is fairly common in headache drugs including Codeine, Panadeine, Veganin, Solpadeine and Codis – you just might find yourself in serious trouble. So check labels carefully.

---

virtue of the E111 form, available from post offices – but "free" means admittance to only the lowest grade of **state hospital** (known as a *yenikó nosokomeío*). In practice, however, hospital staff tend to greet E111s with uncomprehending looks, and you may have to request reimbursal by the NHS upon return home. Basic treatment for cuts, broken bones and emergencies is given, but extended care and nursing will be virtually non-existent; Greek families take in food and bedding for relatives so as a tourist you'll face difficulties.

Rather better are the ordinary **state outpatient clinics** (*yatría*) attached to most hospitals and also found in rural locales; these operate on a first-come-first-served basis, so go early – usual hours are 8am–noon. Again, EU citizens are eligible for free treatment; without an E111, outpatient clinics make a small charge.

INFORMATION AND MAPS

The National Tourist Organization of Greece (*Ellinikós Organismós Tourismóu*, EOT) is the obvious first stop for information on Crete, even though few of their glossy pamphlets apply exclusively to the island. Go armed with specific questions, or you'll simply be given the general leaflet on Crete, which has plenty of pictures, a very small-scale map, and hardly any hard information at all. They may also have up-to-date bus and ferry timetables and prices.

The National Tourist Organization maintains **offices** in most European capitals (though not Dublin), Australia and North America.; see the box on the facing pages for addresses.

TOURIST INFORMATION

On the island, there are EOT offices in Iráklion (p.60), Haniá (p.220) and Réthimnon (p.177). Where there is no EOT office, you can get information (and often a range of leaflets) from municipally run **tourist offices** or from the **tourist police**. The latter are basically a branch (often just a single delegate) of the local police and deal with complaints about restaurants, taxis, hotels and all things tourist-related; call ☎104 for information and help, and see individual towns for local addresses.. They can also sometimes provide you with lists of rooms to rent, which they regulate. In addition, local **travel agencies** are always helpful.

MAPS

Island **maps** are available locally, but you'll almost certainly find a better one at home. None seems to be particularly accurate when it comes to minor roads and footpaths: the *Nelles* and *Freytag & Berndt* (the latter is generally to be

---

EOT OFFICES ABROAD

Australia
51 Pitt St, Sydney, NSW 2000 (☎02/241-1663).

Britain
4 Conduit St, London W1R 0DJ (☎0171/734 5997).

Canada
1300 Bay St, Main Level, Toronto, ON M5R 3K8 (☎416/968-2220).

1223 rue de la Montagne, QCH 3G, Montréal (☎514/871-1535).

Denmark
Copenhagen Vester Farimagsgade 1,2 DK 1606-Kobenhavn V (☎325-332).

Netherlands
Leidsestraat 13, NS 1017 Amsterdam (☎20/254-212).

Norway
Ovre Stottsgate 15B, 0157 Oslo 1 (☎2/426-501).

Sweden
Grev Turigatan 2, PO Box 5298, 10246 Stockholm (☎8/679 6480).

USA
645 Fifth Ave, New York, NY 10022 (☎212/421-5777).

168 N Michigan Ave, Chicago, IL (☎312/782-1084).

611 W 6th St, Los Angeles, CA (☎213/626-6696).

If your home country isn't listed here, apply to the embassy. Note that there are no Greek tourist offices in Ireland or New Zealand.

---

had on the island under the *Efstathiadis Group* imprint) offerings are the clearest for general use.

Until recently more detailed **hiking/topographical maps** were virtually non-existent. The 1:200,000 maps of the National Statistical Service (*Ethnikí Statistikí Ipiresía*), occasionally available in specialist shops, are so out of date as to be almost entirely worthless. However, an enterprising German publisher *Harms-Verlag* has now brought out a **1:80,000 five-map set** (*Crete Tourist Map*) covering the whole island, with footpaths marked and including many topographical features missing from other publications. It seems to have been based on the *Military Geographical Service* maps (see below) and is available from bookshops in Iráklion, Réthimnon and Haniá, or *Stanfords* (see box over) in London by mail order. Mountainous zones are also covered by the Greek mountaineering magazine *Korfés* (16 Platía Ayíou Vlassíou in the Athens suburb of Aharnés; ☎246-1528) which

covers Crete in its 1:50,000 series of alpine areas. More than thirty now exist and a new one is issued every other month as a centrefold in the magazine, which is sold at many newsstands. Recently production of Roman-lettered maps began, but you have to go out to the Aharnés office to get these.

The maps are extremely accurate, based as they are on the generally unavailable maps of the **Hellenic Military Geographical Service**. If you want to try your luck at obtaining these, visit the HMGS at Evelpídhon 4, north of Areos Park in Athens, Monday, Wednesday or Friday from 11.30am to 2pm only. If the officer in charge decides you have a legitimate reason to procure a map or two (not more) he will authorize your purchase, but you must sign a statement declaring that you won't sell, give away, export, photocopy or trace said map(s), under penalty of two years' imprisonment! You'd also better speak good Greek or send a Greek friend to get them for you.

MAP OUTLETS

UK

London

National Map Centre, 22–24 Caxton St, SW1 (☎0171/222 4945);

Stanfords, 12–14 Long Acre, WC2 (☎0171/836 1321);

The Travellers Bookshop, 25 Cecil Court, WC2 (☎0171/836 9132).

Edinburgh

Thomas Nelson and Sons Ltd, 51 York Place, EH1 3JD (☎0131/557 3011).

Glasgow

John Smith and Sons, 57–61 St Vincent St (☎0141/221 7472).

Maps by **mail or phone order** are available from *Stanfords* (☎0171/836 1321).

USA

Chicago

Rand McNally, 444 N Michigan Ave, IL 60611; ☎312/321-1751.

New York

British Travel Bookshop, 551 Fifth Ave, NY 10176; ☎1-800/448-3039 or 212/490-6688.

The Complete Traveler Bookstore, 199 Madison Ave, NY 10016; ☎212/685-9007.

Rand McNally, 150 E 52nd St, NY 10022; ☎212/758-7488.

Traveler's Bookstore, 22 W 52nd St, NY 10019; ☎212/664-0995.

San Francisco

The Complete Traveler Bookstore, 3207 Fillmore St, CA 92123; ☎415/923-1511.

Rand McNally, 595 Market St, CA 94105; ☎415/777-3131.

Santa Barbara

Pacific Traveler Supply, 529 State St, 93101; ☎805/963-4438 (phone orders: ☎805/965-4402).

Seattle

Elliot Bay Book Company, 101 S Main St, WA 98104; ☎206/624-6600.

Washington DC

Rand McNally, 1201 Connecticut Ave NW, Washington, DC 20036; ☎202/223-6751.

Note: *Rand McNally* now has more than 20 stores across the US; call ☎1-800/333-0136 (ext 2111) for the address of your nearest store, or for **direct mail** maps.

CANADA

Montréal

Ulysses Travel Bookshop, 4176 St-Denis; ☎514/289-0993.

Toronto

Open Air Books and Maps, 25 Toronto St, M5R 2C1; ☎416/363-0719.

Vancouver

World Wide Books and Maps, 736A Granville St V6Z 1G3; ☎604/687-3320.

AUSTRALIA

Adelaide

The Map Shop, 16a Peel St, Adelaide, SA 5000 (☎08/231 2033).

Brisbane

Hema, 239 George St, Brisbane, QLD 4000 (☎07/221 4330).

Melbourne

Bowyangs, 372 Little Bourke St, Melbourne, VIC 3000 (☎03/670 4383).

Perth

Perth Map Centre, 891 Hay St, Perth, WA 6000 (☎09/322 5733).

Sydney

Travel Bookshop, 20 Bridge St, Sydney, NSW 2000 (☎02/241 3554).

GETTING AROUND

By Greek standards Crete is pretty well served for roads and transport, and the main towns and resorts along the north coast are linked by an excellent road served by a fast and frequent bus service. To get away from the crowds, though, and see a little of the real Crete, you'll want to get off the main roads – for at least some of your time you should think about renting some transport or, better still, setting out on foot.

The main public transport **routes and timings** are detailed at the end of each chapter in "Travel Details".

BUSES

Buses are the standard – indeed the only – form of public transport on Crete, covering the island remarkably fully. Along the main north-coast road modern, fast and efficient buses run every hour or so. Off the major routes services vary: the ones used primarily by tourists (to Omalós or Hóra Sfakíon for the Samarian gorge, or Festós and Mátala) tend also to be modern and convenient; those that cater mainly for locals are generally older buses which run once daily as transport to market or school – into the provincial capital very early in the morning and back out to the village around lunchtime. This means that for day-trips they are little use. If you are determined, though, there are few places not accessible by bus, and if you combine the services with some walking you'll get about exceptionally cheaply, if not always especially quickly.

Buses on Crete are a turquoise-green colour, and run by a consortium of companies jointly known as **KTEL**. That this is not one single company is most obvious in Iráklion where there are three separate termini, each serving different directions. On the whole, buses serving a given village will run from the provincial capital – Iráklion, Réthimnon, Haniá or, in the case of Lasíthi, Áyios Nikólaos or Sitía – but there are also a number of small-scale services which cross inter-provincial borders.

TAXIS AND TOURS

Local **taxis** are exceptionally cheap, at least as long as the meter is running or you've fixed a price in advance. A good proportion of their business is long-distance, taking people to and from the villages around the main towns (in some places, including the airports, there's a printed list of prices to the most common destinations). If you want to visit somewhere where there's only one bus, or hike somewhere and get a ride back, it's well worth arranging for a taxi to pick you up: for four people this generally costs little more than the bus.

It's also quite easy to negotiate a day's or half-day's **sightseeing** trip, although this does require a certain ability in Greek and faith in the driver, and over long distances can become expensive.

A simpler alternative for a one-off visit is to take a **bus tour**. Travel agents everywhere offer the obvious ones – the Samarian gorge; Vái Beach; a local "Cretan night" – and a few offer much more adventurous alternatives; some of the best are detailed in the *Guide*. They're worth at least considering as a relatively cheap and easy way to see things you might otherwise be unable to get to – a day-trip to the Minoan sites or the gorge, for example; isolationists can always escape from the rest of the group once there.

DRIVING: CAR RENTAL

Cars have obvious advantages for getting to the more inaccessible areas, but this is one of the more expensive countries in Europe to **rent a car**. If you drive **your own vehicle** to and through Greece (not really an option on a short visit to Crete), you'll need international third-party insurance, the so-called **Green Card**, as well as an International Driving Licence and the registration documents. Upon arrival your passport will get a **carnet stamp**; this normally allows you to keep a vehicle in Greece for up to six months, exempt from road tax.

CAR RENTAL

Car rental in Greece starts at £200–230/US$300–345 a week in high season for the smallest model, including unlimited mileage, tax and insurance. Outside peak season, at the smaller local outfits, you can sometimes get terms of about £27/US$40 per day, all inclusive, but three days is the preferred minimum duration.

You may get a better price from one of the **foreign companies** that deal with local firms than if you negotiate for rental in Crete itself. One of the most competitive, which can arrange for cars to be picked up at bith Iráklion and Haniá airports, is *Holiday Autos* (see box for phone number). Most travel agents can also offer car rental in Greece, though their rates are generally higher than the specialist rental agents. **In Greece**, *Payless, Kenning, Thrifty, Ansa* and *Just* are reliable medium-sized companies with branches in many towns; all are considerably cheaper than (and just as reputable) as the biggest international operators *Budget, Europcar, Hertz* and *Avis*.

All agencies will want either a credit card or a large cash **deposit** up front; minimum age requirements vary from 21 to 25. In theory an **International Driver's Licence** is also needed but in practice European, Australasian and American ones are honoured.

Note that initial rental prices quoted in Greece almost never include tax, collision damage waiver fees and personal insurance. These are absolutely vital; the coverage included by law in the basic rental fee is generally inadequate, so check the fine print on your contract. Be careful of the hammering that cars get on minor roads; tyres and the underside of the vehicle are often excluded from insurance policies

DRIVING IN GREECE

Greece has the highest **accident rate** in Europe after Portugal, and many of the roads can be quite perilous – asphalt can turn into a dirt track without warning on the smaller routes. Uphill drivers insist on their right of way, as do those first to approach a one-lane bridge – headlights flashed at you mean the opposite of what they mean in the UK or North America and signify that the driver is coming through. Wearing a **seatbelt** is compulsory and children under ten are not allowed to sit in the front seats. If you are involved in any kind of accident it's illegal to drive away, and you can be held at a police station for up to 24 hours. If this happens, ring your consulate immediately, in order to get a lawyer (you have this right). Don't make a statement to anyone who doesn't speak, and write, very good English.

Tourists with proof of membership of official motoring associations are given free **road assistance** from *ELPA*, the Greek equivalent, which runs breakdown services – there's an office based in Crete. The information number is ☎174. In an **emergency** ring their road assistance service on ☎104, anywhere in the country. Many car rental companies have an agreement with *ELPA*'s competitors, *Hellas Service* and *Express Service*, but they're prohibitively expensive to summon on your own – over 25,000 drachmas to enrol you as an "instant member" in their scheme.

CAR RENTAL AGENCIES

BRITAIN

Avis (☎0181/848 8733).

Budget (☎0800/181 181).

Europcar/InterRent (☎01345/222 525)

Hertz (☎0181/679 1799).

Holiday Autos (☎0171/491 1111).

NORTH AMERICA

Auto Europe (☎1-800/223-5555).

Avis (☎1-800/331-1084).

Budget (☎1-800/527-0700).

Dollar (☎1-800/421-6868).

Europe by Car (☎1-800/223-1516).

Hertz (☎1-800/654-3001; in Canada ☎1-800/263-0600).

Holiday Autos (☎1-800/422-7737).

Thrifty (☎1-800/367-2277).

Petrol/gasoline currently costs around 200dr a litre for unleaded (*amólivdhi*) or super.

BIKES, MOPEDS, SCOOTERS AND CYCLES

Motorbikes, mopeds and Vespa scooters are also widely available in Crete, at prices starting at around £10/US$15 a day, £50/US$75 per week for a moped to about £15/US$23 a day, £75/US$115 a week for a 175cc trail bike.

The smaller bikes are ideal for pottering around for a day or two, but don't regard them as serious transport: Crete is very mountainous and the mopeds simply won't go up some of the steeper hills, even with only one person aboard. Be sure not to run beyond the range of your petrol tank, either, as they're not designed for long-distance travel and there are few filling stations outside the towns. For serious exploration, or to venture into the mountains, you really need a motorbike or a powerful Vespa – the latter is cheaper but much more dangerous. Whatever you rent, make sure you check it thoroughly before riding off, since many are only cosmetically repaired and if you break down it's often your responsibility to return the machine. It's worth taking the phone number of the rental company in case they do give out miles from anywhere, or you lose the ignition key!

Although motorbikes are enormous fun to ride around, you need to take more than usual care: there's an alarming number of **accidents** each year (many fatal) among visitors and locals because simple safety procedures are not followed. It's only too easy to come to grief on a potholed road or steep dirt track – especially at night. Two tips: never rent a bike which you feel you can't handle, and **use a helmet**. The latter will probably be the one item that saves your life in a spill. All operators should have helmets, but only a few will supply them unless you ask and only one or two insist that you wear them; some people now bring their own helmet with them. Quite apart from your own injuries you're likely to be charged a criminally high price for any repairs needed for the bike, so make sure that you are adequately insured, both in the rental agreement and by your own travel insurance – many of these schemes specifically exclude injuries sustained while riding/driving a rented vehicle.

CYCLING

There's no great popularity for **cycling** in Crete, not surprisingly, perhaps, in view of the moun-tainous terrain and fierce summer heat, but again the seat of a bike offers an incomparable view of the island and guarantees contact with locals the average visitor could never meet – provided you are a hardy hill climber. You can bring your own bike in by plane (it's normally free within your ordinary baggage allowance) or train (in which case it should go free on the ferry). On the island you may have difficulty with bus conductors, always protective of their luggage compartments, but if you stick to older buses you can always throw it on top.

In the flatter resorts you'll even find pedal **bikes for rent**: they're very cheap for a few hours' exploration, and child seats are sometimes available too. Some of these outlets are also starting to rent out mountain bikes, and are detailed throughout the *Guide*.

WALKING AND HITCHING

The idea of **walking** for pleasure is one that has yet to catch on widely in Crete, but if you have the time and stamina it is probably the single best way to see the island. There are suggestions for hikes – from easy strolls to serious climbing – throughout the *Guide*, and further tips for hikers in the *Contexts* section. The two Cretan books in the *Landscapes* series (*Landscapes of Eastern Crete* and *Landscapes of Western Crete*, each by Jonnie Godfrey and Elizabeth Karslake, Sunflower Books) make excellent further reading; and see "Information and Maps", pp.28–30, for details of walkers' maps of Crete. If you're plan-ning on doing some serious walking – such as any of the various gorges – stout shoes or train-ers are essential and walking boots with firm ankle support recommended, along with protec-tion against the sun and adequate water supplies.

It's worth noting that Crete also offers some exciting possibilities for **climbers**: contacts for the local mountaineering clubs (*EOS*) in Iráklion, Réthimnon and Haniá are given in their respec-tive listings.

When you get tired of walking, or you're stuck in a place after the last bus back has gone, **hitching** usually recommends itself. This, of course, carries the usual risks and dangers, and is inadvisable for women travelling alone. At its best, though, it's a wonderful way to get to know the island and to pick up some Greek. Your luck hitching in Crete will very much depend on where you are. The main road along the north coast is very fast if you want to travel some distance in a hurry, though drivers are less inclined to stop. In rural areas, hitching is great as long as you're not too pushed for time – most people will stop (the more obscure the road, the better your chance) but there may be little traffic and locals are rarely going further than the next village.

FERRIES

Around the island there are numerous **local ferry services** to offshore islets and isolated beaches; these are detailed throughout the *Guide*. Where there is no ferry service you can often arrange a trip by **kaíki** with local fishermen. An enquiry at the bar in the nearest fishing village will usually turn up someone willing to make the trip – it's always worth trying to knock a bit off the first price quoted. To give some idea of prices, a *kaíki* from Móhlos, near Áyios Nikólaos, to Psíra would cost about 12,000dr return, which includes a couple of hours on the island.

ACCOMMODATION

There are vast numbers of beds available for tourists in Crete, and most of the year you can rely on turning up pretty much anywhere and finding something. In July and August, however, you can run into problems without an advance reservation, especially in the bigger resorts and in Iráklion, Haniá and Áyios Nikólaos. The only real solution is to turn up at each new place early in the day, and to take whatever is on offer in the hope that you will be able to exchange it for something better later.

HOTELS AND ROOMS

Hotels are categorized by the tourist police from "Luxury" down to "E" class and all except the top category have to keep within set price limits.

"D" and "E" class hotels are very reasonable, costing around £9–15/US\$14–22.50 for a double room, £6–9/US\$9–14 for single rooms (where available – in practice they are rare). More luxurious establishments, except perhaps in the centres of larger towns, are often fully booked in advance by foreign tour operators.

Far more often, you'll be staying in "**rooms**" (*dhomátia* – but usually spotted by a *Rooms for Rent* or *Zimmer Frei* sign), which once again are officially controlled and divided into three classes ("A" down to "C"). At the bottom end these are cheaper, and generally cleaner and much more congenial, than hotels of a similar price. These days, most rooms places are housed in new purpose-built apartment buildings but some are still, literally, rooms in people's homes – where you'll often be treated with disarming hospitality. At its most basic, a room might consist of a bare concrete space with a bed and a hook on the back of the door, and toilet facilities (cold water only) outside in the courtyard; at its fanciest it could be a fully furnished place with en-suite marble bathroom. Between these extremes you may well find that you pay extra for a hot shower (or for any shower at all); that there's a choice of rooms at various prices (they'll always offer you the most expensive first); and that price and quality are not necessarily directly linked: always ask to see the room first. A double room could cost anything from £6/US\$9, for a very basic place out of season, to £20/US\$30-plus for high-season luxury in a resort.

As often as not, rooms find you: owners descend on ferry or bus arrivals to fill any space

ACCOMMODATION: ROOM PRICE SCALES

All accommodation establishments in this book have been price-graded according to the scale outlined below. The rates quoted represent the **cheapest available double room in high season**; where possible, a per-person rate is given for dormitory-style accommodation in youth hostels. Out of season, room rates can drop by up to fifty percent, especially if you negotiate rates for a stay of three or more nights. Single rooms, where available, cost around seventy percent of the price of a double.

Rented private rooms on the islands usually fall into the ② or ③ categories, depending on their location and facilities, and the season; a few in the ④ category are more like plush self-catering apartments. They are not generally available from late October through the beginning of April, when only hotels tend to remain open.

① up to 4000dr (£10.50/US$16.50)
② 4000–6000dr (£10.50–16/US$16.50–25)
③ 6000–8000dr (£16–21/US$25–33)

④ 8000–12,000dr (£21–32/US$33–50)
⑤ 12,000–16,000dr (£32–42/US$50–66)
⑥ 16,000dr (£42/US$66) and upwards

they have. In smaller places, simply ask in a taverna or *kafenion* – even if there are no official places around there is very often someone prepared to earn extra money from putting you up. (In the larger places there are now signs posted by the tourist police warning against going with people who offer rooms; some caution is sensible – make sure that you at least know where you're being taken.) It's also wise to be aware of the "airport taxi scam" when you pick up a cab at Iráklion or Haniá airports: a driver will frequently attempt to persuade you to go to a "good" hotel (perhaps after rubbishing the one you have in mind) with which, of course, he has an arrangement.

It has become standard practice for "rooms" proprietors to ask to keep your **passport**; ostensibly "for the tourist police", but in reality to prevent you leaving with an unpaid bill. Some owners may be satisfied with just taking down the details, as in hotels, and they'll almost always return the documents once you get to know them, or if you need them for another purpose (to change money, for example). In the larger resorts, bitter experience has made proprietors wary, and the only way to keep hold of your passport may be to pay in advance.

Prices, for rooms and hotels, should be displayed on the back of the door: if you feel you're being overcharged at a place which is officially registered, it should be enough to threaten to go to the tourist police (who really are very helpful in such cases), although small amounts over the odds may be legitimately explained by tax or out-of-date forms. And just occasionally you may find that you have

bargained so well, or arrived so far out of season, that you are actually paying *less* than you're supposed to.

HOSTELS AND ROOF SPACE

If even rooms are beyond your budget, then an alternative can usually be found. There are eight official youth hostels (*ksenón neótitas*) on Crete, all of which must be among the least strictly run in the world: they're in Iráklion, Haniá, Mália, Áyios Nikólaos, Réthimnon, Sitía, Mírthios and Plakiás. The last four are particularly good. Facilities are basic – you pay around £2–3/US$3–4.50 a night for a dormitory bed on which to spread your sleeping bag – but they usually offer cheap meals and/or kitchen facilities, a good social life and an excellent grapevine for finding work, travelling companions or whatever. They rarely ask to see a membership card, though if you want to be on the safe side, join your home country's hostelling association (see addresses over) before you go.

A few of the cheaper hotels, especially in Iráklion and Haniá, are run on similar lines as unofficial hostels: here or from a sympathetic rooms or taverna proprietor, you may be able to negotiate **roof space**. Sleeping on the tiles is better than it sounds – most Cretan buildings have flat concrete roofs on which will be provided a mattress for you to lay a sleeping bag on; there's also often an awning for shade. The nights are generally warm and the stars are stunning. It's worth asking about roof space wherever you go, though as this practice is now officially illegal and contraveners face losing their licence, it's becoming increasingly rare.

YOUTH HOSTEL ASSOCIATIONS

Australia *Australian Youth Hostels Association*, Level 3, 10 Mallett St, Camperdown, NSW (☎02/565-1325).

Canada *Hostelling International/Canadian Hostelling Association*, Room 400, 205 Catherine St, Ottawa, ON K2P 1C3 (☎613/237-7884 or 1-800/663-5777).

England and Wales *Youth Hostel Association* (*YHA*), Trevelyan House, 8 St Stephen's Hill, St Alban's, Herts AL1 (☎017278/45047). London shop and information office: 14 Southampton St, London WC2 (☎0171/836 1036).

Ireland *An Oige*, 39 Mountjoy Square, Dublin 1 (☎01/363111).

New Zealand *Youth Hostels Association of New Zealand*, PO Box 436, Christchurch 1 (☎03/799-970).

Northern Ireland *Youth Hostel Association of Northern Ireland*, 56 Bradbury Place, Belfast, BT7 (☎01232/324733).

Scotland *Scottish Youth Hostel Association*, 7 Glebe Crescent, Stirling, FK8 2JA (☎01786/51181).

USA *Hostelling International-American Youth Hostels* (*HI-AYH*), 733 15th St NW, Suite 840, PO Box 37613, Washington, DC 20005 (☎202/783-6161).

CAMPING

Official campsites are surprisingly rare – they're mentioned in the *Guide* where they exist – and not, on the whole, very good. They tend to be either very large and elaborate or else nothing more than a staked-out field. Although prices start at around £1/US$1.50 a night per person at the latter (and count on at least double this at the more elaborate places), they begin to mount up once you've added a charge for a tent (about £2.50/US$3.75), a vehicle (£1.50/US$2.25) and everyone in the party. When it's all added up you may feel that a basic room represents better value.

"**Freelance camping**" – outside authorized campsites – has always been the cheapest and in many ways most pleasant means of travel around the Greek islands. In modern Crete, however, it's a dying tradition. For a start, it's officially forbidden – there's been a law since 1977 and once in a while it gets enforced – and, much more significantly, the best sites are gradually being developed, which inevitably means turfing off the "undesirables" (and unfortunately some campers have been undesirable, leaving otherwise scenic sites filthy). Nevertheless, with discretion and sensitivity it can still be done, and just occasionally you may find yourself with nowhere to sleep but the beach. Obviously the police crack down on people camping rough on (and littering) popular mainstream tourist beaches, especially when a large community of campers is developing: elsewhere nobody is really bothered. The ideal is to find a sympathetic taverna near which to sleep out: if you take most of your meals there they'll often be prepared to guard your gear during the day and let you take showers. If you do camp like this, however, take your rubbish away with you.

It's warm enough to sleep out in just a sleeping bag from May until early September, so you don't even need to drag round a tent. A waterproof bag (available from camping shops) or groundsheet is, however, useful to keep out the late summer damp: so too is a foam pad, which lets you sleep in relative comfort almost anywhere. You will always need a sleeping bag, since even in midsummer the nights get cool, but this can be as lightweight as you can find.

APARTMENTS AND VILLAS

Another of the great traditions of Greek travel is finding that perfect villa and renting it for virtually nothing for a whole month. In the Cretan summer, forget it. All the best **villas** on the coast are contracted out to one agent or other, and let through foreign operators. Even if you do find one empty for a week or two, you'll discover that renting it in Crete costs far more than it would have done to arrange from home. See the addresses of specialist operators listed under the "Getting There" sections if you're interested.

Having said that, all hope is not lost if you arrive and decide you want to drop roots for a while. If you don't mind avoiding the coast altogether, then the old cliché might just come true. Pick an untouristy inland village – in the Amári Valley, for example, or up behind Paleohóra – get yourself known and ask about; you might still pick up some fairly wonderful deals. Out of season your chances are again much better – you'd undoubtedly be able to bargain a very good rate even in touristy areas if you wanted to stay anytime between October and March, especially for a month or more on end. Travel agents are another good source of information on what's available locally, and many rooms places have an apartment on the side or may know of friend or relative with one to rent.

One other alternative is to rent a regular **apartment** in one of the larger towns. Most renters would be expecting longer-term tenants, but you might be able to strike a deal: look for a sign saying *Enoikhiázete*, or check classifieds in the local papers.

EATING AND DRINKING

Greek food has a poor reputation which is not entirely deserved. No one would argue that this was one of the world's great cuisines, but at its best it can be delicious – fresh, simple and flavoured with the herbs that scent the countryside. The most common complaint is that food is often lukewarm and always oily. Both are deliberate, and any local will be happy to lecture you on the dangers of consuming too-hot food and on the essential, life-enhancing properties of good olive oil.

BREAKFAST, FAST FOOD AND SNACKS

Breakfast is not a meal normally served in Greek restaurants. In the major resorts there are now plenty of places offering a choice of English or Continental starts to your day, but mostly these are poor and overpriced. Try to search out instead a *galaktopoleío* (milk bar), which serve puddings and yoghurt (many *kafenia* also serve yoghurt with honey), or a **zaharoplasteío** (patisserie) for gorgeously sweet and syrupy cakes and pastries. A combination *galaktozaharopoleío* (quite a mouthful in every sense) is not uncommon.

At **bakeries**, you'll find oven-warm flaky pies filled with *féta* cheese (*tirópita*), with spinach (*spanakópita*), sausage (*louhanikópita*), or better still *bougátsa*, filled with creamy cheese and sprinkled with sugar. *Kafenia* normally make no objections if you eat these at an outdoor table, but politeness demands that you order at least a coffee.

Ubiquitous **fast-food snacks** include *souvláki* – small kebabs most commonly in the form of the doner-kebab type *yíros píta* or chunks of *píta-souvláki*, stuffed into a doughy bread (more like Indian nan than pita bread) along with salad and yoghurt, and quite superb. These are all cheap, and are at their best and most varied in the larger towns. You'll also find places serving varieties of *tost* – bland toasted sandwiches – and pizza; but avoid Cretan hamburgers at all costs.

MEALS: TAVERNAS AND RESTAURANTS

You can get a meal at a **taverna**, an *estiatório* or a **psistariá**. Regular tavernas are by far the most common, *estiatória* are very similar but tend to be cheaper and simpler, perhaps more "Greek". *Psistariés* are restaurants that specialize in fresh prepared plates – predominantly grilled meat but often good vegetables too. A *psarótaverna* is a taverna which specializes in fish. Chic appearance is not a good guide to quality. Often the most basic place will turn out to be the best and in swankier restaurants you may well be paying for the linen and stemmed wine glasses.

Often at traditional tavernas and *estiatória* there are no menus and you're taken into the kitchen to inspect what's on offer: uncooked cuts of meat and fish, simmering pots of stew or vegetables, trays of baked foods. This is a good time to fix prices, since they always seem to turn out higher if you wait until after you've eaten. Even where there is a **menu** in Greek and English it will probably be a standard printed form and bear little relation to what is actually on offer: again, check the kitchen or display case. Where prices are printed you'll be paying the right-hand (higher) set (inclusive of taxes and, usually, service) and often a number of unexpected extras, too. Unless you're feeling overwhelmingly expansive, a **tip** of five percent in most establishments will suffice.

Cretans generally eat late: **lunch** is served at 2–3pm, **dinner** 9–11pm. You can eat earlier than this, but you're likely to get indifferent service at a tourist establishment or find yourself eating alone everywhere else.

DISHES AND SPECIALITIES

A typical Greek **meal** consists of appetizers and main course (only the tourist restaurants serve desserts though there's sometimes fresh yoghurt) – the Greek practice is to visit a *zaharoplasteío* (see previous page) for pastries, coffee and liqueurs if the fancy takes them once the main meal is over.

In tavernas, the courses will often be served at the same time – if you want the main course later, stagger your ordering. The **main course** of meat or fish comes on its own except for maybe a piece of lemon or half a dozen chips/fries; salads and vegetables are served as separate dishes and usually shared. **Vegetable** dishes (often cooked in a tomato sauce) are often very good in themselves and if you order a few between several people can make a satisfying meal. Some of them, like the tomatoes, peppers or aubergines/eggplants stuffed with rice and minced meat (*yemistés*) are basically a main course. And if you're really pushed for money you can always fall back on pasta – macaroni pie and spaghetti are usually available – or soup, which can be filling and delicious.

The **baked dishes** – generally a mixture of meat and vegetables like *moussaká* or *yemistés* – and **stews** – usually some form of lamb with potatoes – are cheaper in general than straight meat or fish dishes. **Meat** usually means lamb, or sometimes pork, often pretty tough but excellent in its various spit-roasted forms.

Fish is varied and delicious, but very expensive. If the prices on the menu seem phenomenally high, that's generally because they are per kilo – you select your fish from the slab and they weigh it to determine the actual price (don't leave it to the waiter, or you'll get the biggest).

VEGETARIANS

If you are **vegetarian**, you may be in for a dull time, and will often have to assemble a meal from various appetizers or *mezédhes* (small snacks). Even the excellent standbys of yoghurt and honey, *tsatsíki* and Greek salad begin to pall after a while, and many of the "vegetable" dishes on the menu are cooked in meat stock or have small pieces of meat added to liven them up. Restaurants catering for vegetarians, especially in areas which see a lot of younger travellers, are on the increase but still need ferreting out.

BUYING YOUR OWN FOOD

Stores and markets open very early and yoghurt, bread, eggs or fruit, as well as picnic foods like cheese, salami, olives and tomatoes are always easy to buy. Remember that Greek cheese isn't all *féta* (salty white sheep's cheese) and, if you ask, there are some remarkably tasty local varieties: though all surprisingly expensive. Beach picnics can be further supplemented by tinned foods such as stuffed vine leaves (*dolmadhes*) or baby squid (*kalamarákia*).

Fruit is wonderful, and seasonal fruits exceptionally cheap – look out for what's on offer in the markets or by the roadside: cherries in spring, melons, watermelons, plums and apricots in summer, pears and apples in autumn, oranges and grapes most of the time. They even grow small bananas on Crete – an endeavour heavily subsidized by the EU.

DRINKING

For ordinary drinking you go to a **kafenion** – simple places filled with old men arguing and playing *távli* (backgammon), a national obsession. Most places will lend you a set if you ask. They start the day selling coffee (*kafé*) until this is gradually replaced by *óuzo* (an aniseed-flavoured spirit, drunk neat or mixed with water) and, later still, brandy (which is usually Metaxa or Botrys and graded with 3, 5 or 7 stars) or *rakí*, a burningly strong, flavourless spirit also known in Crete as *tsípouro* or *tsikoudhiá*. *Rakí* is also Greece's great ice-breaker and the symbol of the hand of friendship being extended: when you're offered one – inside or outside a bar – you are being honoured and it's polite to accept even if you have to force it down.

The miniature Greek **coffee** is what most Westerners would call "Turkish" and is usually

A FOOD AND DRINK GLOSSARY

Basics and terms

Neró	Water	Fitofágos/Hortofágos	Vegetarian
Psomí	Bread	Avgá	Eggs
Sitarénio psomí	Wholemeal bread	Tirí	Cheese
Sikalénio psomí	Rye bread	(Horís) ládhi	(Without) oil
Aláti	Salt	Katálogo/lísta	Menu
Yiaoúrti	Yoghurt	O logariasmós	The bill
Méli	Honey	Sto foúrno	Baked
Kréas	Meat	Psitó	Roasted
Psári(a)	Fish	Sti soúvla	Spit roasted
Lahaniká	Vegetables	Tis óras	Grilled/fried to order

Soups and starters

Soúpa	Soup	Taramósalata	Fish roe paté
Avgolémono	Egg and lemon soup	Tzatzíki	Yoghurt and cucumber dip
Dolmádhes	Stuffed vine leaves		
Fasoládha	Bean soup	Melitzanosaláta	Aubergine/eggplant dip

Vegetables

Patátes	Potatoes	Kolokithákia	Courgette/zuchinni
Hórta	Greens (usually wild)	Spanáki	Spinach
Radhíkia	Wild chicory	Fakés	Lentils
Piperiés	Peppers	Rízi/Piláfi	Rice (usually with sáltsa – sauce)
Domátes	Tomatoes	Saláta	Salad
Fasolákia	String beans	Horiátiki (saláta)	Greek salad (with olives, féta etc)
Angoúri	Cucumber		
Angináres	Artichokes	Yemistés	Stuffed vegetables
Yígantes	White haricot beans	Papoutsákia	Stuffed aubergine/eggplant
Koukiá	Broad beans	Bouréki	Courgette/zuchinni/potato/cheese pie
Melitzána	Aubergine/eggplant		

Meat and meat-based dishes

Kotópoulo	Chicken	Kelftiko	Meat, potatoes and veg cooked together in a pot or foil; a Cretan speciality traditionally carried to bandits in hiding.
Arní	Lamb		
Hirinó	Pork		
Vodhinó	Beef	Pastítsio	Macaroni baked with meat
Moskhári	Veal	Païdhákia	Lamb chops
Sikóti	Liver	Brizóla	Pork or beef chop
Patsás	Tripe soup	Keftédhes	Meatballs
Nefrá	Kidneys	Loukánika	Spicy sausages
Biftéki	Hamburger	Kokorétsi	Liver/offal kebab
Moussaká	Aubergine/eggplant, potato and mince pie	Tsalingária	Garden snails
Stifádho	Meat stew with tomato and onion		

Fish and seafood

Garídhes	Prawns	Glóssa	Sole	Soupiá	Anchovy
Okhtapódhi	Octopus	Barbóuni	Red mullet	Marídhes	Dentex
Astakós	Lobster	Xifias	Swordfish	Gávros	Bogue (cheap!)
Kalamária	Squid	Sinagrídha	Cuttlefish		
Kalamarákia	Baby squid	Gópes	Whitebait		

Sweets and Fruit

Karidhópita	Walnut cake	*Kasséri*	Hard cheese	*Portokália*	Oranges
Baklavá	Honey/nuts pastry	*Graviéra*	Gruyère type	*Pepóni*	Melon
Rizógalo	Rice pudding		cheese	*Karpoúzi*	Watermelon
Galaktobóuriko	Custard pie	*Fráoules*	Strawberries	*Míla*	Apples
Pagotó	Ice cream	*Kerásia*	Cherries	*Síka*	(Dried) figs
Pastéli	Sesame/honey bar	*Stafília*	Grapes	*Fistíkia*	Pistachio nuts

Drinks

Neró	Mineral water	*Rosé/Kokkinéli*	Rosé	*Gazóza*	Generic fizzy
Enfialoméno		*Tsäï*	Tea		drink
Bíra	Beer	*Kafés*	Coffee	*Boukáli*	Bottle
Krasí	Wine	*Gálakakáo*	Chocolate milk	*Potíri*	Glass
Mávro	Red	*Portokaládha*	Orangeade	*Stiniyássas!*	Cheers!
Áspro	White	*Limonádha*	Lemonade	*Yiásou!*	Cheers!

medium sweet or *métrio*. If you want more sugar ask for *glikó* (sickeningly sweet), if none at all *skéto*. Ordinary coffee is also usually available – ask for "Nescafé", which is what it generally is (*Nes me gála* is Nescafé with milk). Iced coffee is known as *frappé*, and is an excellent refresher. *Oúzo* and other drinks are traditionally served with small snacks – **mezédhes** – but nowadays you generally have to order and pay for these. **Tea**, *tsái*, is often available too, usually served black with a tin of milk to add. It often tastes better with lemon, *me lemóni*, instead.

Real **bars** are rare in traditional Crete, though occasionally you'll find an *ouzeri*, which differs little from a *kafenion*. Bars for tourists are common in resorts, though, usually either places where you can sit outside in cushioned armchairs sipping exotic, expensive cocktails or combined with discos and serving less exotic but even more expensive concoctions.

WINE

Wine (*krasí*) on the island comes in many varieties. The house wine offered in most tavernas will normally be the brown and cloudy rosé-style Cretan *kókkino* (red) especially good around Kastélli in the west, or the white which often has a sherry tang. This will not be resinated (if you want to specify this to make sure, ask for *aretsínato*) and restaurants, especially rural ones, will often have a barrel from which jugs are filled. These locally made brews can vary enormously in quality due to the vagaries of the production process, but they're always worth a try. If you want to test it out before committing

yourself to a *karáfa* (which come in kilo or half-kilo measures), most places will be only too pleased to let you try a glass first.

Although not as popular here as on the mainland (it was largely unknown in Crete before World War II), **retsína** is now produced on the island and most commonly comes in half-litre bottles: you may also find it served from the barrel in quarter, half or kilo metal mugs. This resinated wine is an acquired taste, but once you like it you'll start finding some varieties are extremely good. Acquiring the taste is helped by the fact that it is exceptionally cheap: a litre can cost under £1/US$1.50, often less than a litre of beer. The *retsína* produced by the *Central Union of Haniá Wine Producers* is recommended, but stay well clear of the same cooperative's red variety which is quite awful.

Cretan **bottled wine** is rather more expensive – brands like *Minos* red and white, which you can get everywhere, are fine if rather boring. *Mantiko* from the Pezá wine region (one of Crete's two apellation zones along with Sitía) to the south of Iráklion is a full-bodied red with a bit more character, and *Logado* is another red worth trying. The Sitían wines *Topiko* (medium-dry with a hint of sherry) and *Myrtos*, are both good everyday whites to drink with seafood. In the west, *Kissamos* red is another good bet. Keep an eye out too for the wines of Santorini (Thíra), the volcanic island to the north, which are becoming noted; any of the *Santo* vineyard's output are worth a try, particularly the white *Asyrtiko*.

The best mainland brands of unresinated wine are by *Boutari* – especially the whites *Lac des*

Roches and *Rotonda* and the justifiably famous *Náoussa* red. *Marko* and *Cambas* are also drinkable.

BEER

Beer is standard European lager served in half-litre bottles or smaller cans. The locally brewed *Amstel* and *Henninger* are fairly bland versions of their north European counterparts, and imported *Heineken* and *Lowenbrau* are worth the extra few drachmas. Beware of exotic brands or gold-trimmed bottles served by bars in tourist areas (especially if you leave it to the waiter): the mark-up is usually outrageous.

COMMUNICATIONS: POST, PHONES AND MEDIA

POST

Local **post offices** are open from about 7.30am to 2.30pm, Monday to Friday; in big towns and important tourist centres, hours may extend into the evening and weekends. Bigger post offices will change money as well as handle mail. Air mail **letters** take three to six days to reach the rest of Europe, five to eight days to get to North America, and a bit more for Australia and New Zealand. **Aerograms** are faster and surer; postcards can be inexplicably slow although things are gradually improving: up to ten days for Europe, three weeks to the Americas or the Pacific. A modest **express** fee (about 300dr) cuts letter delivery time to two days for the UK and three days for the Americas.

For a simple letter or card, **stamps** (*grammatósima*) can also be purchased at a *períptero* (corner kiosk). However, the proprietors are entitled to a ten-percent commission and never seem to know the current international rates. **Postboxes** are bright yellow: if you are confronted by two slots, *Esoterikó* is for Greek mail, *Exoterikó* for overseas.

If you are sending large purchases home, note that **parcels** should and often can only be handled in sizeable towns, preferably a provincial capital. This way your bundle will be in Athens within a day or two. **Registered** (*sistiméno*) delivery is also available, but it is extremely slow.

RECEIVING MAIL

Receiving mail, the *poste restante* system is reasonably efficient, especially at the big town post offices. Mail should be clearly addressed and marked *poste restante*, with your surname capitalized and underlined, to the main post office of whichever town you choose. It will be held for a month and you'll need your passport to collect it. Alternatively, **American Express** cheque or card holders can use the office in Iráklion as a mail drop: c/o *Creta Travel Bureau*, Epimenídhou 20–22.

PHONES

Making local calls is relatively straightforward. In many hotel lobbies or cafés you'll find fat **red pay-phones** which presently take a ten-drachma coin and are for local calls only – you'll be asked to give an extra 5dr to the proprietor to equal the fee at a street kiosk (see below). Some call boxes work only with **phone cards** (in three sizes: 100, 500 and 1000 units), bought from kiosks, *OTE* offices and newsagents.

If you won't be around long enought to use up a phone card, it's probably easier to make local calls from a *períptero*, or **street kiosk**. Here the phone is connected to a meter, and you pay after you have made the call. Local calls cost just 15dr, but **long-distance** ones add up quickly to some of the most expensive rates in Europe – and utilize some of the worst connections.

For **international** (*exoterikó*) calls, it's better to either use card phones or visit the nearest **OTE** (*Organismós Tiliepikinoníon tis Elládhos*) office, where there's often a slightly better-wired booth reserved for overseas calls. **Reverse-charge (collect) calls** can also be made here, though connections are not always immediate. Be prepared to wait; late evening is usually a quieter time.

In Iráklion and Haniá there are *OTE* branches open 24 hours; in smaller towns, the *OTE* can close as early as 3pm, though in a few resorts there are *OTE* Portakabin booths. Outgoing **faxes** can also be sent from *OTE* offices, post offices and some travel agencies – at a price. Receiving a fax may also incur a small charge.

Other options – and possibly the only one in remoter areas – for calls are from a *kafenion* or bar, but make sure the phones are metered: look for a sign saying *Tiléfono meh metrití*. Avoid making long-distance calls from a hotel, as they slap a fifty percent surcharge onto the already exorbitant rates. If you have access to a private phone you can dial the international operator on ☎161 to get a reversed-charge call put through, or dial direct: ☎00, followed by the country code (see box) and the local number without its initial zero. Calls will cost, very approximately, £2.75 for three minutes to all EU countries and most of the rest of Europe, or US$10 for the same time to North America or Australia. **Cheap rates**, such as they are, apply from 3pm to 5pm and 9pm to 8am daily, plus all weekend, for calls within Greece.

NEWSPAPERS AND RADIO

British newspapers are fairly widely available in Crete for 300–400dr, 700–800dr for Sunday editions. You'll find day-old copies in all the resorts as well as in Haniá and Iráklion. **American** and international alternatives are represented by *USA Today* and the *International Herald Tribune*; *Time* and *Newsweek* can also be found.

Cheaper and more up-to-date, though heavily biased in favour of US press agency reports, the daily *Athens News* and weekly *Kriti News* are also on sale anywhere there might be a market for them: they have selections from the Greek press. *This Month Crete* is a monthly bi-lingual English-German publication which, as well as feature articles on Crete, also carries useful bits of information on food and entertainment. It's free, and available from tourist shops and bars in all the major towns.

If you have a **radio** you may pick up something more interesting. As well as the BBC World Service, there are also regular news bulletins and bouts of tourist information in English on local Greek stations. American Forces' Radio can be picked up through most of the island, too, while on the extreme eastern end of the island you can receive BBC domestic radio programmes on the FM frequency, disseminated from the British base on Cyprus.

PHONING GREECE FROM ABROAD

Dial the international access code (given below) + 30 (country code) + area code (minus initial 0) + number

Australia	☎0011	Canada	☎011	Ireland	☎010
New Zealand	☎00	UK	☎00	USA	☎011

PHONING ABROAD FROM GREECE

Dial the country code (given below) + area code (minus intial 0) + number

Australia	☎0061	Canada	☎001	Ireland	☎00353
New Zealand	☎0064	UK	☎0044	USA	☎001

USEFUL TELEPHONE NUMBERS

Operator (domestic)	☎131	Speaking clock	☎141
Operator (international)	☎161	Tourist police	☎171
Medical emergencies	☎166	Fire brigade	☎199
Police/emergency	☎100	Road assistance	☎174

POLICE, TROUBLE AND HARASSMENT

It's now over twenty years since the Colonels were evicted and Greece ceased to be a police state. As everywhere, there are a few mean characters around, but in general your average Greek policeman is not likely to have too much of a power complex, and you need to do something very insensitive to risk arrest. The most common causes of a brush with authority – all of them technically illegal – are nude bathing or sunbathing, camping outside an authorized site and (a major crime in the Greek book) taking or possessing cannabis products or any other drug.

SPECIFIC OFFENCES

Nude bathing is, currently, legal on only a very few beaches, and is deeply offensive to many more traditional Cretans: exercise considerable sensitivity to local feeling and the kind of place you're in. As a general rule, stay away from families with children, the main entrance of a beach and any tavernas. If a beach has become fairly established for nudity, or is well secluded, it's highly unlikely that the police are going to come charging in. Where they do get bothered is if they feel a place is turning into a "hippy beach" or nudity getting too overt on mainstream tourist stretches. But there are no hard and fast rules; it all depends on the local cops. Most times the only action would be a warning but you can officially be arrested straight off – facing as much as three days in jail and a stiff fine.

Very similar guidelines exist for **camping rough** – though for this you're still less likely to incur anything more than a warning to move on. The only real risk of arrest is if you are told to move on and fail to do so. In either of the above cases, even if the police do take any action against you, at worst it's more likely to be a brief spell in their cells to speed you on your way than any official prosecution.

Drug offences are a far more serious matter. The maximum penalty for "causing the use of drugs by someone under 18", for example, is life imprisonment and a ten million drachma fine. Theory is by no means practice, but foreigners caught in possession of quite small amounts of hash do get jail sentences of up to a year – much more if there's any suggestion they're supplying others. Greek prisons are not to be recommended.

If you get arrested for any offence you have an automatic right to contact your country's **consul**, who will arrange a lawyer for your defence. Beyond this, there is little they can, or in most cases will, do.

SEXUAL HARASSMENT

Many women travel about Greece on their own without feeling intimidated or constantly harassed – but some undoubtedly are. This has little to do with the way individuals look or behave, and only indirectly relates to the way Greek women themselves are treated. What is important is that different assumptions are made about you as a foreign woman depending on where you are.

In most of the **rural areas**, you'll be treated first and foremost as a *xénos* – a word which means both stranger and guest – in much the same way as a foreign man. You can sit and drink *oúzo* in the exclusively male *kafenia* (there's often nowhere else) without always suspecting the hospitality and friendliness that's offered.

In the **large resorts and towns**, however, where tourism has for a long time determined the local culture, things can be very different. Here the myths and fantasies of the "liberated" and "available" woman are widespread: not perhaps to the extent of other Mediterranean countries but oppressive nonetheless. Without a good control of the language it can be hard to deal with: words worth remembering for an unambiguous response are *stamáta* (stop it), *afísteme* (leave me alone) and *fíyete* (go away).

OPENING HOURS AND PUBLIC HOLIDAYS

It is virtually impossible to generalize about Cretan opening hours, except to say that they change constantly. The traditional timetable starts early – stores open at 7am or 8am – and runs through till lunchtime, when there is a long break for the hottest part of the day; things may then re-open in the mid- to late afternoon. In tourist areas, though, stores and offices may stay open right through the day: certainly the most important archeological sites and museums do so.

Matters are further confused by Crete's **public holidays**, during which almost everything will be closed; there's a list of the most important ones in the box below. It's worth bearing in mind, too, that either side of major **festivals** (see next section) many public buildings and banks tend to close, possibly leaving you stranded for days without cash. Keep an eye on the calendar and plan accordingly.

STORES AND BUSINESSES

Store hours are theoretically Monday, Wednesday and Saturday from approximately 8am to 2pm, and Tuesday, Thursday, Friday 8am–1pm and 5–8.30pm, but there are so many excep-

tions to the rule by virtue of holidays and professional idiosyncrasy that you can't count on getting anything done except between Monday to Friday from 9.30am to 1pm or so. Closed pharmacies are supposed to have a sign on their door referring you to the nearest open one.

ARCHEOLOGICAL SITES

Opening hours vary from site to site: as far as possible, individual times are quoted in the Guide, but bear in mind that these change with exasperating frequency and, at smaller sites, can be subject to the whim of a local keeper who may decide to close early, or even leave the gate open after the official closing time or on the official closing day (usually Mon). The times given are generally summer hours, which operate from around April to the end of September. Reckon on similar days but later opening and earlier closing in winter. A list of **current opening hours** is available from the tourist offices in Iráklion or Haniá.

Smaller archeological sites generally close for a long lunch and siesta (even where they're not meant to), as do **monasteries**. Most monasteries are fairly strict on dress, too, especially for women: they don't like shorts and often expect women to cover their arms and wear skirts. They are generally open from about 9am to 1pm and from 5 to 7pm.

PUBLIC HOLIDAYS

January 1
January 6
March 25
First Monday of Lent (Feb or March)
Easter weekend (according to the Orthodox calendar, see opposite)
May 1
August 15
October 28
December 25 and 26.

FESTIVALS AND ENTERTAINMENT

Most of the big Greek popular festivals have a religious base so they're observed in accordance with the Orthodox calendar: this means that Easter, for example, can fall as much as three weeks to either side of the Western festival.

On top of the main religious festivals there are literally scores of local festivals, or **paniyíria**, celebrating the patron saint of the village church: and with some 330-odd possible saints' days you're unlikely to travel round for long without stumbling on something. Local tourist offices should be able to fill you in on events in their area.

EASTER

Easter is by far the most important festival of the Greek year – infinitely more so than Christmas – and taken much more seriously than anywhere in the West. From Wednesday of Holy Week, the radio and TV networks are given over solely to religious programmes until the following Monday. It is an excellent time to be in Crete, both for the beautiful and moving religious ceremonies and for the days of feasting and celebration which follow. If you make for a smallish village, you may well find yourself an honorary member for the period of the festival.

The first great ceremony takes place on **Good Friday** evening as the Descent from the Cross is lamented in church. At dusk, the *Epitáfios*, Christ's funeral bier, leaves the sanctuary and is paraded solemnly through the streets. Late **Saturday** evening sees the climax in a majestic mass to celebrate Christ's triumphant return. At the stroke of midnight all lights in each crowded church are extinguished and the congregation plunged into the darkness which envelopes Christ as He passes through the underworld. Then there's a faint glimmer of light behind the altar screen before the priest appears, holding aloft a lighted taper and chanting "*Avtó to fos . . .*" (This is the Light of the World). Stepping down to the level of the parishioners he touches his flame to the unlit candle of the nearest worshipper – intoning "*Devthe, levethe fos*" (Come take the light) to be greeted by the response "*Hristós Anésti*" (Christ is risen). And so it goes round, this affirmation of the miracle, until the entire church is ablaze with burning candles. Later, as the church bells ring, the celebrations begin with fireworks and the burning of effigies of Judas.

Even solidly rational atheists are likely to find this somewhat moving: the traditional greeting, as firecrackers explode all around you in the streets, is *Hristós Anésti* and the reply *Alithos Anésti* (He is risen indeed). In the week leading up to Easter Sunday, you should wish acquaintances "*Kaló Páskha*" (Happy Easter). The Lenten fast is traditionally broken early Sunday morning with a meal of *mayirítsa* (a soup based on lamb offal), and later the rest of the lamb will be roasted.

LOCAL ENTERTAINMENT

The events of the various festivals aside (and Iráklion's last for much of the summer), Crete can offer little in the way of cultural diversion. **Dancing** is of course a tradition here as throughout Greece, but for the real thing you have to go to a *paniyíri*, or else be exceptionally lucky in falling into the right company. Which is not to say that the stuff put on for the tourists isn't enjoyable – it is – simply that it may not be entirely authentic. With regard to **music** it's worth keeping an eye out in the villages for posters advertising *lyra* and *bouzoúki* concerts. These can be highly entertaining and you will often find that you're the only foreigners present, thus ensuring a warm Cretan welcome.

THE FESTIVAL YEAR

Epiphany (Jan 6) The hobgoblins who run riot on earth during the twelve days of Christmas are rebanished to the nether world by various rites of the Church. Most important of these is the blessing of baptismal founts and all outdoor bodies of water. At lake or sea-shore locales the priests cast a crucifix into the deep to be recovered by crowds of young men. There used to be a substantial cash prize for the winner, but this custom is now honoured more in the breach owing to recent, serious violence between contenders.

Pre-Lenten carnivals These span three weeks, climaxing over the seventh weekend before Easter.

Clean Monday (*Kathará Dheftéra*) The beginning of Lent, a traditional time to fly kites and to feast on all the things which will be forbidden over the coming weeks.

Independence Day (March 25) Parades and dancing to celebrate the beginning of the revolt against Turkish rule in 1821.

May Day The great urban holiday – most people make for the countryside.

Battle of Crete (May 20–27) The anniversary of the battle is celebrated in Haniá and a different local village each year: sporting events, folk dancing, and ceremonies with veterans of the battle.

Summer solstice/John the Baptist (June 24) Bonfires and widespread celebrations.

Naval Week (late June) Naval celebrations culminate in fireworks – especially big at Soúdha.

Réthimnon Wine Festival (July) A week of wine tasting and traditional dancing.

Iráklion Festival (July and Aug) A wide variety of cultural events – from drama and film to traditional dance and jazz – at scattered sites through most of the summer.

Metamórfosi/Transfiguration (Aug 6) Another excuse for feasting.

Sitía Sultana Festival (mid-Aug) Enjoyable, week-long celebration of the local harvest, with plenty of wine.

Assumption of the Virgin (Aug 15) Celebrated in many villages, including the town of Neápoli, though the great event is the pilgrimage to the island of Tínos.

Áyios Títos (Aug 25) Patron saint of the island – big procession in Iráklion.

Cretan Wedding (late Aug) A "traditional" wedding laid on in Kritsá for the tourists – quite a spectacle nonetheless.

Áyios Ioánnis (Aug 29) Massive name-day pilgrimage to the church of St John Giona on the Rodhópou peninsula in Haniá.

Chestnut Festival (mid-Oct) Celebrated in Élos and other villages of the southwest where chestnuts are grown.

Óhi Day (Oct 28) Lively national holiday – parades, folk dancing – commemorating Metaxas' one-word reply ("No") to Mussolini's ultimatum in 1940.

Arkádhi (Nov 7–9) One of Crete's biggest gatherings celebrates the anniversary of the explosion at the Monastery of Arkádhi.

WORK

It's not easy to find work in Crete, and over recent years it has been getting harder, with more people chasing fewer possibilities. Even so, it remains one of the best places in Greece to try your luck at agricultural labour, and there are a few other possibilities. Short-term work will always be on an unofficial basis, the EU freeing-up of employment restrictions notwithstanding, and for this reason it will generally be badly paid and subject, possibly, to police harassment.

TOURISM-RELATED WORK

Casual work in **bars or restaurants** around the main tourist resorts is one of the easiest options, though very much more so for women than for men. If you're waiting/serving, most of your wages will come from tips but you may well be able to negotiate a deal that includes free food and lodging; evening-only hours can leave a lot of freedom, too. The main drawback may be the machismo and/or chauvinist attitudes of your employer. In particular in Haniá, and to a lesser extent elsewhere, many of the bars like to hire young foreign women as decoys, to lure men in and persuade them to drink. This can occasionally lead to confrontation with irate clients, and more frequently to harassment by the bar owner, who expects his employees also to be his harem. A common tactic is to threaten to report you to the police, whom the bar is usually paying off. With this in mind, ads in the local press for "girl bar staff" are certainly best ignored.

On the whole, you should be moderately pleased with landing a washing-up job. Trained chefs or cooks will do better. Start looking, if you can, around April–May: you'll get better rates if you're taken on for a whole season, when you will also have a better chance of finding somewhere affordable to live.

You might be able to get a job touting/selling for **tourist stores**, or if you've got the expertise helping to supervise one of the burgeoning **windsurfing** "schools" or acting as a translator or even a guide for a local travel agent. **Yacht marinas** can also prove good hunting grounds, though less for the romantic business of crewing than for scrubbing down and repainting. Again, the earlier in the year you arrive, the better your chances. One new possibility, if you can handle it, is **touting for time share**, at the new developments along the north coast.

For a full season's work, relatively slim credentials might also get you a job as a **tour-group courier**. Some firms are willing to take on people waiting to go to university or, more promisingly, having just finished. The nominal pay will be appalling but you'll get a place to live and you can make extra money in tips from grateful clients. Scour the brochures as early in the year as possible and turn up at the companies' offices.

Preparations for the tourist season also often require temporary labour, especially if you have a relevant skill: **building**, **painting** or **signwriting**, for example.

AGRICULTURE

Another possible source of income is from casual, unskilled **agricultural** labour – invariably low-paid and usually more so for women, who tend to be paid at a lower rate. Incidentally, the fields are quite a rough scene, and single women labourers are in a distinct minority. Incidents of violence, non-payment or underpayment, abuse by employers and police harassment are commonplace. If you're still intent on doing it, hang around hostels in the appropriate geographical areas and ask other travellers for the current situation. Something is being harvested somewhere in Crete through most of the year, and there are various well-known centres where the farmers come if they need labour.

TEACHING ENGLISH

Long-term work is very unlikely, unless you've fixed it up in advance. The main opportunity is **teaching English** at one of the many language schools (*frontistíria*) around the island. If you're already in Crete and want teaching work it looks difficult on paper since you officially need a licence (a complicated procedure). In practice, however, this is very loosely enforced and you may just strike lucky if you approach schools directly – they're listed in any phone book. The best time of year is from August onwards, as the start of the school year draws near.

Teaching is essentially a winter exercise – the schools close down from the end of May until mid-September, operating only a few special courses in June and July – so it's general practice to supplement your income by giving **private lessons**. For this the going rate is around £5–10/ US$7.50–15 an hour. Some teachers finance themselves exclusively on private lessons and, although you still officially need a teaching permit for this, few people experience any problems over it.

AU PAIR WORK

The popularity and scale of private English-language teaching also means that English-speaking women may be able to find work as **au pairs**. As ever, positions tend to be exploitative and low-paid but if you can use them to your own ends – living reasonably well and learning Greek – there can be mutual benefits. It's unwise to arrange anything until you arrive, so you can at least meet and talk terms with your prospective family. There are a number of specialist agencies in Athens which may be able to help. These include: *International Staff* (Bótasi 12); *Miterna* (Ermóu 28); *Working Holidays* (Níkis 11); *Greek YWCA (XEN)* (Amerikís 11).

DIRECTORY

ADDRESSES in Greek are usually written with just the street name followed by the number (Sífaka 11); numbers outside the city centres usually represent a whole block so you may get an individual building number added in brackets. *Odhós* means street; *Leofóros*, avenue; *Platía*, square. In a multistorey building, the ground floor is the *isóyeio*; there may be a mezzanine (*imiórofos*) before the first floor (*prótos órofos*).

ADMISSION CHARGES All the major ancient sites are now fenced off and, like museums, most charge admission. This ranges from a token 100dr to a hefty 1000dr at the five-star sites such as Knossós, but with an *ISIC* or *FIYTO* youth card you can get up to fifty-percent reductions. Current students of archeology, classics or history of art qualify for a free admission permit – write (well in advance) to the Ministry of Science and Culture (Museums section), Aristídhou 14, Athens. Over-sixties can also get a small reduction. It's worth remembering that entrance to all state-run sites and museums is free to EU nationals on Sundays and public holidays.

BARGAINING is not a regular feature of life though you'll find it possible with "rooms" and some off-season hotels. A nice line is always to offer to use your sleeping bag, saving the washing of the sheets.

BRING . . . film which is expensive in Greece, an alarm clock for early buses and ferries, as well as a flashlight for camping out, coping with power cuts, visiting caves and churches or finding your way to a midnight swim.

CHILDREN Travelling with children presents few problems in Crete, since kids, on the whole, are worshipped and indulged, perhaps to excess. For young children, heat and sun are the worst hazards. Baby foods and nappies are widely available and under-eights travel free on the buses (but over-eights pay full fare). A "rooms" establishment is more likely to offer some kind of baby-sitting service than the more impersonal hotels.

CINEMA You're unlikely to see any very inspiring films in a Cretan cinema, but most English-language titles are subtitled rather than dubbed, and the open-air screens which can be found in all the major towns in summer are wonderful.

CONTRACEPTIVES Condoms (*kapótes*) are available from city kiosks or *farmakía*; the pill, too, can be obtained from a *farmakío* – you shouldn't need a prescription.

ELECTRICITY is 220 volt AC (British appliances should work, US ones need a transformer); plugs are usually the standard European pattern of two round pins. Power cuts are a common feature in Crete, particularly in summer, when generating capacity is stretched to breaking point. Bank computers and cash machines going down, non-functioning fuel pumps at garages and warm beer and wine in restaurants are some of the hassles which affect visitors; many places (especially cinemas) have their own back-up generators.

GAY LIFE There are no overtly gay resorts on Crete but, as throughout Greece, attitudes are relaxed. Homosexuality is legal over the age of 17 and (generally, male) bisexuality quite widely accepted.

LAUNDERETTES Rare, with expensive service laundries only slightly more common, but there's almost always somewhere to wash your own clothes. Ask to use the laundry trough rather than risk destroying your room's plumbing.

PERÍPTERO A *períptero* is a street-corner kiosk. They sell everything – pens, combs, razors, stationery, postcards, soap, sweets, nuts, condoms, *komboloí* ("worry" beads) – double as phone booths and stay open long after everything else has closed.

SKIING Believe it or not, it is possible to ski in Crete in winter, and there's even a tiny ski lift on the Nídha Plain above Anóyia, while the Kalleryi Lodge in the White Mountains may also open for ski parties. Don't come specially.

SPECTATOR SPORTS Soccer and basketball are, along with the rest of Greece, Crete's major sports. *Ofi*, from Iráklion, is Crete's leading first-division football team and, in season, matches – normally played on Sundays – against many of the mainland's other major sides are easy enough to catch at the ground near to the Martinengo Bastion. Warm-up games for the new season in late August often feature visits by foreign teams.

TIME Greek summertime begins on the last Sunday in March, when the clocks go ahead one hour, and ends on the last Sunday in September when they fall back. Be alert to this, as scores of visitors miss planes and ferries every year; the change is not well publicized. Greek time is two hours ahead of the UK, three hours when the respective changes to summertime fail to coincide. For North America, the standard time difference is seven hours for Eastern Standard Time, ten hours for Pacific Standard Time, with again an extra hour for those weeks in April and October. A recorded time message (in Greek) is available by dialling ☎141.

TOILETS Public ones, generally foul, are usually in parks or squares, often subterranean. Otherwise try a bus station. Throughout Greece you toss paper in adjacent wastebaskets, *not* in the bowl: learn this habit, or you'll block the pipes. It's worth carrying toilet paper with you – though it's provided by the attendants at public facilities, there may be none in tavernas or cafés.

HANIÁ

RÉTHIMNON

IRÁKLION

LASÍTHI

0   100 km

CHAPTER ONE

IRÁKLION

The **province of Iráklion** sees more tourists than any other in Crete. They come for two simple reasons: the string of big **resorts** which lie to the east of the city, only an hour or so from the airport, and the great **Minoan sites**, almost all of which are concentrated in the centre of the island. **Knossós, Mália** and **Festós** are in easy reach of almost anywhere in the province and there are excellent beaches all along the north coast. The price you pay are crowds: **Iráklion** is a big, hustling city, the development to the east is continuous and huge, and in summer the great sites are constantly awash with people.

There seems little here of the old Crete, ramshackle and rural, and yet, by taking the less obvious turn, it is still possible to escape. **West and south** of Iráklion the beaches are smaller, and the coastline is less amenable to hotel builders. The south coast in particular is far less peopled: beaches are accessible only in a handful of places (of which only **Mátala** is at all exploited), the interior remains traditional farming country.

IRÁKLION AND THE NORTH COAST

Iráklion itself can at first seem a nightmare. Arrive expecting a quaint little island town and you're in for a big disappointment. You find yourself instead in the fourth-largest city in Greece; ugly, modern, a maelstrom of traffic, building work, concrete and dust. Stay long enough and you can begin to like the place – but it would take a determined tourist to stay that course. You're better off taking the city for what it has – **Knossós** and the **Archeological Museum** most famously, but also snatched visions of another city, of magnificent fortifications, a wonderful market, the occasional ancient alley, curious smaller museums – and getting out as fast as practicable.

Knossós apart, the immediate **surrounds of Iráklion** offer little compensation. If you are based in the city with time on your hands then the Minoan remains at **Arhánes** or the views from **Mount Yioúhtas** are worth taking in, and transport to local beaches is excellent. But this is hardly getting the most the island offers.

East of Iráklion, the startling pace of tourist development is all too plain to see. The merest hint of a beach is an excuse to build at least one hotel, and these are outnumbered by the concrete shells of rivals-to-be. It can be hard to find a room in the peak season in this monument to the package tour, and expensive if you do. Some of the resorts, most notably **Mália** and **Hersónisos**, do at least have good beaches and lively nightlife. They wouldn't be at all bad if you were on a package deal – providing you like crowds, noise and commercialism. But turn

IRÁKLION PROVINCE

Dhía

To Áyios Nikólaos, Rhodes, Cyprus & Israel

Mikarnassós

Gournes
Háni Kokini
Kató Goúves
Finikas
E 75

Cave of
Eileíthyia

Goúves

Cave
(Skotinó)

Hersónisos
(Limin Hersonísou)

Old
Hersónisos
Piskopiano
Koutoulafari

Stalidha

Mália

To Néapoli &
Áyios Nikólaos

Palace
of Mália

Mohós

Potamiés

Krasí
+ Panayía Kardhiótissa

Episkopí

Mirtiá

Apóstoli

Kastélli

Gonies

To Lasíthi

Ayía
Paraskiés

Thrapsanó

Arkalohóri

Panayía

Dhíkti

Mártha

Ano
Viánnos

Amirás

To Ierápetra

Skiniás

Árvi

Keratókambos

Pírgos

Tsoútsouros

N

0   10 km

up hoping to find somewhere to stay on the off-chance and you won't regard them as the most welcoming of places. As a general rule, the further you go, the better things get: when the road veers inland for an all-too-brief while, the real Crete – olive groves and stark mountains – reveals itself.

To the **west** there's much less to detain you, with mountains which drop virtually straight to the sea. There is just one small, classy resort in the bay at **Ayía Pelayía**, a few isolated hotels and, in the hills behind, a number of interesting old villages: at **Fódhele** the birthplace of El Greco, and at **Tílissos** a famous Minoan villa.

Iráklion

The best way to arrive in **IRÁKLION** is from the sea, the traditional approach and still the one which shows the city in its best light, with Mount Yioúhtas rising behind, the heights of the Psilorítis range to the west and, as you get closer, the city walls encircling and dominating the oldest part of town. As you sail in, you run the gauntlet of the great fortress guarding the harbour entrance. Unfortunately the old harbour can't handle ships of this size, and the ferries actually dock at great concrete wharves alongside – a juxtaposition which seems neatly to sum up much about modern Iráklion. What little remains of the old city has been heavily restored, often from the bottom up, but the slick renovations invariably look fake, pristine and polished alongside the grime which coats even the most recent of new buildings.

Iráklion's name is of Roman origin, taken from a port which stood hereabouts and readopted at the beginning of this century. The present city was founded by the Saracens who held Crete from 827 to 961. In those days it was known, after the great ditch which surrounded it, as El Khandak, later corrupted by the Venetians to Candia, or Candy, a name applied also to the island as a whole. This Venetian capital was in its day one of the strongest and most spectacular cities in Europe: a trading centre, a staging-point for the Crusades and, as time wore on, itself the front line of Christendom. When the Turks finally conquered the city it was only after 21 years of war, culminating in a bitter siege from May 1667 to September 1669.

Under its new rulers the city's importance declined in relation to Haniá's, but it remained a major port and the second city in Crete. It was here, too, that the incident occurred which finally put an end to Turkish occupation of the island. In 1898 fourteen British soldiers and the British consul were murdered, the final straw – where the deaths of thousands of Cretans had not been – which persuaded the great powers to insist on the departure of the remaining Turkish troops and administrators.

Finally united with Greece, Iráklion's prosperity was assured by its central position. Almost all that you see, though, dates only from the last few decades, partly through the reconstruction after the heavy bombing it suffered during World War II but also through a boom in agriculture, industry and tourism. In 1971 the city regained the official title of island capital. Its growth continues, as you'll see if you venture to the fringes of town where the concrete spreads inexorably, but it can hardly be said to add to the attraction. Although prosperous, Iráklion must rank among the least charming of all Mediterranean cities.

Orientation, arrival and information

Virtually everything you're likely to want to see in Iráklion lies within the walled city, and even here the majority of the interest falls into a relatively small sector, the northeastern corner. The most vital thoroughfare, **Odhós 25 Avgoústou**, links the harbour with the commercial city centre. At the bottom it is lined with shipping and travel agencies, car and motorbike rental outfits, but as you climb these give way to banks, restaurants and city-centre shops. **Platía Venizélou** (Fountain Square), off to the right, is thronged with cafés and restaurants favoured by Iráklion's youth; behind Venizélou is **El Greco Park**, with the OTE office and more bars, while on the opposite side of 25 Avgoústou are some of the more interesting of Iráklion's older buildings.

Further up 25 Avgoústou, **Kalokerinoú** leads down to Haniá Gate and out of the city westwards; straight ahead, Odhós 1821 goes nowhere very much, but adjacent 1866 is given over to the animated **market**. To the left, Dhikeosínis, a major shopping street, heads for **Platía Eleftherías** (Liberty Square), paralleled by the touristy pedestrian alley Dedhálou, the direct link between the two squares. Eleftherías is very much the traditional centre of the city, both for traffic, which swirls around it constantly, and for life in general: ringed by more expensive tourist cafés and restaurants, and in the evening alive with strolling locals.

Points of arrival

Iráklion **airport**, 4km east of the city, lies right on the coast – you come in to land low over some of the better local beaches. The #1 bus leaves for Platía Eleftherías every few minutes from the car park in front of the terminal; buy your ticket (130dr) at the booth before boarding. There are also plenty of **taxis** outside, and prices to major destinations are posted; it's about 1000dr to the centre of town. Beware if the driver extolls the virtues of a particular place to stay – he may be motivated by the prospect of a kick-back from the proprietors, rather than your best interests.

From the wharves where the **ferries** dock, the city rises directly ahead in steep tiers. If you're heading for the centre, for the archeological museum or the tourist office, cut straight up the stepped alleys behind the bus station onto Doúkos Bófor and to Platía Eleftherías (this will take about 15min). For accommodation, though, and to get a better idea of the layout of Iráklion's main attractions, it's simplest to follow the main roads: head west along the coast, past the major east-bound bus station and on by the Venetian harbour before cutting left towards the centre on Odhós 25 Avgoústou.

There are three main **bus stations**. Services along the coastal highway to or from **the east and southeast** (Hersónisos, Mália, Áyios Nikólaos, Sitía, Ierápetra and points en route) use the terminal just off the main road between the ferry dock and the Venetian harbour; the #2 local bus to Knossós runs from the city bus stop, adjacent to the east bus station. Main road services **west** (Réthimnon and Haniá) leave from a terminal right next to the east bus station on the other side of the road. Buses for the **southwest** (Festós, Mátala or Ayía Galíni) and along the inland roads west (Tílissos, Anóyia and Fódhele) operate out of a terminal just

---

The phone code for Iráklion is ☎081.

IRÁKLION

S. VENIZELOU

Áyios Andréas
Bastion

SKORDHILON

Priuli
Fountain

IYH
Youth H

MAKARIOU

SAVATHIANON

SFAKION

DEDIDAKI

KALOKERINOU

PLA
EKATE
Áyios Minas

Cathedral

Pantokratoros
Bastion

Pórta Haníon

PLASTIRA

South/West
Bus Station

62 MARTIRÓN

KARDIOTISSIS

To Haniá & Festós

TOBAZI

YIANIKOU

THERISSOU

ROMANOU

THENON

PLASTIR

Kazantza
Tomb

KONDILAKI

0   250 m

outside Haniá Gate, a very long walk from the centre up Kalokerinoú (or jump on any bus heading up this street).

Information

Iráklion's **tourist office** (Mon–Fri 8am–2.30pm; ☎228-825) is just below Platía Eleftherías, opposite the Archeological Museum at Zanthoudhídhou 1. The **tourist police** – more helpful than most – are on Dhikeosínos, halfway between Platía Eleftherías and the market.

Accommodation

Iráklion has a distinct lack of decent, reasonably priced **places to stay**, and at the height of summer a severe shortage of anywhere to stay at all. If possible, arrange to arrive early in the day; rolling up after 8pm or so without a reservation, you'd be lucky to find anything at all – though the hostels are always worth a try. In general, if you do find a room – any room – take it. You can always set out early next day to find something better.

Mid-range **hotels** mostly lie closer to Platía Eleftherías. For hotels of C class and above, it's usually simplest to approach the tourist office first – they should know where there are available rooms and if they're not too harassed will make the phone calls for you. A handful of the more central and convenient medium-price places are included below. At quiet times, if you have the time and patience (or just happen to be passing), it's worth trying some of the B and C class hotels "on spec". During slack periods they'll often make you surprising offers – sometimes reducing prices by fifty percent and more.

The greatest concentration of **cheaper rooms** is to be found near Platía Venizélou, around Hándhakos and in the vicinities of the bus stations. There are a few more central, but rather noisy and marginally more expensive places around El Greco Park and by the bottom of the market; and another small enclave of generally less pleasant places towards the bottom of Kalokerinoú, near the Haniá Gate. Few of the cheaper places offer private bathrooms, but they should all be clean and have (some) hot water.

ACCOMMODATION: ROOM PRICE SCALES

All accommodation establishments in this book have been price-graded according to the scale outlined below. The rates quoted represent the cheapest available double room in high season; where possible, a per-person rate is given for dormitory-style accommodation in youth hostels. Out of season, room rates can drop by up to fifty percent, especially if you negotiate rates for a stay of three or more nights. Single rooms, where available, cost around seventy percent of the price of a double.

Rented private rooms usually fall into the ② or ③ categories, depending on their location and facilities, and the season; a few in the ④ category are more like plush self-catering apartments. They are not generally available from late October through the beginning of April, when only hotels tend to remain open.

① up to 4000dr (£10.50/US$16.50)   ④ 8000–12,000dr (£21–32/US$33–50)
② 4000–6000dr (£10.50–16/US$16.50–25)   ⑤ 12,000–16,000dr (£32–42/US$50–66)
③ 6000–8000dr (£16–21/US$25–33)   ⑥ 16,000dr (£42/US$66) and upwards

For more accommodation details, see p.34.

The dusty park between the east-bound bus station and the harbour is always crowded with the sleeping bags of those who failed to find, or couldn't afford, a room; if you're really broke, crashing here has the advantage that local farmers come round recruiting casual labour in the early mornings, but a pleasant environment it's not. Harassment and some robberies have been reported, and the police will certainly move you on during the day.

There are no **campsites** near to Iráklion; the nearest sites are both to the east of the city – *Creta Camping* at Káto Goúves, 16km away, and *Caravan Camping* at Hersónisos, 28km away.

Hotels

Alaira, Epimenidou and Ariadnis 1 (☎227-103). Tastefully furnished modern hotel with character; very popular roof garden. ④.

Daedalos, Dedhálou 15 (☎244-812). Very centrally placed on the pedestrianized alley between Venizélou and Eleftherías. Balcony rooms with bath. ④.

El Greco, Odhós 1821 4 (☎281-071). One of Iráklion's best-known hotels but little to recommend it from any of the others in its price range. ④.

Kris, Doúkos Bófor 2 (☎223-944). Apartment-style rooms with kitchenette, fridge and balconies overlooking the harbour. ④.

Kronos, Agarathou 2, west of 25 Avgoústou (☎282-240). Pleasant, modern hotel with sea view and baths in all rooms. ④.

Lato, Epimenidou 15 (☎228-103). Good facilities. Brilliant views over the old Venetian port and handy for bus station and ferry terminal. ⑤.

Marin, Doúkos Bófor 12 (☎224-736). Similar to the *Kris*, but with fewer facilities; balcony rooms all have showers and harbour view. Very convenient for bus stations and the Archeological Museum. ④.

Metropol, Karterou 48 (☎242-330). Situated in a quieter area near the cathedral, this dated 1960s-style hotel represents good value, especially as room rates include breakfast. ③–④.

Mirabello, Theotokopoúlou 20 (☎285-052). Good-value, family-run place just north of El Greco Park in a quiet street. Rooms with and without bath. ③.

Olympic, Platía Kornárou (☎288-861). Refurbished 1960s hotel overlooking a busy square and the famous Bembo and Turkish fountains. ⑤.

Selena, Andrógeo 11 (☎226-377). Very central but also noisy location – not from traffic but bars. May be worth trying to get reduction on the noisiest rooms. ④.

Hostels and inexpensive rooms

Atlas, Kandanoléon 11 (☎288-989). Rather rundown old pension in convenient but noisy alley between Platía Venizélou and El Greco Park. Pleasant roof garden and freshly squeezed orange juice for breakfast. ②.

Christakos, Evyénikon 12 (☎284-126). One of a number of establishments in the backstreets around Hándhakos; shared facilites and no breakfast. ②.

Cretan Sun, Odhós 1866 10 (☎243-794). Basic hotel right above the market stalls; not especially quiet, but atmospheric. ②–③.

IYH Hostel, Hándhakos 24 (☎280-858). Occupies the small original youth hostel building, with the usual facilities. 800–1300dr per person; private rooms ①.

Lena, Lahana 10 (☎223-280). Around the corner from the youth hostel on Vironos is this quiet hotel with clean rooms and a good reputation. ②–③.

Paladion, Hándhakos 16 (☎282-563). Very basic but cheap hotel close to Platía Venizélou with stuffy rooms upstairs but a pleasant garden at the back with rooms off it. No private facilities. ①–②.

Rea, Kalimeráki 1 (☎223-638). A friendly, comfortable and clean hotel in quiet street. Some rooms with washbasin, others with own shower. ②–③.

Vergina, Hortátson 32 (☎242-739). Basic but pleasant rooms with washbasins set around a courtyard which boasts an enormous banana tree. ②–③.

Youth Hostel, Vironos 5 (☎286-281). This used to be Iráklion's official youth hostel, but was recently stripped of its IYH status. Still a good place to stay, it is family run, very friendly and helpful, with plenty of space and beds on the roof if you fancy sleeping out under the stars. Private rooms as well as dormitories, hot showers, breakfast and other meals available. 900dr per person; private rooms ①.

The City

By far the most striking aspect of Iráklion is its massive Venetian walls; though well preserved and where necessary restored, access is difficult. The obvious starting point for your explorations is the fortress, which stands guard over the harbour.

The fortress and the walls

Built between 1523 and 1540, the **Fort** (Mon–Sat 8am–4pm, Sun 10am–3pm; 400dr, students 200dr, explanatory video 1000dr) was known to the Venetians as the *Rocca al Mare*, to the Turks as *Koule*. Painstakingly refurbished, it now often houses temporary exhibitions which may disrupt the standard opening hours. Taken simply as a structure, it is undeniably impressive: massively sturdy walls command superb views over harbour and town and protect a series of chambers (many still piled with cannonballs) in which the defenders must have enjoyed an overwhelming sense of security. It is easy to see here how Venetian Iráklion managed to resist the Turks so long.

On the other hand there is something unsatisfying about the way it has been so thoroughly scrubbed, polished and cosseted, losing any hint of atmosphere in the process. While you may know, from the Lions of St Mark adorning the exterior and the simple solidity of the stone, that the fort is the genuine sixteenth-century article, it *feels* as if it were built yesterday for some swashbuckling Hollywood production. At night, when the fortress is floodlit, the causeway leading to it is the haunt of courting couples, while the niches in the walls provide temporary accommodation for people awaiting ferries or for fishermen: it's a fine place to watch the ships coming and going.

The only other survivors of the Venetian harbour installations, the vaulted **Arsenali**, are now lost in a sea of concrete and traffic. Here, ships were built or dragged ashore to be overhauled and repaired – close up, you may still find bits of broken boat lying about.

The **walls** themselves are rather harder to penetrate. Perhaps the easiest approach is to follow Odhós Pedhiádhos south from the back of Platía Eleftherías and find your way up one of the dusty tracks which lead to the top of the rampart. With luck and a little scrambling you can walk all the way around from here, clockwise, to Áyios Andréas Bastion overlooking the sea in the west. There are some curious views as you walk around, often looking down onto the rooftops, but the fabric of the walls themselves is rarely visible – it's simply like walking on a dusty path raised above the level of its surrounds. A word of warning, though: usually completely safe in daytime, the walls tend to attract less desirable types from dusk onwards.

On the Martinengo Bastion, facing south, is the **tomb of Níkos Kazantzakís** (1883–1957, see p.83), Crete's greatest writer. Although his works were banned for their unorthodox views, Kazantzakís' burial rites were performed at Áyios Mínos Cathedral, although no priests officially escorted his body up here. His simple grave is adorned only with an inscription from his own writings: "I hope for nothing, I fear nothing, I am free". At the weekend Iraklians gather to pay their respects – and to enjoy a grandstand view of the soccer matches in the football stadium below.

For more impressive views of the defences, from the outside, stroll out through one of the elaborate **gates** – the Pórta Haníon at the bottom of Kalokerinoú or the Pórta Kenoúria at the top of Evans. Both of these date from the second half of the sixteenth century when the bulk of the surviving defences were completed. Originally thrown up in the fifteenth century, the walls were constantly improved thereafter as Crete became increasingly isolated in the path of Turkish westward expansion: their final shape owes much to Michele Sanmicheli who arrived here in 1538 having previously designed the fortifications of Padua and Verona. In its day this was the strongest bastion in the Mediterranean, as evidenced at the Kenoúria Gate, where the walls are over 40m thick.

If you want to follow the walls in the other direction, from the sea up, simply head west along the coastal road from the harbour – a considerable walk – until you reach them. Not far along the way you pass the recently extended **Historical Museum** (Mon–Sat summer 9am–4.30pm; winter 8.30am–3pm; 800dr). The collection is now less confused, and it does help fill that gap which, for most people, yawns between Knossós and the present day, and since it always seems virtually deserted, wandering around is a pleasure. The basement, if you're working chronologically, is where you start, and contains sculptures and architectural fragments from the Byzantine, Venetian and Turkish periods. There are some beautiful pieces, most especially a fifteenth- or sixteenth-century tiered-fountain from a Venetian palace. The ground floor has religious art, wall paintings and documents from the same periods, a reconstruction of a typically domed Cretan church and a work by the Cretan artist El Greco – a view of Mount Sinai painted around 1570. Upper floors bring things to the present with reconstructions of the studies of Níkos Kazantzakís and of the Cretan statesman (and Greek prime minister) Emanuel Tsouderos; photos and documents relating to the occupation of Crete by the Germans plus the odd helmet and parachute harness; and a substantial selection of folk art – particularly textiles. The new extension has also given the museum the space to re-create the interior of a Cretan farmhouse. On your way out, take a look at a charming Venetian fountain opposite the entrance and partly obscured by bushes.

From the harbour to the market

Heading inland from the harbour, Odhós 25 Avgoústou offers a less strenuous walk past more obvious attractions. On the left as you approach Platía Venizélou, the church of **Áyios Títos** commands a lovely little plaza. Originally Byzantine, but wholly rebuilt by the Venetians in the sixteenth century, it was adapted by the Turks as a mosque and rebuilt by them after a major earthquake in 1856. The Orthodox Church renovated it after the Turkish population left Iráklion and it was reconsecrated in 1925. A reliquary inside contains the skull of St Titus, which came here originally from his tomb in Górtys (the rest of the body was never found) and was later taken to Venice, where it stayed from the time of the Turkish invasion until 1966: in the Middle Ages the head was regularly and ceremonially exhibited to the people of Iráklion.

On the top side of this square, abutting 25 Avgoústou, stands the Venetian **City Hall** with its famous *loggia*, reconstructed after the work of earthquakes was compounded by the rigours of World War II. Just past here on the left is **San Marco**, a church very much in the Venetian style which, also restored, is used for exhibitions and occasional lectures or meetings. Under the Venetians it was the cathedral and under the Turks a mosque: nowadays the church steps make a handy overflow for the cafés in **Platía Venizélou**. In the square, the Morosini Fountain (hence "Fountain Square") dates from the final years of Venetian rule. On first sight it's a rather disappointing little monument, but the decoration is fine close up and the lions on guard, which replaced an original statue of Neptune and are two to three hundred years older than the rest of the structure, are wonderful.

Straight across the main crossroads, Odhós 1866 is packed throughout the day with the stalls and customers of Iráklion's **market**. This is one of the few living reminders of an older city, with an atmosphere reminiscent of an eastern bazaar. There are luscious fruit and vegetables, as well as bloody butchers' stalls and others selling a bewildering variety of herbs and spices, cheese and yoghurt, leather goods, souvenirs, an amazing array of cheap kitchen utensils, pocket knives and just about anything else you might conceivably need. At the far end you emerge in a quiet square, **Platía Kornárou**, the focal point of which is a beautiful **Turkish pumphouse**. Heavily restored, this hexagonal building houses a café which serves as a lively meeting place for the male octogenarians of this quarter who converse at the tables under the trees. A small Venetian drinking fountain (the Bembo Fountain) – incorporating a headless Roman torso imported from Ierápetra – stands beside the café.

Churches and icons

Turning right before the market leads you down Kalokerinoú towards the Haniá gate and the main road west. Veer left after about 100m, up Áyii Dhéka or one of the streets immediately after, and you'll reach a large open space beside the **Cathedral of Áyios Mínas**. The cathedral, a rather undistinguished nineteenth-century building, is notable mainly for its size. Just in front, however, stands the tiny original medieval church of Áyios Mínas: the interior is worth a look and contains some interesting icons (if it's closed, ask at the cathedral).

Far more worthwhile, and just at the bottom of the same square, is the church of **Ayía Ekateríni** (Mon, Wed & Sat 10am–1pm, Tues, Thurs & Fri 10am–1am & 4–6pm, closed Sun; 400dr) which houses a **Museum of Religious Art**. This is the finest collection of Cretan icons anywhere, and some Cretan icons are very fine indeed. Built in the fifteenth century, the church was part of a monastic school which in the following centuries – up to the end of Venetian rule – was one of the centres of the "Cretan Renaissance", a last flourish of Eastern Christian art following the fall of Byzantium and mainland Greece. Among the school's students were Vicénzos Kornáros, author of the Cretan classic *Erotókritos*, and many leading Orthodox theologians; most importantly, however, it served as an art school where Byzantine tradition came face to face with the influences of the Venetian Renaissance. Among the greatest of the pupils was Mihailis Dhamaskinos, six of whose works form the centre of the collection. It was the much-imitated Dhamaskinos who introduced perspective and depth to Byzantine art, while never straying far from the strict traditions of icon painting; in his later works he reverts to a much purer, earlier style. The most famous Cretan painter of them all, El Greco, took the opposite course – wholeheartedly embracing Italian styles to which he brought the influence of his Byzantine training. Although there is little evidence, it's generally accepted that these two – Dhamaskinos and El Greco – were near contemporaries at the school. Two further icons now attributed to Dhamaskinos are in the fourteenth-century church of Áyios Mathéos, now sitting below street level on Odhós Taxiárhou Markopoúlou leading southwest from the cathedral.

Alongside Ayía Ekateríni is the church of Áyii Dhéka, a seventeenth-century building which acted as a chapel to the larger church. Turning left from the cathedral before the market brings you quickly up to **Platía Eleftherías**, a confused mass of pavement cafés and whorls of traffic. There's a small bust of Níkos Kazantzakís and a larger-than-life statue of Eleftheríos Venizélos, leading figure in the struggle for union with Greece, staring out over the harbour from the ramparts and looking more like Lenin than ever. Beyond the statue you reach the entrance to the **Public Gardens**, as often as not half taken over by a funfair, but generally relatively peaceful. Above all, however, Platía Eleftherías offers access to the Archeological Museum and the new Battle of Crete and Resistance Museum on the corner of Doukos Bofor and Hatzidaki.

The Archeological Museum

Iráklion's **Archeological Museum** (Mon 12.30–7pm, Tues–Sun 8am–7pm; 1000dr, free on Sun) on Zanthoudhídhou, just off Platía Eleftherías, is one of the major reasons to visit the city. The museum houses far and away the most important collection of Minoan art and artefacts anywhere in the world. There is no doubt that the enjoyment and meaning of a visit to Knossós or the other sites will be greatly heightened if you've been here first – or better still, between two visits. Despite being old-fashioned, poorly displayed and sparsely labelled, it's always crowded (at least in summer) and at times quite overwhelmed by the stampede of coach parties thundering through. Try to see it early, late, or during everyone else's lunch break. The collection is large and will prove a lot more rewarding in small doses: take in the highlights first time around and go back later for whatever you feel you've missed – tickets are valid for re-entry the same day.

Several good museum guides are on sale (the best is probably the glossy one by J. A. Sakellarakis), but the following should give you some idea of what to expect. Basically, the galleries on the ground floor, which you have little choice but to walk through in order, follow a chronological pattern: they run from the Neolithic era right through to Roman times, with the more important Minoan periods also divided according to where the items on display were discovered. Upstairs, larger rooms show the fabulous Minoan frescoes. Due to ongoing renovation and reorganization (partly to move the most popular items to places where crowds cause less of an obstruction), some items may not be precisely where stated below; however, they should still be in the same room.

Room I covers several thousand years, from the earliest signs of human settlement around 6000 BC to the beginnings of Minoan civilization in the Pre-Palatial period. There's a bit of everything here, of interest mainly because it is *so* old: statuettes, including a Neolithic "fertility goddess"; pottery, among which the blotchy **Vasilikí ware** (Case 6) with elegant elongated spouts points to the great things to come; and stone jars from the island of Móhlos (Case 7), displaying an early mastery of the lapidary's craft. Among the miniature sculpture don't miss a

clay bull, in Case 12, with tiny acrobats clinging to its horns: an early sign of the popularity of the bull sports so important later. In the central cases, and typical of what is to be seen later, is a display of some sophisticated early **jewellery** alongside some intricately engraved **seal stones** – among the latter one from ancient Mesopotamia (no.1098), indicative of contacts between the island and its Near Eastern neighbours from very early on.

Room II contains objects from the earliest period of occupation of Knossós and Mália (around 2000–1700 BC), along with items found in various peak sanctuaries of the same era. Archeologically most significant is the **Kamáres ware** pottery, with often-elaborate white and red decoration on a dark ground. For casual visitors, however, the miniature figures are of far more immediate interest, in particular the famous "**town mosaic**" from Knossós in case 25. This consists of a series of glazed plaques depicting multistoreyed Minoan houses, beautiful pieces which probably fitted together to form a decorative scene. There are also some lovely figurines and tiny animals, mostly offerings found in the peak sanctuaries: look out for the three-columned shrine with a dove perched on the top of each column, thought to represent the epiphany, or a manifestation, of the goddess worshipped there. Finally, note the **clay statuettes** (Cases 21 and 24) of sanctuary worshippers – their arms crossed or placed on the chest in reverential attitudes – as well as the *taxímata* or sick-symbols representing parts of the human body the deity was requested to heal, a custom still followed in churches all over Greece today.

Room III is devoted to the same period at Festós. Here the **Kamáres ware** is even more elaborate, and it was at Festós that this art reached its peak – exemplified by a magnificent vase with sculpted white flowers in high relief. In Case 30 you'll find the original pieces, retreived from the cave at Kamáres, that gave the style its name. Nearby in Case 128 there is a unique portrayal of lively dolphins plunging among cockles and seaweed. The celebrated **Festós Disc**, a circular slab of clay upon which hieroglyphic characters have been inscribed in a spiral pattern, resides in Case 41. The disc is frequently described as the earliest-known example of printing, since the impressions of hieroglyphs were made with stamps before it was fired; the various signs are divided up into groups, believed to be words. Interestingly, some of these "words" are repeated, leading scholars to suggest that what is represented on the disc may be some form of prayer or hymn. Despite a plethora of theories – and claims in several books on sale around the island to "reveal the secret" of the disc – this earliest Minoan script remains undeciphered.

Room IV represents the New Palace period (1700–1450 BC) in which the great sites reached their peak of creativity, rebuilt after the first destruction. Kamáres pottery is now replaced by new styles with patterns painted in dark colours on a light background, and themes drawn from nature (in particular marine life) rather than abstract patterns. The **Jug of Reeds** in Case 49 is a brilliant example of this stylistic development. Other objects are more immediately striking: above all in Case 51 the renowned **bull's head rhyton**, a sacred vessel used in religious ceremonial and found in the Little Palace at Knossós. Carved from black stone (steatite) with inlaid eyes and nostrils (the wooden horns are new), the bull is magnificently naturalistic. There are other animal heads here too, including another rhyton in the form of a lioness's head crafted from white limestone and the stunning leopard's-head axe from Mália. In Case 46 are a number of vessels connected with the snake cult; some of them may have been snake containers. These are pertinent to Case 50, where two representations of the **snake goddess** – both wearing tight-waisted, breast-baring dresses and a decorated apron, each with snakes coiling around their hands – may equally be priestesses engaged in sacred rituals. A delicate ivory acrobat, generally accepted to be a bull-leaper, and a faience relief of a *Kri-Kri*, or wild goat, suckling her calf, also stand out. The **gaming board**, in Case 57 from the "Corridor of the Draughtsboard" at Knossós, is beautiful too – made of ivory, blue paste, crystal and gold and silver leaf, with ivory pieces – and a further reminder of the luxurious life which some Minoans at least could enjoy. Room IV also contains a collection of tools and weapons (especially a giant sword from Mália), almost all bronze with decorative work in ivory, gold and semiprecious stones. Finally, in Case 44, two small clay cups may hold important clues to the history of Minoan writing, of which so little survives. These vessels bear inscriptions written in Linear A script – developed from the cumbersome hieroglyphic – using cuttlefish ink. This use of ink suggests the existence of other suitable writing materials (possibly imported papyrus or even domestically produced palm-leaf paper) which have since perished in the Cretan climate.

Room V is devoted to the last period of the palace culture (1450–1400 BC), mainly at Knossós. Already the objects are considerably less exciting. In pottery, similar decorative themes continue to be used, but with a new formalism and on new types of vessel, which has been taken as a sign that Mycenaean influences were beginning to take hold. Such influences are clear on the giant amphorae standing against the walls. The numerous **Egyptian objects** found at Knossós are interesting too: fine in themselves and providing important evidence of the extent of trade between the two civilizations – and for archeologists, vital ammunition in the war over dates. In Case 70a is a clay **model of a modest Minoan dwelling** from Arhánes: with small rooms and tiny windows to keep out the bright Cretan sun and fierce winds, it has a small court in one corner which must have served to let in light. The roof terrace above, with typical tapered columns, is similar to those seen on village houses throughout Crete today. Side by side in Case 69, you can also see examples of both Linear A and Linear B scripts.

Room VI covers finds from cemeteries at Knossós, Festós and Arhánes of approximately the same period. First come some small groups of clay figures from a tomb near Festós, in particular one of a ritual dance inside a circle decorated with horns of consecration – very crude work but wonderfully effective. In Case 75a (against the wall) is the curious horse burial found in a fourteenth-century thólos tomb at Arhánes, and now believed to be an animal sacrifice in honour of the possibly royal personage buried in the same tomb. After slaughter, the beast had been systematically dismembered and its parts carefully placed in the position in which they are now displayed. In the centre of the room is some of the museum's finest **jewellery**: gold signet rings, necklaces of gold and beads, and other gold work demonstrating the fine granulation typical of Minoan style. The martial arts are represented by some fine gold sword hilts and two fabulous **helmets**, one of boar's tusks (reconstructed), the other of bronze with long cheekpieces. The boar's tusk helmet also makes an appearance on a ceramic amphora in Case 82. Taken with the other weapons displayed here, these items can be taken as further proof of the subordination of Minoan culture to the more warlike Mycenaean in this period.

Room VII backtracks slightly in time to include objects from minor sites – mostly small villas and sacred caves, though including the larger complex of Ayía Triádha – throughout the main palace period and beyond (1700–1300 BC). As you enter you'll see great bronze double axes, erected on wooden poles, stone horns of consecration and bronze cauldrons set about the room. In the cases themselves are some very famous pieces, above all the three **stone** (steatite) **vases** from Ayía Triádha and the **gold jewellery** from a grave near Mália. The "Harvesters' Vase" is the finest of the three vases, depicting with vivid realism a procession returning home from the fields; the harvesters are led by a strangely dressed character with long hair and a big stick, possibly a priest, and accompanied by musicians. The other two show scenes from boxing and wrestling matches and a chieftain receiving a report from an official.

The Mália jewellery is to be found in a single case (101) in the centre of the room – worth seeing above all is the stunningly intricate **pendant of two bees** around a golden disc (the latter supposedly a drop of honey which they are storing in a comb). Beside it are a number of other gold animal pendants, as well as necklaces and rings. Some **bronze figurines** in Case 89 depict worshippers making the ritual "salute" gesture to the deity whilst leaning backwards, and there's also a rare depiction of an older man released from the constriction of the usual tight belt – thus demonstrating that not all Minoans had such sylph-like figures as their art would lead you to believe. The enormous bronze cauldrons are worth a closer look; superbly crafted from sheets of metal riveted with nails, their discovery at Tílissos led to the excavation of the villas there. More mundane items in Case 99 include large copper ingots, almost certainly used as a form of currency.

Room VIII is given over to finds from the palace at Zákros (1700–1450 BC) and again includes several superlative items. There's a magnificent **rhyton of rock crystal** with a handle of beads and a collar that hides a join between two pieces encased in gold (Case 109). Its beauty aside, this exhibit is always singled out by guides as an example of the painstaking reconstruction undertaken by the museum – when discovered, it was broken into more than three hundred fragments. Also striking, in Case 111, is the **peak sanctuary rhyton**, a green stone vessel on which a low-relief scene depicts a peak sanctuary with horns of consecration decorated with birds and wild goats. Originally covered in gold leaf, this discovery provided valuable information on Minoan religion. In the case parallel to this is a bull's head rhyton, smaller than but otherwise similar to that in Room IV. Room VIII also has a fine display of pottery from both palace and town, mostly from the zenith of the **marine and floral periods**. Finally, there are some outstanding stone and ceramic miniatures – shells and a butterfly in particular – and an assortment of the craftsmen's raw materials: a giant elephant's tusk, burnt in the fire which destroyed the palace, and unused ingots of bronze from the storerooms.

Room IX contains discoveries of the same period from lesser sites in the east. As usual there is an assortment of pottery and everyday objects, the most important of which are a series of **terra-cotta figurines** from a peak sanctuary at Piskoképhalo (Case 123). These naturalistic figures are fascinating in that they show what ordinary Minoans must have looked like and how they dressed – albeit for worship.

Beside them are some charming miniature animals and models of sanctuaries. In Case 127 you can see a collection of bronze tools and weapons from the workers' village at Gourniá: hammers, picks, cutters and even "razor blades". Also in this room (Case 128) is the museum's largest collection of **seal stones**. Two things stand out about these. Firstly the intricacy of the carving, superbly executed in tiny detail on the hardest of stones, and secondly the abundance of different themes (for obvious reasons, no two seals are the same) relating to almost every aspect of Minoan life, from portraits of individuals (rare) to religious ceremonies, hunting scenes and, most commonly, scenes from nature. The seals were used to fasten parcels or clay amphorae and for signing correspondence – a number of impressions of seals in clay have survived from Minoan times, mostly baked hard in accidental fires. Some of the larger seals, especially those in precious stones or with non-natural designs, may also have seen use as charms or amulets.

Room X begins the museum's post-Minoan collection, covering a period (1400–1100 BC) when Crete was dominated by Mycenaean influences. The stylization and repetition of the themes employed in pottery decoration, coupled with a near-abandonment of the highly skilled craft of stoneworking, are obvious indications of artistic decline. Figurines from the sanctuaries are also far less naturalistically executed; there are many examples of a stereotyped goddess, both hands raised perhaps in blessing. However, an evocative clay sculpture of a **dancing group** with a lyre player from Palékastro (Case 132) does seem to echo past achievements, but even here Mycenaean influences are apparent.

Room XI continues the theme into the period of the arrival of Dorian Greeks (1100–900 BC). Among the Minoans, the goddess with raised hands remained important. The anguished features of the example from Mount Karfí (Case 148) – a remote mountain above the Lasíthi Plateau to where many Minoans fled from the vulnerable coastal areas – seem to foreshadow the end. The newcomers introduced stylistic changes: the clay cart drawn by curiously portrayed bodyless oxen is a new form of ritual vessel. The passing of the Bronze Age can be seen in Case 153: the metal of the new age was iron, which came to be used for the vast majority of weapons and tools. But some Minoan beliefs and traditions survived, such as worship at the cave sanctuary of the Minoan goddess of childbirth, Eileithyia, to the east of Iráklion; Cases 149 and 158 display votive offerings from the cave dating from Hellenistic and Roman times. Some clay figurines portray couples engaged in sexual intercourse, pregnant women or women giving birth – leaving the goddess in little doubt as to what was required of her.

Room XII takes the collection up to about 650 BC. The early part of the period simply shows a development of the art of the previous era; later exhibits betray eastern, notably Egyptian, influences. This is most evident on the pottery, which is decorated with griffins, and with figures who would look at home in Tutankhamun's tomb. An interesting jug in Case 163 is typical of this era: on the vessel's neck two lovers – thought by some to be Theseus and Ariadne – embrace fondly. There are also some fine pottery and bronze figures, and a small treasure of gold jewellery.

Room XIII may well come as a relief, simply because there is nothing tiny or intricate to look at. Instead it contains a collection of **sarcophagi** from various periods, their painted decoration reflecting the prevailing pottery style. The Minoan burial position of knees drawn up to the chest explains the small size of the coffins. They come in two basic shapes: chests with lids and "bathtubs" (which may well have been used as such during their owners' lifetimes). From here stairs lead to the rooms on the second floor.

Room XIV upstairs, the **Hall of the Frescoes**, is perhaps the most exciting in the museum – and warrants another visit if by now you're too weary to appreciate it. Only tiny fragments of actual frescoes survived, but they have been almost miraculously reconstituted, and mounted on backgrounds which continue the design to give as true an impression of the entire fresco as possible. Frescoes are among the greatest achievements of Minoan art: they were originally painted directly onto wet plaster, using mostly plant dyes but also colours from mineral sources and even shellfish – a technique which has ensured their relatively unfaded survival. The job of the restorers was helped to an extent by knowledge of the various conventions, which matched Egyptian practice: men's skin, for example, was red, women's white; gold is shown as yellow, silver as blue and bronze, red.

Most of the frescoes shown in the museum come originally from Knossós, and date from the New Palace period (1600–1400 BC). Along the left-hand wall are four large panels from the enormous fresco which led all the way along the Corridor of the Procession at Knossós; an artist's impression shows how the whole might originally have looked. Two groups of youths are shown processing towards a female figure, presumably a priestess or goddess. Between the doors there's the fresco of griffins from the Throne Room at Knossós, and then on the far side a series from the villa at Ayía Triádha, some blackened by fire. Among these, the animation of the wild cat is especially striking; a floor painting of a seascape is also shown here. The opposite wall signals a return to Knossós, with some of the most famous of the works found there: the shields which adorned the Grand Staircase; the elegant priest-king, or Lily Prince; the great relief of a bull's head; a heavily restored fresco depicting elegantly attired ladies of the court; a beautifully simple fresco of dolphins from the queen's apartment; and the famous depiction of athletes leaping over a bull. Finally, there are two simple pictures of lilies from the walls of a villa at Amnísos (see p.76).

As striking as the frescoes themselves is the **Ayía Triádha sarcophagus**, decorated in the same manner, which stands in the centre of the room. The only stone sarcophagus to have been found in Crete, its unique and elaborate painted-plaster ornamentation has led archeologists to assume that it was made originally for a royal burial and later re-used. On one side is an animal sacrifice, with a bull already dead on the altar and two goats tied up awaiting their fates. On the other are two scenes, perhaps of relatives making offerings for the safe passage of the deceased. The ends feature a scene of goddesses riding in a chariot drawn by griffins, and of two women in a chariot pulled by goats above a procession of men. Also in this room is a wonderful wooden **model of the Palace of Knossós**.

Room XV has more **frescoes** of the same period. The most famous of them is "La Parisienne", so dubbed for her bright red lips, huge eyes, long hair and fancy dress, but in reality almost certainly a priestess or a goddess if her twin image on the next panel has been interpreted correctly.

Room XVI exhibits yet more **frescoes**, the most interesting being the first, the "Saffron Gatherer". Originally reconstructed as a boy, it has since been decided that this in fact represented a blue monkey; the two versions are shown side by side. Here too is "the Captain of the Blacks", a work from the troubled end of the New Palace period. It apparently shows a Minoan officer leading a troop of African soldiers, probably Sudanese mercenaries – a sign of the period's increasing militarism.

Room XVII back downstairs breaks off from the chronological approach to display the accumulations of an Iráklion doctor, the **Yiamalakis Collection**. This covers the entire remit of the museum in a single room, and it has some very fine pieces indeed. Of particular note is a steatopygous ("fat-buttocked" in plain English) Neolithic figurine – perhaps a fertility goddess – from near Ierápetra. There are also stunning gold jewels, especially the bull's head and two other pieces of the "Zákros Treasure"; some fine miniatures, bronze and ceramic; and from later periods, huge Roman figures and a mosaic relaid on the floor.

Room XVIII continues the chronological collection right through from the Archaic period to the division of the Roman empire (c.650 BC–400 AD). There's an enormous variety of styles and objects here – among which a striking terracotta figurine of a spear-bearing Athena and a sensitively worked bronze of a youth in toga and sandals from Roman Ierápetra stand out – but the period was not one of Crete's artistic high points.

Room XIX, downstairs, goes back a little to display larger pieces from the early years of this final period, the Archaic (650–500 BC), in particular three large bronze figurines of Apollo and Artemis with their mother Leto from the early sanctuary of Apollo Delphinios at Dréros. These are impressive in their simplicity, and significant as early examples of works made from sheets of hammered bronze, riveted together.

Room XX is devoted to Classical Greek and Greco-Roman sculpture. Apart from a few good Roman copies of Greek Classical works, and some stern portrait busts of members of the imperial families, it's not a terribly inspiring end to the museum.

Eating

Big city as it is, Iráklion disappoints when it comes to **eating** – and even more when it comes to going out after you have eaten. The cafés and tavernas of the main squares – **Venizélou** and **Eleftherías** – are quintessential places to sit and watch the world pass, but their food is on the whole expensive and mediocre. The cafés and tavernas on **Dedhalou** itself, the pedestrian alley linking the two main squares, are popular with tourists too, but again are not particularly good value.

For better quality and reasonably priced food, you need to get away from the more obvious tourist haunts, although you don't always have to travel very far. A more atmospheric option is to head for the little alley, Fotiou Theodosaki, which runs through from the **market** to Odhós Evans, and is entirely lined with the tables of rival taverna owners, who cater for market traders and their customers as well as tourists.

At the basic end of the scale, **takeaways** are not in short supply. There's a whole group of *souvlaki* stalls, for instance, clustering around 25 Avgoústou at the entrance to El Greco Park; the park itself is handy if you need somewhere to sit and eat. For cheese or spinach pies or some other pastry, sweet or savoury, try the *Samaria zaharoplastío* next to the Harley Davidson shop.

Cafés

Several places in Venizélou and at the top of Dhikeosínis specialize in luscious pastries to accompany a strong mid-morning coffee; local treats include *bougátsa* and *loukoumades*.

Bougátsa Kirkor, by the fountain in Venizélou. The place to sample authentic *bougátsa*, a creamy cheese pie served warm and sprinkled with sugar and cinnamon.

Onar, Hándhakos 36b, north of Venizélou. Café with a small terrace, where a wide variety of teas as well as great ices are served.

Rigas, Kandanoléon 2. A good breakfast place on the southwestern side of El Greco Park – with a wide range of mouthwatering cakes and pastries as well as the usual standards such as *tirópita* and *spanakópita*.

Ta Leontaria, next door to *Kirkor*. Another classic *bougátsa* place with tables on the square.

Themeneopoulos, N. Foká 5, the alleyway between Dhikeonsínis and Dedhalou. This café specializes in *loukoumades*: you can watch the yeasty dough bubbling away before it is dropped to cook in the hot oil, then served with honey syrup, sesame seeds and crushed nuts. These confections are traditionally taken with a glass of cold water.

Restaurants

Good restaurants are scattered across town. Just off Eleftherías at **Platía Dhaskaloyíannis** (where the post office is) are some cheaper, if not exceptional tavernas. The *platía* is a pleasant and relaxing venue – a good place to break your tour of the nearby Archeological Museum; nearby are a couple of authentic *ouzeri* serving up tasty *mezédhes*. Nearer Venizélou, try exploring some of the back streets to the east, off Dedhalou and behind the Loggia.

Down around the harbour, you'll find a number of slightly more expensive restaurants, many specializing in fish. Far more promising just to the south is a line of *ouzeri*, plying fish *mezédhes*, along the narrow Marineli (passage leading into Platía Áyios Dimítrios, with a pint-sized church of the same name.

Curry House, just off Dedhalou. Food with a kick – Mexican and Indian dishes.

Empolo, M. Miliaria 7, a tiny street off Evans, near Platía Kornárou. Pleasant place serving traditional Cretan dishes at tables spread out at the end of a cul-de-sac.

Geroplatanos, in the leafy square fronting the church of Áyios Títos. Taking its name from the great old plane tree beneath which its tables are set out, this is one of the most tranquil lunch spots in town.

Giovanni, on the alley Koraí, parallel to Dedhalou. One of the better tavernas in Iráklion, this friendly place uses fresh, good-quality ingredients to produce a varied menu, including vegetarian dishes. Giovanni's pet parrot, cockatoo and mynah bird certainly add to the atmosphere, although one of his feathered friends recently flew off.

Ionia, corner of Evans and Yiánari. This taverna has been operating since 1923 and is the sort of place to come for substantial, no-nonsense Greek dishes.

Ippokampos, Sófokli Venizélou, just to the west of 25 Avgoústou. The best and least-expensive fish to be had in Iráklion, served in unpretentious surroundings. Deservedly popular with locals, this place is often crowded late into the evening and you may have to queue or turn up earlier than the Greeks eat. Even if you see no space it is worth asking as the owner may suddenly disappear inside the taverna and emerge with yet another table to carry further down the pavement.

Kapetanios, Marineli 1, opposite the tiny church of Áyios Dimítrios. The first in a row of *ouzeris* that line this alley off Vironos, sloping down to the harbour. Good fish dishes and *mezédhes*.

Katsina, Marineli 12. A simple and friendly *ouzeri* at the opposite (seaward) end of the alley from *Kapetanios*. Tasty and economical seafood *mezédhes* served at outdoor tables.

Loukoulos, on the alley Koraí, parallel to Dedhalou. Italian restaurant – in case you need a change of pace.

New China Restaurant, on the alley Koraí, parallel to Dedhalou. Chinese cuisine served in a leafy courtyard.

Rizes, Hándhakos 54. Economical option with a pleasant, quiet courtyard setting.

Tartuffo, Dhimokratias, near the *Galaxy* hotel. The ten-minute walk out along the road to Knossós is worth it for the excellent pizza.

Drinking and nightlife

As for **nightlife**, Iráklion is a bit of a dud when compared to many other towns on the island. Much of what does happen takes place in the suburbs or out along the hotel strip to the west. If you're determined, however, there are a couple of city-centre possibilities – and plenty of options if all you want to do is sit and drink. Indeed there is a new breed of *kafenion* emerging in Iráklion, aimed at younger people: the drinks are cocktails rather than *raki*, the music is western or modern Greek, and there are prices to match.

There are also a number of **cinemas** scattered about: check the posters at the tourist police office for programme details. Most enjoyable is the open-air cinema on the beach to the west of the city.

Bars

Bars congregate in the same areas as the restaurants. Perhaps the most animated are in Platía Koraí, a quiet square behind Dedhalou, while slightly more touristy alternatives are centred around Platía Venizélou and around the fringes of El Greco Park. After ten at night, a lively bar scene also fans out into the streets around Hándhakos and you'll stumble on many places by following the crowds.

Iráklion looks a great deal better than you'd expect from above, and most of the fancier hotels have rooftop bars; the *Alaira* hotel, just above the harbour, has particularly stunning views.

Café Flou, Platía Dhaskaloyiánnis. This laid-back café-bar casts off its daytime serenity after ten when locals gather to sink into the canvas chairs on the square, and sometimes to dance inside when the music gets really raucous.

De Facto, Platía Venizélou. One of the most popular of the fashionable bars in this area.

El Azteca, Psaromilíngon 32, west of Hándhakos. Lively Mexican bar serving tacos and fancy beers, with a garden at the back.

Flash, Platía Koraí. On the same square as *Avgo*, also with outdoor tables, this bar serves a wide variety of exotic (and expensive) beers and cocktails. Those on a tight budget can nurse a *frappé* for hours.

Idaean Andron, Perdhíkari 1, a little way east of Platía Venizélou. A good example of the new-style *kafenion*, with a nice atmosphere.

Jasmin, tucked in an alley on the left midway down Hándhakos. Another good night-time rendezvous, with jazz, soul and latin music and an outdoor terrace. Also serves snacks.

Odysseia, Hándhakos 63. Popular meeting place for Iráklion's younger set, with music and an outdoor terrace.

Piano Bar/Ladies Café Loggia, Platía Venizélou. Pleasant rooftop bar.

To Avgo, Platía Koraí. Trendy little bar frequented by students, on a pleasant square just to the north of Dedhalou.

Clubs and discos

For **discos** proper, there is a greater selection – even if they do all play techno interspersed with Greek music. **Nightclubs** are clustered in two areas: down around the harbour and on Ikarou, downhill from Platía Eleftherías, around twenty minutes' walk apart.

Makao, on the opposite side of the street to *Trápeza*. Has a loyal following, as does the *Genesis* next door.

Trápeza. The most popular of the clubs down towards the harbour at the bottom of Doúkos Bófor, below the Archeological Museum.

Listings

Airlines *Olympic*, on Platía Eleftherías (☎229-191), is the only airline with a permanent office in Iráklion. Charter airlines flying into Iráklion mostly use local travel agents as their representatives. For airport information call ☎282-025.

Airport buses Bus #1 runs from Platía Eleftherías to the airport every few minutes; buy a ticket from the booth on the square first.

Banks The main branches are on 25 Avgoústou, many of which have 24-hr cash machines (not always working); there's also a *Visa* machine at *Ergo Bank* on Dhikeosínis.

Beaches For city beaches take a #7 bus east to Amnísos or a #6 west to Amoudhári: both leave from Platía Eleftherías. The ticket booth is outside the *Astoria Hotel*; see "Buses" section below for details.

Bike and car rental 25 Avgoústou is lined with rental companies, but you'll find cheaper rates on the backstreets and it is always worth asking for discounts. Good places to start include *Eurocreta* (Sapotie 2; ☎226-700) for cars and *Motor Speed* (Ariadnis; ☎224-812) for bikes: near the Archeological Museum and under the same management, they both offer free delivery to hotels and airport. *Blue Sea* (Kosma Zotou 7 near the bottom of 25 Avgoústou; ☎241-097), *Ritz* in the *Hotel Rea* for cars (Kalimeráki 1; ☎223-638), *Sun Rise* (25 Avgoústou 46; ☎221-609) and finally *Motorrad* (Vironos 1; ☎281-670) are also reliable outlets.

Buses See p.57 for locations of bus stations – and p.121 for timetable.

Cinema Check details of what's on at the hoardings along Dhikeosínis near the tourist police office or by the main entrance to the Public Gardens. There's an open-air cinema in the west of the city.

Consulates See *Basics* p.22.

Festivals The Iráklion Summer Festival runs from July to mid-Sept. It includes exhibitions, concerts and plays by groups from around the world, some of which are top-notch, others on the level of concerts by American high-school choirs. Details from the tourist office. August 25 is St Titus' Day, marked by a major procession from the church of Áyios Títos.

Hospitals There are three hospitals. The one on Apollónion southwest of Platía Kornarou, between Alber and Moussoúrou is reasonably central. The others are out of town, including a new modern one, Periferiako Panenistemiako Veniko Nosokomeio Irakleio (PAYNE; ☎269-111) – not one to get your lips around when you're feeling under the weather.

Launderette One can be found in the backstreets below the Archeological Museum. Take plenty of change. Mon–Fri 9am–2pm & 5–7pm, Sat 9am–2pm, closed Sun.

Left luggage There's a left luggage office in the east-bound (A) and southwest (B) bus stations (daily 6am–8pm; 200dr per bag per day) but not at the west-bound. There is also a commercial agency at 25 Avgoústou (daily 7am–11pm; 450dr per bag per day) and you can also leave bags at the *youth hostel*s (even if you don't stay there) for 200–300dr per bag per day. If you want to leave your bag while you go off on a bike for a day or two, the rental company should be prepared to store it.

Mountaineering The local *EOS* is at Dhikeosínis 53 (☎227-609).

Newspapers and books English-language and other foreign newspapers are sold throughout the city centre – best bet is up Dedhálou where you'll find a wide selection of Jackie Collins novels as well as local guides and maps. For a more comprehensive selection of English-language titles including education books, then there is the *Planet International Bookstore* at the corner of Hándhakos and Kidonias (☎287-141) behind Platía Venizélou, with a huge stock of English-language titles. On 5 floors, now considerably expanded from its original premises on Hándhakos 71 which it now uses as a store, this is now reputed to be the largest bookstore in Greece.

Pharmacies Plentiful on the main shopping streets – at least one is open 24hr on a rota basis, check the list on the door of any. Also traditional herbalists in the market.

Post office Main office in Platía Dhaskaloyiánnis, off Eleftherías: open Mon–Fri 7.30am–8pm. There's also a temporary office (a van) at the entrance to El Greco Park (daily 7.30am–7pm), handy for changing money.

Shopping The market is best for food as well as for cheap practical goods and for leatherware and most standard tourist items. Herbs make an unusual souvenir from Crete – one of the best places to buy is at the stall belonging to *Kostas Stathakis* along Odhós 1866, about 50m from the junction with Dhikeosínis, on the right. Saffron is a bargain here, but get the strands and not the powdered stuff. More upmarket tourist shops – jewellery and fabrics especially – can be found down Dedhalou. Everyday shops and embroidered textiles down Kalokerinoú and clothes and shoe shops around Averof are good value in late July sales. Small mini-markets in tourist areas are open every day, and the *Continent* supermarket has recently opened out towards Amoudhári.

Taxis Major taxi ranks in Platía Eleftherías and El Greco Park or call ☎210-102 or 210-168. Prices displayed on boards at ranks.

Telephones OTE head office in El Greco Park – often long queues, efficient 24-hour service.

Toilets There are public toilets in El Greco Park and the Public Gardens and near the cathedral. However toilets are also at the bus stations and the Archeological Museum (no need to pay entrance charge to use them).

Tourist office The NTOG is opposite the Archeological Museum at Zanthoudhídhov 1 (Mon–Fri 8am–2.30pm; ☎228-825). Friendly but overworked.

Tourist police On Dhikeosínis 10 (☎283-130). Better informed and more helpful than most.

Travel agencies 25 Avgoústou is crammed with shipping and general travel agents. Cheap/student specialists include the extremely helpful *Blavakis Travel* (Platía Kallergon 8, just off 25 Avgoústou by the entrance to El Greco Park; ☎282-541) and *Prince Travel* (25 Avgoústou 30, ☎282-706). Ferry tickets also from *Minoan Lines* (25 Avgoústou 78; ☎224-303), or *Kavi Club* near to the tourist office (☎221-166). For excursions around the island, villa rentals etc, the bigger operators are probably easier: *Irman Travel* (Dedhálou 26; ☎242-527) or *Creta Travel Bureau* (Epiménidhou 20–22; ☎243-811). The latter is also the local *American Express* agent.

Amnísos and other local beaches

If all you want to do is escape Iráklion to lie on a beach for a few hours, the simplest course is to head **east**, beyond the airport, to the municipal beach, Amnísos or Tobróuk. All are easily reached by public transport: the #7 bus runs every fifteen minutes or so from the tree-shaded stop opposite the *Hotel Astoria* in Platía Eleftherías.

Leaving the city through its sprawling eastern suburbs and the town of Néa Alikarnassós into which they merge, the bus follows the old road as it skirts around the **airport**. Even in spring this manages to be a wasted and dusty-looking landscape – an impression not helped by the ill-camouflaged bunkers of the Greek air force base which shares the runway. Once past the airport, however, the road swings down to the coast and a narrow patch of level ground between the sea and the hills. First stop is at the **municipal beach**: fenced off (you pay to get in) and provided with showers and changing rooms. There seems little point in paying unless you want to study the undercarriages of incoming planes in intimate detail – this beach tends to be crowded and only marginally cleaner than the free sections.

The next halt is **AMNÍSOS**, where there are a couple of tavernas and food stalls immediately behind the beach, and even a huddle of hotels. Although you're unlikely to want to stay here, it's not a bad beach to find so close to the city. The main drawback is the stream of planes coming in to land: on peak weekends there seems to be one every few minutes, while during the week quiet periods are enlivened by fighters on low-level runs.

The last of these beaches, **Tobróuk**, is perhaps the best, with more tavernas and drink stalls, slightly fewer people, and relative peace to be found if you walk a little way along the sand.

Amnísos and Eileíthyia: two minor sites

Amnísos is also a famous name in Minoan archeology, although today the site is not particularly impressive, and the remains – right by the road down to Amnísos beach, on the low hill to the left – can only be glimpsed through a fence. There was a small settlement here, apparently a port for Knossós, from which the Cretan forces engaged in the Trojan War are said to have set sail, and it was here, in a villa, that the unusual Fresco of the Lilies was found – now on display in the Iráklion Archeological Museum (see p.70). The site is also noted for excavations by Marinatos in the 1930s, when the archeologist's discovery of pumice fragments amongst the ruins prompted him to develop his theory attributing the destruction of Minoan palaces to an eruption of the volcanic island of Thíra (see *Contexts*). The scorch marks on many of the remaining stones testify to the intense fire which destroyed the villa during this period. On the west side of the rocky outcrop behind the villa, new excavations have unearthed the remains of a harbour, possibly verifying the link with the world of Homer.

On the eastern edge of Amnísos, a sign points inland from the main road towards the hills (the turnoff to Episkopí) indicating another significant ancient site, the **Cave of Eileíthyia**, which gets a mention in *The Odyssey* as one of Odysseus's stopovers on his way home from Troy. Just over 1km up the steep road from the junction, the cave's entrance is signed on the left and lies below the road. Eileíthyia was a goddess, primarily of childbirth, of very ancient origin and this cave was a cult centre from Neolithic times. Inside are two large walled stalagmites which were almost certainly regarded as fertility totems. One of these has been worn smooth by the fingers of countless worshippers, who conducted rituals here from Neolithic times until the fifth century AD. The cave itself is now fenced and locked and if you are intent on making a survey (it's about 50m deep), you'll need to get a key from the guardian 7km away at Nirou Hani (see p.90).

Beaches to the west

There are also **beaches to the west of the city**, which are less noisy but also less atmospheric and more touristy. If you take a #6 bus from immediately in front of the *Hotel Astoria*, it will head out through the Haniá Gate and into

Iráklion's more prosperous western extremities. Eventually you'll end up on the road which runs behind the hotel strip, past the *Continent* hypermarket (and a small *Marks and Spencer* department store) and on eventually to the luxury *Creta Beach* hotel complex, unappealingly sited immediately before the power station and cement works. You can get off almost anywhere in this area, and attempt to get to **Amoudhári Beach**, though this is not always easy. Although the beach itself is public, there are very few access roads to it, and the hotels and campsite try hard to prevent non-residents walking through their grounds: you just have to ignore the people shouting at you, or take one of the roads down and put up with the crowds who tend to congregate at these access points.

Knossós

> *. . . a dancing place*
> *All full of turnings, that was like the admirable maze*
> *For fair hair'd Ariadne made, by cunning Daedalus*

Homer, *The Odyssey*

KNOSSÓS (April–Sept Mon–Fri 8am–7pm, Sat & Sun 8.30am–3pm; Oct–March daily 8.30am–3pm; 1000dr, students 500dr, free on Sun) lies some 5km south of Iráklion on a low, largely man-made hill. No matter when you come, you won't get the place to yourself – but exploring on your own does give you the opportunity to appreciate individual parts of the palace in the brief lulls between groups. The best time of day to avoid the crowds in summer is the period two hours before closing time, which also has the advantage of being cooler. If you get the opportunity to come back a second time, it will all begin to make a great deal more sense.

By far the largest of the Minoan palaces, it thrived over three thousand years ago at the heart of a highly sophisticated island-wide civilization. Long after Minoan culture had collapsed, a town on this site remained powerful, rivalling Górtys right into the Roman era. Although only the palace itself is much visited, the hills all around are rich in lesser remains dating from the twentieth century BC through to the second or third century AD.

Yet less than a hundred years ago this was a place thought to have existed only in mythology. Here it was in legend that King Minos ruled and that his wife Pasiphae bore the Minotaur – half-bull half-man. Here the labyrinth was constructed by Daedalus to contain the beast, and youths were brought from Athens as human sacrifice, until finally Theseus arrived to slay the beast and, with Ariadne's help, escape its lair. Imprisoned in his own maze, Daedalus later constructed the wings that bore him away to safety – and Icarus to his untimely death.

The excavation of the palace, and the clothing of these legends with fact, is among the most amazing tales of modern archeology. Today's Knossós, whose fame rivals any such site in the world, is associated above all with Sir Arthur Evans, who excavated the palace at the turn of the century and whose bust is one of the first things to greet you at the site. The autocratic control he exerted, his working standards and procedures, and, above all, the restorations he claimed were necessary to preserve the building as he worked his way through it, have been a source of furious controversy among archeologists ever since. It has become clear that much of Evans's upper level, the *Piano Nobile* – is pure conjecture. Even so, his guess as to what the palace might have looked like is certainly as good as anyone else's, and it makes the other sites infinitely more meaningful if you have seen Knossós first. Without the restorations, it would be hard to visualize the ceremonial stairways, strange top-heavy pillars and brightly frescoed walls that distinguish the site – and almost impossible to imagine the grandeur of the multistorey palace in its original state. To get an idea of the size and complexity of the palace in its original state, take a look at the cutaway drawings on sale outside – they may seem somewhat fantastic, but are probably not too far from reality.

The palace

When you enter the **Palace of Knossós** through its West Court – the ancient ceremonial entrance – you soon discover how the legends of the labyrinth grew up around it. Even with a detailed plan, it's almost impossible to find your way around: the trick is not to try too hard. Wander around for long enough and you'll eventually stumble onto everything; if you're worried about missing the highlights, you can always tag onto one of the guided tours for a while, catch the patter and then hang back to take in the detail when the crowd has moved on.

The remains you see are mostly those of the second palace, which was rebuilt after the destruction of around 1700 BC and was occupied (with increasing Mycenaean influence) through to about 1450 BC. At the time it was surrounded by a town of considerable size. The palace itself, though, must have looked almost as much a mess then as it does now – a vast bulk, with more than a thousand rooms on five floors, which had spread across the hill more as an organic growth than a planned building, incorporating or burying earlier structures as it went. In this the palace simply followed the pattern of Minoan architecture generally, with extra rooms being added as the need arose. It is the style of building still most common on Crete, where finished buildings are far outnumbered by those waiting to have an extra floor or room added when need and finance dictate.

The West Court and first frescoes

The **West Court**, across which you approach the palace, was perhaps a marketplace or at any rate the scene of public meetings. Across it run slightly raised walkways, leading from the palace's West Entrance to the Theatral Area, and once presumably onto the Royal Road. There are also three large, circular pits: originally grain silos or perhaps depositories for sacred offerings, but used as rubbish tips by the end of the Minoan era. If you follow the walkway towards the West Entrance nowadays, you arrive at a typically muddled part of the palace, not at all easy to interpret. First there's a line of stones marking the original wall of an earlier incarnation of the palace, then the facade of the palace proper and beyond that a series of small rooms of which only the foundations survive. When the palace was still standing, you would have passed through a guardroom and then followed the **Corridor of the Procession**, flanked by frescoes depicting a procession, around towards the south side of the palace. This is still the best way to go, though it can be hard to fathom which is the corridor.

Around on the south side of the Central Court, you can climb a flight of stairs to admire the reproduction of the **Priest-King Fresco** (also known as the Prince of the Lilies) and look down over the palace. Apparently a whole series of large and airy frescoed chambers, perhaps reception rooms, once stood up here.

Central Court, Throne Room and Piano Nobile

You can climb from this side of the courtyard to the *Piano Nobile*, the upper floor on the west side, but this is best left till later. Instead, proceed straight into the **Central Court**, the heart of the palace. Aligned almost exactly north–south, the courtyard paving covers the oldest remains found on the site, going back to Neolithic times. Some say this was the scene of the famous bull-leaping, but that seems rather unlikely; although the court measures almost 60m by 30m, it would hardly be spacious enough to accommodate the sort of intricate acrobatics shown in surviving pictures, let alone for an audience to watch. In Minoan times the courtyard would have had a very different atmosphere from the open, shadeless space which survives, with high walls hemming it in on every side.

The entrance to one of Knossós's most atmospheric survivals, the **Throne Room**, is in the northwestern corner of the courtyard. Here a worn stone throne sits against the wall of a surprisingly small chamber: along the walls around it are ranged stone benches and behind there's a copy of a fresco depicting two griffins. In all probability, this was the seat of a priestess rather than a ruler – there's nothing like it in any other Minoan palace – but it may just have been an innovation wrought by the Mycenaeans, since it appears that this room dates only from the final period of the palace's occupation. Overexposure has meant that the Throne Room itself is now closed off with a wooden gate, but you can lean over this for a good view, and in the antechamber there's a wooden copy of the throne on which everyone perches to have their photo taken. Opposite the real throne, steps lead down to a lustral basin (a sunken "bath", probably for ritual purification rather than actual bathing – it has no drain).

Alongside the Throne Room, a stairway climbs to the first floor and Evans's reconstructed **Piano Nobile**. Perhaps the most interesting feature of this part of the palace is the view it offers of the palace storerooms, with their rows of *pithoi* (storage jars) often still in place. There's an amazing amount of storage space here: in the jars, which would mostly have held oil or wine, and in spaces sunk into the ground for other goods. The rooms of the *Piano Nobile* itself are again rather confusing, though you should be able to pick out the Sanctuary Hall from stumps that remain of its six large columns. Opposite this is a small concrete room (complete with roof) which Evans "reconstructed" directly above the Throne Room. It feels entirely out of place: inside there's a small display on the reconstruction of the frescoes, and through to the other side you get another good view over the Central Court. Returning through this room, you could climb down the very narrow staircase on your right to arrive at the entrance to the corridor of storerooms (now fenced off) or head back to the left towards the area where you entered the palace.

The Royal Apartments

Returning to the courtyard allows you to cross to the east side, where the **Grand Staircase** leads into the **Royal Apartments** (currently undergoing restoration), plainly the finest of the rooms at Knossós. The staircase itself is a masterpiece of design: not only a fitting approach to these sumptuously appointed chambers, but also an integral part of the whole design, its large well allowing light into the lower storeys. Light wells such as these, usually with a courtyard at the bottom, are a common feature of Knossós and a reminder of just how important creature comforts were to the Minoans, and how skilled they were at providing them.

For more evidence of this luxurious lifestyle you need look no further than the **Queen's Suite**, off the grand **Hall of the Colonnades** at the bottom of the staircase. The main living room is decorated with the celebrated dolphin fresco and with running friezes of flowers and (earlier) spirals. On two sides it opens to courtyards which let in light and air – the smaller one would probably have been planted with flowers. In use, the room would probably have been scattered with cushions and hung with rich drapes, while doors and curtains between the pillars allowed for privacy, and for cool shade in the heat of the day. Plausible as it all is, this is largely speculation – and some pure con. The dolphin fresco, for example, was found in the courtyard, not the room itself, and would have been viewed from inside as a sort of *trompe l'oeil*, like looking out of a glass-bottomed boat. There are also some who argue, convincingly, that grand as these rooms are, they are not really large or fine enough to have been royal quarters. Those would more likely have been in the lighter and airier rooms that must have existed in the upper reaches of the palace, while these lower apartments were inhabited by resident nobles or priests.

The truth hardly matters, for whether or not you accept Evans's names and attributions, the rooms remain an impressive example of the sophistication of Minoan architecture – all the more so when you follow the dark passage round to the **Queen's Bathroom**, its clay tub protected behind a low wall (and probably screened by curtains when in use), and to the famous "flushing" lavatory (a hole in the ground with drains to take the waste away – it was flushed by throwing a bucket of water down).

On the floor above the queen's domain, the Grand Staircase passes through a set of rooms which are generally described as the **King's Quarters**. These are chambers in a considerably sterner vein: the staircase opens into a grandiose reception area known as the **Hall of the Royal Guard**, its walls decorated in repeated shield motifs. Opening off it is the ruler's personal chamber, the **Hall of the Double Axes** – a room which could be divided to allow for privacy in one half while audiences were held in the more public section, or the whole opened out for larger functions. Its name comes from the double axe symbol, so common throughout Knossós, which here is carved into every block of masonry.

The palace fringes

From the back of the queen's chambers you can emerge into the fringes of the palace where it spreads down the lower slopes of the hill. This is a good point at which to consider the famous **drainage system** at Knossós, some of the most complete sections of which are visible under grilles. The snugly interconnecting terracotta pipes ran underneath most of the palace (here they have come more or less direct from the Queen's Bathroom) and site guides never fail to point them out as evidence of the advanced state of Minoan civilization. They are indeed quite an achievement – in particular the system of baffles and overflows (most clearly seen down by the external walls), designed to slow down the run-off and avoid flooding. Just how much running water there would have been, however, is another matter: the water supply is at the *bottom* of the hill, and even the combined efforts of rainwater catchment and water physically carried up to the palace can hardly have been sufficient to supply the needs of more than a small elite.

From the bottom of the slope you get a fine impression of the scale of the whole palace complex and can circle around towards the north, climbing back inside the palace limits to see the area known as the **Palace Workshops**. Here potters, lapidaries and smiths appear to have plied their trades, and here also are the spectacular **giant pithoi**, where people queue to have their photograph taken with the jars towering over them. There's also a good view of the bull-relief fresco set up by the north entrance.

Outside the main palace, just beyond the North Entrance, is the **Theatral Area**, one of the more important enigmas of this and other Minoan palaces. An open space resembling a stepped amphitheatre, it may have been used for ritual performances or dances, but there's no real evidence of this – and again there would have been very little room for an audience if that was its function.

Beyond it the **Royal Road** sets out: originally this ran to the Little Palace (see over), and beyond that probably on across the island, but nowadays it ends after about 100m in a brick wall beneath the modern road. Alongside are assorted structures variously interpreted as stores, workshops or grandstands for viewing parades, all of them covered in undergrowth. Back down the Royal Road, you can re-enter the palace by its **North Entrance**. Beside the entry is a well-preserved **lustral basin**, and beyond that a guardroom. Heading back to the central courtyard, a flight of stairs doubles back to allow you to examine the copy of the **Bull Relief** close to.

Of the lesser structures which crowd around the palace, a number of houses on the south side are particularly worth noting, although they aren't open to the public. The one known simply as the **South House**, reconstructed to its original three floors, seems amazingly modern, but actually dates from the late Minoan period (c.1550 BC). The dwelling is believed to have belonged to some important official or noble, since it encroaches on the palace domain. In the **Southeast House**, of the same period, were discovered a cult room with a sacred pillar as well as stands for double axes and a libation table. Across a little valley from here, outside the fenced site, was the **Caravanserai** where travellers would rest and water their animals; the restored building contains two elegant rooms, as well as a large stone footbath still running with water from an ancient spring.

Among the other important outlying buildings are the **Little Palace**, on a site which also contains a mansion and many Roman remains (just up the narrow alley which veers off to the left as you head back towards Iráklion), and the **Royal Villa**, facing the palace from the slope to the northeast. Both are occasionally open for special visits.

About 100m along the road to Iráklion from the site entrance lies the **Villa Ariadne**, an Edwardian villa constructed by Evans and where he resided while conducting excavations. Later the house served as a military hospital during the German siege of Iráklion and, following the city's fall, as the residence of the German commander of Crete. It was where General Kreipe was based when he was kidnapped by Paddy Leigh Fermor and others (see "The Historical Framework" in *Contexts*). The villa's dining room was also where the German army signed the surrender on May 9, 1945. Although not open to the public, nobody seems to mind if you walk up the drive past the gatehouse to have a look at the house's exterior and gardens.

Practicalities

Getting to Knossós from Iráklion could hardly be easier. The #2 bus sets out every ten minutes from the city bus stands adjacent to the east-bound bus station, runs up 25 Avgoústou (with a stop just below Platía Venizélou) and out of town on Odhós 1821 and Evans. Taxis run from the city and cost 700dr (see p.75). If you're driving you can take this route, through Evans Gate, or follow the signs from Platía Eleftherías; from anywhere other than Iráklion turn directly off the bypass onto the badly signed Knossós road.

Arriving, you're confronted first by a string of rather pricey tavernas and tacky souvenir stands. There are several **rooms** places here too, and if you're really into Minoan culture there's a lot to be said for staying out this way to steal an early start. Be warned, though, that the site area is expensive and unashamedly commercial. At the end of all the development, on the other side of the road, is the free official car park – although it tends to be inadequate at peak times. This is where the bus drops you, and it's through the car park that you enter the site proper, having first run the gauntlet of map salesmen and tour guides and bought your ticket at the turnstiles. To catch the bus back, you have to walk a short way back up the road; a ruse no doubt designed to force you once again past all those souvenir shops.

South to Mount Yioúhtas

The countryside south of Knossós is dominated by the bulk of **Mount Yioúhtas** (811m), which rises alone from a landscape otherwise characterized by gently undulating agricultural country. Seen from the north, and especially the north-west, the mountain has an unmistakeably human profile identified with Zeus in the post-Minoan period. Underneath the mountain, the ancient Cretans claimed, Zeus lay buried: given that the god is immortal, this furnished proof for other Greeks of the assertion that "All Cretans are liars" – and may, indeed, have been the original basis of this reputation.

Beyond Knossós the nature of the journey is transformed almost immediately – the road gradually empties, the country becomes greener. Almost any of these roads south makes a beautiful drive, past vineyards draped across low hills and through flourishing farming communities. Just a couple of kilometres from the site, at the head of the valley, there's an extraordinary **aqueduct** arching along beside the road. This looks medieval, but is in fact barely 150 years old, having been built during the brief period of Egyptian rule (1832–40) to provide Iráklion with water. Just beyond are a couple of tavernas/cafés beside the road – a convenient escape from the Knossós crowds – and just past them is a turning on the left, clearly signposted to Mirtiá.

Mirtiá and the Kazantzakís Museum

The main reason to visit **MIRTIÁ** is for the Kazantzakís Museum in the village, but you don't need to be a fan of the writer to find the trip worthwhile. Only enthusiasts are likely to spend long over the exhibits, but it's an enjoyable collection to look over quickly and a lovely drive there on almost deserted roads. Mirtiá itself is larger than you'd expect – as indeed are many of these villages – and bright with flowers planted in old olive-oil cans.

The **museum** (March–Oct Mon–Sat 9am–4pm, closed Sun; 400dr) is on the central *platía* (well beyond the multicoloured, multilingual signs on the main street at either end of the village), along with three pleasant *kafenia* where you can stop for a drink. Occupying a house where Kazantzakís's parents once lived – a fine bourgeois mansion – the collection includes a vast quantity of ephemera relating to the great author: diaries, photos, manuscripts, first editions, translations into every conceivable language, playbills, stills from films of his works, costumes and more. There's also a video documentary in Greek.

Briefly, **Níkos Kazantzakís** was born on Crete in 1885, and his early life was shadowed by the struggle against the Turks and for union with Greece. Educated in Athens and Paris, he travelled widely throughout his life working for the Greek government on more than one occasion and for UNESCO, but above all writing: a vast range of works including philosophical essays, epic poetry, travel books, translations of classics (such as Dante's *Divine Comedy*) into Greek and, of course, the novels on which his fame in the west mostly rests. *Zorba the Greek* (1946) was the first and most celebrated of them, but his output remained prolific to the end of his life. Particularly relevant to Cretan travels are *Freedom or Death* (1950), set amid the struggle against the Turks, and the autobiographical *Report to Greco*, published posthumously in 1961 (he died in West Germany in 1957 after contracting hepatitis from an unsterilized vaccination needle during a visit to China). Kazantzakís is widely accepted as the leading Greek writer of the century, and Cretans are extremely proud of him, despite the fact that most of his later life was spent abroad, that he was banned from entering Greece for long periods and excommunicated by the Orthodox church for his vigorously expressed doubts about Christianity – the latter also gained him more recent notoriety when *The*

Last Temptation of Christ was filmed by Martin Scorsese. The church was also instrumental in working behind the scenes to deny him the Nobel Prize, which he lost by one vote to Albert Camus in 1957. Plenty of people now regard his writing as overblown and pretentious, but even they admit that the best parts are where the Cretan in Kazantzakís shows through, in the tremendous gusto and vitality of books like *Zorba* and *Freedom or Death*. He himself was always conscious, and proud, of his Cretan heritage.

Arhánes

Back at the turning to Mirtiá, it's a further 2km through the vineyards on the main road to the junction where you turn right for Arhánes. It was here, in what appears to be a singularly unthreatening spot on a summer afternoon, that General Kreipe was kidnapped on April 26, 1944.

The fork leads for another 2km through Patsídhes and Káto Arhánes to the large agricultural centre of **ARHÁNES** – a town substantial enough to have a one-way traffic system. Arhánes is also served by hourly buses from Iráklion. The centre, with a small square by a restored church and a couple of large, dozy *kafenia*, is on the north-bound side: drive through and double back. The church has an incongruous whitewashed clock tower and a fine collection of icons; elsewhere there are Byzantine frescoes in the church of Ayía Triádha, on the fringes of town and, much more importantly, at the church of **Asómatos**, to the east, where the superb fourteenth-century works include a horrific *Crucifixion*, and a depiction of the fall of Jericho with Joshua in full medieval armour. Before setting out, you'll need to get the key from the *Miriófiton Snack Bar* on the square – leaving a passport with them as a deposit. To get there, follow the road through the town, and then the signs east for a couple of kilometres.

Arhánes was a sizeable **centre of Minoan civilization**, and there are a number of sites roundabout. All of them are relatively recent discoveries – they have been excavated in the last 25 years or so – and not all of the excavations are yet fully published. Consequently they are neither particularly famous nor especially welcoming to visitors, but many of the finds have been important. The largest of the structures is the **Palace**, in reality more likely a large villa, which lies right in the heart of the modern town, signed just off the main road. Through the chain-link fence you can see evidence of a substantial walled mansion, representing only a small part of what once stood here. Piecemeal excavation is still going on, but much is hidden beneath more modern buildings.

The second of the sites is **Foúrni** (daily 8.30am–3pm; free) off to the right as you enter the town (immediately before the school) and about ten minutes' walk up a ferociously rocky, steep trail. What has been unearthed here is a burial ground used throughout the Minoan period, with its earliest tombs dating from around 2500 BC (before the construction of the great palaces), and the latest from the very end of the Minoan era. The structures include a number of early *thólos* tombs – round stone buildings reminiscent of beehives – each of which contained multiple burials in asarcophagi and *pithoi*. Since many simpler graves and a circle of seven Mycenaean-style shaft graves were also revealed at Foúrni, it is by far the most extensive Minoan cemetery known. Its significance was increased by some of the finds made here: most importantly, within *Thólos A*, a side chamber was found which revealed the undisturbed tomb of a woman who, judging by the jewellery and other goods buried with her, was of royal descent and perhaps a priestess. Another recent suggestion is that she was a princess buried here shortly before the final destruction of Knossós Palace. Her jewellery and rings are now on display at the Iráklion Archeological Museum, as is the skeleton of a horse apparently sacrificed in her honour.

The size of Foúrni is further evidence of the scale of the Minoan community that once thrived around Arhánes.

Anemospília

As sites go, **Anemospília**, 2km northwest of Arhánes, is considerably more worthwhile than other sites in the vicinity, and is enlivened by a spectacular setting and a controversial story. The road there heads north from Arhánes: coming from Iráklion you enter the one-way street and turn sharp right, back on yourself, almost straight away, just past a small chapel. Following the best of the roads, you begin to climb across the northern face of Mount Yioúhtas, winding around craggy rocks weirdly carved by the wind (*Anemospília* means "Caves of the Wind") until you reach the fenced site held in a steep curve of the road.

What stood here was a temple, and its interpretation has been the source of outraged controversy among Minoan scholars since its excavation at the beginning of the 1980s. The building is a simple one, consisting of three rooms connected by a north-facing portico, but its contents are not so easily described. The temple was apparently destroyed by an earthquake, which struck during a ceremony that appears to have involved **human sacrifice** – the only evidence of such a ritual found in Minoan Crete. This came as a severe shock to those who liked to portray the Minoans as the perfect peaceable society, but the evidence is hard to refute. Three skeletons were found in the western room: one had rich jewellery, indicative of a priest; another was a woman, presumably a priestess or assistant; the third was curled up on an altar-like structure, and, according to scientists, was already dead when the building collapsed and killed the others. A large bronze knife lay on top of this third skeleton. Outside the western room, another man was crushed in the corridor, apparently carrying some kind of ritual vase. These events have been dated to around 1700 BC, roughly the time of the earthquakes that destroyed the first palaces and, in the circumstances, it seems easy to believe that the priests might have resorted to desperate measures in a final attempt to appease the gods who were destroying their civilization.

To the summit: Vathípetro

Continuing beyond Arhánes you'll see a sign after a couple of kilometres for the **summit of Mount Yioúhtas**, up a track which is a relatively easy drive. You can also climb to the top in little over an hour from Arhánes along the same route, but it seems rather unsatisfying to do this only to discover other people rolling up on their motorbikes or in taxis. The panoramic views are the main lure – back across Iráklion especially, but also west to Psilorítis and east to Dhíkti; the view south is blocked by another peak crowned with a radio mast. On the summit is a small and fairly ordinary chapel, and the trappings of the annual *Paniyíri*, which is celebrated on August 6 and attracts villagers from all around. There was once a Minoan peak sanctuary too, but no significant trace of it remains; on the shoulders of the mountain, not easily accessible, are caves associated with the local Zeus cult.

The main road running beneath Mount Yioúhtas continues south toward **VATHÍPETRO**, which is well signposted along the way. Here, at last, is a site which can be examined close to: a large Minoan **villa** (daily 8.30am–3pm; free), which once controlled the rich farmland south of Arhánes. Inside was found a remarkable collection of everyday items – equipment for making wine and oil and other tools and simple requisites of rural life. Still surrounded by a vineyard, the house was originally a substantial building of several storeys, with a courtyard enclosing a shrine, and fine large rooms – especially on the east. The basement workrooms, however, were the scene of the most interesting discoveries, many of which can still be seen *in situ*: finds included most of the agricultural equipment and a superb **wine press**. When the doors are locked, you can see something of what remains through the barred windows.

West of Iráklion

Heading west from Iráklion the modern E75 highway, cut into the cliffs, is as fast and efficient a road as you could hope to find. In simple scenic terms it's a spectacular drive, but with very little in the way of habitation – only a couple of developed beach resorts and the "birthplace of El Greco" at Fódhele until the final, flat stretch just before Réthimnon. If you go this way, the point where you join the bypass offers perhaps the best view of Zeus's profile on Mount Yioúhtas – open mouth, prominent nose and chin.

If you're in no hurry, forget the highway and try the older roads west, curling up amid stunning mountain scenery. The only specific site on these back roads is the Minoan one at Tílissos (see p.89), but they have the advantage of taking you through archetypal rural Crete, with tracks tramped solely by herds of sheep or goats, isolated chapels or farmsteads beside the road, and occasionally a village. City buses will take you as far as the *Creta Beach* hotel (p.77), but to travel any further west you'll need either your own transport or a KTEL bus from one of the west-bound stations.

The new road

Once past the city beaches, the highway heads north, climbing into the foothills of the Psilorítis range as they plunge straight to the sea. As you ascend, keep an eye out for the immaculately crafted medieval fortress of **Paleókastro**, built into the cliff right beside the road; it's easy to miss, so completely do the crumbling fortifications blend in against the rocks. Just beyond, the road crosses a bridge over the modern village of Paleókastro, nestling in a little gully which leads down to the sea: a beautiful setting, with wealthy suburban homes and restaurants popular for weekend outings.

Ayía Pelayía
As you round the headland, **AYÍA PELAYÍA** is laid out below, a sprinkling of white cubes around a deep blue bay, unbelievably inviting from this distance. Closer to, the attraction is slightly diminished: continuing development is rapidly outpacing the capacity of the narrow, taverna-lined beach, and is beginning to take its toll on the village. Meanwhile, the water is clear and calm, and the swimming excellent;

water-skiing, parasailing and motorboats are all available if you're prepared to pay. There's a superb view, too, of all the ships which pass the end of the bay as they steam into Iráklion – spectacular at night when the brightly lit ferries pass. Although the beach can get very crowded with day-trippers from Iráklion at week-ends, the resort clings to its exclusivity in the shape of two of the best-looking luxury hotels on the island – the *Capsis Beach* (☎081/811-112; ⑤) on the promontory overlooking town and the *Peninsula* (☎081/8111-313; ⑤) over on the headland beyond. If you feel in need of a little more space, you can always head for the nearby beach to the east – Ligaria, which is much more welcoming, but has fewer facilities.

Buses run between the *Capsis Beach* hotel and the *Astoria* in Platía Eleftherías, Iráklion, six times a day. If you take a long-distance bus bound for Réthimnon or Haniá, you face a steep three-kilometre descent from the main road where you'll be dropped – and it's even worse walking back up.

Food is an easier proposition: if you tire of or can't afford the beachfront restaurants, head into the village where there are some more basic takeaways and small supermarkets for the makings of a picnic on the beach. **Accommodation** tends to consist of hotels and studios or apartments with cooking facilities, rather than straightforward rooms. Out of season, these can be excellent value if you're prepared to bargain hard, but through the summer they're mostly block-booked. If you do want to stay, it's a question of wandering around asking at every door with a sign – the owners will usually know who has a room free (if anyone does). Otherwise, try one of the travel bureaus, such as *Diana Tours* (☎081/811-126), just off the beach opposite *Vasilis Supermarket*. For late-night **entertainment**, the *7am–7pm Music Bar*, actually open from 11pm onwards, is on the road from the beach up to the *Capsis Beach* hotel.

Fódhele

Turning **inland from the main road** opposite Ayía Pelayía, an old stretch of paved road runs from Ahládha to Fódhele, connected by rutted, unpaved sections with other old roads inland. Ahládha's spectacular hilltop setting serves to detract from the lack of attractions in the village itself. If you're simply heading for Fódhele, you can get there more efficiently by taking the later turnoff about 3km west, but if you can afford the time to travel at a more leisurely pace, the old route is a great deal more diverting.

FÓDHELE is firmly established on the tourist circuit as the birthplace of El Greco, although there's virtually no hard evidence to substantiate this. The excursion is a pleasant one, in any case: Fódhele lies in a richly fertile valley, surrounded by orange and lime groves. On the far side of the river as you drive up are a couple of small Byzantine chapels, and there's an ancient church in the village. Despite the craft and souvenir shops that line the main street, selling local embroidery, and the café tables ranged along the river bank, Fódhele most of the time is almost preternaturally sleepy – you can sit at one of these shady tables for half an hour before anyone emerges to take your order, and wait as long again before the order has any effect. Meanwhile, take a few minutes to study the plaque in the village square: made of stone from Toledo (where Domenico Theotokopoulos settled to produce the bulk of his most famous works and earn the name El Greco), it was presented to Fódhele in 1934 by the University of Valladolid – an authentication of the locale's claim to fame, which must be responsible in some measure for its current prosperity.

To get to **El Greco's House** you cross the bridge over the river, pass the church (which has copies of many of his works) and follow the clearly signed road which heads northwards out of town. Now heavily restored, the building does not look old enough to have been around when the painter was, but having got this far you might as well see it – especially if plans to incorporate some kind of display have been completed.

A couple of **buses** a day run direct to Fódhele from the Haniá Gate terminal in Iráklion, but the timings aren't really conducive to a quick visit. On the other hand, it's not too far to walk back to the junction, 3km away, so you could catch the direct afternoon bus up (at 2.30pm) and then try flagging down a long-distance bus on the main road. There are also occasional tours from Iráklion.

The old roads

Ignoring the benefits of the modern coastal road and taking the slower, mountain route you run at first through villages, like Gazí, that are mostly industrial and lacklustre. Once under the raised highway, however, you immediately start to climb into the hills. Almost straightaway there's a right turn signed to Rodhiá, a sizeable village looking back down over the city. This is the quieter way to Ayía Pelayía and Fódhele, but to get there you face more than 9km of atrocious road between here and Ahládha.

From Rodhiá a signed detour climbs 5km northwest into the hills to the famous **convent of Savathianá** (8am–1pm & 4–7pm), set in a rock cleft and surrounded by lofty cypresses. Founded in the Venetian period, the diligent nuns here have transformed the settlement into a flower-festooned oasis; a quince orchard behind the convent is the source of homemade jams sold to visitors. The convent gained further celebrity in 1991 when an eighteenth-century icon entitled *Lord Thou Art Great*, and identical to the one at Tóplou (see p.156), was discovered; both were painted by Ioánnis Kornáros.

As you apparently start to leave development behind, you promptly come across it again in the form of **Arolíthos**, a brand new "traditional village", which represents a surprisingly successful attempt to create the atmosphere of traditional Crete in a tourist development. There are craftsmen – potters, weavers, artists, a smith – at work using traditional methods, stores where you can buy their products, a restaurant with wood-fired ovens, and events such as Greek dancing evenings laid on. There are also some upmarket rooms, though no very good reason to stay. For the moment the place seems half empty except when a bus tour calls by, but it's worth a look as you pass.

A little way beyond Arolíthos, the way divides: the road that used to be the main route from Iráklion to Réthimnon is the one which runs through **MÁRATHOS**, 9km beyond Arolíthos. Famous for the honey that seems to be on sale at every house, Márathos is an attractive place with a couple of *kafenia* if you feel like breaking the journey (this road runs through very few other villages of any size). Not far beyond the village, it's possible to cut down by another pretty terrible track to Fódhele (see above).

These days more people travel by the furthest inland of the roads, the one that climbs up through Tílissos and on via **Anóyia** (see p.193). It's a pleasant ride through the Malevísi, a district of fertile valleys filled with olive groves and vineyards renowned from Venetian times for the strong sweet **Malmsey wine** much favoured in western Europe.

Tílissos

The big attraction of the first part of the trip along this inland route is **TÍLISSOS**, a name famous in the annals of Minoan archeology as among the first sites to be excavated. Local archeologist Hatzidakis, working at the beginning of the century, revealed evidence of occupation from the early Pre-Palace period (c.2000 BC), but interest focuses primarily on three large villas (known as Houses A, B and C) from the New Palace era, contemporary with the great periods at Knossós, Festós and elsewhere. They were probably not as isolated in the country-house sense as they seem today, but may well have been part of a thriving community, or even a staging post on the route west towards as yet undiscovered centres there. The existence of a rather simpler villa at Sklavókambos, on the road halfway from here to Anóyia, may lend weight to this latter theory. The site shared in the destruction of the palaces about 1450 BC but new buildings then arose, among which was the cistern in the northeast corner. With the arrival of the Dorians Tílissos developed into a Greek city of the Classical period, issuing its own coinage. This later construction tends to makes it a bit harder to get a clear picture of what's there.

The archeological **site** (daily 8.30am–3pm; 400dr) is signed to the left at the foot of the main street of the modern village. While it's not always the easiest of sites to interpret, it is a lovely place to wander round: it gets few visitors, has pine trees for shade, and boasts some evocative remains including staircases and walls still standing almost 2m tall – alongside some unsubtle restoration. Immediately beyond the fence, vineyards and rich agricultural land suggest a seductive, but probably illusory, continuity of rural life.

Houses A and C are of extremely fine construction and design (C is the more impressive), while little remains of House B apart from its ground plan, but it does contain some of the oldest relics here. A building of finely dressed ashlar stone, **House A** has a **colonnaded court** at its heart with a window lighting the staircase to the west side of this. In **storerooms** on the north side, some of the large reconstructed *pithoi* can be seen with holes near their bases for tapping the contents (probably oil); a number of Linear A tablets also came to light in this area. In the south wing, the main rooms open onto a light well with the **central room** having a **lustral basin** – in this case more of a sunken bath – just off it. A stand for a double axe, similar to finds from Knossós, was found in the **pillar crypt**, along with the three enormous bronze cauldrons (now in the Iráklion Archeological Museum) that originally prompted the site's excavation. Throughout the house, fragments of painted stucco were found, leading archeologists to postulate the existence of a luxurious second storey to this dwelling, which had fallen in over time.

House C contains a **cult room** with a central pillar, **storerooms** and, at its northern end, the **living area**, where a paved **main room** would have been illuminated by a **light well** on its eastern side. At the end of one of many corridors (a Minoan speciality), a staircase would once have led to an upper floor. There is also evidence of a drainage system, while outside the house, beside the **cistern**, is a **stone altar** from the Classical period.

Tílissos village, a pleasant enough place, provides food, drink and even a few **rooms** for its visitors. For a delicious Cretan omelette, made with local *Tirozoúli* cheese, stop at the *Estiatório Akropolis*, 150m up on the left of the main street after the site turnoff. **Buses** run five times daily to the village from the Haniá Gate in Iráklion, and continue towards Anóyia.

East of Iráklion

Beyond the city beach at Amnísos there's almost continuous development all the way to Mália, as what little remains of the coastal landscape is torn apart to build yet more hotels, apartments and beach complexes flanking the main E75 highway; you'll need to turn off to reach the places below.

The first distinct centre is **HÁNI KOKKÍNI**, a grubbily nondescript resort with a long but rather scrabbly beach. There's a **Minoan villa** here – known as *Nirou Hani* – which must have been beautifully sited when it stood alone. With the road immediately outside and traffic roaring by, however, it is harder to appreciate. Excavations of the villa revealed the foundations of a two-storey building dating from the New Palace period (c.1550 BC). All the usual Minoan architectural features – light well, storage rooms, connecting corridors, decorative paving – are present and the site was particularly rich in religious paraphernalia, including tripod altars and some striking bronze double axes now on display in the Iráklion Archeological Museum. These finds led the excavators to name it the "House of the High Priest". The site is now open on a regular basis (Tues–Sun 8.30am–3pm) but the guardian is often available after this – enquire at the nearby cafés if he's not immediately apparent; the guardian also holds the key to the Cave of Eileíthyia (see p.76).

Through **GOÚRNES** and **GOÚVES** things get even worse. At Goúrnes a giant US air force base has now closed; the Greek government have not yet decided what to do with the base, and it may be their own planes that buzz the coast in the future. The beach stretches unbroken for several kilometres, but for the most part it's a narrow strip of dirty pebbles, windy and exposed. The picture is completed by giant radar dishes overlooking it all from the hills. At Káto Goúves, just east of Fínikas, there's a campsite, *Camping Creta* (☎0897/41400) which shares a boundary with the base. Some shelter is provided by the small tamarisk trees. Apart from the beach there is little here to warrant a special stop, although it is the nearest site to Iráklion.

About 6km inland by car from the junction with the E75, up the turning to Goúves proper, is the **Skotinó Cave**, one of the largest and most spectacular on the island. You can walk there along 3km of unsigned tracks from Goúves if you're feeling adventurous. It's a pleasant walk of some 45 minutes from the coast road, passing through Goúves village, which makes an encouragingly complete contrast to the coastal strip. You can stop here for refreshment and to check directions before continuing to the signed turnoff, on the right, for Skotinó (which means "dark"). Driving, head through Goúves, then take a right turn to Skotinó village. About a kilometre out of the village, take a track downhill on your right after a hairpin bend and the cave is a further kilometre; there's a sign off the road but it's not the most obvious. From here, follow the track that eventually leads to a broken gate – the white chapel ahead marks the beginning of a path that descends to the cave entrance. Divided into four levels with an awesomely huge main chamber, the cave is 160m deep. It was first investigated by Evans and more scientifically explored in the 1960s by French and Greek archeologists. A considerable number of bronze and ceramic votive offerings were found here (the earliest dating back to early Minoan times), suggesting that this was an important sacred shrine. The cave remained in use well into the Greek and Roman eras, when the fertility goddess Artemis was worshipped in what is thought to have been a substitution for an earlier Minoan female fertility deity, possibly Brytomartis.

Hersónisos (Límin Hersonísou)

Continuing east along the main coast road, the turning for the direct route up to the Lasíthi Plateau is signed 3km beyond the bridge over the Apsolémis winter torrent. Shortly after this, you roll into the first of the really big resorts, **HERSÓNISOS** (or, more correctly, Límin Hersonísou; Hersónisos is the village in the hills just behind). A brash, sprawling and rather seedy resort, Hersónisos is replete with all the trappings of mass tourism. If you're looking for tranquillity and Cretan tradition, forget it; this is the world of concrete high-rise hotels, video bars, English breakfasts and Eurodisco nightlife. That said, there are enough restaurants to keep prices down, and plenty of sand to escape the crowds – the one thing you won't find in high season is a room.

Along the modern seafront, a solid line of restaurants and bars is broken only by the occasional souvenir shop: in their midst you'll find a small pyramidal fountain with broken mosaics of fishing scenes. This dates from Roman times and is the only real relic of the ancient town of **Chersonesos**, a thriving port from Classical Greek through to Byzantine times, handling trade from Lyttos, which once lay inland near Kastélli. Around the headland above the harbour and in odd places along the seafront you can see remains of Roman harbour installations, mostly submerged, and on the headland above the more modern church is the fenced and locked site where an early Christian basilica, probably the seat of a bishop, has been excavated. But in the main the new port covers the old.

There is little more of historic interest to keep you occupied in the town, but if you want something to do to ring the changes from beach and bar then there are other distractions nearby. A short distance inland are the three **hill villages** of Koutoulafári, Piskopianó and "Old" Hersónisos – worth searching out for accommodation and for their good selection of tavernas. Despite restoration and their increasing use by tour operators, the villages still maintain a reasonably traditional atmosphere. Piskopianó has a **Museum of Rural Life** (10am–1pm & 4–8.30pm; 300dr), situated in one of the narrow streets, which makes for a welcome break from the hustle and bustle of Hersónisos below. The olive press and the *raki* still in the courtyard outside act as reminders to search out the village *kafenion* afterwards.

If you begin to get withdrawal symptoms from a lack of contact with water, try the **Star Water park** on the beach to the eastern side of the resort: admission is free, but you do pay to indulge in the range of water sports on offer, which include scuba-diving lessons (also available at *Scubakreta* at the *Nana Beach Hotel* (☎22950).

Arrival and Information

Every thirty minutes from 7.30am to 10.00am **buses** run between Hersónisos and both Iráklion and Áyios Nikoláos. For shorter hops around town, **taxis** gather next to the *Aria* disco and the *Creta Maris* hotel, or can be called on ☎22-186 or 22-622. The **OTE** office, on Elefthériou Venizélou 65, is open from mid-June to mid-September (Mon–Fri 7.30am–10.00pm, Sat & Sun 7.30am–3.00pm). The very helpful **tourist office** on Giaboúdaki, down towards the harbour, makes a good starting point, and can offer guidance in the search for somewhere to stay.

> The phone code for Hersónisos is ☎0897.

Accommodation

Although you should have little problem finding somewhere to stay outside the peak season of July and August, much of the **accommodation** is allocated to package-tour operators and what remains is not cheap – you are unlikely to find anything less than 5000–7000dr per night for a double room. The proliferation of places to stay means that your best option is to call in at the **tourist office** (see above), or one of the travel companies on the main street, such as *Zakros Tours*. A word of warning: hotels in the centre are subject to a fair amount of noise; for more peaceful surroundings, head inland or towards Sarandáris. Providing you don't mind a short taxi-ride or twenty-minute walk, the pleasant hill villages of

Piskopianó or Koutouloufári are useful options – as is "Old" Hersónisos, although this is not within walking distance.

Caravan Camping (☎22-025), by the beach at the eastern end of town, has ample places to camp in the shade, although the pitches can be extremely close to one another. If you crave more comfort, reed-roofed bungalows (①–②), with sea views, are also available.

Creta Maris (☎22-115). One of the ritziest places in the resort; good range of facilities. ⑥.

Crystal, Giaboudaki (☎22-546). Reasonable, centrally located hotel. ③.

Nancy, Ayía Paraskevís (☎22-212). Decent hotel, also in the town centre. ③–④.

Selena Apartments, Maragáki 13 (☎22-412). Clean, family-run establishment on a quiet street. ②.

Youth Hostel, Eleuthériou Venizélou (☎23-674). Situated across from *Caravan Camping*, this hostel is well run by a helpful and friendly American-born Greek; meals and laundry facilities available. (1400dr per bed).

ACCOMMODATION: ROOM PRICE SCALES

All accommodation establishments in this book have been price-graded according to the scale outlined below. The rates quoted represent the cheapest available double room in high season; where possible, a per-person rate is given for dormitory-style accommodation in youth hostels. Out of season, room rates can drop by up to fifty percent, especially if you negotiate rates for a stay of three or more nights. Single rooms, where available, cost around seventy percent of the price of a double.

① up to 4000dr (£10.50/US$16.50)	④ 8000–12,000dr (£21–32/US$33–50)
② 4000–6000dr (£10.50–16/US$16.50–25)	⑤ 12,000–16,000dr (£32–42/US$50–66)
③ 6000–8000dr (£16–21/US$25–33)	⑥ 16,000dr (£42/US$66) and upwards

For more accommodation details, see p.34.

Restaurants

Despite the abundance of **places to eat**, there are few worth recommending in the resort itself, with the vast majority being very average; the tavernas down on the harbour front are generally best avoided. The hill villages have the greatest selection and a more relaxed atmosphere – particularly Koutoulafári where, among others, there's a nameless, unpretentious family-run taverna with a small garden courtyard in the centre of the village near *Koutoulafari Apartments*. Restaurants also cluster around the main square of "Old" Hersónisos, while Piskopianó has a good *kafenion* and a number of tavernas.

Chicken Georges, 2km out, on the road to Lasíthi. Worth visiting for tasty and cheap chicken, although it can be rather quiet on some nights, presumably because of the extra distance involved.

Copper Kettle, Eleuthériou Venizélou. Take your pick from a fairly standard international menu.

Fegari Taverna, on the Piskopianó road near the junction to Koutoulafári. Friendly taverna serving good Greek food at reasonable prices. Entertainment is provided by the steady stream of clubbers heading down the hill to the bars and nightclubs of Hersónisos.

Kavouri, Arxéou Théatro. A good but pricey traditional taverna, whose decor boasts a diverting mural of inebriated crab, octopus and other seafood; the house speciality is lamb with garlic and lemon wrapped in paper.

Pithari, in the central square of Koutoulafári. Popular, but a little on the expensive side.

Tria Adelphi, just off the square in "Old" Hersónisos. This stands out as a more authentic taverna among the mass of more touristy places in the vicinity.

Nightlife

Hersónisos is renowned for its **nightlife** and there's certainly no shortage of it; the place to be seen is along Eleuthériou Venizélou, where most of the better bars and clubs are. If you fancy a quiet drink, you've come to the wrong resort, but you could seek refuge at the open-air cinema attached to the *Creta Maris* hotel.

Aria. Perenially popular glass-fronted disco – reputedly one of the biggest on Crete.

Hard Rock Café. Live music on Sun.

La Luna. A lively venue, with up-to-date music.

Stalídha

STALÍDHA is something of a Cinderella, sandwiched in between its two louder, brasher and, some would say, uglier sisters of Mália and Hersónisos. This rapidly expanding beach resort can offer the best of both worlds: a friendlier and more relaxed setting, a better beach with the usual array of water sports, and easy access to its two livelier neighbours. Don't be misled, though – Stalídha itself is not exactly quiet and undeveloped.

Finding **accommodation** can be difficult as most rooms are block-booked by package companies, and most rooms and studios fall into the ③–④ range; travel agencies often know what is available. **Eating** is less likely to be a problem, but don't expect anything particularly special. *Maria's* in the centre of the resort, where the road in from the main highway joins the coastal strip, is one of the better and more popular tavernas. The **nightlife** scene in Stalídha is low-key – compared to its neighbours, anyway. There are a few discos, including *Bells*, on the main coast road, and *Rhythm*, on the beach, while *Sea Wolf Cocktail Bar* and *Akti Bar*, near each other along the beach, play music to accompany your drink.

Although Stalídha doesn't have a bank, there are exchange offices, and a mobile yellow **post office** on the beach (Mon–Sat 9am–1pm).

Mália

Large enough to be a substantial town in its own right, **MÁLIA** is undeniably commercial, and its beach, long and sandy as it is, becomes grotesquely crowded at times. If you're prepared to enter into the holiday spirit, however – party all night and sleep all day – it can be very enjoyable. And, of course, there's a Minoan palace just down the road.

The town consists of two distinct halves, fanning out to the north and south of a T-junction where the main **bus** from Iráklion or Áyios Nikólaos drops you. The more raucous side of town lies along the **Beach Road**, which snakes for a good kilometre towards the sea. Here you'll find supermarkets, souvenir shops, tour agents, cafés, restaurants, video bars and nightclubs. To walk the length of this will take you about fifteen minutes – longer if you allow yourself to be enticed by the sales patter along the way. At the end there's a car park, a small harbour and a couple of beaches to the west. The **main beach**, however, stretches away to the east; in summer, you'll need to walk through the mass of bodies for about another fifteen minutes before you find somewhere to spread out. At this eastern end of the beach is a small church backed by dunes and patches of marshy ground alive with frogs. For entertainment, you can swim out to a tiny **offshore islet**: the rocks here are sharp for barefoot exploring, but your efforts will be rewarded by a (perpetually locked) white chapel and rock-pools alive with crabs, shellfish and sea urchins – on the islet's seaward side. To find a trace of real Cretan life in all of this, turn inland to the north of the main road. Here in the **old town**, with its narrow, twisting alleyways and white-washed walls, old Mália determinedly (if not always successfully) clings to its self-respect.

In terms of both action and accommodation, Mália has a great deal more to offer than any of its rivals along the north coast, and the practical matters are easily attended to, with a **post office**, a couple of banks and an **OTE** right in the centre; good exchange rates can also be had at the three-storey tourist emporium called *Mália Maria Market*, a little way down the Beach Road. The best place for **bike rental** is *Moto Euro Tours* (☎31-636), back along the main road going west, where the owner, Pit Frankoulis, will tell you of his lifetime love affair with the motorcycle if you give him the chance. Or **rent a car** from *Athena* (☎31-705) nearby, who do special offers. And, if you're shopping for food, look out for bananas: chances are they'll have been grown under plastic sheets in the fields around the town.

Accommodation

As in Hersónisos, many rooms are taken up by the package industry, so in the peak season finding somewhere to stay is not always easy. Your best bet, especially if you want any sleep during the night, is to try one of the numerous **rooms** (③–④) signed in the old town; most of the cheaper hotels around the T-junction are invariably full. Backtracking from here along the main Iráklion road there are a number of reasonably priced **pensions** on the left, including *Argo* (☎31-636; ②), and further along, on the right, opposite the Mobil filling station, is the **youth hostel** (☎31-555; 800dr per bed) – sadly, rather rundown and unwelcoming these days.

To save time, call in at one of the travel and tourist companies, such as *Foreign Office* on the main road, which, in addition to giving information on bus excursions and car rental, can also give details of accommodation availability.

Restaurants

Restaurant owners jostle for your custom at every step in Mália, especially along the Beach Road; none are particularly good, but they know their clientele – *moussaká* and pie and chips abound. Incidentally, the Beach Road also has a reputation for poisonous *souvláki*. One way of avoiding this would be British-style fish and chips, authentically wrapped in newspaper, from the *Electra Café* at the bottom of the Beach Road near the sea; at least as good as the real thing – and cheaper.

But the best places to eat are in the **old town**, to the inland side of the main road: wander up to Platía Áyios Dhimítri, a pleasant square beside the church, where you can sample a meal at *Taverna Minos Knossos*, after an aperitif of excellent local wine from the barrel at the *Ouzeri Kapilla*. Other welcoming tavernas just off the square include *Yiannis, Kalimera, Petros* – and the *Romantic Raphael Restaurant*, which, in defiance of low-cholesterol diets, proudly proclaims that all their dishes (including Thai, Chinese and Indonesian) are prepared in butter and not oil.

Nightlife

The Beach Road is transformed during the hours either side of midnight when the profusion of bars, discos and **clubs** erupt into a pulsating cacophony. The aptly named *Zoo* is a popular new club where, after midnight, great excitement is generated as one of the internal walls parts to reveal an even larger dance area. *Zig Zag* and *Cloud 9* are the other really popular spots, while *Desire*, further along the Beach Road, concentrates on live rock music. Unfortunately, a good night out is frequently spoilt by gangs of drunken youths pouring out of the bars: a great battle a few years back between hundreds of drunken English, German and Dutch visitors resulted in deaths and mayhem. To avoid the seafront brawls, stick to the old village.

If all you want is a **quiet beer**, try *Bar Epsilon* on the main road near the bus stop, or the *Stone House* café-bar in the old town. Both also have good live music some nights, but of a gentler variety with acoustic guitars.

For *après*-club refuelling, *Kipouli Bar* might be your place: situated in the old town, it proudly advertises the fact that it opens from "5.50 o'clock in the morning", and is instantly recognizable from the spectacle of a red plastic panda, half-way up a tree, clutching a case of Heineken while astride a brightly painted and fairy-lit mountain bike – only in Mália.

The Palace of Mália

The **Palace of Mália** (Tues–Sun 8.30am–3pm, closed Mon; 400dr, Sun free) lies forty minutes' walk east of the town, just off the main road. Any bus bound for Áyios Nikólaos will stop, or rent a bicycle – it's a pleasant, flat ride. Much less imposing than either Knossós or Festós, Mália in some ways surpasses both. For a start, it's a great deal emptier and you can wander among the remains in relative peace. And while no reconstruction has been attempted, the palace was never reoccupied after its second destruction, so the ground plan is virtually intact. It's a great deal easier to comprehend than Knossós, and if you've already seen the reconstructions there it's easy to envisage this seaside palace in its days of glory. Basking on the rich agricultural plain between the Lasíthi mountains and the sea, it retains a real flavour of an ancient civilization with a taste for the good life.

From this site came the famous gold pendant of two bees which can be seen in the Iráklion Archeological Museum or on any local postcard stand. It was allegedly part of a horde which was plundered and the rest of which now resides (as the Aegina Treasure) in the British Museum. The beautiful leopard's-head axe, also in the museum at Iráklion, was another of the treasures found at Mália. Of the ruins, virtually nothing stands above ground level apart from the giant *pithoi* which have been pieced together and left about the palace like sentinels: the palace itself is worn and brown, blending almost imperceptibly into the landscape. With the mountains behind, it's a thoroughly atmospheric setting.

First discovered by Joseph Hatzidakis early this century, in 1922 the site passed to the French School at Athens. As at Knossós and Festós, there was an earlier palace dating from around 1900 BC, which was devastated by the earthquake of about 1700 BC. The remains you see today are those of the palace built to replace this, and which functioned until about 1450 BC, when it was destroyed for the last time in the wave of violence which swept across the island (see "The Historical Framework" in *Contexts*).

PALACE OF MÁLIA

Paved Road

Storerooms (pithoi)

North Court

Processional Way

Lustral Basin

Royal Apartments

Archive Room

West Court

Pillared Hall

Lodge

Pillar Crypt

Storerooms (covered)

Storerroom

Central Court

Entrance

Altar

Storage pits

South Entrance

0   25 m

Entering the palace: the West Court

You enter the site through the **West Court**. As at the other palaces, there are raised pathways leading across this, with the main one heading south towards the area of the eight circular **storage pits**. These probably held grain – the pillars in the middle of some would once have supported a protective roof. In the other direction the raised walkway takes you to the building's north side, where you can pick up the more substantial paved road that apparently led to the sea.

Entering the palace itself through a "door" between two rocks and jinking right then left, you arrive in the **North Court** by the storerooms and their elaborately decorated, much-photographed giant *pithoi*. Off to the right were the so-called Royal Apartments, on the far side of which is a well-preserved **lustral basin**. Nearby lay the **Archive Room** where a number of Linear A tablets were unearthed. Straight ahead is the **Pillared Hall** – which the excavators, encouraged by the discovery of some cooking pots, think may have been a kitchen – with a grand dining room on the floor above, looking out over the courtyard. Incidentally, if they're correct, the relative location is almost exactly the same as that of the palace kitchen at Zakrós.

The Central Court and Royal Apartments

Mália's **Central Court**, a long, narrow area, about 48m in length by 22m wide, is only slightly smaller than the main courtyards at Knossós and Festós. Look out for the remains of the columns which once supported a portico at this northern end, and for traces of a similar portico down the eastern side. Post-holes were discovered by the excavators between these columns, suggesting that the court could be fenced in – possibly to protect the spectators during the bull-jumping games. Behind the eastern portico are more storerooms, now under a canopy. In the centre of the court is a shallow pit which may have been used for sacrifices; if this was indeed its purpose then, along with Anemospília, these are the only such Minoan sacrificial areas to have been discovered.

On the west side of the courtyard are the remains of two important stairways. The first led to the upper floor beside what is termed the **Royal Lodge** or Throne Room, which overlooks the courtyard. The second, in the southwest corner, comprises the bottom four steps of what was the main ceremonial stair to the first floor, still impressive in its scale. Beside this is the curious *kernos*, or **altar**. The purpose of this heavy limestone disc, with 34 indentations around its rim and a single one in the centre, is disputed: one theory has it as an altar where, at harvesttime, samples of the first fruit of the Cretan crops would be placed in the hollows as offerings to a fertility goddess; other theories have it as a point for tax collecting or even an ancient gaming board.

The rooms along the west side of the court also merit exploration. Between the two staircases ran a long room which may have gone straight through to the upper floor, like a medieval banqueting hall. Behind this is the **Pillar Crypt**, where the double-axe symbol was found engraved on the two main pillars. Behind that runs yet another corridor of **storerooms**: only accessible through areas which had some royal or religious significance, these would doubtless have been depositories for things of value – the most secure storage at the palace.

New discoveries

The excavations at Mália are by no means complete. Inside and beyond the fenced site to the north and west digs are still going on, as an apparently sizeable town comes slowly to light. Beneath a canopy to the west of the northern end of the palace lies the **Hypostyle Hall**. This building consists of a number of storerooms and two interconnected halls of uncertain function. Benches run round three sides of the halls, leading some to speculate that this was some form of council chamber. Five hundred metres to the north, close to the sea, is the *Chrysolakkos* or **Golden Pit**, which appears to have been a large, multi-chambered mausoleum dating from the Old Palace period. Its elaborate construction suggests a royal burial place, as does the wealth of grave goods discovered here – among them the gold honeybee pendant mentioned above.

Back to town – the beach

Leaving the site the same way you came in, a dirt track (50m back) runs around the fence to the right, leading eventually to a lovely stretch of deserted **sand** which, considering its position, is amazingly little-visited. If you're prepared for the total lack of facilities, it makes a fine place to camp out, picnic or simply have a swim. **Moving on**, you can easily walk along the shore to Mália itself, or to the main road where buses pass every half hour – either back to Iráklion or on towards Áyios Nikólaos.

Inland: the Pedhiádha

The hinterland east of Iráklion and south of Hersónisos consists mainly of hilly farm country, with large, widely scattered villages. Known as the *Pedhiádha*, this region is quietly prosperous but sees few visitors. Indeed if you're reliant on public transport, there's little opportunity to take in a great deal: most villages see just their daily market bus. But with your own transport, it makes for enjoyably aimless touring; certainly the inland roads are far more attractive than the coastal one.

Frescoed churches and potteries

The area's chief village, **KASTÉLLI**, or Kastélli Pedhiádhos, is a pleasant place to pull over for a while, with a number of tavernas and *kafenia* around the crossroads in the centre of town. There are even some comfortable modern **rooms**, *Veronica* (④), located above a bar on the road which leads out to the east. Excitements, however, are few. The main attraction is the countryside itself, with its winding lanes traced by elderly oak and plane trees, and the many smaller villages, often with frescoed medieval **churches**. Look out, as you drive, for signs to such churches, which are usually worth seeking out simply for the journey off the main routes, even if very often you can find no one to let you in.

One of the more famous is the fifteenth-century **Isódhia Theótokon**, with fine Byzantine frescoes, near the village of Sklaverohóri just a couple of kilometres west of Kastélli. Six kilometres further west again, and down a side road beyond Apostolí, the **Moní Angaráthou** is another pleasant location. Although the monastery's church dates from the last century, the surrounding buildings are mainly sixteenth-century and include a picturesque white-walled courtyard with palms, orange trees and cypresses. Another church is **Áyios Yióryios** at Ksidhás (confusingly also known as Lyttos), about 3km east of Kastélli, which not only has frescoes of its own but also incorporates part of a much earlier basilica, the latter probably associated with ancient **Lyttos**, which once occupied the high ground immediately above the village. An important city in Classical times, Lyttos was eventually destroyed by the rival city-state of Knossós in 220 BC, but enjoyed a small-scale renaissance under the Romans through to Byzantine times. What little remains is likely to be of interest to specialists only and detailed investigations have just started, and are expected to reveal the largest Roman theatre on the island.

A personal favourite among the churches is **Áyios Pandheleímon**, off the road back to Hersónisos just before the village of Piyí. To get there, set off north and not far out of Kastélli you'll see a sign directing you onto a dirt track to the right. There are several alternative trails but, providing you don't mind bumpy driving, it doesn't seem to matter which one you take: they all seem eventually to pass the church – just stick to the side of the valley, parallel with the paved road.

The way is shaded with huge old trees and the church itself, which is surprisingly big, is set in a grove of ancient oaks around a spring. This idyllic spot shelters a small taverna where you can sit with the local farmworkers while you wait to see if anyone turns up with a key, which is by no means certain (he's usually either "just left" or, worse, "on his way") and hardly vital. If you do get in, you'll find that the frescoes are weathered almost beyond recognition but the structure, probably early thirteenth-century, is interesting for the way it incorporates parts of the original tenth-century basilica and uses as columns some much older fragments, possibly scavenged from Lyttos. The aqueduct that once transported water to the ancient city passes close by, and you may spot parts of it as you drive around looking for the church.

To the southwest of Kastélli is the large village of **Thrapsanó**, for centuries an important pottery-making centre in eastern Crete. Workshops still thrive in the village itself and towards Voni and Evangelimos, and all welcome visitors if you want to admire the potters' skills. There is a good range of earthenware, and the large jars or *pithoi* are evident throughout Thrapsanó, not only in workshops but upturned in its main square and on the backs of parked pickup trucks.

Towards Lasíthi

The one inland route which visitors follow in any numbers is the drive **up to Lasíthi**. Once again the attractions are charmingly simple: scenery which becomes increasingly mountainous as you climb towards the plateau, spreading old trees beside the road, and still older churches in the villages. Starting from Iráklion the normal route is to follow the coast road until just before Límin Hersonísou, where you turn inland towards Kastélli and then east through the Aposelémis valley to Potamiés and Goníes. Before reaching the turnoff on the right for Kastélli (you continue left), look out for the ruins of the **Roman aqueduct** which carried water from springs in the hills near ancient Lyttos to its port at Hersónisos, visible in a ravine below the road.

Approaching Potamiés you'll see the small Byzantine frescoed chapel of **Sotíros Christos** (locked) to the left; soon after this a signed track, also on the left, heads for the tenth-century monastery of the **Panayía Gouverniótissa** (Assumption of the Virgin), one of the oldest in Crete. The track climbs through olive groves to a shaded parking space next to the deserted, partly ruined and rather eerie monastery buildings. The enormous ovens that once fed the brethren are still in evidence, and precarious staircases (not for the fainthearted) climb to the dormitories above. The tiny **chapel**, which still attracts visitors and the faithful, stands close by in a peaceful garden with a shady lemon tree. Inside are restored frescoes dating from the fourteenth century with a fine *pantokrátor* in the dome. The chapel will probably be locked (key available from the *kafenion* at the edge of the village), but a restricted view of the frescoes inside can be had through a small glassless window in the apse.

Five kilometres further on is Avdhoú, where there are more fine, if faded, frescoes from the fourteenth and fifteenth centuries in three churches: Áyios Andónios, Áyios Constantínos and Áyios Yióryios. The churches should be open; if not, enquiries in the village cafés should produce the necessary keys.

The Lasíthi plateau itself is covered on pp.128–132

Mohós

Starting **from Mália,** or on a round trip from Áyios Nikólaos, you can take a short cut, turning inland at Stalídha and following the road signed for Mohós. This route is probably the most dramatic of the three approaches to the plateau (the third is from the other end, Neápoli – see p.127), with **spectacular views** back over the coast as the road climbs dizzily above the Gulf of Mália. After crossing a pass, you arrive at the village of **MOHÓS,** which boasts a pleasant leafy square edged by tavernas and cafés, and a major festival – albeit rather touristy – on August 15 every year. The late Swedish prime minister Olof Palme was a regular summer visitor here, and when he was cruelly murdered in a Stockholm street in 1986, Mohós was plunged into mourning. His simple house, just behind the church on the main square, has been turned into a shrine (ask to be directed to the **Villa Palme**), and the street in which it stands has been renamed Odhós Olof Palme. The mainly Swedish visitors to the house have filled two books with their heartfelt comments.

Krási and Panayía Kardhiótissa

Three kilometres beyond the point where the roads from Hersónisos and Stalídha join, a loop off the main route will bring you to the curiously named village of **KRÁSI.** Curious because Krási translates as "wine", but the village's fame is in fact based on water, in the form of a curative spring. This is situated under stone arcading in the shade of an enormous plane tree, which is claimed to be two thousand years old and the largest in Europe, with a girth that cannot be encircled by twelve men. The waters are reputed to be especially good for stomach complaints – worth noting if you have fallen foul of the Mália *soúvlaki* poisoner.

Not much further on, just before the village of Kerá, the convent of **Panayía Kardhiótissa** (Our Lady of the Heart) lies immediately below the road and is one of the most important places of worship on Crete, with an annual celebration on September 8. The buildings date from the twelfth century, and though the outside of the monastery looks like whitewashed concrete, the interior is undeniably spectacular, with restored frescoes throughout. These came to light only in the 1960s, when they were discovered beneath accumulated layers of paint. There is also a copy of a famous twelfth-century icon of the Virgin, the original of which was taken to Rome in 1498. According to legend, successive attempts to steal the icon were thwarted when it found its way back to Kerá, despite being chained to a marble pillar; the pillar is now in the monastery yard, while the chain (kept inside the church) is believed to alleviate pain when wrapped around the bodies of the afflicted. In a peaceful garden outside the church, one of the three remaining nuns will probably be on duty at the stone table in the shade of a mulberry tree or in the shop. If you wanted to try out your Greek, you could ask Sister Theophilate, Sister Dionysia or Sister Theodoti to tell you of how they came to "enter" the order at the age of ten – a story that reveals a darker side to the smiling face of the Orthodox Church in Greece.

The mountains

After the village of Kerá, the road winds on into the Dhiktean mountains, and the views become progressively more magnificent. To the left, **Mount Karfí** looms ominously, its summit over 1100m above sea level. This spire-like peak (*karfí* means "nail" in Greek) was one of the sites where the Minoan civilization made its last stand, following the collapse of the great centres after the twelfth century

BC. In the face of Dorian advances, the last of the Minoans fled to remote refuges such as this, keeping alive shadowy vestiges of their culture. The solitary peak, now identified as a Minoan sanctuary, stands as a silent witness to the end of Europe's first great civilization.

The road continues to climb until, at Séli Ambélou, you approach a dramatic pass flanked by stone windmills on the ridges above. Once through the rocky outcrops, the Lasíthi plateau suddenly unfolds before you. Beyond, almost straight ahead, the highest peaks of the range dominate the landscape, including **Mount Dhíkti** itself – all 2148m of it. The *Séli* taverna, here at the pass, often serves barbecued roast lamb, and makes a good place to stop and take in the sights (though it's surprisingly cool once you start sitting around); don't neglect the view seawards, either – on clear days you can see as far as the island of Thíra (Santorini), over 100km distant.

On the ridge behind the car-parking area, a couple of the windmills have been restored and pressed into use as souvenir shops. There's a path from here leading to still higher viewpoints and eventually the site of ancient **Karfí**, a five-kilometre hike away, but this is probably better approached from Tzermiádho (see p.129) on the plateau.

ACROSS THE ISLAND

There are a number of roads that run from Iráklion towards **the south coast**, but almost all the traffic seems to follow the one which heads slightly southwest, **towards Festós and Mátala**. Plenty of buses come this way too, leaving from the Haniá Gate terminal and heading for Festós, Mátala, Léndas or Ayía Galíni via Timbáki. Míres, in the heart of the Messará plain, is the southern junction for switching between these various routes. The only other regular bus service across the island from Iráklion runs southeast **towards Ierápetra**, via Áno Viánnos and Mírtos.

The southern half of the province is very different from the north: there's just one resort of any size, **Mátala** – and a day-trip route that takes in the sites of **Górtys**, **Festós** and **Ayía Triádha**. The rest is countryside with few concessions to tourism, which is not to say that the area is undeveloped: on the contrary, it represents the island's single most important location for agriculture. The **Messará plain**, in particular, has always been a vital resource, and its importance is reflected in widely distributed and wealthy villages.

The coast, with the exception of Mátala, is relatively little visited, and indeed a good part of it is quite inaccessible: east of **Léndas** (where there's excellent sand) stretches well over 30km of shore that simply can't be reached overland; even beyond this, **Tsoútsouros** and **Keratókambos** are accessible only by steep, rough tracks.

Towards Festós

Crossing the island from Iráklion is not, on the whole, the most exciting of drives: you leave the city westwards (through the Haniá Gate) and on the outskirts turn south, under the highway, following the signs to Festós. From the beginning the road climbs, heading up to the island's spine, through thoroughly business-like countryside. This is more of what traditionally was the Malevísi, or Malmsey, wine producing region: though some wine is still made, most of the grapes you'll see now are table grapes, grown for eating rather than pressing.

Moní Palianí and Ayía Varvára

Just beyond a turn off for Dáfnes – a village noted for its wine – at the twenty-kilometre marker in the village of Veneráto there's the option of a two-kilometre detour to the **Moní Palianí**, an ancient monastic foundation and now a nunnery. After leaving the road on the left (signed), keep your eyes skinned for another sign directing you right; the road then crosses a valley before climbing gently towards the nunnery gates. Founded as early as the seventh century, the place today is an oasis of tranquillity where the nuns' cells surround a courtyard filled with oleanders, geraniums, vines and palms with a thirteenth-century church at its centre. Unlike many religious communities in Crete, this one is a viable concern, supporting itself through sales of lace and embroidery, which the nuns will be only too pleased to show you in their small shop.

AYÍA VARVÁRA, 8km further on, is the main village of this area, a place known as the *Omphalos* (navel) of Crete. The great chapel-topped rock which you see as you arrive is held to be the very point around which the island balances, its centre of being. Not that this makes for any great tourist attraction. There are plenty of cafés and shops, but they cater mostly for local farmers in search of a bag of fertilizer or a tractor part.

Zarós and around

On the southern fringe of Ayía Varvára a turning takes off to the west, following the flank of the Psilorítis range **towards Kamáres** (p.196) and eventually on to Réthimnon or down to Ayía Galíni. This is a beautiful drive and a relatively good, empty road: **ZARÓS** is a particularly attractive village famous for its spring waters, which are now bottled and sold all over Crete. Well-appointed hotels are rare inland, making the *Idi Hotel* (☎0894/31-302; ④ including breakfast) a lovely place to get away from it all, despite its discovery by the package companies. The hotel has information on several scenic walks on the Psilorítis range, and the taverna next door makes a speciality of the locally farmed trout.

Along the way there are a number of ancient churches, the first being **Moní Vrondísi**, above the road about 3km beyond Zarós. Here there are fourteenth-century frescoes in the church and a collection of icons taken from the nearby church of Áyios Fanoúrios – Vrondísi itself has given up the finest of its artworks, the six great panels by Dhamaskinos, to the icon gallery of Ayía Ekateríni in Iráklion (see p.64). Even without them, though, this is a wonderful setting, with trees for shade, cool water, a gushing fifteenth-century fountain in the elaborate Italian style, and views towards Festós and the Gulf of Messará. Áyios Fanoúrios, all that survives of the **Moní Valsamónero**, is reached by a track from the next village, Vorízia. The frescoes in this church are among the best in Crete: painted in the fifteenth century by Konstantínos Ríkos, they depict scenes from the life of the *Panayía* (Virgin Mary) besides images of various saints and a fine *pantokrátor*. The guardian is on site most weekdays (official opening hours 8am–3pm daily), but if not he can be found in the village.

There's also a great **gorge walk** to be had just outside Zarós. Five hundred metres west of the village, turn right up a track signposted to Áyios Nikólaos (another frescoed church), which ends after about 2km in a car park. Above the church is the cave of St Euthymios, an old hermitage. You can continue to climb, on foot, for a further 2km to the entrance to the Gorge of Zarós, whose three-kilometre length is negotiated by a path, including steps and bridges for the difficult bits, which takes much of the strain. The gorge is rarely visited, and your exertions will be rewarded by spectacular views of the Psilorítis range and – depending on the time of year – plenty of bird, plant and even animal life.

The Messará plain

Continuing by the main road south from Ayía Varvára the way becomes genuinely mountainous, and after 7km you cross the Pass of Vourvoulítis (650m) and the watershed of the Messará. The **Messará plain**, a long strip running west from the Gulf of Messará, is the largest and most important of Crete's fertile flatlands. Bounded to the north by the Psilorítis range and the lower hills which run right across the centre of the island, to the east by the Dhiktean mountains, and in the south by the narrow strip of the Kófinas hills, it is watered, somewhat erratically, by the Yeropótamos. Heavy with olives, and increasingly with the fruit and vegetable cash crops that dominate the modern agricultural economy, the plain has always been a major centre of population and a mainstay of the island's economy. There is much evidence of this, not only at Górtys, Festós and Ayía Triádha but at a wealth of lesser, barely explored sites; today's villages exude prosperity, too, surrounded by neat and intensive cultivation.

As you descend to the plain by a series of long, looping curves, the main road heads west through Áyii Dhéka. A left turn, eastwards, takes you across far less travelled country and (see p.119) all the way to Ierápetra.

Áyii Dhéka

ÁYII DHÉKA, served by frequent buses from Iráklion, is the first village you reach on the Messará, and the most interesting. The place takes its name from ten early Christians who were martyred here around 250 AD, at the behest of the emperor Decius. The **Holy Ten** are still among the most revered of Cretan saints: regarded as martyrs for Crete as much as Christianity – the first in a heroic line of Cretans who laid down their lives opposing tyrannical occupation. On the southwestern edge of the village are two churches associated with them: the older, originally Byzantine, has an icon portraying the martyrs and the stone block on which they are supposed to have been decapitated. Steps beneath the more modern chapel nearby lead to a crypt where you can see six of their tombs. Other reminders of the village's ancient past include the Roman statues, pillars and odd blocks of masonry scavenged from Górtys that are much in evidence: re-used in modern houses, propping up walls or simply lying about in yards. In the centre there are a number of roadside cafés and restaurants and a few signs offering **rooms** – a pleasant place to break your journey.

Górtys

The remnants of the ancient city of **GÓRTYS** (known traditionally as Gortyn or Gortyna) are scattered across a large, fragmented area, covering a great deal more than the fenced site by the road that most people see. The Italian Archeological Institute is currently carrying out extensive excavations that it hopes will eventually link the disparate elements of the ancient city. The best way to get some idea of its scale is to follow the path through the fields from the village. This heads off, more or less parallel to the road, opposite the chapel of Áyii Dhéka: it's an easy walk to the main site, and along the way you'll skirt most of the major remains.

Settled from at least Minoan times, when it was a minor subject of Festós, Górtys began its rise to prominence under the Dorians. By the eighth century BC, it had become a significant commercial power and in the third century BC, it finally conquered its former rulers at Festós. The society was a strictly regulated one, with a citizen class (presumably Dorian) ruling over a population of serfs (presumably "Minoan" Cretans) and slaves. Even for the citizens, life was as hard and orderly as it was in Classical Sparta.

Evidence of early Górtys has survived thanks largely to the remarkable law code found here (see over) and to a lesser extent through treaties known to have existed between the Górtys of this era and its rivals, notably Knossós. Hannibal fled to Górtys briefly after his defeat by Rome. The city also helped the Romans to conquer Crete, and it was during the ensuing Roman era that the city reached its apogee, from 67 BC on: as the seat of a Roman praetor it was capital of the province of Crete and Cyrenaica, ruling not only the rest of the island but also much of Egypt and North Africa. It was here that Christianity first reached Crete, when St Titus was despatched by St Paul to convert the islanders. After the

Saracen invasion in the ninth century, when much of the city was razed, Górtys was abruptly abandoned.

South of the road

In the fields en route to the site, it is the **Roman city** that dominates: this once stretched from the edges of Áyii Dhéka to the far banks of the Mitropolitanos (then known as the *Lethe*) and from the hills in the north as far south as the modern hamlet of Mitrópolis (where a small Roman basilica with good mosaics has been excavated). For most people, though, the ruins along the main path, others seen standing in the distance, and the tantalizing prospect of what lies unexcavated beneath hummocks along the way, are quite enough. In another setting, or individually, these might seem unimpressive, but with so many of them, abandoned as they are and all but ignored (fenced to keep souvenir hunters out, but not guarded nor advertised) they are amazing – you feel almost as if you have discovered them for yourself.

The **Praetorium** (governor's palace) is the most extensive remain, a vast pile built originally in the second century AD, rebuilt in the fourth, and occupied as a monastery right up to the time of the Venetian conquest; within the same fenced area is a courtyard with fountains and the **Nymphaeum**. Somewhere near here, too, was the terminus of the main aqueduct that brought water from the region of modern Zarós. Further on, the **Temple of Pythian Apollo** was the most important of the Roman city's temples, again later converted to a church, while the **Theatre**, though small, is very well preserved.

Áyios Títos and the law code

From the theatre you can cut up to the road and cross to the parking area which marks the entrance to the main, fenced **site** (daily 8.30am–3pm; 400dr, free on Sun). As you enter, it is the church of **Áyios Títos** which immediately grabs the eye, the back of its apse rising high in front of you. This is the only part of the church that survives intact, but the shape of the rest is easy enough to make out. When it was built (around the end of the sixth century), it would have been the island's chief church, and is the best remaining example of an early Christian church in the Aegean: you can see the extent to which it is still revered from the little shrine at the end of one of the aisles. The church's capitals bear the monogram of the sixth-century Byzantine emperor Justinian.

Beyond the church lies an area that was probably the ancient forum, and beyond this the most important remain of ancient Górtys, the **Odeion** (or covered theatre) and its **law code**. The law code – a series of engraved stones some 9m long and 3m high – dates from around 500 BC, but presumably codified laws long established by custom and practice. It provides a fascinating insight into a period of which relatively little is otherwise known; the laws are written in a very rough Doric Cretan dialect and inscribed alternately left to right and right to left, so that the eyes can follow the writing continuously (a style known as *boustrophedon*, after the furrows of an ox plough). The code is not a complete system of law, but rather a series of rulings on special cases, and reflects a strictly hierarchical society in which there were at least three distinct classes – citizens, serfs and slaves – each with quite separate rights and obligations. Five witnesses were needed to convict a free man of a crime, one could convict a slave; the rape of a free man or woman carried a fine of a hundred *staters*, while the same offence committed against a serf was punishable by a mere five-*stater* fine. The laws also cover subjects such as property and inheritance rights, the status of children of mixed marriages (that is, between free people and serfs) and the control of trade.

The panels on which the law is inscribed are now incorporated into the round Odeion, which was erected under Trajan around 100 AD and rebuilt in the third or fourth century (the brick terrace which protects the inscriptions from the elements is modern). The Odeion is just the latest incarnation of a series of buildings on this site, in which the code had apparently always been preserved – obviously this was a city which valued its own history. When they were discovered in the late nineteenth century, these ruins were entirely buried under eroded soil washed down from the hills behind.

In a small pavilion backing onto the site **cafeteria** there's a collection of **statuary**, demonstrating the high standard of work being achieved here during the city's halcyon days.

West of the river

Beside the fenced site the river runs by an abandoned medieval mill and on the far bank you can see a larger **Theatre**, in rather poor repair, set against the hillside. In Roman times the river ran through a culvert here and you could have walked straight across; nowadays, you have to go back to the roadbridge to explore this area. The guard at the site – who, though he speaks no English, is very keen to encourage people to explore the outlying areas – will give you directions to the easiest path up to the **Acropolis** on the hilltop above the river. Hardly anyone makes it up there, shying away from such a stiff climb in the heat, but the ruins are surprisingly impressive, with Roman defensive walls and a building known as the *kástro* (though apparently not a castle) still standing to a height of 6m in places. The lesser remains are among the earliest on the site, and include scant relics of a Greek temple that was later converted to a church. From this hilltop vantage point, you also get a fine overview of the layout of Górtys and can trace the line of the aqueducts coming in from the north.

Míres

From Górtys it's about 6km to **MÍRES**, a bustling farming town of some size and the transport centre for the area. If you are changing **buses** – and you can get to Léndas or Mátala on the coast from here, to Zarós and Kamáres in the mountains (very occasionally), through Timbáki to Ayía Galíni or Réthimnon and even (once a day) to Réthimnon via the Amári Valley – watch out for the fact that there are two termini some distance from each other along the main road. One serves the Iráklion-based routes, the other those into Réthimnon province: check well in advance which you need. Heading direct for Festós there's usually no need to stop.

Míres could hardly be described as attractive, but as a centre for local commerce as well as passing tourists, it at least has plenty of life, with scores of places to eat and drink, the only bank for miles around, and cheap **rooms** that are easy to find, if you happen to be stranded between buses. The *Hotel Olympic* (☎0892/42-777; ②) is characterless but clean; among a few places to eat nearby there's *Pizzeria Bambola*, where the chef leaves pizzas to cook in the oven while he leaps aboard a powerful Honda to deliver telephone orders. On Saturday mornings the town is enlivened by a busy market.

Three kilometres beyond Míres a turning on the right leads to the **Moní Kaliviani**, an impressive monastic complex which today serves as an orphanage, boarding school and sanitorium. Inside the gates, the buildings fronting the central avenue shower cascades of magenta bougainvillea down their exteriors in summer, and everywhere there are plants sprouting more blooms. Behind the modern church there is a tiny fourteenth-century chapel, dedicated to the Panayía Kalivianís, with ancient frescoes. The nuns support themselves by weaving, embroidery and making handicrafts, which they sell at their store opposite the church.

Festós and Ayía Triádha

Set in a wonderfully scenic location on a ridge at the eastern end of the Messará plain with fine views towards the encircling mountains, the **palace of Festós** and its neighbouring "summer palace", the charming **Ayía Triádha**, are Minoan sites ranking second only to Knossós on the island.

Bus services to the Festós site are excellent, with some nine a day to and from Iráklion (the last leaves just before the site closes), but rather fewer on Sunday, five of which continue to, or come from, Mátala; there are also services direct to Ayía Galíni. All buses stop right by the Festós parking area. If you're arriving in the afternoon, plan to visit Ayía Triádha first, as it closes early. The **Tourist Pavilion** at Festós serves drinks and food and also has a few beds, though these are very rarely available (thanks to advance bookings) and pricey when they are. There are a few more **rooms** (☎0892/99-494; ②) to be found in the nearby village of Áyios Ioánnis, at the picturesque *Taverna Áyios Ioánnis* on the main road, which also makes an excellent **lunch**-stop, with tables under the trees; *kounéli*, the house speciality of charcoal-grilled rabbit, is recommended. There are also places offering **accommodation** along the road towards Mátala or, alternatively, you should be able to find something in the first larger place you strike in almost any direction – Míres, Tímbáki or Pitsídhia.

Festós

The palace of **FESTÓS** (Mon–Fri 8am–7pm, Sat & Sun 8.30am–7pm; 800dr, free on Sun) was excavated by Federico Halbherr (also responsible for the early work on Górtys), at almost exactly the same time as Evans was working at Knossós. The style of the excavations, however, could hardly have been more different. Here, reconstruction has been kept to an absolute minimum, to the approval of most traditional archeologists: it's all bare foundations, and walls that barely rise above ground level.

As at Knossós, most of what survives is what the excavators termed the Second Palace, rebuilt after the destruction of c.1700 BC and occupied to c.1450 BC. But at Festós the first palace was used as a foundation for the second, and much of its well-preserved floor plan has been uncovered by the excavations. Fascinating as these superimposed buildings are for the experts, they help make Festós extremely confusing for more casual visitors to interpret. Combined with a distinct lack of elaboration, at least in the decoration of the palace, this adds up to considerable disappointment for many. Since much of the site is also fenced off, it becomes almost impossible to get any sense of the place as it once was.

Only Knossós was more important and although there are major differences between Festós and the other palaces, these are in the end outweighed by the

Tourist Pavillion

Lustral Basin

Royal Apartments

Archive

Entrance

Peristyle Hall

Peristyle House

Theatral area
and West Court

Propylon

Grand
Stairway

Workshops

Storerooms

Office

Furnace

Storage Pits

Prince's
rooms

Steep bank

Central
Court

First Palace Remains

Classical Temple

0   25 m

Steep bank

PALACE OF FESTÓS

multitude of similarities. The rooms are set about a great central courtyard, with
an external court on the west side and a theatral area north of this; the domestic
apartments are, as usual, slightly apart from the public and formal ones; there are
the same lines of storage magazines and pits for grain; and on the east side are
workshops for the palace craftsmen. While no traces of frescoes were found, this
doesn't imply that the palace wasn't luxurious: the materials – marble, alabaster,
gypsum – were of the highest quality; there was sophisticated drainage and bathing facilities; and remains suggest a large and airy dining hall on the upper floors
overlooking the court. Bear in mind, as you explore, that part of the palace is
missing: there must have been more outbuildings on the south side of the site
where erosion has worn away the edge of the ridge and a corner of the central
court itself has collapsed.

Entry: the West Court and Grand Stairway
You enter the palace from above, down steps leading past a **Tourist Pavilion** and
approaching the northwest corner of the complex through the Upper Court. Step
down first into the **West Court** and integral **Theatral Area**: as at Knossós there
are raised walkways leading across the courtyard, and here one of them runs
right up the steps that form the seats of the Theatral Area (accorded this title by

archeologists who supposed it was used for viewing some kind of performance or spectacle). On the west side of the court are circular walled pits, probably for storing grain. The West Court itself is a rare survival from the original palace – the main walkway leads not up the stairs into the new palace but past them and into the entrance to the old. From there, much of the facade of the old palace can be seen as a low wall in front of the Grand Stairway which leads into the new. When the palace stood, of course, this would not have been apparent; then the court was filled with rubble and levelled (though not paved) at the height of the bottom step of the stairway.

The **Grand Stairway** was a fitting approach to Festós, a superbly engineered flight of twelve shallow stone steps, 14m wide. Some of the steps are actually carved from the solid rock of the hill, and each is slightly convex, higher in the middle than at the ends, in order to improve the visual impact – a remarkable architectural innovation, anticipating similar subtleties on the Parthenon at Athens by twelve centuries. The entrance facade was no doubt equally impressive – you can still see the base of the pillar which supported the centre of the doorway – but it's hard to imagine from what actually survives. Once inside, the first few rooms seem somewhat cramped: this may have been deliberate – either for security purposes, to prevent a sudden rush, or as a ploy to enhance the larger, lighter spaces beyond. At the end would have been a blank wall, open to the sky, and a small door to the right which led out onto stairs down towards the Central Court. Standing in the entrance area now, you can look down over the **storerooms**, and going down the stairs you can get closer to them through a larger room that once served as an office. Exposed here is a storeroom from the old palace, with a giant jar still in place. At the far end, more *pithoi* stand in a room apparently used to store olive oil or other liquids; there's a stool to stand on while reaching in and a basin to catch spillage, while the whole floor slopes towards a hole in which any slops would collect.

The Central Court and Royal Apartments

From the stores "office", quite an elaborate room, you can pass into the **Central Court**, which is by far the most atmospheric area of the palace. In this great paved court, with its scintillating views, there is a rare sense of Festós as it must have been. Look north from here in the direction of the Psilorítis range and you can make out a black smudge to the right of a saddle between the two peaks. This marks the entrance to the Kamáres Cave (see p.196), a sacred shrine to the Minoans and the source of the great hoard of elaborate Kamáres ware pottery now in the Iráklion Archeological Museum. Even without the views – which would have been blocked by the two storeys to either side when the palace was standing – the courtyard remains impressive. Its north end, in particular, is positively and unusually grand: the doorway, flanked by half-columns and niches (possibly for sentries) covered in painted plaster, can be plainly made out. To the left as you face this are a couple of *pithoi* (left there by the excavators) and a stepped stone that some claim was an altar, or perhaps a block from which athletes would jump onto bulls; the equally unlikely and unprovable counter-theory has it, more prosaically, as a base for a flowerpot.

Along each of the long sides of the courtyard ran a covered **portico** or veranda, the bases of whose supports are still visible: in the southwest corner are various rooms which probably had religious functions; beyond these, and hard to distinguish from them, are parts of the old palace which are mostly fenced off.

Also here, right at the edge of the site, are the remains of a **Greek temple** of the Classical era, evidence that the site was occupied long after the Minoans and the destruction of the palace.

Heading up through the grand north door – notice the holes for door pivots and the guardroom just inside – a corridor leads through the **North Court** toward the **Royal Apartments**. These have been covered and shut off to prevent damage from people walking through, and it's hard to see a great deal of the queen's rooms, or the king's behind them. Above the king's quarters is a large **Peristyle Hall**, a colonnaded courtyard much like a cloister, open in the centre. On the north side this courtyard was open to take in the view of Psilorítis: it must have been a beautiful place, and perhaps also one of some religious significance. Staircases linked the hall directly with the Royal Apartments (and the **lustral basin** on the north edge of the king's rooms); nowadays it is easier approached from the palace entrance, turning left up the stairs from the Propylon.

Palace dependencies

Continuing past the royal quarters on the other side, you come to the dependent buildings on the northeast side of the palace, which almost certainly predate much of the palace itself. Among the first of these is the so-called **Archive**, where the famous Festós disc (see p.66) was discovered in one of a row of mud-brick boxes. A little further on is the **Peristyle House**, probably a private home, with an enclosed yard similar in style to the Peristyle Hall. From here, stairs lead back down to the level of the Central Court, into the area of the palace **workshops**. In the centre of another large courtyard are the remains of a furnace, probably used for metalworking or as a kiln. The small rooms roundabout were the workshops, perhaps even the homes, of the craftsmen. Walking back to the central court, another suite of rooms – usually described as the **Prince's Rooms** – lies on your left, boasting its own small peristyle hall.

Ayía Triádha

AYÍA TRIÁDHA (daily 8.30am–3pm; 400dr, free on Sun) lies about 3km from Festós on the far side of the hill, an easy drive or a walk of about 45 minutes by a well-signed road around the south slope. Avoid the approach from the main road by car – the track up the hill is liable to rip your exhaust off. (There is also an old footpath around the north side, but it seems to have fallen into disuse – check with the guards at Festós about the current feasibility of the walk.) The site – discovered and excavated at the turn of the century by the Italian School – remains something of an enigma: nothing to compare it with exists in what is known of Minoan Crete, nor does it appear in any records; even the name has had to be borrowed from a nearby chapel.

In sharp contrast with unadorned Festós, however, Ayía Triádha has provided some of the most delicate Minoan **artworks** found. From this site came the three vases of carved black steatite – the Harvester Vase, the Boxer Vase and the Chieftain Cup – on display in the Iráklion Archeological Museum (see p.68), as well as some of the finest works in the Fresco Hall there, including the unique painted sarcophagus. Yet again, the ruins enjoy a magnificent hillside site, looking out over the Gulf of Messará. The modern view takes in the coastal plain with Timbáki airstrip in the foreground (built by the Germans during the war, its runways are now more often used for motor races), but in Minoan times the sea

AYÍA TRIÁDHA

0   25 m

To tombs

Town Area

Market

Fresco Room

Stairs to ramp

Ramp

Queen's Room

Entrance

Chambers with Hall over

Courtyard

Ayios Yioryios

Storerooms

Shrine

would have come right to the base of the hill. Despite this beauty and wealth, Ayía Triádha is plainly not a construction on the same scale as the great palaces: the most commonly accepted explanation is that it was some kind of royal villa or summer retreat, but it may equally have been the home of an important prince or noble, or a building of special ceremonial significance.

You approach the site from the car park above. Predictably, the remains, in which buildings of several eras are jumbled, are confused and confusing. This matters much less here, however, for it is the atmosphere of Ayía Triádha that really makes the place – the absence of crowds, the beauty of the surroundings and the human scale of the villa with its multitude of little stairways and paved corridors between rooms.

The site

To your left as you climb down are the bare ruins of a Minoan house older than most of the other remains (the villa was broadly contemporary with the new palace at Festós) and beyond them a **shrine** which contained a frescoed floor and walls now on show in the Iráklion Archeological Museum. If you keep to the higher ground here you come into the courtyard of the villa, perhaps the best place to get an impression of its overall layout. L-shaped, the building enclosed the courtyard only on its north and west sides, and the north side is further muddled by a much later hall – apparently a Mycenaean megaron – built over it. To the south of the courtyard is the early fourteenth-century chapel of **Áyios Yióryios** (key available from the guardian), in which there are fragments of some fine frescoes.

The **Royal Villa** now lies mostly below the level of the courtyard, but in Minoan times it would not have appeared this way: the builders made use of the natural slope to create a split-level construction, and entrances from the court would have led directly into upper levels above those you see today. The finest of the rooms were those in the corner of the "L", looking out over the sea; here were found the best of the frescoes, including that of the famous stalking cat – now preserved in the Iráklion Archeological Museum. The quality of workmanship can still be appreciated in these chambers with their alabaster-lined walls and gypsum floors and benches. Beside them to the south is a small group of storerooms with a number of *pithoi* or large terracotta jars still in place. Some bear scorch marks from the great fire which destroyed the palace about 1450 BC. From the hall and terrace out front you can walk around the **ramp** that runs beneath the north side of the villa. The Italian excavators named this the *Rampa dal Mare* and claimed that it once ran down to the sea, though there seems little evidence for this.

Follow it the other way instead and you can head down to the lower part of the site, the **town area**. By far the most striking aspect of this is the **market**, a row of stores which are once again unique in Minoan architecture. The stores, identically sized and fronted by a covered portico, run in a line down the hill; in front of them is an open space and, across that, the houses of the town. Only one problem mars the easily conjured image of the Minoan populace milling around the market while their rulers looked benignly on from above: this area apparently dates only from the declining years of the Minoan culture and is contemporary not with the villa, but with the megaron erected over it. Beyond the stores (and outside the fence) lies the **Cemetery**, where remains of two *thólos* tombs and many other graves were found, including the one containing the Ayía Triádha sarcophagus.

West towards Timbáki

Continuing west from Festós, towards Ayía Galíni or Réthimnon, the final stretch of the Messará plain, with its acres of polythene greenhouses and burgeoning concrete sprawl, must be among the ugliest places in Crete. **TIMBÁKI** may also be the drabbest town. It's a place of some size, which means there are cafés and restaurants along the main street, stores and banks, and even a couple of hotels, but there's no reason to stay here longer than you have to.

Just beyond, a turning leads to **KÓKKINOS PÍRGOS** on the coast. Here, too, plastic and concrete are the overwhelming images, and the place is barely redeemed by a plentiful supply of cheap **rooms** and the lack of crowds on the none-too-beautiful beach.

Inland: Vóri to Kamáres

Having dismissed this part of the island, it's worth remembering that – as is often the way on Crete – all you have to do is turn off the main road to escape altogether. **VÓRI** lies only a very short distance north and, despite being quite a big place, is far more pleasant: a working village almost entirely off the beaten track, and with a couple of *kafenia* in the village square if you need refreshment before heading on your way. That some tourists do come here is largely due to the excellent new **Museum of Cretan Ethnology** (daily 10am–6pm; 500dr), advertised by large signs along the main road. Hidden behind the church, it's worth seeking out for a comprehensive survey of traditional country life in Crete, and compares favourably with the equivalent museum in Réthimnon (see p.183); the museum won a special commendation in the European Museum of the Year award in 1992. The collection itself is a miscellany of agricultural implements, building tools and materials, domestic utensils, furniture, basketware, pottery, musical instruments, weaving and embroidery, all well labelled and fascinating. The collection of baskets is especially interesting, with 25 different designs reflecting their uses as beehives, eeltraps, cheese-drainers, animal muzzles and snail containers.

If you're heading for Ayía Galíni you have little choice but to return to the main road, but for the Amári Valley and Réthimnon it's also possible to take the new road up to Kamáres for another lovely, climbing drive.

Mátala

MÁTALA is much the best known of the beaches in the south of Iráklion province, and was once one of the chief ports of Górtys. You may still meet people who will assure you that, with its cave-dwelling hippy community, this is *the* travellers' beach on Crete. But that's now history – and bears about as much relation to modern reality as Mátala's role in legend as the place where Zeus swam ashore in the guise of a bull with Europa on his back.

The entry to the village should prepare you for what to expect, as you drive in past a couple of kilometres of new hotels, "Welcome to Mátala" signs and extensive car-parking areas on the roadsides all the way into town. It does get better, and development is still relatively small-scale, but the town never feels anything other than wholly touristy: bus-tour arrivals in the afternoon take up every inch of sand and prices, for rooms especially, are high. For all practical purposes, Mátala consists virtually of a single street, the continuation of the main road into town as it curves round behind the beach. The "market" and many of the places to eat lie to the right, between the road and the beach; the "old town", such as it is, is crammed against the rocks to the left. Almost every other practical need is easily taken care of: **car and bike rental** and **currency exchange** are all around the main square or up the single main street, and there are also a couple of **travel agents**. There's a **post office** van parked throughout the summer at the entrance to the beach car park, with competitive exchange rates as well as stamps for your postcards; the **OTE** also occupies a temporary building, this time in the middle of the car park behind the beach. The covered "**market**" still has a couple of authentic market stalls selling fruit and veg, but these are rapidly being displaced by souvenir stores, general stores and travel agents. Finally, if you want to escape, there are **boat trips** from the harbour (in addition to all the usual bus excursions on offer at the travel agents): a taxi service to Red Beach and Kómmos, and twice-weekly trips to Ayía Galíni and Préveli.

On the plus side, Mátala beach really is quite spectacular: a curving swathe of sand tucked under the cliff in which the notorious caves are carved; if you are prepared to walk, there are other beaches with far fewer people on them. The town crowds – there are always crowds – are relatively young, the atmosphere is boisterous and you will never be short of somewhere to enjoy a cocktail at sunset. If you enjoy that, Mátala has something to offer; if you're after solitude or a cheap room, try somewhere else.

Caves and beaches

The **caves** started it all. Nobody knows quite who started the caves, which are entirely man-made, but it seems likely that the first were Roman or early Christian tombs: they have since been so often re-used and added to that it is virtually impossible to tell. The cliff in which they are carved, an outcrop of compacted sand, is soft enough to allow surprisingly elaborate decor: some caves have carved windows and doorways as well as built in benches or beds (which may originally have been grave slabs); others are mere scooped-out hollows. Local people inhabited the caves, on and off, for centuries, and during the war they made a handy munitions dump, but it was in the Sixties that they really became famous, attracting a large and semi-permanent foreign community. Name a famous hippy and there'll be someone who'll claim that he or she lived here too – Cat Stevens and Bob Dylan are only the most frequently mentioned. It has, however, been a very long time since the caves were cleared out; nowadays they're fenced off, open by day but searched by the police every night.

The **beach** below the caves is the focus for most of the town's activity, and during the day everyone hangs out either on the sand or in the tavernas overlooking it. The swimming is great – if surprisingly rough when the wind blows – with gently shelving sand in the centre, underwater remains of the Roman port around the base of the rocks on both sides (watch out for sea urchins), and multicoloured fish everywhere. If the crowds on this town beach get too much, you can head south, climbing over the rocks behind town in about twenty minutes, to another excellent stretch of sand known locally as **Red Beach**, but be warned that the track can be quite hard going and you may end up scrambling over loose scree on the way down. Usually half empty, this beach has curious dark reddish-brown sand and wonderfully clear water. On the way you pass more caves, many of which *are* inhabited through the summer; indeed, when you know where to look, it turns out that there are a number of cave dwellings around, all some way from the village and the exact whereabouts of the better ones a closely guarded secret.

Accommodation

Finding a **room** should be no problem with so many alternatives, and travel agencies should be able to help if you can't face the trawl. Out of season, you may well be in a position to bargain; but Mátala does have a very long season – it's a popular Easter destination for Greek families. The most attractive place to stay would undoubtedly be in the old town on one of the little backstreets, but there are very few places here. More realistic, and still right at the centre of things, is to take the little street to the left immediately after *Hotel Zafiria* (☎0892/42-112; ③–④), along a road signed "Hotels and Real Rooms", which is almost entirely lined with purpose-built rooms places. Among the first and best of these is the *Hotel Sofia* (☎0892/42-134; ④), although rooms facing towards the town square can be very noisy. Quieter and mostly cheaper alternatives further up the street include *Matala View* (☎0892/42-114; ②), *Fantastik* (①), *Red Beach* and *Silvia*. There's a **campsite** above the beach car park, *Matala Camping* (☎0892/42-720), which is fine and convenient if you like camping on sand. If you don't mind being further from the beach then *Camping Kómmos* (☎0892/42-596) is a better bet, with an on-site swimming pool and taverna; buses between Pitsídhia and Mátala stop nearby.

Restaurants and nightlilfe

Finding something to **eat** is the least of your worries. Tavernas fringe the bay, with sufficient competition to keep prices reasonable; menus are generally very similar. The smallest and least pretentious is the *Skala* fish taverna with superb views across to the cliffs. It is also the furthest away and is approached through the bar of *Neosicos* – make sure of your steps across the cliffs, especially on the way back. Takeaway food and ingredients for picnics can be found in the stalls of the "market".

The chief **entertainment** in the evening is watching the invariably spectacular sunset: almost every bar and restaurant has a west-facing terrace. Although there are a couple of **discos** such as *Neosicos* and *Scorpios* (next to the beach car park), nightlife is generally low-key. The two most popular music bars are the *Marinero* and the *Rock Bar*, while the *Zwei Brüder* bar/taverna, in the main square as you arrive in town, is the longest-established meeting place, with music and reasonably cheap food.

Pitsídhia, Kalamáki and Kómmos

An alternative base to Mátala, and a good way of saving some money and also enjoying rather more peace, is to stay at **PITSÍDHIA**, sprawling around the main road about 5km inland. This is already a well-used option, so Pitsídhia is no unspoilt village, and nor is it quite as cheap as you might expect, but there are plenty of rooms, lively places to eat, and an affable young international crowd.

KALAMÁKI, which is right on the beach a similar distance from Pitsídhia as Mátala, is another possibility. At the moment it seems unfinished, a dusty, ugly place caught halfway between being a beach with a taverna on it and a full-blown resort, but there's plenty of accommodation in half-built rooms places, several bike rental companies with hardly any customers, a number of places to eat, and a long, empty, windswept beach. The road down there seems to run out halfway (unless they've finally completed the new paved one), but any of the dusty tracks seems to find its way to the coast eventually.

Kómmos

At the southern end of the long beach that starts in Kalamáki, almost halfway to Mátala, lies the archeological site of ancient **KÓMMOS**, a Minoan harbour town which was probably the main port for Festós and Ayía Triádha. The site can also be approached from Pitsídhia by a track signed "to *Camping Kómmos*" on the right, 1km west of the village.

Sir Arthur Evans was the first to report signs of Minoan occupation here, but real excavation started only a decade ago when Joseph Shaw began work, funded by the American School of Classical Studies. The work carried out in the seasons since then has made it clear that Kómmos is destined to become a major site of the future. Meanwhile, the excavations are fenced off and not strictly open to visitors – but this does not prevent you taking a look at what's been uncovered.

There are three main **excavation areas** to the north, centre and south; none of them more than a stone's throw behind the beach. It is thought that the whole area will eventually yield evidence of occupation. The **northern area**, on a low hill close to the sea, contains domestic dwellings among which is a large house (on the south side) with a paved court and a limestone winepress. The **central group** – behind a retaining wall to prevent subsidence – has houses from the New Palace era, with well-preserved walls and evidence, in the fallen limestone slabs, of the earthquake around 1600 BC which caused much destruction here. A rich haul of intact pottery was found in this area, much of it in the brightly painted Kamáres style.

The most remarkable finds to date, however, came in the **southern sector** where what you see is partly confused by being overlaid by a Classical Greek sanctuary. Minoan remains here include a fine stretch of limestone **roadway**, 3m wide and more than 60m long, heading away inland, no doubt towards Ayía Triádha and Festós. The road is rutted from the passage of ox-drawn carts and would also have been pounded by the feet of countless Minoan mariners. Note the drainage channel on its northern side. To the south of the road one building contains the longest stretch of Minoan wall on the island: over 50m of dressed stone. The function of this enormous building isn't known but it may well have had a storage purpose connected with the port. Just south of this was another large building (now partly overlaid by a later Greek structure – probably a warehouse), 30m long and 35m wide, divided into five sections with its seaward end open to the sea. This was a shipshed or **dry dock** where vessels were stored out of the water during the winter (or non-sailing) season.

An interesting **temple** lies to the western side of this area, nearest the sea. Here an early tenth-century BC Dorian temple – one of the earliest in the whole of Greece – was replaced by a later one, apparently devoted to a pillar cult similar to that of the Phoenicians who had founded a trading empire based upon modern Lebanon. The excavators think that the Phoenicians may have erected the temple here for use by their sailors, who would have made frequent trading missions to Kómmos. The other remains and altars in this area date from the Hellenistic period when the site became a revered sanctuary. When fully excavated and opened to the public, Kómmos may well emerge as among the most important Minoan sites yet explored.

Léndas and Kalí Liménes

South of the Messará, two more beach resorts – Léndas and Kalí Liménes – beckon on the map. Léndas has a couple of buses a day from Iráklion and in an undeveloped way is quite a busy place. Kalí Liménes, 20km south of Míres, for reasons which will become apparent, is hardly visited at all. If you have your own transport, the roads around here are all passable but mostly very slow: the Kófinas Hills, which divide the plain from the coast, are surprisingly precipitous and even on the paved roads you have to keep a sharp eye out for sudden patches of mud, potholes and roadworks (the only halfway decent road to the coast here is the 25-kilometre route from Górtys to Léndas via Mitrópolis; follow the signs carefully). Other than the direct Léndas–Iráklion service, public transport is very limited indeed – you'll almost always have to travel via Míres.

Léndas

Many travellers who arrive in **LÉNDAS** think they've come to the wrong place. The village at first looks filthy; the beach is small and rocky; and the rooms are frequently all booked. Quite a few leave without ever correcting that first impression. For the real attraction of Léndas is not here at all but beyond the point to the west, 3km or so along the coast road. Here you come upon an enormous sandy beach, where three good taverna/bars, each with a few basic rooms, overlook the sand from the roadside and tents and makeshift shelters provide accommodation for many more down on the sand. This beach is almost entirely nudist, and largely German-speaking (all the menus are written in German). Once you've discovered why Léndas is so popular, the village itself begins to look slightly more welcoming – in a rather scrappy and primitive sort of way. The bus drops you in a sandy yard which also serves as a car park for those who drive – from here you pick your way down to the beach as best you can. There is no proper street, and the few paths which look promising mostly end up in someone's back garden to the outrage of a barking dog or rooting piglet.

At least the village has most of the facilities you'll need, including a store which will change money and sells newspapers and souvenirs, a couple of food stores, numerous places to eat (including *Taverna Iris*, with a long-distance phone available 8am–noon & 2–10pm), and several bars (the *Pink Panther* serves pizzas and cocktails). Perhaps the nicest of the **tavernas** is the light-blue place around to the far right of the beach. You'll see all the **accommodation** options pretty soon – some of them, like *Léndas Bungalows* on the village "square", are relatively luxurious. Out at the good beach (if you're walking, you can save time by cutting across the headland), *Taverna Sifis* has the best rooms, though it's also the most expensive.

East of Léndas, you can also explore some smaller, near deserted beaches, and the hilltop remains of ancient **Levín** (or Leben) overlooking them from immediately outside the village. This was an important healing sanctuary, with at its centre an *Asklepion* by a spring of therapeutic waters; people were still coming here for cures as recently as the 1960s when the spring was diverted and the site became neglected. At its height, from the third century BC on, the sanctuary maintained an enormous temple and was a major centre of pilgrimage. You can still see ruins spread over an extensive area, but sadly, little of their nature can be discerned. There's an arch through which the water once flowed, otherwise only the odd segment of broken wall survives, along with a few severed columns or statue bases, and isolated fragments of mosaic. Much closer in, just above the main part of the village, are the more substantial remains of an early Christian basilica, with a much smaller eleventh-century chapel still standing in their midst.

Kalí Liménes

Leaving Léndas **to the west**, past the beach, you can follow a mostly unpaved road along the coast all the way to Kalí Liménes. It's a very bumpy drive, but far from impossible, and on the way you'll pass a number of smaller beaches. The only one of these with any sort of permanent habitation is Platiá Perámata, a sandy little village with a couple of stores, a few basic rooms and usually the odd camper. It's really not the best of beaches, though. In each of the last two bays before Kalí

Liménes small rooms places have recently opened above little beaches; the first a very basic affair of bungalow/shacks, the second slightly bigger.

KALÍ LIMÉNES itself was an important port in Roman times, the main harbour of Górtys and the place where Saint Paul put in, as a prisoner aboard a ship bound for Rome, in an incident described in the Bible in *Acts 27*. He wanted to stay the winter here, but was overruled by the captain of the ship and the centurion acting as his guard: setting sail they were promptly overtaken by a storm, driving them past Clauda (the island of Gavdhós) and on eventually to shipwreck on Malta.

Today Kalí Liménes is once again a major port – for oil tankers. Which has rather spoilt its chances of becoming a resort, although it's peculiarly appealing. The constant procession of tankers gives you something to look at (they discharge their loads into tanks on an islet just offshore); there are a number of places offering **rooms** (including the excellent *Kanavourissia Beach*, a kilometre or so east of the main village where the road from Pómbia arrives); the coastline is broken up by spectacular cliffs; and, as long as there hasn't been a recent oil spill, the beaches – lined by shacks, a couple of which serve simple food and drinks – are reasonably clean and almost totally empty. But it has to be said that it's a long way from the postcard image of Crete.

Back towards Míres

Heading **back to the Messará** you're in for a bit of mountain driving, and total contrast once you hit the plain on the far side. Leaving Kalí Liménes, don't attempt to drive out of the west end of the village or you'll soon grind to a halt on precipitous rocks: the road inland heads off a short way east, back towards Léndas. At Pigaidákia you rejoin tarmac for the very steep hairpin descent to Pómbia, a large agricultural centre. Beyond here you can either head straight on to Míres or take a left turn for Petrokefáli (where there's a simple pension should you want to stay) and the short route towards Mátala. Touring around here, through quiet and prosperous villages surrounded by their crops of oranges, pomegranates or olives, is a wonderfully peaceful contrast to the traffic of the main road.

Across the south: to Áno Viánnos and Árvi

The road **east across the Messará**, from Áyii Dhéka through Asími to Áno Viánnos in the shadow of the Dhiktean mountains is now paved all the way – a feat which has taken many years. Now an enjoyably empty drive through fertile farming country – there are no buses across, very little transport of any kind, in fact – and, although there's not a great deal to stop for along the way, a visit to the secluded **monastic community** of the Moní Koudoumá is an escapist's dream. If you're looking for a slightly less spartan seaside stopover, the low-key coastal settlements of **Keratókambos** and **Árvi** each have their respective delights, while the more substantial village of **Áno Viánnos** has plenty of places for a lunch break and a couple of churches to see.

From Iráklion the road cuts across the centre of the island, through Arkalohóri, to join this route at Mártha and continue through Áno Viánnos towards Ierápetra. In this direction there are a couple of daily buses, but you'll still have to change buses if you hope to hit the coast before Mírtos.

The coastal route

Coming across the island, access to the coast becomes a realistic proposal only beyond Pírgos, a sturdy farming village 10km down the road from Asími. However, for those looking for adventure there is a fine walk from here to the remote **Moní Koudoumá** set in a spectacular seaside location. The monastery nestles in a cove, surrounded by pinewoods, at the foot of a cliff down which descends a dizzying track with endless switchbacks. Arriving here is a distinctly end-of-the world experience and the few monks remaining have only a couple of nearby dwellings inhabited by elderly women for company. The monks see few visitors, but are extremely welcoming to those that do turn up and will offer you food and a mattress in one of the dormitories set aside for "pilgrims"; while the monks will not accept payment for their hospitality, a donation to "monastery funds" is unlikely to be refused. If you think the magic of the place may persuade you to prolong your stay, you should bring supplies with you. The nights here – illuminated by oil lamps in the absence of mains electricity – are exquisitely serene, broken only by the sound of the sea splashing against the rocks.

On foot, the easiest route from Pírgos (about 20km) is to leave the village by the Priniás road that winds down through the hamlet of Trís Ekklisíes, before it degrades into a dirt track. By road, your best bet is to double back to Stérnes and head south along a slightly better (but still unpaved) surface. Be warned, though, that the final cliff-face section is particularly hazardous – not the kind of thing to be attempted lightly in a rented car. Should you need to spend a night in Pírgos before setting out, *Rooms Tzaridakis* (☎0893/22-238; ①), just off the main street, is pleasant enough, and there are also a couple of decent tavernas nearby.

Tsoútsouros and Keratókambos

A much less arduous route to the sea comes 12km beyond Pírgos at Kató Kastilianá: 13km of trail which wind alarmingly down to Tsoútsouros. This is not an effort to be recommended for **TSOÚTSOUROS**, despite its apparent isolation, is amazingly developed. The source of the crowds that flock here and how they reach it is a mystery; nevertheless, the small grey beach can barely cope.

Far better to hold out for **KERATÓKAMBOS**, a tranquil fishing village 10km along a terrible coastal trail from here – or a similar distance by a much better route from the main road. The road down, via the highly picturesque village of Hondrós, is now paved – no doubt a portent of development. For the moment, though, Keratókambos remains tiny and quiet, very much a locals' resort. A single street of houses interspersed with cafés and tavernas faces a tree-lined sand and shingle beach with a shower on it. Two of the tavernas rent out a few **rooms** (②) which must be among the most basic in Crete: stone cells with a couple of cots and no washing facilities at all. For more luxury you could retrace your steps 2km or so to the point where the road emerges at the coast – this is Kastrí Keratókambos and here you'll find *VE Rooms* (②). If you do stay, or you want to **camp** in isolation, you could explore better patches of deserted sand along the coast road in either direction.

Áno Viánnos

Moving on, the **coast road** gets better as you head towards Árvi, passing beneath a great crag of rock with a ruined castle perched upon it. Again, however, the direct approach is the turning off the main road, heading first through the large village of **ÁNO VIÁNNOS**, clinging to the southern slopes of the Dhíkti range. The air is much sharper up here, even in high summer, and the eating fare more substantial than on the sweltering beaches far below. The traditional centre of this part of southeastern Iráklion province, Áno (or upper) Viánnos' importance has waned as the coastal settlements have grown. But it's still a substantial village with a couple of interesting churches containing well-preserved fourteenth-century frescoes. These, Ayía Pelayía (with a magnificent, if damaged, image of the Crucifixion on the back wall) and Áyios Yióryios, are located up a narrow, stepped side street close to the enormous plane tree on the village's eastern extremity.

The Ierápetra road leads east out of the village, skirting an alarming precipice, and continues on through Amirás, where you turn off for Árvi by a giant memorial to Cretans killed in World War II. A paved road winds gradually down to sea level and emerges on the coast through the gorge of a stream which waters the exotic fruits grown around Árvi.

Árvi

Standing on the site of the ancient Roman town of Arvis, and hemmed in by rock cliffs which trap the heat – creating a microclimate among the hottest in Crete – **ÁRVI** has surprisingly not been overwhelmed by development. This may have something to do with a long but pebbly beach and the villagers' greater interest in the wealth to be made from growing bananas, oranges and pineapples in this near-tropical environment. There are **rooms**, but not always enough in high season: try the *Hotel Ariadne* (☎0895/71-300; ③), near the entrance to the village with balcony sea views, or the slightly cheaper *Gorgona* or *Rooms Galaxy* (☎0895/71-373; ②), towards the centre. Failing these, follow the usual street-corner signs. Once you've settled in there's not much else to do apart from baking in the sun, which is something you can often do comfortably here even when the rest of the island is too cold to contemplate it. When you need shade, there are numerous stores, bars, cafés and tavernas behind the beach; there's even a **bank**. On the hillside overlooking the village is the monastery of Áyios Andónios, which now has only a couple of monks in residence.

Along a bumpy track **to the east** lie more isolated beaches leading eventually to the coastal hamlets of Faflángos and, after 6km, Akrotíri Sidonía, which has a superb beach but no rooms or other facilities. It should be possible to **camp** here, but be aware of local sensitivities: these are not resorts but ordinary villages on the sea. Some maps don't mark it, but the dirt track continues to Tértsa and Mírtos (p.174), some 12km in all, which makes a pleasant walk.

travel details

Buses

Iráklion to: Áno Viánnos (2 daily; 6.30am and midnight; 2hr 30min/3hr); Anóyia (6 daily; 6.30am–4.30pm; 1hr); Arhánes (12 daily; 7am–8.30pm; 30min); Ay. Galíni (7 daily; 6.30am–4.15pm; 2hr 30min); Áy. Nikólaos (24 daily; 6.30am–7.30pm; 1hr 30min); Ay. Pelayía (6 daily; 8.15am–7pm; 30min); Festós (9 daily; 7.30am–5.30pm; 2hr); Fódhele (2 daily; 6.30am and 2.30pm; 1hr); Haniá (25 daily; 5.30am–8.30pm; 1hr 30min/3hr) Hersónisos (every

30min; 6.30am–7.30pm; 45min); Ierápetra (7 daily; 7.30am–6.30pm, via Ay. Nikólaos; 2hr 30min); Lasíthi plateau (2 daily; 8.30am and 3pm; 2hr); Léndas (1 daily; 1.15pm; 3hr); Mália (every 30min; 6.30am–7.30pm; 1hr); Mátala (7 daily; 7.30am–5.30pm; 2hr); Milátos (2 daily; 7am and 3pm; 1hr 30min); Omalós (daily at 5.30am; 4hr 30min); Réthimnon/Haniá (29 daily; 5.30am–8.30pm, a couple via the old road; 1hr 30min/3hr); Sitía (6 daily; 7am–5.30pm; 3hr 30min).

Mália/Hersónisos to: Lasíthi plateau (1 daily; 8.45am; 1hr 30min).

Some of these services are restricted on Sundays

Ferries

To the Cyclades daily to Thíra, Íos and Páros; most days to Míkonos and Náxos; at least 2 weekly to Tínos, Skíros, Skíathos and Anáfi.

To Kárpathos/Rhodes Wed 7am, Sat 5.30pm and Sun 11pm (10hr/12hr).

To Pireás 2 daily, at 7.15pm and 7.30pm (12hr).

To Thessaloníki Tues 7.30pm, Thurs 8pm and Sat 11pm.

To Thíra 2 daily, early morning and late afternoon (2hr 30min fast boat/4hr).

These are summer timetables – schedules severely restricted in winter

International ferries

To Alexandria Every 8 days; currently suspended (27hr).

To Ancona Wed 10pm and Sun 9pm (56hr).

To Çeşme and İzmir (Turkey) Mon midnight (39hr).

To Limassol (Cyprus) and Haifa (Israel) Tues 11am (28hr/36hr).

To Venice Every 8 days (63hr).

Flights

To Athens 7 daily (50min).

To Páros 3 a week (45min).

To Rhodes 4 a week (40min).

To Thessaloníki 3 a week (1hr 30min).

To Thíra/Míkonos 2 a week (40min/30min).

Summer timetables – no island flights and others restricted in winter

ΑΓ ΠΕΛΑΓΙΑ	Αγ Πελαγία	Ay. Pelayía
ΑΜΝΗΣΟΣ	Αμνήσος	Amnísos
ΑΝΩ ΒΙΑΝΝΟΣ	Ανω Βιάννος	Ano Viánnos
ΑΡΒΗ	Αρβή	Arví
ΑΡΧΑΝΕΣ	Αρχάνες	Arhánes
ΒΑΘΥΠΕΤΡΟ	Βαθύπετρο	Vathípetro
ΓΙΟΥΧΤΑΣ	Γιούχτας	Yioúhtas
ΓΟΥΡΝΕΣ	Γούρνες	Goúrnes
ΓΟΡΤΥΣ	Γόρτυς	Górtys
ΗΡΑΚΛΕΙΟ	Ηράκλειο	Iráklion
ΚΑΛΟΙ ΛΙΜΕΝΕΣ	Καλοί Λιμένες	Kalí Liménes
ΚΕΡΑΤΟΚΑΜΠΟΣ	Κερατοκάμπος	Keratokámbos
ΚΝΩΣΟΣ	Κνωσός	Knossós
ΛΕΝΤΑΣ	Λέντας	Léndas
ΜΑΛΙΑ	Μάλια	Mália
ΜΑΤΑΛΑ	Μάταλα	Mátala
ΜΟΙΡΕΣ	Μοίρες	Míres
ΤΣΟΥΤΣΟΥΡΟΣ	Τσούτσουρος	Tsoútsouros
ΤΥΛΙΣΟΣ	Τύλισος	Tílissos
ΤΥΜΠΑΚΙ	Τυμπάκι	Timbáki
ΦΑΙΣΤΟΣ	Φαιστός	Festós
ΦΟΔΕΛΕ	Φόδελε	Fódhele
ΧΕΡΣΟΝΗΣΟΣ	Χερσόνησος	Hersónisos

CHAPTER TWO

LASÍTHI

E astern Crete, at least in the minds of most visitors, is dominated by **Áyios Nikólaos** and the mass tourism it attracts. Travellers who come here to see a more traditional face of the island tend not to look on the area with much favour. Áyios Nikólaos itself is less crowded these days than it once was, though it still makes a lively and exciting base, whilst the surrounding countryside – the **Lasíthi plateau** and **Krítsa** in particular – is worth a few days of anyone's time.

Things improve, too, as you move towards the **far east** of the island, which is under the sway not of Áyios Nikólaos but of **Sitía**, a large and traditional town where tourism has had little outward effect. At the eastern tip, the Minoan palace at **Zákros** and the laid-back beaches around **Vái** offer wildly contrasting escapes.

Along the **south coast**, there is generally far less development, though **Ierápetra** and its environs would win few beauty prizes. Not far away, however, at **Mírtos** and **Makriyialós** for example, there are beaches as good as any in the province.

ACCOMMODATION: ROOM PRICE SCALES

All accommodation establishments in this book have been price-graded according to the scale outlined below. The rates quoted represent the cheapest available double room in high season; where possible, a per-person rate is given for dormitory-style accommodation in youth hostels. Out of season, room rates can drop by up to fifty percent, especially if you negotiate rates for a stay of three or more nights. Single rooms, where available, cost around seventy percent of the price of a double.

Rented private rooms usually fall into the ② or ③ categories, depending on their location and facilities, and the season; a few in the ④ category are more like plush self-catering apartments. They are not generally available from late October through the beginning of April, when only hotels tend to remain open.

① up to 4000dr (£10.50/US$16.50)
② 4000–6000dr (£10.50–16/US$16.50–25)
③ 6000–8000dr (£16–21/US$25–33)
④ 8000–12,000dr (£21–32/US$33–50)
⑤ 12,000–16,000dr (£32–42/US$50–66)
⑥ 16,000dr (£42/US$66) and upwards

For more accommodation details, see p.34.

THE LASÍTHI PLATEAU AND ÁYIOS NIKÓLAOS

The **northwestern corner of Lasíthi** may be the gathering ground for almost all the province's visitors, but it's not just about resorts. Stay for a few days in the **Lasíthi plateau** and you experience a very different world; make your way east

LASÍTHI PROVINCE

To Rhodes

Dionysades
Islands

To Kásos

Ítanos

Vái

M. Faneroméni

Sitía

M. Tóplou

Paléokastro

Petrás

Minoan Site

Móhlos

Hamézi

Skopí

Zoú

Karídhi

Sfáka

Sítanos

Zákros

Káto
Zákros

Órnó

Askordaliá
(1237m)

Présos

Aféndis
vroménos
1476m)

Lamnóni

Handhrás

tís

Orinó

Lithínes

Etiá

Zíros

Xerókambos

Análipsi

Makriyialós

M. Kápsa

Goúdhouras

Koutsourás

Ayía Fotiá

N

0   10 km

along the coast to **Goúrnia** and you can enjoy one of the best minor Minoan sites in near isolation. And at **Áyios Nikólaos**, of course, there is genuine fun to be had, in what is perhaps Crete's most cosmopolitan enclave.

Transport, at least along the main roads, is excellent. There's a constant stream of buses between Iráklion and Áyios Nikólaos, stopping at major points en route, and good local services from both Áyios Nikólaos and the inland centre of Neápoli.

Mália to Áyios Nikólaos

Driving into Lasíthi from Mália there's a choice of routes. The wide, fast **new road** leaves the palace at Mália behind and embarks almost immediately on the long climb inland – rising at first through the **Gorge of Selinári** where travellers would traditionally stop at the chapel and pray to St George for safe passage. There's still something of a truckstop here, but most traffic roars straight past and on through the tunnel blasted beneath the old pass. It's a tremendous engineering achievement, though beyond here – having bypassed Neápoli – there's little else to see until you emerge high above Áyios Nikólaos to encounter spectacular views of the Gulf of Mirabéllo.

Sísi

The **old road** follows the coast for a while longer, rolling on through Sísi with a branch off to Mílatos (see below). **SÍSI** is becoming developed, but for the moment this amounts only to scattered apartments, and the local beaches remain quiet and small-scale. **Epáno Sísi**, the inland part of the village, has one or two possibilities for rooms but a more tempting stop is **Sísi Paralía**, 2km away on the coast. Here a picturesque tiny harbour is overlooked by some slow-moving tavernas: try *Koursaras* or *Miramare* which have views of the harbour and sell fresh fish. However, new construction has undermined the village's erstwhile tranquillity and as well as a large new holiday complex, *Kalimera Krita*, a couple of kilometres to the east, there's now also the usual array of bike rental offices, souvenir stores and bars.

Scattered around the village are numerous **rooms**, or there's *Camping Sísi* (☎0841/71 247), just over 1km to the west, with its own swimming pool and plenty of shade.

Mílatos

MÍLATOS remains less developed, possibly because of its uncomfortable pebble beach (though there are sun beds for hire). Once again **rooms** are available both in the village and at the beach settlement 2km away. Here, tavernas, cafés and stores cluster around a small church on the waterfront, the tavernas specializing in fresh but expensive fish.

Although you'd never guess from what remains today, **ancient Mílatos** has a distinguished story and the glory of a mention by Homer in the *Iliad* as one of the seven Cretan cities that sent forces to fight at Troy. In mythology (backed up by recent archeological finds) it was from Mílatos that Sarpedon, King Minos's brother whom the king had defeated to take the throne, sailed to found Miletus –

destined to become one of the greatest of all the cities in Asia Minor. Unlike its namesake in modern Turkey, however, little has survived on the site to the east of the beach. The city faded into obscurity in antiquity and by Roman times no longer existed.

There's more recent history to be seen at the **Mílatos Cave**, 3km east of the village and signposted up a good dirt road. More a series of caverns than a single cave, this appears to go back for miles: with adequate lighting you might be able to discover just how far. Less adventurously, there's a small chapel to explore right at the entrance, a memorial to the events which earned the cave its notoriety. Here in 1823, during one of the early rebellions against the Turks, some 2700 Cretans (that at least is the number claimed) took refuge, were discovered and besieged in the cave. Eventually, having failed to break their way out, they were offered safe conduct by the Turkish commander – only to be killed or taken away into slavery as soon as they surrendered.

Beyond the cave, you could continue around the Áyios Ioánnis peninsula, or across to Neápoli, by a variety of dirt roads. Back through Mílatos village, however, the scarcely used, paved road to Neápoli is an equally beautiful, and certainly an easier way to zigzag through the mountains.

Neápoli

NEÁPOLI, despite its size, history (Pope Alexander V was born here) and location, sees virtually no tourists other than those who stop for a coffee in the square between buses or as they drive through. A charming provincial town, it was formerly the capital of Lasíthi (a role now usurped by Áyios Nikólaos) and remains the seat of the local government and of the provincial courts; there's one **museum**, dedicated to folklore (Tues–Sun 10am–1pm & 6–9pm; 300dr), at the south end of the main square.

Facilities include a cheap **hotel**, the *Neapolis* (☎0841/33-268; ①), various other **rooms** to rent, and, around the square, tavernas, *kafenia* (try *soumadha*, a local almond drink), post office and banks. It's a peaceful place to stay, and it is from here that one of the roads up to the Lasíthi plateau (see following section) sets out.

Dríros

Continuing instead towards Áyios Nikólaos, there's soon a turning signed towards **Dríros**, a route that curls steeply up above the old and new roads (which here run almost exactly parallel). Following the signs you eventually come to a dead end beneath a rocky hillside, and scrambling up you'll find ruins of the ancient city – its earliest remains dating back to the eighth century BC. A canopy covers the **Temple of Apollo Delphinios**, one of the earliest temples known in all of Greece. It was dedicated to a cult that celebrated Apollo transformed into a dolphin, a guise the god used when guiding Greek sailors. That the chief sanctuary of Miletus in Asia Minor was devoted to the same cult is further evidence of a link between this area and the founding of the colony there. In the centre of the temple can be seen the remains of a sunken hearth. Here were found three hammered bronze statuettes (among the earliest known) as well as two Eteocretan inscriptions (Greek letters used to write a Cretan, possibly Minoan tongue). It's hard to believe that this temple once lay on the edge of the bustling *agora*, or main square, and was approached by a flight of steps – visible in the gorge fronting the temple, now crammed with fig trees.

Finding anything else of note among the thorny bushes and ruined dry-stone walls roundabout is virtually impossible, and deciphering it once you do is even harder. Nevertheless, if you make it to the top of the hill – topped by a charming barrel-vaulted chapel – the views make the climb worthwhile, whilst the drab desolation all round is a startling contrast to the green country around Neápoli.

North and east of Dríros

To the **north of Dríros**, a series of twisting (mostly asphalt) roads link a string of remote farming villages which rarely see visitors. Many of the windmills you'll see perched along the heights are still functioning and used to grind flour. One, at Vrouhas, actually welcomes visitors.

If you want to continue east by the least arduous scenic route, however, take the road through **KASTÉLLI**, **FOURNÍ** – with its dramatic entry road lined with severly pruned eucalyptus trees – and **PÍNES**, which winds down to Eloúnda with yet more wonderful views of the Gulf of Mirabéllo. The characteristic landscape of this part of Crete still remains with its stone walls and stone windmills, which hug the steep hillsides and summits.

Worth a detour, near the village of **KARÍDI**, is the impressive **monastery of Areti** which is currently being restored. Ask the builders if they mind you wandering around, and look out for the large cisterns where rainwater was stored (there was no spring in the area).

The Lasíthi plateau

Scores of bus tours toil daily up to the **Lasíthi plateau** to view its famous sea of white cloth-sailed windmills. Most must leave disappointed, for few of the mills remain in operation, and those that do operate only for limited periods. Others are found next to tavernas and used as a feature to attract people. Nevertheless, even if you see none unfurled at all, the trip is still worth making for the drive alone.

From Neápoli a long and winding road, twenty slow kilometres of it, climbs into the mountains which ring the plain. When you think you have arrived, another village appears around the corner and the road climbs again. Before you reach Ámigdáli there are a couple of roadside tavernas which have stunning views into the hills. Stock up on handmade wooden spoons which hang outside the craftsman's house at Zénia, or call in at the small taverna at Exo Potámi. At Mesa Potámi, 4km further, you are almost on the plateau, but there are more tavernas to entice you, in addition to roadside stalls selling honey or whatever fruit is in season. When you finally come upon the plateau laid out below you, it seems almost too perfect – a patchwork circle of tiny fields enclosed by the bare flanks of the mountains. Closer to it's a fine example of rural Crete at work, with every inch given over to the cultivation of potatoes, apples, pears, cereals and almost anything else that could conceivably be grown in the cooler climate up here.

The area has always been fertile, its rich alluvial soil washed down from the mountains and watered by the rains which collect in the bowl. In spring there can be floods, which is why the villages all cluster on the higher ground around the edge of the plain, but in summer the windmills traditionally come into use pumping the water back up to the drying surface. Although the plateau was irrigated in

Roman times – and inhabited long before that – this system was designed by the Venetians in the fifteenth century, bringing the plain back into use after nearly a century of enforced neglect (during which time cultivation and pasture had been banned after a local rebellion). Where they survive, the windmills have barely changed since then. In the past twenty years or so, however, most have been replaced by more dependable petrol-driven pumps. The other windmills – the 26 stone ones standing guard on the ridges above the plain, also mostly ruined – were traditional grain mills. Today, only two of these are left in use.

Come on a day-trip and you will see all this. **Stay overnight** and you'll see a good deal more, as the tourists leave and a great peace settles over the plateau. The excesses of Mália or Hersónisos seem a world away as you climb into your cot to the sound of braying donkeys and a tolling church bell outside, and wake to the cock's crow the next morning. If you feel inclined to rise with the lark you'll see a diaphanous white mist floating over the plain and its windmills in the sparkling early morning sun. Ideally you'd arrive at either end of the season: in late spring the pastures and orchards are almost alpine in their covering of **wild flowers**, an impression reinforced by the snow lingering on the higher peaks; in autumn the fruit trees can barely support the weight of their crop. Whatever time of year, though, bring some warm clothing. The nights get extremely cold.

A paved circular road links the **villages** on the plateau's edge. Whichever village you stay in you can catch the **bus** as it circles the plain, or more enjoyably walk through the fields from one to another. The path is rarely direct, but it's easy enough to pick your way by the trails – even right across the plain, from Psihró to Tzermiádho, is a bare hour-and-a-half's walk. Whichever point you arrive at on the circuit you'll be assailed by villagers encouraging you to buy their handmade **rugs and embroidered work**. If you're tempted to buy, don't jump at the first opportunity. And don't be afraid to bargain.

Tzermiádho

TZERMIÁDHO, the largest and most important village on the plateau's northern edge, comes complete with post office, OTE, bank, garage, a number of cafés and tavernas, and even a couple of **hotels**. The *Kri Kri* (☎0844/22-170; ①) in the centre of the village is relatively comfortable and there is also *Hotel Kourites* (☎0844/22-194; ①) on the western edge of the village – both have restaurants. The "bakery" next to the *Kronia Taverna* in the centre sells extremely hot and fresh *tirópita*, some of the best to be had.

From the road in the centre of Tzermiádho there's a sign up to the **Trápeza Cave**, in which Evans and Pendlebury discovered assorted remains and tombs going back to Neolithic times. If you don't take up the offer from one of the many elderly "guides" who may accost you en route, you'll need to look out for a slope on the left where the track narrows. Follow this to the top and be alert for the narrow, unmarked cave entrance. As you wander in the murky darkness (a flashlight is essential) it's easy to imagine that this is where Crete began: Stone Age peoples huddled around fires no doubt telling stories in the manner of surviving tribal groups today. From these modest beginnings sprang the Minoans and then, under their tutelage, the Greeks.

The ascent to Karfí

From Tzermiádho there's also an ascent to the ancient Minoan site of **Karfí**, one of the most dramatic places in Crete, perched on the southeast slope of Mount Karfí, with an opportunity to see some spectacular birds of prey. The climb will take about an hour on foot – less if you drive the first part; you'll also need sturdy footwear and, in summer, plenty of water. There are a number of shady places for a picnic on the way up, or even at the site itself, but remember to take all rubbish away with you.

The start of the track up is located on the village's western edge at the side of the district health centre, opposite a blue sign marked in English "To the Tinios Stavros church." Follow this as it winds gently up to the Níssimos plateau (also accessible by car), a twenty- to thirty-minute walk offering fine views over the Lasíthi plain. Once on the plateau you will arrive at a fork where three dirt tracks diverge. Leave any transport here and take the left track, aiming for a saddle between two peaks. You will soon spot the red waymarks at the start of the ascent, followed fairly soon by the name, Karfí, daubed in Greek on various rocks. It's an easy and well-marked thirty-minute climb from here through a rocky landscape patrolled by agile goats.

At the end of the climb, after taking in the magnificent views over the coast and distant Hersónisos to the north, you'll come to the **archeological site** spread across a saddle between the summit of Mount Karfí (the location of an ancient peak sanctuary) to the east and the pinnacle of Mikre Koprana (topped by a trig point) to the west. Founded in the twelfth century BC, in this enclave Minoan refugees fleeing from the Dorian advance attempted to preserve vestiges of their ancestral culture. The settlement consists of a cluster of stone-built single-storey dwellings, a rather crude imitation of the site at Gourniá. For the three thousand or so inhabitants that lived here prior to the site's peaceful evacuation around 1000 BC life must have been a grim struggle, lashed by the winds and prey to the vicious winter elements. But this very inaccessibility was of great defensive value and preserved the settlement from attack, whilst the cultivation of the Níssimos plateau below provided food and pasture for livestock.

Among the ruins, excavated in the 1930s by John Pendlebury, the easiest building to identify is what the archeologist described as the **Great House**, an important building still retaining its walls and where a number of bronze artefacts were turned up. Behind this, just to the north, and in an area covered with a carpet of ancient potsherds, was the **shrine** where were found the remarkable metre-high terra-cotta goddesses with arms raised in blessing, now in the Iráklion Archeological Museum. The remainder of this desolate village, intersected by a number of paved alleyways, isn't easy to make sense of, except for the dwelling thresholds and the odd evocative hand-grindstone lying among the collapsed piles of stones. But this remote eyrie, with all its historical associations, is one of the most haunting places on the island.

Whilst you're up here, there's a good chance you'll see the odd **griffon vulture** gliding majestically overhead; maybe even the much rarer **lammergeier**, or bearded vulture, now down to a few isolated pairs. There are few more dramatic sights than this raptor hoisting the leg bones of its victims into the air to dash them onto a rock below (nearly always the same one) – once broken the bird extracts the marrow with its specially adapted tongue.

Áyios Konstantínos and Áyios Yióryios

Clockwise from Tzermiádho, the next village of any size is **ÁYIOS KONSTANTÍNOS**, which is where the Neápoli road emerges on the plain. Here, too, you could find a **room** if you wanted one, and because it is the first (and last) village most people visit, it is packed with souvenir stores. Watch out particularly for a priest and his wife selling embroidered fabrics: these two could sell ice to Eskimos. You may also see Maria working her antique family "heirloom" in the doorway of her store. Natural dyes from onions, walnuts and other sources are still used by some.

ÁYIOS YIÓRYIOS, next in line, is larger and less commercial. There's a small and entertaining **Folk Museum** (summer only, daily 10am–4pm), which also contains a fascinating photo-biography of Crete's great writer, Níkos Kazantzakís. Excellent-value **rooms and food** (and home-made wine) are to be had at the *Hotel Dias* on the village's main street (☎0844/31-207; ①), or try the *Hotel Rea* (☎0844/31-209; ①), further along the street, if this is full.

Psihró

Most people's main destination is **PSIHRÓ**, the base for visiting Lasíthi's other chief attraction, the Dhiktean Cave (see below), known as the birthplace of Zeus. The village itself is another simple plateau community strung out along a tree-lined main street. There are a couple of tavernas as well as some traditional (if rather dingy) **rooms** at the *Dikteon Andron* (☎0844/31-290; ②), in the upper part of the village, near the church. Better facilities are available at the not overly-friendly *Hotel Zeus* (☎0844/31-284; ②), a little way beyond the village towards the Dhiktean Cave. If you find everything full – as is likely during the big local festival over the last three days in August – try the unofficial **campsite** by the *Taverna Panorama* (you're expected to eat there) at the western end of the village.

The birthplace of Zeus

The **Dhiktean Cave** (daily 10.30am–5pm; 400dr, car park 300dr) lies just past Psihró, up a trail for which mules are on offer but which is in reality neither particularly long nor dauntingly steep. According to legend it was in the Dhiktean Cave that Zeus was born to Rhea. His father, Kronos, had been warned that he would be overthrown by a son and accordingly ate all his offspring. On this occasion, however, Rhea gave Kronos a stone to eat instead and left the baby concealed within the cave, protected by the Kouretes, who beat their shields outside to disguise his cries. From here Zeus moved to the Idean Cave, on Psilorítis, where he spent his youth (p.195). That at least is the version generally told here, and though there are scores of variations on the myth, it is undeniable that the cave was a cult centre from the Minoan period on, and that explorations around the turn of the century retrieved offerings, to the Mother Goddess and to Zeus, dating through to Classical Greek times.

If you resisted the guides at the bottom of the path you'll find them more persistent still at the entrance to the cave. Whatever they say, a guide is not compulsory, and in the middle of the day there are so many tours going through that there is plenty of light and commentary to be had without one. However, if you have neither flashlight nor an extremely lurid imagination, a guide is not a bad investment (around 2000dr for 2 people including lamps, or 500–600dr each if part of a larger group). It takes long experience and a Cretan eye to pick out such intimate details as the nipples the baby Zeus sucked on from the rest of the stalactites and stalagmites. Hokum aside, though, when you look back from the depths of the cave towards the peephole of light from the world you have left behind, framed in a blue haze caused by the damp atmosphere, it's not hard to believe that this may well have been the infant Zeus's first sight of the world destined to become his kingdom.

Two general points. To avoid the crowds and savour the cave's mystical qualities to the full, try to arrive before noon. Also watch out for damp and extremely
slippery stones underfoot on the way down: non-slip shoes are essential. If this
has given you a taster to explore more of the countryside around then one of the
guides, Petros Zarvakis, takes people into the hills at the weekend, with an overnight stop, sleeping rough. Ask for details at the car park – he usually leaves from
there on Saturday at (very roughly) around 5pm.

Áyios Nikólaos

Sited on the picturesque Gulf of Mirabéllo, "Ag Nik", as **ÁYIOS NIKÓLAOS** is
known to the majority of its English-speaking visitors, was originally the ancient
port for Lató, one of the dominant cities of this area in Hellenistic times. This settlement faded in the Roman period and seems to have been abandoned in Byzantine
times. The Venetians built a fortress here – of which nothing remains – and gave
the surrounding gulf its name, Mirabéllo (lovely view). The town came slowly back
to life and by the nineteenth century the port was again busy. After union with
Greece in 1913, Áyios Nikólaos was confirmed as the capital of Lasíthi province.

A quiet harbour town for most of this century, it was discovered in the Sixties by
international tourism. The attractions were – and are – obvious: a setting on a
small, hilly peninsula around a supposedly bottomless lake, now connected to the
sea to form an inner harbour. It is wonderfully picturesque, and it knows it. The
lake, the harbour and the coast all around are fought over by restaurants, bars and
hotels, charging well above the odds. The town's reputation did take a nosedive
some years ago when it became too crowded and too boisterous for its own good.
However, the worst of the holiday excesses now occur at Mália, up the coast, and
Áyios Nikólaos has emerged without any lasting damage. But if you're looking for
a beach, forget it – the few small patches of sand are either closely guarded by
expensive hotels or standing room only by the time you've finished breakfast.

> The phone code for Áyios Nikólaos is ☎0841.

Arrival, orientation and information

You get the best impression of all of Áyios Nikólaos if you arrive by **ferry**; the
dock is on a tiny peninsula, a couple of minutes' walk from the lake and the pretty
town centre. The **bus station** is very much on the low-rent, southern side of
town, where the concrete modernity is at its most apparent and the traffic noise
never stops. Arriving here – or **driving** in on the one-way system – head up the
hill to Platía Venizélou, and then down into the picturesque areas past the souvenir stores which line both Koundoúrou and 28 Oktovríou. The lake marks the
centre of town in every way, and the narrow bridge over its channel is a notorious
bottleneck for traffic and strolling visitors. From here, Aktí Koundoúrou curves
around the sides of the harbour, and M. Sfakianáki strikes over a small hill to the
cove of Kitroplatía. Almost all the action in Áyios Nikólaos takes place around
these streets.

You'll probably want to visit the **tourist information office** (daily 8.30am–
9.30pm; ☎22-357) at some stage (see "Accommodation" opposite), situated

ÁYIOS NIKÓLAOS

between the lake and the port. The **tourist police** are at K. Paleológou 17 (☎22-321), north of the lake

For **departure information**, and details of **bike rental** and **boat trips**, see "Listings" on p.136.

Accommodation

It's actually become much easier to find a room in Áyios Nikólaos in recent years, though in peak season you may still struggle for choice. Nevertheless, there are

literally thousands of rooms scattered all over town and the best move is to visit
the tourist information office, which normally has a couple of boards with cards
and brochures about hotels and rooms, including their prices. If the prices seem
very reasonable it is because they are for the low season.

The **youth hostel** has now closed and it seems that there may not be a replace-
ment for some time to come. The nearest **campsite** (*Gournia Moon*) is 17km
away (see p.144).

Adonis Pension, Salaminos 4 (☎22-931). Overlooking the sea across the harbour, though a
little noisy as it's above the road. Visit in low season and share a shower and the price drops
by almost 50 percent. ③.

Atlantis Hotel, Metamorfoseos (☎28-964). One block east of the bus station, this is nothing
special but is handy enough and has a snack bar below with breakfast for 500dr. ②.

The Green House, Modatsou 15 (☎22-025). Probably the best cheap place to stay in town,
this clean pension has shared bathrooms, but there is a garden. ②.

Katerina Pension, Stratigou Koraka 30 (☎22-766). Near the *Marilena* and another good
choice in the same price bracket – some rooms have their own balcony. ②.

Linda Hotel, Salaminos 3a (☎22-130). This friendly place has 22 rooms all with shower,
balcony and a partial sea view; it's located just off Akti Koundourou. ③–④.

Loukas, Platía Venizelou 13 (☎23-169). A very central location in the heart of the shopping
area of Áyios Nikólaos. ③.

Mantraki Apartments, Kapetan Tavla (☎28-880). A possible choice in one of the town's
quieter backstreets behind the bus station. Best for 3 or 4 people sharing, the apartments
include a kitchen. ④.

Marilena Pension, Erithrou Stavrou 14 (☎22-681). One of the main budget options, the
Marilena is a clear winner, with a friendly proprietor and some rooms with sea view and
balcony. ②.

New York Pension, Kontoyianni 23 (☎28-577). Rough-and-ready place on a noisy street,
close to the bus station – which is about the only reason for its popularity. ②.

Perla Pension, Salaminos 4 (☎23-379). Basic family-run place, next door to the *Adonis*, on a
hill to the north of the harbour. Front rooms have sea-view balconies. ③.

Sgouros Hotel, Kitroplatia (☎28-931). Modern hotel next to one of Áyios' few beaches and
close to loads of tavernas. ③–④.

The Town

Things to do in town by day are pretty limited – you're not supposed to have
recovered from the night before so soon. A couple of museums (see opposite)
hold some interest, but for most visitors the days are taken up strolling the area
around **Lake Voulisméni** – allegedly over 60m deep – nosing around in the
shops, and heading for the strips of **beach**. In the little cove at Kitroplatía there's
a rocky foreshore from which you can swim; north of town by the *Dolphin*
taverna you'll find a narrow length of gritty sand; or there's a municipal beach
(with entry fee) beyond the bus station on the south side of town. This at least is
clean and sandy, but again it's terribly crowded.

Most people simply end up diving off the rocks which line the foreshore north
of town, or else they get out altogether: the sandy beach of Almirós is 2km south
and there's a constant stream of people walking there; further in this direction by
bus or bike there are good beaches around Kaló Hório, or in the other direction
around Eloúnda (see following sections). The **boat trips** to beaches around the
bay are also popular; see "Listings" for details.

The Folk Museum

The **Folk Museum** (daily except Sat 10am–1.30pm & 6–9.30pm; 200dr) is opposite the bridge and housed on the ground floor of the Harbour Masters Office, across from the tourist office. It has a small but interesting display of handicrafts (especially embroidery), costumes, pottery and cooking utensils. Scots should resist the temptation of trying out the old Cretan goats leather bagpipe.

The Archeological Museum

There's more interest in the modern and well laid-out **Archeological Museum** (Tues–Sun 8.30am–3pm; 400dr) on Paleologou, north of the lake, which as ever will mean a lot more after you've visited a few sites in the area.

Following some interesting Neolithic finds in Room 1, you come to Room 2 and the museum's star exhibit, the extraordinary **Goddess of Mírtos**. This goose-necked early Minoan (c.2500 BC) clay figurine – actually a jug – was found in the excavation of the superbly sited Bronze Age settlement at Fournoú Korifí, near Mírtos. Note the pubic triangle, breasts and the square panels thought to portray a woven garment. The beak-spouted jug she's holding (which is also the vessel's mouth) is similar to vases in the museum from the same period. Elsewhere in Rooms 1 and 2 are displayed some fine examples of **Vasilikí ware**, named after the early Bronze Age site on the isthmus of Ierápetra where it was first discovered. The lustrous mottled finish of this pottery was achieved by uneven firing, an effect which obviously pleased its creators. Even more remarkably, these flawless artefacts – including a "teapot" and a beak-spouted ewer dating from around 2500 BC – were made not with the wheel, but on the clay "turntables" exhibited in Room 2. The potter's wheel only reached Crete some six hundred years later and you can see an early example in Room 2 from a tomb at Kritsá.

Room 3 displays some fine Marine-style pottery which, although found in a villa near Makriyialós, is thought to have come from the Knossós workshop. Also here is some interesting **jewellery**, including a beautiful gold pin bearing an intricately crafted bramble motif and a long inscription in Linear A on the reverse. In the same room is a wonderful collection of Late Minoan **clay sarcophagi** or *larnakes* decorated with birds, fish and the long-tentacled octopus which seems to have delighted the Minoan artists. The archeologists assumed, when they turned up these items, that they were all burial chests. But when they found more of these painted tubs, with clearly identifiable plug-holes in the bottom, the Minoans had the last laugh – they were obviously avid bathers.

Room 4 contains a rare Minoan infant burial displayed exactly as found at its site at Kryá, near Sitía. Dating from the Late Minoan period, the transferring of the whole thing from site to museum by Costis Davaras "without displacing a single stone" must have been some headache. Finally, in Room 7, there's an eerie grinning skull from the Roman cemetery at Potamós, on the edge of Áyios Nikólaos, to send you on your way. A wreath of gold olive leaves is still in place about its crown as was the silver coin – originally in the mouth of the deceased – now displayed separately in the case. This was the traditional fare paid to the boatman Charon, who ferried the dead across the River Styx to the underworld.

Eating

There are tourist-oriented **tavernas** all around the lake and harbour and little to choose between them apart from the different perspectives you get on the passing fashion show. Have a drink here perhaps or a mid-morning coffee and choose somewhere else to eat. The places around the Kiroplatía are generally fairer value, but again you are paying for the location. For a change from Greek food consider trying one of the good Italian restaurants at the north end of Kiroplatía such as the *Casanova*. It's also worth visiting *Dimitri Spices* along the waterfront, a little way past the *Loukakis* taverna, especially if you're after an unusual gift to take home – it sells henna red and black sesame tea, along with the usual range.

Ellinikon, Kapetan Kozyri. A small café with loads of character that serves traditional mountain dishes, made freshly every day, with village *raki* or wine. The list of drinks and *mezédhes* available are chalked up inside on a board.

Itanos, Kyprou. On a side street off the east side of Platía Venizelou, this serves Cretan food and wine and has a terrace across the road opposite. It's popular with the locals.

Loukakis and **Ikaros**, Akti. S. Koundouro. Two good-value tavernas, a few minutes' walk away from the port along the Elounda road, next to each other along the waterfront.

Pelagos, Koraka, set just back off the lake behind the tourist office. A stylish fish taverna, with good food but at a price.

Taverna Auoas, Paleológou. On the way to the Archeological Museum, this serves good traditional Cretan food in and under a plant-covered trellised courtyard.

Trata, at the beach end of Sfakianáki. Slightly more expensive than usual but with a tempting roof garden for sultry nights.

Drinking, nightlife and entertainment

After you've eaten, you can start to get into the one thing which Áyios Nikólaos undeniably does well: **bars and nightlife**. Not that you really need a guide to this – the bars are hard to avoid, and you can just follow the crowds to the most popular places.

For a quieter **drink**, the *Hotel Alexandros* on Paleológou has a rooftop cocktail bar overlooking the lake and frequent live music sessions. The *Creta Café*, among the disco bars on Koundoúrou harbourside, is a surprisingly civilized haven of sanity where Greek professionals unwind at various hours of the working day. Also, try *Yiannis* further down the harbour or, further still, the new bar *Porto*, where the ferry boats arrive. If you feel like a drink on the harbour itself then there is always the floating café-bar, the *Armida*, to consider. Finally, around midnight, when the crowds have gone, the cafés along the lakeside are pleasant places to linger.

Quiet drinking, however, is not what it's all about in the **disco bars**. *Lipstick* and *Bora Bora*, on Koundoúrou harbourside, are very popular, and there are more bars to try at the bottom of 25 Martíou (known as "Soho Street") where it heads up the hill – like *Rififi*, *Captain Sky* and *Club Scorpio*.

Each year Áyios Nikólaos mounts a summer-long **cultural festival**, "the Lato", which includes music, dance and theatre from Crete, Greece and elsewhere. Keep an eye out for posters advertising the various events or ask at the tourist office.

Listings

Airlines *Olympic Airways*, Plastira 20 (☎22-033).

Bike rental Available from dozens of outlets, mainly in the harbour area – it's very expensive in high season, though outside the summer months shopping around might bring you a real bargain. Try *Adonis* on Akti Koundoúrou or *Mike Manolis*, who has a pitch at the junction of 25 Martíou and Sfakianáki near the OTE, for cheaper alternatives.

Boat trips Trips to points around the gulf mostly leave from the west side of the harbour, near the tourist office, and if you walk around here and along Akti Koundoúrou northwards you'll be accosted by their operators.

Bus station For route information, call ☎22-234. Buy tickets on the bus for services to Elounda (180dr), Kritsa (180dr), Lasíthi (1600dr) and Vai (1700dr).

Ferries The main agent is *Massaros Travel*, Koundoúrou 29, not far from the post office (☎22-267); other travel agents, for local tours, are all around.

Hospital The town hospital (☎22-369) is at the northern end of Paleológou, one block beyond the Archeological Museum.

Left luggage Facilities are available at the bus station from 6am–9pm, but as there is little control of who goes into and out of the area reserved it's not really worth taking the risk.

OTE On N. Sfakianáki just above 25 Martíou (☎28-099); open June–Oct daily 6am–midnight, rest of the year from 6am to 10.30pm

Post office 28 Oktovriou, above the lake (Mon–Sat 7.30am–2pm; ☎22-276).

Taxis There's a rank in the main square, or call ☎24-000.

The Gulf of Mirabéllo

North of Áyios Nikólaos the swankier hotels are strung out along the coast road – flashest of them the *Minos Beach* (☎0841/22-345; ⑤) with its bungalows, private pools and jealously guarded beach – with upmarket restaurants, discos and cocktail bars scattered between them. Among them, and by way of contrast to this hedonistic beach life, a signposted road leads off to the right towards the sea and the Byzantine church of **Áyios Nikólaos**, from which the modern resort takes its name. To get in you'll need to ask at the nearby *Minos Palace Hotel* for the key, which will be handed over in return for the deposit of a passport. The trouble is worth it to see some of the earliest fresco fragments found in Greece, dating back to the eighth or ninth century. The geometric patterns and motifs that survive are the legacy of the Iconoclastic movement, which banned the representation of divine images in religious art.

Soon after this the road begins to climb above the **Gulf of Mirabéllo**: looking across, Psíra and Móhlos can be made out against the stark wall of the Sitía mountains, while nearer at hand mothballed supertankers are moored among the small islands sheltering in the lee of the peninsula. One of the largest of these islets, Áyios Pándes, is a refuge for the island's wild goat, the *kri-kri*. The animals have an elusive reputation, carefully avoiding the cruise parties from Áyios Nikólaos which put in to see them.

Oloús

The road drops back down to sea level as it approaches Eloúnda (see over). Before you reach the centre of the village, however, there's a track signed off to the right to the "sunken city" of **Oloús**. This leads down to a natural causeway which is the only link between the peninsula of Spinalónga (often known as "big Spinalónga" to distinguish it from the more famous island of the same name) and the mainland. All around the causeway on both sides you'll find people swimming from small patches of beach or basking on flat rocks. Protected by it are the remains of Venetian salt pans, now fallen into disrepair but which are worth checking for migrating birds in the spring.

Oloús itself lay around the far end of the causeway and along the coast to the right. Though it is known chiefly for having been the port of Dríros, what little remains is Roman: there's a fenced enclosure behind the popular *Canal Bar* in which you can see the floor of a Roman basilica with an odd, almost patchwork-style black and white mosaic; and among the rocks a little further round (watch out for sea urchins) are the sunken traces of harbour installations. The site has never been excavated, however, and this is about the extent of what survives, but the excursion is worth it for the setting – the beaches, causeway, "French" canal and stone windmills. On the far side of the peninsula there are better beaches still – tough to get to except by boat.

Eloúnda

ELOÚNDA, though it's a fair-sized resort these days, with one very exclusive hotel (the *Elounda Beach*; ☎0841/41-812; ⑤) and scores of new apartment developments, is a very different proposition from Ag Nik – low-key and slow moving. At its heart is an enormous square with cafés, stores and hotels on three sides, the seafront promenade on the fourth. This is where you park if you've driven, it's where the bus stops, and it's also where the boats to Spinalónga leave from. Just about everything else in Eloúnda is in the immediate vicinity. Post office, OTE (Mon–Sat 8am–11pm, Sun 10am–3pm & 5–10pm), bank and car rental office can all be seen as you stand in the square.

There are even a few **rooms** available, most at the far end of the village behind the church: try those above *Kalimera* (②) or – further out – at *Pension Oasis* (③). Chronis Daskalakis, the manager of *Olous Travel* (☎0841/41-324), next to the post office, can also find rooms for you, while the travel agency serves as a local information office. *Hotel Calypso* has a poular **restaurant** and *Nikos'* fish taverna on the square has a good selection of fish and Greek food at reasonable prices.

Spinalónga

The great majority of people visiting the fortress rock of **Spinalónga** leave from Eloúnda (though there are also boats direct from Áyios Nikólaos and from Pláka) and it is certainly the most convenient way of getting there, with reasonably priced caiques making the trip every half hour or so.

The islet was fortified by the Venetians in 1579 to defend the approach to the gulf and more particularly the sheltered anchorages behind the peninsula of Spinalónga. Like their other island fortresses it proved virtually impregnable and was handed over to the Turks only in 1715, by treaty – some fifty years after the rest of Crete had surrendered. The infamous part of the island's history is much more recent, however. For the first fifty years of this century, Spinalónga was a leper colony, the last in Europe. Lepers were sent as outcasts – long after drugs to control their condition had rendered such measures entirely unnecessary – to a colony primitive in the extreme and administered almost as if it were a detention camp. Its jail was frequently used for lepers who dared complain about their living conditions.

Even today there's an unnerving sense of isolation when the boat leaves you here, at a jetty from which a long tunnel leads up into the fortified centre. There are still just two easily sealed entrances: this tunnel, and a jetty on the seaward side (which you see if you approach from Áyios Nikólaos) which leads up to the old castle gate with its Lion of St Mark. Around the base of the castle a real town grew up – Turkish buildings mostly, adapted by the lepers using whatever materials they could find. Although everything is in decay, you can still pick out a row of stores and some houses which must once have been quite grand.

Pláka

The colony's mainland supply centre was at **PLÁKA**, about 5km north of Eloúnda, and if you ask at *Manoli's Taverna* there you can still get someone to run you across to the island (1000dr). This is a better bet if you fancy having Spinalónga to yourself and don't want to share it with hundreds of others. Pláka itself remains a very quiet spot. There are several **tavernas**, of which *Manoli's* serves fresh fish at reasonable prices, while a couple of the others rent out **rooms** such as *Taverna Castello* (②) and *Rooms Margarita* (②). There's beautifully clear water and a beach on which the pebbles are rather too large for comfort.

Only at weekends, when locals come to escape the crowds elsewhere, does the place lose its tranquillity – and even then it's quieter than anywhere else around. Walking, you could continue to the point of the cape in around an hour and a half, following the road which climbs almost as far as the next village, Vrouhás, before taking off along a track above the sea.

Kritsá and Lató

The other excursion everyone from Áyios Nikólaos takes is inland to Kritsá, a "traditional" village about 10km away. Despite the commercialization, this is a trip well worth making for a break from the frenetic pace of Ag Nik; buses run at least every hour from the main station. Along the way two sites delay you, each worthy of a visit.

Panayía Kirá

About 1km before Kritsá, the road runs straight past the lovely Byzantine church of **Panayía Kirá** (Mon–Sat 9am–3pm, Sun 9am–2pm; 400dr), inside which is preserved perhaps the most complete and certainly the most famous set of Byzantine frescoes in Crete. Of the three naves (the buttresses and lantern are later additions), the larger, central one is the oldest, though the frescoes have all been retouched and restored to such an extent that it is impossible to say with certainty which is the most ancient. All of them originate from the fourteenth and perhaps early fifteenth centuries. Those in the south aisle, through which you enter, depict the life of Ann, mother of Mary – her marriage to Joachim, the birth of Mary – and the early life of the Virgin herself up to the Journey to Bethlehem. In the centre of the church Mary's story is continued and there are scenes from the life of Christ including the Nativity, Herod's banquet and a superb Last Supper. And in the final aisle there are vivid scenes of the Second Coming and Judgement, along with the delights of Paradise and assorted interludes from the Lives of the Saints (especially St Anthony). Throughout, the major scenes are interspersed with small portraits of saints and apostles. Alongside the church are a couple of tavernas and a store selling excellent, but expensive, reproduction icons.

Lató

Just beyond the church you can turn off towards the archeological site of **Lató** (daily except Mon 8.30am–3pm; free), about 3km up an asphalted road; the gate is often left considerably open after the official closing time. Although there's as much to be seen here as in many of the more celebrated sites it's very little visited: presumably because most visitors' interests are directed to the Minoans, and this was a much later settlement, Doric in origin but flourishing through to Classical times. Even the archeologists shared this lack of curiosity, for systematic excavation of the site started only in 1967 under the French School.

The city's name derives from a Cretan Doric corruption of Leto, the mythical mother of Artemis and Apollo. Homer relates in the *Odyssey* how Eileithyia (the Minoan goddess of childbirth) attended Leto when she gave birth to the god Apollo on the island of Delos: it is thus fitting that Eileithyia became the patron goddess of Lató, as coins turned up in the excavations here proved. That it was an important city is clear from the sheer extent of the ruins, which spread in every direction. It is a magnificent setting – this city of sombre grey stone sprawled across the saddle between the twin peaks of a dauntingly craggy hill – and standing on the peak you can look down onto the white cluster of Áyios Nikólaos (Lató's ancient port), with the bay and Oloús, a major rival of Lató in its heyday, beyond, or inland to the valleys and climbing peaks of the Dhiktean mountains. Ruins aside, these views would be worth the sweat getting up. The exposed position can't have been all that practical, however, and wearing a toga must have been a hazardous business in the fierce summer winds which gust from all directions.

You enter the city, artificially, by stepping straight over the broken defensive wall into its very heart. The open area of the **agora** is an interesting fusion of early Greek and older Minoan influences. This pentagonal space was a meeting place for citizens but also incorporates a tier of steps on its northern side, reminiscent of the theatral areas at Minoan sites such as Knossós and Festós. The steps ascend between the remains of two towers to the **prytaneion**, or town hall, with small rooms at the rear which held the city's archives. In the centre of the agora is a deep square cistern and a shrine, flanked on the western side by a colonnaded **stoa**, a shady place to converse or shelter from the elements. The southern end of this has been cut through by a relatively modern circular threshing floor. The **exedra** nearby was a sort of public seating area. In the southeast corner of the site is another exedra with what is termed a "theatral area" beside it – a broad flight of steps again similar to the Minoan style – which leads to a raised terrace containing a well-preserved fourth-century BC temple with a stepped altar just before it.

To the east, a stepped path leads downhill to a rectangular area with a gateway which would have been the original entrance to Lató. Climbing back up the street you can see the stores and workshops abutting the city wall on the right, with defensive towers and gateways into the residential areas on the left.

Kritsá

If you wanted, you could retrace your steps from Lató to where the track divides, and then turn right to head down to Flamouriá on the Lakonía plain, from where there's a paved road (and buses) back to Áyios Nikólaos. Most people head for **KRITSÁ**, however. Always a sizeable place (known as "the largest village in Crete"), its popularity and its fame as a handicrafts centre have not really spoilt the place. Nowadays it feels more like a small town, with the main street lined with tourist stores selling (mostly) leather goods or embroidery. Despite the commercialism, prices are a great deal better than in Áyios Nikólaos – though you can still pay as much as £400/US$650 for some of the wonderful, elaborately woven rugs – and if you manage to avoid the tour-bus crowds (early morning and mid-afternoon are the best times) the place reverts to a friendly semi-somnambulance in which you're free to wander and browse under no pressure at all.

Kritsá's other chief claim to fame lies in its situation, with views back over the green valley up which you arrived and the mountains rising steeply behind. You get little impression of this at street level, other than an awareness that you are climbing quite steeply, so try to get out onto one of the balconies at the back of the cafés along the main street, where you can look back over the town and towards Áyios Nikólaos.

Practicalities

Staying in Kritsá is a surprisingly easy and attractive option. There are usually beds to be found – certainly more chance than on the coast – and it's an ideal place to experience something approaching a genuinely Cretan atmosphere.

A number of places offer **rooms**. One of the best is *Argyro,* on your way into the village (☎0841/51-174; ②), which is clean and friendly, has rooms with and without private shower, and its own café. *Pension Kera* (②), up the hill from the bus stop, is a slightly cheaper alternative; if this is full, any of the textile sellers opposite will put you in touch with family-run rooms nearby.

There are a number of **cafés** in the centre of Kritsa, including *Sareithakis*, a cool place to sit out under a plane tree. Otherwise, head for the bakers for tempting cheese pies or currant breads. One of the best-situated tavernas is *Castello*, in the centre, and there are a few others near where the bus stops.

As it is impossible to park in the village, car parks are provided at the top and bottom of the village.

Around Kritsá

If you want to explore further, you'll find more frescoed churches here and in the immediate surroundings. **Áyios Yíoryios**, for example, is on the edge of the village, signed uphill to the left as you walk through: the frescoes here are contemporary with those at the Panayía Kirá, though in a very much worse state of preservation. Further in this same direction, **Áyios Ioánnis** lies a kilometre or so down the road to Kroústas. These churches will probably be locked – enquire as to accessibility from the guardian at the Panayiá Kirá.

South to the isthmus

The main road south and then east from Áyios Nikólaos is not a wildly exciting one – a drive through barren hills sprinkled with villas and above the occasional sandy cove. Beyond the reed-fringed beaches at Almirós and Amoudhára there's little temptation to stop until you reach the cluster of increasing development around **KALÓ HÓRIO**. Here there are several tavernas and mini-markets, OTE and mobile post office. Below them paths wind down, quite steeply, to a couple of excellent small beaches. On the first of them there's a taverna by the outflow from a small river. Immediately beyond is **ÍSTRO**, a burgeoning resort in its own right, just beyond which the *Istron Bay Hotel* (☎0841/61-303; ⑤) hangs from the cliff above a spectacular cove with a fine sandy beach. If you walk confidently through the hotel grounds you can get down to enjoy this and the hotel's beach bar: there's no such thing as a private beach on Crete, but apparently nothing to prevent all the approaches being privately controlled. Unfortunately, like all the beaches in this part of the bay, much rubbish is washed up although this is regularly cleaned away by the hotel.

Five kilometres further on, a track is signed on the right for the **Moní Faneroméni**. The track is a rough one and climbs dizzily skywards for 6km, giving spectacular views over the Gulf of Mirabéllo along the way. The view from the monastery itself, when you finally arrive there, must be among the finest on Crete. To get into the rather bleak-looking monastery buildings, knock loudly (and repeatedly if necessary). When you gain entry you will be shown up to the chapel, built into a cave sanctuary where a sacred icon of the Virgin was miraculously discovered, the reason for the foundation of the monastery in the fifteenth century. The frescoes, although late, are quite brilliant – especially that of the Panayía Theotókou, the Mother of God. The monk who unlocks the chapel has been known to be a little mean with the time (and electric light) you need to view the artworks – more time can usually be "purchased" with a discreet contribution to monastic funds.

Gourniá

Back on the coast road, another 2km brings you to the site of **GOURNIÁ** (daily except Mon 8.30am–3pm, 400dr), slumped in the saddle between two low peaks. A look at the map tells you much about ancient Gourniá's strategic importance, controlling the narrow isthmus with its relatively easy communication with the southern seaboard at modern Ierápetra. The overland route avoids a hazardous sea voyage around the eastern cape – a crucial factor in ancient times, especially in winter when sailing usually stopped because of rough seas.

This is the most completely preserved of the Minoan towns, and in its small scale contains important clues about the lives of ordinary people and perhaps about the nature of the communities from which the palaces evolved. The desolation of the site today – you are likely to be alone save for the sleeping guard – only serves to heighten the contrast with what must have been a cramped and raucous community three and a half thousand years ago.

There is evidence of occupation at Gourniá as early as the third millennium BC, but the remains you see today are those of a town of the New Palace period (c. 1500 BC). Around 1450 BC, as happened elsewhere, the town was destroyed by fire. A limited rebuilding occurred during the era of Mycenaean rule at Knossós and the shrine may date from this late period. But the site was soon abandoned again and disappeared beneath the soil where it lay unsuspected until the awakening of archeological interest in the nineteenth century. Evans, as usual, was the first to scent Minoan occupation of this area and then a young American, Harriet Boyd-Hawes, started digging in 1901. The site, a budding archeologist's dream, made her reputation.

The narrow, cobbled alleys and stairways – built for pack animals rather than carts – intersect a throng of one-roomed houses centred on a main square and the house of a local ruler or, more likely, governor. The settlement is not a large place, nor impressive by comparison with the palaces at Knossós and elsewhere, but it must have been at least as luxurious as the average Cretan mountain village of even 25 years ago. Among the dwellings to the north and east of the site are some which have been clearly identified, by tools or materials discovered, as the **homes of craftsmen**: a carpenter, a smith and a potter. It's worth remembering that the rooms may not have been as small as they appear – many of these are in fact basements or semi-basements reached by stairs from the main rooms above, and the floor plans of those did not necessarily correspond with what you see today. The houses themselves were mainly built of stone on the lower courses and mud brick above, with plaster-daubed reeds for roofing.

The **palace** (or governor's quarters) occupied the highest ground, to the north of a courtyard containing a familiar L-shaped stairway. With a smaller court at its heart, the whole is a copy in miniature of the palaces at Knossós or Festós. About 20m to the north of the palace a **shrine** was discovered. It is easily identified by the sloping approach path paved with an intricate pattern of evenly matched cobbles. The shrine itself, up three steps, is a small room with a ledge for cult objects. Here were unearthed a number of terra-cotta goddesses with arms raised, as well as snake totems and other cult objects, now on display in the Iráklion Archeological Museum.

Across the island: Pahiá Ámmos and Vasilikí

It is tempting to cross the road from the Gourniá site and take one of the paths through the wild thyme to the sea and a swim. Don't bother – this seemingly innocent little bay acts as a magnet for every piece of floating detritus dumped off Crete's north coast. If you backtrack a little you could head instead to the **campsite** of *Gournia Moon* (☎0842/93-243), with its own small cove and beach; there is a bus stop directly above the campsite on the main road. There's almost as much junk washed up in the cove here, but at least the people who run the site make an effort to clear it up. The campsite has a taverna and store, and if you don't like the look of the sea, a swimming pool.

Pahía Ámmos

There is a much larger beach, as well as rooms to rent and tavernas, at **PAHIÁ ÁMMOS** in the next valley. As you climb the road above Gourniá, be sure not to miss looking back over the site, its street plan laid out like a map. Even its best friends wouldn't describe Pahía Ámmos as an attractive town, but this windswept mess of concrete does possess an eccentric Greek charm. However, the **pollution** problems mentioned above are, sad to say, even worse here. Local political battles have stymied a grand clean-up plan (with huge moles to keep out the junk) and much of the time it is positively dangerous to swim here. A close look at the sea should convince doubters. That said, should you still wish to stop over, Pahía Ámmos at least has every basic facility you're likely to need, including a line of seafront **tavernas**. *Taverna Aiolus* is outstanding – one of the best fish restaurants for miles around – and you'll struggle to beat the locals to a table in high season.

This is the narrowest part of the island, and from here a fast new road follows the ancient route through the Monastiráki gorge **towards Ierápetra** in the south. To the left the awesome slopes of the Thriptí range bear down on the road until some 3km along it you reach a turn-off for Vasilikí on the right.

Vasilikí

The archeological site of **Vasilikí** is visible from the main road, with an entrance from the side road a short distance down on the left. There is no obvious place to park off the road, and neither is the sign to the site apparent. Although Vasilikí is fenced the gate is always left open.

This Pre-Palatial settlement, dating from about 2650 to 2200 BC, may not be much to look at, but it's important for the light it throws upon the hazy millennium preceding the Minoan great period. Remains from this period occur at Knossós and other palaces but cannot be properly excavated because of the important buildings constructed on top of them. Vasilikí was the first of these early sites to be found in a pristine condition, due to its being abandoned after a fire about 2200 BC.

The site contains two main buildings, originally surrounded by numerous smaller (and simpler) dwellings. The remains of the edifice nearest to the entrance, on the lower slope of the hill, are slightly earlier than that on the crown. The **Red House**, as the former is named, has a number of interesting features. It is oriented with its corners towards the cardinal points of the compass, a practice normal in Mesopotamia and the Near East but alien to Egypt and the Aegean (a clue to Minoan origins?). In the southern corner deep basement rooms allow you to gain an idea of early Minoan building techniques: holes to support the absent wooden beams are visible as well as large patches of hard, red lime plaster, the forerunner of what later artists were to use as the ideal ground for the wonderful palace frescoes. This material gives the dwelling its modern name. The pottery known as Vasilikí ware, orange or red with dark, blotchy decoration, takes its name from this site where the fine examples on display in the archeological museums at Iráklion and Áyios Nikólaos were discovered. New excavations on the southern flank of the Red House have revealed a bath, a stretch of roadway and more dwellings.

Episkopí

Unless you wish to continue on up the lane into the village of Vasilikí, for another glimpse of rural Crete, the main road continues towards Ierápetra via **EPISKOPÍ**, almost exactly halfway across the isthmus. Here, below the road beside a pleasant raised *platía* where old men play *távli* in the shade of eucalyptus trees, lies a charming blue-domed Byzantine church. The arched drum dome with elaborate blue-tile decoration, together with an unusual ground plan, make this church unique on the island. Entry to view a rather bare interior with a late *ikonstásis* is difficult due to the frequent absences of the *papás* who apparently possesses the only key, but anyway it's the church's exterior which gives it its standing in Byzantine architecture.

The road's next stop is Ierápetra, 7km further (p.169).

AN AIRPORT FOR THE EAST

The tranquil isolation of this strip may be about to end if plans for a new international airport – sited to the south of Vasilikí – are finalized. Due to take up a tract 5km long, archeologists are worried about potential damage to as yet undiscovered sites in an important historical area. There's also a rumbling row between the rival towns of Áyios Nikólaos and Sitía, the latter believing it, and not Áyios Nikólaos/Ierápetra, should get the east's first major airport. It seems, however, that the provincial capital, Áyios Nikólaos, is set to win the argument and the airport, which is intended to open up the east of the island to the development of package tourism.

THE FAR EAST

The **far east** of Crete marks yet another dramatic change in scenery and tempo. Although much of it is rocky, barren and desolate, it is an area of great natural beauty. With the exception of **Ierápetra**, the towns and villages are slower and quieter, life conducted at an easier pace. **Sitía**, in particular, seems a contented city unperturbed by its visitors. The north coast has few beaches, and in the main the mountains drop straight to the sea (the drive towards Sitía is as dramatic as any in Crete), but there are a couple of coves which are just about accessible, and beyond Sitía, as the heights tail away, there's more opportunity for swimming. The far east is much visited only in two spots – the overrated palm beach at **Vái** and the superb Minoan palace at **Zákros**. Away from these it's a great area for escapists. On the south coast there are a number of excellent sandy beaches: at **Makriyialós**, at **Ayía Fotiá** and the coast east of Ierápetra, and at **Mírtos**.

Bus connections and main roads continue to be good: there are frequent rapid services from Áyios Nikólaos to Ierápetra, and good connections along the north coast to Sitía. Onwards from Sitía it's easy enough to continue to Vái or Zákros or to cut back south to Ierápetra; from Ierápetra, rather less readily if you're relying on public transport, you can carry on west, across the centre of Crete, to Iráklion.

The road to Sitía

Beyond the isthmus, the tawny bulk of the Sitía mountains makes a formidable barrier to further progress and the road at first is carved into the cliff face, teetering perilously above the gulf. The views back become more expansive all the time, until at **PLÁTANOS** you reach a famous viewpoint, with a couple of tavernas, *Panorama* and *Skinoseli* further on, where you can sit and stare down on the island of Psíra, the site of a Minoan settlement, or west across the gulf to Áyios Nikólaos to watch the sunset. Past here the road runs further inland, emerging only occasionally to glimpses of the sea far below.

Of the tempting beaches you see many are inaccessible, although **THÓLOS**, where there's a quiet beach and chapel but not much else and similar pollution problems to Pahía Ámmos, can be reached 4km down an asphalted road. The *Tholos Beach* taverna, apartments and rooms are about halfway down. **KAVOUSI** with its Byzantine churches and main tree-lined street of oleanders and mulberry trees would be a better place to stay.

Móhlos and its islet

A more inviting alternative is **MÓHLOS** – though getting there involves tackling 5km or more of dusty hairpin bends. There is no bus connection down to the coast, which leaves you with the options of a taxi or walking. Shortest of the routes down is a road signposted soon after Plátanos, but you may have difficulty persuading the bus to stop here, at San Pandelémas, and it is also the least attractive route, past a large quarrying operation. There are equally obvious ways to follow down (in one and a half hours or less) from the villages of Sfáka, Tourlotí (a trail not marked on the maps) and Mirsíni, all of which are standard halts for the bus. The Sfáka road is now asphalted and the way to go if you have transport. You could also get to Móhlos by boat from Áyios Nikólaos – a regular trip in summer which includes a stop at Psíra, ask at the bus station in Áyios Nikólaos for details. Heading back from Móhlos to the main road involves a more serious walk, of two hours or more, which you might want to bypass by taking a taxi.

Tiny and out of the way as it is, Móhlos has plenty of **tavernas**: *Ta Kokília* is the best on the seafront, while *Sta Limenária* in a cove to the west has interesting "specials" and vegetarian dishes. There are also two small **hotels**, *Sofia* (☎0843/94-179; ③) and *Mochlos* (☎0843/94-205; ②–④) – the cheaper rooms at the latter don't have sea views – as well as numerous houses which rent out **rooms**. Try *Rooms Limenária* (☎0843/94-206; ②), close to the *Mochlos*, or *Pension Ermis* (☎0843/94-074; ②), just behind the *Mochlos*. There are some new hotel developments, too, but fortunately these are far enough out not to affect the character of the village much.

Obviously, the place is not wholly unspoilt: rooms are surprisingly expensive and often booked up in high season, and some of the bars and tavernas much fancier than you'd expect. This appears to be mainly because American and Greek teams are still excavating on the islet offshore, and they and their followers often spend whole summers here, occupying much of the available space. No matter, the atmosphere remains sleepy, there's plenty of space if you need to camp out, and plenty of rather rocky foreshore to swim off during the day. Keep an eye out for sea urchins while bathing here (the mini-market sells plastic shoes); they flourish in the clear, unpolluted water. In the mornings, you'll see divers collecting them for restaurants along the coast, which serve up the female ovaries as *achinosalata* – a much-prized delicacy.

The islet

The **islet** looks within swimming distance – and it is when the weather is calm – but it's easier to arrange a ride with a local fisherman if you want to go over. A return trip will cost around 2000dr for the boat – ask at *Ta Kokília* taverna, where many fishermen hang around after work.

Inhabited from the Pre-Palatial period, in Minoan times this barren rock was almost certainly a much less barren peninsula, and the sandy spit linking it to the mainland would have been used as a harbour (anchorages which could be approached from either side were a great advantage for boats that could sail only before the wind). You can see remains of late Minoan houses on the south side of the island, and there are more below the current sea level where recent excavations have also identified remnants of the ancient harbour. But the important discoveries at Móhlos were in the much more ancient tombs built up against the cliff. Here were found very early seal stones (including one from Mesopotamia), some spectacular gold jewellery (now in the Iráklion Archeological Museum), and a fine collection of marble, steatite and rock crystal vases (in the Áyios Nikólaos and Sitía archeological museums).

Psíra

The larger island of **Psíra**, this time genuinely offshore, was also a Minoan port, and here the remains are of a town a little like Goúrnia but built amphitheatrically around a good natural harbour. It was first excavated in 1907 by an American, Richard Seager, who revealed a settlement which again was occupied from the early Minoan era. During the Neo-Palatial period, this community of merchants, sailors and fishermen shared in the general prosperity of the time.

A long, stepped street climbs away from the harbour and most of the dwellings here have a hearth in one of their rooms. No palaces or obvious public buildings were discovered but the site has produced rich finds of painted pottery. One jar, now on display in the Iráklion Archeological Museum, is noted for its decoration of bulls' heads interspersed with the double axe symbol. Trading with overseas areas such as Egypt and the Levant must have been necessary to import the essential requirements of life to such a parched, infertile place. The remains of what is thought to be an ancient well have been found – although the island is completely dry these days. The site was another of those destroyed about 1450 BC: later the Romans used the island for strategic and navigational purposes, and you can still make out the remains of their lighthouse and military settlement on the island's crown. As with the islet, you should be able to arrange a ride over to Psíra with a fisherman, or you could take a more organized visit from Áyios Nikólaos for around 500dr per person.

East to Mirsíni

From Móhlos to Sitía the road, lined with a riot of pink oleander flowers in summer, continues to toil through villages clinging to the mountainside, now high above a deserted bay, now enfolded by mountains, until the final approach to the city, and a descent in great loops through softer hills. As you progress, the familiar olive groves are increasingly interspersed with vineyards and there are some fine and highly regarded local wines to be had in the village cafés (especially in **ÉXO MOULIANÁ**). Wine under the *Agrilos* label is bottled in nearby Sitía. Most of the grapes, however, go to make sultanas: in late summer, when they are laid out to dry in the fields and on rooftops all around, the various stages of their slow change from green to gold to brown make a bizarre spectacle.

Mirsíni

Of the villages en route, **MIRSÍNI** has an attractive church built around, and entirely enclosing, a frescoed fourteenth-century chapel. You'll need to find the priest if you want to look inside, but no matter if you can't track him down – apart from the church, and a small pottery and weaving workshop, Mirsíni also has a taverna whose terrace has stunning views across the coast below.

Hamézi

Near to the ruined stone windmills on the final crest before the Bay of Sitía, a track is signed on the right for the ancient site of **Hamézi** (the village of the same name is further on). The track will eventually lead you to a Minoan site with a spectacular hilltop setting after about a fifteen-minute walk. Once on the track, take the second turning right, the one just beyond the windmills – this should bring you to a beekeeper's hut with hives stacked beside it. The fence circling the site on its conical hilltop is visible from here. Should you get lost on the way – which isn't difficult – head for the nearby village of Paraspóri (see below), where the boys at *Yiordanis' Bar* will be only too pleased to direct you. "Archaeológiki anaskafí" are the words you need, but make sure you are heading for the hilltop site or they may think you want Ahládia (see below).

Dating from the Pre-Palatial period (c.2000 BC), this grey stone ruin has a unique importance in Minoan archeology, for it is the only known structure to have had an oval ground plan, possibly dictated by the conical shape of the hill. It was thought at first to be a peak sanctuary, but the discovery of a cistern made a dwelling, or even a fortress, seem more likely. The ground plan sketched out by the walls – more than 1m high in places – consists of a number of rooms grouped around a central courtyard where the cistern is located. A paved entrance is visible on the south side. Whatever the building's function, it certainly had a commanding view over the surrounding terrain. While you're taking this in, keep an eye out for the rare Eleanora's falcon which breeds on the offshore island of Paximádha – the valley to the east is one of its favourite hunting grounds. **HAMÉZI** proper is a sleepy little village where plants festoon over buildings and down white-washed steps. The folk museum is at the church, but if it is closed ask at the café back on the main road.

Ahládia and Paraspóri

If you still have the appetite for more ruins, nearby at **Ahládia** are the remains of an impressive *thólos* tomb dating from the Mycenaean period, as well as a Neo-Palatial Minoan villa. The **tomb** lies 2km to the east of the village of **PARASPÓRI** up a track to the right, whilst the **villa** lies up another track (also on the right) 1km beyond Ahládia.

Moní Faneroméni

Further along the main Sitía road, just beyond Skopí, you'll come to a track signed on the left for the **Moní Faneroméni**. Partly asphalted, this five-kilometre track leads to a picturesque cove lapped by a turquoise sea. From here, the track climbs inland to the monastery, which can also be approached by another track 5km closer to Sitía.

What you'll find when you reach it is a charming monastic church overlooking a gorge near to the sea. In many ways a metaphor for more recent Cretan history, the church has been battered but still stands unbowed. In 1829 the monastery and tiny church were looted and burned by the Turks, and most of the frescoes destroyed. The beauty of what was lost is visible from one scarred remaining fragment depicting a saint reading. The three indentations across his face are bullet holes, again Turkish. By the iconostasis hangs a curtain embroidered with a gold Greek cross which you may be tempted to peer behind. The remains of the founder here are not for the squeamish. The shoals of silver *taxímata*, or sick symbols, hung on the icon of the Virgin to implore her miraculous intervention attest to the importance of the shrine locally today – a tradition stretching back to Minoan times and probably beyond. There's a path from here, which would take you on foot to Sitía in less than two hours.

Sitía

After the excesses of Mália or Áyios Nikólaos, arriving in **SITÍA** can seem something of an anticlimax, even dull. But don't be fooled; Sitía's charms are subtle. Allow yourself to adjust to the more leisurely pace of life here and you may, like many other visitors before you, end up staying much longer than intended. The town certainly makes an ideal base from which to visit the other attractions in the region. Not even Sitía, of course, can entirely escape the tourist boom, and the increasing number of tourists attracted to the port has led to a great deal of new development at the fringes. Many of the new visitors are French or Italian, a legacy perhaps of the French troops who garrisoned the place under the Great Power protection at the end of the nineteenth century, and the Italians who occupied it during World War II.

This area was settled, as *Eteia*, in Classical times but may be identified with the Minoan *se-to-i-ja* inscribed on clay tablets found locally. That there was a substantial Minoan presence in the area is borne out by the excavations at Petrás, the town's southern suburb, where a settlement dating to the early second millenium has been unearthed and where, in the later Neo-Palatial period, there was a fine town with sophisticated buildings and roads. Details concerning the subsequent Greek and Roman settlements are sketchy and little tangible evidence, apart from some tombs and fish tanks (see p.153), survives. It was under the Venetians that the port really took off (they called it *La Sitia* – hence Lasíthi), as part of a conscious attempt to exploit the east of the island. For all their efforts, the area remained cut off by land from the rest of Crete and although what was in effect a separate fiefdom developed here, it never amounted to a great deal. Perhaps the most significant event of this era was the birth of Vicenzo Kornaros, author of the epic Cretan poem, the *Erotókritos*. More physical remains are few, prey to earthquakes and the raids of Barbarossa. Where once there was a walled city, now you'll find only the barest remains of a fortress.

The town is set on a hill tumbling down towards the western end of the picturesque Bay of Sitía. Its oldest sections, hanging steeply above the harbour, look

---

The phone code for Sitía is ☎0843.

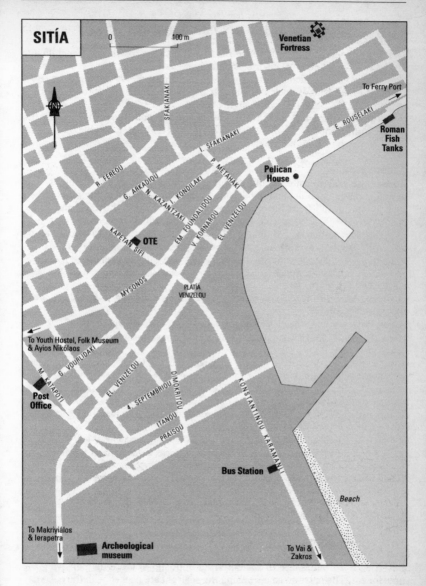

SITÍA

0   100 m

Venetian Fortress

To Ferry Port

E. ROUSELAKI

Roman Fish Tanks

SFAKIANAKI

I. SFAKIANAKI

P. METAHAKI

Pelican House

R. FEREOU

G. ARKADIOU

N. KAZANTZAKI

KONDILAKI

EM. FOUNDALIDOU

V. KORNAROU

EL. VENIZELOU

KAPETAN SIFI

OTE

MYSONOS

PLATÍA VENIZELOU

To Youth Hostel, Folk Museum & Ayios Nikólaos

G. VOURLIDAKI

M. KAPAPOTI

Post Office

EL. VENIZELOU

4. SEPTEMBRIOU

DIMOKRITOU

ITANOU

PRAISOU

KONSTANTINOU KARAMANLI

Bus Station

Beach

To Makriyiálos & Ierapetra

Archeological museum

To Vai & Zakros

east over the bay and the long ribbon of new development along the coast. Life concentrates on the waterfront, around Platía Venizélou in the corner of the bay. North towards the port and ferry dock is a seafront promenade crowded with the outdoor tables of rival tavernas. South, the main road runs behind the beach, flanked for miles by a rambling jumble of development.

Arrival, information and accommodation

The **bus station** is on Konstantinou Karamanli (aka the Beach Road) and though there's a left-luggage area of sorts, it's hardly secure. Leaving the station, turn left along the seafront which will bring you into the centre. **Ferry** arrivals from Áyios Nikólaos or the islands dock at the port at the northeastern end of town; it's a ten-minute walk (or 2-min taxi ride) into the centre.

The tourist office has inexplicably closed and the none-too-competent **tourist police**, at Mysonos 24 (daily 7.30am–2.30pm; ☎24-200), may be able to come up with a town map, though little else.

Accommodation

Rooms are rather scattered, but except at the busiest times you should be able to find something. Quiet and good-value places can be found in the older streets leading up the hill from the waterfront, especially behind the OTE and in the nearby streets off Kapetan Sifi. Odhos Kondhilaki, which runs down the side of the OTE, has numerous possibilities. If you are at a loss where to begin then try one of the helpful travel agencies, who can suggest possible options.

Arhontiko, Kondhilaki 16 (☎28-172). One of the most pleasant budget hotels, with a mature orange tree in the front garden. If full, then Apostolis Kimalis, the owner, has a few other (more expensive) rooms around the corner. ②.

El Greco, Arkadiou (☎23-133). Serviceable hotel, a couple of blocks in from the seafront, with en-suite rooms. ④.

Itanos, Platía Venizélou. Smart, mid-range hotel on the town's main square. ④.

Maria Hamilaki, Kondhilaki 35 (☎22-768). Clean, simple rooms, overseen by friendly proprietress. ①.

Nora, Rouselaki 31 (☎23-017). Near the ferry port, this is a friendly hotel run by women proprietors, with fine views over the harbour; the rooms have balconies and showers. ②.

Pension Venus, Kondhilaki 60 (☎24-307). Comfortable, recommended place, run by an ebullient English-speaking owner. ②.

Rooms Ariadne, Katapoti 49 (☎22-418). Good, family-run place with rooms at the back overlooking a garden. It's 3 blocks north of the post office. ②.

Rooms Elena, Kondhilaki 58 (☎24-844). Try here if the *Venus*, next door, is full. ②.

Rooms Iris, Riga Fereou 15 (☎22-494). A couple of blocks to the north of Kondhilaki, the pleasant rooms here have the use of a shared kitchen. ①.

Youth hostel, Odos Therisou 4a (☎22-693 or 28-062). One of the better ones around, at 1200dr a night – you pass it on the right as you drive into town. The walls of the room adjoining the kitchen contain much learned writing from around the world, including the "Hitchhiker's Guide to Youth Hostels."

The Town

Sitía is an absorbing place to wander around, doing no more than enjoying the atmosphere. The narrow streets behind the seafront are packed with the everyday happenings of a Cretan provincial town: villagers in to stock up on news and necessities and stores which cater to their every conceivable need, from steel drums to wooden saddles, seed to pick-up trucks. While you're people-watching, one thing not to be missed, especially on Sundays, is the *vólta*, when the whole town puts on its finery to parade in front of their neighbours. Get a seat around six in the evening at a table adjacent to the road behind the waterfront for the show.

You'll not be in town long, especially around the harbour area, before you bump into **Níkos**, a resident pelican who is also the town's pampered mascot. When he was first trapped in fishermen's nets some years ago, Níkos's wings were clipped to force him to stay. Now that his wings have grown again he shows no signs of wanting to leave. This may have something to do with the town council providing him with his own purpose-built house on the harbourside together with a daily supply of fresh fish. When not waddling proprietorially along the seafront greeting visitors, Níkos indulges a delinquent streak by dive-bombing bathers from a great height (he rarely hits them!), and flopping onto the sails of capsized windsurfers, making them impossible to right. Níkos now has a friend Alítis, to whom he appears to be teaching his roguish antics.

In spite of the potential hazards posed by Níkos and his sidekick, the heat will eventually propel you towards the beach: the **town beach** is attractive and swimmable and windsurfers are on hire along the beach road. However, the better beaches are a few kilometres further east towards Ayía Fotiá – the bus to Vái will drop you off.

Aside from wandering the streets, sitting in the cafés or lying on the beach, things to do are limited. The **Folk Museum** at Therisou 13, near the youth hostel (Tues, Thurs & Fri 9am–1pm & 5–8pm, Wed 5–8pm, Sat 9am–1pm; 200dr), offers an entertaining look at traditional life: Adam Hopkins's book *Crete* includes a wonderful section on his stay with a family in Sitía, revealing the extent to which the old lifestyle survives to this day. If you continue north to the end of the same street you'll arrive at the restored **Venetian fort**, now used as an open-air theatre. Climbing down towards the port from here, you can see the ruined remains of some **Roman fish tanks**, just along the harbour front from the pelican's house. In these semicircular constructions, freshly caught fish were kept until they were needed.

The Archeological Museum

To gain a clearer picture of the past, however, the **Archeological Museum** (Tues–Sat 8.45am–3pm, Sun 9.30am–2pm; 400dr), on the Ierápetra road, sandwiched in between builders yards, contains an interesting collection of finds from the surrounding area and the palace at Zákros. You enter by the main room, where finds from the early Minoan cemetery at nearby Ayía Fotiá are displayed, as well as some fine stone vases from Móhlos and its island neighbour, Psíra. A new case here contains recent finds from Petrás, Sitía's southern suburb, where important buildings from the Minoan Neo-Palatial period have been unearthed. One large building has a magazine for storing *pithoi* (the large earthenware jars), similar to that at Knossós. The archeologists are hesitant to describe this as a palace until more work has been done, but the early signs seem promising.

The **Zákros section** comes next: interesting exhibits here include a bronze saw, a winepress from a Minoan villa near the palace and a collection of sea shells. Archeologists claim these had a sacred function, but it would be nice to think that the Minoans used them for decorative purposes as we do today – perhaps they even put them to their ears to listen to the sea.

Further on lies one of the museum's great treasures, a case full of **Linear A tablets** – so rare that many of the world's leading museums don't even have one. They were discovered by archeologist Nikólaos Pláton in the archives room at the palace – note how the Minoan characters have been delicately scratched into the soft clay. Some show evidence of being burned by the fire which destroyed the palace, and in fact it was the fire that preserved them, for as unbaked clay tablets they would have crumbled to dust. A nearby case illustrates the **domestic life** of the kitchen, the only one so far positively identified at any palace. Among the cooking pots and other utensils there's a superbly preserved terra-cotta grill, probably used for cooking some form of *souvláki* – a method used in the Greek world since pre-Mycenaean times and mentioned by Homer.

After the Hellenistic and Roman sections, don't miss the barnacle-encrusted tangle of Roman pots (probably from a wreck) which has been preserved by placing it inside a fish tank of salinated water. This artistically stunning idea was the brainwave of the museum's founder, the eminent Cretan archeologist Níkos Papadákis: his guide to the monuments of Sitía and Eastern Crete is on sale at the museum and is recommended.

Eating

A line of enticing outdoor **tavernas** crowds the harbour front, many with a display of dishes and fresh fish out front to lure you in. Tempting as they are, eating at these seafront places can work out very expensive if you're not careful. Cheaper (and more interesting) eats are available away from the water. If you're just looking for a **snack**, the *Picadilly* pastry shop, on the corner behind *Zorba's*, sells excellent *tirópita* and delicious-looking chocolate cakes. Bakeries and cake stores are something of a local attraction, in fact, and there are a couple more good ones along Venizélou: try the bakery at no. 49 or, for more mouthwatering delights, *Zacharoplasteion Kalambokis* at no. 95.

Arkhontiko, Rouselaki 155. Classy place near the Roman fish tanks, with a superb belvedere sea view, where the octopus is recommended.

Kali Kardia, Foundalídhou. The "Good Heart", 2 blocks in from the waterfront, is an *ouzeri* where you can wash down a fish *mezé* with house retsina – a good place to mix with the locals

Mixos, Kornárou 117. Traditional charcoal cooking on a spit in the street, served up with a very strong local wine.

Neromilos, off the road to Ayía Fotiá, 4km from Sitía. Housed in a converted mill high above the bay, this offers magnificent views as well as a good selection of *mezédhes*, and grilled meat and fish. Take a taxi, as the road down can be pretty tortuous in the dark.

Panorama, off the road to Ayía Fotiá. Further up the hill from the *Neromilos*, this taverna also serves up decent food from a charcoal grill.

Psistaria, Itanov. Opposite *Knossos* bike rental – popular with locals and good value.

Remegio, at the harbour. One of the longest established (1941), just along from *Zorba's*, which serves excellent food at average prices.

Zorba's, at the harbour. Biggest and most popular place on the seafront, and the only restaurant in town open all year round. It's good for standard dishes, like swordfish.

Drinking, nightlife and entertainment

Nightlife, mostly conducted at an easy Sitían pace, centres around drinking and disco-bars. These are concentrated in two areas: up at the north end of Kornárou, and out along Beach Road (officially named Karamanli). In the first group there's the *Glyfada* – on the seafront after the pelican's house – whose terrace has a great view over the bay, and the stylish *Di Settia* nearby. Closer in along the harbour, try the *Time In* cocktail bar or *Skala*. At the other end of town, young Sitían professionals gather at their own open-air hideaway, *Status*, on the Ierápetra road, 100m past the Archeological Museum. Here, beneath a giant palm tree – which is spotlit at night – you can sip cocktails and dance to a disco on a crazy-paving floor; don't arrive before 10pm. Back at the north end of town, a couple of kilometres beyond the ferry port, is the *Planetarium* disco, a large new venue catering for up to a thousand people and playing a wide range of music including rock, jazz and Greek.

During the middle of August (16–20) the annual *Sultanina* or **sultana festival** marks the start of the grape harvest. The local export is celebrated with traditional music and dancing, and all the locally produced wine you can consume is included in the entrance fee to the fairground beyond the ferry port. Tickets for this are sold at a booth on the corner of the harbour, which also has tickets and information for the summer-long **cultural festival** – concerts, dance, theatre – the *Kornaria*.

Listings

Airlines *Olympic* are at Venizélou 56 (☎22-270), just off the *platía*, for local flights to Kásos, Kárpathos and Rhodes; there's also a twice-weekly (Tues and Sat) service to Athens.

Banks and exchange There's a branch of the *National Bank* (Mon–Thurs 8am–2pm, Fri 8am–1.30pm) at the bottom of Odhós Sífi, facing Platía Venizélou. There are also ATM cash machines at two banks close to Venizélou: *Ethniki Bank* on the platía and, just south, *Ionian Bank* at Venizélou 47.

Bike rental Outlets are on Itánou below the bus station, best of the bunch being *Petras Moto* (☎24-849), which provides helmets; or *Kazamias* (☎24-074) and *Knossós* (☎22-057), both near each other on Itánou. Mike Fabrikarakis at *Knossós* may also be able to help you find somewhere to stay.

Books and newspapers *Tsirilakis*, Kornarou 49, close to the *platía*, has English-language books (with a second-hand section) and newspapers.

Bus station At Karamo 4 (☎22-272), at the southern end of the waterfront. Services to Áyios Nikólaos (8 daily; 2hr), Iráklion (5 daily; 3hr 15min); Ierápetra (5 daily; 1hr 30min); Vái (4 daily; 1hr); Káto Zákros (2 daily; 1hr).

Ferries The ferry agent (for boats to Kásos and the Dodecanese) is *Tzortzakis* (☎25-080), on the harbour front down towards the dock.

Hospital Kapetan Sífi, at the junction with Arkadiou (☎24-311).

Laundry Self-service launderette, *Wash & Go*, at Kornarou 118, behind the seafront.

OTE On Kapetan Sífi, 2 blocks west of Platía Venizélou (Mon–Fri 7.30am–9.45pm).

Post office Platía Ethnikis Antistasis 2 (Mon–Fri 7.30am–8pm, Sat 7.30am–2pm).

Towards the east: Vái and Palékastro

Vái beach, with its famous grove of palm trees and silvery sands, features alongside Knossós, the Lasíthi plateau and the Samarian gorge on almost every Cretan travel agent's list of excursions. For years it was a popular hang-out for backpackers, but repeated fires followed by a clean-up campaign to attract a more well-heeled crowd have resulted in a ring fence around the beach with a guard to enforce the new regulations which prohibit overnight stays. People still claim to be able to sleep there, but it hardly seems worth the hassle. If you're looking for more to do than simply sizzle on the sands, there are a number of likely sights within striking distance of Vái. With your own transport, the beaches and archeological sites at Ítanos and Palékastro are within reach, while the scenically sited ancient monastery at Tóplou is one of the most revered on the island.

Ayía Fotía

From Sitía the road runs along the beach, tracking a rocky, unexceptional coastline past **Ayía Fotía**, a small cove that now supports a cluster of new development. Here, in 1971, the largest Minoan graveyard yet found in Crete was excavated, revealing over 250 chamber tombs from the early Pre-Palatial period. Among the outstanding finds of vases, fish hooks, daggers and stone axes (now in the Sitía and Áyios Nikólaos archeological museums) were a number of lead amulets which suggest that these early Minoans regarded lead as well as silver as a precious metal. To reach the cemetery, keep your eyes skinned on the eastern edge of the village for a rough track descending sharply to the left immediately after the *Sitían Arts Pottery Garden* (blue sign). This leads (after 200m) to the fenced-off cemetery, close to the sea.

After some 7km the road turns inland, climbing into quite deserted, gently hilly country, the slopes covered in thyme, heather and sage with the occasional cluster of strategically sited beehives. In summer the deep violet thyme flowers prove an irresistible attraction for the bees which feed on them almost exclusively, creating the much sought-after *thimárisio* (thyme honey). Pick a sprig for your buttonhole.

Tóplou Monastery

Not long after you leave the coast, there's a road signposted up to the **Monastery of Tóplou** (daily 9am–3pm & 4–6pm; free, museum 300dr), which is also the short way to Vái. As you approach, the monastery looks more like a fortress, standing defiant in landscape almost empty, save for a line of intrusive wind turbines along the ridge behind. The name Tóplou is Turkish for "with a cannon" – a reference to a giant device with which the monks used to defend themselves and uphold the Cretan monastic traditions of resistance to invaders. And they needed it. The monastery was sacked by pirates and destroyed in 1498, and in the 1821 rebellion it was captured by the Turks, who hanged twelve monks from the gate as an example. In World War II it again served as a place of shelter for the resistance. The opening above the main gate harks back to these troubled times: through it the monks hurled missiles and boiling oil on those attempting to gain entry.

Its forbidding exterior and grim history notwithstanding, Tóplou is startlingly beautiful within: a flower-decked, cloister-like courtyard with stairways leading up to arcaded walkways off which are the cells. The blue-robed monks keep out of the way of visitors as far as possible, but their cells and refectory are left discreetly on view. And in the church is one of the masterpieces of Cretan art, the eighteenth-century **icon** *Lord Thou Art Great* by Ioannis Kornaros. This is a marvellously intricate work, incorporating 61 small scenes full of amazing detail, each illustrating, and labelled with, a phrase from the Orthodox prayer which begins "Lord, thou art great . . .". Outside you can buy enormously expensive reproductions of the icon, as well as postcards and books.

As you leave the church, take a look at the stone **inscription** set into the exterior wall. It records an arbitration by Magnesia, a city in Asia Minor, dating from the second century BC, concerning a territorial dispute between nearby

Ítanos and Ierápytna (modern Ierápetra). At this time, when the Romans held sway over Crete, these deadly rivals clashed constantly and finally Rome, unable to placate the two, called in the Magnesians to act as honest brokers. The inscription records part of their judgement (in favour of Ítanos) and was placed in the monastery wall at the suggestion of the English traveller and antiquarian Robert Pashley, when he found it being used as a gravestone in 1834.

The monastery is reputed to be incredibly wealthy – it owns most of the northeastern corner of the island – and this is no doubt how they can afford the endless and extensive restorations which seem set to destroy the romance of the place. The sheer weight of numbers visiting doesn't help either. The **museum** – which now incorporates the church and the icon – has also been extended. Apart from a handful of superb icons, the main addition is a collection of tedious religious engravings which fill the wall space, alongside a niche devoted to weapons and battle paraphernalia dating from the Cretan War of Independence to World War II. Beyond Tóplou the road descends towards Vái through the same arid, rock-strewn landscape as before. This area is another where you might catch a sighting of the rare **Eleonora's falcon**, which breeds on the Dionysádes islands to the north – Tóplou and Cape Síderos (a closed military zone) are regular hunting grounds.

Vái

Vái beach makes for a thoroughly secular contrast to the spiritual tranquillity of Tóplou. Famous above all for its palm trees, the sudden appearance of what is claimed to be Europe's only indigenous wild date-palm grove is indeed an exotic shock. Lying on the fine sand in the early morning, the dream of Caribbean islands is hard to dismiss. During the day, however, the sand fills to overflowing as buses – public ones from Sitía and tours from all over the island – pour into the car park in numbers which really can't be justified by a few palm trees. The boardwalks laid out across the sand are not there only to protect feet from the burning sand, but also to guarantee a route through the mass of baking bodies. Even the adjoining beaches, where those in the know used to hide out to escape the swarm, get pretty crowded nowadays.

The buses are packed, the beach is worse, the café and taverna charge over the odds once you've endured the long queue, you pay to have a shower or use the toilet, and still people come here to camp rough. As everywhere, notices warn that "Camping is forbidden by law", and for once they really do seem to mean it – at least within the confines of the park which protects the palm trees. However, you can climb the steps cut into the rock behind the taverna to the cove to the south, or with rather more difficulty clamber over the rocks to that to the north, and join thriving little communities at either. If you do sleep here, watch your belongings: rip-offs abound. Having endured all this you may just, for a couple of hours at each end of the day, be able to enjoy Vái the way it ought to be. Alternatively, avoid the high season if you can.

Ítanos

The sand may be less good, but the emptiness of the three small beaches at **ÍTANOS**, 1.5km north of the turning to Vái, makes them far more enjoyable. There's still the odd palm tree scattered around, and if you're at a loss for something to do you can explore the remains of the ancient city here. Inhabited from Minoan times, Ítanos became important later, flourishing through the Classical Greek and Roman eras when she vied with Ierápytna (modern Ierápetra) for control of eastern Crete. One twenty-year squabble between these two led to the Arbitration of Magnesia in 132 BC, part of the stone record of which is preserved at Tóplou Monastery. The settlement here remained prosperous until the medieval Byzantine era when it was destroyed, most likely by Saracen pirates. All sorts of messy ruins strewn with potsherds survive beneath the twin acropolis, but little which retains any shape. There are two early basilicas you might be able to make out, as well as the beautifully cut lower courses of a Hellenistic wall on the western hill.

Palékastro

The main road to Vái, and all the public buses, run via **PALÉKASTRO**, 9km south. It's a pleasant little farming village and a good place to stay close to the beaches – with a couple of excellent tavernas on the main square which are worth breaking your journey for if you're simply passing through. However, the place is now starting to realize the potential of its position and tourism is expanding – there's even a rather incongruous nightclub.

The **OTE** office (Mon–Fri 9.30am–9.30pm, Sat 9.30am–1.30pm), up a passage-way opposite the main door of the church, helps with finding rooms as well as having exchange facilities, stamps and phonecards. For **accommodation**, try *Hotel Itanos* (☎0843/61-205; ②) on the main square (not connected with the restaurant below it – ask instead at the supermarket next door), *Hotel Hellas* (☎0843/61-240; ②) or the *Palekastro* (☎0843/61-235; ②), 100m along the road to Sitía on the left. Don't be misled by a drab exterior here: the pleasant new rooms lie beyond a courtyard behind. There are also plenty of signs indicating **rooms**, including some at the next small village of Angathiá, like the *Vaios Taverna* (②). The best place to eat in Palékastro is the **restaurant** at the *Hotel Hellas*.

The ancient site

The **Minoan site of Palékastro** lies towards the beach, about twenty minutes' walk from the village. Follow the signs to the *Marina Village Hotel* and then to the beach at Chiona. For archeologists this was a very significant place, the largest Minoan town yet discovered and the source of much information about everyday Minoan life. It is an obvious site to settle, a broad and fertile agricultural plain set on an excellent bay beneath the protection of a high, flat-topped bluff: and indeed the area was extensively inhabited both before and after the Minoan era. Much of the site is disappointing for the casual visitor, with only a few odd walls lost among the fields: many of the excavations were later infilled to protect them. Still, some of the latest excavations are open to view and offer fascinating glimpses of dwellings, stairways and streets. Try to resist entering the excavation areas through the broken fences as the delicate walls are still being made safe for posterity by the archeologists.

Local beaches

When you've had your fill of wandering among the olive groves seeking out some of the further-flung remnants, there are some excellent **beaches** not far beyond where you could easily camp out. The better sands are around the bay further to the south, but the only facilities are on the first stretch of beach you reach: a taverna by the makeshift car park where the track arrives at the coast, and another around to the left, in the shadow of the bluff. Between Palékastro and Vái, a number of other good beaches are signed off the road, including **Kouremenos**, which is one of Crete's best windsurfing areas.

Zákros and the far southeast

Palékastro is also the crossroads for the road south to **Zákros**, a beautiful drive through country where the soil is a strange pinkish-purple colour, as if indelibly stained with grape juice (although actually it's olives which grow around here). The few hamlets you pass on the way are so small that they make Zákros (or more properly Áno Zákros) seem positively urban when finally you get there.

Áno Zákros

A slow-moving little town, **ÁNO ZÁKROS** boasts three or four **restaurants** around the square and a small **hotel**, the *Zakros* (☎0843/61-284; ③), which despite rickety rooms and frequent lack of hot water manages to hold onto its C-class status; the rooms at the back have good views over the gorge behind. What little trade these establishments see, however, is almost exclusively passing through, since Káto (or lower) Zákros, and the palace, are on the coast 8km further on. Locally, Zákros enjoys a certain fame for its numerous springs which feed the lush vegetation hereabouts and which were also an attraction for the Minoans. If you follow the sign up to the right as you come into the town, or simply climb the hill from the centre, you'll reach a little chapel from where in five minutes a path leads beside the stream to its source and some pleasant, shady picnic spots.

Leaving the village by the Káto Zákros road, you'll soon pass the remains of a **Minoan villa** dating from the late Neo-Palatial period (c.1500 BC); here was turned up a winepress which is now in the Sitía Archeological Museum. Pressing on towards the coast, a good new road winds spectacularly down to approach the small bay from the south. There are even better views if you turn left down the purple track which runs straight into the back of the village, past the palace.

Káto Zákros

KÁTO ZÁKROS is a delight. There's a pebbly sand beach, three good tavernas and a few places offering **rooms**, of which *Poseidon* (☎0843/93-316; ②) – on a rocky outcrop with spectacular sea view – is the best. A new place, *George Village* (☎0843/93-316; ②) – ask at *Taverna Akrogiali* on the seafront – has rooms 200m back from the sea, while *Rooms Alex* (☎0843/93-338; ②) is another possibility, though it's 2km (and not 500m as their publicity says) back towards Áno Zákros. It's worth bearing in mind, however, – especially if you're arriving by bus – that accommodation is severely limited (due to building restrictions surrounding the archeological site) and during high season you will rarely find a room on spec; you may be able to sleep under the trees or on the beach but the patience of the villagers is wearing thin towards people doing this.

Along with a tiny harbour with a few boats in it, this is about all the place amounts to. Everything you really need you can find – they'll change money in the tavernas and you can even make long-distance phone calls – but there is absolutely nothing else, not even a store. Ideal if it's tranquillity you're after.

Although in summer a couple of daily buses do run all the way to Káto Zákros, most transport still stops in the upper village. From here you could hitch the rest of the way quite easily, but it's also worth considering the **walk**, less than two hours to the palace via a beautiful ravine known as the **Valley of the Dead**. The easiest route traces the road for almost 2km, before turning left (signposted) onto a track which brings you out above the ravine. Getting to the bottom is something of a scramble, which may need hands as well as feet, but once you're down the trail is easy to follow along the left-hand side of the stream bed, marked by the usual red waymarks in case of confusion. It's a solitary but magnificent walk, brightened especially in spring by plenty of plant life. High in the cliff walls you'll see the mouths of caves: it is these, used as tombs in Minoan times and earlier, which give the ravine its name. At the bottom you rejoin the dirt road, which runs through groves of bananas and olives and into Káto Zákros past the palace. As an alternative you can follow the waymarked path all the way from Áno Zákros, avoiding the road altogether. This is more easily attempted on the way back, when getting lost is difficult; to find the way down, you'd have to get someone to guide you through the fields behind the village and onto the start of the trail.

The Palace of Zákros

The valley behind Káto Zákros was explored by a British archeologist, David Hogarth, at much the same time as the other great Cretan palaces were being discovered, around the turn of the century. But Hogarth gave up the search, having unearthed only a couple of Minoan houses, and it was not until the 1960s that new explorations were begun by a Greek, Nikólaos Pláton. Pláton found the palace almost immediately, just yards from where Hogarth's trenches ended. The **Palace of Zákros** (Tues–Sun 8.30am–3pm, 400dr) thus benefited from the most modern of techniques in its excavation and, having been forgotten even locally, it was also unlooted. The site yielded an enormous quantity of treasures and everyday items, including storerooms with all their giant *pithoi* still in place and a religious treasury full of stone vases and ritual vessels.

For the amateur, Zákros is also full of interest, and a great deal easier to understand than many of the other Minoan sites. Here the remains are of one palace only, dating from the period between 1600 and 1450 BC. Although there is an earlier settlement at a lower level, it is unlikely ever to be excavated – mainly because this end of the island is very gradually sinking. The water table is already almost at the palace level, and anything deeper would be thoroughly submerged. Even the exposed parts of the palace are marshy and often waterlogged – there are terrapins living in the green water in the cistern. When it is really wet you can keep your feet dry, and get an excellent view of the overall plan of the palace, by climbing the streets of the town which occupied the hill above it.

Though the palace is a small one, it can match any of the more important Minoan centres for quality of construction and materials. And it is unique in the way that so much of the town – a place very like Gourniá – can still be made out all around. The original destruction of the palace appears to have been a very violent one, with only enough time for the inhabitants to abandon it, taking

0   25 m

Upper Town

Magazines

Portico

Light Well

Central Shrine

Archives Room

Latrine

Dye House

Kitchen

Storerooms

Entrance

Bathroom

Courtyard

Main Gate

Foundry

Altar Base

Entry to West Wing

Queen's Megaron

Treasury

Lustral Basin

Workshop

Banquet Hall

Central Court

Ceremonial Hall

Light Well

Cistern

Well

Workshops

Well

Portico

King's Megaron

Royal Apartments

PALACE OF ZÁKROS

almost nothing with them. This again contributed to the enormous number of artefacts found here, but more importantly the nature of the destruction, in which the palace was flattened and burnt, is an important prop in the theory that it was the explosion of Thíra which ended the Minoan civilization. Large lumps of pumice found among the ruins are supposed to have been swept there by the tidal wave which followed the eruption. However, many archeologists take issue with this hypothesis and question both its chronological accuracy and the type of destruction (for example fire), seeing the palace's demise as being more consistent with human rather than natural causes.

Entrance

A paved **road** led from the site to its **harbour**, the chief reason why a palace existed here at all. The harbour installations have disappeared beneath the sea, but two large houses excavated along the road are enough to show that this must have been a significant port: the first landfall on Crete for trade from Egypt, the Nile Delta and the Middle East. Among the ruins were found ingots of copper imported from Cyprus, elephant tusks from Syria, and gold and precious materials from Egypt.

The road nowadays forms the **entrance** to the site, leading directly towards the main gateway of the palace in its eastern corner. Before entering the palace proper the remains of a foundry dating from the Old Palace period can be seen beneath a protective canopy on the left. The road then curves round into the town, passing the palace entrance to the left. Entering the palace, the **main gate** leads to a stepped ramp followed by a **courtyard** which may have served as a meeting place between the palace hierarchy and the townspeople. Here in the northeast corner is a **bathroom** where visitors to the palace may have been required to wash or purify themselves before proceeding further. To the west of the courtyard lies the main or **Central Court**, a little over 30m by 12m, or about a third the size of that at Knossós. Crossing the north edge of the court you come to an **altar base**, with the lower courses of the west wing wall in grey ashlar stone beyond.

The west wing

The **west wing*** is entered between two pillars and this is where, as usual, the chief ceremonial and ritual rooms were located. A **reception room** leads into a colonnaded **light well**, the hallmark of Minoan architecture. The light well's black stone crazy paving survives, as do the pillar bases and a drain in the northwest corner. It was here that the excavators unearthed what is arguably Zákros's single most important find: the **peak sanctuary rhyton**, a carved stone vase depicting a peak sanctuary with wild goats from which was gleaned valuable information about Minoan religion. The light well illuminated the **Ceremonial Hall** beyond which lay the **Banqueting Hall**, originally a lavish room with frescoed walls and an elaborate floor. Pláton gave the room this name because of the large number of cups and drinking vessels discovered scattered about the floor.

At the heart of a complex of rooms behind the Banqueting Hall is the **Central Shrine** which contains a ledge and niche, similar to the shrine at Gourniá, where idols would have been placed. Nearby is the **lustral basin**, necessary for purification before entering the shrine. Here, too, was the **Treasury**, probably the most important discovery from the excavators' viewpoint as it is the only one so far positively identified. In a number of box-like compartments (which have been partially restored) were discovered almost a hundred fine stone jars and libation vessels including the exquisite rock crystal rhyton – crushed into more than three hundred fragments – with its delicate crystal bead handle and collar that the Iráklion Archeological Museum is so proud of. Next to the treasury in the **Palace Archive**, hundreds of Linear A record tablets had been stored in wooden chests. Sadly, only a handful of the top layers survived the centuries of rain and flooding; the rest had solidified into a mass of grey clay, depriving the archeologists of potentially priceless clues in their attempts at deciphering the script. On the opposite side of the treasury is a **workshop** where pieces of raw marble and

---

*Actually the northwest wing, as Zákros is not truly aligned north–south. None of the major palaces, in fact, were exactly laid out on compass bearings – though others were closer than this – but for convenience the excavators always refer to the rooms on each side of the Central Court as the north, south, east and west wings.

steatite were found. The remaining stone slabs most likely supported a crafts-man's workbench. More workshops and storerooms lay to the west of the shrine, and one of these has been identified as a **dye-house**. And if you were wondering where the occupants of this end of the palace answered the call of nature, a lava-tory with a cesspit outside the wall was found nearby. Further west, beyond the palace confines, new excavations are still going on.

North, south and east wings

On the **north** side of the Central Court was the palace **kitchen**, the first to be positively identified at any of the palaces. Bones, cooking pots and utensils were found strewn around the floor both here and in the storeroom or pantry next door. The **south** wing was devoted to **workshops**: for smiths, lapidaries, potters and even, according to Pláton, perfume makers – possibly a borrowing from Egypt. The **well** that serviced this area still flows with drinkable water and close to the steps leading down into it was found an offering cup containing olives preserved by the waters. Pláton and his team devoured the three-and-a-half-thousand-year-old olives, which shrivelled upon contact with the air, and said that they tasted as fresh as those in the nearby tavernas.

Two large rooms regarded as **Royal Apartments** flank the **eastern** side of the Central Court behind a portico. The larger of the two, to the south, is called the King's Room and the smaller is claimed to be that of the queen. However, one of these may have been the throne room and there would have been elaborate rooms on the first floor, possibly with verandas overlooking the courtyard below, which might more realistically have been where the rulers lived. Next to a light well in the eastern wall of the King's Room lay the colonnaded **Cistern Hall** which, with its eight steps leading down to the water contained in a plaster-lined basin, may have served as a royal aquarium or even a swimming pool (if so, the only one known). It is ingeniously designed to maintain the water at a constant level with the excess draining into the **well** to the south, which lay outside the palace wall and was probably used by the townsfolk. The water from the spring was, as at Knossós, piped throughout the palace and traces of the pipework are still to be seen around the site.

Beyond these royal apartments lay other **residential areas**, but much has been destroyed by centuries of ploughing combined with frequent waterlogging of the land here. At nearby Pelekita, on the coast 3km to the north, was recently discovered the quarry from where the tufa limestone used to build the palace was taken.

Onwards: the coast

Hardly any tourist ever ventures **south of Zákros**, and indeed there's little in the way of habitation in the whole of the southeastern corner of the island, nor any public transport whatsoever. Even the boulder-strewn dirt roads seem to be left in this condition to discourage the adventurous. A little effort, however, is rewarded with excellent beaches – mostly deserted – and a challenging route by which you can circle back to Sitía, taking in an archeological site at Présos along the way.

Leave Áno Zákros on the new road (towards Káto Zákros) and you'll shortly reach a track to the right, with a hand-painted sign for "Ambelos and Liviko View". It's not a bad surface, descending through olive groves and giant greenhouses to run along a deep ravine. After 10km, and just when you're convinced you're lost, a brilliant turquoise sea and white sandy beaches divided by rocky outcrops appear below. The tiny village of **KSERÓKAMBOS**, a short way inland, is the place to make enquiries if you want a **room**. The village consists of one street, two tavernas and a mini-market which sells basic foods. Both tavernas will provide information and keys for rooms (if available, which they may not be in Aug). Try ringing ahead to secure space at *Liviko View* (☎0843/91-473; ②), run by a couple of Greek-Australians, Ioannis and Katerina Hatzidakis. The cooking here is recommended and at weekends they even put on the occasional *lyra* concert.

Archeologists argue as to whether Kserókambos is the site of ancient Ambelos (in spite of a location of this name nearby): artefacts discovered in the area and a looted peak sanctuary certainly suggest there was a settlement of some kind here in ancient times.

Completing the circle: Zíros and Handhrás

If you are unfazed by Cretan dirt roads you can complete a circle back to Sitía via Zíros, although as the road climbs inland the going does get a good deal rougher. Make certain your vehicle is up to it – it's not the sort of area to be stranded in. As the hills enfold you, all views are dominated by a giant radar dome on the mountain top, and the road itself is surrounded by "No Photography" signs. At the top of the climb the road, now tarmac, levels to a plateau surrounded by rock cliffs in the midst of which lies the fair-sized farming village of **ZÍROS**. Tumbling down a hillside towards a busy centre, it's a welcoming place, with a neat *platía* circled by willow and acacia trees with whitewashed trunks. There's even an occasional bus to Sitía. If you come in late July, you may be lucky enough to catch the annual festival – something not to be missed. Then the women of the village produce huge trays of delicacies, which are laid out on tables in the square and washed down with gallons of *rakí* to the accompaniment of *bouzouki* and *lyra*. For quieter times there are sixteenth-century frescoes to be seen in the church of Ayía Paraskeví, but you may prefer to lazily soak up the atmosphere of this stone-country with a drink at a table in the square. In the early evening, when the rocky heights crowd in on all sides, it seems that places like Zíros are the real heart of Crete.

Gluttons for punishment could turn back onto the dirt and head down to the south coast at Goúdhouras (see over), but the easy way is via Handhrás, past the sail-less and derelict irrigation windmills. The reasons for Zíros's size and prosperity are evident along the road out, as it cuts through olive groves and vineyards said to be among the best on the island.

A turning at Handhrás leads after 4km to **ETIÁ**, a hamlet where a ruined **Venetian mansion** stands in memorial to the glory days of the Italian city's power in Crete. Built by the Di Mezzo family in the late fifteenth century, this once elegant edifice was badly damaged in 1828 when the local populace vented their rage on the Turks who had been using it as an administrative base; nowadays the ground floor, with its impressive entrance hall and vaulted ceiling, is all that remains of the three-storey building. Because few country houses of the Venetian period survive on Crete, however, the mansion has been declared a national monument under the care of the Greek Archeological Service. The mansion lies 100m up a track, behind the roadside church with an elegant carved stone tower.

Continuing along the Handhrás–Présos road, a lane just outside Handhrás is signed on the right for **VOILÁ**, a ruined medieval village that you can just see at the foot of the hill. With its gothic arches and silent paved streets, this is a distinctly eerie place to wander round; two ornamental drinking fountains (one at each end of the village) with beautiful brass taps – a Turkish contribution to this Venetian stronghold – are still functioning. The twin-naved Áyios Yióryios church, usually locked, but with an interesting sixteenth-century gravestone fresco in an interior recess, and a tower of the Turkish period, dominate the site. If you still have the energy, you can climb to a ruined Venetian fort on top of the hill above the village.

Ancient Présos

The archeological site of **PRÉSOS** lies close to the modern village of the same name. This is another of those sites where what you see – in this case very little – cannot begin to match the interest and importance of the history. But even without ruins it would be worth taking the walk around the site for the scenery alone. From the centre of the village, opposite a *kafenion* with a raised terrace, a dirt road is clearly signposted downhill. After about 1.5km you'll come to a signed gate for the "First Acropolis". This is where to leave your vehicle if you have one.

Présos first came to light in 1884, when the Italian archeologist Federico Halbherr turned up a large number of clay idols and some unusual inscriptions written in an unknown tongue – very likely the same as that of the Linear A tablets – using Greek characters. Set out with lines reading alternatively right to left and left to right, these Eteocretan (true Cretan) inscriptions are now believed to be evidence of the post-Bronze Age Minoans who fled the Dorian invasions to these remote fastnesses in the east of the island in an attempt to preserve their civilization. Présos seems to have been one of their principal towns, controlling the sanctuary of Dhiktean Zeus at Palékastro, probably an earlier Minoan shrine. With harbours on the north and south coasts of the island her power eventually led to conflict with the leading Dorian city of the region, Ierápytna (modern Ierápetra). Following final victory about 155 BC, Ierápytna razed Présos to the ground and the city was never rebuilt. With this defeat the long twilight of Minoan civilization, lasting more than a thousand years after the palaces had fallen, came to an end.

From the entrance follow the path west to a saddle between the two hills where the ancient city lay. On the summit of the **First Acropolis** you can make out the foundations of a temple. On the western slope of this hill are the remains of a substantial **Hellenistic house** excavated by the British archeologist Bosanquet at the turn of the century. Dating from the third century BC, the outer walls of superbly cut stone define the main living rooms at the front of the house with workrooms at the rear. In the largest workroom was found an olive press together with a stone tank for storing the oil. A stairway to the left of the main door led down to a cellar.

A hundred-metre walk across the saddle to the **Second Acropolis** will reveal cuttings in the rock on the south side which formed the foundations of dwellings. The defensive wall which encircled these two hills can still be made out in places.

Sitía to Ierápetra

The main road across the island **from Sitía to the south coast** cuts between the east and west ranges of the Sitía mountains, giving some fine views in the hill country of the central section before descending towards the sea plain. There are a number of sturdy hamlets along the route, such as Áyios Yeorgíos and Lithines, good places to stop for a snack and a beer.

South to the coast

Just before Piskokéfalo, less than 2km out of Sitía, Minoan enthusiasts may want to pause at the remains of a **Minoan villa** (signed) cut through by the road. Dating from the late Neo-Palatial period (1550–1450 BC), it had two floors and is terraced into the hillside with the well-preserved staircase giving access to an upper floor. The villa's view would have encompassed the river valley below the road, where its farm lands were probably located.

At the entrance to Piskokéfalo itself a dirt road is signed to the left for **ZOÚ**, 6km further on, where there's another **Minoan villa** of the same period. Follow the road, which crosses a dry riverbed and then turns right (signed), eventually becoming asphalt as it winds up into the hills towards Zoú. The villa – not easily spotted and with no sign – lies on a high bank to the right of the road just before the village. Excavated by Nikólaos Pláton, the excavator of the palace at Zákros, this is more a farmhouse – cultivating the land in the valley to the east – than simply a country dwelling. The rooms seem to be divided between those for domestic life and others for work and storage of farm equipment. A pottery kiln (perhaps used for making olive oil containers) was discovered in one room, while two deep pits near the entrance probably stored grain.

Back on the main Sitía–Ierápetra road, it's a long climb to the island's spine, past Epáno Episkopí and the turning to Présos (see previous page), before the road dips towards **LITHÍNES**. Just after this the islands of Koufonísi, to the east, and Gaidhouronísi, to the west, become visible beyond the coastal plain out in the Libyan Sea. You emerge, eventually, on the south coast at **PILALÍMATA**. For empty beaches you should get off just past here, where a track on the left is signed for the Moní Kápsa and Goúdhouras. There's a fair stretch of rather pebbly grey beach – known as **Kaló Neró**, with a couple of cafés – no more than 1km from the road. If you have transport, however, there are better strips of sand to be found scattered all along this rocky foreshore.

East: Moní Kápsa and Goúdhouras

The **Moní Kápsa** enjoys a spectacular setting on a ledge in the cliffs just above the road, and an abiding reputation for miracles. The original monastery, probably founded in the early Venetian period, was destroyed by Turkish pirates in 1471. It was rebuilt, but most of the present buildings were constructed in the nineteenth century, thanks to the energies of "Yerontoyiannis", a monk who earned himself a name as a Robin Hood-style hero as well as a healer. Locally he is revered as a saint, and although he never conducted a single service due to his illiteracy, and is denied canonization by the Church, Cretans flock in to leave their offerings beside his silver encased cadaver in the monastery chapel. You may also visit the cave behind the church to where he often retreated. As you enter the monastery, pairs of baggy trousers and other battered old items of clothing are hung on pegs by the door, for use by anyone who turns up in shorts or otherwise "unsuitably" attired. But most times of the year you will have the place to yourself, and the people around the monastery, lay workers mostly, always seem to have time to sit you down for a chat and a cold drink.

Further along the same road, now asphalt, you come to the best beach of all, just before **GOÚDHOURAS**. There should be little problem camping around here, taking advantage of three or four tavernas in the village. It has to be said, though, that Goúdhouras itself is an exceptionally unattractive, plastic-wrapped little place.

West: Makriyialós and beyond

Westwards, the route to Ierápetra passes Análipsi and **MAKRIYIALÓS**, villages which have merged into each other along the road. Makriyialós has one of the best beaches at this end of Crete, with tavernas and sand which shelves so gently you begin to think you are going to walk the 320km to Africa. But while it is by no means overrun, heavy building has ensured that it's no longer exactly pretty either – and in any case it's not somewhere you're likely to find a very cheap room. Try *Irini Rooms* (☎0843/51-422; ②) on the main road, or the slightly quieter *Villa Stars* (☎0843/51-920; ②) or *Katerina* (☎0843/51-558; ②), all within easy walking distance of where the bus drops you.

As you leave Makriyialós, you pass yet another **Minoan villa** (signed only from the western approach), 200m inland from the road. Leave any transport and follow the level track starting to the west of the sign; this eventually climbs up to the site beside a farmhouse. It was long suspected that such a tempting area would not have escaped the attentions of the ancient peoples and in 1971 Costis Davaras began excavations which eventually unearthed an important villa of the late Neo-Palatial period (1550–1450 BC). As can be seen from the remains, it had strong outer walls and some fine stone-flagged floors. The ground plan is not unlike that of the palaces, with rooms situated around a central court, where an altar was also identified. The excavation also revealed that the house was destroyed by fire – yet more evidence for the endless debate over what caused the downfall of the Minoans.

There's a second bay immediately beyond Makriyialós, with a smaller, emptier beach, and the road then runs along what is for the most part an exposed and rocky coast, with only the occasional scrubby beach. **KOUTSOURÁS**, the main village hereabouts, has little to commend it, although *Pension Gorgona* (☎0843/23-935; ③) is a reasonable seafront place.

Dásakis Butterfly Gorge

Things look up 2km further on, where a hand-painted sign on the right announces **Dásakis Butterfly Gorge**. *Dásakis* (small forest), is an embryonic national park administered by the forestry department of Áyios Nikólaos: embryonic because it has not yet reached the minimum size to be granted full national park status. Surprisingly, this is the only pine forest in Crete which starts from the beach and continues uninterrupted to the mountains – and if it looks a bit threadbare today, that's because it was burnt down by the German army in World War II in order to root out resistance forces. It was further affected by a serious forest fire in 1993, which left much of the pinewood as blackened stumps and devastated the flora and fauna in the gorge, including the butterflies, which are, however, expected to return in numbers in the coming years.

Leave your vehicle by the café at the entrance and walk the 500m through the woods to the gorge entrance. In late spring and summer, fluttering Cardinal, Cleopatra and Swallowtail **butterflies** drift past visitors. The gorge is also a haven for blue-rock thrushes, griffon vultures, crag martins and other interesting bird life. The café manager, Yiorgos Yeorgamlis, is a committed Green and a fount of information on the park. He has recently built a water garden next to the café, which has already attracted wild flamingos, and it's worth a stop for a frappé just to marvel at the dragonflies around the water. Local attitudes, however, are not in accord with the park, and many of the nearby villagers would prefer to see olives planted here or some other "sensible" utilization of the land.

The more energetic may wish to **walk** up the gorge into the mountains of the Thriptí range, ending up at the picturesque village of Orinó (sturdy footwear required). Alternatively, there's a **scenic road** there, signed 2km further along the main road.

THE FIRES OF CRETE

Recent years have seen appalling **forest fires** throughout Crete, the latest devastation occurring in and around the hill villages to the north of Sóuyia and at the Ayía Iríne gorge in western Crete; terrific blazes in the hills surrounding Kalamáfka to the northwest of Ierápetra in the east also did enormous damage to the landscape.

Depressingly, these fires are not always the accidents they seem to be. Figures from the Greek Agricultural Ministry for the period 1968–93 attribute the cause of no less than 57 percent of all fires to unknown causes or arson. A survey of fires throughout Greece by the *I Koinonía* newspaper showed a dramatic increase in their number over the last decade and further sharp escalations prior to general elections. This, of course, is when the politicians – in a desperate scramble for votes – are willing to recognize the claims to land of those who may have started the fires in the first place. Under Greek law there is no organized system of land registry for publicly owned land, which means that if an area of woodland is burned down, the barren territory left behind becomes a no-man's-land which can be claimed under squatters' rights. Once olives or other crops have been planted, a foothold towards possession has been attained, with local politicians often smoothing over the obstacles to the ownership of the land being transferred. This callous attitude to the environment, where trees are little regarded for their beauty, has a long history. In his book *Wild Flowers of Crete*, biologist George Sifkas writes that "the Greek holds the deeply rooted view that a green wood is useless because the trees drink valuable water and don't produce anything". Until this attitude is combatted and reversed the fires will continue to transform the island from one of the most fertile in the Mediterranean into one of the most barren.

Ayía Fotiá and beyond

For a while after this there's a genuinely mountainous stretch, until the road dips down to a beach with a taverna on it, and in the following bay a poorly signed track leads down to **AYÍA FOTIÁ**. Hidden from the road in a wooded valley, Ayía Fotiá has its attractions: cheap **rooms** in the village; an excellent beach just a couple of minutes' walk away down the stream bed; cafés and tavernas with good music; and places to camp out if that's what you're looking for.

Ayía Fotiá is, sadly, the last place from here to well beyond Ierápetra which could be described as inviting. The final 10km of road runs fast across a flat plain, unimaginatively developed for tourism along the coast and for hothouse agriculture inland. Neither **FÉRMA** nor **KOUTSONÁRI** has much to offer, despite the latter's much vaunted "tourist village", a group of abandoned houses which have been restored to rent as holiday villas. Just past here, however, is the **campsite** – *Camping Koutsounari* (☎0842/61-213) – which is the only campsite nearby if you want to be based at Ierápetra. It has a taverna and store, and plenty of shade. This is also the beginning of the aptly named **Long Beach**, a windswept line of sand (and the wind can really blow here) which stretches virtually unbroken along the final 5km of shore to Ierápetra.

Ierápetra

IERÁPETRA has various claims to fame – the largest town on the south coast of Crete, the southernmost in Europe – but charm is not one of them. It's a sprawling place; a supply centre for the region's farmers which until recently attracted an amazing number of package tourists and not a few backpackers looking for work. But the boom years appear to be on the wane: some of the package companies have pulled out, the tourist office has closed down and the town seems to

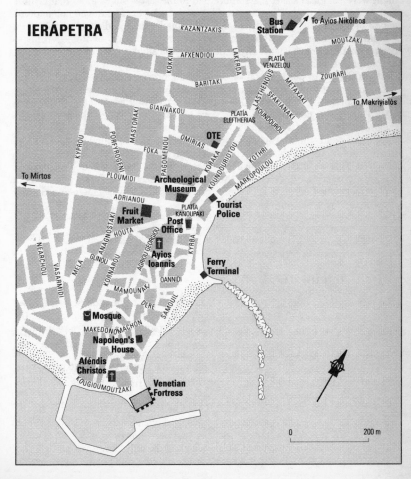

have given up trying. Even the excellent beach – which used to be Ierápetra's saving grace – is no longer the great attraction it once was.

Although you'd never know it to look at the town today, Ierápetra has quite a history. Early knowledge is sketchy, but it's almost certain that there was a settlement, or at least a port, here in Minoan times. A look at the map suggests a link across the isthmus with Gourniá and it was probably from Ierápetra and other south-coast harbours that the *Keftiu*, as the Egyptians called the Cretans, sailed for the coast of Africa. However, it was as a Doric settlement that **Ierápytna**, as the place was then known, grew to real prominence. By the second century BC it occupied more territory than any other Cretan city.

Ierápytna became a bastion of the Greek Dorians against their bitter enemies the Eteocretans: the final victory over Eteocretan Présos in 155 BC ended the last Minoan presence in eastern Crete. Those Eteocretans not killed in battle or put to flight were sold into slavery, a sombre end to the last vestiges of a great civilization. Only Ítanos, near Vái, now stood between Ierápytna and the complete domination of the eastern end of the island. Prolonged wars and disputes rumbled on for almost a century, and were finally brought to an end only by Rome's ruthless conquest of the entire island. Even then Ierápytna stubbornly resisted to the last, becoming the final city to fall to the invading legions. When Rome then joined Crete to Cyrene in northern Libya, forming the province of Cyrenaica, Ierápytna embarked on a new career as an important commercial centre in the eastern Mediterranean – trading with Greece and Italy as well as Africa and the Near East. During this period much impressive building took place – theatres, amphitheatres, temples – of which virtually nothing survives today, save for piles of fractured pillars and column capitals scattered in odd corners around the town. From the Romans to the tourists is a chronicle of steady decline. The Venetians (who favoured Sitía as their administrative centre in the east) left behind a small **fortress**, now restored, defending the harbour entrance. The Turks, under whom Ierápetra languished as a backwater, are represented by a nineteenth-century **mosque** and nearby Ottoman fountain.

> The phone code for Ierápetra is ☎0842.

Arrival and information

The **bus station** is just up from Platía Plastíra on Lasthenou – the Áyios Nikólaos road – around five minutes from the centre. It's convenient for a couple of the better budget places to stay (see below), though for a better impression of the town head down towards the water, past the souvenir stores and stalls selling German newspapers, to the seafront and promenade. Here, with a string of restaurants and bars stretching out in either direction – to the left behind the beach, right towards the fortress and the harbour – Ierápetra can be genuinely picturesque.

The **tourist police** (☎22-560) are located on the waterfront, across the square from the Archeological Museum. The most you'll get from them, however, is a few blank looks and, if you're lucky, a town map. If you're really stuck for information, try the helpful *Ierapetra Express* agency on Platía Eleftherías (see "Listings", over).

Accommodation

There are cheap choices near the bus station and in the centre, though the hotels fronting, and set behind, the north and easterly beach are more modern and pricey. There is no youth hostel and the only nearby **campsite** is *Camping Koutsounari*, 7km out of Ieráptera on the Sitía road (see "Áyia Fotiá and beyond" on p.168), though if you stay there you'd have to come into town in the evenings for food and nightlife.

Coral, Ioannidou 18 (☎22-846). The cheapest of the lot, behind the beach and tavernas along Samouil, to the north of the Venetian fort. Rooms are clean and fairly quiet, and an apartment with a kitchen and shower will only set you back another 1000dr or so. ②.

Cretan Villa, Lakerda 16 (☎28-522). Close to the *Four Seasons*, with rooms in a beautiful 180-year-old house. It's just a couple of minutes' walk from the bus station. ②.

Ersi, Platía Eleftherías 20 (☎23-208). Hotel with superb views out to sea. Look out for the switchboard in the lobby – it must be worth a fortune these days. ②.

Four Seasons, Kazantzakis (☎24-390). A couple of hundred metres up the road from the bus station, this is one of the older properties in the town, built in 1866. There's a friendly atmosphere, while one of the rooms on the ground floor has lovely painted designs on its wooden ceilings. ③.

Ligia, Kyrba (☎28-881). In the centre, this hotel is spacious and reasonable value. It's down a narow street, just behind the post office. ③.

The Town

Things to do in Ierápetra by day – apart from lie on the beach – are severely limited. The morning **fruit market** near the museum on K. Adrianou can provide a colourful and entertaining half-hour; get there before noon on weekdays or come on Saturday for the rather bigger affair. The **Archeological Museum** itself is rather less colourful. Its dusty rooms (officially open Tues–Sat 9am–3pm; 400dr) are known to close at a moment's notice, but it's probably worth the effort if only to see a fine Minoan terra-cotta **larnax**, excavated at nearby Episkopí. Dating from the very end of the Neo-Palatial period (c.1300 BC) the *larnax*, or clay coffin, has fascinating painted panels, one of which depicts a mare suckling her foal. Other scenes revel in the stalking of the *kri-kri* or wild goat by hunting dogs. If he's in the mood, the guardian (on request) will raise the *larnax* lid to enable you to see the remains of the three corpses still entombed inside. The Greek and Roman section contains a selection of statuary, mostly headless because iconoclastic Christians tended to regard the stone craniums as places where the spirit of the devil was lurking. One recent discovery, however, managed to hang on to hers: a wonderful second-century statue of the fertility goddess, Demeter, holding an ear of corn in her left hand. Her head is crowned by a small altar encoiled by two serpents, symbols of her divinity.

Elsewhere in town, two churches which stand out from a miscellaneous collection are the twin-domed **Aféndis Christos** (near the fort), a fourteenth-century building with a fine carved and painted wooden iconostasis (key from the house to the left of the entrance); and **Áyios Ioánnis**, an equally ancient, but now restored, former mosque. The Tzami, or Turkish **Mosque**, has now been painstakingly restored and retains a substantial chunk of its minaret and – inside – the original *mihrab*. There's also an old house in which locals claim that **Napoleon** spent the night of June 6, 1798, on his way to Egypt.

Out of town

If you're staying in Ierápetra and it finally becomes too much, there are a number of ways out. Simplest is the day-trip by caique to **Gaidhouronísi** (Donkey Island), some 10km offshore. A real desert island, with a fine cedar forest and a couple of tavernas, Gaidhouronísi has some excellent sandy beaches and plenty of room to escape – although you wouldn't want to miss the boat back. Boats leave from the jetty on the seafront at 10.30am, returning at 4.30pm.

Alternatively, there are more **beaches** along the coast a few kilometres in either direction, with good bus services along the main road behind them.

Eating and entertainment

When it comes to **eating and drinking** Ierápetra's scorecard starts to improve. Along Markopoulou, the seafront promenade stretching north of the tourist police office, there's a string of restaurants with outdoor seating – try the *Argo* or the *Acropolis*. On the Samonil promenade to the south of the ferry terminal another line of restaurants faces the sea. The better ones are found towards the Venetian fortress, like the *Kyknos* or *Gorgona*. If it's just a drink you're after then *Ouzeri Manos* or *Kafenion E. Manthourares* are the ones to go for.

The **bars and discos** are concentrated in the streets immediately behind the seafront, mainly along Kyrba, which is also the area to find more basic food and takeaways. *Politikos Syllogos Ierapetrou* is an interesting, offbeat bar, down a side street off the north side of Kyrba. Music bars are commonplace, with those playing Greek music found on the beach road, those favouring mainstream European sounds a street inland. Along and around Kyrba, *Saxo, Medusa, Diagoras* and *Le Figaro* are popular as is the disco *Zanadu*, which is nearby on the waterfront. *VIP's* nightclub, 4km out of town on the Sitía road, has live *bouzouki* action but isn't cheap.

Listings

Banks *Ionian Bank* on Platía Venizélou has an ATM cash machine.

Bike rental The best deal is at *Moto Cross* (☎23-432) at Kothri 36, just behind the waterfront. They provide helmets and also goggles, which you'll appreciate when the sand starts to fly in the summer winds (the proprietor also has rooms to rent). Alternatives are *Galaxie* (☎25-374) at Metaháki 1, or *Omega Motors* (☎28-995) at Lampraki 1.

Bus station On Lasthenous; information on ☎28-237. Services to Iráklion, Áyios Nikólaos, Sitía and Mírtos.

Post office Stilianou Hota 3; open Mon–Sat 7.30am–2pm.

Telephones OTE at Koraka 25; open Mon–Fri 8am–2pm & 5–8.30pm.

Travel agency *Ierapetra Express* (☎22-411) on the central Platía Eleftherías is a helpful source of travel information, and also provides general information about the town and local festivals and events.

West to Mírtos

Heading **west from Ierápetra**, the first stretch of coast is grey and dusty, the road jammed with trucks and lined with drab ribbon development. Where the concrete runs out, the plastic greenhouses start. However, if you're travelling under your own steam, there are a couple of **scenic detours** worth taking at Gra Ligiá.

Into the hills

From **GRA LIGIÁ**, the first detour winds upwards past a dam, followed by an unsightly quarrying operation, before climbing again – with fine views over the Libyan Sea – to the charming hamlet of **KALAMÁFKA**, tucked into a mountain cleft. The bars along the tiny main street provide a good excuse to stop for a while. From here, you could reach the north coast and Áyios Nikólaos via the village of Prína or, by taking the road to Anatolí, pick up the second detour. This also starts from Gra Ligiá, a hundred metres beyond the first, and is signed for Anatolí, eventually climbing to **MÁLES**, a village clinging to the lower slopes of the Dhíkti range. Here would be a good starting point if you wanted to take a **walk** through some stunning mountain terrain. Otherwise, the dirt road down (signed for Míthi) has spectacular views over the Libyan Sea and eventually follows the Mírtos river valley down to Mírtos itself.

Two Minoan sites: Néa Mírtos and Pírgos

Continuing along the coast road at Gra Ligiá, it's 8km further to **NÉA MÍRTOS**, where a Minoan site excavated in the Sixties by a British team yielded important evidence concerning early Minoan settlements. Known locally as **Fournoú Korifí** (Kiln Hill), the site is located beyond the village on the peak to your right, just after a chapel on the coastal side of the road. Immediately after the hill you'll see a sign for "Minoan Villa". Follow a level track 50m inland and leave your vehicle. A path to the right will eventually lead you up to the site; there are thorns for the last 50m.

The excavations – which are not always easy to make sense of – revealed not a villa but a much earlier stone-built village of nearly one hundred rooms spread over the hilltop. Probably typical of numerous other settlements sited on the coast of eastern Crete during the early Pre-Palatial period (c.2500 BC), these rooms contained stone and copper tools, carved seals and over seven hundred pottery vessels. Some of these were Vasilikí-type jugs with their intriguing mottled finish, and many were no doubt used to store the produce of the surrounding lands, then less arid than today – olives, vines and cereals. In a room in the southwest corner of the site was located the oldest known Minoan domestic shrine which produced the most important of the finds: the goddess of Mírtos, a clay idol with a stalked neck and carrying a ewer. (It's now in the Áyios Nikólaos museum, along with the rest of the finds from this site and Pírgos.) Around the goddess broken offering vessels were strewn about the floor, many of them charred by the fire which destroyed the site about 2200 BC. The riddle of the fire, which seems to have left no casualties and provoked no rebuilding, is yet another of the unresolved Minoan questions. However, the site of Pírgos may offer a few clues.

Pírgos

PÍRGOS, just 2km further on, is considerably easier to get to and has a superb view over the coast. The sign to this Minoan villa comes immediately before a large bridge across the Mírtos river and leads into what appears to be a quarry, which makes it hard to work out the way up. Once you spot it, though, the trail to the top (waymarked with whitewashed stones) is obvious and it's a bare ten-minute walk to the site.

The settlement here was inhabited at much the same time as Fournoú Korifí and was also destroyed by fire around 2200 BC. Unlike Fournoú Korifí, however, Pírgos was reoccupied and rebuilt following its destruction, when it appears to have incorporated the former's lands. By the time of the Neo-Palatial period (c.1600 BC), the community occupying the lower slopes was dominated by a two- or three-storey country villa spread over the crown of the hill. A **stepped street** flanked by some well-cut lower courses of the villa's outer wall leads into a **court-yard** partly paved in the purple limestone of the region. At the rear of the villa (furthest away from the sea) on the west side, it's possible to make out a **light well** floored with the same purple limestone. Many of the walls carry marks of the ferocious blaze which destroyed the villa around 1450 BC, lending credibility to the Thíra explosion theory, especially when volcanic material was discovered amidst the rubble. But it now seems that whilst the villa was burned, the surrounding settlement was untouched – another puzzle to contemplate as you savour the magnificent sea view from the courtyard.

On your way down, take a left turn at the bottom of the stepped street and follow the hill around to see the remains of an enormous plastered **cistern** dating from the Pre-Palatial era (c.1900–1700 BC), the largest found in Minoan Crete. When it burst over the northern side of the hill in ancient times it was not repaired. Beyond this a fine stretch of **paved road** survives from the early period: this led to a burial pit, now excavated.

Mírtos

Across the bridge, the main road turns sharply inland, while a turn-off cuts back down to the coast and **MÍRTOS**. Razed to the ground by the German army in 1943 as a punishment for resistance activities, Mírtos today is an unexpected pleasure after the drabness of what has gone before. This charming white-walled village is kept clean as a whistle by its house-proud inhabitants, and most of the summer you'll find space to breathe on the long shingle beach. Behind the beach lies a short promenade lined with bars and tavernas: *Votsalo* is a good bet, while the foreign-run (and more expensive) *Bel Ami*, nearby, does vegetarian dishes..

In August the place can get pretty full, often with young travellers who sleep on the beach to the irritation of the authorities. But Mírtos takes all this in its easy stride and refuses to be overwhelmed to the point where it is taken over – and so long as there are no big hotels it doesn't seem likely to be. Most of the time there are plenty of **rooms** advertised throughout the village, on every street it seems. Try *Rooms Agelos* (☎0842/510-106; ②) or *Rooms Mertini* (☎0842/51-386; ②). There's also a small hotel, the *Mírtos* (☎0842/51-215; ③). **Information** about rooms can also be had from *Aris Rent-a-Car Travel*, just up the street from *Hotel Mírtos*. The proprietor does sell boat and plane tickets, changes money and operates a taxi service to Iráklion and Haniá airports.

There are more good **beaches** and a pleasant **walk** out along the dirt track which follows the coast west to **TÉRTSA**, 6km away, and then on to Árvi (p.121). Head out here also to find places to **camp**, where you should be undisturbed.

Inland, the character of the main road, now heading towards Áno Viánnos (p.120) and Iráklion, changes immediately as it begins to climb around the south side of the Dhíkti range. Here you're back into the traditional Crete of small mountain villages and alarming precipices.

travel details

Buses

Some of these services are restricted on Sun

Áyios Nikólaos to: Eloúnda (20 daily; 5.30am–9pm; 30min); Ierápetra (10 daily; 6.30am–8pm; 1hr); Iráklion (27 daily; 6am–9pm; 1hr 30min); Kritsá (13 daily; 6am–7.30pm; 30min); Lasíthi plateau (2 daily; 8.15am and 2pm; 2hr); Mália (27 daily; 6am–9pm; 30min); Sitía (7 daily; 6.30am–7pm; 2hr).

Ierápetra to: Áno Viános (Mon–Fri 2 daily; 6am and 4.30pm; 30min); Áy. Nikólaos (8 daily; 6.30am–8pm; 1hr); Iráklion (8 daily; 6.30am–8pm; 2hr 30min); Makriyialós (8 daily; 6.15am–8pm; 30min); Mírtos (6 daily; 6am–8pm; 30min).

Sitía to: Áy. Nikólaos (6 daily; 6.30am–7.15pm; 2hr); Ierápetra (15 daily; 6.15am–7.45pm; 2hr); Iráklion (6 daily; 6.30am–7.15pm; 3hr 30min); Kato Zákros (2 daily; 11am and 2.30pm; 1hr 30min); Makriyialós (15 daily; 6.15am–7.45pm; 1hr); Vái (5 daily; 9.30am–4pm; 1hr).

Ferries

To the Dodecanese *Sifnos Express* leaves Áy. Nikólaos Wed morning for Sitía, Kásos, Kárpathos, Hálki, Rhodes, Sími, Tílos, Nísiros, Kós, Kálimnos, Astipalía, Amorgós, Páros and Pireás; Sat morning to Sitía, Kásos, Kárpathos, Hálki and Rhodes. *Lasithi* sails Sat afternoon from Áy. Nikólaos to Rhodes.

To the Cyclades *Sifnos Express* sails Sat afternoon from Áy. Nikólaos to Anáfi, Thíra, Folégandros, Mílos, Sífnos and Pireás.

These ferries operate very infrequently in winter

Flights

From Sitía Once weekly to Kásos (summer only) and Kárpathos (summer only), twice a week to Athens (all year).

ΑΓΙΟΣ ΝΙΚΟΛΑΟΣ	Αγιος Νικόλαος	Áyios Nikólaos
ΑΓΙΑ ΦΩΤΙΑ	Αγία Φωτιά	Ayía Fotiá
ΒΑΙ	Βάι	Vái
ΓΟΥΡΝΙΑ	Γούρνια	Goúrnia
ΕΛΟΥΝΤΑ	Ελούντα	Eloúnda
ΖΑΚΡΟΣ	Ζάκρος	Zákros
ΙΕΡΑΠΕΤΡΑ	Ιεράπετρα	Ierápetra
ΚΡΙΤΣΑ	Κριτσά	Kritsá
ΛΑΣΙΘΙΟΥ	Λασίθιου	Lasíthi
ΜΑΚΡΥΓΙΑΛΟΣ	Μακρύγιαλος	Makríyialos
ΜΙΡΤΟΣ	Μίρτος	Mírtos
ΜΟΧΛΟΣ	Μόχλος	Móhlos
ΝΕΑΠΟΛΗ	Νεάπολη	Neápoli
ΠΑΛΑΙΚΑΣΤΡΟ	Παλαίκαστρο	Palékastro
ΣΗΤΕΙΑ	Σητεία	Sitía
ΣΠΗΝΑΛΟΓΚΑ	Σπηναλόγκα	Spinalónga
ΤΖΕΡΜΙΑΔΟ	Τζερμιάδο	Tsermiádho
ΨΥΧΡΟ	Ψυχρό	Psihró

CHAPTER THREE

RÉTHIMNON

Réthimnon province is dominated by mountains, its borders defined to the east by the island's highest peaks, including the looming mass of Psilorítis, and to the west by the outflung reaches of the Lefká Óri. The towns, even the provincial capital Réthimnon, feel compact and hemmed in, and so do many of the beaches – especially along the often wild and inaccessible southern coast.

Not surprising, then, that it is **the interior** which offers the greatest attractions – in the villages ranged around the **Psilorítis massif** and in a series of wilderness hikes originating from them. A few days here are strongly recommended, for casual ramblers and committed hikers alike. The peaks themselves are approached most easily from **Anóyia**, a high mountain town with a reputation for homespun weaving and embroidery. From here, you can hike across to the south side of the mountains or down, via the **summit of Psilorítis**, to the villages of the **Amári valley** – some of the least visited and most traditional places in Crete.

On the north coast, **Réthimnon** is at the centre of some of Crete's most drastic resort development, with hotels and apartments spreading ever eastwards along a narrow strip of plain. The town, though, has just about managed to keep its priorities straight, and a core of life continues relatively unaffected. To the west, a sandy coastline, still not greatly exploited, runs all the way to the borders of Haniá. But for time by the sea, it's across the island, on the **south coast**, that the province has most to offer. Here there are just two resorts of any size, overblown **Ayía Galíni** and its fast-emerging rival, **Plakiás**. Away from these enclaves is the Crete of old: little-known pockets of sand, hard of access but well worth it.

Réthimnon

Although the third largest town in Crete, **RÉTHIMNON** never feels like a city, as Haniá or Iráklion do. Instead, it has an air of the provincial: a place that moves slowly and, for all the myriad bars springing up along the seafront, preserves much of its Venetian and Turkish appearance. Arriving, especially if you approach from the east in the evening, it looks exactly as it does in old engravings or in Edward Lear's watercolours – dominated by the bulk of a Venetian fortress, the skyline picked out with the delicate spires of minarets.

All of this is increasingly under commercial threat, but for the time being it's an enjoyable place to spend some time, with a wide, sandy beach and palm-fringed promenade right in front of the tangled streets of the old town. There are hundreds of tavernas, bars, cafés and discos, but the big hotels are all out of town, stretching for miles along the shore to the east. Staying in town, away from the front, you'll find things relatively quiet at night, though noisily animated during the day.

Arrival and information

Most people arrive in Réthimnon by road, turning off the main E75 north coast highway (aka the New Road) and descending the 1km into the town. If you're driving, you should head straight for the waterfront, which is the easiest place to find and to park. The two **bus stations** are diagonally opposite each other, at the corner of Dhimokratías and Moátsou, one for the long-distance and north-coast services, the other for trans-island and village buses. If you come in on the **ferry** you'll arrive more centrally still, at the western edge of the harbour; simply walk into the old town directly ahead of you. If you're **leaving from the airport at Hanía**, a bus leaves from the *Olympic Airways* office in town (see "Listings", p.186) to connect with flights, two and a quarter hours before departure.

To get your bearings from the bus station, walk straight down towards the front, following Dhimokratías and then Kalérgi or one of the narrower alleys of the old town. You'll emerge on the beach, virtually opposite the **tourist office** (Mon–Fri 8am–2.30pm; ☎29-148), where you can pick up maps, timetables and accommodation lists. When closed, the tourist police in the same building will provide maps and basic information until 11pm. Alternatively, turn left on Arkadhíou to head straight for the centre and most of the accommodation.

> The phone code for Réthimnon is ☎0831. Note that the Réthimnon phone system is currently being modernized and some numbers may change. The tourist office should have the latest listings.

Accommodation

There's a great number of places to stay in Réthimnon, with the greatest concentration of **rooms** in the tangled streets west of the inner harbour, between the Rimondi fountain and the museums: there are also quite a few places on and around Arkadhíou. The cheap **hotels** are, on the whole, less good value than the rooms places, but on the other hand they are more likely to have space; there are

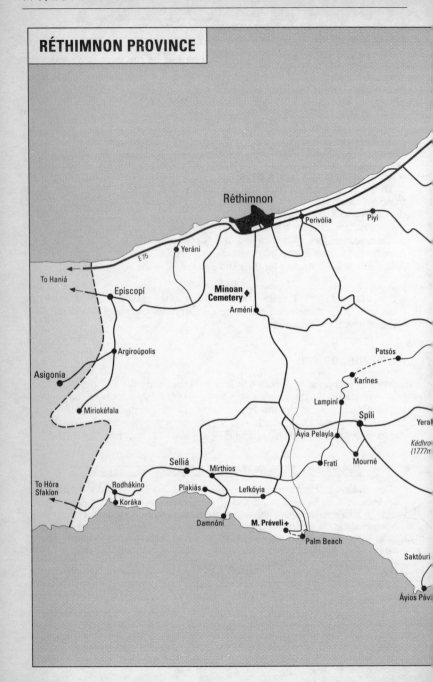

RÉTHIMNON PROVINCE

Réthimnon

Perivólia

Piyí

Yeráni

E 75

To Haniá

Episcopí

Minoan
Cemetery

Arméni

Argiroúpolis

Patsós

Asigonía

Karínes

Miriokéfala

Lampiní

Spíli

Yeral

Áyia Pelayía

Kédhro
(1777m

Selliá

Fratí

Mourné

Mírthios

To Hóra
Sfakion

Rodhákino

Plakiás

Lefkóyia

Koráka

Damnóni

M. Préveli ✝

Saktóuri

Palm Beach

Áyios Páv.

several along or just off Arkadhíou. The higher-category hotels are all modern and businesslike. The two nearest **campsites** are 4km east of town; if you're looking for central, rock-bottom budget accommodation, the only option is the **youth hostel** (see "Seafront and behind", below).

Fortezza and harbour area

Anna, Katehaki 5 (☎25-586). Comfortable pension in a quiet position on the street which runs straight down from the entrance to the fortress to Melissinou. All rooms have bath, and some have a kitchen, too. A couple more new rooms places are very close by. ③.

Atelier, Himáras 32 (☎24-440). Pleasant rooms close to the *George* in a place run by a talented potter who has her studio in the basement and sells her wares in a store on the other side of the building. ②.

Barbara Dokimaki, Platía Plastíra 7 (☎22-319). Strange warren of a rooms place, with one entrance at the above address, just off the seafront behind the *Ideon*, and another on Dambergi, opposite *Corina*. The nearby Platía Frakidaki has more cheap rooms. ②.

Corina, Dambergi 9 (☎26-911). Very friendly pension with a couple of airy, balcony rooms out front, several darker ones behind. ②.

Fortezza, Melissinou 16, near the Fortezza (☎55-551). Stylish, top-of-the-range hotel with everything you'd expect for the price, including a pool and restaurant. ⑤.

Ideon, Platía Plastíra 10 (☎28-667). Brilliant position just north of the ferry dock; the balcony rooms have a sea view. There's little chance of space in season, though, unless you've booked in advance. ④.

Lefteris, Platía Plastíra 26 (☎23-803). Clean, pleasant pension rooms, with and without bath. They will allow one-night stays, but would rather rent by the week. ②.

Rent Rooms Garden, Nikifourou Foka 82 (☎26-274). Good-value rooms with bath in an ancient Venetian building in the heart of the old town. ①.

Rooms George, Makedonias 32 (☎27-540). Decent rooms, some with fridge, near the Archeological Museum. ③.

Rooms Isidora, Mavili 1 (☎26-293). Comfortable rooms in a quiet location, a couple of blocks below the Fortezza. ③.

Seeblick, Platía Plastíra 17 (☎22-478). On the seafront as you walk round from the inner harbour towards the outer wall of the fortress. Rooms with sea view cost more, but are good value for the position; some cheaper rooms are available without views. The owners prefer to rent by the week and won't even consider a single-night stay in season. ③.

Stelios Soumbasakis, Nikiforou Foka 98, corner of Koronaíou. This taverna has some rooms to rent, and contacts with many small rooms places in the surrounding streets. ②.

Seafront and behind

Ahillion, Arkadhíou 151 (☎22-581). Rambling and very run-down hotel (worn lino, sagging furniture), but clean and in a good position. Some rooms have a sea view. ①.

Leo, Vafe 2 (☎29-851). This hotel has lots of wooden decor and a traditional feel. The price includes breakfast, and there's a good bar. ③.

Minoa, Arkadhíou 60 (☎22-508). Basic hotel rooms but clean and central. ②.

Olga's Rooms, Souliou 57 (☎29-851 or 23-493). Nice old building on this touristy street with some very good rooms with bath overlooking the sea, some cheaper without. Several other relatively upmarket rooms places can be found on Souliou. ①–②.

Rethimnon, V. Kornarou 1 (☎23-923). Very pleasant rooms of a high standard in an old building just off Arkadhíou. Bar downstairs. ②.

Vrisinas, Heréti 10 (☎26-092). In a narrow street parallel to Kalérgi, this pension is worth checking as you walk in from the bus station, but it's often full. Lovely rooms, though some are noisy. ②.

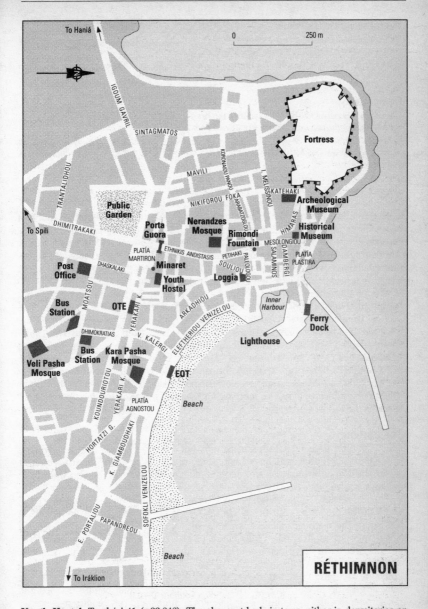

Youth Hostel, Tombázi 41 (☎22-848). The cheapest beds in town, either in dormitories or on the roof. The hostel is large, clean, very friendly and popular, and there's food, showers, clothes-washing facilities and even a library of books in an assortment of languages. ①.

Zania, Pavlou Vlastou 3 (☎28-169). A refurbished old house, right on the corner of Arkadhíou by the old youth hostel building, but with only a few rooms available. ②.

Near the Public Gardens

Brascos, Dhaskalaki 1, corner Moatsou (☎23-721). B-class hotel comfort, international bland-ness, but often has space when everywhere else is full. ③.

Byzantine, Vosporou 26, near the Porta Guora (☎55-609). Spotless rooms with bath in a renovated old Byzantine palace. The tranquil patio bar is open to all. ③.

Campsites

Camping Arkadia (☎28-825). Only a few hundred metres from *Elizabeth*, further east along the beach. Bigger and slightly less friendly, similar prices.

Camping Elizabeth (☎28-694). Pleasant, large site on the beach about 4km east of town; all facilities. Take the bus for the hotels (marked *Scaleta/El Greco*) from the long-distance bus station to get there.

The City

Réthimnon is a thoroughly enjoyable place to wander around. Although much of it has succumbed to the commercial reality of fast-food outlets and supermarkets, the buildings themselves have changed little, and there's still the odd corner where English or German are not automatically spoken, a few curious old stores and craftsmen working away in their traditional get-up of high boots, baggy trousers (*vrákes*) and black headscarves (*tsalvária*).

The monuments described below don't amount to a great deal on paper, but walking between them is often every bit as interesting as getting to them. The streets themselves are a fascinating mix of generations of architecture, the Venetian buildings indistinguishable most of the time from the Turkish and all of them adapted and added to by later generations. Ornate wooden doors and balconies are easily spotted, ancient stonework crops up everywhere, and there are a number of elaborate **Turkish fountains** hidden in obscure corners: one by the Kara Pasha mosque, another below the south side of the fortress at the corner of Smírnis and Koronaíou, two more on Patriárhou Grigoríou leading up from here towards the Public Gardens.

The harbour

Most people's time in Réthimnon is split between the beach and the tavernas immediately behind it, with an occasional excursion as far as the inner harbour or up to the Rimondi fountain and another cluster of tavernas. So the waterfront seems a logical place to start.

The impressive breakwaters, which are constantly being extended, reveal some of the problems with the **harbour**. Originally created by the Venetians, it has spent the centuries since constantly silting up, and until very recently had given up on trying to handle really big ships or ferries: when the locals decided to set up their own ferry service to Pireás (the *Arkadhi* was bought by public subscription) the whole thing had to be completely cleared out, and only a constant dredging operation keeps it open. Even now, the ferry is virtually the only large ship to call here: the inner harbour is for small fishing caiques and pleasure craft only; the outer part is given over almost entirely to tourists.

The Fortezza

If you follow the shoreline round to the west you'll emerge beneath the walls of the massive **Venetian Fortress** (daily 9am–4pm; 200dr). Said to be the largest

Venetian castle ever built, this was a response, in the last quarter of the sixteenth century, to a series of pirate raids (by Barbarossa in 1538, Uluch Ali in 1562 and 1571) which had devastated the town. Whether it was effective is another matter – the Venetian city fell to the Turks in less than 24 hours (they simply bypassed the fort); and when the English writer Robert Pashley visited in 1834 he found the guns, some of them still the Venetian originals, entirely useless. Walk around the outside, preferably at sunset, to get an impression of its vast bulk and fearsome defences. There are great views along the coast and a pleasant resting point around the far side at the *Sunset Taverna*.

The **entrance**, however, is not on the seaward side but in the southeastern corner, opposite the new Archeological Museum. As you walk in through the walls there's a small café/bar in what must have been some sort of guardhouse within the bastion, and then you emerge into the vast open interior space, dotted with the remains of barracks, arsenals, officers' houses, earthworks and deep shafts. At the centre is a large domed building which was once a church and later a mosque, designed to be large enough for the entire population to take shelter within the walls. Although much is ruined now, the fort remains thoroughly atmospheric, with views from the walls over the town and harbour, or in the other direction along the coast to the west.

Among the most impressive remains are the **cisterns** where rainwater would have been collected: deep and cool, and dimly lit by slits through which shafts of sunlight penetrate. The church/mosque, recently restored, has a really fabulous dome and a pretty carved *mihrab* (a niche indicating the direction of Mecca and sadly defaced by graffiti), both of which are Turkish additions. Just to the north of this are some fine arched foundations and a stairway leading down to a gate in the seaward defences. This was in theory for resupplying the defenders, but in practice it was through here that the Venetians fled from the Turkish attack.

Archeological and Historical museums

Réthimnon's **Archeological Museum** (Tues–Sun 8.30am–3pm; 400dr, Sun free) occupies a building almost directly opposite the entrance to the fortress. This was built by the Turks as an extra defence for the entry, and later served as a prison, but it's now entirely modern inside: cool, spacious and airy. It's worth a look, especially if you're going to miss the bigger museums elsewhere: there's Minoan pottery and sarcophagi, and lots of Roman coins, jewellery, pots and statues, all of them from Réthimnon province. Take a look beneath the central atrium at an unusual unfinished Roman **statue of Aphrodite**. The sculptor's chisel marks are plainly visible, allowing you to glimpse the goddess's features – never completed – emerging from the stone.

The **Historical and Folk Art Museum** (Mon–Sat 9am–1pm & 7–9pm; 200dr), not far away on Mesolongíou, is even smaller but a good deal more enjoyable. Inside, in just two not particularly large rooms, are gathered musical instruments, old photos, basketry, farm implements, an explanation of traditional bread-making techniques, smiths' tools, traditional costumes and jewellery, lace, weaving and embroidery, pottery, knives and old wooden chests. Much of this looks as if it has just come out of someone's attic – as it sometimes has – and the displays include explanations (most of them translated) of how they've gathered the items, often as a result of a traditional craft workshop, farm or bakery closing down. It's a fascinating insight into a fast disappearing rural (and urban) lifestyle, which had often survived virtually unchanged from Venetian times to the 1960s.

The Rimondi fountain and city centre: some mosques

The centre, at least as far as tourists are concerned, is probably the area from the Loggia to the Rimondi fountain; with streets of shops, restaurants and bars radiating in every direction. The seventeenth-century Venetian **Loggia** is currently being converted into a library. The **Rimondi fountain**, at the other end of Paleológou, is also seventeenth-century Venetian. Half-hidden under a blocked-off arcade, the fountain's lion-head spouts still splash water down to a marble bowl, and nowadays they look out over one of the liveliest areas in Réthimnon – Platía Petiháki. Straight up from the fountain, a line of cafés and tavernas leads into Ethníkis Andistásis, the **market** street. Turn right just before this and the backstreets will lead you to the **Nerandzes Mosque**, whose minaret (daily 11am–7pm; closed Aug), ascended by a steep spiral stair, has the best views in town. The body of the mosque is now a meeting hall, often used for concerts.

Up through the market area, the old city ends at the only surviving remnant of the city walls, the **Porta Guora**. Through the gate you emerge into the Platía Tessáron Martíron with its ugly, unfinished modern church. Almost directly opposite are the quiet and shady **Public Gardens**, a former Turkish cemetery now laid out with a fine variety of palms and other trees. In July, the gardens play host to the festivities of the **Réthimnon Wine Festival** (see "Drinking, nightlife and entertainment" over).

Wandering further afield into the newer parts of town, two more **mosques** almost complete the roll of Réthimnon's acknowledged "sights". **Veli Pasha**, up behind the bus station, has a fine minaret whilst **Kara Pasha** by Platía Iróon is older, but only part of the facade survives, with a small garden planted in front.

The beach

To find the **beach** you hardly need a guidebook: the broad swathe of tawny sand in the centre of town advertises itself. There are showers and cafés here, and the waters protected by the breakwaters are dead calm (and ideal for kids). Sadly they are also crowded and none too clean. Outside the harbour, less sheltered sands stretch for miles to the east, only marginally less crowded but with much cleaner water. Interspersed among the hotels along here is every facility you could need – travel agents, bike rental, bars and restaurants.

Eating

Immediately behind the town beach are arrayed the most obvious of Réthimnon's **restaurants**, all with illustrated menus out front and most with waiters who will run off their patter in English, German, French, Swedish or whatever else seems likely to appeal. These places are not always bad value – especially if you hanker after an "English breakfast" – but they are all thoroughly touristy. Look out, here and throughout town, for the wonderful fresh fruit juices and shakes which have become a local speciality: melon is particularly good. Around the **inner harbour** there's a second, rather more expensive group of tavernas, specializing in fish and an intimate atmosphere – though as often as not this is spoilt by the stench from the harbour itself.

Although they lack the sea views, the cluster of *kafenia* and tavernas **by the Rimondi fountain** and the newer places spreading into the streets all around generally offer better value. There are a couple of good pizza places here, too, and a number of old-fashioned *kafenia*, a couple of which serve magnificent yoghurt and honey.

Takeaway food means either *souvláki* – there are numerous stalls including a couple on Arkadhíou and Paleológou and *O Platanos* at Petiháki 44 – or buying your own. **Market** stalls are set up daily on Andistásis below the Porta Guora and there are small general stores scattered everywhere, particularly on Paleológou and Arkadhíou; east along the beach road you'll even find a couple of mini supermarkets. The **bakery** *I Gaspari*, on Mesolongíou just behind the Rimondi fountain, sells the usual cheese pies, cakes and the like, and it also bakes excellent brown, black and rye bread. There's a good *zaharoplasteío* on Petiháki, and another at Koundouriotou 49, west of Platía Martíron.

Tavernas and restaurants

Agrimi, Platía Petiháki. Just one of the places queuing for your custom as you walk up from the fountain. It's a good place to sit outside and the food is usually reliable.

Alana, Salaminas 11. A romantic, tree-filled courtyard setting for candlelit tables and (mostly) non-Greek food. High prices, however.

O Gounas, Koronaíou 6. In the old town. Hearty, no-frills cooking. The family running this bar/restaurant perform *lyra* every night. When things get really lively, the dancing starts.

Kyria Maria, Moshovitou 20. Pleasant small restaurant tucked down an alley behind the Rimondi fountain – after the meal everyone gets a couple of Maria's delicious *tiropitákia* topped with honey on the house.

Palazzo, at the inner harbour. One of the nicest on the harbour, with rooftop tables, but overpriced for what you get.

O Pontios, Melissinou 34. A tiny place near the Archeological Museum and the Fortezza, this is run single-handedly by Katerina, the charming proprietor. A good lunchtime stop.

Stelios Soumbasakis, Nikiforou Foka 98. A very friendly, simple taverna, on the corner of Koronaíou.

Sunset Taverna, on the west side of the Fortezza. Mostly visited for its views rather than the food, but the meals aren't bad and the tables are right by the edge of the sea – the waiters have to cross the road to the kitchen.

Taverna Kargaki Haroulas, Melissinou by Mesolongíou. Big, cheap Greek breakfasts plus standard taverna dishes at reasonable prices.

Taverna Kombou, edge of Atsipópolou village, 3km southwest of town. An excellent garden taverna, this is where the locals go. The Cretan specialities on offer include *spilogáradouma* (a type of lamb sausage) which should be eaten with *áfogalo*, a creamy sauce. Take a taxi there and back.

Taverna Petrino, junction of Salaminas and Diakou, behind the inner harbour. Small family-run neighbourhood taverna, less commercialized than those on the harbour.

Taverna Samaria, Venizélou, almost opposite the tourist office. One of the few seafront places trusted by locals; well-prepared food at fair prices.

To Rempetiko, Koronaíou 11. Laidback place with a limited menu, though served at outdoor tables.

O Zefyros, at the inner harbour. Less outrageously priced and among the more reliable of the fish tavernas here.

Drinking, nightlife and entertainment

Bars and nightlife are concentrated in the same general areas as the restaurants. At the west end of Venizélou, approaching the inner harbour, a small cluster of noisy **music bars** rock the beach. Up around the corner of Arkadhíou and Paleológou are some slightly quieter places, with candle-light and acoustic guitar. Larger **discos** are mostly out to the east, among the big hotels, but there are one or two in town as well.

Each August the town puts on its **Anagennisiakó** or **Renaissance Festival**. Held in the Fortezza, it includes classical and folk concerts, and theatrical events as well as performances of Classical tragedies and comedies. A full programme is available from the tourist office. There's more public entertainment on offer at the annual **Wine Festival**, staged in the Public Gardens in the second half of July. The entrance fee includes all the wine you can drink from barrels set up around the gardens, and there are also food stalls and entertainment laid on. You'll need to take your own cup or else buy one of the souvenir glasses and carafes on offer outside. Although it's touristy, the locals go too, and as the evening progresses and the barrels empty the organized entertainments give way to spectacular displays of the local dance steps.

Cafés, bars and discos

Café Bals, Himáras 1. Stylish, popular garden bar, west of the Rimondi fountain.

Delfini Club, Venizélou, below the eastern harbour mole. Beachside open-air disco which incorporates a pool and features go-go dancers. All very Sixties.

Fortezza, inner harbour. Big, glitzy disco-bar, where there's not much action till midnight.

Galera, Platía Petiháki. Large beers, toasted sandwiches and snacks. *Basiliko*, next door, offers the same sort of thing.

Metropolis, Nearchou. Just round the corner from the *Fortezza*, on an alley which connects with Arkadhíou. A loud rock-music bar with other bar-discos nearby.

Odysseas, Venizélou, right by the inner harbour. Touristy Cretan music and dancing place, with live performances every evening from 9.30pm.

Rouli's, Venizélou, behind the end of the beach. One of the cheapest and liveliest of several noisy bars here.

Zanafoti, Platía Petiháki. Long-established *kafenion* overlooking Rimondi fountain. Prices are higher than average, but it's a great place to people-watch over a coffee; good yoghurt and honey, too.

Listings

Airlines *Olympic Airways,* Dhimitrakáki 6 (☎22-257), facing the Public Gardens.

Banks *National Bank* is at the foot of Dhimokratias near the bus station and has a 24-hr ATM which takes *Mastercard* and *Eurocard*. Over the road, the *Interamerican Bank* has a cash-exchange machine. *Commercial Bank* on Platía Agnostou, near the seafront, *Credit Bank* at Koundouriotou 29, and *Ionian Bank* at Koundouriotou 134 all have *Visa* ATMs.

Bike and car rental There are several competing outlets on Paleológou: try *Stavros* (☎22-858) or *Katridizaki* (☎29-263), which also rents out mountain bikes. Other possibilities are around Platía Agnostou, and out along the beach road. For cars, try the very reliable *Direct* (☎25-110) at Platía Agnostou 31; *Arkadi* (bikes; ☎29-134) at Venizélou and Papandreou, and *Pioneer* (cars; ☎20-312) at Venizélou 64, are other places in the same zone.

Boat trips The *Scorpios* offers day-trips to Pánormos, Balí and the Skaléta caves or to Yeoryioúpouli, as well as evening cruises and fishing expeditions. The *Pirate* does similar trips in a more touristic "Jolly Roger" vessel, complete with sails, which you may feel embarrassed boarding; great for kids, though. Both tout for custom around the inner harbour.

Cinema There are several, including the open-air *Astoria* on Melissinou beneath the south side of the Fortezza (lovely place, poor films) and *Cinema Pandelis* on the main road out towards Iráklion (new films, many in original version).

Ferries The agent for the Réthimnon–Pireás ferry, *Rethymniaki*, is at Arkhadíou 250 (☎55-518). The *Arkadi* sails to Pireás on Tues, Thurs, Sat and Sun at 7.30pm. A new boat (the *Préveli*) is due to come into operation soon making the service a daily one. The *Artemis* also makes a daily one-day cruise to Santorini (Thera).

Laundry Launderette at Tombázi 45, by the youth hostel (daily 9am–2pm & 5–9pm).

Left luggage The long-distance bus station has a small and chaotic office; *Direct Cars* also has an office at Platía Agnostou 31.

Mountain climbing and walking The local EOS is at Dhimokratias 12 (☎22-655); besides advice on climbing it also organizes walking tours (contact Sifis Spandidakis). Walking tours (from 1 day to 2 weeks) are offered by *The Happy Walker*, Tombázi 56 (☎52-920), a Dutch operation located near the youth hostel.

Newspapers and books Foreign newspapers are sold at several places along the seafront. Best for these, and for a wide selection of new books in English, is *International Press* at the junction of Venizélou and Petiháki. Good places for second-hand English-language books are *Palaiobibliopoleío* at Soulíou 43 in the old town, and *Direct Cars* on Platía Agnostou which offers 50 percent of the cover price for unwanted paperbacks.

Pharmacies Scattered about the main shopping streets, especially Koundouriótou and Arkadhíou. Check the rota on the door for late/weekend opening. The tourist office has a list of English-speaking doctors.

Post office The main post office (Mon–Sat 7.30am–2pm, Sun 9am–1.30pm) is in a smart new building on Moátsou, opposite the *Hotel Brascos*. There's also a temporary office, in season, just behind the beach at the bottom of the eastern breakwater (on S. Venizélou; Mon–Sat 8am–8pm, Sun 9am–6pm).

Shopping Most of the souvenir stores are along Arkadhíou, Paleológou and Souliou; the market is on Andistásis, while more general stores line Arkadhíou and Koundouriótou. There's also a market on Thurs along Dhimitrakaki, near the Public Gardens. Souliou has the most upmarket and varied tourist stores (including one store that sells nothing but herbs and herbal remedies), but prices throughout town are markedly higher than in Haniá. For beach games and fishing or diving gear, try *Spiros Spor* on Petiháki. Official shop hours are Mon, Wed & Sat 8am–2pm, Tues, Thurs & Fri 8am–1pm & 5–8pm.

Taxis Ranks in Platía Tessáron Martíron and Platía Iróon. Call ☎22-316 for a radio taxi.

Telephones The OTE office at Koundourióti 28 (daily 7am–midnight).

Toilets Public toilets on the beach by the tourist office (clean!), opposite the Loggia and in the Public Gardens.

Travel agents Several along Paleológou, Arkadhíou and Koundouriótou, and also around Platía Agnostou and along Venizélou. *Aloha Travel* (Paleológou 25; ☎21-537), *Rethymno Tours* (Yerakari by Hortatzi; ☎55-179; open daily 8am–midnight), *Creta Tours* (Venizélou; ☎22-915) and *Caroline Tours* (Platía Agnostou; ☎24-351 for boats from Kastélli Kisámou–Gythion) can all arrange excursions and ferry tickets; though for flights home you'd be better off in Haniá or Iráklion.

Out from Réthimnon: Monastery of Arkádhi

Of all the short trips which could be taken out of Réthimnon, the best known is still the most worthwhile. This is to the **Monastery of Arkádhi** (daily 6am–8pm), some 25km southeast of the city. Immaculately sited in the foothills of the Psilorítis range, Arkádhi is something of a national Cretan shrine. During the 1866 rebellion the monastery served as a Cretan strongpoint in which, as the Turks took the upper hand, hundreds of Cretan guerrillas and their families took refuge. Here they were surrounded by a Turkish army until, after a siege of two days, the defences were finally breached on November 9, 1866.

As the attackers poured in, the ammunition stored in the monastery exploded: deliberately fired, according to the accepted version of events, on the orders of the abbot. Hundreds (some sources claim thousands) were killed in the initial blast, Cretan and Turk alike, and most of the surviving defenders were put to death by the enraged assailants. The following year the British philhellene J. Hilary Skinner, fighting with the insurgents, could still describe "scores of bodies unburied, half-buried, sun-dried, and mangled, to be seen within the monastery". That he was here at all is proof of the international sympathy for the cause of Cretan independence which this ultimate expression of the cry of "*Freedom or Death*" did much to promote. Figures as disparate as Victor Hugo, Garibaldi and the poet Swinburne were moved to public declarations of support, and in Britain money was raised for a ship (the *Arkádhi*) to run the Turkish blockade. Though Crete's liberty was still some way off, the monastery remains the most potent symbol of the struggle. There are celebrations of the anniversary of the blast every November, from the seventh to the ninth.

The buildings

Nowadays you can peer into the roofless vault beside the cloister where the explosion took place, and wander about the rest of the well-restored grounds. Despite the carnage, the bulk of the monastery buildings, including the others around the central cloister, were relatively unscathed and Arkádhi is still a working monastery. Before its notoriety, indeed, it was one of the richest in Crete and already a well-known stopover for travellers (Edward Lear spent one of his better-tempered nights here) and a centre of resistance. Pashley relates a story of events over forty years prior to the famous blast, when eighty Muslims, who had occupied the monastery to pacify local rebels, were captured and put to death: in retaliation, many of the buildings were burnt. More recently the monastery lent assistance to guerrilla fighters during World War II: George Psychoundakis, for example, describes handing over to the monks supplies from a parachute drop.

Of the surviving buildings the **church** is much the most impressive, with a rich mix of styles which places it among the finest Venetian structures left in Crete. Its highly decorative facade, dating from 1587, features on the 100-drachma note – isolated here in the Cretan countryside, it seems startlingly out of place. The rest of the monastery is mainly seventeenth-century (though it was originally founded as early as the eleventh) and more familiar in layout and style. Across the courtyard from the scene of the explosion a small **museum** devoted to the exploits of the defenders of the faith contains a variety of mementoes and tributes, bloodstained clothing and commemorative medals.

Getting there

Getting to Arkádhi is straightforward. In addition to all the tours, there are **buses** from Réthimnon at 6am, 10.30am, noon and 2.30pm, returning at 7am, 11.30am, 1pm and 4pm. Going up at 10.30am and back at 1pm gives you about the right amount of time, but these are the most popular buses, and consequently can be crowded; alternatively hitching a lift down should be no problem – the road ends here and the only place any traffic can go is back down to the coast. You could also try walking on to Thrónos in the Amari valley (p.199) – get someone at the monastery to set you on the right track.

The **road up** is attractive in itself: if you're driving take the old route out of Réthimnon via Perivólia and then follow the signs at Plataniás which lead under the highway towards the monastery via Ádhele and Piyí. Five kilometres beyond Piyí you'll come to Loutrá where, on the right the *Taverna Panorama*

(☎0831/71- 339; ①) makes a good lunch or drink stop. They make their own wine here in five-, ten- and even twenty-year-old vintages which you can buy. The panorama is at the back where a terrace looks out over groves of olives towards the sea. Should the ancient vintages prove too potent, they also have **rooms**.

As you climb into the lower reaches of the mountains the road, and the valley through which it runs, gradually narrow until at the end it's a real ravine. This opens out quite suddenly into the small plain at whose centre stands the monastery: you'll pass a modern monument to the martyrs of independence – with displayed human skulls – and arrive at a huge spreading tree where the bus stops and cars park. There is **food** available, but this is also a quiet place to picnic, either on benches around the outside of the monastery or walking out into the meadows which surround it.

With your own transport you could take an **alternative route back to the coast** through some picturesque wooded hill country dotted with interesting villages. Directly in front of the monastery a dirt road cuts away to the northeast and soon becomes paved before it reaches Eléuthérna, 5km away, and ancient Eléutherna, followed by Margarítes (both covered on pp.191–192).

West towards Haniá

Heading west from Réthimnon the roads are easy and efficient, but they offer little in the way of diversion. As you leave the city, you immediately start to climb; within a couple of kilometres the **old road** peels off to head inland, while the **highway** carries on above the coast.

The highway
Following the highway, you drop back to sea level at **YERÁNI**, 6km from Réthimnon, with a rocky cove good for a swimming break. There's a sign here to the Yeráni cave, site of a Neolithic cult rediscovered when the road was built, but the cave is not actually open to the public. Beyond, after another brief flirtation with the hills, the road finally levels out beside the **Gulf of Almirós**, from where it traces the shore, flat and straight, the rest of the way to Yeoryióupolis (pp.239–40). A long and windswept sandy beach follows it all the way, separated from the road by straggling bushes of oleander: there are frequent spaces to pull over and park if you want a swim, and just a few new developments beginning to spring up. The beach itself is virtually deserted much of the way, but there can be dangerous currents so don't venture too far out: it gets further from the road and considerably more sheltered as you approach the development at Yeoryióupolis.

The old road
The **old road**, much more scenic, is by comparison quite populous. You'll pass through five or six prosperous little villages before arriving at **EPISKOPÍ**, something of a local market centre. Here you're approaching the fringe of the White Mountains, which rise with increasing majesty ahead. To the left a road runs up to some of the smaller villages, a rarely travelled route where the old life continues little affected.

A turn-off 4km beyond Episkopí brings you to **ARGIRÓUPOLIS**, a scenic hamlet with **rooms** and a couple of tavernas, while the more direct route countines to **ASIGONÍA** at the end of a perpetually cloudy cul-de-sac. This isolated settlement has been a particular favourite of students of traditional Cretan culture, partly, perhaps, because it was the home village of George Psychoundákis (see "Books" in *Contexts*). There's an interesting local festival, on April 23, when flocks of sheep are brought at dawn to the church to be milked, sheared and dedicated to Áyios Yioryios, their patron saint and protector. The road south from Asigonía soon degrades to a track which snakes through a valley to Kallikrátis before doubling back towards **MIRIOKÉFALA** whose monastery church of the Panayía has ancient Byzantine **frescoes**, among the earliest on the island.

Continuing west, beyond Episkopí, the old road soon divides, the main way descending steadily towards Yeoryióupolis (pp.239–40), a secondary route climbing through the village of Kournás (p.241) and then dropping steeply to the lake.

East by the coast road

Leaving Réthimnon to the **east**, you can strike almost immediately onto the new road, which runs fast, flat and dull along the coastal plain, or follow the old road, squeezed into the narrow gap between this and the sea. This way you'll pass through a string of village suburbs, connected now by an almost continuous string of hotel development for some 10km. At Stavroménos the old road cuts under the highway and heads inland; the new road continues to hug a featureless coastline, now with barely any development at all, past the odd rocky beach.

Pánormos

PÁNORMOS marks a distinct break (still more marked if you are coming the other way, suddenly to emerge on the flat): the end of the level ground and the start of a spectacular, swooping mountain drive which continues virtually all the way to Iráklion. Here, too, is the last of the large hotels for some time, curving round a headland above a small bay and beach.

The tiny village of Pánormos is just a short detour off the road, a pretty little place with a couple of bars and tavernas perched above the harbour and a small, sandy beach. Surprisingly, this is an ancient settlement (a miniscule river runs through to the sea) with the ruins of what was once a large sixth-century basilica, probably destroyed in the ninth-century Saracen invasion, and of a later Genoese castle. Unfortunately, there are also lots of new **rooms** places as well as the large hotel, and combined with the boat tours from Réthimnon this can mean that the place is swamped in midsummer. Out of season, though, it wouldn't be a bad place to stay for a few days. The *Taverna Restaurant* (☎0834/51-209; ②) and *Lucy's Pension* (☎0834/51-212; ①) are both decent places.

Balí

The next stop you might consider making is at **BALÍ**, a small resort set around a series of small coves. Here the road drops down briefly from the heights to a desolate patch of low ground behind a bay. There's a large garage (where the bus will drop you), opposite which a road runs around the bay towards the village. On foot, this last stretch is further than it looks – a couple of kilometres to the village, more to the best beach. What you see first, though, is a fair-sized scrabbly beach at the end of the bay: grey and stony, this often shelters a considerable collection of camper vans and tents. Sadly, it's no longer really worth the effort of walking any further: although the beaches are still spectacular, they're very much over-run, and Balí has become a package resort too popular for its own good. Only well out of season, when there are bound to be bargains given the number of rooms here, is it worth staying; then, you could try *Mira Mare* (☎0834/94-256; ③) which has a sea view.

Balí proper consists of three coves. The first has a pebbly beach and a couple of tavernas and rooms places: here, too, is the *Bali Beach Hotel* (☎0834/94-210; ⑥), the first and still much the most luxurious hotel. In the second cove is the original village, with most of the local stores as well as more hotels, rooms and tavernas. One side of this cove has been concreted to form a harbour (there are day-trips by boat from Réthimnon), on the other you can swim, though rarely with much space. The third cove is known as Paradise Beach, and though it's still much the best for swimming – with a patch of sand and, on either side, crags of rock with level places to sunbathe – it's too crowded and overlooked to really deserve the name any more. Just outside the cove, but still well sheltered within the larger bay, are a couple of rocks to dive from. It's a beautiful place to splash about, surrounded by mountains which seem to rise direct from the sea to impressive heights.

Beyond Balí
After Balí, the next access to the coast is at Ayía Pelayía, 25km further on (p.86). Nor is there much else to stop for: **SÍSES** has wonderful views from its perch beside the highway, and a few rooms, but little else. From the village a track with an appalling surface cuts up to the old road. Don't be deceived by maps which show some kind of way through above Balí – there is no other practicable route inland between Pánormos (from where there's a good road to Pérama) and Fódhele.

East on the mountain roads

Taking the old roads east, inland through the fringes of the Psilorítis range, there are a variety of alternate routes and a number of interesting detours off them. The old main road, through Dhamásta, has least to offer, though it's a pretty enough drive. Striking higher **into the mountains** is more rewarding. For a combination of relatively easy driving and interest, perhaps the best option is the road up through Garázo and Axós to **Anóyia**, though you can also reach Axós on an even higher road from Pérama.

Margarítes and Eleútherna

Whichever route you follow, you'll leave the coast at Stavroménos and head up through Viranepiskopí. The first potential detour comes some 5km further on, a right turn to **MARGARÍTES** and Archéa Eleútherna (formerly Prinés). Margarítes, 4km beyond the turnoff, has a long tradition of pottery manufacture and workshops are scattered throughout the village and along the steep main street where you can buy the results. Truth to tell, though, most of the output is fairly unsophisticated, but one of the most authentic places is the workshop of Nikos Kavgalakis on the village's southern edge. Jovial Nikos not only turns out pots, but also the the enormous Ali Baba jars similar to those found in the Minoan palaces and still used throughout agricultural Crete today. There are cafés at the top of the village, pleasant places to sit outside and rest awhile.

Ancient Eleúctherna

Beyond here the road climbs for 4km to the village of **ARCHÉA ELEÚTHERNA** where, opposite a fountain, a paved way on the right leads after 200m to a parking place with a taverna and a track to **ancient Eleúctherna**. The city that stood here in ancient times was one of the most important of eighth and seventh century BC Dorian Crete. When the Romans came in search of conquest in 67 BC it put up a stiff resistance, and later flourished as the seat of a Christian diocese. The Saracen invasions finished it off, however, and only recently has excavation of the site recommenced (by the University of Crete) after British archeologists packed up and left in 1929.

Imposingly situated on a ridge between two watercourses, the city was originally approached on a road cut from the rock, at the town end of which stood (and in large part still stands) a hefty **tower**. Apart from some fragments of the massive walls there are few other significant remains on the acropolis but the setting is tremendous and if you find the remnants of several pillared cisterns cut into the rock on the west side of the ridge, you may be able to spot the remains of the aqueduct which fed them. By following the continuation of the path running north through the site which descends below the acropolis and continues for 500m along the stream bed, you'll come to a magnificent **Hellenistic stone bridge**.

Recently, archeologists made a potentially very significant discovery here: traces of a human sacrifice made in front of the funeral pyre of some local magnate. It apparently dates from the late eighth century BC, about the same time that Homer was describing very similar sacrifices of Trojan prisoners in front of the funeral pyre of Achilles. The victim, who was bound hand and foot and had died in a ritual during which his throat was cut, may well have been expected to serve the dead man in the next world – also found in front of the pyre were sacrificed animals and offerings of perfume and food. Other cremations on the site (some 20 have been found, though only one human sacrifice) had offerings including gold, jewellery and fine pottery, as well as four tiny, superbly crafted ivory heads: among the best work of their time (c.600 BC) yet discovered anywhere. There's said to be a practicable walk from Eleúctherna to the monastery at Arkádhi, less than 5km away as the crow flies, but you'll have to check out the route locally. Otherwise you've little choice but to retrace your steps to the main road.

Pérama to Axós

PÉRAMA is a substantial place, an agricultural centre which also has a little light industry, and its businesslike main street is lined with banks, stores and cafés. The chief interest in this is the rarity value of seeing a town of such size in Crete that owes nothing whatever to tourism. Even if you do no more than drive through it's a refreshing sight, and you may well find yourself passing this way more than once if you take one of the local detours available.

The Melidhóni Cave

The most obvious of these is to **MELIDHÓNI**, a bare 5km from Pérama. The village itself is unremarkable, but a half-hour's walk (or a short drive, signed from the village) leads to a great **cave**, whose series of chambers are thick with stalactites and stalagmites. This was the legendary home of Talos, a bronze giant who protected the coasts of Crete by striding around the island thrice daily (or perhaps only 3 times a year) hurling rocks at unfriendly ships: the Argonauts were greeted thus when they approached the island. Far more infamously, however, the Melidhóni cave was also the setting for one of the most horrific atrocities in the struggle for Cretan independence. Here, in 1824, around three hundred local villagers took refuge, as they had often done before at time of war, in the face of an advancing army. This time, however, the Muslim commander demanded that they come out: when the Cretans refused, and shot two messengers sent to offer safe conduct, he attempted to force them out by blocking the mouth of the cave with stones, and cutting off the air supply. After several days of this, with the defenders opening new air passages every night, the troops changed their tactics, piling combustible materials in front of the cave and setting light to them. Everyone inside was asphyxiated*.

The bodies were left where they lay for the cave to become their tomb. Ten years later Robert Pashley became one of the first to enter since the tragedy, to find in places "the bones and skulls of the poor Christians so thickly scattered, that it is almost impossible to avoid crushing them as we pick our steps along". A shrine near the entrance to the cave today commemorates the dead.

Garázo and Axós

Back through Pérama, the main road wends along the valley of the Yeropótamos all the way to the turning for **GARÁZO**, a small village where hardly anyone seems to stop. If you do, you'll find that the simple roadside cafés are friendly and exceptionally good value.

AXÓS, especially if you arrive at lunchtime, makes a surprising contrast. Where the main road passes through, it is lined with weaving and embroidery for sale (mostly rather poor) and with tavernas crowded with tourists. This is largely because the village serves as a lunch stop for "Photo-Safari" day-trips from Iráklion and Réthimnon. If you catch it without the crowds, Axós is undeniably attractive; there's a small (and locked) frescoed church and the site of a post-Minoan settlement, also called Axós, barely accessible on a ridge above the village. The upper road from Pérama, via Livádá and Zonianá, emerges in Axós by the church.

Anóyia

The focus of this route is **ANÓYIA**, a small town perched beneath the highest peaks of the Psilorítis range. It is the obvious place from which to approach the Idean Cave and, for the committed, the summit of Psilorítis itself. The weather, refreshingly cool when the summer heat lower down is becoming oppressive, is one good reason to come, but most people are drawn by the proximity of the mountains or by a reputation for some of the best woven and

---

*This grisly event was far from unique – numerous other caves around the island have similar histories, although none claimed so many victims.

embroidered work in Crete. The last is greatly exaggerated but the town still makes a very pleasant break from the coast.

As you drive through, it seems that Anóyia has two quite distinct halves: from what appears to be the older, lower part, the road takes a broad loop around, to re-emerge in the modern looking *platía* of the upper town. In many ways this appearance is deceptive. A series of steep, sometimes stepped alleys connect the two directly, and however traditional the buildings may look, closer inspection shows that most are actually concrete. This reflects a tragic recent history – the village was one of those destroyed as reprisal for the abduction of General Kreipe (see p.201) and at the same time all the men who could be rounded up here were killed. The local handicrafts tradition is in part a reflection of this history, both a conscious attempt to revive the town and the result of bitter necessity with so large a proportion of the local men killed. At any rate it worked, for the place is thriving today, though there do still seem to be large numbers of elderly widows anxious to subject any visitor to their terrifyingly aggressive sales techniques.

The impression of an old and a new town persists even when you know it to be false. The upper half of the village has almost all the **accommodation** as well as the **bank** (no foreign exchange), **post office** (reluctant foreign exchange), police, most of the non-tourist stores and a large *platía* where the younger residents hang out. The more antique feel of the lower half is reinforced by the elderly men, baggy trousers tucked into their black boots, moustaches bristling, who sit at the *kafenia*, and by the black-clad women sitting outside their stores. In the square in the lower half of town stands a statue and next to it a wooden carving of Venizélos, arm in a sling – the carver's workshop is nearby, full of similar bizarre works. Walk the lanes between the two halves of town and there's a real country feel: empty houses and garages closed up with wire and used to stable livestock; goats grazing in vacant lots; and more workshop/homes where the craftswomen have set up showrooms in their front parlours.

Anóyia sees a lot of day-trippers, but most stay only an hour or so. Linger a while, or stay overnight, and it's surprisingly uncommercial. It shouldn't normally be hard to find a **room** in the upper half of town, where you'll see signs leading off all along the main street. The one drawback to staying is that there's hardly anywhere to **eat**: one taverna on the main road where it loops out of the lower village (*Prásini Foliá*, with a large open-air space for dancing which occasionally hosts "Cretan Evening" tours) and a *souvláki* place near the top of the town. Neither of these seems to serve anything other than the excellent barbecued lamb which is a local speciality, though the local cheese is also excellent.

Psilorítis and its caves

Heading for the mountains, a rough track leads the 13km from Anóyia to the **Nídha plateau** at the base of Mount Psilorítis. It's a steady climb most of the way, and a road travelled little except by the shepherds who seasonally pasture their sheep up here (and who nowadays travel back and forth by pick-up). Along the way you'll pass some of the stone huts – many of them ruinous – in which traditionally the sheep's milk yoghurt and cheese would be made. Somewhere near the highest point a track leads off to the **ski area**: an unlikely thought in summer, although it does see plenty of snow in season. Soon after, the small plateau and its bare summer pastures fan out below you, and the road drops to skirt around its western edge.

Zeus and the Idean Cave

At what is effectively the end of the road (shortly beyond, it peters out in a net of trails across the plateau), a modern **taverna** stands looking over the plain. Since this was the only place for miles which offered rooms or sustenance it seems both unfortunate and surprising that it should have been forced to close. But it has, and the rooms and kitchen are now used only by private climbing groups. Opposite the taverna, a short path leads up to the celebrated **Idean Cave** (*Idhéon Ándhron*), a rival of that on Mount Dhíkti (p.131) for the title of Zeus's birthplace. Although scholarly arguments rage over the exact identity of the caves in the legends of Zeus, and over the interpretation of the various versions of the legend, locals are in no doubt that the Idean Cave is the place where the god was brought up, suckled by wild animals.

Certainly this hole in the mountainside, which as Cretan caves go is not especially large or impressive, was associated from the earliest of times with the cult of Zeus, and at times ranked among the most important centres of pilgrimage in the Greek world. Pythagoras visited the cave, Plato set *The Laws* as a dialogue along the pilgrimage route here, and the finds made within indicate offerings brought from all over the eastern Mediterranean. Current excavations have revealed that the cave cult had a much longer history than this, too. First signs of occupation go back as far as 3000 BC, and though it may then have been a mere place of shelter, by the Minoan era it was already established as a shrine, maintaining this role until about 500 AD. Sadly for visitors, a major new dig is still going on inside, which means the whole cave is fenced off: there has even been a little railway constructed to carry all the rubble out. Unless you befriend an archeologist, you can do no more than stand outside and stare at the blank mouth.

To the summit

The taverna also marks the start of the way to the **summit of Psilorítis** (Mount Ida), at 2456m the highest mountain in Crete. Though it's not for the unwary or unfit, the climb should present few problems to experienced, equipped climbers. The route, which diverts from the path to the cave just beyond the small spring and chapel, is marked with red dots: a guide who knows the mountain would be useful, since it's not always obvious which is the main trail, but is by no means essential. Don't attempt it alone, however, as you could face a very long wait for help if you ran into trouble. If you do make the climb, it should be a seven-to-eight-hour return trip to the chapel at the summit, though watch out in spring for thick snow which will slow you down. It's wise to carry enough food, water and warm gear to be able to overnight in one of the shelters should the weather turn on you – in any event a night at the top, with the whole island laid out in the sunset and sunrise, is a wonderful experience.

For the first half-hour or so **the climb** trails south across the mountainside, a gradual ascent until you reach a gully where it starts in earnest. Head west here, away from the plain, on a rocky path up the left-hand side of the gully. After about an hour and a quarter of this you reach an open height with a stone shelter and good views back the way you came: do not follow the most obvious trail at this point, which leads only to one of the lesser peaks (Koussákas, 2209m), but follow the ridge *downhill* and south instead, unlikely as this may look. After barely fifteen minutes you reach a basin where several trails meet, and where there is spring water and stone huts for shelter. Turn right, northwest, and an obvious uphill trail will take you all the way to the summit, though it is only in the last twenty minutes that the peak itself becomes visible and the ground starts to fall away to reveal just how high you are. The summit itself is marked by another shelter and the chapel of **Tímios Stavrós** (a name by which the peak is sometimes known locally); nearby there's water in a cistern, which you are advised to boil or purify before drinking. When it's clear, the panoramas from the top make the climb well worthwhile. Usually, though, conditions are very cold and windy and the views are spoilt by cloud or heat haze.

Other routes: the Kamáres Cave

While the route outlined above is probably the easiest to follow without a guide, there are any number of **alternate routes** up and down.

From the west you can climb from virtually any of the Amári villages below the peak (especially Fourfourás, p.201), but although this is relatively straightforward in the sense that you can see the peak almost all the way, there are no real trails and you may run into difficulty with patches of thorny undergrowth or loose scree. **South**, Vorízia and Kamáres also make possible starting/finishing points. If you want to descend towards **KAMÁRES**, the trail divides in the basin mentioned above, about halfway from Nídha to the summit. It's not hard to follow, heading south from the basin, but is a good deal steeper and longer than anything outlined above: perhaps six hours down to Kamáres, seven to eight hours for the ascent. About halfway, there's a junction with a trail to the huge **Kamáres Cave**, in which the first great cache of the elaborate pottery known as Kamáres ware was found (it's now in the Iráklion Archeological Museum). From the cave you either backtrack to this trail to continue to the village or carry on east to another trail, equally steep.

If you're prepared to camp on the plateau (there's plenty of water but conditions can be very cold) or can prevail on the taverna to let you in, an even more attractive option is to tackle the peak in one day, and continue south next day **from the Nídha plateau**. This is a beautiful hike – at least, as long as the road they're attempting to blast through here is out of sight – and it's also a relatively easy one, four hours or so down to **VORÍZIA**, five or six to Kamáres. For either, track around to the southern edge of the plateau, where a gully (soon to become a considerable ravine) leads off. Large red arrows direct you towards Kamáres on the trail which passes east of the cave. For Vorízia, you follow the ravine for about an hour until a faint trail climbs out on the left (soon after this, the stream bed becomes impassable). Above the ravine there are fine views and a heady drop for another hour, when you must turn left (east) again. This is not obvious, but you should begin to see signs of life – goat trails and shepherds' huts. You cut past the top of a second, smaller ravine to a stone hut and then descend, zigzagging steeply, to a dirt road and Vorízia.

Vorízia and Kamáres both have **rooms and food** and at least one **bus** a day to Míres. Hitching to Míres should also be simple enough.

Across the island

Heading south across the island, towards Plakiás or Ayía Galíni, the road takes off from the very centre of Réthimnon, running along the side of the Public Gardens and then climbing rapidly above the town. Look back from the final bend and you have the city, its castle and harbour laid out like a map below you, but once the view has been blocked out, and you've passed the large service station which marks the end of the populated north coast, there's very little to stop for before the Libyan Sea. It's a scenic drive, though, on a good road.

Arméni Minoan cemetery

A little under 10km from Réthimnon, just before the village of **ARMÉNI**, a sign to the right points the way to a remarkable **Minoan cemetery** (officially Mon–Fri 9am–3pm, but there's often an attendant on hand at other times willing to show you around for a consideration). Important discoveries have been made here in over two hundred rock-cut tombs dating from the Late Minoan period, after the fall of the great palaces. Pleasantly sited today in a shady oak wood, most of the tombs are of the *dromos* (passage) and chamber type. One large tomb on the south side of the site which the guide will point out – giving him an excuse to hand out candles for the descent – has a spectacular *dromos* and finely cut chamber and may well have belonged to a royal personage. Some other tombs had only the *dromos* cut and work on them seems for some reason to have been abandoned. Many *larnakes* (clay coffins) and grave goods, including weapons, jewellery, vases and a rare helmet made from boar's tusks, found in the tombs are now on display in the archeological museums at Réthimnon and Iráklion. One mystery yet to be solved regarding the cemetery remains: the location of the no doubt sizeable settlement which provided this necropolis with its customers.

Onward routes

Another 10km takes you to the first of the turn-offs **towards Plakiás**: this one on a new road through Áyios Ioánnis and down the Kotsifoú gorge. Just by this turning there's a café/truck stop which is the best place to change buses if you are travelling between Ayía Galíni and Plakiás or vice versa (there's a timetable posted outside). There's also a good chance here of a lift with passing tourists or a local truck. Only a little further the alternative route to Plakiás takes off – through Koxaré and the Kourtaliótiko gorge. Either way, the drive is a pretty spectacular one.

Spíli

Sticking to the main route south, **SPÍLI** is 30km from Réthimnon: the one place on this road where you might spend some time for its own sake. The town doesn't look much as you drive through – although the mountainside which hovers over the houses is impressive – but if you get off the main road, into the alleys which stagger up towards the cliff, it is wonderfully attractive. A sharp curve in the road marks the centre of town, by a small *platía* with a broken statue. Just above there's a charming Venetian fountain, with a long row of lions' heads splashing cold water into a trough, and above this begins a steep mosaic of flowered balconies, cobbled lanes, shady archways and giant urns and chimney-pots. On occasion, Spíli can become quite crowded – many of the bus tours passing along the road make a brief stop here, usually for lunch – but between times and in the evenings it is quiet and rural. Stay overnight and you'll be woken early by the sounds of the farmyard and an agricultural community starting work.

Practicalities

There are numerous places offering **rooms** spread out along the main road – the flower-decked *Green Hotel* (☎0832/22-225; ③) at the north end of town is good, although not the oasis it once was since its discovery by organized tour groups. Just behind it, however, is a delightful smaller (and cheaper) pension, *Heracles* (☎0832/22-411; ①) with spotless balcony rooms with bath. Right on the corner by the fountain, a new establishment offers comfortable but (during the day anyway) rather noisy accommodation.

The few places to **eat** (local yoghurt and honey are excellent) and most of the local stores and businesses cluster close around the central square: there's a post office and bank on the main road, and a metered phone in the souvenir/newspaper store on the corner by the fountain.

Walks around Spíli

If you can stay longer there are some challenging **hikes** which start in Spíli across to Yerakári in the Amári valley for example. However, the new road – spectacular drive though it is – linking the two places makes this seem less of an achievement than it once was.

A less taxing four-kilometre hike would bring you to the pretty village of **LAMPINÍ**, to the northwest, and its domed Byzantine **church of the Panayía**, sited above a valley. This was the scene of a terrible massacre in 1827 (marked by a plaque) when the Turks locked the congregation inside the church before setting fire to it. All perished and only fragments of the fourteenth- and fifteenth-century frescoes survived the blaze. To get there follow the main road back to Mixórrouma, turning right in the village on a road signed for Karínes.

To extend this walk, you could continue 5km beyond Lampiní to **KARÍNES** itself, another attractive village with a friendly *kafenion* in the midst of gently terraced hills. A further 7km brings you to Patsós with a turn on the left 1km before it (and a 10-min walk) to the Áyios Andónios **cave**, a Minoan and later Dorian and Roman sanctuary. From Patsós, Thrónos (see facing page), 9km away and reached via the hamlets of Pandánasa, Apostoli and Kalóyeros, becomes a realistic end destination with the possibility of a bed and a meal (but ring ahead to make sure in high season).

Heading in the other direction, a **walk** encompassing Mourné, Fratí and Ayía Pelayía takes in some superb scenery with views of the Psilorítis and Lefká Óri ranges besides four ancient churches (fine frescoes at the last one) and offers opportunities for birdspotting. Take the road from Spíli to Mourné, beyond which a paved road – along which you'll see the churches – heads southwest in the direction of Fratí, approached by a stiff descent. From here there's an easy route above the Kissanos river valley to Ayía Pelayía and the main road back to Spíli.

Beyond Spíli, the road towards Ayía Galíni follows a long valley between Mount Kédhros and the lesser summit of Sidhérotas. Apart from the odd patch of extremely bad road surface it holds few excitements.

The Amári valley

An alternative route south from Réthimnon, and a far less travelled one, is the road which turns off on the eastern fringe of town to run via the **Amári valley**. Amári is one of those areas, like Sfakiá, which features large in almost everything written about Crete – and especially in tales of wartime resistance – yet which is hardly explored at all by modern visitors. Shadowed by the vast profile of Psilorítis, its way of life survives barely altered by the changes of the last twenty, or even fifty years. Throughout the valley, isolated hamlets subsist on the ubiquitous olive, with the occasional luxury of an orchard of cherries (especially around Yerakári), pears or figs, and throughout there are a startling number of richly frescoed churches. It's an environment conducive to slow exploration, with a climate noticeably cooler than the coast: in midsummer the trees, flowers and general greenery here make a stunning contrast to the rest of the island.

Three **buses** a day run from Réthimnon to the crossroads at Ayía Fotiní: onwards from there the service is sporadic to non-existent. It's best to explore on foot – in which case a water bottle and the best map you can find are essential equipment – but the main roads are fine if you have your own transport. As for staying in the valley, there are officially **rooms** only in Thrónos and Yerakári, but don't let this deter you from asking in other villages: villagers are often only too happy to have a paying guest for a night or two, and traditional hospitality here has not yet been killed by abuse.

Whenever you come, but in July or August especially, you may be lucky enough to stumble on a village **festival** in honour of the local saint, the harvest or some obscure historical event. They're worth going out of your way for, so keep an eye out for notices pasted to *kafenion* windows with details of when and whereabouts. Beginning in a distorted cacophony of overamplified Cretan music, the celebrations continue until the participants are sufficiently gorged on roast lamb and enlivened by wine to get down to the real business: the dancing. Cretan dancing at an event such as this is an extraordinary display of athleticism and, as often as as not, endurance. If the party really gets off the ground locals will dig out their old guns and rattle off a few rounds into the sky to celebrate. It should prove an experience not swiftly forgotten.

The eastern slope

There are two roads through the Amári valley, one following the eastern side and clinging to the flanks of the Psilorítis range, the other tracing the edge of the lesser Kédhros range on the western side. Both are scenically spectacular, but the **eastern route** probably has the edge in terms of beauty and places of interest.

Thrónos

Going this way, the first of the real Amári villages is **THRÓNOS**, situated just off the main road at the head of the valley beneath the site of ancient Sybritos. Like so many others here, Thrónos seems lost in the past, with its beautifully frescoed **church** – Panayía – and majestic views across the valley and up to the mountains. There are more ancient remains, too. In the Byzantine era this was the seat of a bishop (hence *Thrónos*, throne) and these early Christian days are marked by the remains of a mosaic which spreads under the village church and oozes beyond its walls, with traces both inside and out. The new building, in fact, is only about a quarter the size of the original church, whose floorplan, guarded by a low rail, can be clearly seen. The elderly keeper will usually appear with the key as soon as you start to take an interest in the church; if not, ask the local kids, who will no doubt be watching your every move, or in the café/store alongside. On the hill above the village are still earlier remains of the acropolis.

If you want to stay, simply follow the crude "Rent Rooms" signs through the ramshackle streets to *Rooms Aravanes* (☎0833/22-760; ①), a modern concrete structure with pink cinderblock balconies. The building is an aberration, but once inside it's out of sight and the balconies have the best view in the village. The rooms are pleasant and there's a taverna on the ground floor, which is just as well for the only other place in the village offering food is a basic *kafepantopolíon*. The *Aravanes*'s yard outside is also pressed into use for periodic big *bouzouki* get-togethers, with dozens of tables put out and fires lit for barbecueing; keep an eye out for the posters, as these are well worth attending.

From Thrónos a relatively easy path leads north through the foothills in a couple of hours to the Moní Arkádhi (p.187) where you can pick up buses again; but get directions, as the way divides more than once. South, a paved road runs back into the main valley via Kalóyeros, also an extremely easy stroll from Thrónos. Fifteen minutes' walk beyond this village, a narrow path on the left leads uphill to the small stone church of **Áyios Ioánnis Theológos**, whose fine frescoes date from 1347 – ask about the key in the village on the way.

The Moní Asomáton and Amári

From here, back on the main road, the **Moní Asomáton** is only 1km further. The buildings are Venetian, though the monastery itself is older; having survived centuries of resistance and revolution it finally became an agricultural school in 1931. It's not open to the public, but no one seems to mind if you wander in and look over the lovely old buildings, with a weed-infested central courtyard containing a church, a fountain, two retired old buses and – at the rear – a prodigious plane tree.

Outside and beside a friendly taverna, a line of fir and eucalyptus marks the beginning of the five-kilometre paved road to the village of **AMÁRI**, the chief village of the valley. This is another beautiful drive or manageable walk, although the second half climbs quite steeply up the hill of Samítos which rises right in the middle of the valley. On the way you pass through two picturesque villages, Monastiráki and Opsigiás, but Amári itself outdoes them: it looks like nothing so much as a perfect Tuscan hill village – note the steeply sloping roofs to cope with the winter snows and the chimneys for wood fires. There's really nothing to do here – even the couple of *kafenia* seem to close for a siesta in the afternoon – but there are scintillating views across to Psilorítis, which seems really close here. For a bird's-eye view, climb the Venetian clock tower which dominates the narrow alleyways (the door is always open). It's not immediately obvious how to get here, but keep climbing and circling the hill and you'll make it eventually. Just outside town, the church of **Ayía Ánna**, reached down a track opposite the police station, has some extremely faded frescoes – and well they might be: dated 1225, they have a fair claim to being the oldest on Crete. As well as a police station, Amári also boasts an OTE and post office, and there's a daily bus at about 4pm for Réthimnon.

Fourfourás and beyond

Continuing south to **FOURFOURÁS** and beyond, there are more lovely villages, with the peak of Psilorítis now almost directly above and the softer lines of Mount Kédhros behind the Samítos hill on the other side. Fourfourás is a traditional place to begin the climb of Psilorítis, although no one seems to tackle the peak from here any more (Anóyia and Kamáres are more convenient); it is also the trailhead of some arduous hikes to the lesser peaks. At **NÍTHAVRIS** the road divides. South, with the coast coming into view, you can head down to Ayía Galíni (see over) or follow the flank of the mountains around through Kamáres (p.196). Turn off west and you can curve round to complete a circle of the valley through the villages on the lower slopes of **Kédhros** (1777m).

The western side

The villages on **the western side** of the valley look little different, but in fact they are almost entirely modern – rebuilt after their deliberate destruction during World War II. George Psychoundákis watched the outrage from a cave on the slopes of Psilorítis:

> *I stayed there two or three days before leaving, watching the Kedros villages burning ceaselessly on the other side of the deep valley. Every now and then we heard the sound of explosions. The Germans went there in the small hours of the twenty-second of August and the burning went on for an entire week. The villages we could see from there and which were given over to the flames were: Yerakari, Kardaki, Gourgouthoi, Vrysses, Smiles, Dryes and Ano-Meros. First they emptied every single house, transporting all the loot to Retimo, then they set fire to them, and finally, to complete the ruin, they piled dynamite into every remaining corner, and blew them sky high. The village schools met the same fate, also the churches and the wells, and at Ano-Meros they even blew up the cemetery. They shot all the men they could find.*

Officially these atrocities – other villages around Psilorítis, from Anóyia to Kamáres, were also burned – were in reprisal for the kidnap of General Kreipe, four months earlier. But Psychoundákis, for one, believed that it was a more general revenge, intended to destroy any effective resistance in the closing months of the German occupation. Today the villages of Méronas, Elénes, Yerakári, Kardháki and Vrísses mark the southward progress of the German troops with etched stone **memorials** dated one day apart. Áno Méros has a striking war memorial of a woman wielding a hammer.

Even here, a number of frescoed **churches** survived the terror. Between Vrísses and Kardháki one such lies off to the right of the road, lying low in a field of grain and apparently forgotten. Push the door aside, however, and the gloom gradually reveals beautiful Byzantine paintings around the altar.

Yerakári

YERAKÁRI is a bigger, more modern and prosperous-looking village than most, with several places to stop for a drink or some food, and **rooms** (①) available above an unnamed taverna. The bubbling Kiría Despina is the proprietor here and her rooms seem to be only a sideline, for the taverna's kitchen is a veritable pickling and bottling factory for the fruits of the region, especially cherries – for which the village is famous – and which she spreads out to dry on every available neighbour's rooftop during the picking season. Her cheeses, *thimarísio* (thyme honey) and pickled cherries are all for sale and recommended, although the cherry brandy is probably an acquired taste.

With transport you have the option of taking the spectacular **new road** heading west from Yerakári to Spíli with tremendous **views** along a valley between the heights of Kédhros and Sorós towards the distant and magnificent Lefká Óri. The way to it lies up the hill at the end of Yerakári's main street. Starting out unpromisingly as a rough dirt track, almost before you know it you're bowling along a superb asphalted highway thoroughly out of synch with what has gone before.

Áyios Ioánnis Theológos
Just to the south of the Yerakári you'll pass the unusual **Monastery of Áyios Ioánnis Theológos**, with a spreading oak tree in front providing shade for a tapped spring. There are thirteenth-century frescoes in an exposed side chapel, and slightly later ones as you enter the church, all very battered and exposed to the elements. Traces of the medieval stone road or track on which the church was originally aligned can still be made out behind it.

Méronas
Continuing along the road north to complete the Amári valley's western flank, beyond Mesonísia and Elénes comes **MÉRONAS** where, to the right of the road, a soft pink Venetian-style **church of the Panayía** shelters frescoes from the fourteenth century; you'll need to ask for the key across the road. Again, it takes time to adjust your eyes to take in the painstaking detail of the artwork, darkened with age as it is; a torch would allow you to see a great deal more than the candles or nightlights which usually provide illumination.

Ayía Galíni

Twenty years ago **AYÍA GALÍNI** must have been an idyllic spot: an isolated fishing community of some five hundred souls nestling in a convenient fold of the mountains which dominate this part of the south coast. The village itself is barely a hundred years old, its inhabitants having moved down from the mountain villages of Mélambes and Saktoúria as the traditional threat of piracy along the coast receded. Catch it out of season and the streets of white houses, crowded in on three sides by mountains and opening below to a small, busy harbour, can still appeal. But this is a face which is increasingly hard to find. Packed throughout the season with package tourists, and confined by the limits of its narrow situation, the village's old houses are rapidly being squeezed out by ever larger apartment buildings and concrete hotels. Since the beach was never up to much anyway, there's little reason to stay here long in summer. The lack of a decent beach is a shame, for otherwise there's something appealing about Ayía Galíni's relatively staid and respectable brand of tourism. It's a nicer place than it looks, or than you'd expect from first impressions; largely because despite the development the people have stayed friendly and the atmosphere Cretan.

Practicalities

Buses to Ayía Galíni terminate at the bus station by the church, near the top of the village proper. It's a handy spot to get your bearings since few of the streets are named and such names as there are seem rarely used. The nucleus of the place is built around three streets which run down to the harbour. The first of these (technically Venizélou) is a continuation of the main road into town: along it you'll find post office, bakery, doctor and a couple of car rental places. In the narrow street parallel to this to the east is the garage and stores; the next street along is packed with tavernas (and known locally as "Taverna Street"). All of this falls within an extremely small area where nothing is more than a couple of minutes' walk away.

Many places near and including the post office (below the bus station towards the harbour) **change money**; when the latter is closed try the *Opsis Tourist Office* (☎0832/91-115) opposite, which gives bank rates. *Opsis* is also a good place for **bike and car rental** or there's the equally reliable *Soulia Car Rental* (☎0832/91-347) a little nearer the harbour, and *Biggis Bikes*, more or less opposite the bus stop. Travel information and tickets are available from *Candia Tours* on Taverna Street. The OTE has a phone cabin on the harbour (daily 8am–2pm & 4–10pm); **telephones** can also be found in *Minos* store on Taverna Street (near the top) and at the nearby kiosk.

Accommodation

Rooms are equally tightly packed, and there are so many that you can usually find something – though for much of July and August all but a handful are pre-booked by tour operators. Prices are very closely linked to demand: for most of the summer both are high, but away from peak seasons you may get an exceptional bargain.

Probably the best place to start looking is at the top of the town, either walking down to the left from the main road, or up Taverna Street and round to the right. The latter is the best way to the friendly *Hotel Minos* (☎0832/91-292; ①), an excellent-value place with sea-view rooms, all with bath, and open all year. Also here is *Rent Rooms Acropol* (☎0832/91-273; ①), a very basic place with an unbeatable location right on the edge of the cliff. The daughter of the people here runs the *Hotel Acropolis* (☎0832/91-234; ①), not far away on the main road, which is much more likely to have a room but also less well positioned. Between these you'll pass dozens of other possibilities – *Rooms Candia* (☎0832/91-203; ①) and *Rooms Dedalos* (☎0832/91-214; ①) are promising – and you'll need to ask at each one. Check the room before taking it as some of these places have seen better days. A number of newer places are in the streets on the other side of the main road, west of where the bus drops you.

There's also a **campsite**, *Camping Agia Galini*, to the east near the mouth of the river, reached either by a dirt track which takes off from the main road about 1km outside the village, or by walking out along the beach. The campsite itself may be full in midsummer, in which case, despite official discouragement, there's rarely any shortage of people sleeping on the beach.

Eating

One major and undeniable benefit which the crowds have brought to Ayía Galini is a vast range of **food and drink**: much of it excellent and, thanks to the competition, not overpriced. The bulk of the tavernas are located, surprisingly enough, along Taverna Street, which in the evening is choked with pedestrian traffic. There are plenty of good places here with tables spilling out into the street. Good value for a great setting is the *Restaurant Onar*, overlooking the harbour from a rooftop at the bottom of the street. Near here, *Madame Ordans* is another splendid rooftop place with a similar view.

Other places which are not on Taverna Street, and hence less easy to find, include *Horiatis Taverna* opposite the bus stop, quiet and out of the way, and *Stelios Café*, on the square below this on the main road, where they have drinks and breakfasts and occasionally serve freshly made *loukoumadhes*. Among the indifferent and overpriced harbourside places *Taverna Rockas*, at the western end and facing the OTE kiosk, serves the usual standards at reasonable prices.

Drinking and nightlife

There are plenty of **bars and discos** where you can carry on after you've eaten, mostly around the bottom of Taverna Street and near the harbour. *Zorba's*, where dancing starts after midnight, is a long-established favourite and *Whispers*, at the foot of Taverna Street, is another option. Just opposite, *Juke Box* is currently the resort's liveliest disco.

Ayía Galíni also has one of the island's rarities: a genuine **jazz bar**. *Jazz 'n Jazz* (up a flight of steps off Taverna Street – ask any local for directions) is the creation of jazz aficionado Costa Spanos whose philosophy is proclaimed on a sign outside: "If you don't like jazz, don't come in." In a cellar stuffed with jazz memorabilia the trilby-hatted Costas serves up drinks behind the bar to the cool sounds of Miles, Dizzy, Charlie et al. He's even got pool tables in the back and sometimes there's live stuff, too.

Beaches and day-trips

The **beach** at Ayía Galíni is astonishingly small when you consider the number of people who expect to use it. It's not even very sandy or attractive – once the few patches of soft sand have been claimed you have to rent a chair if you hope to lounge in any comfort. It lies to the east of the village, reached by a narrow path that tracks around the cliff from the harbour front, or by one that descends from the top of the town (or you can drive round and park by *Camping Agia Galini*). Walking round by the cliffs, you'll pass caves which in Worlds War II served as gun emplacements. You can get food and drink at a number of places immediately behind the beach.

Further afield **to the west** are some much better patches of sand. **Boats** from the harbour (details from any travel agent, or get your tickets when boarding) make daily day-trips to the beaches of Áyios Yióryios and Áyios Pávlos (3000dr per person) as well as to the Paximádia islands 12km offshore, which have wonderful fine sand beaches but little shade, making a sun umbrella a must.

Áyios Yióryios is also fairly easily reached on foot: take the main road up past the bus station and at the crown of the first bend follow a left turn towards a group of apartments. Just beyond these, cross a dry river bed and head up the hillside on a well-worn path marked with splashes of red paint. The beach is almost two hours away, a shingly cove with two tavernas, one of which, *Nikos*, has rooms (②); there are a couple of other, less attractive coves along the way.

Áyios Pávlos is even further, but also much more attractive, with some striking rock formations around a sheltered bay, and excellent snorkelling. In addition to the people arriving by boat from Ayía Galíni, Áyios Pávlos has now attracted a colony of New Age yoga practitioners who fly in stressed-out executives for two weeks of muscle stretching at their centre, the *Practice Place*. The boat is the easiest way to get here, but you can also drive via Saktóuria, with the final 6km on a very rough, unsurfaced road. The quicker route is to take the main road towards Spíli out of town and then turn left (signed) after about 12km, but the old road via Mélambes has been newly sealed and is an excitingly winding route with great views. Once there, you'll find two taverna/rooms places, *Áyios Pavlos* (②), immediately above the beach, and the *Hotel Livikon* (①), a little way up the road, as well as a couple of modest apartment developments.

Plakiás and around

Thirty kilometres west, Plakiás is beginning to rival Ayía Galíni as a south-coast resort. Commercialized as it is, though, it still has a very different feel: accommodation is simpler, less of it is booked in advance, and the nearby beaches are infinitely better. The people who stay here are on the whole much younger, too.

There are two main approaches to the area, both off the Réthimnon to Ayía Galíni road. The first is on a newly surfaced road down through the **Kotsifóu gorge**; the second, just a few kilometres further on, via the even more impressive **Kourtaliótiko gorge**. Either way, it's worth pulling over in the gorge to take time to appreciate the scenery and the wildlife (from snakes by the water to birds of prey soaring above). On the first route the gorge eventually opens out to leave you on the main coast road west of Plakiás: turn right for Sellía, left for Mírthios and Plakiás. On the second there are parking places about halfway through the gorge and steps leading down to the chapel of Áyios Nikólaos near the bottom. Further on you have a choice of turning right for Lefkóyia and Plakiás or continuing to follow the course of the stream all the way down to Préveli.

Mírthios

MÍRTHIOS hangs high above the Bay of Plakiás, with wonderful views down over it. It's a small village but, thanks to a large and friendly **youth hostel** (☎0832/31-202; ①), one which sees a fair number of young travellers. The hostel is hard to miss, lying just above the road in the very centre of the village with a fantastic view that any five-star hotel would envy. Facilities are pretty basic (though you can cook), but it's a popular meeting place and a good source of local information; if you want more luxury, several other places offer **rooms**. Along the road opposite the hostel are a few tavernas with terraces hanging over the hillside, and a general store. *Plateia Taverna*, right under the youth hostel, is particularly friendly and recommended.

There's a post office for changing money, but for other facilities you have to go down to Plakiás (see over), about twenty minutes' steep downhill walk on a path which sets off from the *platía*/car parking space opposite the hostel. The long walks to the beach (and much longer climbs back) are the chief disadvantage of staying here, but you are rewarded with considerably lower prices and friendlier atmosphere – locals still just about outnumber visitors. And, of course, if you're a keen walker it's heaven: ask at the youth hostel about some of the more substantial hikes, to almost entirely deserted coves to the west, or up into some of the gorges. The Plakiás bus usually comes up to Mírthios after it has dropped most of the passengers, but check with the driver. You may get left by the junction, about ten minutes' walk away, on the way in.

Plakiás

PLAKIÁS itself is growing all the time, and it's no longer the unspoilt village all too many people arrive here expecting. Even so, it's still some way from the really big league, and if it's not that attractive in itself it does make a good base for the beautiful countryside and excellent beaches all around. The road comes in from the east, behind the beach, and heads straight into the heart of things along the harbour front. There's basically just a single street that runs inland, rapidly deteriorating into paths which wind up towards Selliá and Mírthios; otherwise everything is strung out in a line facing the sea or in tiny new streets, no more than three or four houses long, built off the main road. The coast road very rapidly becomes an extremely rough track west of the last houses, eventually ending altogether at Souda Beach after 3km or so.

There are relatively few facilities in Plakiás, but there's at least one of every-thing you could need. A **post office** van is parked by the harbour, and although there's no bank you can **change money** here or at many of the travel agents (try *Creta Tours* on the seafront) or supermarkets. Also right in the centre are a couple of **bike rental** places (like *Motoplakias*; ☎0832/31-400) and numerous **travel agencies** (*Plakias Tours* also rents cars) offering boat trips to Souda Beach, Préveli and even Loutró. There's a **launderette** (Mon–Sat 10am–1.30pm & 5.30–9pm) at the western edge of town near *Julia's Place*. Some of the tackiest souvenirs in all Crete can be bought at the *Forum* **supermarket**, in the new development on the road in; it also sells books, sunscreen and some food.

Accommodation

There are loads of new hotels and **rooms** in Plakiás. Indeed there's little else, but even so you may have difficulty finding a vacancy in high season. As ever, it's a question of wandering around and asking everywhere: those places up the back-streets lack the sea views but are quieter and usually the last to fill.

Among the better possibilities are *Pension Asteria* (①) and *Garzonieres* (①), both up the main inland street near the *Secret Nest Taverna* (☎0832/31-235; ②) which also has a few rooms. East of here, at the end of the street which runs inland from *Candia Tours*, *Rooms Nefeli* (②) is a friendly new place with well-equipped rooms, including fridges. The slightly more expensive *Hotel Livikon* (☎0832/31-216; ②) is right by where the buses stop along the seafront and can be noisy. This is also the problem with rear-facing rooms at *Christos Taverna* (☎0832/31-472; ①), at the western end of the seafront, although the balcony front rooms above the sea are fine. Across the road, *Stefanakis Rooms* (☎0832/31-066; ②) also has balconies, is slightly less expensive and offers discounts out of season. The more luxurious *Hotel Lamon* (☎0832/31-279; ②), at the other end of the seafront, is less pricey than it looks and in addition to balcony rooms with sea views in its main building, has cheaper rooms in a building behind. Another pleasant place near the youth hostel (see facing page) is *Pension Afroditi* (☎0832/31-266; ②), in a gleaming white building with spotless rooms and lots of cascading bougainvillea.

Various other peaceful places can be found off the road before you really arrive in town: look for the signs to *Panorama* and *Finikas* (both ①), each a five-minute walk or so from the centre. In the other direction new places are starting to open along the coastal track to the west of town, and if you have a vehicle it's worth driving through to check these out. *Geronimos* taverna/rooms (②) is set some way above the road, while even further out near Souda Beach (see "Beaches" below) the modern *Hotel Phoenix* (☎0832/31-331; ③) has good-value rooms with breakfast included.

The relaxed **youth hostel** (☎0832/31-560; ①) has moved to the rear of the town (follow the signs from the road heading inland next to *Candia Tours*) where its buildings are surrounded by an olive grove. There's also a **campsite**, *Camping Apollonia*, on the right as you enter the town, which although small and cramped has good facilities and a pool. Wherever you stay, be warned that Plakiás is periodically plagued with **mosquitos**: the pyrethrin coils or electric devices sold locally are the most effective deterrent.

Eating and drinking

Right on the front at the centre of town is a little row of **tavernas** and bars with tables right out by the water, none of them terribly cheap (in fact food is generally costly here by Cretan standards). *Sofia's* here is just about the longest-established place in town, serving huge portions of reasonably good food. *Gorgona* next door is very similar; *Christos*, a few doors down, is slightly cheaper, with a pleasant tree-shaded terrace and usually at least one vegetarian dish. Back towards the bridge at the entrance to the town, *Zorba's* serves pizzas and pasta as well as the usual staples (and a huge chef's salad); on the other side of the bridge, set down a bit, *Lysseos* strives for a more romantic atmosphere. The ambience and food seem rather more authentically Cretan at another cluster of places round the corner from *Christos*, facing west along the shore: *Apanemo* next door to the *On the Rocks* bar, *Kedros*, *Glaros* and *Taverna Sunset* each have their devotees. On the way here you pass *Julia's Place*, English-run with a wide range of dishes, including vegetarian and curries – owner John Heath claims it's the only "balti" house in Crete. You might want to share your chapatis with a bunch of quarrelsome geese which live in the cove just opposite. Finally, behind the seafront the *Secret Nest Taverna* has fish dishes and *Nikos Souvlaki*, up the street behind *Candia Tours*, dishes out the cheapest meals in town often with some impromptu *bouzoúkia* thrown in as well.

The **bars** don't take much finding, since the music will lead you there. Most are lined up on the waterfront, keeping people who stay here awake. Real late-nighters can move on to the fancy *Hexagon Club*, on the seafront, or to the far less pretentious *Meltemi* disco, in a wooden hut out near *Camping Apollonia*. Things don't start to liven up here till midnight or so.

Beaches

Getting to the **beach** need involve no more than a two-minute walk. The town is set at the western end of the bay, and east of the paved harbour grey sand curves around in an unbroken line to the headland 1km or more away. Unfortunately this beach is not as good close up as it appears from a distance. The long open sweep of the bay means it can be exposed and windy, and the strong summer **winds** do seem to affect Plakiás more than other places along this coast. There's plenty of space – especially towards the far end where there's a large hotel and a beach bar – but you'll find much better sands beyond the headland at Damnóni (over), or to the west at Souda Beach.

Souda Beach is just over half an hour's walk west of town, past signs of encroaching development, and there are places to stop for a swim along the way. The sand is grey and coarse, but there's plenty of room and the water at the far end is reasonably sheltered. Above the very end of the beach, the *Galini* taverna enjoys a lovely position in a miniature palm grove.

Damnóni and Lefkóyia

Just to the east of Plakiás Bay, beyond a headland riddled with caves and wartime bunkers and gun emplacements, lie some of the most tempting beaches in central Crete, albeit ones which are already a very poorly kept secret. Three splashes of yellow sand, divided by rocky promontories, go by the general name of **Damnóni**. To get there on foot, follow the main road east and turn right just after the "Welcome to Plakiás" sign, where a track leads through the olive groves. After a while you'll see the beach below you and a path which runs down to it – about thirty minutes in all. Alternatively, but slightly longer, you can walk right to the end of the beach, past the big hotel, and on over the headland. Driving, you have to go much further round: follow the road towards Lefkóyia and turn down at the sign for Damnóni or, much further on, for Amoúdhi.

Damnóni Beach itself is the first you reach, and the only one that has so far really seen the beginning of the development: work on a big new hotel, the *Minoan Prince*, going up on the heights behind, is currently stalled whilst the western half of the beach has been colonized by a German-owned holiday village and piles of concrete boxes are now stacked up the hill overlooking what was once a beautiful bay. On the road in, the original rooms place here, *Pension Sokrates* (☎0832/31-480; ②) is still going and surrounded by a (diminishing) oasis of greenery. Whether you want to make use of its undeniably pleasant rooms, studios and more expensive apartments will depend on your attitude to the concrete invasion. There are still two **tavernas** on the beach, a wonderfully long strip of yellow sand and super-clear water. The *Taverna Damnoni*, fronting the beach, always seems very unfriendly; they have some particularly dank rooms to rent but will generally let you camp, which is more pleasant, although for how much longer is doubtful. The *Taverna Akti*, just behind, is a better bet for food and service.

At the far eastern end of Damnóni Beach you'll still find a few people who've dispensed with their clothes, and the little cove which shelters the middle of the three beaches (a scramble over the rocks, or there's a just-passable track) is entirely nudist. This little enclave can get very crowded, and at times looks like an illustration from *Health and Efficiency* magazine – blow-up beach balls and all – but it's a good-humoured crowd and, exceptionally, there are usually quite a few Greek naturists, too. Again, the water is beautiful and there are caves at the back of the beach (around which people camp) and rocks to dive from. There's some great snorkelling to be had around these rocks with their caves and passages. Continuing over the rocks you pass another tiny pocket of sand (also nudist) before **Amoúdhi Beach**, where there's a rather more sedate atmosphere and another taverna (very friendly, with much better rooms for rent).

If lying on beaches was your only plan, you'd have less far to walk, and probably spend less, staying in the village of **LEFKÓYIA** rather than Plakiás. Lefkóyia is barely twenty minutes' walk from Amoúdhi and has a couple of supermarkets, four or five pleasant rooms places, and a couple of tavernas (try *Stelios*) by the main road: its chief disadvantage is that it is not itself on the coast, and that it has no other facilities at all. For the people who stay here, these are also its chief advantages. Don't, incidentally, try to walk to the *Beach Hotel* signposted from the village – it is an extremely long way.

Moní Préveli and "Palm Beach"

Some 6km southeast of Lefkóyia the celebrated **Monastery of Préveli** (daily 8am–1pm & 3–7pm; 200dr) perches high above the sea. Its fame was capped in World War II when the monks provided shelter for Allied troops stranded on the island after the Battle of Crete, feeding the soldiers and organizing them into groups to be taken off nearby beaches by submarine. There's a monument commemorating the evacuations and alongside the icons in the church a number of offerings from grateful individuals and governments. The church also houses a cross said to contain a fragment of the True Cross; there's a small museum with other relics and religious vestments; and a fountain in the courtyard with the Greek inscription "Wash your sins, not only your face". There are also fine views out to sea towards the distant and chunky looking Paximádia islands which have lent their name to the tooth-cracking lumps of twice-baked bread served up with *mezédhes* in the island's *kafenions*.

The road to Préveli turns off the main road between Lefkóyia and Asómatos, now a paved surface which descends into the fertile valley of the River Megapótamos – unusually for Crete flowing throughout the year – before it eventually climbs towards the monastery. A couple of kilometres before the Préveli monastery you pass the ruinous **Monastery of Áyios Ioánnis** (called Kato, or lower, Préveli) the site of the original sixteenth-century monastery. It was used by the community prior to the Abbot Préveli's decision during the following century to seek out the greater safety of the monastery's present site. Torched by the Turks in the last century and long abandoned, only the church now stands complete amid the broken walls, cattle mangers and derelict dwellings once used by the monks. Nevertheless it's an atmospheric place to wander around: the church is open and retains its wooden *ikonostásis*, whilst nearby is a beautiful courtyard with a sweet vine trellis still providing plenty of shade.

Palm Beach

Earlier still you'll have passed an ancient-looking bridge (actually a nineteenth-century copy of a Venetian original), where a sign indicates a left turn to a taverna and Palm Beach. Almost immediately you turn right, shortly crossing another cobbled Venetian bridge, beyond which the track leads eventually (after perhaps 20 minutes' tortuous, rough driving) to *Amudi* rooms/taverna (②), one of two on a not terribly attractive beach alongside Palm Beach. From here it's a ten-minute scramble around the cliff, a narrow, slippery path for which you need decent shoes and at least one hand free to hold on with – though once you've managed the first bit it gets a lot easier. Alternatively, you can head down the cliffs from Préveli, which is even tougher: a track (barely driveable, or a 15-min walk) takes off about 1km before the monastery, and at the end a marked path clambers steeply down over the rocks, for about half an hour. If you don't feel confident of climbing, the boat will get you here with a great deal less fuss.

Sadly, **Palm Beach** is no longer worth all this effort – at least not if you're here in the middle of the season. It still looks beautiful – a sand-filled cove right at the end of the Kourtaliótiko gorge, where a freshwater estuary feeds a little oasis complete with palm grove and cluster of oleanders – but too many visitors have ruined it. On any given day you may have three or more day-trip boats, plus people who've walked in and a sizeable community of campers. The worst problem is that there's no toilet for any of them, so almost every sheltered corner stinks, and despite attempts to dispose of it there are also vast piles of accumulated rubbish, mostly plastic water bottles. If you do come (and at the beginning of the season it's still lovely), take all your rubbish away with you. Behind the beach, you can walk up the palm-lined riverbanks or paddle through the icy water upstream. Lots of people camp along the banks, a lovely setting, but again they have no way of disposing of their rubbish and sewage. Further upstream, before the gorge becomes too steep to follow, are a couple of deep pools nice to swim in. On the west edge of the beach, a small bar sells drinks and a few basic provisions, mostly tinned. A strange thought as you lie on the crowded sands here is that it was from here, forty years ago, that many of the soldiers who sought refuge at the monastery were eventually evacuated by submarine.

West of Plakiás: Sellía and Rodhákino

Heading west from Plakiás, towards Frangokástello, it's a stiff climb up towards Mírthios and then round, hugging the mountainside, to **SELLÍA**. Looking up from Plakiás or across from Mírthios you would imagine that Sellía had the best views of all over this area, but if you do no more than drive through you see nothing – it is the backs of the houses which face out towards Africa. If you want to stop and take a look it's easy enough to find a path through or, better still, head for the church and cemetery at the western edge of town. There's a track from the centre of the village down to Plakiás, about half an hour's walk steeply below, and there's a pleasant long circular hike from Plakiás up here and then back down via Mírthios. Drivers and bikers heading west from here would be advised to check their fuel as there is no official garage before Hóra Sfakíon.

Beyond Sellía the nature of the country changes and there's a real feeling of the approach of western Crete. The road runs high above a series of capes and small coves, quite a good surface all the way apart from a brief unpaved section just outside Argoulés. The only village of any size is **RODHÁKINO**, set on steep streets above a ravine which leads down to the small, grey sand and shingle beach of Koraka, where General Kreipe was finally taken off the island after his kidnap in 1944. There are a couple of good **rooms** places here, both offering studio-style facilities with kitchenette. One, *Rooms Yiannidakis* (☎0832/31-663; ②), is set back from the beach near a new chapel, whilst the other, *Sunrise* (0832/31-787; ②) has a taverna with a rooftop terrace and fine view. A little to the west of here, Polirizio beach in the next bay along has another rooms place, *Panorama* (☎0832/31-788; ①), together with a taverna.

Beyond Rodhákino on the main road west, a number of beaches look incredibly tempting far below, but only one seems at all easy to get to: heading down a vertiginous dirt track just before the tarmac on the main road runs out near to Argoulés.

travel details

Buses

Ay. Galíni to: Festós (7 daily; 8am–8pm; 30min); Hóra Sfakíon (1 daily at 7am; 2hr 30min); Iráklion (7 daily; 8am–8pm; 2hr); Plakiás (daily at 7am, 9am and 3pm; 1hr 30min); Réthimnon (daily at 7am, 10.30am, noon, 2.30pm, 4pm and 6.30pm; 1hr 30min).

Plakiás to: Ay. Galíni (daily at 10.30am and 7pm; 1hr 30min).

Réthimnon to: Amári (2 daily; 1hr); Anóyia (2 daily; 5.30am and 2.30pm; 1hr 30min); Arkádhi (daily at 6am, 10.30am, noon, 2.30pm and 5pm; 50min); Ay. Galíni (6 daily at 7am, 9am, 10.30am, 12.45pm, 2.15pm and 5pm; 1hr 30min) ; Haniá (30 daily; 6.15am–10pm; 1hr 30min–3hr); Iráklion (29 daily; 6.30am–9.45pm; 1hr 30min–2hr); Omalós (daily at 6.15am and 7am; 2hr 30min); Plakiás (8 daily; 6.15am–5.30pm; 45min); Spíli (daily at 7am,

9am, 10.30am, 12.45pm, 2.15pm and 5pm; 40min).

Some of these services are restricted on Sun

Ferries

To Pireás Tues, Thurs, Sat and Sun 7.30pm

To Thíra Sun 7am, plus seasonal day-trips.

ΑΓ ΓΑΛΗΝΗ	Αγ Γαλήνη	Ay. Galíni
ΑΝΩΓΕΙΑ	Ανώγεια	Anóyia
ΑΣΙΓΩΝΙΑ	Ασιγωνία	Asigonía
ΑΞΟΣ	Αξός	Axós
ΕΠΙΣΚΟΠΗ	Επισκοπή	Episkopí
ΘΡΟΝΟΣ	Θρόνος	Thrónos
ΚΑΜΑΡΕΣ	Καμάρες	Kamáres
ΛΕΥΚΟΓΕΙΑ	Λευκόγεια	Lefkóyia
Μ. ΑΡΚΑΔΙΟΥ	Μ. Αρκαδίου	Arkadhi Monastery
ΜΠΑΛΙ	Μπαλί	Balí
ΜΥΡΘΙΟΣ	Μύρθιος	Mírthios
ΠΕΡΑΜΑ	Πέραμα	Pérama
ΠΛΑΚΙΑΣ	Πλακιάς	Plakiás
ΠΡΕΒΕΛΙ	Πρέβελι	Préveli
ΡΕΘΥΜΝΟ	Ρέθυμνο	Réthimnon
ΣΠΗΛΙ	Σπήλι	Spíli
ΦΟΥΡΦΟΥΡΑΣ	Φουρφουράς	Fourfourás
ΨΗΛΟΡΕΙΤΗΣ	Ψηλορείτης	Psilorítis

CHAPTER FOUR

HANIÁ

Haniá, Crete's westernmost province, is still its least visited, which alone is a significant part of its attraction. And although tourist development is spreading fast, and has already covered much of the coast around Haniá, the west is likely to remain one of the emptier parts of the island, partly because there are no large sand beaches to accommodate resort hotels, partly because the great archeological sites are a long way from here. In their place are some of the most classic elements of the island: scattered coves, rural, unexploited villages, and a spectacular vista of mountains.

The city of **Haniá**, island capital until 1971, is reason in itself to come: unequivocally the most enjoyable of Crete's larger towns, it is littered with oddments from its Venetian and Turkish past, and bustles with harbourside life. To either side, almost along the whole **north coast** of the province, spreads a line of sandy beach – at times exposed, and increasingly developed, but still with numerous reaches where you can escape the crowds. The expanse of sand is broken by three peninsulas: **Akrotíri**, enclosing the magnificent natural harbour of the **Bay of Sóudha**; **Rodhópou**, a bare and roadless tract of mountain; and, at the western tip of the island, **Gramvoúsa**, uninhabited and entirely barren. Akrotíri is overshadowed by NATO, with air bases on land and naval installations in the bay (Haniá itself is often crowded with servicemen and buzzed by low-flying aircraft), but it's still worth a day-trip, with a couple of excellent beaches, **Stavrós** above all, and two beautiful monasteries. Most of the region's tourists stay to the west, on the coast between Haniá and Rodhópou, in one of a number of villages now joined together by a string of low-key development through **Ayía Marína** and **Plataniás**, with the villas and apartments thinning out as you head further from the city.

The south is overshadowed by the peaks of the **Lefká Óri** – the **White Mountains** – whose grey bulk, snowcapped from January through to June, dominates every view in western Crete. Although marginally less high and considerably less famous than the Psilorítis range, they're far more rewarding for walking or climbing. Along the south coast the mountains drop straight to the Libyan Sea and the few towns that exist here do so in their shadow, clinging to what flat land can be found around the bays. Through the heart of the massif there's no road at all, nor is there any driveable route along the south coast: unless you want to travel back and forth across the island you'll have to rely on boats here, or your feet. Despite the summer hordes who thunder through the National Park in the **Gorge of Samariá**, Europe's longest gorge, the hike is still a stunning experience. With a little spirit of adventure and preparation there are scores of other, deserted **hiking** routes to take.

The south coast communities beneath the mountains see plenty of visitors, mostly gorge trippers passing through, but none could really be described as a resort. **Ayía Rouméli** and **Loutró** can be reached only on foot or by boat, although this hasn't prevented Ayía Rouméli, the end-point of the Samarian gorge walk, from becoming crowded and somewhat overdeveloped; if you want somewhere to unwind after your exertions, the serenity of Loutró is a much better bet. **Hóra Sfakíon**, the capital of the wild region known as Sfakiá, is a pleasant enough place to stay if you can handle the influx of day-trippers; far more peace is to be found down the coast a little, at the superb beaches by the Venetian castle of **Frangokástello**.

The west end of the island, beyond Rodhópou, is very sparsely populated. The port of **Kastélli** is the only town of any size, and there's a growing resort at **Paleohóra** in the south. **Soúyia** may be the next in line, but for the moment it seems in a rather curious state of limbo. The whole of the mountainous south-western corner, an area known as **Sélinos**, is worth exploring: with rough roads leading to untouched mountain villages and little-known ruins and churches. On the west-facing coast – hard to get to but well worth the effort – are two of Crete's finest beaches, **Falásarna** and **Elafonísi**.

THE NORTH COAST

Using **Haniá as a base**, getting around the **north coast** is easy enough: it's a heavily populated region with excellent roads and a stream of buses along the main routes. Trying to get off the beaten track presents more of a problem if you're dependent on public transport. On Rodhópou, for example, there are no services at all, and while most inland villages are served by at least a couple of daily buses, it can be frustrating if you want to get to several in a day.

Renting a vehicle or motorcycle, then, is a good investment, and there are plenty of outlets in Haniá (see "Listings" on p.231). Just remember that this is mountainous country – the smaller mopeds are (more or less) all right for one person but with two people on board they simply won't make it up many of the hills.

Haniá

HANIÁ, as any of its residents will tell you, is the spiritual capital of Crete, even if the title is officially bestowed on Iráklion's urban sprawl. With its shimmering waterfront, crumbling masonry and web of alleys, it is an extraordinarily attractive city, especially if you can catch it in spring when the Lefká Óri's snowcapped peaks seem to hover above the roofs. The permanent population – fast expanding into hill and coastal suburbs – always outnumbers the tourists and visitors, many of whom are sailors or airmen from the NATO bases at Soúdha or Akrotíri. It all adds up to a city worth getting to know, where you'll almost certainly stay longer than intended, making use of plentiful accommodation, excellent markets, stores and nightlife, and most other facilities you could hope for.

Haniá's recent history, in which it has featured as a hotbed of nationalist sentiment under the Turks, and its proximity to the scene of most of the heavy fighting in the Battle of Crete, has left it with little in the way of monuments. Yet it's one of the longest continuously inhabited city sites anywhere in the world, and remains an enticing place to wander round, with odd reminders of the past at every pace, and antiquities in the most unlikely settings.

To Kithira

Diktynna

Rodhópou

Agria Gramvoúsa

Cape Voúxa

N. Gramvoúsa

Áyios Ioánnis Giónis +

Afráta

Ayía Iríni

Rodhopós

+ M. Goniá

Kolimbári

Áyii Theó

Gramvoúsa

Tavronítís   Méleme   Plataniás

Yeráni   Ma

Falásarna ◆ Kaliviani

Noríyia   Nochiá

E 65

Koléni

Dhrapaniás

Kaloudhianá

Kastélli
Kisámou

Plátanos

Voukoliés   Alikianó

Voulgháro

Polyrínia ◆

Topólia   Skin

Ayía Sofía Cave ∩   Nísi

Sfinári   Koutsomátados

Roúmata

Kámbos   Flória   Prasés

Kefáli   Élos   Stróvles   Omalós

Perí**v**ólia

Váthi   Ayía Iríni

Kándhanos

Kámatera   Plemenianá

+ M. Hrissoskalítissa   Máza   Moní   Gír
[2(

Voutás   Kakadíki   Témenia

Azoyirés   Koustoyérako

Elafonísi

Anídri   Soúyia

Yialós   Lissós ◆

Paleohóra

0   10 km

To Gávdhos

HANIÁ PROVINCE

To Piréas

M. Katholikó
+
Stavrós
+ M. Gouvernetou
Horafákia
M. Ayía Triádha
+
Kalathás   *Akrotíri*
Kounoupidhianá   Pervolítsa
Haniá   Stérnes

tás
Perivolia   Mourniés   Soúdha   Kalámi
Kalíves
Aptera   Kókkino Horió
Almirídha
ournés   Stílos
Neo Horió   Gavalohóri
Mesklá   Vámos   Kefalás
Thériso   Samonas
kki   Kámbi   E 75
Sóurva   Tsakístra   Kálamitsi Amigdáli
Ramní   Vrísses   Exópolis
Yeoryioúpolis

Alíkambos
Mávri   Moúri
(2069m)   *Lake Kournás*   To Réthimnon

e f k á   Ó r i
riá   Kournás

Samarian Gorge   Pahnes
(2453m)   Ammoudhári

Imbrós

Ayía Rouméli

Anópoli   Hóra
Fínix   Sfakíon   Patsianós
Loutró   Komitádhes   Argoulés   To Plakiás
Líkkos   *Sweetwater Beach*
Frangokástello

As **Kydonia**, it was a Minoan community of obscure status: only scattered remnants have so far been brought to light, but many believe that there's a major palace still to be discovered somewhere in the vicinity. After the collapse of the Minoan palace culture, it grew into one of the island's most important cities – well enough known for its citizens to warrant a mention in Homer's *Odyssey* – and remained so through the Classical Greek era. When Rome came in search of conquest, the city mounted a stiff resistance prior to its eventual capitulation in 69 BC, after which it flourished once more. The hillside area known as Kastélli served as the city's acropolis, but dwellings spread at least as far as the extent of the walled city which can be seen today. Roman mosaics from this era have been discovered beneath the Cathedral Square and up near the present market.

In early Christian times, Kydonia was the seat of a bishop, and under the protection of Byzantium the city flourished along with the island. As the Byzantine Empire became increasingly embattled, however, so its further outposts, Kydonia (and Crete) included, suffered neglect. Not until the thirteenth century is much heard of the place again, when the Genoese (with local support) seized the city from the Venetians and held it from 1263 to 1285.

When the Venetians finally won it back they acted quickly to strengthen the defences, turning the city – renamed **La Canea** – into a formidable bulwark in the west. The city walls were built in two stages. In the fourteenth century Kastélli alone was fortified: within these walls stood the original cathedral and the city administration. Later, in the sixteenth century, new walls were constructed as a defence against constant raids by pirate corsairs – in particular against the systematic ravages of Barbarossa. It is these defences, along with the Venetian harbour installations, that define the shape of Haniá's old town today. Within the walls, meanwhile, a flourish of public and private construction left La Canea perhaps the island's most beautiful city.

In 1645, after a two-month siege with terrible losses (mostly on the Turkish side – their commander was executed on his return home for losing as many as 40,000 men), Haniá fell to the **Turks**. It was the first major Cretan stronghold to succumb, becoming the Turkish island capital and seat of the pasha. Churches were converted to mosques, the defences more or less maintained, and there must have been at least some building: today it is barely possible to distinguish Venetian buildings maintained by the Turks from originals of Venetian or Turkish workmanship.

For the rest, it is a history of struggle: for independence during the **nineteenth century**, then in **resistance** against the Germans in World War II. In the independence struggle, the city's most dramatic moment came in 1897, following the outbreak of war between Greece and Turkey, when the Great Powers (Britain, France, Russia and Italy) imposed a peace and stationed a joint force in the waters off Haniá. From here, in one famous incident, they bombarded Cretan insurgents attempting prematurely to raise the flag of Greece on the hill of Profítis Elías (see p.232). When the Turkish administrators were finally forced to leave, Prince George, the high commissioner chosen by the powers, established his capital here for the brief period of regency before Crete finally became part of the Greek state. During **World War II**, with most of the German landings and the bulk of the fighting on the coast immediately west of the city, Haniá suffered severe bombardment, this destruction eventually compounded by a fire which wiped out almost everything apart from the area around the harbour. In the final six months of their occupation of the island, the Germans withdrew to a heavily defended perimeter centred on the city. In the post-war period, the town was rebuilt and sprawling, traffic-congested suburbs now encircle the ancient core. The arrival of **tourism** has inspired the will – if not the resources – to save and restore much of the city's crumbling architectural heritage, and Haniá is currently enjoying a period of peace and prosperity unrivalled in its modern history.

Orientation, arrival and information

The **old city** clusters around the harbour and most tourists rightly confine themselves to this area or the fringes of the new town up towards the bus station. You may get lost wandering among the narrow alleys, but it's never far to the sea, to one of the main thoroughfares or to some other recognizable landmark.

The major junction at the south end of Hálidhon, as much as anywhere, marks the centre of town. To the east, Odhós **Yianári** leads past the market and, if you follow it round, either to the main coast road or out onto the Akrotíri peninsula. **Skalídhi**, westwards, leads eventually out of town towards Kastélli Kisámou. North, straight ahead, Hálidhon descends to the harbour and into the heart of the old town. As you stand at this junction, everything in front and below you is basically the old, walled city – behind and to either side lie the newer parts. Much of your **shopping** and other **business** will take place around the border of the old and new represented by the main Hálidhon junction: down towards the market you'll find pharmacies, newspaper stores and banks. **Tzanakáki** and **Konstantínou** (which later becomes Dhimokratías), opposite, represent modern Haniá, full of clothes stores, car-rental places and more banks.

Hálidhon is perhaps the most commercially touristic street in Haniá: walk down here and you pass the Cathedral Square, about halfway down on the right, and the Archeological Museum, just beyond on the left, before reaching a square by the harbour – officially called Platía Sindriváni, it is known by everyone simply as **Harbour Square**. To the left, Aktí Koundouriótou circles around the outer harbour, crowded with outdoor cafés and tavernas. Straight ahead is the strange, squat Mosque of the Jannissaries, while on the little bluff that rises behind is the area known as **Kastélli**, site of the earliest habitation in Haniá.

Carry on past here and you'll curve round to the right to the **inner harbour**, where ruinous Venetian arsenals look out towards the breakwater. Behind is the most run-down, and in some ways the most atmospheric, part of the old town – alternatively approached by turning right off Hálidhon before reaching the harbour. To the left of Hálidhon, in the relatively narrow strip between the outer harbour and the wall, the alleys are narrower, the houses older and more attractive: here, though, they have been very much taken over by the tourist trade.

Points of arrival

Arriving **by boat**, you'll anchor at the port and naval base of **Sóudha**, at the head of the magnificent Bay of Sóudha, an approach which offers unparalleled views of the Lefká Óri as you near the island. Sóudha itself is about 10km from Haniá and there are city buses approximately every fifteen minutes from here to Haniá marketplace, although these can be swamped when the ferries arrive – you might be better off taking a taxi from the square right by the dock. You wouldn't choose to stay in Sóudha – the hotels are sited right above the constant traffic of the main road and it's a grubby, dusty, concrete little place – and fortunately there's no real

HANIÁ

Lighthouse

Firkas and
Naval Museum

ANGELOU

Mosque of the
Janissaries

AKTI TOMBAZI

LITHINON

AKTI KANARI

To Nea Hora beach

APOSTOLIDHOU

THEOTOKOPOULOU

AKTI KOUNDOURIOTOU

Renieri
Gate

ZAMBELIU

SKUFON

KONDILAKI

PLATIA
SINDRIVANI

E DOROTHEU

Archeological
Museum

Cathedral

PARDHALI

HALIDHON

BOTOLO

SKRIDLOF

Schiavo
Bastion

METAIAKI

MANOUSOYANAKIDHOU

KIRILOU

SKALIDHI

EOT

PLATIA
1866

KRIA

KISSAMOU

KIDHONIAS

Bus
Station

ZIMVRAKAKIDON

SFAKIANAKI

SMIRNIS

To Kastélli

need to do so: most ferries arrive first thing in the morning and leave in the evening. If you are stuck you'll find just about everything on the square right by the ferries: stores, a bank, a post office, a couple of bars and restaurants and two inexpensive hotels.

The tiny, no-frills **airport** is about 15km out, in the middle of the Akrotíri peninsula, and doubles as a NATO air base – so no picture-taking allowed. *Olympic* flights are met by a bus; otherwise there are plenty of taxis, for which official prices to most popular destinations are listed at the rank.

The **bus station** is on Odhós Kidhonías, within easy walking distance of the centre. There's a left-luggage facility here if you want to leave your bags while you find a room.

Information and getting around

The **EOT** (Mon–Fri 8.30am–2pm; ☎26-246) is at Kriári 40, just east of Platía 1866, on the fourth floor of the Mégaro Pántheon building, and there's an extremely helpful **municipal tourist office** (Mon–Fri 8.30am–1.30pm; ☎59-990), more centrally sited at Sífaka 22, below Kastélli. For ticket and **departure information**, see the relevant entries in "Listings", pp.231–2.

You're going to want to walk around much of the city, but the terminus for most **city buses**, especially those heading west, is at Platía 1866: for Sóudha and the eastern side of town you may find it easier to get on at one of the stops by the market.

The phone code for Haniá is ☎0821. The Haniá phone system is currently being modernized and some numbers listed may have changed by the time you read this. Contact the tourist office for the latest details.

Accommodation

There must be thousands of **rooms to rent** in Haniá and, unusually, quite a few comfortable **hotels**, though you may face a long search for a bed at the height of the season. Perhaps the most desirable rooms are those **overlooking the harbour**, west of Hálidhon, though be warned that these can be noisy at night. Most are approached not direct from the harbourside itself but from the alley behind, Zambelíu, or from other streets leading off the harbour further round (where you may get more peace). The nicest of the more expensive places are here too, usually set back a little way (and thus quieter), but often still with good views from upper storeys.

In the **eastern half of the old town** rooms are far more scattered, and in the height of the season your chances of finding somewhere are much better over here. Immediately east of the harbour and reached via the alleys that lead north off Kaneváro, **Kastélli** has some lovely places with views, although they are very popular and often booked up.

There's really not much reason to stay in the **modern part of town**, unless you arrive late and need to find somewhere near the bus station on your first night. The hotels are, on the whole, soulless business establishments, and many of the rooms are noisy and grimy. The other possibility is to stay in one of the streets leading back off the town beach; quieter and not unpleasant, although there are only a few places from which to choose.

ACCOMMODATION: ROOM PRICE SCALES

All accommodation establishments in this book have been price-graded according to the scale outlined below. The rates quoted represent the cheapest available double room in high season; where possible, a per-person rate is given for dormitory-style accommodation in youth hostels. Out of season, room rates can drop by up to fifty percent, especially if you negotiate rates for a stay of three or more nights. Single rooms, where available, cost around seventy percent of the price of a double.

Rented private rooms usually fall into the ② or ③ categories, depending on their location and facilities, and the season; a few in the ④ category are more like plush self-catering apartments. They are not generally available from late October through the beginning of April, when only hotels tend to remain open.

① up to 4000dr (£10.50/US$16.50) ④ 8000–12,000dr (£21–32/US$33–50)
② 4000–6000dr (£10.50–16/US$16.50–25) ⑤ 12,000–16,000dr (£32–42/US$50–66)
③ 6000–8000dr (£16–21/US$25–33) ⑥ 16,000dr (£42/US$66) and upwards

For more accommodation details, see pp.34–7.

Around the harbour: west of Hálidhon

Amirilis, Skúfon 6 (☎56-797). On a street running inland from Zambelíu, a lovely old house with tasteful antique decor in rooms. ①.

Amphora, Theotokopóulou 20 (☎93-224). Fourteenth-century Venetian building, beautifully renovated with some interesting features such as spiral staircases and 4-poster beds. Balcony rooms with harbour view are the best value. ⑤.

Artemis, Kondiláki13 (☎91-196). One of many clean but basic places in this touristy street running inland from Zambelíu. ①.

Contessa, Theofánous 15 (☎98-566). Another renovated hotel close to *Amphora* and *Amirilis* with harbour views from some rooms. ④.

El Greco, Theotokopóulou 49 (☎90-432). Comfortable hotel with decent rooms in a quiet street; roof garden with harbour view. ②.

Eugenia, Theotokopóulou (☎54-357). Pleasant rooms with bath, at the top of Angélou. ①.

George, Zambelíu 30 (☎43-542). Old building with steep stairs and eccentric antique furniture – rooms vary in price according to position and size. ①–②.

Ireni, Theotokopóulou 13 (☎50-011). Clean, simple rooms without bath; near *Eugenia*. ①.

Lucia, Aktí Koundouriótou (☎90-302). Harbourfront hotel with balcony rooms. Less expensive than you might expect for one of the best views in town, although rooms at the back are less inviting. ③.

Meltemi, Angélou 2 (☎40-192). First in a little row of possibilities well located on the far side of the harbour, this pension may be noisier than its neighbours, but has fabulous views and a good café downstairs. ③.

Piraeus, Zambelíu 10 (☎94-665). One of the oldest hotels in Haniá; basic and somewhat run-down but friendly, English-speaking and excellent value even for a room with a balcony over the harbour. ②.

Porto del Colombo, Theofánous and Moschon, near the Renieri Gate (☎70–945). Similar to the *Amphora*, though slightly darker and more old-fashioned, this hotel occupies a building they claim was once the French Embassy and later home of Eleftheríos Venizélos. ④.

Stella, Angélou 10 (☎73-756) Creaky eccentric old house close to the *Hotel Piraeus*, with plain, clean rooms above a ceramics shop. ②.

Thereza, Angélou 8 (☎40-118). Beautiful old pension in great position with stunning views from its roof terrace and some rooms; classy decorations, too. More expensive than its neighbours but deservedly so; you'd be well advised to book ahead in high season. ③.

The old city: east of Hálidhon

Apartments Anastasia, Kandanoléon 41 (☎50-709). Worth a try for longer stays or if you want to self-cater. ②–③.

Cleopatra, Botolo 51 (☎45-489). New pension in lively but rather noisy area, just north of Cathedral Square. ②.

Fidias, Sarpáki 8 (☎52-494). Signposted from the cathedral. This pension is a favourite back-packers' meeting place: rather bizarrely run, but extremely friendly and with the real advantage of offering single rooms or fixing shares. ①.

Kastelli, Kaneváro 39 (☎57-057). Not the prettiest location, but comfortable, modern, reasonably priced, and very quiet at the back. Alex, who runs this pension, is exceptionally helpful and also has a few apartments and a beautiful house (for up to 5 people) to rent. ②.

Kydonia, Isódhion 15 (☎57-179). Between the Cathedral Square and Platía Sindrívani, in first street parallel to Hálidhon. Rather dark, but good value for so central a position. ①–②.

Lito, Epískopou Dorothéou 15 (☎53-150). Very near the cathedral; another street with several options – this one with simple rooms, with shared bath. ②.

Marina Ventikou, Sarpáki 40 (☎57-601). Small, personally run rooms place in a quiet corner of the old town. ①.

Monastiri, Áyios Markou 18, off Kaneváro (☎54-776). Simple rooms, some with sea view and bath, in the restored ruins of a Venetian monastery. Roof terrace with view, too. ②–③.

Navarino, Sarpáki 67 (☎56-598). Pleasant, good-value rooms with shared bath. ①.

Nikos, Dhaskaloyiánnis 58 (☎54-783). One of a few places down near the inner harbour; relatively modern rooms, all with shower. ②.

Rooms 47, Kandanoléon 47 (☎53-243). Quiet, traditional rooms place on street leading up from Kaneváro into Kastélli. Some rooms have balconies with great sea views. ①.

Stoa, Lithínon 5 (☎26-879). One of the cheapest of several on this street; rooms at the back look over the harbour from above. ①.

The modern city

Helen Bambakaki, Moní Gonías, corner of Akti Papanikóli (☎53-572). Rooms with shared bath right on the beachfront road, behind the town beach, which means some way from everything else. ①.

Lato, Ioánias 8 (☎95-088). Hotel with good rooms and very handy for the bus station. ②.

Manolis, Smírnis 23 (☎24-110). An ordinary rooms place near the bus station. ①.

Tina, Boniali 3 (☎45-527). Backstreet location just off Tzanakáki near the Public Gardens. Quiet and comfortable, and may have rooms when other places are full. ①.

Hostel and campsites

Youth Hostel, Dhrakoniánou 33 (☎53-565). A long way from anywhere and not much of a place – 4 or 5 rooms with metal bunks in each – but at least cheap (850dr) and friendly, with a good view inland. You get here on the *Áy. Ioánnis* bus (every 15min; last, they claim, at midnight) from the square opposite the market – ask for Platía Dhexamení. The hostel organizes budget guided tours to the Samarian gorge and other places.

Camping Hania (☎31-686). Behind the beach, 4km west of Haniá, just about walking distance if you follow the coast around, but much easier reached by taking the local bus (see "The beaches", pp.226–7). There's a large sign to tell you where to get off; walk down towards the sea for about 5min through a patch of new development. The site itself is rather basic, but lovely: small, shady, and just a short walk from a couple of the better beaches.

Camping Ayía Marína (☎68-555). A much bigger and more expensive site, 4km or so further west on an excellent beach at the far end of Ayía Marína village. This is beyond the range of Haniá city buses, so to get here by public transport you have to go from the main bus station. Check before turning up, because the site is earmarked for redevelopment.

The harbour and around

The **harbour** comes into its own at night, when the lights from bars and restaurants reflect in the water and the animated crowds – locals as much as tourists – parade in a ritualistic *voltá* of apparently perpetual motion. There are stalls set up on the waterside, and buskers serenading the passers-by. By day, especially in the hot, dozy mid-afternoon, it can be less appealing: deserted and with a distinct smell of decay from the rubbish washing up against the quayside. You could always escape on a carriage ride around town behind one of the poor nags that stand waiting in the square all day, sweating beneath their straw hats.

Walk straight on from Platía Sindriváni, past the *Plaza Bar*, and you chance upon the curious, domed profile of the **Mosque of the Janissaries**. Built in 1645, the year Haniá fell to the Turks and thus the oldest Ottoman building on the island, it has been well restored – apart from the jarring concrete dome – and was used to house the EOT office until further repairs meant they had to move to less-convenient Odhós Kriári.

Kastélli

The buildings on the height above the mosque occupy the site of **Kastélli**, the oldest part of the city. Favoured from earliest times for its defensive qualities, this little hill takes its name from a fortress which originally dated from the Byzantine era. Later it was the centre of the Venetian and of the Turkish towns, but very little survived a heavy bombardment during World War II.

Walking up Kanaváro from the harbour square you'll pass various remains, including – at the corner of Lithínon – the fenced-off site where a **Minoan house** is being excavated. Further up Lithínon, towards the top of the rise, are various Venetian doorways and inscriptions and, at the end of the street, a fine old archway. On the next corner, with Kandanoléon, is a larger area of excavation identified simply as "Minoan Kydonia". Neither of these digs is open to the public, though you can see a fair amount through the fence. Swedish archeologists excavating here have traced the outline of a building engulfed by a violent fire about 1450BC, similar to that which destroyed Knossós. It was later rebuilt and, given its proximity to the mainland, may well have been the focus of Mycenaean power on the island. Among pottery finds here were some dating back to the Neolithic era, but the greatest prize uncovered was an archive of clay tablets bearing Minoan Linear A script (see "The Historical Framework", p.251), the first to be found so far west in Crete.

The inner harbour

Back at the bottom of the hill the waterfront curls round to the right along Aktí Tómbazi, into the **inner harbour**, where pleasure boats, private yachts and small fishing vessels are moored. Much of it, including the sixteenth-century Venetian arsenals and various traces of the ancient defensive bastions, has recently been refurbished, and in the evenings this is now a fashionable part of town. Just on the corner past the Mosque of the Janissaries is the local **handicraft cooperative** (Mon–Sat 9.30am–10.30pm), with a permanent exhibition of goods for sale, though not everything is of particularly high quality. In the line of old buildings facing the water beyond this, by the port police, are a couple of unusual antique stores, one full of wonderful old junk – albeit priced for tourists.

Beyond all this are the Venetian arsenals, a cluster of restaurants and bars, and the modern *Porto Veneziana* hotel. From here you can follow the sea wall round as far as the minaret-style **lighthouse**, where there's a bar and an excellent view back over the city.

The outer harbour and city walls

In the other direction from Platía Sindriváni is the **outer harbour**, with its broad promenade fronted by pavement restaurants and bars. The hefty bastion at the far end houses Crete's **Naval Museum** (Tues–Sun 10am–2pm; 300dr), which is of little interest unless you're heavily into naval warfare or seashells (one small room is full of them). It consists mainly of poorly labelled models and pictures of ships, diagrams of naval battles, and assorted memorabilia going back to the times of Classical Greek triremes. Go through the main gate, however, into the compound of what is apparently a small naval garrison (open museum hours, but no need to pay the admission fee) and you can climb onto the seaward fortifications of the **Fírkas**, as this part of the city defences is known. Here the modern Greek flag was first raised on Crete – in 1913 – and there are more fine views. Every Monday and Thursday evening at 9pm there's a Greek dancing display here (adults 200dr, children 100dr).

Carrying on round the outside of the Fírkas, which has been well restored, you can peer through loopholes at the great vaulted chambers within. On the far side is the *Hotel Xenia*, itself raised up on part of the fortifications, and beyond this you can cut inland alongside the best-preserved stretch of the **city walls**. Following the walls around on the inside is rather trickier, but worth a try for the chance to stumble on some of the most picturesque little alleyways and finest Venetian houses in Haniá. Keep your eyes open for details on the houses, such as old wooden balconies or stone coats of arms. The arch of the **Renieri Gate**, at the bottom of Moschón, is particularly elegant. There are also a number of good craft stores around here: a couple of the best, along with an expensive antiques store, are on Angélou just round from the Naval Museum entrance; several newer ones line Theotokopóulou, the delightfully old-fashioned street that runs behind.

The old city

South from the harbour square, up Hálidhon, lie the less picturesque but more lively parts of the old city. First, though, just a short way up on the right, is Haniá's **Archeological Museum** (Mon–Fri 8.30am–3pm; 400dr), housed in the Venetian-built church of San Francesco. Though it doesn't look much now, with its campanile gone and a crumbling facade, this building was once one of the island's grandest: inside, where there has been substantial restoration, you get a better sense of its former importance. The Turks converted the church into a mosque, from which a beautiful fountain and the base of a minaret have survived in the pungent, flowery garden alongside.

Large quantities of Minoan pottery, including a few of the huge Minoan storage jars or *pithoi*, dominate the front part of the museum. In the centre is a collection of Minoan clay tombs (*larnakes*), some wonderfully decorated, and one still containing two small skeletons. For archeologists, the most important items are the inscribed tablets excavated in Kastélli: this is the only place other than Knossós where examples of Linear A and Linear B script have been found together. Towards the back of the church, the collection is arranged chronologically, progressing through a large group of Classical sculptures, a case full of Greco-Roman glassware and some recently discovered third-century Roman mosaics reassembled on the floor. These are really lovely, particularly those of Dionysos and Ariadne, and of Poseidon and Amymone. Outside in the garden courtyard (often enlivened by classical music drifting over the wall from a café outside) are other assorted sculptures and architectural remnants, including a lovely one-legged, headless lion.

Cathedral Square and "Leather Street"

Just past the museum, on the other side of Hálidhon, the **Cathedral** sits at the back of a small square. Given Haniá's history and importance, you might expect this to be rather impressive: in fact it's a singularly unattractive little building, dating only from the last century. Nor is the square, which must once have been at the heart of life in Haniá*, particularly lively any more except as a taxi rank; to one side, above a *períptero* or street kiosk, are the ramshackle domes of a former Turkish bath.

The street just above, **Odhós Skridlóf**, is considerably more interesting and animated. Here traditional leathermakers still ply their trade, and although many are now geared to tourists, prices for leatherware remain the best in Crete – and there are still a few shops which ignore sandals and bags in favour of traditional high Cretan boots and hefty work shoes.

As a final gesture to Hálidhon, take the last right before the top and walk down beside a high stretch of wall into the vicinity of the **Schiavo Bastion**. There's not a great deal to see here, but it's strange to find yourself so suddenly out of the crowds and among the scruffy yards and inquisitive dogs of the backstreets.

The market and points northeast

In the other direction, continuing to the end of Skridlóf or up behind the cathedral, you reach the back of the **market**. An imposing and rather beautiful cross-shaped structure, this dates from the beginning of the century, when it was supposedly modelled on the market at Marseilles. At the back is a small shaded square where locals sit outside a couple of *kafenia*. As you wander round these streets, a minaret keeps appearing above the rooftops, only to disappear when you head towards it: actually located on Dhaliáni, it seems to be part of a carpenters' workshop, but is fenced off and closed to visitors.

A second minaret (this one missing its top) adorns the church of Áyios Nikólaos in **Platía 1821**, further over to the east. Built by the Venetians, the church was converted to a mosque under Sultan Ibrahim and reconverted after Crete's reversion to Greek authority, but has been so often refurbished that there's nothing much to see. The square itself, whose name recalls the date of one of the larger rebellions against Turkish authority, after which an Orthodox bishop was hanged here, is another pleasantly shaded space set with café chairs. Nearby are two more old churches: San Rocco, just a pace towards the harbour, is small and old-fashioned, while Áyii Anáryiri, which retained its Orthodox status throughout the Turkish occupation, has some very ancient icons. Again the area as a whole – known as **Spiantza** – is full of unexpected architectural delights:

---

*The rebel Dhaskaloyiánnis (see p.260) was tortured to death in the square around 1770.

carved wooden balconies and houses arching across the street at first-floor level. Many of the streets between here and the inner harbour have recently been recobbled and generally refurbished, and they're among the most atmospheric and tranquil in the old town.

Continue **eastwards**, past another section of ruinous wall stretching round from the inner harbour, and you'll hit the sea again. From here you can follow the coast round into the smarter areas of the modern city.

The new town

Modern Haniá sprawls in every direction, encircling the old: with time on your hands, there are parts that are worth the walk. Starting in front of the market, the areas to the southwest, on the way to **Platía 1866** and the bus station, have an attractively old-fashioned commercialism about them, full of general stores stocking the essentials of village life.

Heading southeast from the market, Tzanakáki leads to places of more specific interest. First of these is the **Public Gardens**, a few hundred metres up on the left. Laid out by a Turkish pasha in the nineteenth century, they include a few caged animals (not really enough to call a zoo, but there are *kri-kri*, ponies, loud monkeys and birds), a café where you can sit under the trees, a children's play area and an open-air auditorium. The latter, often used as a cinema, is also the setting for local ceremonies and folklore displays which can be really enjoyable – look in to see what's on.

Carry on down the street, then take the second left onto Sfakianáki and you come to the **Historical Museum and Archives** (Mon–Fri 9am–1pm; free), which consists of a couple of gloomy rooms in a small and undistinguished grey building, with poorly labelled photos, a few revolutionary arms from the struggle against the Turks and relics of Venizélos, and many more rooms filled with musty papers and books.

At the end of Sfakianáki is **Platía Eleftherías**, with a statue of Venizélos in the centre and an imposing court building along the south side. This court house was originally the government building built for Prince George's short-lived administrations. From here Dhimokratías leads back to the centre, running past the rear of the Public Gardens and ending (as Konstantínou) opposite the market again. Alternatively, follow **Iróon Politehníou**, which runs due north from Platía Eleftherías down to the sea. A broad avenue divided by trees and lined with large houses, interspersed with several (expensive) garden restaurants and a number of fashionable café/bars where you can sit outdoors, it makes for an interesting walk in a part of the city very different from that dominated by the tourist crowds of Hálidhon.

The beaches

Haniá's beaches all lie to the west of the city. The **bus for the beaches** leaves Haniá from the east side of Platía 1866, about halfway up, and runs along the main road towards Kastélli. This means that if you get off anywhere much before Kalamáki you face quite a walk down to the sea. It's easier to hang on, and get off either by the large Oasis Beach sign or at Kalamáki itself, the next stop. Buses run every twenty minutes or so throughout the day, from around 8am to 9pm.

Néa Hóra to Golden Beach

The **city beach** at Néa Hóra is about a ten-minute walk from the harbour along Aktí Koundouriótou, round past the Fírkas and the *Hotel Xenia*, and on by the city's open-air swimming pools (often drained) and a small fishing-boat harbour. The beach starts in a very crowded section with showers, cafés and restaurants, among these an outstanding fish taverna, *Akrogiali* (see "Eating and drinking" over). Offshore is a tiny islet with a sandy beach large enough for about five people at a time, but it's an unnervingly long swim – better to rent a pedalo or canoe if you want to explore.

If you continue west you can walk – for some twenty minutes – over a stony, scrubby stretch of sand where quite a few people camp or seek out isolation for nude sunbathing. It's a dirty and rather exposed length of gritty sand, though new apartment buildings behind are beginning to provoke a clean-up. **Áyii Apóstoli**, at the end of this walk, amid a clutch of restrained development, is much more agreeable: there's an excellent bungalow/hotel development (*Aptera Beach Bungalows*) with a beachside bar, a restaurant which serves a delicious lunchtime buffet, and a good long slather of yellow sand. The only drawback is the crashing breakers, which can become vicious at times. At the end of Apóstoli's beach a barbed-wire fence attempts to prevent you getting onto the next section, but if you want to continue on foot it's worth clambering over the rocks: going round to the road involves a long detour and something of a climb over a low hill. At the next section, known as **Hrissí Aktí** (Golden Beach), there's more good sand which has attracted the apartment-builders. But it's not yet overcrowded, has a good taverna and is popular with locals.

To get to either of these sections **from the road**, head down the track signed to the *Aptera Beach Bungalows* (for the beginning of the first beach) or past *Camping Hania* to approach from the other end. There's quite a bit of new development around, mostly apartments but also a number of restaurants – *Jetée*, to which you'll see signs, is good, if a little pricier than most. At the far end, as the beach curves round to a little headland, another taverna is set out on stilts over the water.

Oasis Beach to Kalamáki

Beyond the Golden Beach headland lies a tiny sand cove, another small promontory, and then the long curve of **Oasis Beach** running on round to **Kalamáki**. This is crowded, and justly so – the swimming is probably the best in the area, with a gently shelving sandy bottom and a fossil-covered (and very sharp) rocky islet/reef that fends off the bigger waves. There's also a string of cafés and tavernas, and other facilities including windsurf rental or lessons. Kalamáki is the furthest beach accessible by city bus, and it's right by the road. To walk this far would probably take a little over an hour non-stop, but it makes far more sense to dawdle and enjoy the empty beaches along the way, arriving at Kalamáki in time to get the bus back.

Eating and drinking

Evenings in Haniá centre around the harbour, and you need not stray far from the waterfront walk to find a cocktail before dinner, a meal, a late-night bar and an all-night disco. The most fashionable area these days, particularly with locals, is towards the far end of the inner harbour, around Sarpidóna. If you're on a tight budget, however, you'll need to steer clear of the waterfront.

Tavernas and restaurants

Platía Sindriváni is a good starting point: spanning out from here, in a circle round the **harbour**, is one restaurant, taverna or café after another. They all have their own character, but there seems little variation in price or what's on offer, although the inner harbour is a little less frantic. Places away from the water are generally a little cheaper, with plenty of possibilities on Kondiláki, Kanenváro and most of the streets off Hálidhon. Alternatively, striking out a little further afield can take you off the tourist trail altogether and the more local restaurants to the east and west of the centre can make a refreshing change from the touting and brashness of many harbourfront places.

Aerikó, Aktí Míaouli, on the bay to the east of the inner harbour. Good selection of well-prepared dishes on a pleasant seaside square.

Akrogiali, Akí Papanikoli 19 on the Néa Hóra seafront. Worth a taxi trip to this excellent and fair-priced fish taverna with friendly service, pleasant terrace and outstanding seafood – which explains why it's always packed.

Amphora, Akti Koundouriótou, outer harbour. The restaurant of the hotel of the same name (restaurant entrance on the harbour) is one of the more reliable places to eat fish on this strip; serves a range of Cretan specialities.

Dino's, inner harbour by bottom of Sarpidóna. One of the best choices for a pricey seafood meal with a harbour view.

Emerald Bistro, Kondiláki 17. Irish-run place for the homesick, with Irish stew, Guinness, veggie food, and kids' menu of sausage, beans and chips, as well as Greek staples. Friendly and fairly priced.

Karnáyio, Platía Kateháki 8, set back from the inner harbour near the port police. Not right on the water, but one of the best harbour restaurants nonetheless; its touristy looks belie very good food, friendly atmosphere and prices certainly no higher than surrounding restaurants. *Faka*, on the other side of the square, is also good.

Kings, Kondiláki. The first of numerous places as you head up Kondiláki from Zambelíu. Better than most on this touristy street and serves some vegetarian food.

Lukulos, Hálidhon, opposite the Archeological Museum. Italian restaurant with reasonably priced pizzas and spaghetti.

Nikteridha, out of town in the village of Korakiés. Head for Akrotíri and at the top of the hill, after the Venizélos tombs, follow the signs to the left for the village. Delightful garden setting for this traditional taverna, especially worthwhile at weekends when there's often music and dancing. You'll pass a couple of other places with outdoor grills and views over Haniá – as well as more music and dancing – as you climb up the road out of town.

Pafsilipon, Sífaka 19. Good, reliable taverna. Tables on the street and also on the raised pavement opposite. House speciality is *toúrta*, a cheese and meat pie.

Pension Lito, Epískopou Dorothéou 15. Café-taverna with live music (usually Greek-style guitar), one of several in this street.

Retro, Platía Venizélou in Halepa. Fashionable and fairly expensive place set in the former Russian Embassy – a beautiful setting, though the food's not always up to scratch. It's just off the road to Akrotíri but not easy to find, so a taxi might be a good idea.

Le Saladier, Kanenváro just off Platía Sindriváni. French-run joint specializing in salads of every kind.

Tamam, Zambelíu 49, just before the Renieri Gate. Young, trendy place with adventurous Greek menu including much vegetarian food. Unfortunately, has only a few cramped tables outside, and it can get quite hot inside.

Taverna Ela, top of Kondiláki. Standard taverna food, with live Greek music to enliven your meal.

Tholos, Ágion Dhéka 36. Good restaurant with lots of seafood options, in a small street just to the east of Hálidhon.

To Dhiporto, Skridhlóf 40. Very long-established, very basic place amid all the leather stores whose multilingual menu still offers such delights as Pigs' Balls – or, more delicately, *Testicules de Porc*.

To Hani, Kondiláki 26. Claims to be a "garden restaurant" aren't strictly true, but there are tables at the back in a very quiet dead-end alley (as well as less inviting ones out front in Kondiláki); food is run-of-the-mill, but reasonably priced.

Cafés, bars and snacks

The abundance of **cafés** round the harbour tend to serve cocktails and fresh juices at exorbitant prices, though breakfast (especially "English") can be good value. There are more traditional places around the market (including a couple of *zaharoplasteía*, one on Tsoudherón, the other on Mousoúron, down the steps from the side entrance and along Dhaskaloyiánnis. **Fast food** is also increasingly widespread, with numerous *souvláki* places and even a couple of burger joints (on Kalergón by the top of Sarpidóna). *Souvláki* places congregate on Karaolí; round at the end of the outer harbour, near the Naval Museum; and around the corner of Plastíra and Yianári, across from the market.

If you want to get stuff together for a **picnic**, head for the market, which offers vast quantities of fresh fruit and vegetables as well as meat and fish, bread, dairy stalls for milk, cheese and yoghurt, and general stores for cooked meats, tins and other provisions. Several small stores down by the harbour square sell cold drinks and a certain amount of food, but these are expensive (though they do open late): better to head for the shops in the new town where locals go. A couple of large **supermarkets** can be found on the main roads running out of town – particularly *Nea Agora* and *Inka* on the way to Akrotíri. A specialist **mountain-cheese** shop can be found on Sífaka, near where it joins Karaolí

Bougatsa, Sífaka 4. Tiny place that serves little except the traditional creamy cheese pie – *bougátsa* – to eat in or take away.

Ideon Andron, in an alleyway off Hálidhon, next to the Archeological Museum. Classy café/bar, rather slow and expensive, but in a charming garden with piped classical or jazz music and, occasionally, something live.

Meltemi, Angélou 2. Slow, relaxed place for breakfast; later on, locals (especially ex-pats) sit whiling the day away or playing *tavli*.

Mitropolitikon, Cathedral Square. Pleasant setting with tables out on the square in front of the cathedral. Good juices.

Neorion, Sarpidóna. The place to sit and be seen in the evening, in an area packed with bars where everyone is doing the same; some tables overlook the harbour. Try an expensive but sublime lemon *granita*.

Oblomov, Kondiláki. Touristic, trendy little cocktail bar/café with classical music, brown bread and laid-back atmosphere.

Pili Tis, Porta Sabioyera. A superb outdoor bar sited in a garden on top of the eastern harbour bastion, near to the *Porto Veneziano Hotel* and reached through a deceptively small doorway. Great in the evening with lights dangling from the tamarisk trees and views over the Sarpidóna district, as well as out to sea.

Singanaki, Dhaskaloyiánnis. Traditional bakery serving *tiropitta* and the like, with a cake store next door.

Tasty Souvláki, Hálidhon 80. Always packed, despite being cramped and none-too-clean – a testimonial to the quality and value of the *souvláki*. Take-away might be a better option.

Vasilis, Platía Sindriváni. Reasonably priced breakfasts.

Nightlife and entertainment

The presence of NATO air force and navy bases out on Akrotíri means that the
scene in some of the city's **bars** is a lot heavier than you'd expect. In recent
years, though, many of these places have been tamed; tourists and young locals
now predominate. The smartest **clubs** are on and around Sarpidóna.

A few places offer more authentic entertainment, including **rembétika**, which
crudely approximates to Greek blues, and traditional **dancing**. If this appeals, it's
worth checking for events at the open-air auditorium in the Public Gardens and
for performances in restaurants outside the city, which are the ones locals go to.
The hoardings in front of the market usually have details of these, together with
programme information for the couple of **open-air cinemas** that show English-
language films with subtitles (rather than dubbed versions): the *Kipos*, in the
Public Gardens, and the *Attikon*, on Elefthérias Venizélou out towards Akrotíri,
about 1km from the centre. The latter has a great atmosphere, but be sure to sit
near a speaker since they sneakily reduce the sound level as the evening
progresses so as not to offend the neighbours.

The main annual **festival** in Haniá is the commemoration of the Battle of Crete
in the last week of May, with folklore and other events mostly in the Public
Gardens. June 24, St John's Day, is also celebrated. Check with the tourist office
for details of these and others in villages roundabout.

Late bars and discos

Agora Club, Tsoudherón behind the market. Big, bright disco where not much happens
before 2am – at midnight it's still deserted.

Anayennisi, Schiavo Bastion, junction of Skalídhi and Hálidhon. Tucked down a passage
near the bastion, this is a new disco that gets pretty frenetic after midnight.

Berlin Rock Café, Radimanthus. Round the corner at the top of Sarpidóna, a late-night
disco-bar.

Disco Ariadne, inner harbour just off Akti Tobázi. The most central disco; opens at
11.30pm, but doesn't get busy until later.

El Mondo, Kondiláki. A survivor from the days when this street was very rowdy, and still
popular with servicemen.

Fagotto, Angélou 16. Very pleasant laid-back jazz bar, often with live performers in high
season.

Fedra, Ágion Dhéka. Near the *Tholos* restaurant (see previous page), this is another good
jazz place.

Fraise, Sarpidóna. Sit inside for the music, or outside and watch the crowds go by.

Fortetza, sea wall, near the lighthouse. Strange hybrid restaurant/café/nightclub on the far
side of the harbour near the lighthouse. A ferry shuttle takes people across from outside the
port police – a good gimmick, though you could easily walk. Most popular late at night; there
are queues for the boat at midnight.

Four Seasons, inner harbour. Very popular bar by the port police, where the town's youth
gather to size each other up.

Plaza, outer harbour. Quayside bar converted from former landmark hotel, with loud music.

Remember, outer harbour, behind the *Plaza*. "English-style pub", quite pleasant if you like
that sort of thing.

Rudi's Bierhaus, Sífaka 24, next door to the municipal tourist office. Haniá's beer shrine:
Austrian Rudi Riegler stocks almost 100 of Europe's finest beers and will explain the story
behind each one if you have the time and inclination.

Traditional music

Café Kriti, Kalergón 22, at the corner of Andrógeo. Basically an old-fashioned *kafenion* where there's Greek music and dancing virtually every night.

Skala, Kalergón 12. Haniá and Crete's only *rembétika* venue. This place opens at midnight and the show goes on with the same musicians right through until dawn without a break – a memorable experience.

Fírkas; see p.224. Stages Greek traditional dancing at 9pm each Mon and Thurs – pricey but authentic entertainment in full costume.

Haniá by Night, on the new Iráklion road. An enormous modern dance hall that attracts many of Greece's best singers.

Tutti Frutti, in Ayiá, 7km to the southwest. Another regular venue for big-name events; at other times it's a popular disco venue.

Listings

Airlines *Olympic*, the only people with scheduled flights to or from Haniá, have an office at Tzanakáki 88 (Mon–Fri 9am–4pm; ☎57-701 or 57-702 or 57-703), opposite the Public Gardens.

Airport There's a bus from the *Olympic* office, connecting with their flights. For airport information phone ☎63-264.

Banks The main branch of the *National Bank of Greece* is directly opposite the market and has a 24-hr ATM that accepts *Mastercard*. *Credit Bank*, Hálidhon 106, and the *Ionikhi Bank* on Yianári, at the junction with Hálidhon, also have ATMs (*Visa* and *American Express*). Smaller banks offering exchange facilities are next to the bus station, and there are a couple of after-hours exchange places on Hálidhon and a post-office van parked in Cathedral Square throughout the summer.

Bike and car rental For cars try *Hermes* (Tzanakáki 52; ☎54-418), which is friendly and efficient; for bikes and cars, *Duke of Crete* (Sífaka 3, ☎21-651; Skalídhi 16, ☎57-821; and branches in Ayía Marína and Plataniás; 15 percent discount for cash). Others include *Summertime* (Dhaskaloyiánnis 7; ☎28-918), *Zeus* (Karaolí 38; ☎57-457) and *Cornaros* (Hálidhon 86; ☎73-131). *Hertz*, *Avis* and other big companies mostly have offices on Tzanakáki.

Boat trips Various boat trips are offered by travel agents around town, mostly round Soúdha Bay or out to beaches on the Rodhópou peninsula. *Domenico's* on Kanekáro offers some of the best of these; for details of trips (1–3 days) on a small yacht with an English skipper, call at the jewellery shop at Hálidhon 3 or at *E. Barbopoulos* (Tsoudherón 1; ☎22-244, 23-394).

Ferry tickets The *Minoan* line office is at the corner of Dimokratias and Yianári (☎23-939); *ANEK* is nearby on Venizélou, right opposite the market (☎53-636).

Hospital On the east side of town at the junction of Dragoúmi and Kapodístriou (☎27-231).

Launderette There are 3, at Kanekáro 38 (9am–10pm), Epískopou Dorothéou 7 and Áyii Dhéka 18; all do service washes.

Mountain climbing and walking The local EOS, at Tzanakáki 90 (☎24-647), provides information about climbing in the Lefká Óri and takes reservations for the mountain refuge at Kallergi, near the Samarian gorge. It also produces a leaflet on the new E4 hiking route across the island. *Trekking Plan*, Karaolí Dimitríou 15 (☎44-946) organize pricey 1- to 5-day guided treks into the Lefká Óri.

Newspapers and books English- and other foreign-language newspapers are sold at 2 places on Odhós Yiánari, one right by the corner of Hálidhon, the other towards the market. There are 2 bookshops on Hálidhon which stock a fair range of foreign material: one (*Pelekanakis*) near the top, the other at the bottom in the square. For guides and maps you could also try the kiosk in the market or the one by Cathedral Square.

Pharmacies Several on Yiánari between the market and Platía 1866; more up Tzanakáki.

Post office The main post office is at Tzanakáki 3 (Mon–Fri 8am–8pm, Sat 8am–2pm), augmented by a handy summer-only branch set up in Cathedral Square.

Shopping Stores aimed at tourists are found in the old town, especially jewellery and souvenirs on Hálidhon and all around the harbour. The leather goods on Skridlóf are excellent value. On Potié is a place selling nothing but chess and *tavli* sets in all shapes and sizes. Other interesting places to look include the handicraft centre and antique stores on the inner harbour, and various art-craft stores on Zambelíu, Kaneváro and Theotokopóulou.

Taxis The main taxi ranks are in Platía 1866. For radio taxis, try ☎98-700.

Telephones OTE at Tzanakáki 5, just past the post office (daily 6am–11pm), or phone from any *períptero*; the one by the *Hotel Lucia* is quieter than that in the harbour square.

Tourist police Kareskáki 44 (☎94-477). Town and harbour police are on the inner harbour.

Travel agencies *Bassias Travel* (Skridhlóf 46; ☎44-295) is a good bet for cheap bus tickets, flights and standard excursions. Other agents for tours and day-trips are everywhere – one of the biggest is *Interkreta* (Kaneváro 9; ☎52-552).

Work If you're looking for work picking oranges or on other harvests, join everyone else in *Costa's* on the harbour square first thing in the morning.

Akrotíri and the Bay of Sóudha

The hilly peninsula of **Akrotíri** loops round to the east of Haniá, protecting the magnificent anchorages of the Bay of Sóudha. It's a somewhat strange amalgam, with a couple of developing **resorts** on the north coast, several ancient **monasteries** in the northeast, and military installations and the airport dominating the centre and south. Leaving town, the roads are good but as you progress the surfaces become worse and the signs more confusing: heading for the more distant monasteries you wind up on a really narrow track and, eventually, are reduced to walking.

The Venizélos Graves

Following the Akrotíri signs east out of Haniá you embark on a long climb as you leave the city. At the top there's a sign to the **Venizélos Graves**, the simple stone-slab tombs of Eleftheríos Venizélos, Crete's most famous statesman, and his son Sophocles. The setting, looking back over Haniá, is magnificent and also historic – the scene in 1897 of an illegal raising of the Greek flag in defiance of the Turks and the European powers. The flagpole was smashed by a salvo from the European fleet, but the Cretans raised their standard by hand, keeping it flying even under fire. Two stories attach to this: one that the sailors were so impressed that they all stopped firing to applaud; the second that a shell fired from a Russian ship hit the little church of Profítis Elías, which still stands, and that divine revenge caused the offending ship itself to explode the very next day.

The beaches: Stavrós

The road divides by the graves. Straight ahead takes you to the airport and to Korakiés, very close by, where there's an excellent taverna, *Nikteridha*; the northern branch, to Horafákia and Stavrós, is the road to the **beaches**. This is pleasant country to drive around, gently rolling and dotted with villages that are clearly quite wealthy – many city workers live out here or build themselves country villas. About 5km along the northern road, past the village of Kounoupidhianá, the road suddenly plunges down and emerges by the beach at **Kalathás**, two little patches of sand divided by a rocky promontory, with a couple of tavernas on the road behind. This makes a fine place to spend a lazy day, marred only slightly by the proximity of the road. Two kilometres beyond Kalathás on the Ayía Triádha road out of Horafákia, there's an excellent **zaharoplasteío** called *Stavros Bakery,* whose *baklavá* variations are terrific: try their *karída baklavá*, made with coconut.

Carry on to the end of the road, another 3km beyond Horáfakia, and you'll find a near-perfect beach at **STAVRÓS**: an almost completely enclosed circular bay, the sea is dead calm with a gently shelving sand underfoot, making it ideal for kids. It's an extraordinary-looking place, too, with a sheer, bare mountainside rising just 100m away from you on the far side of the bay. This is where the cataclysmic climax of *Zorba the Greek* was filmed (the hill is known locally as Zorba's Mountain) and is also the site of a cave, whose entrance can just about be seen from the beach, in which there was an ancient sanctuary.

The beach is often crowded – it doesn't take many people to fill it up – but even so it's a pleasant place to bask for a few hours, and is the one place near Haniá that's easily accessible by bus (6 daily). There are tavernas behind the beach if you want to make it a meal break; *Mama's* also rents simple rooms without bath, and there's some scattered building, mostly apartments. Nearby **Blue Beach**, with a tiny sand beach in a cove that is largely artificial (though you wouldn't know it), has one of the best apartment/rooms places, *Blue Beach* (☎0821/64-140); pricey but worth it for its spotless rooms and cliff-top position above the sea. Another good contact for apartments in the Stavrós area is a shop in Haniá at Tsoudherón 1 (☎0821/22-244).

The monasteries

For the **monasteries** at the northern end of the peninsula the most direct approach is to branch right in Kounoupidhianá and follow the signs to Ayía Triádha, though there's also a road up from the airport and a dusty track which cuts across from the Stavrós road. If you follow the signs, you should make it eventually.

Ayía Triádha
Ayía Triádha (daily 7.30am–2pm & 5–7pm; 200dr), sometimes known as *Moní Zangarólo* after its founder, was established in the seventeenth century and built in Venetian style. Today, while not exactly thriving, it is one of the few Cretan monasteries to preserve real monastic life to any degree. Its imposing ochre frontage is approached through carefully tended fields and olive groves – all the property of the monastery. Close up, though, some of the buildings themselves are distinctly dilapidated and, despite an ongoing programme of renovation, at least half of the premises lie redundant and empty. Some of the halls at the back have been given over to the stabling of the monks' goats, and skinny cats wander seemingly at will.

You can walk right through the complex, though the monastic cells are locked, and sit on benches shaded by orange trees on the patio. The church, which appears strangely foreshortened, contains a beautiful old gilded altarpiece and, around the walls, ancient wooden stalls; it is built, like most of the monastery, from stone that glows orange in the afternoon sun. By the entrance is a small museum with vestments, relics and ancient manuscripts, mostly dating from the eighteenth or nineteenth centuries, and a few icons which are considerably older. Above, you can climb up beside the campanile to look out over the monastery's fields and beyond. In the courtyard there's a water cooler, and if you're lucky the traditional hospitality will extend further, to a glass of *rakí* and a piece of *loukoum* in the hall where you sign the visitors' book.

Gouvernétou and Katholikó

Outside Ayía Triádha a sign directs you towards **Gouvernétou** (daily 8am–noon & 3–7pm) – about 4km away, first on dirt track ascending through a biblical landscape of rocks and wild olives, and then up a paved but twisting and rutted road through a rocky gully; a spectacular but not a particularly easy drive. The monastery itself is a simple square block of a building, older than Ayía Triádha, with the usual refreshingly shaded patio and ancient frescoes in the church; there's a tiny museum, too. The few visitors here, and the stark surroundings, help to give a real sense of the isolation that the remaining monks must face for most of the year.

Beyond you can follow (on foot) a path which leads towards another monastery, Katholikó, and the sea. After about ten minutes you reach a **cave** in which St John the Hermit is said to have lived and died – a large, low cavern, stark, dank and dripping, with hefty stalactites and stalagmites. Small outbuildings surround the entrance.

Thus far the walk has been easy, along an obvious path, but as you continue to descend the going gets steeper, rockier and sharper, and in places you have to look for the red paint daubed on the rocks to confirm that you are still on the right trail. In a further fifteen minutes you reach the amazing ruins of the **Monastery of Katholikó**, built into the side of, and partly carved from, a craggy ravine of spectacular desolation. This is older still – it was abandoned over three hundred years ago when the monks, driven by repeated pirate raids, moved up to the comparative safety of Gouvernétou. The valley sides are dotted with caves which formed a centre of still earlier Christian worship, at least one of which (just before the buildings) you can explore if you have a torch.

Spanning the ravine by the ruins is a vast bridge leading nowhere. Cross it and you can scramble down to the bottom of the ravine and follow the stream bed all the way to the sea – about another fifteen minutes. There's a tiny natural **harbour**, a fjord-like finger of water pushing up between the rocks, where remains of a port can still be made out. Hewn from the rock, and with part of its roof intact, is what appears to be an ancient boathouse or slipway. There's no beach, but it's easy enough, and delightfully welcome, to lower yourself from the rocks straight into the astonishingly clear green water.

The walk **back up** takes considerably longer – perhaps an hour in all – and is much more strenuous than it might have seemed on the way down.

Sóudha Bay

On the **south side of Akrotíri** there are beaches near Stérnes, but in practice it's not worth the effort to get there. Almost all of this part of the peninsula is a military zone and the only coast you can reach is a small and rather scrubby stretch of sand. The one consolation is the view of the bay as you go down towards Maráthi: above all of the little island (Néa Sóudha) bristling with Venetian and Turkish fortifications which, from a distance at least, appear miraculously well preserved. It proved as impressive a defence as it looks, holding out as a Venetian stronghold for over thirty years after the rest of the island had fallen, before eventually being voluntarily abandoned.

For an alternative route back, you can cut around the other side of the neck of the peninsula, following the road which curves round to Sóudha town. This again affords spectacular views of the bay (there are signs prohibiting photography of the military secrets therein), down over the villas built into the hillside.

The Allied war cemetery

Just before Sóudha, at the water's edge, you pass the superbly sited **Allied war cemetery**. Surrounded by eucalyptus trees, it lies 1km before the town, down a lane signed "Sóudha cemetery" close to the *Paloma* taverna (which is good and cheap). With its row upon row of immaculately kept headstones, many of them to unknown soldiers and others to men disturbingly young, the serene and dignified cemetery brings home with some force the scale of the calamity of the Battle of Crete in which most of them perished. Grave 10E on the cemetery's northern side holds the remains of the distinguished archeologist John Pendlebury, who took over at Knossós after Evans retired; he died in 1941 fighting alongside Cretans during the German assault on Iráklion.

From here the main Sóudha road heads back to Haniá or you can join the E75 highway and continue east.

East to Yeoryióupolis

Heading directly east out of Haniá you can either pick up the main E75 road where it starts, on the south side of town, or follow the buses and most of the other traffic to Sóudha and join it there. As it climbs above the edge of the **Bay of Sóudha** the E75 follows the track of the old; at the point of the bay stands an old fortress, originally the Turkish bastion of **Izzedin**, now pressed into service as a prison.

The new road is fast, but you'll see little through the screen of trees and flowering shrubs until you emerge on the coast just past Yeoryióupolis. Once you set off down the hill past Izzedin there are a couple of turn-offs to villages but just one junction of any size, between Vrísses and Yeoryióupolis, signed to both of them. If you're in no hurry, or you simply want an attractive circular drive, then the minor roads that head inland or out onto the Dhrápano peninsula have much more to offer.

Áptera and inland

Shortly before the fort, roads lead off left and right: left is signed to Kalámi (just a few hundred metres away, immediately below the prison) and Kalíves (which you can see on the coast way below); turn right and you climb to Megála Horáfia and, turning off again, ancient **ÁPTERA** (Tues–Sun 10am–3pm; free). Áptera occupies the table top of this mesa-like mountain, about 3km from – and a good climb above – the new road. From the fifth century BC well into early Christian times this was one of the island's most important cities: substantial ruins remain, although since their excavation early this century they have deteriorated considerably. Among the more obvious relics are the massive walls, almost 4km long, which predate everything else at the site; the large L-shaped Roman cisterns and other buildings scattered around the abandoned monastery which marks the centre of the site; and a Classical Greek temple and theatre in the south. There is more, but since it's all hidden behind fences the excitement is limited, and the countryside is rough, barren and hot for exploring on foot. A much greater attraction of the setting is another crumbling Turkish fort – substantially shored up with reinforced concrete – on the lip of the hilltop, with the best of all the **views** across Sóudha and the Akrotíri. Immediately below is the Izzedin fortress, and below that the three small islands, including heavily fortified Néa Sóudha, which protect the narrow entrance to the bay. From here its superb strategic qualities are plain, with the deep-water anchorages accessible only by running the gauntlet of these forts and fortified islands. According to legend the islands were formed after a musical contest between the Muses and the Sirens on the height near the ancient city: defeated, the Sirens plucked off their wings, flung themselves into the bay, and were transformed into the islands. Áptera, literally translated, can mean "featherless" or "wingless" – one derivation of the city's name.

At the foot of the hill which ascends to the site, the *Taverna Aptera* makes up with its culinary skills for what it lacks in shade.

Stílos and Samonás

From Áptera you can retrace your steps back to the main road, or continue inland to circle round via the Dhrápano peninsula, a very attractive drive. In Megála Horáfia, right opposite the Áptera turn-off, there's a large taverna which is frequently the venue of *bouzouki* nights – look out for posters.

The first place of any size south of here is **STÍLOS**, which is where the Australian and New Zealand rearguard made their final stand during the Battle of Crete (this was then the main road south), enabling the majority of Allied troops to be evacuated while they themselves were mostly stranded on the island. Many found refuge in the villages in the foothills around here and were later smuggled off the island – some of these villages were destroyed in retribution. Today Stílos is an unremarkable agricultural centre, but there are a couple of *kafenia* with shady tables beside the road where you can pull over for a drink.

Not far beyond comes the turning to **SAMONÁS**, a narrow road winding steeply up through 180-degree hairpins, with better views at every turn. The reason to take this detour is to visit the isolated Byzantine church of Áyios Nikólaos at Kiriakosélia, which you'll see signed beyond Samonás. The church, nestling in a valley, has recently been restored and contains fantastic **medieval frescoes**, as good as any on Crete. Painted in the thirteenth century, these have not been touched by the restorers – at least not recently – and are patchy and faded against their deep-blue background, but parts still seem as vivid as the day they were created: in particular a *Madonna and Child*, at eye level on the left-hand side and a dramatic Christ *pantokrátor* in the drum dome. To see them, however, you really need a car, because the keyholders (Kostas or Roussa) live in Samonás – you pick them up there and drive on to the church, a couple of hilly kilometres further (half on a bumpy dirt road). Head for the *kafenion* in Samonás – preferably in the afternoon – and they'll ring for someone to take you, and cheerily overcharge for a drink while you wait. By contrast Kostas or Roussa (or one of their daughters) always seem to refuse money for their time.

The Dhrápano peninsula and Vrísses

A multitude of roads crisscross the **Dhrápano peninsula**, almost all of them scenic and well surfaced. This is rich agricultural land, a countryside of rolling green, wooded hills interrupted by immaculately whitewashed, and obviously wealthy, villages. Nowhere are there individual attractions to detain you long, but all these settlements have *kafenia* where you can sit awhile and wonder at the rural tranquillity away from the main-road traffic. Coming from Stílos you can either head through Néo Horío to Kalíves on the coast, or turn off later for Vámos at the centre of the peninsula. The direct approach, however, is from the E75 highway below Áptera.

Kalíves, Almirídha and the coast

From Kalámi, the old road drops rapidly down to the coast at **KALÍVES**, an agricultural market centre of some size. Approaching, you pass a long sandy beach in the lee of Áptera's castle-topped bluff which looks attractive but is hard to reach. The main beach stretches west from the centre of the village, curving round at the far end by a small harbour where it's more sheltered – you're better off swimming at this end since at the other, just before the beach, what appears to be an open sewer flows past the public toilets and into the sea (a small river also empties at Kalíves). The village itself is still in the early stages of gearing up for tourism, with a scattering of apartments and studios, and a few rooms. The apartments can be great value, but since they tend to be spread out at either end of the village it's easiest to start at one of the travel agencies in the centre – they should know where the vacancies are. You'll find several places to eat on the main road through, but the best spot is occupied by the *Mini-Golf Bar* (which really does have crazy golf as well as over-priced cocktails and snacks), overlooking the western (town) end of the beach.

ALMIRÍDHA, the next village along the coast, is smaller, marginally more of a resort, and considerably more attractive. Again there are far more apartments than rooms (but less chance of finding space here), and there's a row of tavernas behind a couple of small patches of sand in a sheltered little bay. The lovely beach is a popular spot for windsurfing, with a fairly reliable breeze once you're slightly offshore, and, like Kalíves, is popular with local families who drive down to swim and enjoy a leisurely lunch. The fish tavernas, *Dimitri's* and *Manoli's*, as well as *Thalami* offering standard Greek dishes, are all worth a try. The *Enchanted Owl* is an English-run newcomer with an international menu and serves – if you can face it – a "real English breakfast".

Beyond Almirídha the coast becomes increasingly rocky, with cliffs almost all the way round to Yeoryioúpolis denying access to the sea. The roads also deteriorate if you go this way, but as you climb the views become increasingly worthwhile. There are more beaches below **PLÁKA**, a postcard-picturesque hamlet (with rooms) which, like Kókkino Horió on the steep height above it, served as a set for the filming of parts of *Zorba the Greek*. **KEFALÁS**, with views over the sea on both sides, is a prettier village still.

Gavalohóri and Vámos

An excellent new road runs inland from Almirídha towards Vámos. Immediately inland you pass below **ASPRÓ**, a tiny, ancient hamlet looking down over the coast. This is the old Greek village as you've always imagined it: a couple of lucky foreigners have snapped up the only empty houses.

GAVALOHÓRI, further on, offers something more tangible to stop for, in the shape of a small but excellent **folklore museum** (daily 10am–1pm; 300dr; when closed, enquire at the women's cooperative mentioned below) in a beautifully restored Venetian building with Turkish additions. The history and culture of the village is documented in the various rooms, with items clearly labelled in English as well as Greek. Of particular interest are the examples of stone-cutting, wood-carving and *kopanéli* (silk lace made by bobbin-weaving), which is now being revived in the village. The mulberry trees planted around the village by the Turks still produce silk from the silkworms that feed on their leaves. Evidence that this is an ancient settlement is scattered throughout the village's narrow, winding streets: there are Byzantine wells on the outskirts, and on the corner by the museum you can see the remains of a Turkish coffee shop with inscriptions and old jars. In the central square there is a store run by the *Women's Agrotourism Cooperative*, an organization dedicated to reviving many of the disappearing arts and crafts of the region, and the results of their work – glass, ceramics and *kopi-néli* – are on sale. At nearby Kálamitsi Amigdáli, 8km to the southwest, another women's craft cooperative has been set up: they haven't got a store as yet, but they are already weaving silk to sell. Maria Kakotislakis is currently acting as their "marketing manager" – ask for her at the *kafenion* on the main square.

VÁMOS is the chief village of the region, complete with a big new health centre. Only size really distinguishes it from all the other villages, however, and the *kafenia* round the crossroads are as peaceful as any you'll find.

Vrísses

Almost whichever route you follow, you'll end up approaching **VRÍSSES**, a major junction of the old roads and still, though bypassed by the new, the cross-roads for the route south. If you're travelling between Hóra Sfakíon and Réthimnon or anywhere else to the east, you usually have to change buses here. Set on the banks of the Almirós (or *Tris Almiri*) river, Vrísses is a wonderfully shady little town, its streets lined with huge old plane trees. On the riverside are a couple of tavernas by a bridge and a monument to the independence settle-ment of 1898; plenty of smaller cafés line the main street, many of them offering good local honey and yoghurt which is said by many to be the best on the island. There are also **rooms**, should you want one, though they're not desperately attractive.

Heading back towards the coast from Vrísses, the road cuts under the E75 once again, following the river valley down to Yeoryióupolis. This is another lovely stretch, through well-watered fields and woods. About halfway you can pull over to a picnic spot shaded by cypress trees, with a whitewashed chapel by the roadside, fresh spring water and huge picnic tables.

If you're **driving to Sfakiá**, incidentally, it's a good idea to fill up here: fuel is available at a couple of villages en route, but there are only sparse, expensive supplies in other villages along the south coast. About 4km along the road to Hóra Sfakíon, and worth a look if you're passing, the village of Alíkambos lies just off the road. In its church of Panayía there are good frescoes by the fourteenth-century master, Ioánnis Pagomenos; they are remarkably well preserved, which is surpris-ing in view of the way the locals prod them vigorously with their fingers when point-ing out images or the names of the saints. The church lies down a track off to the left just before the village and near a Venetian fountain. Should you miss the unsigned turn-off, the *kafenion* in the village square, fronted by a couple of unexploded bombs from World War II, will provide directions. At Máza, 3km northeast of here, there's another frescoed church, although this is not quite so good nor as well preserved. (The rest of the route south to Hóra Sfakíon is covered on pp.262–63.)

Yeoryióupolis

YEORYIÓUPOLIS (or Georgioupolis) lies at the base of Cape Dhrápano where the Almirós flows into the sea. Like Vrísses it's a beautiful old place, with a tree-lined approach and ancient eucalyptus trees shading the huge square in the centre. Unlike Vrísses it's now an established resort, although on a small enough scale to remain an extremely pleasant place to spend a few days.

The main course of the river runs into the Gulf of Almirós on the northern edge of Yeoryióupolis, by a small harbour protected by a long rocky breakwater, and there are numerous smaller streams running into the sea all around. The main town **beach** heads off to the south, curving round to join the continuous stretch which runs alongside the Réthimnon road for miles. Close to town it shelves very gently and enjoys the protection of the breakwater, and so is popular with Greek families. Showers are provided here, and there are more showers further round, by *Mike's Oasis* (good ice cream and cocktails). At the far end, there are new hotels and beach bars, but there are also **dangerous currents** offshore: don't venture too far out, and take heed of any warning notices on the beach. Windsurfers can be rented by the *El Dorado* hotel. Streams crossing the beach create little quicksands in places (only knee-deep), but most of these have wooden bridges to let you cross without getting your feet wet.

A second, much more sheltered beach lies to the north of the river in a small bay. Swimming here is safer and there are generally fewer people, but the water can be extremely cold, owing to the rivers emptying at each end of the sand. There are a couple of simple bar/tavernas behind this beach. At the far end, beyond the smaller stream, you can follow a path over sharp rocks, past an old chapel and various caves, but in the end it leads only to more sharp rocks and eventually peters out above the cliffs.

Arrival, information and services

Buses drop you on the main road, just a couple of minutes' walk from the square and crossroads at the centre of town. There are several local **travel agents** and **car-rental** places: *Geo Travel* (on the square near *Sun Set* bar, ☎0821/61-206) is one of the best, with services including **money exchange** at decent rates. You can buy newspapers and attempt to make **phone calls** from a *perίptero* kiosk on the square, and a couple of small **stores** and a fruit stall here stock all the basics. A kiosk at the bus stop on the main highway (opposite the *Blue Sky* disco-bar) sells inclusive tickets for the **Samarian gorge return-trip**; buses leave daily at 6.35am and 7.20am.

Accommodation

There are **rooms** to rent everywhere, it seems, and only at the height of season are you likely to have any trouble finding a vacancy; even then you should be all right if you arrive early in the day.

Some of the better places to stay, and also the first to fill up in high season, are to the right from the square, down the lane which heads towards the beach. *Zorba's Taverna* and *Andy's Rooms* (both ②) are possibilities here, but further on are places where the views and sounds are of the sea rather than the street – *Rooms Irini*

(☎0825/61-278; ②) and *Pension Cactus* (②), for example. Another cluster of rooms places lies inland, to the west of the square: *Taverna Paradise* (☎0825/61-313; ②) has rooms above a restaurant and nearby, surrounded by lofty plane trees, there's the pleasant *Hotel Drosia* (☎0825/61-326; ②). Off the square's southern end on the left is the cheaper *Rooms Voula* (☎0825/61-359; ①) above a souvenir store, which also allows use of a kitchen. To the north of the square where the road crosses the river there's the appropriately named *The Bridge* (②) on the near side, and *Anna* (②) on the far side. Mosquitos can be a problem by the river, but the wildlife on the banks is some compensation. Kingfishers can often be seen here.

If you still have trouble finding space, two basic hotels right on the square, the *Amfimala* (☎0831/61-362; ①) and the more recently renovated *Penelope* (☎0831/61-370; ②), are often the last to fill, probably because of the noise at night. With your own vehicle, you could consider a trip to the charming hill village of Exópolis, 3km out of town, where excellent-value studio rooms are to be had at *Marika Studio Apartments* (☎0821/58-831; ①); there are also a couple of tavernas nearby.

Eating, drinking and nightlife

Restaurants in Yeoryióupolis are concentrated round the square, and there are plenty to choose from. The *Café Georgiouopolis Pub* is a fine place for breakfast or to sit over a long drink, watching the world go by; *Samaria*, nearby, is similar. *Hotel Amfimala* has the square's most authentic *kafenion* with outdoor tables and, just west of the square, *Taverna Paradise* is another good place, with tables in a garden. East of the square and out a bit to where the E75 passes the village's edge, *Taverna Georgis* cooks excellent meat and fish dishes on a charcoal fire and in a wood-fired oven; it's set slightly back from the street, approached through a bower, and not to be confused with the dreary place next door. Another good alternative, away from the rush, is *To Arkadi*, on a point by the mouth of the river, on the far side. The *Hotel Gorgona*, on the town beach, also has a decent taverna looking out to sea, while the new *Manoussos*, between the village and the main highway, has an interesting menu and good house wines

Bars again crowd around the square and out towards the main road – *Sun Set* serves poor cocktails but has good music and atmosphere. Alternative entertainment is on offer at a tiny, open-air **cinema**, where they show a different film every night, usually subtitled; programme details are pinned to a tree in the square. There's a choice of two **discos**: the raucous *Time*, across the river bridge and then right after 500m, with a free mini-van service from the square; or the *Blue Sky* disco-bar in the opposite direction, on the E75 highway. Should you get bored here, they also have floodlit mini-golf as a sideline.

Lake Kournás

Four kilometres inland from Yeoryióupolis, the island's only freshwater lake, **Lake Kournás**, shelters in a bowl of hills – an easy if unexciting walk.*

As lakes go, it's small and shallow, but it nevertheless makes for an interesting afternoon's excursion. The appearance of the lake varies greatly according to

---

*There are more rewards in hiking up the Almirós valley towards Vrísses or tackling the steep climb to Exópolis on the road to Vámos where there are two wonderfully sited tavernas with magnificent views.

when you visit: during the day its colours change remarkably as the sun shifts around the rim of the bowl, and its size alters over the course of a year. In late summer, the level drops to reveal sand (or dried mud) beaches all around and a number of popular camping spots. Earlier in the year, the water comes right up to the tidal ring of scrubby growth and it's much harder to find anywhere to camp or to swim from. The lake and the hills around it are also a good place to seek out some of the more unusual island wildlife (see pp.313–21). There's a path which makes a circuit of the lake, about an hour's walk. On the bank where you arrive there's the *Panorama* **taverna** – a popular place for locals' outings, with lamb barbecued on spits – and a few pedaloes and canoes for rent. Upstairs the taverna has about six new **rooms** (③), overpriced and gnat-infested but immaculately sited, looking out over the water, and very comfortable if you have repellent coils to burn. If these are full, you could try at the village of Mourí, which is straight up from the junction with the path that leads down to the banks.

The village of **KOURNÁS** is another 4km beyond the lake, a stiff climb which reveals nothing very exciting – a tranquil, medium-sized village with a couple of sleepy cafés. From here you could follow the poorly maintained road to rejoin the old Haniá–Réthimnon road somewhere before Episkopí (see p.189).

Inland: walks and Venizélos country

The country behind Haniá, a small agricultural plain into which the foothills of the White Mountains intrude, is not the most thrilling in Crete, but with a day to spare it does deserve exploration – especially if you're prepared to embark on some serious hiking. For the most part they grow oranges here, oranges which are the best in Crete and hence, as any local will tell you, the finest in the world. Many of the villages are also associated with **Eleftheríos Venizélos**, the revered Cretan statesman who, as prime minister of Greece for most of the period from 1910 to 1932, finally brought Crete into the modern Greek nation.

Thériso

Perhaps the most attractive journey is the fourteen-kilometre drive up to **THÉRISO**, hometown of Venizélos' mother and one of the cradles of Cretan independence. Here in 1905 was held the Revolutionary Assembly (all baggy black shirts and drooping moustaches, as depicted in so many Cretan museums) that ousted Prince George and did much to precipitate union with Greece. The trip out to the little house, with its plaque commemorating the famous son, is an all but obligatory one for Cretans, and the village seems frequently to find itself crowded with busloads of battling schoolkids. There's actually little to see apart from a traditional country village, but it's worth going anyway for the drive up **Thériso gorge**. In terms of spectacle this can't, of course, compare with Samariá and, in any case, the bed of the ravine is given over to the (mostly paved) road. But it is exceedingly pretty in the lower reaches, gentle and winding with the stream crossed and recrossed on rickety bridges, and surprisingly craggy towards the top where the walls are cracked and pocked with caves.

If you want to continue and complete a circle round to Mesklá (see over), you face a heady climb into the foothills of the mountains and over what feels like an impressively lofty ridge. This road is narrow, rocky and punctuated by gates to prevent livestock straying, and it's not always obvious which way to go, but it's not too bad a drive. Alternatively, it makes a wonderful long hike, occasionally traversed by organized rambling groups but quite possible on your own – as long as you check the route beforehand, ask the way if in doubt, and check bus times to get you home again. There are **buses** to both Thériso and Mesklá from Haniá, and the walk between the two takes less than three hours. Given the vagaries of the timetable, though, the trip is liable to take all day if you do it by bus.

On to Mesklá

Right at the top lies **SÓURVA**, a cluster of whitewashed houses with stupendous views over the surrounding valleys. There's nothing to do here – a lone *kafenion* is tended by a menacing guard dog – but it is a hell of a setting. From Sóurva the way spirals slowly down to **MESKLÁ**, another beautiful village set on a swift-flowing brook and surrounded by lush agricultural land and orange groves; there are several small café/tavernas here. Under the Venetians, Mesklá was a place of considerably more importance than it is now, as indicated by the tiny chapel at the bottom of the village (a turn up to the left if you are approaching from the Fournés end) containing the remains of fourteenth-century **frescoes**. The chapel itself is unprepossessing, and many of the paintings have been severely damaged by damp and mould, but parts remain clearly visible and are all the more remarkable for their ordinary surroundings. There's another chapel alleged to contain the remains of a fifth- or sixth-century Roman mosaic, alongside a modern church at the top end of the village. Since church and chapel both seem permanently locked, however, there's no way of knowing.

Mesklá was also the centre of one of the great legends of Cretan resistance, the **Kandanoleon revolt**. According to the story (which is certainly not historically accurate, though it probably has some basis in fact), much of western Crete rose against the Venetians early in the sixteenth century. They elected as their leader one George Kandanoleon who established a base in Mesklá and from here ran a rebel administration, collecting taxes and effectively controlling much of the west. It was only by treachery that he was finally brought to heel. In order to legitimize his authority, Kandanoleon arranged for his son to marry the daughter of a Venetian aristocrat. The marriage took place and the celebrations began, with Kandanoleon and several hundred of his supporters eating and drinking themselves to a stuporous standstill. At which point, by pre-arranged signal, a Venetian army arrived and captured the Cretans as they slept; their leaders were hanged at villages around the countryside, and the revolt was over.

Fournés and Mourniés

Continuing on foot you could tackle the steep climb to Lákki (see p.249) on the main road to Omalós and the Samarian gorge. The road, however, and the direct route to Haniá, head down to **FOURNÉS** and join the main road there. Fournés is a very much larger place, with stores lining the road (good for stocking up if you're doing this circuit in reverse), heavily cultivated fields roundabout and a large producers' cooperative.

If you want to complete your Venizélos pilgrimage you should also visit **MOURNIÉS**, where the great man was born in 1864. Immediately south of Haniá, this is easiest reached by heading out towards the main E75 highway. Mourniés is just a couple of kilometres southwest off this and, Venizélos' birthplace aside, has little to see, but it's another pleasant drive out of the city, along a road lined with ancient plane trees.

The coast west of Haniá

West from Haniá the main E65 road follows the coastline more or less consistently all the way to the base of the Rodhópou peninsula. Occasionally it runs right above the water, more often 100m or so inland, but never more than easy walking distance from the sea. The coastal route is well served by buses, running every thirty minutes between Haniá and Kolimbári, early morning to late evening. As always, though, you'll really need your own transport to explore the remoter areas inland.

In the early stages the various villages have merged into an almost continuous string of ribbon development – not exactly ugly, but not particularly attractive either. There are villas, hotels and sporadic pensions or rooms to rent all the way, though little in the budget range, and vacancies are often scarce in season. As you leave the city behind, this development thins, giving way between towns to orange groves protected from the *meltémi* by calamus-reed windbreaks, where only the occasional path penetrates down to the sea. There is **beach** of sorts almost all the way, though much is windswept, dirty and subject to crashing breakers; for secure swimming you're better off closer to Haniá – at the city beach of Kalamáki, at Ayía Marína, or at Plataniás.

This coastline was the scene of the fiercest fighting in the **Battle of Crete**, and the bridgehead from which the Germans established their domination. There's a reminder of this almost immediately you leave the city, in the form of an aggressive swooping eagle, erected beside the road by the Germans as a memorial to their paratroops. Passing this, you're into the stretch of coast along which are ranged the town beaches (pp.226–7), though the road here actually veers away from the sea as much as it does anywhere. Frequent minor roads run either down to the beach or up into the hills, where there are some pleasant villas and small hotels looking down over the coastline, and a great deal of development going on.

Galatás and around

Villages like Dharátsos, **GALATÁS** and places even less well defined seem thoroughly unattractive as you drive along the main road, but in most cases there is a real village, up in the hills inland. Galatás actually turns out to be a fair-sized place, in whose village hall is a small Battle of Crete museum, basically a collection of rusty guns and helmets. Outside is a memorial to those who died here, including 145 New Zealand soldiers. *Uncle John's*, opposite, is a good place for a snack if you're passing.

Four kilometres to the southwest of Galatás village on the outskirts of Ayía lies a reservoir renowned for its birdlife. Despite being flanked by a couple of unsightly factories, the marshland itself is home to a rich variety of species, including Crakes, Avocet, Marsh Harrier, Spotted Flycatcher and Squacco Heron in season. The best approach is by a track which descends between a church and a service station on the village's eastern perimeter. It then turns right, flanked by rushes to the edge of the marsh where the low, bevelled concrete roof of an old building makes an ideal "hide".

Ayía Marína and Plataniás

Kalamáki, where the road finally comes in sight of the beach, marks the limit of the local bus service from Haniá and also the end of this strip of sand. Beyond, low hills drop straight to the sea round a couple of bends and then you emerge at

Káto Stalós, which runs into **AYÍA MARÍNA**, the first substantial village along this stretch: in fact, there's virtually no break in the development from Káto Stalós to Plataniás, creating the most developed strip in the west of the island, with stores, restaurants, hotels, rooms for rent, travel agents, tavernas, discos and bike-rental places. This is better than it sounds: it's all fairly low-rise, there's a decent beach almost all the way along (with facilities including jet-skis, windsurfers and parascending) and, by resort standards, it's all pretty quiet.

Ayía Marína itself is distinguished by a small brick factory and, towards the end of the village, *Camping Ayia Marina*, proudly guarding a beautiful sector of beach. Curving round a little promontory, this has a fine view of the sunset and of **Áyii Theódori**, the island offshore which is now a sanctuary for *kri-kri* or wild goats (you're not allowed to land on the island). From the west of the islet a great cave gapes like the jaws of a beast; indeed, legend has Áyii Theódori as a sea-monster which, emerging from the depths to swallow Crete, was petrified by the gods. Remains found in the cave suggest that it was a place of Minoan worship in antiquity, while in more recent times the Venetians turned the whole island into a fortress against the threat of piracy and Turkish invasion.

Heading west again, **PLATANIÁS** follows seamlessly, boasting a delightful old quarter perched high on an almost sheer bluff above the road. There are a number of tavernas which attract evening and weekend trippers from Haniá, notably *O Milos* towards the west end of the village. Specialities here, and elsewhere in the village, are *yíros* and *kokorétsi* – meat or offal cooked on huge spits over charcoal – but the *Milos* has extra attractions in the form of an old millstream with ducks in it running through a walled garden at the back where you eat. *The Carob Tree*, halfway up the hill to the village, has a more varied menu and views way along the coast, while the *Margarita*, a little way back down the hill, serves a memorable tuna steak.

Yeráni to Tavronítis

Beyond Plataniás, things change little all the way to the Rodhópou peninsula, though signs of tourism get fewer the further you go, with lots of isolated villas and one or two slightly more concentrated developments in places such as Yeráni. These on the whole are pleasantly low-key, but the beach is rarely that great, being very open to wind and waves and with rather gravelly, grey sand. Frequent paths and tracks lead down from the road to the sea.

MÁLEME is perhaps the place you're most likely to stop. Just beyond lies the airfield which saw much of the early fighting in the Battle of Crete and where the German invasion began on May 20, 1941; the loss of this airfield in controversial circumstances was crucial to the German success. Although it's a restricted military zone no one seems to mind if you wander just inside the gate to have a peek. Just before the airfield the giant *Crete Chandris* hotel lies to the right of the road, dominating the only bit of sandy beach around. If you're feeling brazen you can walk through to this: the hotel also has a pool and a couple of bars in luxurious grounds.

Almost directly opposite the hotel, a narrow lane leads up to the **German war cemetery**, set on a hillside below the ridge known as Hill 107, which played a crucial role in the defence of, and the battle for, the airfield. Now overlooking the battleground where so many of those buried here lost their lives, the lines of flat headstones each marking a double grave lend a sombre aspect to an otherwise peaceful scene. In a piece of almost grotesque irony its keepers, until recently, were George Psychoundákis (author of *The Cretan Runner*, when offered the job, he was allegedly told, "You looked after the Germans while they were alive, why not look after them now they're dead?") and Manoli Pateraki, who played a leading role in the capture of General Kreipe (see p.299).

In a bizarre twist of fate, the discovery in 1966 of a splendid **Late Minoan tomb** nearby demonstrated that this area had already been a graveyard for over three thousand years. To reach it, follow the lane leading down from the cemetery to the first left bend, where a track signed on the right leads 100m along a terraced hillside to the tomb, again on the right. The *dromos* or entrance passage of the stone-built tomb and its heavy lintel are well preserved.

There's a final reminder of Máleme's significance in the Battle of Crete as you cross the River Tavronítis on a long modern bridge: beside it, twin pontoon bridges survive from the war. **TAVRONÍTIS** itself is still a traditional farming centre, with fruit for sale at stalls beside the road, and marks the junction with the road across the island to Paleohóra (p.275).

Kolimbári and Moní Gonía

Continuing west, **KOLIMBÁRI**, at the base of the Rodhópou peninsula, has far more appeal than anything that has preceded it along this coast. If there were a sandy beach, it would be a perfect resort: as it is there's a long strip of pebbles and clear water looking back along all the coast towards Haniá in the distance. It's little spoiled, and behind the narrow main street with a few tavernas there's a concrete promenade lined with more tavernas and a small harbour. The place is tranquil and, should you want to stay, there are a few places offering **rooms**: for rooms with baths, try the good-value *Hotel Dimitra* (☎0824/22-244; ①) at the end of the village, set slightly back from the sea. A good place for a drink is *Mylos*, a stylish bar converted from an old olive oil mill, with a pleasant sea-view terrace. **Tavernas** also cluster around the seafront and at the top of the 500-metre-long tree-lined avenue which separates the village from its junction on the main road (and where some buses may drop you). Here there's a cluster of hotels, bars and restaurants serving the passing trade, as well as a couple of grill tavernas that are favourites with the locals. One of these, *Macarona*, is sited on a concrete terrace and the exuberance of its owner, Eleni, makes up for what it lacks in finesse. They serve hefty *souvláki* and roast chicken, provided by the adjoining family butchers which seems to stay open as late as the restaurant.

Out onto the peninsula, it's only a few minutes' walk to the **Moní Gonía** (closed from 2 to 5pm; the strict "no shorts" signs outside apply only to beachwear). The monastery occupies a prime site, with stupendous views and a scramble down to what appears to be a sandy cove – rumoured to be the monks' private beach. Founded at the beginning of the seventeenth century, the monastery perhaps has less to show than some, but has stirring tales to tell of resistance to the infidel Turk. Here they can point to the cannonballs still lodged in the walls to prove it – a relic they seem far more proud of than any icon. Which is not to say there are no worthwhile icons: the church has a fine series of post-Byzantine ones dating from the seventeenth and eighteenth centuries (plus a few modern ones), of which Áyios Nikólaos, in a side chapel, is particularly fine. More are kept in the small **museum** (200dr), along with assorted vestments and relics. Although there are (or were) only six monks left, they remain very hospitable and there's even a "tourist monk", Brother Andonios, who has been pointing things out to visitors for years, often treating them to a glass of *rakí* and a look at his treasured stamp collection (all contributions welcome).

Opposite the monastery and beside a fountain, a steep track climbs the cliff in five minutes to the tiny fourteenth-century church that was attached to the original monastery. The church has fragmentary frescoes, and from its terrace there's a wonderful **view** over the monastery and the Gulf of Haniá beyond.

The Rodhópou peninsula

The road that extends onto the **Rodhópou peninsula** goes nowhere in particular, petering out into a dirt track beyond Afráta and then circling back, but the first part at least is a superb drive. Just beyond the monastery is a modern Orthodox academy and from here the road follows the coast for a short way and then begins to climb, hairpinning its way to a dizzy height above the sea before turning inland. The views are magnificent – not only back along the coast you have traversed but also down into the translucent green sea.

AFRÁTA is a tiny place, little visited, with a few simple *kafenia*. Carry on down the hill past the first two of these and you'll come to *Taverna Roxani*. Roxani speaks no English, but she serves good, simple food – including fresh fish: try the *fagrí* (sea bream) if available – in a lovely setting. Below *Roxani's*, keep right on a paved track which drops steeply and after little more than 1km you'll reach a rocky cove, at the far end of the gorge you can see from the village. The exceptionally clear water here offers great swimming, often with no one else about, though you need to watch out for sea urchins and sharp rocks. In the other direction from Afráta, an unsurfaced road is signed to Astrátigos and Áspra Nerá. This is not too bad a drive, and shortly after Áspra Nerá you can rejoin the paved Rodhopós road to head down to the base of the peninsula again.

Towards the tip of the peninsula you'll find no more driveable roads, though there are a couple of sites you might consider undertaking a major hike or a boat trip to reach. The latter is certainly the easier option – in summer the terrain is frighteningly hot, barren and shadeless for walking – especially as day-trip boats from Haniá quite often make for **Diktynna**, almost at the top of the peninsula above a little bay on the east side. An important Roman sanctuary to the goddess of the same name, this was probably built over more ancient centres of worship, and though it has never been properly excavated there's a surprising amount to be seen. The boats come here mainly because it's a sheltered spot to swim (when the sea is rough, fishing boats often shelter here, too), but they allow plenty of time to explore.

On the other side of the peninsula, the isolated **Church of Áyios Ioánnis Giónis** can make a challenging hike and, on August 29 (St John the Baptist's Day), is host to a major pilgrimage and a mass baptism of boys called John, marking one of the most important festivals of the Cretan religious calendar. At this time the two- to three-hour walk (each way), among crowds of people, is definitely worth it. Although you can approach from Afráta, the main path up the spine of the island starts in Rodhopós, which you reach via the first turn off the main road after Kolimbári, and to where there is an occasional bus (from Kolimbári).

SFAKIÁ AND THE LEFKÁ ÓRI

South of Haniá loom the **Lefká Óri**, or White Mountains – a formidable barrier to progress. Just a couple of metres short of the highest point of the Psilorítis range, these are in every other way more impressive mountains: barer, craggier and far less tamed. There is just one road into the heart of the mountains, climbing up to the cold, enclosed plateau of Omalós. From here any further progress south-wards is on foot – most obviously the spectacular, and spectacularly popular, descent through the great cleft of the **Samarian gorge**. Famous as it is, this is just the largest of a series of ravines by which streams make their escape to the coast. Far less beaten tracks lead, for example, down the **Ímbros gorge** towards Hóra Sfakíon, or from Ayía Iríni to Soúyia. With more preparation you could also go climbing among the peaks – there's a mountaineering hut above Omalós – or undertake an expedition right across the range.

Walks also thread their way along the south coast, although it's a great deal easier to get around by boat. Regular summer services link **Ayía Rouméli**, at the bottom of the Samarian gorge, with **Loutró** and Hóra Sfakíon; in the other direc-tion, there are less frequent connections to Paleohóra and Soúyia. **Hóra Sfakíon** is the capital of this region – **Sfakiá** – which for all its desolation and depopula-tion is perhaps the most famous, and certainly the most written about, in Crete. It is an area notorious for its fierceness: harsh living conditions; unrelenting weather; warlike people. Most men here, it is claimed, still carry a weapon of some kind concealed about their person.

Historically, the region was cut off and barbaric, almost a nation apart which, as occupying armies came and went, carried on with life – feuding, rustling, rear-ing sheep – pretty much regardless. Most of the great tales of Cretan resistance, of *pallikari* fighters and mountain guerrillas, originate in Sfakiá or in Sélinos, west of the mountains. The local version of the Creation reveals much of the Sfakiot spirit. As recounted in Adam Hopkins' book (see p.323), it begins:

> *...with an account of all the gifts God had given to other parts of Crete – olives to Ierapetra, Ayios Vasilios and Selinou; wine to Malevisi and Kissamou; cherries to Mylopotamos and Amari. But when God got to Sfakia only rocks were left. So the Sfakiots appeared before Him armed to the teeth. "And us Lord, how are we going to live on these rocks?" and the Almighty, looking at them with sympathy, replied in their own dialect (naturally): "Haven't you got a scrap of brains in your head? Don't you see that the lowlanders are cultivating all these riches for you?"*

Stealing was a way of life and so was feuding and revenge – with vendettas on a Sicilian scale continuing well into this century, and occasionally rumoured even now.

The Venetians had plans to pacify the region, but their castle on the coast at **Frangokástello** was rarely more than an isolated outpost. The Turks did more, imposing taxation on Sfakiá, for example, but they also provoked more violent revenge, notably in the revolt of Dhaskaloyiánnis (see p.260) and many which succeeded it. The mountains were always a safe refuge in which bandits and rebels could conceal themselves while armies took revenge on the lowlands. In World War II Sfakiá resumed this traditional role: when the Germans invaded, King George was rushed across the island and down the Samarian gorge to be evacuated, and it was from Hóra Sfakíon that the bulk of the Allied forces were evacuated (see p.264). Throughout the war, the mountain heights remained the realm of the resistance, and in the late Sixties two ex-civil war guerrillas were found still hiding out here, twenty years on.

Nowadays all of this seems very distant. There are frequent buses to Hóra Sfakíon and Omalós and a constant stream of people trekking between the two, but you don't have to get far off this path to realize how the reputation grew, and why it still holds such sway.

THE GEOLOGY OF THE LEFKÁ ÓRI

The Lefká Óri take their name from the pale-coloured limestones of which they are formed. These rocks were laid down between 150 million and 40 million years ago, when the region which is now Greece and the Aegean Sea featured a different pattern of land and water, dominated by a large landmass called Apulia.

Material eroded from Apulia was transported southwards and deposited in the sea as a series of limestones which are now seen over much of western Crete: they are known as the Plattenkalk or Ida limestones. The nature of the limestone varied according to the distance from the Apulian coast: those deposited close to the coast were coarse and contained quite large pebbles, while those further away were much finer and were often arranged in thin layers alternating with a flint-like rock called chert.

To understand how these limestones were formed into the mountains seen today it is necessary to understand something of the theory of "plate tectonics". This states that the earth's crust is composed of a number of large, very slowly moving plates, which are added to at "Mid Ocean Ridges" and destroyed again in ocean trenches at "subduction zones". About 35 million years ago the plate containing Africa began to move northwards relative to the plate containing Europe, forcing the Plattenkalk limestones up, and eventually causing slices of the Apulian rocks from the north to be pushed over them. This buried and deformed the Plattenkalk limestones – the results of which can now be clearly seen in the walls of the Samarian gorge, where bands of light limestone and dark chert are intensely folded.

Eventually the movement of African plate caused some of the old sea floor to the south to be pushed under all these rocks and initiated a "subduction zone" running along the southern margin of Crete; further movement has since been taken up by subduction of the sea floor. This process has caused continued slow uplift of Crete, particularly in the south close to the subduction zone. As the Lefká Óri have been pushed up in this manner the slices of Apulian rocks on top of them have been eroded away. (Although old Apulian rocks can still be seen to the north of the mountains where the uplift has been less pronounced.)

As the mountains move upwards only very slowly, streams flowing from the centre of Crete have been able to follow their original courses and cut through the mountains, causing the spectacular gorges now seen. This process has been going on for about the last 25 million years and is still continuing – hence gorges such as that at Samariá are getting deeper as the White Mountains continue to rise at the rate of about 2m every thousand years.

Omalós and the heart of the mountains

The little plateau around **Omalós** lies pretty much at the heart of the Lefká Óri, surrounded by the highest peaks of the range. Between several hundred and a couple of thousand people head up here daily to join the stampede down the Gorge of Samariá, but only a handful stop to see anything on the way, and very few indeed take any of the more adventuresome routes into the mountains. The gorge route is described in detail on the following pages, and while mountaineering doesn't really fall within the scope of this book, a few starter suggestions are also included. Bear in mind that this is a genuinely wild mountain zone – venture nowhere alone or without adequate equipment.

The road up

The **road up to Omalós** turns inland from Haniá's western outskirts, heading at first across a rich but rather dull countryside of orange groves and vineyards interrupted by large modern villages. Shortly before Alikianós (see p.279), the large white building bristling with TV aerials is a prison with a fairly open regime (its inmates work in the fields). This is the building after which the Battle of Crete's "Prison Valley" was named, and at the Alikianós turn-off there's a large memorial to local members of the wartime resistance.

Soon after Fournés (p.242) you begin to climb in earnest to the Lefká Óri through a series of sweeping great loops with increasingly alarming drops. **LÁKKI**, the only village of any size you pass, is a bracingly green-and-white place looking back down over the plain; delicious honey is sold here by local producers. In spring, especially, it's an attractive setting. It has a few rooms to rent (try *Kri-Kri* ☎0821/67-316; ①) and a couple of **tavernas** which cater heartily for appetites generated by mountain air and whetted with the prospect of strenuous activity.

Omalós and the plateau

Leaving Lákki the road climbs on, past another memorial at the spot where Kapetan Vasilios (Sergeant. Major Dan Perkins) and a Cretan colleague were ambushed (a story recounted in *The Cretan Runner* – see p.324 – and elsewhere), to a pass at a little over 1200m, before dropping suddenly to the flat expanse of the **Omalós plain**. If you've caught the dawn bus up from Haniá, it's only now that there's enough light properly to take in your surroundings of an eerily deserted, enclosed little world – and to acknowledge your gratitude at being spared the details of your bus's flirtations with the void at every curve of the ascent. At over 1000m the Omalós plateau is cold, its vegetation stunted, and its enclosing ring of stone is clearly visible all around.

Omalós

There's just one small village on the road, **OMALÓS** itself. Here a couple of brand new **hotels** and several tavernas look very out of place alongside the chapel and few crude stone houses of the original settlement. The *Hotel Koutrouli*, in particular, is a large, modern building entirely out of keeping with its surroundings; the *Neos Omalos* (☎0821/67-269; ②) is flash, too, though marginally less so, while relatively ordinary rooms are available at *Samaria* (①) and *Drakoulaki* (☎0821/67-269; ①).

Scattered about the plain are other settlements, but none have the aura of permanent habitation. In winter everything is deep in snow and deserted. In spring the land is marshy and waterlogged – almost becoming a lake if there's a sudden melt. Only in summer do people live here full time, moving up from Lákki and other villages on the lower slopes roundabout (Ayía Iríni, Zóurva, Prasés) to pasture sheep and goats or to cultivate, on a small scale, cereals and potatoes.

Walk out into the plain in almost any direction and within five minutes you'll have left all traces of modern life behind, with only the jingling of the occasional goat's bell or the deliberate piling of stones to remind you of human presence. If you do spend the night, there are fabulous starry skies up here.

Scaling the peaks

If you need more of a reason to stay at the top, you could hike the couple of hours (7km) up to the EOS (Greek Mountain Club) **Kallergi Hut** (May–Oct, occasional winter opening for determined skiers; ☎0821/54-560). At 1677m, this acts as the base for climbing into the peaks, and is reached by following the road on from Omalós for about half an hour, then turning left onto the dirt track signed to the hut, a further hour's walking; you can also take a path from the top of the Samarian gorge, which cuts the hike to a little over 3km (about 1hr 15min). The hut itself – with no prizes for a friendly welcome – is probably the best source of information on tackling the peaks. **Beds** are cheap (①), but **meals**, served morning and evening, are not (and you're pretty much obliged to eat at least one).

For adventurous walkers, there's a two-day hike from here through the heart of the range to Anópoli and Hóra Sfakíon. This would take you right past **Páhnes**, the highest summit in the west and, at 2453m, just 3m short of Psilorítis for the title of loftiest in Crete: Haniot mountaineers regularly add stones to the cairn on the peak in an attempt to catch up. With less commitment you could follow the beginning of this trail for two or three hours for some scintillating views down into the gorge and across the seas to the south and west. The hut itself is perched high over the gorge, but it looks even more impressive from the isolation of these bare stone peaks, a slash of rich green in an otherwise unrelenting landscape of grey and brown.

You'll get more of a sense of achievement – and certainly impress others more – if you tackle the climb to the peak of **Mount Gíngilos** (2080m), beginning from the top of the Samarian gorge. Its north face, the one everyone sees, is a near-vertical slope of solid rock; round the back, though, you can reach the summit with only a little scrambling. It's hard work and you need confidence with heights, especially if it's windy, but no special mountaineering skills are necessary. A large yellow sign points the way from the back of the *Tourist Lodge* at the top of the gorge and the path, though not marked with the usual paint splashes, should be easy enough to follow for the two and a half hours to the top. At first you track around to the west, climbing above the plain, before cutting south, downhill slightly, towards the back of the mountain. Here, almost exactly halfway, amid bizarre rock formations which include an arch across the path, there's a spring of ice-cold water (drinkable). Beyond, you begin to climb in earnest until for the final half-hour the ascent is signalled with red paint – stick to the path as there are hidden hazards and even the official route needs hands as well as feet. The rewards are an all-round panorama from the summit and, with luck, the chance to spot some of the rarer animal life which crowds have driven from the gorge itself.

The Gorge of Samariá

The one trip that every visitor – even those eminently unsuited to it – feels compelled to make is the hike down the **Samarian gorge**, now a national park. At 18km in length, the gorge (or *farángi*) is the largest in Europe. Descending dramatically from the Omalós plateau, this natural wonder was formed by a river which flows between Mount Volakiás to the west and the towering bulk of the Lefká Óri to the east which, over time, has sliced a steep, cavernous ravine between the two. In summer the violent winter torrent reduces to a meek trickle

0   2 km

Omalós

Melíntaou
△ 2133 m

2000 m

1500

Kallergi Hut

Tourist Lodge

Áyios
Nikólaos

1500 m

Xilóskalon

1000 m

500 m

1000 m

1500 m

Samariá

Gíngilos
△ 2080 m

Volakiás
△ 2116 m

2000 m

1500 m

Kéfala
1700 m △

1500 m

Sidherespórtes

1500 m

Katsoprínes
△ 1400 m

1000 m

1000 m

1000 m

Road
Footpath

500 m

Old
Ayia Roúmeli

1000 m

500 m

500 m

Ayía Roúmeli

Site of
Tarrha

Áyios Pávlos

500 m

Ferry to Paleohóra

Ferry to Hóra Sfakion

SAMARIAN GORGE

and this is when the multitudes descend. So if you're expecting a wilderness experience, an opportunity to commune peacefully with nature, think again. On the other hand, this is not a Sunday afternoon stroll to be lightly undertaken; especially in spring when the river is roaring, or on a hot midsummer day, it can be a thoroughly gruelling test of fitness and stamina. The mules and helicopter standing by to rescue the injured are not mere talk: anyone who regularly leads tours through the gorge has a stack of horror stories to regale you with – broken legs and heart attacks feature most frequently. To undertake the walk you need to be reasonably fit and/or used to lengthy walks; and you should have comfortable, sturdy shoes that will stand up to hot, sharp rocks.

Gorge **wildlife** means most famously the *kri-kri* (variously the *agrimi, Capra Aegagrus*, the Cretan wild goat or ibex), for whose protection the park was primarily created. You are most unlikely to see one of these large, nimble animals with their long backswept horns, though you may well see ordinary mountain goats defying death on the cliff faces. More likely candidates are the local birds and reptiles. Almost four hundred varieties of **birds** are claimed to have been seen here, including owls, eagles, falcons and vultures; bird-watchers after a coup should look out for the endangered *Lammergeier* (or bearded vulture). On the ground lizards abound and there's also the odd snake, but the multifarious trees and the wild flowers and herbs are more rewarding finds. There are wild irises and orchids, thyme, sage, oregano and Cretan dittany, a celebrated medicinal herb referred to by Aristotle and Hippocrates and taken by women in ancient times as a method of abortion.

The gorge walk

The gorge begins, with startling suddenness, on the far side of the plain. After the dull tranquillity of the plain you are faced with this great cleft opening beneath your feet and, across it – close enough to bounce stones off, it seems – the gaunt limestone face of Mount Gíngilos. Most walkers head down (rather than up) the gorge, and it would be a daunting start were it not for the well-worn trail leading clearly down below you and the dozens of people hanging around ready to set off. Here **at the top** there's a large area where cars and buses park, with a couple of mobile stalls doing a brisk trade in hot coffee (first thing, the air is breath-foggingly cold up here) and supplies for the journey. This is a fine place for a spot of contemplation before heading down, allowing the crowds to disperse if you've arrived with a mob. There are maps showing the path and facilities en route, others with the vegetation zones marked, and lists of park regulations.

The gorge hike itself is some 16km long and **the walk** down takes between four and seven hours, depending on your level of fitness, and how often you stop to admire the scenery, bathe your feet and take refreshment. Be wary of the kilometre markers – these mark only distances within the park, not the full extent of the walk. At the park entrance, you'll be given a date-stamped ticket (1000dr) which should be kept and handed in at the gate by which you leave; this is partly to make sure no one tries camping in the park, partly to check that nobody is lost inside.

The descent begins on the **Xilóskalon** (wooden stairway), a stepped path cut from the rock and augmented by log stairs and wooden handrails, which zigzags rapidly down to the base of the gorge, plunging 1000m in the first 2km or so of the walk. Near the bottom the chapel of Áyios Nikólaos stands on a little terrace of coniferous trees: there are benches from which to enjoy the view, and fresh water. Beyond, the path begins gradually to level out, following the stream bed amid softer vegetation which reflects the milder climate down here. In late spring it's magnificent, but at any time of year there should be wild flowers and rare plants (no picking allowed), including the endangered large white peony, *paeonia clusii*. The stream itself is less reliable: there are places where you can be sure of icy fresh water and pools to bathe sore feet all year round (particularly in the middle sections), but what starts in spring as a fierce, even dangerous torrent has dwindled by autumn to a trickle between hot, dry boulders, disappearing beneath the surface for long stretches.

The abandoned village of **SAMARIÁ** lies a little under midway through the walk, shortly before the 7km marker. One of the buildings here has been converted to house the wardens' office, another has been pressed into (inadequate) service as a public toilet, but for the most part the remains of the village are quietly crumbling away. Its inhabitants, until they were relocated to make way for the park in 1962, were predominantly members of the Viglis family, who claimed direct descent from one of the twelve aristocratic clans implanted from Byzantium. Certainly this settlement, as isolated as any in Crete and cut off by floodwater for much of the year, is a very ancient one: the church of Óssia María, from which both gorge and village take their name, was founded in the early fourteenth century.

After Samariá the path is more level, the walls of the gorge begin to close in and the path is often forced to cross from one side of the stream to the other, on stepping stones which at times may be submerged and slippery. Beside you, the contorted striations of the cliffs are increasingly spectacular, but the highlight comes shortly after the Christos resting point with the *Sidherespórtes* (**Iron Gates**) where two rock walls rise sheer to within a whisker of a thousand feet: standing at the bottom, one can almost touch both at once. For this short stretch, there's a wooden walkway raised above the stream, whose swirling waters fill the whole of the narrow passage. Almost as suddenly as you entered this mighty crack in the mountain you leave it again, the valley broadens, its sides fall away, and you're in a parched wilderness of rubble deposited here by the spring thaw.

Before long – 8km beyond Samariá – you reach the fringes of Ayía Rouméli, where there's a gate by which you leave the park and a couple of stalls selling cool drinks at crippling prices. Frustratingly, however, this is not the end of the walk: old Ayía Rouméli has been all but deserted in favour of the new beachside community, a further excruciatingly hot, dull twenty minutes away. Arriving finally in **Ayía Rouméli** proper (see over), you face the agonizing choice between plunging into the sea or diving into one of the tavernas for an iced drink – though in the event it takes a strong will to walk past the rows of enticingly dew-dropped cans of chilled fruit juice and ice-cold beers set out to divert you from your course to the water. Once your senses adjust, Ayía Rouméli is a pretty unattractive place – but that drink, and the first plunge in the sea, are likely to live in the memory as the most refreshing ever.

Walking up the gorge
Starting from the bottom, the hike up to Omalós is not as hard as some imagine, though it will take rather longer – six to seven hours at a reasonable, steady pace. Few people do it all the way, which means that at the top you may well find the gorge almost empty; on the way up, however, you'll have had to pass

all the hordes charging down. You could also walk a short way up and come back – an outing offered as a day-trip known as "Samariá the Lazy Way". This will show you the Iron Gates, the most spectacular individual section, but it means a lot of walking in the dullest parts down by the coast and none of the almost alpine scenes nearer the top.

Practicalities

Conditions permitting, the gorge is **open** between the hours of 6am and sunset, from May 1 to October 15 inclusive; entrance to the national park costs 1000dr. If you enter after 3pm, you're only allowed into the first couple of kilometres from each end. During winter the hike is dangerous and often impossible, and even early and late in the season flash floods are a real possibility and not to be taken lightly; in 1993 a number of walkers perished when they were washed out to sea. If in doubt, the Haniá Forest Service has a **gorge information number** (☎0821/ 67-140) and the gorge office at the entrance (☎0821/67-179) will also provide advice. Outside the official season, and at the discretion of the wardens, you may be allowed through if the weather is good, but there will be very little transport.

There are a whole series of national park rules (posted at the entrance), but the most important are **no camping**, no fires (or smoking), no hunting and no interfering with the wildlife. There are wardens who patrol to ensure these are obeyed, that no one wanders too far from the main path (another breach of regulations) and that no stragglers are overtaken by nightfall.

As for **supplies** for the walk, you want to carry the minimum possible. On a day-trip you needn't necessarily carry anything, though a water bottle and something to munch on the way are probably worthwhile (there are springs at regular intervals and ice-cold water in the stream, but for long periods you'll find neither – especially over the last, hottest hour) as is some means of carrying clothes you discard en route (7am at the top feels close to freezing; 1pm at the bottom may hover around 100°F – approximately 38°C). If you plan to stay a day or two at the bottom you'd do better to leave your pack at Haniá's bus station for collection later, taking only what's essential. As far as **food** is concerned, you needn't worry about starving: you can find enough for breakfast in the stalls at the top (or sit down properly for a meal in the *Tourist Lodge*), and Ayía Rouméli is more than equipped to feed everyone arriving at the bottom.

Buses and boats

The vast majority of people who walk through the gorge do so as part of a **day-trip**: a very early bus to the top, walk down by early afternoon, boat from Ayía Rouméli to Hóra Sfakíon and bus from there back home. Most go with one of the **guided tours** offered by every travel agent on the island – and certainly if you're staying in a hotel anywhere in the east of Crete this is much the simplest method, and probably the only way of doing it in a single day. Most tours will include all bus and ferry connections, but not food or the entrance fee to the park itself. (If you're planning to stay on the south coast, the tour bus can save you the effort of carrying your bags; simply stow them underneath and retrieve them in Hóra Sfakíon. Do let them know your plan, though, both to guard against an unexpected switch of bus and to prevent search parties being sent out.) If, however, you are staying in Haniá, or marginally less straightforwardly in Iráklion or Réthimnon, you can save money and avoid having to walk in a large group by taking the **public bus**.

From Haniá there are four departures a day, at 6.15am, 7.30am, 8.30am and 1.30pm, arriving at the top about one and a half hours later. You'll normally be sold a return ticket, including the return leg from Hóra Sfakíon (which needn't necessarily be used the same day), so if you don't want this you'll have to make your intentions very clear; the bus station is in total chaos when the first buses leave. There's a lot to be said for taking the earliest bus: more of the walk can be completed while it's still relatively cool; there's no need to force your pace, and if you're planning to stop over anywhere at the bottom you've more chance of being among the first to arrive. On the other hand, everyone now does this – there's often a procession of as many as five full buses leaving Haniá before dawn, the bus station is in turmoil, there are queues and confusion when you arrive, and you're unlikely to escape from crowds the whole way down. It may be hotter, but it's also quieter if you set out later. The first buses of the day **from Iráklion** (5.30am) **and Réthimnon** (6.15am and 7am) to Haniá continue direct to Omalós.

Heading back, at least five **boats** a day leave Ayía Rouméli for Hóra Sfakíon through most of the summer, with four of them calling at Loutró; there's a slightly reduced service from May to mid-June and from mid-September to the end of October, and hardly any boats from November to April when the gorge is closed. The trip takes around an hour and you should check current times when you arrive: at the time of writing there are boats at 9.30am and 2.30pm, 3.45pm and 5pm prior to the **last ferry** at 6pm. You need to leave by 6pm to be sure of connecting with the last Haniá bus. **For Soúyia and Paleohóra** there's a daily sailing at 4.30pm between May and September. **Buses** from Hóra Sfakíon back to Haniá leave at 7am, 11am, 4pm, 6pm and 7pm; for Réthimnon there's a direct one at 6.30pm (otherwise you change at Vrísses), and for Plakiás and Ayía Galíni at 5.30pm.

Accommodation

If you want to make the gorge part of a longer excursion, there are several accommodation options. You could **stay at the top**, at the *Tourist Lodge* (☎0821/93-237; ④), where there are just seven beds, for which you'll need to book ahead, or at one of the places in Omalós (see p.249), or simply sleep out (there are usually quite a few people trying to find a flat space for their sleeping bags around the entrance). This has few practical advantages – you'd have to be up very early to steal a march on the first arrivals from Haniá (for much of the year this would mean setting off before daylight) and from Omalós you face an extra five-kilometre walk to reach the top of the trail – but it does make quite a change to stay up here and freeze for a night and of course it gives you the opportunity to explore more than just the gorge.

Staying **on the south coast** for a night or more after your exertions makes more sense: there are rooms at Ayía Rouméli (see below), Loutró (pp.256–7) and Hóra Sfakíon (p.264) or westwards in Soúyia (pp.280–1) and Paleohóra (pp.275–7).

Ayía Rouméli

Once you've drunk and eaten your fill, plunged into the sea and out again, lain on the pebbles for a while and rested, **AYÍA ROUMÉLI**'s attractions soon begin to pall. It's a singularly unattractive example of over-rapid development, with a rash of concrete tavernas and rooms for rent spreading over a shingly beach. By local standards it's expensive, too, although given the difficulties of transport this is perhaps not altogether surprising. Ayía Rouméli does have its good points, though – mainly the sheer number of places to eat and to stay – and at night it's very peaceful. Should you be tempted, try the tranquil *Livikon* (①) at the rear of the village, or the sea-view rooms attached to tavernas *Tara* (①) or *Zorba's* (①); you can also book ahead at the *Hotel Agia Roumeli* (☎0825/91-241; ③). The village is even attempting to be environmentally conscious: the pile of huge concrete tank traps behind the beach shields an experimental solar energy plant; at night, or other times when this system can't cope, a diesel generator cuts in.

The kiosk which sells **boat tickets** is plainly marked down by the beach: if you're catching the bus back from Hóra Sfakíon, get a ticket when you emerge from the gorge for the last connecting boat, and spend the afternoon on the beach; if you plan to stay elsewhere on this coast, take the first boat available for the best chance of finding a room at your destination. Given the choice, Ayía Rouméli is the least attractive of the places you could stay, though it does at least have a fair number of rooms and a surprisingly large beach if all you want to do is crash out on the pebbles (a couple of the tavernas have showers which they'll let you use if you eat there). Just to the east of the village (near the solar plant) is a clump of trees among which a few people are usually camped, and on the beach in this direction are some caves, also sometimes used to sleep out in.

Finding anything much to do apart from laze on the beach takes some ingenuity. Although there was an ancient settlement here – *Tarra*, inhabited probably from the fifth century BC through to the fifth AD – and more or less constant later habitation, very little remains to be seen. The ruined Turkish fort, under which you pass as you emerge from the gorge onto the beach, doesn't really justify the scramble up to see it. *Tarra* straddled the stream where it ran into the sea, just to the east of the present village – the only obvious remains are the foundations of an early Christian basilica by the present church of Panayía, around which you may also spot a few tiny fragments of mosaic. This, supposedly, was the site of a much earlier Temple of Apollo.

Loutró and south-coast walks

Of all the south-coast villages, **LOUTRÓ** perhaps best sums up what this coast ought to be all about. It's an incredibly soporific place, where there's absolutely nothing to do but eat, drink and laze – and where you fast lose any desire to do anything else. The big excitements of the day are the occasional arrivals and departures of the ferries. The days start bright and are soon lost in an overpowering heat shimmer; evening comes cool and darkness falls fast – by 10pm the place is virtually asleep. All this despite the fact that it has been entirely taken over by tourists. The waterfront consists of a row of perhaps six tavernas and a similar number of rooms places plus one small hotel; behind the waterfront the mountains rise immediately. There's no road in, and everyone here has either come on the boat or walked, which helps to keep things very low-key, prices reasonable, big groups rare, and the people genuinely friendly.

Perhaps Loutró's main drawback is its lack of a real **beach**. There's a small stretch of pebbles in front of the eastern half of town, with large signs asking bathers to remain respectable. Try lying topless here and you'll be told none too politely to cover up; those who persist risk being catcalled by the village children. But the sheltered little bay is otherwise ideal for swimming, clear and warm, and people bask nude on the rocks around the point, far enough out to avoid offence. The good news is that there are other beaches in walking distance (see below), with small boats ferrying visitors to the best, at Sweetwater and Mármara.

Rooms in Loutró seem uniformly basic and comfortable, though to be sure of finding one you should arrive as early as possible – an increasing number seem to be pre-booked through enterprising travel agencies. Try for one with a balcony (the *Porto Loutro* and *Blue House* offer top-floor rooms with huge roof terraces); the quietest places are generally the furthest round to the east, such as *Keramos* (②); others are right above the tavernas but nowhere is exactly loud or stays open late. The only place with pretensions is the *Hotel Porto Loutro* (☎0825/91-091; ③–④), right in the middle of the village above the beach, whose white cubes fit in surprisingly well with the surroundings; it's lovely and not outrageously expensive, though since the rooms are pretty accurate reproductions of a simple Greek room you may question whether it's worth paying the extra. Even here you may find yourself showering in salt water if there's a shortage (as there is most summers these days). A cheaper option is *The Blue House* (☎0825/91-127; ①–②), whose rooms are pretty good – the less expensive ones come without private bath. If you can't find anywhere to stay, you could hike or take a boat over to Fínix or Líkkos (see over). You could also consider **camping** out by the castle, on the headland or on Sweetwater Beach (see over) but you should be aware that freelance campers are not very popular in the village.

The Blue House, recognizable from its blue-checked tablecloths rather than a sign, is also arguably the best **restaurant** in Loutró, and the owner, Vangelis, one of the friendliest characters. There's usually a fair vegetarian selection here, and at several other places. The only place open late is the *Café Bar Maistrali*, the westernmost building in Loutró (alongside the concrete jetty), where everyone heads in the evening. Its cocktails and music – they also serve exotic breakfasts – may seem a bit slick in this setting, but it's certainly a pleasant way to wind up your day. The **practicalities** are easily taken care of: you can change money and buy supplies at the mini-market, and a second store a little further on (immediately before the beach) has a good selection of second-hand books and also changes money. *The Blue House* has a public phone, and **canoes** can be rented from waterfront owners for expeditions to the nearby coves and beaches.

Boat tickets are sold from a kiosk at the end of the dock, but they only go on sale a few minutes before departure; try to have the right change. The smaller boats tie up at this dock, but the *Samaria* sails straight up to the beach, lowering its bow onto the pebbles. (Occasionally it comes to the dock to unload supplies – a truck drives off onto the jetty, which is barely large enough to contain it, is unloaded and filled with empties and drives back onto the next ferry. There are no more than a few feet of space for it to drive up and down.)

The coast around Loutró: Sweetwater to Mármara

Anyone who spends any time at all in Loutró is eventually taken with the urge to explore – even if it's just climbing up to the ruins on the headland. There are plenty of long, tough walks available (see the following section), but there are also easier hikes to nearby beaches. Some of these can also be reached by boat.

Sweetwater Beach

Sweetwater Beach lies approximately halfway between Loutró and Hóra Sfakíon, in the middle of a barren coastline. From the sea, as you pass on one of the coastal boats, it appears as a long, extremely narrow slice of grey between sheer ochre cliffs and a dark, deep sea. Closer up, the beach seems much larger, but there's still a frightening sense of being isolated between unscaleable mountains and an endless stretch of water.

The beach takes its name from the small springs which bubble up beneath the pebbles to provide fresh, cool drinking water. You can dig a hole almost anywhere to find water; there are plenty already made, but you should take care not to pollute the groundwater with soap. For years there was a little enclave of nudist campers here, their idyll interrupted only by the occasional intrepid cliff walker. Over the last couple of years, though, daily boat services have started from both Loutró and Hóra Sfakíon, bringing a lot more people. So far these have not spoilt the place – the beach is easily big enough to absorb everyone – and the campers are still here, for once doing a good job of keeping the place pristine: there are signs up warning against leaving rubbish, and people regularly make an effort to pick up any junk that is left behind. The long-term residents tend to monopolize the only shade, in the caves at the back of the beach, but you can always escape the sun at the small bar/taverna which sits on a lump of concrete just off the western end of the beach, reached by a rickety plank. You can get cold drinks and simple meals here and they also rent out sun umbrellas. There are no other facilities beyond the boats, which come once in the morning and again in the late afternoon. Walking here is also a possibility, though a very hot and shadeless one: about 45 minutes to Loutró, an hour to Hóra Sfakíon (see following section). On a calm day, you could even paddle a canoe over from Loutró. The path runs along behind all the houses in Loutró – to join it from there, climb up behind the beachside kiosk and church.

Fínix

Immediately to the west of Loutró, in the little bay on the other side of the promontory, stood **ancient Fínikas**, now known as **FÍNIX** or Phoenix. This was a major town during the Roman and Byzantine periods, and a significant port long after that: it was the harbour at Fínix, a more comfortable place to wait out the winter storms than Kalí Liménes, which St Paul's ship was hoping to reach when it was swept away (see p.119). A local story has the saint actually landing here and being beaten up by the locals he tried to convert: given the attitude to Cretans revealed in Paul's epistle to Titus, it is, as Michael Llewellyn Smith points out, "safe to say that if he *had* landed here they *would* have beaten him up".

Yet again there is very little to be seen. These days the bay, with its rocky beach, has just one taverna, the *Finix* (☎0825/91-257; ②), an exceptionally languid place, with simple food and rooms – the epitome of a tranquil hideaway, in fact.

It's hard to believe there could ever have been a population of any size. Up on the headland, though, there's certainly evidence of later occupation, principally in the form of the Venetian fortification on the point. Nearby are traces of a Byzantine basilica and other scattered remains; most curiously, however, there's a building, very much in the form of a Venetian church, sunk entirely below ground level. Its arched roof is intact, the interior entirely full of water. Nowadays it is deliberately flooded and used as a storage cistern, but its original purpose remains a mystery. It could always have been a cistern, of course, but it seems too elaborate for that; an alternative theory suggests it was an underground arsenal attached to the castle.

To get to Fínix by the most direct route, join the path that runs behind Loutró, up behind the beachside kiosk and the church. This will lead you straight up, past the castle and directly over the headland, in around ten minutes; if you're continuing beyond Fínix, you don't have to go down to the water as a path continues straight past the back of the bay, but it's only marginally shorter. It's also possible to get there by walking out past the last house in Loutró and simply following the rocky coast around. This is a much longer and tougher walk, but it does have the compensation of passing plenty of good rocks to swim from, and extensive remains of old buildings which you can imagine are, and may indeed be, ancient Fínikas. Boats to Mármara also regularly call in at Fínix, bringing supplies.

Líkkos and Mármara
Beyond Fínix, the path continues to another, much longer bay, **LÍKKOS**, with three rather poorly patronized taverna/rooms places. *Yioryio's* (①), the last of them, right in the middle of the beach, is very friendly and quiet. Now that electricity has finally reached here, the place is also very comfortable – and there's plenty of fresh water too, which there may not be in Loutró. Unfortunately Líkkos is not a very attractive beach, with rocks and pebbles, and is awkward to swim from unless you wear shoes. Behind, you can look up and see the village of Livanianá, perched on the eastern flank of the Arádhena gorge (see over).

The gorge emerges at the sea in the next bay along, **Mármara** (or marble) **Beach**. This is another fairly small cove, with a sandy beach surrounded by interesting rock formations full of caves and slabs to dive from or sunbathe on. Unfortunately it also sees at least three boats a day from Loutró, which in summer bring more people than can comfortably be accommodated. So although out of season it might be more attractive than Sweetwater, at peak times it is far less so – and it has the additional disadvantages of no one to keep it clean and no fresh water (or anything else, so bring plenty to drink with you). Some people do camp here, but to do so you have to make a very long hike for supplies, or regularly take the boats to and from Loutró. Walking to Mármara takes a little over an hour in all, and the second half, from the far end of the beach at Líkkos, is hot and exposed, climbing high onto the cliff.

More challenging hikes

Loutró lies close to the heart of the network of coastal paths linking Ayía Rouméli to Hóra Sfakíon and, in the absence of a road, is an important junction. Most real traffic nowadays goes by boat, of course, and the last inland hamlets have finally had a driveable track built to them. But the paths and tracks remain, to give a variety of possible hikes, even the easiest of which can be demanding in the heat of high summer. You'll need, at the very least, decent shoes to cope with rough, rocky terrain and a water bottle, which you should fill at every opportunity. You should also have a companion, since some of these paths are pretty isolated, and outside help cannot be relied upon.

Ayía Rouméli to Hóra Sfakíon: the coastal route
The **coastal path** is the most obvious, the most frequently used by tourists and, in terms of not getting lost, the simplest to follow. There's not a great deal to see en route, however, and nor is it an easy walk – the path is often frighteningly

narrow and uneven as it clings to the cliff face, and in summer it is very, very hot, offering no shelter at all from the sun.

From **Loutró to Hóra Sfakíon** this is barely a problem: it's the most heavily travelled part, the whole walk takes less than two hours (8km), and there's a rest stop at Sweetwater Beach halfway. Loutró to Sweetwater is straightforward and fairly well beaten: beyond here the path clambers over a massive recent rockfall and then follows the cliffs until it eventually emerges on the Hóra Sfakíon–Anópoli road about half an hour's walk above Hóra. This is easy to find in the other direction too, the path (to the left) leaving the road at the first hairpin bend.

In the other direction, **Loutró to Ayía Rouméli** is an altogether tougher proposition. For a start you can expect to be walking for four hours solid, and for seconds there's no chance of refreshment between the tavernas at Líkkos and Ayía Rouméli. The path has already been described as far as Mármara Beach (see previous pages). Afterwards you climb again to track along the exposed cliff face for around an hour before reaching the first sign of civilization, a solitary cottage and a few trees. In about another hour, you'll arrive at the chapel of **Áyios Pávlos**, yet another site where Saint Paul is supposed to have landed. Here he allegedly christened locals in a nearby spring. The chapel itself is ancient and rather beautiful, set on a ledge above the water, and surrounded by dunes. You could cool off in the sea here before setting out on the final hour to Ayía Rouméli.

Coming from Ayía Rouméli this path is well marked, heading east out of the village. Ten to fifteen minutes after Áyios Pávlos it splits, left to climb inland to Áyios Ioánnis and Anópoli (for more on these, see the following sections), right to continue along the coast.

On to Anópoli

If you're hiking for its own sake, or for that matter if you want to take the easiest way from Ayía Rouméli to Hóra Sfakíon without necessarily calling at Loutró, then the **inland routes** centring on Anópoli have a great deal to be said for them (see "Anópoli to Ayía Rouméli" opposite).

ANÓPOLI itself is a quiet country town, not much used to visitors, dominating a small upland plain with a few, rare vestiges of forest. There are a couple of *kafenia* and a small general store on the square, and if you want to stay away from all the hustle of the coast you should be able to find somewhere. There are several **rooms** places scattered along the road back towards Hóra Sfakíon; the rather tatty-looking one with green paint is actually quite comfortable (the more expensive place opposite is more so, with showers) and serves fabulous home-made yoghurt.

Anópoli was the home of the first of the great Cretan rebels against the Turks, **Dhaskaloyiánnis** – the subject of a celebrated epic poem. To cut a very long story extremely short, Dhaskaloyiánnis, a wealthy ship-owner, was promised support by Russian agents if he raised a rebellion in Sfakiá, support which in the event never materialized. (The Russians hoped only to create a diversion for their campaigns against the Ottoman Empire elsewhere.) The revolt, in 1770, was short-lived and disastrous for Sfakiá, which for the first time was brought well and truly under the Turkish heel: Dhaskaloyiánnis gave himself up and was executed. There's now a statue of him in the square.

Getting to Anópoli, which is high above the coast, more or less directly above Loutró, is not easy unless you have a car. **From Hóra Sfakíon** it's 12km up a very steep, winding road – you wouldn't really want to walk this but you might not have much choice, since the lone daily bus drives up at 4pm and down again at 6.30am. The walk up **from Loutró** looks terrifying – you can see the path tracking back and forth across an almost vertical cliff – but is in fact far less bad than it seems: about an hour and a half, climbing steeply most of the way (this is best done very early, before the sun gets too powerful; at the top you're on the fringes of Anópoli – turn left for the centre).

Anópoli to Ayía Rouméli

To head for Ayía Rouméli, follow the road through to the far end of town, where it becomes a little-used, dusty jeep track, signed to Arádhena. There may be shorter ways on the old paths than this track (ask in town if you're determined), but there's so little traffic that following the road makes little difference. It is just over an hour to the edge of the **Arádhena gorge**, on the far side of which is the virtually abandoned hamlet of Arádhena.*

Right on the opposite rim of the gorge here is a Byzantine church, with a strangely phallic dome standing proud against the Lefká Óri's heights. Inside, if you can find someone to show you, there are frescoes, and roundabout are a few traces of ancient Aradin, from whose stones the church is said to be built. A new bridge now takes the road across the gorge, with dizzy views down into it, and looking inland you can see the old path, negotiable on foot or by pack animals only, zigzagging down to the bottom and back up the other side. Incidentally, this is still the path you take to follow the gorge down to the sea (see below).

The road now ends at **ÁYIOS IOÁNNIS**, beneath the massed peaks of Páhnes, Troharís and Zaranokefála, 5km or another hour or so beyond. A rather larger village, this goes so far as to have a taverna where you can rest up for a while. There are more Byzantine frescoes in the church here and several impressively large caves nearby. You should ask to be put on the right track from here, as work on the road means that the path may change course. Generally, you have to head to the left, between two chapels, after which the path becomes hard to follow for a while until it emerges on top of the cliffs. From here it loops down a rough but obvious path to join the coast trail before the chapel of Áyios Pávlos. You should be able to complete the approximately seventeen-kilometre walk from Anópoli to Ayía Rouméli in about five hours, though with rest stops and wrong turnings it could well take much longer: leave plenty of leeway if you need to catch a boat back. If you are undertaking this walk in reverse, start early so as to complete the climb of the cliffs before it becomes too hot.

The Arádhena gorge

A retrun trip from Loutró, up to Anópoli and down to Mármara Beach (where you can get a boat back; last at 4pm) via the **Arádhena gorge** makes a challenging excursion. You must be fit to tackle this, as the gorge involves some scrambling and climbing – there are ropes and rope-ladders to help you over the worst parts.

---

*Adam Hopkins claims that the people left to escape with their lives from a series of Sfakiot vendettas. He's probably right, but in the light of what is happening elsewhere, such depopulation seems commonplace. With the new road, one or two people have moved back and started to restore some of the crumbling buildings.

Although this doesn't really need any special mountaineering skills, it can be pretty scary – a feeling not helped by the ominous presence of picked-clean skeletons of goats, which presumably have either fallen from the top or been washed away in spring floods.

The sense of achievement, however, is immense, and the gorge, though far smaller, is in physical terms almost as impressive as that of Samariá. There isn't much in the way of wildlife, but the rocky river bed is forced into an extremely narrow gap between sheer walls almost all the way down – and there'll be hardly anyone else around. Allow six hours at least from Loutró to Mármara (two and a half to the top of the gorge, three and a half down); eight may be more like it once you've stopped a few times.

You set off by turning right off the road and onto the old path, 600m before you reach the gorge, then following the stepped path down to the bottom (the track is deteriorating fast now it's not used much, but this side is better than the other). This and the first stretch, with its relatively flat bottom as you head under the bridge through an impressively deep section, conspire to lull you into a false sense of security: as it gets steeper further down, you find yourself jumping from rock to rock or lowering yourself carefully down dry cascades. Look out as you go for the paint marks indicating the route – these often seem to take you over unnecessarily tricky terrain, but you usually discover the reason further on when you reach an impassable portion. Fill up with water at every opportunity, as there's none towards the end of the gorge or at the beach.

If all this sounds too tough there is an **easier alternative**, though not tried and tested. Head out past Fínix (follow the upper path, bypassing the cove) and you'll come to a fork in the path: the lower one goes to Líkkos, the upper to Livanianá, which you can see above you. From here a path leads down into the gorge, emerging fairly near the bottom having bypassed all the really difficult bits. The Ímbros ravine (see below) is another slightly softer option, with more wildlife but less dramatic terrain.

The road south: to Hóra Sfakíon and Frangokástello

The easy way **into Sfakiá** is by a good road which cuts south from Vrísses (pp.238–9), almost immediately beginning to spiral up into the mountains, towards the Plateau of Askífou. The climb seems straightforward from a bus or car, but the country you drive through has a history as bloody as any in Crete: you pass first through a little ravine where two Turkish armies were massacred, the first during the 1821 uprising, the second in 1866 after the heroic events at Arkádhi (p.187); the road itself is the one along which the Allied troops retreated at such cost in the final stages of the Battle of Crete. This chaotic flight has been described in detail in just about all the books covering the battle (and also in Evelyn Waugh's *Officers and Gentlemen*) – it makes for strange reading from the comfort of a modern journey.

Askífou Plateau

The **Plateau of Askífou** offers the relief of level ground for a while, now as it did then. The plain is dominated by a ruined Turkish castle on a hill to the left of the road – a hill so small and perfectly conical it looks fake, put there expressly to raise the castle above its surroundings. There are several small villages up here, chief of them **AMOUDHÁRI**, with a couple of small tavernas and the chance of a room if you wanted to stay (one place, over the bakery, tends to be noisy in the morning; the only other disturbance to the peace here is the twice-daily convoy of buses, arriving empty and returning with sated gorge-walkers).

For keen walkers, a path leads from Amoudhári to Anópoli, a long day's hike (18km) through the mountains via the hamlet of Kalí Láki, which is not terribly easy to follow. You should attempt to get thorough directions locally before trying this, though this may not be easy unless you speak fluent Greek. Less taxing hikes are to be had by following any of the tracks which climb westwards from the village into the foothills of the Lefká Óri (with good opportunities for birdspotting) or, in the other direction, east of the nearby village of Goní where a track heads west for 10km to the hamlet of Asigonía.

The Ímbros ravine

On the far side of the Askífou plateau lies the village of **ÍMBROS**. Beyond, the road climbs briefly again out of the plain and then begins gradually to descend to the south coast. This stretch is lovely: an excellent, winding track which follows dramatically one side of the **Ímbros ravine**, tracking high through conifer-clad slopes with the cleft always dizzily below. As you approach the coast, still high above it, you begin to glimpse distant sparkles of water until finally the road breaks out of its confinement, way above the sea, with a broad plain to the east (and Frangokástello hazy in the distance), steeper drops to the west, and immense vistas out towards Africa ahead. Hóra Sfakíon is out of sight until you are almost upon it, an alarming plunge down through hairpin bend after hairpin bend. Driving, you need to watch out for buses: it can be alarming in the evening meeting the vast convoy coming the other way on these relatively narrow curves, and in the afternoon you'll pass them parked in every available spot since they can't all squeeze into Hóra Sfakíon.

It is also possible to **walk down the Ímbros ravine**, following a track which, until the completion of the new road, was the district's main thoroughfare. This is easily enough done – in less than three hours – and it's a wonderfully solitary walk, a spectacular contrast to the crowds at Samariá. The only problem is that you miss the wonderful views from above. In its own way the ravine is as interesting as its better-known rival, albeit on a smaller scale: narrow and stiflingly confined in places, speckled with caves in others and at one point passing under a monumental, natural stone archway. The path starts from the southern fringe of Ímbros village, close by a blue shrine near a *kafenion* (excellent cheese omelette with honey), where a well-trodden trail leads down to the stream bed. Through the ravine you simply follow the stream until, emerging at the lower end, an obvious track leads away again towards the village of Komitádhes. Unfortunately, the last 5km west to Hóra Sfakíon makes a hot, boring anticlimax to your walk. It's also easy enough to walk the gorge as a half-day trip from Hóra Sfakíon (or Loutró, by getting the first boat from there): simply take the early bus to Haniá, and get off at Ímbros.

Should you be arriving here by car and the needle is quivering around empty, a **garage** is sited just after where the road turns west along the coast towards Hóra Sfakíon.

Hóra Sfakíon

Squeezed between the sea and the mountains, **HÓRA SFAKÍON** (often known simply as Hóra) couldn't grow even if it wanted to. Nevertheless it's a surprise to find the capital of Sfakiá quite so small. It is, too, a thoroughly commercial centre these days: restaurants cram the seafront promenade between the square where the buses stop and the pier where the boats dock, and every house in town seems to display a large "Rooms" sign. Although it is cheap and pleasant enough if you do decide to stay, and relatively quiet by the end of the day, the beach is small and pebbly and there is little else to distract you.

Supposedly, Hóra once had as many as a hundred churches and chapels, built for one reason or another by devout Sfakiots, but few survived the wartime bombardments. There are a couple of ancient-looking examples on the road as you curve down into Hóra, but all seem permanently locked. As for other monuments, a plaque on the waterfront, between the restaurants, commemorates the Dunkirk-style wartime evacuation when some ten thousand men were taken off the island: almost as many were left behind to be bombed as they waited to be taken prisoner or to escape as best they could. Many of the inhabitants who aided the operation were later dealt with brutally by German execution squads. A memorial opposite *Rooms Panorama* on the bend above the town commemorates their bravery; as is the custom here, the skulls of the dead are visible behind a window in the monument's base.

If you have time to kill you're probably best off getting out, to **Sweetwater Beach** (p.258) an hour along the coast path west (or accessible by twice-daily boat), or to Frangokástello (see opposite), 14km east. The coast road to the east runs some way from the sea through a series of small, little-visited villages: Komitádhes has a couple of tavernas and even a few rooms, but Vraskás and Voúvas can offer no more than a *kafenion* and a general store each. It's also possible to visit the **Cave of Dhaskaloyiánnis**, one of several large caves in the cliffs to the west of Hóra. Always a hideout in times of trouble, this was where the rebel leader (see p.260) set up a mint to produce revolutionary coinage. The tourist office (see below) will provide directions on how to reach it, and also has information about local boats which can take you there if you don't fancy the hike.

Practicalities

Rooms are better and cheaper if you avoid the obvious places right on the front or the main road. Good places to try are *Panorama* (☎0825/91-296; ①) on the bend as you descend into the town, and with some rooms overlooking the eastern harbour; or the central *Hotel Stavris* (☎0825/91-220; ①–②), in the street behind the waterfront tavernas, where some rooms have private bath.

There are a couple of good **supermarkets**, which even sell new and second-hand books in English, and some excellent **restaurants** along the seafront promenade: *To Limani* is worth trying for its seafood special which includes five kinds of fish; it also has a good array of vegetarian food, such as *bouréki* and vegetable-stuffed aubergines. The backstreet parallel to the waterfront is also where almost all the other facilities are. Practically the first building is an excellent bakery, and there's also a large supermarket with better prices than those on the front, a dairy shop for local cheese, yoghurt and honey, several exchange places, the post office and a small **tourist office**. The **OTE** (7am–3pm) is on the main square.

Boat tickets for the coastal ferries and also to the island of Gávdhos are sold from a hut at the bottom of the jetty: check which boat you'll be getting as the *Samaria* is too big for the dock and comes in instead right on the other side of town, quite a long way to run if you're waiting in the wrong place. **Bus tickets** are sold from a wooden hut on the square: for Haniá, most people already have tickets and the important thing is to get on the bus in order to secure a seat. The south-coast bus to Plakiás leaves at 4.30pm, and this is often even more crowded.

Frangokástello

FRANGOKÁSTELLO lies 3km off the main road, just under 10km from the junction with the Hóra–Vrísses road (buses divert along the new road through the village): the castle makes an easy target to aim for.

For peaceful lassitude on the beach Frangokástello is still among the best spots in Crete, with fine sand, crystal-clear water (with good snorkelling opportunities), and very little effort required either to get here or to find food and drink once you've arrived. If you want company you'll find it around the castle where the best part of the sand is, sheltered and slowly shelving; for solitude head westwards along the shoreline – less soft sand and more wind, but still very pleasant. There are beaches to the east, too: follow the coastal path for ten to fifteen minutes and you'll arrive at the top of a low cliff overlooking perhaps three-quarters of a mile of beautiful, deserted sand and rocks. Lying in the sun here the only thing to disturb the afternoon tranquillity is the occasional muffled crump of an explosion offshore, emanating from the home-made depth charges of local fishermen going about their business in the time-honoured and highly illegal way. Watch closely, and you'll see the sudden spout of water near the boat before the noise of the explosion reaches you.

The **castle**, so impressively four-square from a distance, turns out close up to be a mere shell. Nothing but the bare walls survive, with a tower in each corner, and over the seaward entrance an escutcheon, which can just be made out as the Venetian Lion of St Mark. Still, it's some shell. The fortress was originally built in 1371 to deter pirates and in an attempt to impose some order on Sfakiá: a garrison was maintained here throughout the Venetian and Turkish occupations, controlling the plain as surely as it failed to tame the mountains (even today, the orange-pink walls look puny when you see them with the grey bulk of the mountains towering behind). In 1828, Frangokástello was occupied by Hadzimihali Daliani, a Greek adventurer attempting to spread the War of Independence from the mainland to Crete. Instead of taking to the hills as all sensible rebels before and since have done, he and his tiny force attempted to make a stand in the castle. Predictably, they were massacred and their martyrdom became the fuel for yet more heroic legends of the *pallikari*. Locals will claim that to this day, on or around May 17, the ghosts of Daliani and his army march from the castle: they are known as *dhrossoulítes*, or dewy ones, because they appear in the mists around dawn.

Just below the castle, before the beach, there's a patch of greenery which shades a taverna and a tiny freshwater creek with thoroughly incongruous ducks on it: between the road and sea to the west are more little streams and marshy patches like this, home to terrapins and some type of water snake or eel.

Practicalities

The first turning off the road takes you straight down to the sea where a left turn along the shore leads past just about all the places which offer **rooms**. There are several places right on the beach below the castle, well located but subject to mosquitos, and lots more possibilities along the road westwards. There's also good **camping** among the dunes, both right by the castle and along the longer beach to the west, with plenty of ruined walls and bamboo groves for shelter – if you do camp here, respect local sensitivities and take your rubbish away with you. Set back from the sea, the lone **disco**, *Blue Sky*, is run by a couple of friendly Germans who live in the house behind. They also rent out mountain **bikes**, scooters and cars and can provide information on renting **apartments** for longer stays (☎0825/92-095; ②).

Tavernas cluster around the beach to the right, on the promontory, while others straggle along the road. None are particularly sophisticated but they're friendly and, barring the extortionate *Dhrossites* opposite the castle, reasonably priced; the *Fata Morgana* taverna on the beach has the best reputation. There are also a couple of **mini-markets**, selling most things you're likely to want.

An early morning **bus** (6.30am) runs to Hóra Sfakíon to connect with the first bus from there, and buses running between Plakiás and Hóra Sfakíon also pass through.

For a description of the road **east to Plakiás**, see p.206.

THE FAR WEST

Crete's far west has, to date, attracted surprisingly little attention from tourists or developers, though inevitably that is beginning to change. The one town of any size west of Haniá is **Kastélli Kisámou**, a port with a twice-weekly ferry service to the Peloponnese, very regular buses to Haniá, and little else to attract visitors. Beyond, Crete's west-facing coast remains remote: west of a line between Kastélli and Paleohóra there's little public transport, no more than a handful of rooms to rent, and absolutely nothing in the way of luxurious facilities. Yet here you'll find two of the finest beaches on the island – **Falásarna** and **Elafonísi** – both of them, sadly, beginning to suffer from overexploitation. For longer stays in this part of Crete it's important to carry all the money and most of the supplies you'll need – there are some facilities at the beaches, but the villages are few and far between, and have only the most basic of shops.

On the **south coast**, good roads and several buses a day run to **Paleohóra** and **Soúyia**. The former is already a resort of some size – surprisingly large given its isolation, but far from totally despoiled – the latter is smaller and less attractive but still inexpensive and friendly. Regular boats connect the two places, or there's a footpath by way of the ruins of ancient **Lissós**, on the coast just west of Soúyia. Moving between them by road is rough and sometimes impossible unless you're prepared to backtrack most of the way to the north coast; the only properly paved roads are those which run north–south. Along the way, there's spectacular mountain scenery in which frescoed medieval churches are liberally scattered.

Kastélli Kisámou and the north coast

Kastélli lies some 20km beyond the crossroads at Kolimbári (p.245), and the new E65 highway which runs across the bottom of the Rodhópou peninsula has now cut journey times considerably. It has also left the **old road** – always a beautiful drive – as a delightful backwater. Going this way you wind steeply up a rocky spur thrown back by the peninsula and emerge through a cleft in the hills to a magnificent sunset view of the Gulf of Kisámou, with Kastélli in the middle distance. With the sun setting behind the craggy heights of Cape Voúxa at the far west of Crete, this is a memorable panorama. There's a roadside restaurant from which you can enjoy the view, and further along a number of quite large, entirely unvisited villages, such as Nochiá, Koléni or Kaloudhianá, where you could also stop for a drink or a bite to eat at a number of inviting tavernas.

As it leaves the height, the road loops back out of the hills onto the fertile plain of Kastélli. Almost as soon as you hit level ground there's a sign to a **campsite**, *Camping Mithymna* (☎0822/31-444), on the coast about 1km from the road. It takes its name from the ancient town of *Mithymna*, thought to have been approximately where the nearby village of Noríya now stands. Well equipped, and reasonably priced, you'll generally find it fairly empty since a new campsite opened up in Kastélli itself (see below). The village of Kaloudhianá, 4km further along, is also the place to turn for the inland route to Topólia and Elafonísi.

Kastélli Kisámou

Heading for the west coast, you'll pass through **KASTÉLLI KISÁMOU** (mostly known simply as Kastélli), which at first sight seems to offer little to get excited about. It's a busy little town and port with a rather rocky beach. But this very ordinariness has a real charm once you get over your initial reaction: it's a working town full of stores that the locals use and cafés not entirely geared to outsiders.

On the western outskirts the old and new roads join forces to head straight through the town, by-passing the centre: parallel to this road, towards the sea, runs the main street – with stores and banks – leading into the central square, Platía Kastellioú. A block to the southwest of this is another square where the **buses** pull in. There's a second cluster of development along the **waterfront**, directly down from the main square, with a short promenade and the small **folklore museum**, housing an interesting collection of household miscellany.

All the facilities you're likely to need lie on or near the main square. **Ferry tickets** for boat connections with Elafonísos, Kíthira, Yíthio and Monemvassía are on sale at *Xirouchakis Travel* (☎0822/22-655) on the square itself or from *Horeftakis Tours* (☎0822/23888); the **ferry dock** is some 2km west of town – a significant walk if you're heavily laden, or a cheap taxi ride. The **post office** (Mon–Fri 7.30am–2pm), which also changes money, and the **OTE** (same hours) are both on the main street to the east of the square. For **bike and car rental**, try the reliable *Motor Fun* (☎0822/23-440) on the main square.

Accommodation

Accommodation options include the *Castelli Hotel* (☎0822/22-140; ②), on the square, with rooms at the cheaper end of this price band, although it's not the friendliest of places. Close by, towards the sea, *Rooms Koutsounakis* (☎0822/23-416; ①) is another possibility and has rooms with private bath. On the seafront at the western end, *Maria Kastanaki Beach* (☎0822/22-610; ①–②) has balcony rooms with and without private bath, and similar facilities are on offer at the nearby *Argo* (☎0822/23-563; ②). Slightly to the east, *Manty Apartments* (☎0822/22-830; ③) also has balcony rooms with separate kitchen/diner, worth considering for a longer stay – those on higher floors tend to escape the late-night noise from the terrace bar downstairs.

A quieter option, accessible only with your own transport, is the *Hotel Playies* (☎0822/23-404; ②), set on a hill above town, along the road to Polyrínia (see below); all rooms have private bath and balconies with good sea views, and it should be possible to bargain when business is slack. West of the square, 150m down the main street, you'll find the town's **campsite**, *Camping Kissamou* (☎0822/23-443), with some shade and a nice pool, although this does tend to be an obvious first stop for people who bring cars and campervans across on the ferry from Yíthio.

Eating and drinking

The best **restaurants** are also along the seafront: try the reasonably priced *Papadakis* at the western end for seafood, or the nearby *Makedonas*. A little way back from the sea, *Taverna Piccadilly* has a mainstream menu and lower prices than the waterfront places, while among another group of restaurants at the opposite end of the promenade, *Salt and Pepper* caters for northern European tastes, with a variety of ". . . and chips" possibilities. In the centre of town, *Restaurant Agrimi* to the west of the main square serves traditional Cretan dishes. Wherever you eat, you'll probably be offered some of the **local red wine**: made from the *roméiko* grape, which is believed to have been brought to the island by the Venetians, it is as good as any produced on Crete.

Although the seafront area often has a listless, end-of-season air by day, it comes to life at night when the locals pile in to drink at the numerous **bars**.

Polyrínia

Kastélli Kisámou (also sometimes known simply as Kisámou or Kísamos) is so named to distinguish it from the other Kastéllis scattered around Crete. The name is taken from ancient *Kíssamos*, which once stood here and served as a port for the sizeable ancient city of **Polyrínia**. About 7km inland, above the village of Paleókastro (confusingly also known as Polirinía), vestiges of the ancient settlement can still be seen. There are **buses** up from Kastélli Kisámou (Mon, Wed & Fri 7am & 2pm; returning 30min later), but the walk is perfectly feasible; your best bet is to take a bus or taxi up, and walk back down.

It's something of a climb from the village to the hilltop site, where ruins are scattered across two horns of high ground which seem to reach out to enclose the Gulf of Kisámou. Originally an eighth-century BC Dorian colony from the Peloponnese, Polyrínia – a name meaning "rich in lambs" – remained a prosperous city down to Roman times and beyond. One of its main claims to fame, however, would not endear it to most Cretans: an inscription found here and dated to 69 BC tells of how the Polyrinians created a statue in honour of the Roman conqueror of Crete, Quintus Metellus, referring to him as the "saviour and benefactor of the city". It seems that Polyrínia did not join in the resistance put up by Haniá and other cities to the Roman invasion, and as a result was spared destruction.

The most obvious feature when you reach the site is the **Acropolis**, which is in fact almost entirely a Venetian defensive structure, but there are all sorts of foundations and obscure remains, including Roman and Greek masonry incorporated into the church that now stands on the site. The church is itself constructed on the base of what must have been an enormously impressive Hellenistic building. The sheer amount of work involved in cutting and dressing these stone blocks and transporting them to places as inaccessible as this makes you wonder at the phenomenal scale of manpower at the service of these towns in antiquity. The unsightly breeze blocks used for the cemetery wall of the modern church makes a starkly ironic contrast.

On the way back from the site, the pleasant *Taverna Polyrinia* in the village of Áno Paleókastro has views almost as good as those from the top.

The west coast: Falásarna

Leaving Kastélli Kisámou for the west, the road climbs back into the hills again, cutting south across the base of the Gramvoúsa peninsula. The paved road now continues all the way down to the beautiful beach at **FALÁSARNA** (note that the signs in Plátanos seem designed to confuse – you need to turn right fairly early, and the road should be good and new), with two buses a day direct from Haniá. The last part snakes down a spectacular series of hairpin bends before turning north onto the narrow coastal plain, where farmers have discovered the benefits of plastic greenhouses for forcing tomatoes, melons and the like. The end of the asphalt is marked by two tavernas just above a sublime beach, a broad crescent of yellow sand edged by turquoise waters. Although the beach can occasionally be afflicted by washed-up oil, tar and discarded rubbish, this doesn't detract from the overall beauty of the place. Besides, if it gets too crowded here, there are two more beaches within easy walking distance, as well as others further south which can be reached along rough tracks.

There are an increasing number of **rooms** places here, some of them quite good; try *SunSet* (☎0822/41-204; ①), which has excellent balcony rooms with sea views and private baths as well as a good **restaurant** below. Many of the people who stay here **camp** at the back of the beach, either in a couple of small caves or beneath makeshift shelters slung between a few stumpy trees; take your rubbish away with you.

Ancient Falásarna and Gramvoúsa

The **ancient city** and port of Falásarna lies just to the north of the beach. If you follow the main dirt track for 1km past the tavernas and through the olive groves, at the edge of the archeological site you will pass the large stone "**throne**" that has puzzled experts for decades – there is still no satisfactory explanation for its function.

The westernmost of the cities of ancient Crete, and now undergoing systematic excavation, Falásarna was founded prior to the sixth century BC and remained the sworn enemy of nearby Polyrínia (see above). What you are now able to see are the scattered remains of a city built around a large depression (its inner harbour) and the bed of a canal that once joined this to the sea. All of the site is now high and dry, offering conclusive proof that Crete's western extremities have risen at least 8m over the last 24 centuries or so. The excavators discovered large stone blocks thrown across the entrance to the old harbour; current thinking suggests that this was done by the later Romans to prevent ships using the port as the base for a "pirates' nest". The harbour was defended by part of the city wall linked by a number of towers to a harbour

mole, with the **South Tower**, the nearest to the sea, a formidable bastion built
of huge sandstone blocks. More ruined structures are to be seen ascending the
acropolis hill behind, and near to the chapel of Áyios Yeóryios (beneath a
canopy) a recently excavated building revealed a number of well-preserved
terra-cotta baths.

Continue on the best of the roads past the throne and you pass under
Cyclopean walls to emerge above another small bay. Tempting as it is, this is too
sharp and rocky for you to be able to get to the sea, but it does give you views to
the north, over **Cape Voúxa**, which are shielded from Falásarna itself. Towards
the top you can see the island of **Gramvoúsa** (not to be confused with the unin-
habitable rock of Pontikonísi, a more distant islet which can sometimes be seen
from the beach at Falásarna) on which the Venetians built an important castle.
Along with the fortified islands of Néa Sóudha and Spinalónga, this was one of the
points that held out against the Turks long after the Cretan mainland had fallen.
When the Venetians left, the fort was allowed to fall into disrepair until it was
taken over by Greek refugees from other Turkish-occupied islands (notably
Kásos) who used it as a base for piracy. It took a major Turkish campaign to
wrest the fortress back, and thereafter they maintained a garrison here. In the
War of Independence it became a base for the Turkish ships attempting to maintain a blockade of the coastline. Another slightly larger and wilder island, Agría
Gramvoúsa, lies to the north just off the cape.

It's possible to visit these islands by renting a **boat** in Kastélli (or Haniá for a
cruise of several days), and there are also rumours that you can wade across to
one of them if you hike up the peninsula. This seems unlikely, but certainly if you
fancy some wild and lonesome walking, **the peninsula** fits the bill – being
extraordinarily barren and quite unpopulated. A path of sorts runs up the eastern
side from the village of Kaliviani and about three hours' walk will take you to a
really spectacular white-sand beach (sadly with an even worse tar problem than
Falásarna) more or less opposite Gramvoúsa. Bear in mind that there are no
tavernas or shops at Kaliviani and, although the friendly *Kafenion Siponitakis*
(facing the start of the path) will make you a tasty potato omelette and salad,
provisions for the hike should be purchased ahead. In high summer, you'll also
need water – which can be replenished at a spring near to the chapel of Ayía Iríni,
about 6km out.

Routes to the southwest

Heading for the **southwest**, the normal way is to follow the inland route by turning off the north-coast highway at Kaloudhianá, before Kastélli. This is a lovely
rural drive up the valley of the Tiflós, and follows a reasonably good road as far as
Váthi. In the sturdy farming villages of this unusually green part of Crete there
are plenty of opportunities to take in the local wildlife, or to do some walking in
the oleander- and chestnut-wooded hills and along numerous gorges.
Alternatively, the **coast road** southwest of Plátanos, although lacking greenery,
is often spectacularly scenic and, despite lengthy unpaved sections between
Sfinári and Kefáli, makes a perfectly easy drive. Both roads eventually end up at
the romantically sited monastery of **Hrissokalítissa** and the idyllic beaches of
Elafonísi, a little to the south. If you have your own transport, try to go out one
way and return the other.

The inland route

The area of the far west between Topólia in the northeast and Vathi to the south-west includes some of the most fertile lands on the island. Here, lush woodland watered by tumbling streams emanating from the mountains is a haven for a rich variety of flora and fauna. Water is so plentiful around places such as Élos and Kefáli, in fact, that tourism comes a very poor second to agriculture. Everyone it seems has a *kípos*, or smallholding, with a couple of dozen olive trees or a vegetable patch. The life of these villages is dictated by the needs of the farmers, a hard-working and laconic bunch who dress in sturdy boots and lumberjack shirts and greet one another with gruff cries of "*yia!*" (abbreviated from *yia sou*) from the open windows of Japanese pick-up trucks – the ultimate status symbol around these parts, as you need a permit to import one.

Following the **inland route**, after some 4km of ascent you reach the village of **VOULGHÁRO**, where you could stretch your legs in search of two ancient frescoed churches, Áyios Yióryios and Áyios Nikólaos – in the satellite villages of Mákronas across the valley and Mourí along a track 2km further south, respectively. Just south of Mourí you could also descend into the ravine (see below) making for the village of Koutsoumátados, a **walk** of about 5km. By road you'll continue climbing to **TOPÓLIA**, 3km after Voulgháro, whose church of Ayía Paraskeví has more frescoes, this time from the late Byzantine period. South of here the road enters a tunnel before skirting the edge of the dramatic **Koutsoumátados ravine**, one of the most imposing on the island. Nearing the middle of the ravine you'll come to a signed stairway cut into the rock on the right, and a muscle-taxing short climb to the **cave of Ayía Sofía**. This is one of the largest caves on Crete and remains found here date its usage back to Neolithic times; it now shelters a small chapel, along with stalactites, stalagmites and its present residents, a colony of bats.

Proceeding along the ravine you will soon reach the hamlet of **KOUTSOUMÁTADOS** where the roadside *Rooms Taverna Panorama* (☎0822/51-163; ①) is a possible stopping place for a meal, or even **rooms**, should you decide to get into more detailed exploration of the area. Its friendly owner Manolis Motakis and his Dutch wife are keen to put up walkers, and will advise on various hiking routes around the ravine as well as climbing Koproula, the highest peak hereabouts.

Élos and Pervólia

Beyond Koutsoumátados the road continues for 3km to where, on the right, there's a potential detour through the charming villages of Vlátos, Rogdiá and Límni, set in the midst of more verdant countryside. This turning is quickly followed by one on the right which heads southwest to pick up the road to Paleóhora (see pp.275–7). The direct route passes slopes covered with magnificent stands of chestnut, planes and other deciduous trees. Chestnuts, in fact, are a major local crop around here and **ÉLOS**, 4km along, is the centre of the chestnut-growing region known as the *Enneachora* (nine villages). This is a wonderfully refreshing place, even at the height of summer, and it's easy to forget just how high you are here – the mountains to the south rise to about 1200m. In the village's square, shaded by plane, eucalyptus and, of course, chestnut trees, *Rooms Kastanofolia* (chestnut den, ☎0822/61-258; ①) is a clean and simple place with **rooms** above a good taverna, run by the young and tireless Kiría Kokolakis who serves a daily special fresh from the oven. There are ducks in a pool filled by a stream running beside the taverna's terrace and directly opposite, over the road, you can stroll along a track that leads a couple of kilometres into the chestnut forests. Behind the taverna there is also an impressive old arch which was probably once part of a Turkish aqueduct. The great event in Élos's year is the annual **chestnut festival** in late October.

Five kilometres further, a turn on the left indicates a sharp descent to the picturesque hamlet of **PERVÓLIA** tucked into the folds of a high gorge beneath the northern flank of Mount Áyios Díkeos Ióv (Job the Just). The village is another verdant oasis with charming narrow streets punctuated by simple whitewalled dwellings and smallholdings overflowing with vigorously growing vegetables. Continue to the foot of the village and a fountain, near a recently erected bust to one of the noted local *pallikári* of the last century, Anagnostis Skalidis, and at the house opposite you will find a small **museum** assembled by one of his descendants, Zacharia Skalidis. An amiable man who speaks only Greek, he will be delighted to show you around his collection, which includes lots of atmospheric photos from a Crete long gone, as well as old guns, letters and coins.

Kefáli and Váthi

Barely 2km beyond Pervólia, another charming *Enneachora* village, **KEFÁLI**, has a fine fourteenth-century frescoed **church**, Metamórphosis tou Sotirís (Transfiguration of Christ), down a track on the left as you enter the village. Inside, the church has some interesting and apparently genuine early graffiti, scratched across the paintings. An Englishman, Francis Lerfordes, has marked his contribution with the date 1553, while Turks later inscribed their blasphemous thoughts along with the crescent symbol – to the further detriment of the art works. The main street has simple **rooms** above *Taverna Polakis* (☎0822/61-260; ①), with a splendid balcony view over the Bay of Stomíou. The owner, Yeorgos Polakis, is a fount of local knowledge and will direct you to the church should you encounter difficulties. The aptly named *Panorama* taverna, opposite, provides meals with a view.

Nearby **VÁTHI**, 1km or so after Kefáli, is another of the *Enneachora* villages with two more ancient **churches** for enthusiasts: the thirteenth-century Áyios Yióryios off the central square, and Mikhaíl Arkhángelos, just to the south, with fourteenth-century frescoes.

The coast road

If you were to carry straight on in Kefáli, you'd be on the coast road back around to Plátanos. Just out of Kefáli magnificent coastal **views** unfold, with the distant beaches of Elafonísi shimmering mirage-like in a turquoise sea. The road winds towards the coast, sometimes paved and sometimes not, but always with stunning views over the Mediterranean. Around you, olives ripen on the terraced hillsides and the villages seem to cling desperately to the high mountainsides, as if miraculously saved from some calamitous slide to the sea, glittering far below.

By **KÁMBOS** you've descended enough for there to be an excellent beach below the village, albeit an hour's hike down a superb gorge inhabited by colonies of doves. Should you want to try this at a more leisurely pace, **accommodation** and **food** is available at *Rooms Hartzulakis* (☎0822/41-445; ①) where the friendly owner, Lefteris Hartzulakis, will advise on walking the gorge and seeking out the *dictamus* herb (Cretan dittany) that grows there – used as a panacea by the Cretans since ancient times. **SFÍNARI**, a tortuous 7km north and slightly inland from a quiet pebble beach, is more developed, with several houses offering **rooms** for rent, plus a couple of decent **tavernas**: try *Phidias* towards the beach, which also has rooms.

Hrissoskalítissa

HRISSOSKALÍTISSA lies some 10km southwest of Váthi, on a road which deteriorates rapidly. There are a couple of tavernas on the way down here, but otherwise little beyond the monastery (now, in fact, a nunnery), beautifully sited but today barely functioning, reduced from some two hundred residents to just one often grumpy nun and one monk, whose main task seems to be keeping the place acceptable for tourists. The present church dates only from the last century, but the monastery building is an ancient foundation: the first church was built in a cave here in the thirteenth century. Look out for the ninety steps that lead to the top of the crag around which the place is built: one of them appears golden (*Hrissí skála*) to those who are pure in spirit – a fact which the authors are unable to verify.

Elafonísi

For **ELAFONÍSI** you've another 5km of very dusty, bumpy road to traverse, but it's worth it. The almost tropical lagoon of white-sand beaches tinged pink by shells, aquamarine waters, salt-encrusted rock pools and bright red starfish is still, despite increasing exploitation, as idyllic a spot as any in Crete. The water is incredibly warm, calm and shallow and Elafonísi – actually an island just offshore – is a short wade across the sandbar. There are more beaches on its far side (with waves), along with the odd ruined wall, seashells and a monument to Australian sailors shipwrecked here in 1907. A couple of simple **cafés** stand on the road as you arrive.

Not surprisingly, all this has not gone undiscovered, and there are now two **boats** a day from Paleohóra, a daily **bus** from Haniá, and often at least one bus tour. The chief result of this is that there are often piles of rubbish on the mainland beach, but for now the water, and the island, remain pristine, and there are rarely so many people that the island can't absorb them. Note, however, that change is in the pipeline (literally) for this area: water is being piped in from the north, soon to be followed by electricity and an asphalted road, while German and Greek consortia (one of the latter headed by the Cretan former prime minister of Greece, Constantine Mitsotakis) have bought up large tracts of land. Plans for development are well under way and it's to be hoped that something of the natural beauty of this place will survive the concrete mixers.

Moving on

Continuing south from Elafonísi is no easy matter, though you could catch the boat if you were heading for Paleohóra. There's a coastal path, reasonably well marked, via which you should be able to reach Paleohóra in about six hours. Be sure to get some accurate directions before setting out, however, as this coastline is barely inhabited and a wrong turn could lead you a very long way astray in hostile terrain.

If you're driving, there is a road which turns off the inland route between Élos and Topólia, cutting down to Paleohóra. This soon becomes dirt track and splits:

the easiest way is to keep left, through Aligí and Drís, to meet the main road at the village of Plemenianá. This is rough, but not too bad, while the routes that bear directly south are really atrocious in places: if you're feeling brave, though, it is a rewarding venture. Along the way scores of little streams cascade beside, under, or sometimes across, the road. Hardly any traffic passes, and the rare villages are ancient and rustic; their inhabitants stand and stare as you drive through, but are extremely welcoming if you stop.

The southwest

The **direct route to Paleohóra** has to negotiate the same mountains, but it's a well-surfaced road and takes the line of least resistance: it feels a great deal less intimidating. From the turning at Tavronítis the road traces a long valley fingering its way beneath the hills as far as Voukoliés, a large village with a crowded Saturday morning market (all over by about 10am). Hereafter you begin to climb in earnest, through several much smaller villages, towards the **eparchy (province) of Sélinos**.

Sélinos

Sélinos, the southwestern corner of Crete, is famous these days mainly for its Byzantine churches, of which every village seems to offer at least one example. **FLÓRIA**, almost exactly halfway across the island, has two: **Áyios Yióryios** with fine fifteenth-century frescoes, reached by a track which descends to the right of the second café, and Áyii Patéres in the upper village, although only fresco fragments remain. Near to the first café, two war memorials – one German, one Greek – face each other across the road, serving as grim reminders of the terrible atrocities that happened here during World War II when, locals will tell you, they saw their parents and relatives gunned down in the self-same road.

If you take the short detour from Kándhanos up to **ANISARÁKI** you'll find more fresco traces in the churches of Ayía Ánna, Panayía and Ayía Paraskeví. The next two villages on the main road are also worth a look: Áyios Yióryios in **PLEMENIANÁ** has paintings dating from the fifteenth century, while **KAKODHÍKI**, known for its curative springs, has several churches nearby. These include the very ancient chapel of Mihaïl Arhángelos, probably early thirteenth-century, beside the modern church of Ayía Triádha, and the hilltop Áyios Isidhóros, with magnificent views and frescoes defaced by the Turks. Many more small churches can be found throughout the area, particularly if you get off the road into the smaller villages. Few, if any, of them will be open when you arrive – but express an interest at the nearest *kafenion* or to a local passer-by and it rarely takes long to hunt out the priest or someone else with a key.

KÁNDHANOS, though it's a great deal smaller than Paleohóra these days, is the chief village of the eparchy and makes a pleasant, quiet place to stop for a coffee. Despite the existence of as many as fifteen Byzantine churches in the vicinity, the village buildings are almost entirely new, for the place was razed to the ground by the Germans for its role in the wartime resistance. The original sign erected then is today preserved on a war memorial in the square. In German and Greek it reads, "Here stood Kándhanos, destroyed in retribution for the murder of 25 German soldiers".

Paleohóra

PALEOHÓRA was known originally as Kastél Selínou – the castle of Sélinos – and for much of its history was no more than that, a castle. Built by the Venetians in 1279, the fort was destroyed by Barbarossa in 1539 and never properly reconstructed even when the small port grew up beneath it. The ruins are still perched at the bulbous end of the headland now occupied by the settlement of Paleohóra – at its narrowest a bare four blocks across from the harbour on one side to the beach on the other.

The village is rapidly growing, and its facilities can barely cope with the ever-increasing volume of visitors. For the time being, though, it retains an enjoyably laid-back, end-of-the-line feel, helped out by superb and extensive sands. Warm right through the winter, this out-of-season backwater makes an excellent place to rent an inexpensive apartment long-term. A eucalyptus-lined avenue leads into the single main street, Venizélos, lined with taverna after café after bar. Although not particularly attractive by day, this is the soul of the village, and in the evening it is filled to overflowing as the restaurants' tables spill across the pavement and encroach onto the road, creating total chaos when the bus arrives or a truck tries to squeeze through, as one invariably does. Chaos tends to reign anyway, as the waiters and cooks keep up voluble arguments with each other and their customers, or vie to outdo the sales pitches of their rivals: it's an enjoyable madness as long as you're in no hurry to eat or go anywhere.

Not that you're likely to have far to go, since nothing is more than five minutes' walk away. The better **beach** (called "Sandy Beach"), magnificently broad and sandy, lined with tamarisks and supplied with showers, is on the west side of town, facing a bay with excellent easy windsurfing (good boards for rent). People still camp all along here under the trees, though these days you're likely to be moved on in high summer to the official campsite (see over). There's more – but much less attractive – beach, pebbly at first but sandy further out, at the base of the peninsula on the east side.

The oldest parts of town, if you want to explore, are on the east side around the harbour: from here you can clamber up into the **castle**, for the views back over town, or walk right around the end of the promontory to return to the beach on the other side. Neither of these options are as appealing as they might be, since the fortress itself is little more than a hillock ringed with broken walls, while a new marina dominates the point; there are some very much more attractive **walks** to be had inland, to charming villages like Ánidhri and Azoyirés (see pp.277–8), or along the coast in either direction.

Information and services

The municipal **tourist office** (Mon–Fri 10am–1pm & 5–8pm) on Venizélos can give you a copy of their town map, and advise about likely rooms places, as well as apartment lets should you be interested in a longer sojourn.

Several **travel agents** are dotted around the town: *Interkreta Travel*, close to the junction of Kontekaki and Venizélos, is the best for boat tickets, and gives out information on just about everything else, as well as changing money. It also sells tickets for local **ferries** – to Elafonísi (daily except Wed and Sat at 10am and 2pm), Gávdhos (Wed, Sat and Sun at 8.30am) and along the coast to Soúyia and Ayía Rouméli, Loutró and Hóra Sfakíon (daily at 8am). You can also pick up tickets at the ferry company offices, on the road down to the jetty. A reliable **car and**

bike rental place is *Sirocco*, on Venizélos, opposite the town hall, with *Paleohóra Moto Rent*, round the corner from *Interkreta Travel*, a possible alternative.

There are two **banks** on Venizélos, just north of the town hall, and the **OTE** (Mon–Fri 7.30am–3.10pm) is immediately south. There are also phones next door, at the nearby kiosk, and down by Sandy Beach. The **post office** (Mon–Fri 8am–2.30pm, Sat 9am–1.30pm), which also changes money, is out on the road behind Sandy Beach, and there's a **health centre** in the street parallel to Venizélos to the west (daily 8.30am–2pm & 5–8pm).

Accommodation

Finding a **room** is unlikely to be a major problem outside August. Inexpensive places are mostly found in the backstreets behind Venizélos, but you'll see signs everywhere. Good possibilities include *Hotel Oasis* (☎0823/41-328; ①), with balcony rooms overlooking a garden, or the nearby *Hotel Rea* (☎0823/41-307; ②). *Marina Devoga Rooms* (☎0823/41-564; ①) on Kontekaki, the street heading west from the lower end of Venizélos, has clean, budget rooms within easy distance of Sandy Beach, while *Rooms Oriental Bay* (☎0823/41-322; ①), at the northern end of the pebble beach, has pleasant rooms over a seafront taverna. *Rooms Anonymous* (①), just behind Venizélos on the street heading inland to the cinema, is another economy place with good-value rooms and an unusual garden; more modern accommodation is on offer at the *Beach Hotel* (☎0823/41-512; ③), with sea-view rooms fronting Sandy Beach.

Out-of-town possibilities are listed in the "Around Paleohóra" section opposite. *Camping Paleohóra* (☎0823/41-120) lies 2km northeast of the centre, reached along the road running behind the pebble beach. Sited in an olive grove close to the beach with plenty of shade, the only drawback is the bonehard terrain.

Eating, drinking and nightlife

Apart from the beach, entertainment in Paleohóra is confined mainly to the **tavernas** and bars. There are numerous choices along the main street, Venizélos: *Dionisos* is a straightforward taverna where you choose from the kitchen, which usually comes up with some vegetarian options; *Savas* has good swordfish; and there are a couple of old-fashioned café/*ouzeris* for good-value drinks.

Paleohóra's first **grill-restaurant** hugs the junction of Kontekaki and Venizélos, and has since been joined by *Akrogiali*, down by the pebble beach; other places are strung out along both shores and the streets leading down to them. In a backstreet off Kontekaki, near *Interkreta Travel*, is a friendly little restaurant called *The Third Eye*; run by a Greek/New Zealand couple, it serves all kinds of local dishes, as well as Asian specialities, and offers some imaginative **vegetarian** specials. Nearby, *Pizzeria Niki*, on Kontekaki itself, has excellent pizzas cooked in a wood-fired oven. Across the junction east of here, *Pelican*, fronting the boat jetty, has a reasonable menu but its reputation is based on the visits of an enormous (but now elderly) pelican who often puts in personal appearances. A good bet for salads and omelettes (try the "special omelette") is the *Seagull Snack Bar*, further along behind the pebble beach. Also close by, and facing the beach, is *The Wave*, a tranquil place serving good seafood, enhanced by an evening view of the moon rising behind the mountains. Another, slightly pricier, meal-with-view option is *Fortessa Bar-Restaurant*, just below the fort, with excellent views over the bay and decent food. Along the road to the campsite is *Vrissali*, a pleasant taverna which serves traditional Greek dishes on a shady garden terrace.

By the pebble beach are several places specializing in **breakfast**, although the "all-in" breakfasts tend to be a severe rip-off in most of them. For cakes and sweets, *Notos Coffee Shop*, just up the road heading south from the boat jetty, is the best choice.

Bars along Sandy Beach on the west side of town enjoy particularly good sunsets and there are numerous quite fancy places here, like *Jetée*, where you can linger over a sundowner. Back at the pebble beach, *Caravela* is a good spot for an evening drink, as is the more expensive *Skala Bar*, near the boat jetty.

There's also a **disco**, imaginatively called the *Paleohora Club*, on the east side of town close to the campsite. Nightly showings at the open-air **cinema**, *Cine Attikon*, tucked away in the northern backstreets, are also worth knowing about; most of their films are in English and programmes change daily.

Around Paleohóra

Follow the coast either way from Paleohóra and you'll find more beaches. To the **west** it's not a terribly pretty coastline, marred by plastic greenhouses, but there are some excellent beaches along the way. A paved road along the coast leads after 5km to **Grameno Beach** on a small peninsula which, although pebbly, has trees for shade. On the landward side of the road here, *Taverna Grameno* is a good place to eat, and has a play area for kids; nearby there's a decent rooms place, *Grameno Rooms* (②). Continuing along the road will quickly bring you to **YIALÓS** (Koundourá on some maps), which also has rooms but is spoiled by more greenhouses: you could try *Vienna Rooms* (②) with a pool and sea views if you are running out of options. The paved road peters out – 4km beyond Yialós – at **Kriós**, another pebble beach where the water can be incredibly cold due to underwater springs. The dirt road from here on continues to several shingly, deserted bays, where some people camp beside beautifully clear water. In theory you can continue on foot right around this coast to Elafonísi (see p.273), but check first for an exact route and ascertain the state of the path – there have been tragic incidents involving walkers getting into difficulties on this stretch.

To the **east**, things are simpler: a footpath traces the shore for miles beyond the campsite, passing a succession of grey pebble strips with fewer people clad in fewer clothes the further you venture. This path continues to Lissós (3hr) and Soúyia (4hr 30min), and if you time it right you can return to Paleohóra by boat (currently leaving around 5.30pm in summer). Again you should carefully check out both the route and the boats beforehand, as the service deteriorates rapidly out of high season. The path is waymarked, but it doesn't simply follow the coast all the way, and there are one or two steep scrambles. Since the most scenic section is through the gorge between Lissós and Soúyia, it might be easier to do it from there. An alternative, easier walk would take you down from Prodhrómi, inland, but you'd have to take a taxi to the starting point. The village of **ÁNIDHRI**, en route, is particularly beautiful, with a fourteenth-century church, Áyios Yióryios, which has an unusual double altar and frescoes by Ioánnis Pagoménos (John the Frozen), the most prolific of several painters whose signatures appear frequently around Sélinos.

Finally, with your own transport, you could follow a **spectacular drive** along the road which heads northwest from the town and tracks the valley of the River Pelekaniotikos, calling at a string of charming Sélinos hamlets such as Voutás, Kámatera and Arhondíko, en route to Stróvles and Míli 25km on, where it joins up with the road south to Elafonísi. With substantial chunks still unpaved, some parts are slow going, but the dramatic mountain scenery more than makes up for the time lost. To join the road, head west out of Paleohóra along the coast, turning right after 500m into the hills in the direction of Voutás.

Azoyirés

Other villages in **the interior** are equally unspoilt and, if you have transport, almost any of the tracks into the hills are fascinating. Heading north out of Paleohóra on the main road, you'll soon reach a couple signs to **AZOYIRÉS**: one official, the other extolling the virtues of "Azoyires, Paradise Village", with its museum and caves. The road up to the village – set amidst woods of cypress and pine – is a very rough 8km. Head straight for the centre of the village (ignoring the sign for the museum, which will almost certainly be closed), where there are two **taverna/rooms** places, *Mihailis* and *Alpha* (both ①), though neither is that special and a better alternative would be to take a packed lunch to enjoy under the trees on the banks of the nearby stream.

The **museum** (officially Sat & Sun 9am–2pm) is a single-room record of the Turkish occupation, full of fascinating old stuff. Outside the opening hours, the curator can usually be found if you ask at *Alpha*, right at the bottom of the village, by a chapel built into a cliff and the old olive-oil factory: a pretty path leads down there, above a lovely tree-filled ravine where pine, cypress, olive and maple grow. The **cave** is in the other direction, on a road which sets off opposite *Mihailis* and winds steeply upwards for nearly 2km (keep climbing and turning where there's any doubt about the way). At the top you have to park and there's an obvious path leading on – look up and you'll see a cross, which marks your destination. Approaching the cave, some 200m above, you may disturb quail (sometimes on the menu at *Alpha*) – the eerie sounds in the cave itself emanate from more birds, mostly pigeons, bizarrely amplified by the cave. Going down, there's a steep metal stairway and rock-cut steps descending 50m or so to a little shrine lit from above by dim, reflected light. If you have a powerful torch, you can continue a fair way, although there's no proper path here: frankly, it's not that impressive.

Beyond Azoyirés you can continue for a further 10km or so – on a road no worse than you've already endured – to Teménia, where there's another medieval frescoed church and on a nearby hilltop scant remains of the ancient city of Yrtakína. At Teménia you rejoin a good, newly surfaced road which cuts through from Kandános to the Soúyia road at Rodováni; in this direction, Máza is a particularly attractive village.

Haniá to Soúyia

Although you can cut through by the route outlined above, the main road to Soúyia (see pp.280–1) is the one which runs right **across the island from Haniá**. This follows the route to Omalós for about 13km before turning off through Alikianós to skirt west of the highest mountains. Beside this turning there's a large war memorial. The Cretans it remembers were mostly local members of the irregular forces which defended the area known as "Prison Valley" in the Battle of Crete (you've already passed the prison, see p.249). Cut off from any other Allied units – who indeed believed that resistance here collapsed on the first day of the battle – the Greeks fought on even as everyone else was in full retreat. By doing so they prevented the Germans getting around the mountains to cut the road and guaranteed that the evacuation from Hóra

Sfakíon could go ahead. In much earlier history, Alikianós was also the site of the wedding massacre which ended the Kandanoleon revolt (p.242).

In **ALIKIANÓS** itself, the fourteenth-century church of Áyios Yióryios has well-preserved fifteenth-century frescoes. After **SKINÉS**, a large village with several tavernas and *kafenia*, set among extensive orange groves, the road starts to climb out of the valley into the outriders of the Lefká Óri. Here the citrus trees give way to leafier, deciduous varieties – chestnuts and planes especially – and the villages are a great deal smaller. Just over halfway across the island, near Ayía Iríni, there's a road signed to Omalós: the asphalt lasts only a few hundred metres, though it's gradually being extended, and beyond that becomes just another track. But it's an exhilarating drive over extremely high mountains, with wonderful views and plenty of vegetation. **AYÍA IRÍNI** is also a very green village, with lots of old chestnut trees, although it still suffers the aftermath of a **great fire** in the late summer of 1994, which devastated a vast tract of land between the Ayía Iríni gorge and Soúyia, and set fire to many villages en route. Continuing south, you start gradually to descend, looping down to occasional views of the Libyan Sea and, in the last few kilometres, tracing a gorge with Soúyia framed at the far end. Beyond Rodhováni are the remains of ancient **Elyrós**, the most important city in southwest Crete in Roman times and earlier, but now offering very little to see.

In **MONÍ**, the last village before the coast, the delightful fourteenth-century **church of Áyios Nikólaos** has frescoes by Ioánnis Pagaménos, including a huge and striking image of St Nicholas himself. Outside the church, take a look at the **campanile** or free-standing bell tower – it's the only one known on the island. Before setting out for the church, ask in the first bar you pass on entering the village for the key: it's actually kept at a house a few doors along but they'll sort you out. The church lies along a track which descends from the road on the right about 50m beyond the bar.

Koustoyérako

Only about 5km short of Soúyia, a road cuts back to the ancient Sélinos villages of Livadás and Koustoyérako, some 8.5km away at the end of the road. **KOUSTOYÉRAKO** is a very ancient village that was, and still is, the home of the Paterakis family, famed in the annals of resistance to German occupation. Manoli Paterakis was one of those who took part in the capture of General Kreipe (see p.299). He died some years ago, at the age of 73, when he fell while chasing a wild goat through the mountains.

The village, like so many, has a long history of resistance to foreign occupation, and was destroyed by Venetians, Turks and Germans alike. In 1943, German troops entered the village, which the men had deserted, and rounded up the women and children in the village square:

> *They lined them all up, and, as they refused to speak, prepared to execute the lot. But, before they could press the trigger of their heavy machine-gun, ten Germans fell dead. For some of the village men – about ten – had taken up position along the top of a sheer cliff above the village, from where they could watch every detail, and, at just the right moment, had opened fire. Not a bullet went wide. Terrified, the Germans took to their heels. . . .*
>
> George Psychoundákis, *The Cretan Runner*

Next day the Germans returned, but by then the village was deserted; they blew up the empty houses in frustration. Costas Paterakis, who fired the first shot and killed the machine-gunner (Patrick Leigh Fermor has described this as one of the most spectacular moments of the war), still lives here.

While the villagers have no desire to become tourist attractions, the village itself is a lovely and very friendly one, set beneath the heights of the Lefká Óri looking out over the Libyan Sea. At the entrance to the village there's a striking modern war memorial, and a simple taverna, next to the school and village playground. Further along, you reach the square, with a couple of *kafenia*. The famous shot was fired from the rocky cliffs above, to your right as you face inland. At the top of the village, to your left from the square, is a tiny Byzantine **chapel**, Áyios Yióryios, inside which are some beautiful remains of frescoes, with sixteenth-century graffiti carved into them. The chapel itself may be as early as tenth-century in origin: the inscription inside the door dates from sixteenth-century restorations and records various generations of the Kandanoleon family – the last named is one Maria Theotokopoulos. From this tenuous connection comes the claim that El Greco (Domenico Theotokopoulos) came originally from Koustoyérako.

In summer French groups frequently camp by the school, and from here climb – with a guide – to Omalós and the gorge. If you ask permission, and take your meals at the taverna, you'd probably be allowed to **camp** here, too.

Soúyia

SOÚYIA is a small village on its way to becoming a big resort. For the moment, though, there are no big hotels, no major tour operators, just lots of rooms, simple restaurants and bars, and general stores which double as travel agents, phone offices and banks. In front there's an enormous swathe of bay and sparklingly clean, clear sea, and a long pebbly beach. None of it is particularly attractive – the village has an untidy, half-built feel to it, the beach is not always especially clean – but it is a very welcoming place, with plenty of room to spread out. You could camp here under a few scraggly trees if you wanted, and around at the east end of the bay there's something of a nudist community – known locally as the Bay of Pigs.

The village church, down by the beach, seems symptomatic of the local lack of concern about the beauty of the environment. The story goes that it was built after a villager slept here and dreamt that an ancient church lay beneath him and that he was being summoned to erect a new one on the site. Sure enough the ancient church was found and the new one built. Unfortunately the new building was far smaller than the old and at a different angle: as a result the sixth-century Byzantine mosaic which formed the floor of the original stuck out beyond the walls of the new one. Although much of the original mosaic has been taken away for "restoration" and seems unlikely to return, you can still see where it was. The original church was a part of ancient Syía, a port for Elyrós which flourished through the Roman and early Christian eras: other remains can be seen in the village and around to the east of the bay.

Practicalities

Rooms are everywhere in Soúyia, and the place is small enough to discover them all in a few minutes. Some of the best are to the left of the main street as you come in, overlooking where the gorge opens out on the coast. In the same street on the edge of town are *Paradisos* (☎0823/51-358; ①), *Lissos* (☎0823/51-244; ②) and *Filoxenia* (①), all with very pleasant rooms. *Zorba's* (②), on the seafront to the right from the bottom of the main road, is German-run and rather more expensive, but boasts a great position.

Places to eat include the *Hotel Pikilassos*, just off the main street, with taverna-style dishes served on a little terrace where a tame pelican lives; the *Paradisos* café/pizzeria, in the same building as the eponymous rooms place; and several along the front, where *Liviko* is one of the most popular, a bar-restaurant which is as much a place to hang out as to eat. At the eastern end of the seafront, the pricier, Dutch-run *Omikron* has a more north European flavour, and some vegetarian choices.

At night, there are a couple of **disco bars** which sometimes attract a crowd: the first, *Alabama*, is sited among the trees on the far side of the stream to the east of the village, whilst the other, *Fortuna*, is at the northern edge, on the left as you come in.

The local **travel agent**, *Syia Travel* (money exchange daily 8.30am–12.30pm & 4.45–8.45pm), is also on the *Paradisos* premises, and there's a **phone** in the minimarket where the main road joins the seafront.

Lissós

The archeological site of **Lissós** is a great deal more rewarding than anything you'll see in Soúyia itself. The four-kilometre walk there, a little over an hour (90min if you dawdle), is part of the pleasure: you set out on the road which heads west, behind the beach, and at the harbour turn right (there's a rusty old sign marked "Lisos") onto a track leading slightly inland. The route is well marked once you're on it, leading up a beautiful echoing gorge, which you follow for about half an hour, and then climb steeply out of towards the sea. After a short level stretch the sea comes into view, followed almost immediately by Lissós, below you at the back of the little bay of Áyios Kiriákos.

The site

Originally a Dorian city, Lissós grew through the Hellenistic and Roman eras and continued to thrive, along with its neighbours Syía and Elyrós, right up to the Saracen invasion in the ninth century, when they were all abandoned. These places have little history, although it is known that they joined together around 300 BC – along with Yrtakína in the hills behind, Pikilássos on the inaccessible coast between here and Ayía Rouméli, and Tarra, at modern Ayía Rouméli – to form the Confederation of Oreioi, and were later joined by Górtys and Cyrenaica (the latter in North Africa). The remains at Lissós are mostly Classical Greek and Roman.

The most important survival is an **Asklipion**, or temple of healing, built beside a curative spring against the cliffs on the east side of the site. The temple probably dates from the third century BC, although the mosaic floor which is its most obvious feature was added later, in the first century AD: notice also the marble altar-base which would have supported a statue, and the "snake pit" (or hole to place sacrifices) next to it. On the gentler, western slope of the valley, opposite, are a group of tombs that look like small stone huts, with barrel-vaulted roofs – hardly the best advertisement for the healing temple. You'll also find a small ruined theatre and two thirteenth-century churches, Áyios Kiriákos and Panayía, which reused older material from the site.

When you've completed your explorations of the site, a small pebble **beach** provides solace in the form of a swim, and a hut, occupied by the site's guardian, where you can get a drink. Ask here if you find the site locked or if you need directing onto the continuation of the path westward towards Paleohóra.

Gávdhos

Gávdhos, the southernmost point of Europe, is the largest of Crete's offshore islands and the only one with any significant population. Plain and somewhat barren, its attraction lies in its enduring isolation. The 50km of rough sea separating it from the coast of Crete frequently prove too much for the kaíkia, and the ports they serve have themselves only begun to see tourists in the last few years. Consequently – and despite the fact that it's now possible to get a very basic package tour to Gávdhos – the trip to the island remains one more talked about than done. Not that you can expect complete solitude: in summer, there's a semi-permanent community of beach-campers who often outnumber the local population of little over fifty.

In the north and east, the low coast features a number of deserted beaches; in the southwest the island rises to 384m, its shoreline rocky and barely accessible. The interior, with four distinct settlements, is carpeted with pines and scrub and rich with the scent of wild thyme, but it can still be a pretty inhospitable environment, with summer temperatures which frequently climb well beyond 38°C (100°F).

To the northwest of Gávdhos (and passed en route from Paleohóra) lies the flat little islet of **Gavdhopoúlo**, inhabited only in summer by the occasional shepherd taking advantage of the grazing. If you wanted to visit, you'd have to arrange a trip with one of the local fishermen.

The island

As you approach, the harbour is hidden behind a headland, and the island looks totally uninhabited – only with the aid of binoculars might you pick out one or two isolated homes. The port at **Karabé** is minute. Lost in a drab expanse of rock and scrub, two *kafenia* sit alongside a stubby concrete breakwater, and a few ramshackle houses and a church squat behind in silent support. It's normally possible to find a boat here if you want to get to one of the **beaches** the easy way, or you could take one of the vehicles (tractors with trailers or minibuses) that usually meet the ferry. Some people bring rented scooters and bikes across on the ferry with them – it certainly facilitates island exploration. Forty minutes' stiff walk will take you north across the headland, past the pretty little church of Áyios Yioryios, to Sarakiníkos, one of the best of the strands, a broad strip of golden sand where there are eight or nine very basic tavernas. It's a fair-sized track that leads here, but the only real road – a dirt track built in 1980 for the benefit of Gávdhos' four vehicle-owners – runs inland from Karabé. You could also head south, a similar distance, to Kórfos beach, the second most popular.

Kastrí

KASTRÍ, the island capital, is an hour's walk along this steadily climbing dirt track – a ghostly sort of place where only a handful of houses remain inhabited

GÁVDHOS

while the majority gradually crumble away to become one with the weathered and fissured rock on which they stand. Depopulation here has been acute and constant. In the Middle Ages Gávdhos is said to have had eight thousand residents and had a bishop of its own: even in 1914 there were 1400 souls living here. Given the isolation and the stark severity of island life the drain is hardly surprising, but it has undoubtedly made conditions harder for the members of the six families who remain. Not far from the village there is a minor (unfenced) archeological site from which some derive proof that the island was settled as far back as Neolithic times. What is certain is that Gávdhos was inhabited in the Classical Greek era (some claim that this was the island of *Calypso* visited by Odysseus) and well known to the Romans, who christened the place Clauda or Kaudos – Saint Paul was blown past Clauda in the storm which carried him off from Kalí Liménes (see p.118).

In Kastrí you'll find the island **post office** (incorporating the telephone office, store and occasional taxi service) which along with a number of other very basic stores also serves as a café and meeting place. On the outskirts stands a substantial two-storey building where between the wars political prisoners were incarcerated: there have been attempts since to convert it to a hotel and a sanatorium, but currently it stands empty.

Ámbelos and Vatsianá

Climbing out of Kastrí the track reaches the ridgeline and divides. Close to this junction is the island school with its one pupil and one teacher – a facility jealously guarded by the islanders. The left branch leads to the tiny settlement of VATSIANÁ, the right to the equally sparse hamlet of ÁMBELOS. From the latter there's a particularly fine view towards North Africa, a sealane ploughed constantly by enormous supertankers.

Kórfos and Triití

From either village you can continue by narrow paths to some great beaches: north from Ámbelos to Potámos, behind which you can explore a couple of spectacular ravines. Heading east from Vatsianá will bring you to KÓRFOS where there's a good beach (known locally as Yorgo's beach, after the man who lives here with his family over the summer at the taverna on the hill behind). They have a couple of basic **rooms** (①) to rent or you can camp nearby (but ask first). Depending on the water situation, it may also be possible to use the showers here. You might even be able to persuade Yorgo to make a boat trip to TRIPITÍ (rather a long hike from Vatsianá), to the most southerly point of Europe. The beach here is pebbly with no shade but the water is brilliantly clear and a snorkeller's paradise, with lots of aquatic life to be seen. When you need a break, you can climb the famous **three-holed rock** and sit pondering life on the edge of a continent.

Practicalities

Ferry connections aren't bad in summer: **from Paleohóra** via Soúyia (June–Sept leaves Paleohóra 8.30am Wed, Sat and Sun, Soúyia 9.30am, returns at 2.45pm; May and Oct Fri and Sun 8.30am, returns 2.30pm); **from Hóra Sfakíon** (July to mid-Sept, Fri 6pm, Sat and Sun 9am; June, late Sept and Oct, Sat only at 9am); **from Gávdhos to Hóra Sfakíon** (July to mid-Sept, Sat 6am and 4pm, Sun 4pm; June, late Sept and Oct, Sat only at 4pm). Outside these months things are much less certain – there are occasional sailings all year round taking essential supplies across (mostly from Paleohóra) but these are dependent on the weather (unpredictable even in high summer) and other circumstances. The only accurate information can be had on the spot. Whatever time of year, this crossing can be rough, so take precautions if your seaworthiness is in doubt.

The most obvious sign of the hardship of Gávdhos life is the paucity of **food** available. With the exception of a few basic vegetables, and the occasional feast when someone slaughters a sheep or goat, almost everything has to be imported from the mainland and there is little choice in any of the island's stores or eating places. (Karabé and Sarakiníkos have the best options, with at least a chance of fresh fish.) It makes sense to bring some supplies with you, especially fresh bread and fruit, although visitors who fail to spend anything at all not surprisingly irritate locals somewhat. The local honey is wonderful, and watch out for the island wine, which is vicious.

Water is also in short supply. There is very little springwater and most fresh water has to be drawn from wells or collected in rainwater cisterns; check with locals before drinking from any of them. Don't expect to find too many showers or modern plumbing, and don't join those thoughtless visitors who insist on contaminating the limited fresh-water supply with soap. There is no mains electricity either, though generators are fairly widespread, as can be seen from the number of TV aerials.

Rooms are most obviously available in Karabé, though they can also be had in Kastrí and elsewhere if you ask around, and there are now a couple on each of the main beaches. It's even possible to book ahead from Paleohóra (try *Interkreta Travel*, p.275). If you're prepared to **camp** you can pick your spot just about anywhere, on the beaches or in any number of sheltered locations inland, though be aware of local sensibilities.

In **emergencies** there should be a doctor in Kastrí during the summer and there's also a telephone line to the mainland, with a phone in each of the four main settlements. The best advice, however, is not to tempt fate – especially as an accident could mean being airlifted by army helicopter, incurring a hefty bill which your insurance may not cover. At least a few words of **Greek** would be extremely useful, though locals try their best with all visitors.

travel details

Buses

Haniá to: Ay. Marína (every 15min; 8.15am–7.15pm); Elafonísi (1 daily; 7.30am; 3hr); Falásarna (2 daily; 8.30am and 3.30pm; 2hr); Foúrnes (7 daily; 6.45am–8pm; 30min); Gavalohóri (1 daily; 2.15pm; 45min); Hórafakia/Stavrós (5 daily; 7am–8pm; 30min); Hóra Sfakíon (4 daily; 8.30am, 11am, 2pm and 3.30pm; 2hr); Iráklion (26 daily; 5.30am–8.30pm; 3hr), a couple via the old road (5hr); Kalíves (5 daily; 7am–7.30pm; 45min); Kastélli (15 daily; 6am–8.30pm; 1hr 30min); Kolimbári (29 daily; 6am–10.30pm; 1hr); Máleme (every 15min; 8.15am–7.15pm); Omalós/Samarian gorge (4 daily; 6.15am, 7.30am, 8.30am and 1.30pm; 90min); Paleohóra (5 daily; 8.30am–5pm; 2hr); Réthimnon (26 daily; 5.30am–8.30pm; 1hr 30min), a couple via the old road (2hr); Skalóti (for Frangokástello) (1 daily; 2pm; 2hr 30min); Soúyia (2 daily; 8.30am and 1.30pm; 2hr); Vámos (5 daily; 7am–7.30pm; 30min).

Hóra Sfakíon to: Plakiás/Ayía Galíni (daily; 4.30pm; 1hr 30min–3hr).

Kastélli to: Elafonísi (1 daily; 8.30am; 1hr 30min); Omalós (3 daily; 5am, 6am and 7am; 3hr).

Ferries

Gávdhos to: Hóra Sfakíon (July to mid-Sept, Sat at 6am and 4pm, Sun 4pm; June, late Sept and Oct, Sat only at 4pm).

Hóra Sfakíon to: Gávdhos (July to mid-Sept Fri 6pm, Sat and Sun 9am, returning 4pm; June, late Sept and Oct Sat only at 9am).

Kastélli to: Kalamáta (2 weekly; Tues 11pm, Sat 2.30pm); Kíthira (3 weekly; Tues 8am, Thurs 5pm, Sun 9am); Monemvassía (2 weekly; Thurs 5pm, Sun 9am); Neápoli (2 weekly, Thurs 5pm, Sun 9am); Pireás (2 weekly; Thurs 5pm, Sun 9am); Yíthio (1 weekly; Fri 8am).

Paleohóra to: Gávdhos (June–Sept Wed, Sat and Sun 8.30am, returning 2.45pm; May and Oct Fri and Sun 8.30am, returning 2.30pm); all weather permitting.

Sóudha to: Pireás (*ANEK Line* daily at 7pm; *Minoan* 3 weekly, Tues, Thurs and Sat 6.30pm).

Kaíkia **(caiques)** also run along the south coast, daily from Paleóhora to Soúyia and Ayía Rouméli (depart 8am, return 5.30pm); at least 4 times a day in season (May–Oct) from Ayía Rouméli to Loutró and Hóra Sfakíon.

Flights

To Athens 5 daily (45min).

To Thessaloníki 1 weekly; Tues 8.40pm (1hr 15min).

ΑΓ ΜΑΡΙΝΑ	Αγ Μαρίνα	Ay. Marína
ΑΓ ΡΟΥΜΕΛΗ	Αγ Ρουμέλη	Ay. Rouméli
ΑΚΡΩΤΗΡΙ	Ακρωτήρι	Akrotíri
ΑΛΙΚΙΑΝΟΣ	Αλικιανός	Alikianós
ΑΠΤΕΡΑ	Απτερα	Áptera
ΑΛΜΥΡΙΔΑ	Αλμυρίδα	Almirídha
ΑΝΟΠΟΛΗ	Ανόπολη	Anópoli
ΒΑΜΟΣ	Βάμος	Vámos
ΒΡΥΣΕΣ	Βρύσες	Vrísses
ΓΑΥΔΟΣ	Γαύδος	Gávdhos
ΓΕΩΡΓΙΟΥΠΟΛΗ	Γεωργιούπολη	Yeoryióupoli
ΕΛΑΦΟΝΗΣΗ	Ελαφονήση	Elafonísi
ΕΛΟΣ	Ελος	Élos
ΘΕΡΙΣΟ	Θέρισο	Thériso
ΚΑΛΑΜΙ	Καλάμι	Kalámi
ΚΑΛΥΒΕΣ	Καλύβες	Kalíves
ΚΑΝΤΑΝΟΣ	Κάντανος	Kándanos
ΚΑΣΤΕΛΛΙ	Καστέλλι	Kastélli
ΚΟΛΥΜΒΑΡΙ	Κολυμβάρι	Kolimbári
ΚΟΥΡΝΑΣ	Κουρνάς	Kournás
ΛΑΚΚΟΙ	Λάκκοι	Lákki
ΛΟΥΤΡΟ	Λουτρό	Loutró
ΜΑΛΕΜΕ	Μάλεμε	Máleme
ΜΕΣΚΛΑ	Μεσκλά	Mesklá
ΜΟΥΡΝΙΕΣ	Μουρνιές	Mourniés
ΟΜΑΛΟΣ	Ομαλός	Omalós
ΠΑΛΑΙΟΧΩΡΑ	Παλαιοχώρα	Paleohóra
ΠΕΡΙΒΟΛΙΑ	Περιβόλια	Perivólia
ΠΛΑΤΑΝΟΣ	Πλάτανος	Plátanos
ΠΟΛΥΡΡΗΝΙΑ	Πολυρρηνία	Polirinía
ΡΟΔΩΠΟΣ	Ροδωπός	Rodhopós
ΣΑΜΑΡΙΑ	Σαμαριά	Samariá
ΣΟΥΓΙΑ	Σούγια	Sóuyia
ΣΟΥΔΑ	Σούδα	Sóudha
ΣΤΑΥΡΟΣ	Σταυρός	Stavrós
ΣΦΑΚΙΑ	Σφακιά	Sfakiá
ΣΦΗΝΑΡΙΟ	Σφηνάριο	Sfinári
ΦΑΛΑΣΑΡΝΑ	Φαλάσαρνα	Falásarna
ΦΟΥΡΝΕΣ	Φουρνές	Fournés
ΦΡΑΓΚΟΚΑΣΤΕΛΛΟ	Φραγκοκάστελλο	Frangokástello
ΧΑΝΙΑ	Χανιά	Haniá
ΧΡΥΣΟΣΚΑΛΙΤΙΣΣΑΣ	Χρυσοσκαλίτισσας	Hrisoskalítissa
ΧΩΡΑ ΣΦΑΚΙΩΝ	Χώρα Σφακίων	Hóra Sfakíon
ΧΩΡΑΦΑΚΙΑ	Χωραφάκια	Horafákia

PART THREE

THE

CONTEXTS

THE HISTORICAL FRAMEWORK

The people of Crete unfortunately make more history than they can consume locally.

Saki

The discovery of the Minoan civilization has tended to overshadow every other aspect of Cretan history. And indeed it would be hard for any other period to rival what was, in effect, the first truly European civilization. It was in Crete that the developed societies of the east met influences from the west and north, and here that "Western culture", as synthesized in Classical Greece and Rome, first developed.

Yet this was no accident or freak one-off: Crete's position as a meeting place of east and west, and its strategic setting in the middle of the Mediterranean, has thrust the island to the centre-stage of world history more often than seems comfortable. Long before Arthur Evans arrived to unearth Knossós, and for some time after, the island's struggle for freedom, and the great powers' inactivity, was the subject of Europe-wide scandal. The battle for the island when the Turks arrived had similarly aroused worldwide interest, and represented at the time a significant change in the balance of power between Islam and Christianity. In fact from Minoan times to World War II, there has

rarely been a sustained period when Crete didn't have some role to play in world affairs.

THE STONE AGE

Crete's first inhabitants, **Neolithic cave dwellers**, apparently reached the island around 7000 BC. They came, most probably, from Asia Minor, or less likely from Syria, Palestine or North Africa, bringing with them the basics of Stone Age culture – tools of wood, stone and bone; crude pottery; and simple cloth. A possible clue to the origins of these peoples may lie in the importance of bull cults at certain centres in Neolithic Anatolia (see below).

Development over the next three thousand years was almost imperceptibly slow but gradually, whether through new migrations and influences or internal dynamics, advances were made. Elementary agriculture was practised, with domestic animals and basic crops. Pottery (the oldest samples of which were found beneath the palace at Knossós) became more sophisticated, with better-made domestic utensils and clay figurines of humans, animals and especially of a fat mother goddess or fertility figure. Obsidian imported from the island of Mílos was used too. And though caves continued to be inhabited, simple rectangular huts of mud bricks were also built, with increasing skill and complexity as the era wore on. One of the most important of the Neolithic settlements was at Knossós where two remarkable dwellings have been revealed below the Central Court, and there is abundant evidence that many other sites. of later habitation were used at this time – Mália, Festós, Ayía Triádha, the Haniá area – as were most of the caves later to assume religious significance.

THE BRONZE AGE: MINOAN CRETE

Minoan Crete has been the subject of intense and constant study by archeologists since its emergence from myth to archeological reality at the beginning of the century. Yet there is still enormous controversy even over such fundamental details as who the Minoans were and what language they spoke. No written historical records from the time survive (or if they do, they have not yet been deciphered) so almost everything we know is deduced from physical remains, fleshed out somewhat by writings from Classical Greece, almost one thousand years after the destruction of Knossós. Nevertheless it is not hard to forge some kind of consensus from the theories about the Minoans, and this is what is set out below: fresh discoveries may yet radically change this view.

One of the central arguments is over **dating**. The original system, conceived by Sir Arthur Evans, divided the period into Early, Middle and Late Minoan (see p.307), with each of these again divided into three sub-periods – a sequence that has become extremely complicated and cumbersome as it has been further qualified and sub-divided. Arcane distinctions between the pottery styles of Early Minoan IIa and IIb have no place in a brief history and used here is a simpler system (following the archeologist Nikolaos Platon) of four periods: **pre-palatial**, proto-palatial or **First Palace**, neo-palatial or **New Palace**, and **post-palatial**. This has the additional advantage of avoiding many of the niceties of exact dating and of uneven development across the island. However, as many archeological texts and guides, as well as numerous museums on the island use the Evans system, the approximate corresponding periods – Early, Middle and Late Minoan – are given in brackets below.

PRE-PALATIAL: 3000–1900 BC (EM–MMI)

Among the more important puzzles of Minoan society is its comparatively sudden emergence. During the centuries before 2600 BC there were important changes on the island, and thereafter very rapid progress in almost every area of life. Villages and towns grew up where previously there had been only isolated settlements, and with them came craft specialists: potters, stonecutters, metalworkers, jewellers, weavers. Many of these new settlements were in the east and south of the island, and there was for the first time significant habitation on the coast and near natural harbours.

It seems safe to assume that these changes were wrought by a new migration of people from the east, bringing with them new technologies, methods of agriculture and styles of pottery, but most importantly, perhaps, a knowledge of seafaring and trade. The olive and the vine – which need little tending and therefore help free a labour force – began to be produced alongside cereal crops. Copper tools replaced stone ones and were themselves later refined with the introduction of bronze. Art developed rapidly, with characteristic Vasíliki ware and other pottery styles; gold jewellery; and stone jars of exceptional quality, based originally on Egyptian styles. Significantly, large quantities of seal stones have been found too, almost certainly the mark of a mercantile people. They were used to sign letters and documents, but especially to seal packets, boxes or doors as proof that they had not been opened: the designs – scorpions or poisonous spiders – were often meant as a further deterrent to robbery.

At the same time new methods of burial appear – *Thólos* and chamber tombs in which riches were buried with the dead. These appear to have been communal, as, probably, was daily life, based perhaps on clan or kinship groupings.

THE FIRST PALACES: 1900–1700 BC (MMI–MMII)

Shortly before 1900 BC the first of the palaces were built, at **Knossós**, **Festós**, **Mália** and **Zákros**. They represent another significant and apparently abrupt change: a shift of power back to the centre of the island and the emergence of a much more hierarchical, ordered society. The sites of these palaces were also no accident: Festós and Mália both dominate fertile plains whilst Zákros had a superbly sited harbour for trade with the east. Knossós, occupying a strategic position above another plain to the south and west of Iráklion, was perhaps originally as much a religious centre as a base of secular power: certainly at this time religion took on a new importance, with the widespread use of mountain-top peak sanctuaries and caves as cult centres. At the same time much larger towns were growing up, especially around the palaces, and in the countryside substantial "villas" appeared.

The palaces themselves are proof of the island's great prosperity at this period, and the artefacts found within offer further evidence. Advances were made in almost every field of artistic and craft endeavour. From the First Palace era came the famous **Kamáres Ware** pottery – actually two distinct styles, one eggshell thin and delicate, the other sturdier with bold-coloured designs. The true potter's wheel (as against the turntable) was introduced for the first time, along with a simple form of hieroglyphic writing. Elaborate jewellery, seals and bronzework were also being produced.

Cretan bronze was used throughout the Mediterranean, and its production and distribution were dependent on a wide-ranging **maritime economy**. For though Crete may have produced some copper at this time, it never yielded tin, the nearest significant sources of which were as distant as Iran to the east, central Europe in the north, Italy, Spain, Brittany and even Britain in the west. While some claim that Minoan ships actually sailed as far afield as the Atlantic, it seems more likely that the more exotic goods were obtained through middlemen. Nevertheless, in the Mediterranean Crete controlled the trade routes, importing tin, copper, ivory, gold, silver and precious stones of every kind, exporting timber from its rich cypress forests, olive oil, wine, bronze goods and its fine pottery, especially to Egypt. Minoan **colonies** or trading posts were established on many Cycladic islands as well as the island of Kíthira off the Peloponnese, Rhodes and the coast of Asia Minor; a fleet of merchant vessels maintained regular trade links between these centres and, above all, with Egypt and the east.

Around 1700 BC, the palaces were destroyed for the first time, probably by earthquake, although raiders from the early Mycenaean Greek mainland may also have seized this opportunity to raid the island whilst it was temporarily defenceless; this may well account for the wealth of gold and other treasure – much of it obviously Cretan – found in the later royal shaft graves at Mycenae.

THE NEW PALACES: 1700–1450 BC (MMIII–LMI)

Though the destruction must have been a setback, Minoan culture continued to flourish, and with the palaces reconstructed on a still grander scale the society entered its golden age. It is the **new palaces** which provide most of our picture of Minoan life and most of what is seen at the great sites – Knossós, Festós, Mália, Zákros – dates from this period.

The **architecture** of the new palaces was of an unprecedented sophistication: complex, multistorey structures in which the use of space and light was as luxurious as the construction materials. Grand stairways, colonnaded porticoes and courtyards, brightly frescoed walls, elaborate plumbing and drain-

age, and great magazines in which to store the society's accumulation of wealth, were all integral, as were workshops for the technicians and craftsmen, and areas set aside for ritual and worship.

Obviously it was only an elite which enjoyed these comforts, but conditions for the ordinary people who kept Minos* and his attendants in such style appear to have improved too: **towns** around the palaces and at sites such as Gourniá and Palékastro were growing as well.

Very little is known of how the **society** was organized, or indeed whether it was a single entity ruled from Knossós or simply several city states with a common cultural heritage. However, in an intriguing reference to Crete in his *Politics* Aristotle implied that a caste system had operated in the times of Minos. Clearly, though, it was a society in which **religion** played an important part. The great Corridor of the Procession fresco at Knossós depicted an annual delivery of tribute, apparently to a Mother Goddess; bull leaping had a religious significance too; and in all the palaces substantial chambers are set aside for ritual purposes. Secular leaders were also religious leaders.

That Minoan society was a very open one is apparent too. There are virtually no **defences**, internal or external, at any Minoan site, and apparently the rulers felt no threat either from within or without, which has induced scholars to emphasize a military strength based on seapower. As far as internal dissent goes it seems safe to assume that the wealth of the island filtered down, to some extent at least, to all its inhabitants: the lot of a Minoan peasant may have been little different to that of a Cretan villager as little as fifty years ago.

Externally, maritime supremacy was further extended: objects of Cretan manufacture turn up all over the Mediterranean and have even been claimed as far afield as Britain and Scandinavia (amber from the Baltic certainly found its way to Crete). Behind their seapower the Minoans clearly felt safe, and the threat of attack or piracy was further reduced by the network of colonies or close allies throughout the Cycladic islands – Thíra most famously but

---

*Arthur Evans named Minoan society after the legendary King Minos, but there is little doubt that Minos was in fact the title of a dynasty of priest/kings, a word rather like Pharaoh.

also at Mílos, Náxos, Páros, Mikonós, Ándhros and Dílos – and in Rhodes, Cyprus, Syria and North Africa. Nevertheless, this appears to have remained a trading empire rather than a military one.

Cultural advances

If the New Palace period was a high point of Minoan power, it also marked the apogee of **arts and crafts** in the island: again, the bulk of the objects you'll admire in the museums date from this era. The **frescoes** – startling in their freshness and vitality – are the most famous and obviously visible demonstration of this florescence. But they were just the highly visible tip of an artistic iceberg. It was in intricate small-scale work that the Minoans excelled above all. Naturalistic **sculpted figures** of humans and animals include the superb ivory bull-leaper, the leopard-head axe and the famous snake goddesses or priestesses, all of them on show in the Iráklion Archeological Museum. The carvings on seal stones of this era are of exceptional delicacy – a skill carried over into beautifully delicate gold jewellery. Examples of **stone vessels** include the bull's head rhyton from Knossós and the three black vases from Ayía Triádha which are among the museum's most valuable possessions. And **pottery** broke out into an enormous variety of new shapes and design motifs, drawing their inspiration especially from scenes of nature and marine life.

The other great advance was in **writing**. A new form of script, Linear A, had appeared at the end of the First Palace period, but in the new palaces its use became widespread. Still undeciphered, Linear A must record the original, unknown language of the Minoans: it seems to have been used in written form almost exclusively for administrative records – stock lists, records of transactions and tax payments. Even were it understood, therefore, it seems unlikely that the language would reveal much in the way of history. The pieces which have survived were never intended as permanent records, and have been found intact only where the clay tablets used were baked solid in the fires which destroyed the palaces. It is possible that a more formal record, an abstract of the annual accounts, was kept on a more valuable but also more perishable material such as imported papyrus or even a paper produced from native date palm leaves.

The end

Around 1600 BC the island again saw minor earthquake damage, though this was swiftly repaired. But in about 1450 BC came **destruction** on a calamitous scale: the palaces were smashed and (with the exception of Knossós itself) burned, and smaller settlements across the island devastated. The cause of this disaster is still the most controversial of all Minoan riddles, but the most convincing theory links it with the explosion of the **volcano of Thíra** in about 1500 BC: a blast which may have been five times as powerful as that of Krakatoa. The explosion threw up great clouds of black ash and a huge tidal wave, or waves. Coastal settlements would have been directly smashed by the wave, and perhaps further burnt by the overturn of lamps lighted on a day made unnaturally dark by the clouds of ash. Blast, panic and accompanying earth tremors would have contributed to the wreck. And then, as the ash fell, it apparently coated the centre and east of the island in a poisonous blanket under which nothing could grow, or would grow again, for as much as fifty years.

Only at Knossós was there any real continuity of habitation, and here it was with **Mycenaean Greeks** in control, bringing with them new styles of art, a greater number of weapons, and above all keeping records in a form of writing known as **Linear B**, an adaptation of Linear A now used to write in an early Greek dialect. In about 1370 BC, Knossós was itself burnt, whether by rebellious Cretans, a new wave of Mycenaeans, or perhaps as a result of another natural disaster on a smaller scale.

Such at least is the prevailing theory. But it has its problems – why, for example, should Festós have been burnt when it was safe from waves and blast on the south side of the island? And why should the eruption that vulcanologists now date to 1500 BC have had such a dramatic effect only fifty years later – indeed there are signs that away from the worst effects of the devastation many areas on Crete experienced comparative prosperity after it. As the debate continues the best that can be said currently is that the volcano theory fits the available evidence better than most of its rivals. But many scholars still claim that the facts are more consistent with destruction by human rather than natural causes. The main counter-theory assumes an invasion by the Mycenaeans, and points to some evidence that Linear B was in use at Knossós *before* 1450 BC. But if the Mycenaeans came to conquer, they would have gained nothing by destroying the society already flourishing on Crete; nor would they have subsequently left the former population centres deserted for a generation or more.

A third theory attempts to answer these inconsistencies suggesting that an internal revolt by the populace against its rulers (possibly in the wake of the chaos caused by the Thíra eruption) could provide an explanation. This theory would fit the evidence from sites such as Mírtos Pírgos on the south coast, where a villa dominating the site was burned down whilst the surrounding settlement remained untouched. Needless to say this theory does not find favour with those who see Minoan civilization as a haven of tranquil splendour, but it does fit with the later Greek tradition of a tyrannical Minos oppressing not only his own people but those abroad as well. Further archeological investigation both on Crete and other islands in the Aegean may ultimately resolve this Minoan mystery.

POST-PALATIAL: 1450–1100 BC (LMII–LMIII)

From their bridgehead at Knossós, the Mycenaeans gradually spread their influence across the island as it became habitable again. By the early fourteenth century BC they controlled much of Crete, and some of the earlier sites, including Gourniá, Ayía Triádha, Tílissos and Palékastro, were reoccupied. It is a period which is still little-known and which by the early Minoan scholars was written off almost entirely. More recent excavations are revealing, though, that the island remained productive, albeit in a role peripheral to the mainland.

In particular **western Crete** now came into its own, as the area least affected by the volcano. **Kydonia** became the chief city of the island, still with a considerable international trade and continuing, in its art and architecture, very much in the Minoan style. But Kydonia lies beneath modern Haniá and has never been (nor is ever likely to be) properly excavated – another reason that far less is known about this period than those which preceded it. In

central Crete the main change was a retreat from the coasts, a sign of the island's decline in international affairs and trade and perhaps of an increase in piracy. Even here, however, despite the presence of new influences, much of the art is recognizably Minoan. Most of the famous clay and stone *larnakes* (sarcophagi) – which were a distinctly new method of burial – date from this final Minoan era.

More direct evidence of the survival of Crete comes in Homer's account of the **Trojan War**, when he talks of a Cretan contingent taking part under King Idomeneus (according to him, the grandson of Minos). The war and its aftermath – a period of widespread change – also affected Crete. In the north of Greece the Mycenaeans were being overrun by peoples moving down from the Balkans, in particular the **Dorians**. Around 1200 BC the relative peace was disrupted again: many sites were abandoned for the last time, others burnt. Briefly, Mycenaean influence became yet more widespread, as refugees arrived on the island. But by the end of the twelfth century BC Minoan culture was in terminal decline, and Crete was entering into the period of confusion which engulfed most of the Greek world. Some of the original population of the island, later known as **Eteo-Cretans** (true Cretans), retreated at this time to mountain fastnesses at sites such as Présos and Karfí, where they survived along with elements of Minoan culture and language for almost another millenium.

THE IRON AGE: DORIAN AND CLASSICAL CRETE

The bulk of the island, however, was taken over by the Dorians: there may have been an invasion, but it seems more probable that the process was a gradual one, by settlement. At any event over the succeeding centuries the Dorians came to dominate the central lowlands, with substantial new cities such as Láto.

Dorian Crete was not in any real sense a unified society: its cities warred with each other and there may, as well as the Dorians and Eteo-Cretans, have been other cultural groupings in the west, at Kydonia and sites such as Falásarna and Polirinía. Nevertheless the island saw another minor artistic renaissance, with styles now mostly shared with the rest of the Greek world, and in tools and weapons iron gradually came to replace bronze.

Much the most important survival of this period, however, is the celebrated **law code from Górtys**. The code (see p.106) was set down around 450 BC, but it reflects laws which had already been in force for hundreds of years: the society described is a strictly hierarchical one, clearly divided into a ruling class, free men, serfs and slaves. For the rulers, life followed a harsh, militaristic regime similar to that of Sparta: the original population, presumably, had been reduced to the level of serfs.

As mainland Greece approached its **Classical Age**, Crete advanced little. It remained a populous island, but one where a multitude of small city-states were constantly vying for power. Towns of this period are characterized by their heavy defences, and most reflected the Górtys laws (Górtys remained among the most powerful of them) in tough oligarchical or aristocratic regimes. At best Crete was a minor player in Greek affairs, increasingly known as the den of pirates and as a valuable source of mercenaries unrivalled in guerrilla tactics. The island must have retained influence, though, for it was still regarded by Classical Athenians as the source of much of their culture, and its strict institutions were admired by many philosophers. In addition, many Cretan shrines and caves show unbroken use from Minoan through to Roman times, and those associated with the birth and early life of Zeus (the Dhiktean and Idean caves especially) were important centres of pilgrimage.

The multitude of small, independent city-states is well illustrated by the Confederation of Oreii, an accord formed around 300 BC between Élyros, Lissós, Írtakina, Tarra, Syía and Pikílassos: six towns in a now barely populated area of the southwest. They were later joined in the Confederation by Górtys and Cyrenaica (in North Africa). Meanwhile Roman power was growing in the Mediterranean, and Crete's strategic position and turbulent reputation drew her inexorably into the struggle.

ROME AND BYZANTIUM

From the second century BC on, **Rome** was drawn into wars in mainland Greece and the involvement of Cretan troops on one or often both sides became an increasing irritation. Hannibal was staying at Górtys at the time of one Roman attempt to quiet the island, around 188 BC. More than a century passed with only

minor interventions, however, before Rome could turn her full attention to Crete – the last important part of the Greek world not under her sway.

In 71 BC Marcus Antonius (father of the famous Mark Antony) attempted to invade but was heavily defeated by the Kydonians. In 69 BC a fresh attempt was made under **Quintus Metellus** (afterwards called Creticus). This time a bridgehead was successfully established by exploiting divisions among the Cretans: Metellus was supported in his initial campaign against Kydonia by its rivals at Polirinía. The tactic of setting Cretan against Cretan served him well, but even so it took almost three years of bitter and brutal warfare before the island was subdued in 67 BC. It was a campaign marked by infighting not only among the Cretans – Górtys was among those to take Metellus's side – but also between Romans, with further forces sent from Rome in an unsuccessful bid to curb Metellus's excesses and his growing power.

With the conquest complete, peace came quickly and was barely disturbed even in the turbulent years of Julius Caesar's rise and fall. Perhaps in part this was because there was little immediate change in local administration, which was simply placed under Roman supervision. At the same time, the end of the civil wars brought much greater prosperity: Crete was combined with Cyrenaica (in North Africa) as a single province whose capital was at **Górtys**, and though there was little contact between the two halves of the province, both were important sources of grain and agricultural produce for Rome.

Through the first and second centuries AD important **public works** were undertaken throughout Crete: roads, aqueducts and irrigation systems; important cities at Knossós, Áptera, Lyttos and others as well as considerable grandeur at Górtys. **Christianity** arrived with Saint Paul's visit around 50 AD – soon after, he appointed Titus as the island's first bishop to begin the conversion in earnest. Around 250 AD, the Holy Ten – *Áyii Dhéka* – were martyred at Górtys.

With the split of the Roman empire at the end of the fourth century, Crete found itself part of the eastern empire under **Byzantium**. The island continued to prosper – as the churches which were now built everywhere would testify – but in international terms it was not important and Byzantine rule, here as everywhere, imposed a stiflingly ordered society, hierarchical and bureaucratic in the extreme. Of the earliest churches only traces survive, in particular of mosaic floors like those at Soúyia or Thrónos, though there are more substantial remains at Górtys, of the basilica of Áyios Titos.

Then in 824 Crete was invaded by a band of **Arabs** under Abu Hafs Omar. Essentially a piratical group who had been driven first from Spain and then Alexandria, they nevertheless managed to keep control of the island for well over a century. There was not much in the way of progress at this time – for its new masters the island was primarily a base from which to raid shipping and launch attacks on the Greek mainland and other islands – but there was a fortress founded at al-Khandak, a site which later developed into Iráklion. At the same time Górtys and other Byzantine cities were sacked and destroyed.

After several failed attempts, the Byzantine general **Nikiforas Fokas** reconquered Crete in 961, following a siege at Khandak in which he catapulted the heads of his Arab prisoners over the walls. For a while the island revived, boosted by an influx of colonists from the mainland and from Constantinople itself, including a number of aristocratic familes (the *Archontopouli*) whose power survived throughout the medieval era. By now, however, the entire empire was embattled by Islam and losing out in trade to the Venetians and Genoese. Frescoed churches continued to be built, but most were small and parochial.

Ironically enough it was not Muslims who brought about the final end of Byzantium, but Crusaders. The **fourth Crusade** turned on Constantinople in 1204 (perhaps at the instigation of the Venetians) sacking and burning the city. The leader of the Crusade, Prince Boniface of Montferrat, ceded Crete to the Venetians for a nominal sum.

VENETIAN CRETE

Before Venice could claim her new territory, she had to drive out her chief commercial rivals, the **Genoese**, who had taken control in 1206 with considerable local support. By 1210 the island had been secured, though for more than a century thereafter the Genoese pursued

their claim, repeatedly siding with local rebels when it looked like there was a chance of establishing a presence on the island.

The **Venetians**, however, were not going to surrender the prize lightly. Crete for them was a vital resource, both for the control of eastern Mediterranean trade routes which the island's ports commanded, and for the natural wealth of the agricultural land and the timber for shipbuilding. The Venetian system was rapidly and stringently imposed, with Venetian overlords, directly appointed from Venice, administering what were effectively a series of feudal fiefdoms.

It was a system designed to exploit Crete's resources as efficiently as possible, and not surprisingly it stirred up deep resentments from the beginning. There were constant **rebellions** throughout the thirteenth century, led as often as not by one or other of the aristocratic Byzantine families from an earlier wave of colonization. Certainly the wealthy had most to lose: it was their land which was confiscated to be granted to military colonists from Venice (along with the service of the people who lived on it) and their rights and privileges which were taken over by the new overlords. The rebellions were in general strictly noble affairs, ended by concessions of land or power to their Cretan leaders. But there were more fundamental resentments too. Heavy taxes and demands for feudal service were widely opposed – by the established colonists almost as much as by the natives. And the **Orthodox Church** was replaced by the Roman as the "official" religion, the senior clergy expelled and much Church property seized. Local priests and monasteries which survived helped fuel antagonism: even from this early date the monasteries were becoming known as centres of dissent.

In the mid-fourteenth century, one of the most serious revolts yet saw Cretans and second-generation Venetian colonists fighting alongside each other, in protest at the low fixed prices for their produce, steep taxes, and the continued privileges granted to "real" Venetians. Although on this occasion the revolt was put down in a particularly fierce repression, the end result of this and the other rebellions was a gradual relaxation of the regime and integration of the two communities – or at least their leaders. The **Middle Ages** were perhaps the most productive in Crete's history, with exports of corn, wine, oil and salt, the ports busy with transshipment business, the wooded hillsides being stripped for timber.

After 1453, and the final fall of Constantinople, Crete saw a spectacular **cultural renaissance** as a stream of refugees arrived from the east. **Candy** – as the island and its capital were known to the Venetians – became the centre of Byzantine art and scholarship. From this later period, and the meeting of the traditions of Byzantium and the Italian Renaissance, come the vast majority of the works of art and architecture now associated with the Venetian era. The great icon painter Dhamaskinos studied alongside El Greco in the school of Ayía Ekaterini in Iráklion; the Orthodox monasteries flourished; and in literature the island produced, among others, what is now regarded as its greatest work – the *Erotokritos*.

But it was the growing **external threat** which stimulated the most enduring of the Venetian public works – the island defences. Venice's bastions in the mainland Middle East had fallen alongside Constantinople, and in 1573 Cyprus too was taken by the Turks, leaving Crete well and truly in the front line. Large-scale pirate raids had already been common: in 1538 Barbarossa had destroyed Réthimnon and almost taken Haniá, and in the 1560s there were further attacks. Across the island, cities were strengthened and the fortified islets defending the seaways were repaired and rebuilt. As the seventeenth century wore on, however, Venice herself was in severe decline: weakened by the Thirty Years War; her Mediterranean trade overshadowed by a pre-occupation with the New World, a business dominated by the Spanish, English and Dutch.

Finally in 1645 an attack on an Ottoman convoy provided the excuse for an all-out **Turkish assault** on Crete. Haniá fell after a siege which cost forty thousand Turkish lives, and Réthimnon rapidly followed. By 1648 the Turks controlled the whole island except **Iráklion**, and they settled down to a long siege. For 21 years the city resisted, supplied from the sea and with moral support at least from most of Europe. The end was inevitable, though, and from the Turkish point of view there was no hurry: they controlled the island's produce, they were well supplied, and they enjoyed a fair degree of local support, having relaxed the Venetian rules in, for example,

allowing Orthodox bishops back into Crete. By 1669 the city was virtually reduced, and in a final effort the pope managed to persuade the French to send a small army. After a couple of fruitless sorties involving heavy losses, the French withdrew in an argument over the command. On September 5, the city surrendered, leaving only the three fortified islets of Soúdha, Spinalónga and Gramvoúsa in Venetian hands, where they remained until surrendered by treaty in 1715.

TURKISH CRETE

It is arguable whether the **Turkish occupation** was ever as stringent or arduous as the Venetian had been, but its reputation is far worse. In part this may simply be that its memory is more recent, but Turkish rule was complicated too by the religious differences involved, and by the fact that it survived into the era of resurgent Greek nationalism and Great Power politics.

If on their arrival the Turks had been welcomed, it was not a long-lived honeymoon. Once again Crete was divided, now between powerful pashas, and once again it was regarded merely as a resource to be exploited. The Ottoman Empire was less strictly ordered than the Venetian, but it demanded no less: rather than attempt to take control of trade themselves, the Turks simply imposed crippling **taxes**. There were fewer colonists than in the Venetian era, and they took far less interest in their conquest so long as the money continued to come in. Very little was re-invested: outside the cities there was hardly any building at all, and roads and even defences fell into gradual disrepair. As far as local administration went, it was left to local landlords and the mercenary *Janissaries* they controlled to impose. At the local level, then, there was a further level of exploitation as these men too took their cut. Stultified by heavy taxes and tarriffs, slowed by neglect, the island economy stagnated.

One way to avoid the worst of the burden was to become a Muslim and, gradually, the majority of the Christian population was **converted to Islam** – at least nominally. Conversion brought with it substantial material advantages in taxation and rights to own property, and it helped avoid the worst of the repression which inevitably followed any Christian rebellion. These Greek Muslims were not particularly religious: even among the Turks on the island, Islamic law seems to have been loosely interpreted and many continued to worship as Christians in secret, but the mass apostasies served to further divide the island. For those who remained openly Christian the burden became increasingly heavy as there were fewer to bear it. Many took to the mountains, where Turkish authority barely spread.

As the occupation continued, the Turks strengthened their hold on the cities and the fertile plains around them, while the mountains became the stronghold of the Christian *pallikares*. The first major **rebellion** came in 1770, and inevitably it was centred in Sfakiá. Under **Dhaskaloyiánnis** (p.260) the Cretans had been drawn into Great Power politics; drawn in and abandoned, for the promised aid from Russia never came. With the failure of this struggle, Sfakiá was itself brought under Turkish control for a while. But a pattern had been set, and the nineteenth century was one of almost constant struggle for independence.

The beginning of the century saw the Ottoman Empire under severe pressure on the Greek mainland, and in 1821 full scale revolution, the **Greek War of Independence**, broke out. Part of the Turkish response was to call on the pasha of Egypt, **Mehmet Ali**, for assistance: his price was control of Crete. By 1824, in a campaign which even by Cretan standards was brutal on both sides, he had crushed the island's resistance. When in 1832 an independent Greek state was finally established with the support of Britain, France and Russia, Crete was left in the hands of the Egyptians, whence it reverted to Turkish control within ten years.

From now on guerrilla warfare in support of union with Greece (*Enosis*) was almost constant, flaring occasionally into wider revolts but mostly taking the form of incessant raids and irritations. The Cretans enjoyed widespread support, not only on the Greek mainland but throughout western Europe and especially among expatriate Greek communities. But the Greeks alone were no match for the Ottoman armies, and the Great Powers, wary more than anything of each other, consistently failed to intervene. There was a major rising in 1841, bloodily suppressed, and in 1858 another which ended relatively peacefully in the recall of the Turkish governor and some minor concessions to the Christian population.

In 1866 a Cretan Assembly meeting in Sfakiá declared independence and union with Greece, and Egyptian troops were recalled to put down a further wave of revolts bolstered by Greek volunteers. Again the Egyptians proved ruthlessly effective, but this campaign ended in the explosion at **Arkádhi** (p.187), an act of defiance which aroused Europe-wide sympathy. The Great Powers – Britain above all – still refused to involve themselves, but privately the supply of arms and volunteers to the insurgents was redoubled. From now on some kind of solution seemed inevitable, but even in 1878 the Congress of Berlin left Crete under Turkish dominion, demanding only further reforms in the government. In 1889 and 1896 there were further violent encounters, and in 1897 a Greek force landed to annex the island. Finally, the Great Powers were forced into action, occupying Crete with an international force and dividing the island into areas controlled by the British, French, Russians and Italians.

INDEPENDENCE AND UNION WITH GREECE

The outrage which finally brought about the expulsion of Turkish troops from Crete in 1898 was a minor skirmish in Iráklion which led to the death of the British vice-consul. A **national government** was set up, still nominally under Ottoman suzerainty, with Prince George, younger son of King George of Greece, as high commissioner: under him was a joint Muslim-Christian assembly, part elected, part appointed.

Euphoria at independence was muted, however, for full union with Greece remained the goal of most Cretans. A new leader of this movement rapidly emerged – **Eleftheríos Venizélos**. Born at Mourniés, outside Haniá, Venizélos had fought in the earlier independence struggles and become a member of the Cretan Assembly and minister of justice to Prince George. Politically, however, he had little in common with his new master, and in 1905 he summoned an illegal Revolutionary Assembly at Thériso. Though the attempt to take up arms was summarily crushed, the strength of support for Venizélos was enough to force the resignation of Prince George. In 1908 the Cretan Assembly unilaterally declared *Enosis* – much to the embarrassment of the Greek government. For meantime the "Young Turk" revolution looked set to revitalize the Ottoman Empire, and the Great Powers remained solidly opposed to anything which might upset the delicate balance of power in the Balkans.

The failure of the Greek government to act decisively in favour of Crete was one of the factors which led to the *Military League* of young officers forcing political reform on the mainland. With their backing, Venizélos became premier of Greece in 1910. In 1912 Greece, Serbia and Bulgaria declared war on the Ottoman Empire, making spectacular advances into Turkish territory. By the peace of 1913, Crete finally and officially became **part of the Greek nation**.

Though Greece was politically riven by World War I, and succeeding decades saw frequent, sometimes violent changes of power between Venizelist and Royalist forces, Crete was little affected. On just one further occasion did the island play a significant role in Greek affairs before the outbreak of war in 1940: in July 1938 there was a popular uprising against the dictator Metáxas and in favour of Venizélos. But it was swiftly put down.

The island was, however, hit hard by the aftermath of the disastrous Greek attempt to conquer Istanbul in pursuit of the "Great Idea" of rebuilding the Byzantine Empire. As part of the peace settlement which followed this military debacle, there was a forced **exchange of populations** in 1923: Muslims were expelled from Greece, Orthodox Christians from Turkey. In Crete many of these "Turks" were in fact Muslim Cretans, descendants of the mass apostasies of the eighteenth century. Nevertheless they left – some thirty thousand in all – and a similar number of Christian refugees from Turkey took their place.

WAR AND OCCUPATION

In the winter of 1940 Italian troops invaded northern Greece, only to be thrown back across the Albanian border by the Greek army. Mussolini's humiliation, however, only served to draw the Germans into the fight, and although an Allied army was sent to Greece, the **mainland** was rapidly overrun.

The Allied campaign was marked from the start by suspicion, confusion and lack of communication between the two commands. On the Greek side Metáxas had died in January, and his successor as premier commit-

ted suicide, leaving a Cretan – **Emanuel Tsouderos** – to organize the retreat of king and government to his native island. They were rapidly followed by thousands of evacuees, including the bulk of the Allied army, a force made up in large part of Australian and New Zealand soldiers. Most of the native Cretan troops, a division of the Greek army, had been wiped out in defence of the mainland.

According to the Allied plan, Crete should by now have been an impregnable fortress. In practice, though, virtually nothing had been done to improve the island defences, there were hardly any serviceable planes or other heavy equipment, and the arriving troops found little in the way of a plan for their deployment.

On May 20, 1941 the **invasion** of the island began, as German troops poured in by glider and parachute. It was at first a horrible slaughter, with the invaders easily picked off as they drifted slowly down. Few of the first wave of parachutists reached the ground alive and many of the gliders crashed. The main German force was smashed before it ever reached the ground. In the far west, however, beyond the main battle zone, they succeeded in taking the airfield at Máleme. Whether through incompetence (as much of the literature on the Battle of Crete suggests*) or breakdown of communications, no attempt to recapture the field was made until the Germans had had time to defend it and, with a secure landing site, reinforcements and equipment began to pour in. From now on the battle, which had seemed won, was lost, and the Allied troops, already under constant air attack, found themselves outgunned on land too.

Casualties of the **Battle of Crete** were horrendous on both sides – the cemeteries are reminiscent of the burial grounds of World War I victims in northern France – and the crack German airborne division was effectively wiped out. No one ever attempted a similar assault again. But once they were established with a secure bridgehead, the Germans

---

*Recent theories stress the importance of intelligence. Not long before the battle, the German codes had been cracked, and General Freyberg therefore knew in detail exactly where and how the attacks would come. Whether because he didn't trust the info, however, or because of the need to keep secret the intelligence breakthrough, he did not redeploy his troops.

advanced rapidly, and a week after the first landings the Allied army was in full retreat across the mountains towards Hóra Sfakíon, whence most were evacuated by ship to Egypt. On May 30, the battle was over, leaving behind several thousand Allied soldiers (and all the Cretans who had fought alongside them) to surrender or take to the mountains.

THE RESISTANCE

One of the first tasks of **the resistance** was to get these stranded soldiers off the island, and in this they had remarkable success, organizing the fugitives into groups and arranging their collection by ship or submarine from isolated beaches on the south coast. Many were hidden and fed by monks while they waited to escape, especially at the monastery of Préveli. In this and many other ways the German occupation closely mirrored earlier ones; opposition was constant, reprisals brutal. The north coast and the lowlands were, as in the past, easily and firmly controlled, but the mountains, and Sfakiá above all, remained the haunt of rebel and resistance groups throughout the war.

With the boats which took the battle survivors away from Crete were landed intelligence officers whose job it was to organize and arm the resistance: throughout the war there were a dozen or so on the island, living in mountain shelters or caves, attempting to organize parachute drops of arms and reporting on troop movements on and around the island.

How effective the sporadic efforts of the resistance were is hard to gauge: they had one spectacular success when in 1944 they kidnapped **General Kreipe**, the German commander, outside Iráklion, and succeeded in smuggling him across to the south coast and off the island to Egypt. Among this group were the author Patrick Leigh Fermor and Stanley Moss (whose *Ill Met by Moonlight* describes the incident in detail). The immediate result of this propaganda coup, however, was a terrible vengeance against the Cretan population, in which a string of villages around the Amári valley were destroyed and such menfolk as could be found slaughtered (see p.201). Harsh **retribution** on Cretan civilians, indeed, was the standard reaction to any success the resistance had.

At the end of 1944, the German forces withdrew to a heavily fortified perimeter around Haniá, where they held out for a final seven months before surrendering. In the rest of the island, this left a **power vacuum** which several of the resistance groups rushed to fill. Allied intelligence would no doubt claim that one of the achievements of their agents in Crete was the virtual avoidance of the civil war which wracked the rest of Greece. On the mainland the organization of the resistance had been very largely the work of Greek communists, who emerged at the end of the war as much the best organized and armed group. On Crete, groups in favour with the Allies had been the best armed and organized, and certainly in the latter stages of the war, communist-dominated organizations had been deliberately starved of equipment. There were only a few, minor incidents of violence on the island, and these were swiftly suppressed.

MODERN CRETE

In avoiding the civil war, Crete was able to set about **reconstruction** some way in advance of the rest of Greece, and since 1945 it has become one of the most prosperous and productive regions of the nation. The really spectacular changes, however, date from the last 25 years, fuelled above all by a tidal wave of tourism.

Politically, post-war Crete remains a place deeply mistrustful of outside control, even from Athens. At the local level above all, loyalties are divided along clan and patronage lines rather than party political ones, and leaders are judged on how well they provide for their areas and their followers. This is exemplified by **Kostas Mitzotakis**, former head of the right-wing Néa Dhimokratía (ND) party and prime minister until his defeat by PASOK (the socialist party) in the 1993 election: a Cretan, many islanders respected his ability to get things done on Crete even if his party was not much liked.

Cretan politicians at the local level (there is no overall island government, only a regional administration controlled by appointees from Athens) continue to take an almost universal joy in standing up to central authority. In one famous incident the mayor of Iráklion organized a sit-in at the Archeological Museum to prevent artworks being taken abroad for an exhibition: fifty thousand turned out to support him, and though President Karamanlis ordered his arrest, the national government was eventually forced to back down.

Rivalries within Crete are fierce, too, most notably between Haniá, the traditional capital, and upstart Iráklion which nowadays is richer and politically more important. This factionalism results in all sorts of anomalies and compromises: symptomatic was the thoroughly impractical decision to spread the University of Crete across three campuses, at Iráklion, Réthimnon (which has always considered itself the most cultured town in Crete) and Haniá.

In **national politics**, the island presents a more unified front as the upholder of Venizélos liberal tradition. After the overthrow of the Colonels in 1974, Crete voted heavily against a restoration of the monarchy and for a republican system; in the presidential election which followed, support for the right-winger Karamanlis was less than half as strong on Crete as it was in the rest of Greece. This has been an abiding pattern. Pasok has consistently polled twice as many Cretan votes as ND.

Increasingly, however, the hold of the powerful old families (Mitzotakis is a member of one such long-established clan) and traditional loyalties are crumbling as their power-broking becomes less effective. The day-to-day reality of control from Athens cannot be denied even by the most fervent Cretan nationalist. It first flexed its muscles under the Colonels, when the major tourist developments were got underway, brushing aside local qualms over planning or the desirability of mass tourism. Nowadays the EU, through directives and grants, has also started to affect Crete, above all her farmers. But central power – and the increasing importance of issues over personalities – perhaps manifests itself most clearly with regard to **NATO**.

Crete is home to numerous American and NATO bases, a couple of which are believed by local activists to store atomic weapons. The missile base on Akrotíri is the chief suspect – its missiles (you can see them test firing most Wednesdays) are certainly capable of carrying nuclear warheads. At Sóudha, as well as extensive naval installations, the US marine corps has its Mediterranean ammunition store in submarine pens. Also based on Crete is the most advanced listening station in the Mediterranean, monitoring transmissions from the Middle East. On a slightly crazier level, Crete is earmarked as a potential emergency landing site for the space shuttle. None

of this is popular locally, and again the extent of it is a legacy of the Colonels: the Americans are singled out as the butt of most protests because of their part in the 1967 coup and their role (or lack of one) in the Cyprus affair. Crete's all too recent past of military occupation does nothing to make the presence of foreign troops easier.

In June 1981 a massive demonstration, supported among others by Iráklion's mayor and bishop, blockaded Sóudha with people and slow-moving vehicles. Andreas Papandreou's Pasok, which won sixty percent of the total Cretan vote in 1985, promised that all US bases in Greece would be closed by 1988. In 1993 the base at Goúrnes shut down but there seems little prospect of all the bases closing: too much has been invested. Around $1000 million annually in rent and military aid is hard to give up, to say nothing of the other pressures applied. Above all is the fear that if they were thrown out, both bases and aid would simply be transferred to Turkey. But at least plans for expansion seem to have been shelved: there was to have been another base on the Méssara plain, possibly at Timbáki where the Germans had a big wartime base and where new barracks have been built but never occupied.

In the late Eighties and early Nineties Crete shared in the Greek and European economic downturn as a split developed between state employees (two-thirds more than in any other EU country) and the Mitzotakis government armed with a Thatcherite austerity programme to cut public expenditure. Strikes and mass protests ended with Nea Dhimokratía's crushing defeat in the general election of October 1993, and the **return to power of a Pasok government** still led by the ageing and ailing Andreas Papandreou. The austerity programme of Mitzotakis was halted (an election promise) but there are as yet no answers as to how the nation with the lowest productivity, highest inflation and largest external debt in the EU will raise its living standards, another election promise. In Crete itself the age of mass market tourism is beginning to pall as the attractions of sun, beach, cheap drinks and little else along much of the coast attract mainly younger holidaymakers who will move on when prices rise. As tourist numbers decline, efforts to build a market in "green tourism" are in their infancy, held back by an indifference to environmental concerns by politicians, farmers and a populace who have yet to realise that environmentally organized tourism – for which the island with its rich variety of flora and fauna is an ideal location – can be enormously profitable. The island has faced up to invaders throughout its history, but the tourist invasion presents it with a new dilemma: to submerge its traditional ways in the pursuit of ever greater numbers or to try to raise the quality of development and at the same time preserve Crete's unique character. How the island tackles this challenge will significantly determine the economic and social future as Crete enters the next millennium.

MONUMENTAL CHRONOLOGY

STONE AGE 6000 BC	First inhabitants arrive from east.	Neolithic habitation of caves, and later more settled centres at Knossós and elsewhere.
PRE-PALATIAL 2600 BC	New migration brings more sophisticated culture and larger settlements: first Minoans.	Settlements especially in the south: Vasíliki, Móhlos and Mírtos among the best known.
PROTO-PALATIAL 2000 BC	Emergence of a more formally structured society.	First palaces built at most of the famous sites.
1700 BC	Earthquake destroys the palaces.	
NEO-PALATIAL 1700 BC onwards	The Minoan Golden Age.	Great palaces at Knossós, Festós, Mália, Zakrós; thriving towns at Gourniá, Palékastro. Most of the Minoan remains date from this era.
1450 BC	Final destruction of the palaces.	Many earlier sites reoccupied. Kydonia the island's chief city.
POST-PALATIAL	Gradual revival under Mycenaean influence.	Eteo-Cretans keep Minoan culture alive at Présos and Karfí.
1100 BC	Mycenaean control giving way to Dorian.	
DORIAN	Island divided between rival groups, gradually emerging as constantly warring city-states.	Hundreds of small towns: Láto, Falásarna, along the south coast, Knossós and, above all, Górtys.
300 BC	Cities on south coast form Confederation of Oreii.	
71 BC	Failed Roman invasion.	
69–67 BC	Romans subjugate the island.	
ROMAN		Górtys the chief Roman city. Others include Lyttos, Áptera, Knossós. Public works across the island.
325 AD	Empire split, Crete ruled from Byzantium.	
BYZANTINE		Traces of early churches at Górtys, Soúyia, Thrónos.

824	Arab invasion.	
ARAB		Górtys sacked. al-Khandak, later Iráklion, the Arab base.
961	Liberation by Nikiforas Fokas.	
BYZANTINE		Small churches throughout Crete.
1204	Fourth Crusade, Byzantium sacked, Crete sold to Venice.	
VENETIAN		Very extensive building. Early remains are mostly in the form of churches and monasteries.
1453	Fall of Constantinople, renaissance of Byzantine art on Crete.	Later works include the shape of most major towns and defences all over the island. The cities of Iráklion, Réthimnon and Haniá owe much to the Venetians; castles include Frangokástello and the fortified islets; other reminders in the shape of saltpans (for example Olóus) and deforested hillsides.
1645	Turks capture Haniá.	
1669	Iráklion surrenders.	
TURKISH		Mosques and fountains in the cities, especially Haniá and Réthimnon, but few public works undertaken in the rest of the island.
1770	Revolt of Dhaskaloyiánnis.	
1821	Greek War of Independence.	
1866	Explosion at Arkádhi.	
1897	Great Powers occupy Crete.	
1898	Independence under Prince George.	
INDEPENDENT		New government buildings at Haniá.
1905	Revolutionary Assembly at Thériso, prince abdicates.	
1908	Crete declares *Enosis*.	
1913	Union of Greece and Crete formally declared.	
1941	German invasion.	Cemeteries and war memorials.
1945	Liberation.	
1960s		Tourist boom starts.

THE DISCOVERY OF BRONZE AGE CRETE

The story of the discovery of Bronze Age Crete – dominated by two larger-than-life characters in Heinrich Schliemann and Arthur Evans – is almost as fascinating as that of the Minoans themselves. Long before the appearance of these two giants, however, others had taken soundings and laid the foundations for their discoveries.

Already in antiquity ancient Crete had disappeared into the mists of Greek mythology and Homeric legend, and it was only during the Venetian period that curiosity about the island's illustrious past was re-awoken. In 1422 a Florentine monk, **Buondelmonte**, visited Crete and reported that he had seen over two thousand columns and statues at Górtys. More monuments and inscriptions were recorded by **Honorio de Belli** in 1596. In 1675, the Dutchman **Johann Meursius**, in his book *Creta*, sifted through the Classical references relating to the island.

In the eighteenth century a French explorer and botanist, **Joseph Tournefort**, described Crete in his *Voyage au Levant* of 1717; and the English navigator **Richard Pococke** also took an interest, documenting his findings in the second volume of his *Description of the East* published in 1745. But these were largely superficial observations and early in the nineteenth century it fell to another Dutchman, **Karl Hoeck** (who never actually visited the island) to write the first scholarly account of ancient Crete.

THE NINETEENTH CENTURY: TRAVELLERS AND TRADITION

A more genuinely first-hand record, and the best description of Crete's monuments and sites so far, was provided by Cambridge scholar **Robert Pashley** who, in the early 1830s, travelled extensively throughout the island in what can only have been a rugged journey. Pashley allied a Classical education to a keen eye and seems to have had an uncanny knack when it came to identifying ancient sites, written up in his entertaining *Travels in Crete* (1837). A century later, Pendlebury, the eminent British archeologist, paid Pashley fulsome tribute when he credited the traveller-scholar with identifying most of the important Cretan sites, including Knossós.

It was probably as well for those who were to come after him that it never occurred to Pashley to take up the spade. That he came near to doing so is borne out by his prophetic comments on Knossós: "The mythological celebrity and historical importance of Cnossus, demand a more careful and minute attention than can be bestowed on them in a mere book of travels".

During the years 1851–3 **Captain (later Admiral) Spratt** surveyed the Cretan coastline for the British admiralty. Taking an interest in the island's archeological remains, Spratt imperiously shipped quite a few of these back to the British Museum – often against the wishes of the local population. In an attempt to move a stone sarcophagus on board ship at Ierápetra he describes how one of his officers had to sleep in the sculptured coffin on the beach overnight " . . . to prevent it being injured wantonly or by local enemies (there was a party there who were opposed to our removal of the relic) . . . yet it did not wholly escape mischief, for some wanton hand destroyed what remained of the face of Hector".

Spratt also studied the island's natural history and geology, and it was the latter pursuit which earned him a footnote in Cretan archeology. His work for the British navy enabled him to demonstrate that, as a result of a geological convulsion in the sixth century AD*, the whole island had been tilted upwards at its western end by as much as 8m while the eastern end had sunk down: something clearly visible in the marshy swamps at the eastern site of Zákros.

THE AGE OF SCHLIEMANN

None of these early visitors to Crete, however, were concerned with pre-Classical history. The discovery of the great **Bronze Age** Minoan civilization was the almost single-handed achievement of Arthur Evans.

---

*Spratt was probably wrong about the cause, but his observations remain valid.

An important clue had been found as early as 1878. Digging at Knossós a Cretan merchant, with the appropriate name of **Minos Kalokairinos**, had uncovered a number of large storage jars mixed in with Mycenaean pottery fragments – something that was to confuse later investigators. This find attracted the attention of **Heinrich Schliemann**, who had already excited world interest by his excavation of ancient **Troy** in northwest Turkey, followed by the fortresses at **Mycenae** and **Tiryns** in the Greek Peloponnese. The son of a poor German pastor who filled his son's head with the fabulous tales of Homeric Greece, Schliemann left school without completing his studies to set up in business. In the course of a highly successful commercial career in which he amassed a fortune based on military contracts in the Crimean war and participation in the California gold rush, Schliemann never lost sight of the goal that he had set himself as a boy: to prove that the world of Homer was not mere myth as the majority of scholars then believed and to discover the fabulous places mentioned in the *Iliad* and the *Odyssey*.

When he finally embarked on this quest in his late forties, Schliemann taught himself Latin and Greek which he used to dissect his Homer before setting out for Turkey and then Greece. To the chagrin of the professional classicists, he was later to claim that it was a thorough reading of Homer which had led him to his discoveries. In fact, Schliemann became so besotted with his Hellenic vision that he not only took a Greek wife, but did so after a public competition in which the celebrated archeologist offered his hand in marriage to the first Greek girl who was able to render a faultless recitation of the entire *Iliad* from memory. Given Schliemann's luck it was inevitable that the first woman to achieve this was also an outstanding beauty and **Sofia Schliemann** became as enthusiastic as her husband in the pursuit of Greece's Bronze Age past.

Schliemann arrived in Crete in 1887, made a visit to the site at Knossós, and became convinced that a substantial palace, equivalent to those he had discovered on the mainland, lay waiting to be unearthed. But Crete was still under the subjection of Turkey and the authorities were often indolent and obstructive. In addition, when Schliemann attempted to negotiate the purchase of some land at Knossós, the

Turkish owners proved impossible to deal with and finally, with his patience exhausted and his health declining, Schliemann departed. A chill, caught after an ear operation in Naples, led to his sudden death in 1890. It was this twist of fortune which was destined to make Arthur Evans the discoverer of Knossós and Minoan Crete.

THE FIRST EXCAVATIONS

Meanwhile, others had also begun to take an interest in the island's past. During the twilight period of Turkish rule there was some relaxation of the iron grip, and the sultan gave permission to a Cretan archeologist, **Joseph Hatzidhakis**, to set up the **Cretan Archeological Society**, the forerunner of the Iráklion Archeological Museum. In 1884 an Italian scholar arrived in Crete, became friends with Hatzidhakis, and the two men began to search for ancient sites.

The scholar was **Federico Halbherr**, whose name was also destined to become prominent in Cretan archeology. It was on one of their expeditions in 1885 that the **first recorded discovery of Bronze Age artefacts** was made at the **Psihró Cave** above the Lasíthi plateau. The following year the chance unearthing of a tomb near **Festós** gave Halbherr the idea that there was probably a settlement nearby. Preliminary excavations revealed substantial buildings as well as prehistoric pottery, but the political turmoil leading up to the end of Turkish rule postponed further progress.

Another important clue to what was to come had also been found on the volcanic island of **Thíra** in the 1860s. During quarrying operations for the enormous amounts of pumice needed to make cement for the construction of the Suez Canal, a buried settlement was revealed. Here whole rooms had been preserved intact, their walls covered with remarkable fresco paintings. Although it's now understood to be a colony or outpost of Minoan civilization, this was long before any comparable Minoan remains had been discovered on Crete itself.

ARTHUR EVANS

In 1882 a meeting occurred at one of Athens' most elegant mansions which was to have an enormous importance for Cretan archeology.

The host was the famous archeologist Heinrich Schliemann, his guest a young scholar and journalist – **Arthur Evans**. Born in 1851, the son of a wealthy and distinguished numismatist, Evans's upbringing could hardly have differed more from that of the self-made German businessman. Educated at Harrow and then Oxford, Evans was always to have the time and financial security to pursue his interests wherever they might lead him.

Schliemann was digging again at Troy and regaled his guest with the story of his excavations both there and at Mycenae. But Evans displayed more interest in Schliemann's extensive collection of ancient artefacts, particularly some **engraved seals** bearing an octopus design which he felt must be of Aegean, possibly Cretan, origin. Schliemann then announced to Evans that his next project was to be the excavation of another Mycenaean fortress at Tiryns following which he would dig at the site in Crete from where, as Homer put it in the *Iliad*, "came forth the men from Knossós". Little can he have realized the frustration of this goal that lay ahead, or that his attentive guest would himself be the recipient of this great archeological prize.

For the time being, Evans returned to England to take up a post as keeper of the Ashmolean Museum at Oxford, although he continued to pay visits to the Balkans and Greece. Evans's studies during this period, allied to the discovery of more seal stones bearing **pre-alphabetical writing**, led him to the proposition that Crete had been an important centre of Mycenaean culture, possibly even its birthplace. When, in 1893, a great hoard of **painted pottery** was discovered by Italian archeologists at the **Kamáres Cave** on Mount Ida (Psilorítis), Evans's mind was made up: he would visit Crete to search for more seal stones and, if circumstances allowed, make a fresh attempt to carry out the excavations at Knossós which had been denied to Schliemann.

Evans arrived in Crete for the first time on March 15, 1894. Typically, in spite of an horrendously rough voyage from Pireás lasting 24 hours, no sooner had he set foot on the island than he records in his diary that he has toured the Candia bazaar and purchased "twenty-two early Cretan stones at about one and a half piastres apiece". Evans had started out as he

meant to continue, and once the initial obstacles had been overcome the pace was hardly to slacken over the next thirty years.

With the assistance of Joseph Hatzidhakis, now curator as well as president of the Cretan Archeological Society, Evans began to negotiate for the **purchase of the land at Knossós** with its Turkish owners. He became bogged down in the same protracted wrangles that had forced Schliemann to despair. But Evans was a man who usually got what he wanted. Even so it took five years, some valiant efforts from Hatzidhakis, and a stroke of the kind of luck that some people seem to attract. In this case it was the lifting in 1898 of the Turkish yoke which had burdened Crete for 230 years. Evans, possessing a Liberal political outlook, had worked with Hatzidhakis to raise funds in Britain and Crete for the victims of the insurrections during this period. But finally the major obstacle to starting excavations at Knossós had been removed.

KNOSSÓS: THE EARLY YEARS

In 1899 the new government changed the law and most of the restrictions on foreign excavators were cleared away. Evans's purchase of the land at **Knossós** went through and work started on March 23, 1900. Interestingly for the future, the team that Evans assembled for the dig included an architect, **Theodore Fyfe**, from the British School at Athens. As the excavations progressed Evans soon realized that he was dealing with a site far older than the Roman, Greek or even Mycenaean periods. Then out of the earth came **frescoes**, **pottery** and what came to be known as **Linear B** tablets bearing the ancient Minoan script. On April 10 the throne room was discovered with its elegant **gypsum throne** – named at first the "throne of Ariadne" by Evans who thought it too dainty to hold the manly posterior of Minos himself – flanked by stone benches and frescoed walls.

During the first five years of the excavations, in which most of the palace was revealed, Evans made a number of innovations. In his magisterial style he named the new civilization "**Minoan**" after the legendary Cretan king. He then proceeded to delineate his division of the island's Bronze Age into **Early**, **Middle** and **Late Minoan** based on pottery styles found at Knossós (see box).

EVAN'S DATING GAME

Early Minoan 3000–2000 BC
Middle Minoan I & II 2000–1700 BC
Middle Minoan III + Late Minoan I & II 1700–1400 BC
Late Minoan III 1400–1100 BC

In spite of problems later encountered with this system – for example, not all contemporary sites went through the same artistic developments in similar timescales – Evans's system remains the one used by archeologists and scholars if only because no one has yet bettered it.

RESTORATION AND CONTROVERSY

Another of Evans's early decisions was to prove far more controversial: he determined that he would not only reveal the palace of Minos but that he would also **restore** large parts of it (he insisted on the word "reconstitute") to the splendour prior to its final destruction around 1400 BC. That Evans was able autocratically to decide this rested on his personal ownership of one of the major sites of antiquity, something that would be unthinkable today. "I must have sole control of what I am personally undertaking ... my way may not be the best but it is the only way I can work," he said revealingly about this decision in a letter to his father.

What Evans had now embarked upon was one of the most expensive enterprises in the history of archeology, and in the early years funds were often stretched. But fortunately or otherwise for Knossós – depending on your viewpoint – two large legacies fell into Evans's lap eight years into the mammoth task, as a result of the deaths of both his father and his uncle (John Dickinson the paper millionaire) within months of each other in 1908. Evans's plans for Knossós, destined to last for a further 23 years, were now financially secure.

With the assistance of Theodore Fyfe and later **Piet de Jong**, the architects, Evans first roofed the throne room and then reconstructed the **grand staircase**, replacing the **tapered columns** with his speculative concrete reconstructions (none of the wooden originals was ever found). Two Swiss artists then began to repaint the reconstructed walls with **copies of** the frescoes now in the Iráklian Archeological Museum. In 1930 the almost entirely conjectural upper storey (or **Piano Nobile** as Evans fancifully termed it) was added using reinforced concrete. Next, the **Central Court** was extensively restored as the archeological site became a building site. Evans attempted to deflect criticism of his methods as he imposed his own grand design on the work of architects and artists by saying that he wanted to recreate the "spirit" of the palace structure and decor rather than create a literal reconstruction. This was where many scholars parted company with him. Pendlebury, who was to be Evans's successor at Knossós (see over), put aside earlier reservations and defended Evans in a guidebook to the site stating that "without restoration the Palace would be a meaningless heap of ruins". Others furiously disagreed and the debate is no less heated today. One thing, however, is certain: no professional archeologist would be allowed or would expect to carry out such a work again.

In his views on Minoan scholarship Evans could be equally autocratic and blinkered. When **Alan Wace**, director of the British School at Athens, excavated a number of tombs on the site of Mycenae in the Greek Peloponnese in the early 1920s, his findings led him to conclude that Mycenae had not only been a culture independent from that of Crete – Evans stated that it had been a colony of Crete ruled by Cretan overlords – but that in the later period Mycenaeans had been in control at Knossós. For Evans this was heresy and he used his considerable influence to attack Wace, get him sacked, and stop him carrying out any further work at Mycenae. Evans went to his grave believing he was right, but in the light of the decipherment of Linear B and later investigation, it is Wace's views that are generally accepted today.

THE END OF AN ERA

During the long periods that Evans spent working at Knossós he lived in some style at the villa he had constructed for himself overlooking the palace site. The **Villa Ariadne**, as he typically named it, became the focus of scholarly life of a slightly stuffy, Victorian kind. Evans revelled in the stream of distinguished visitors to Knossós – who were met at the harbour by his chauffeur-driven limousine – and the house's servants would ply them with French champagne following a guided tour of the site. His relationship with the Greeks, not to say the native Cretans, seems to have been scratchy by comparison. A crusty, aloof man by nature, he seems never to have been able to relax with them and certainly would never be seen around a table at the *kafenion*, as Pendlebury later was. Evans's lack of fluency in modern Greek – in spite of the time he spent on the island – was also taken by many as a sign of his disdain for the degenerate latterday occupants of such ancient lands.

In 1924 Evans donated the Knossós site and the Villa Ariadne to the British School at Athens – it was only in 1952 that the site was to become the property of the Greek government – and in the early Thirties, approaching his eightieth year, he handed over the reins at Knossós to a young English archeologist, **John Pendlebury**, and retired to his home near Oxford to complete the final volumes of his monumental work *The Palace of Minos*. It was the end of an era. Sir Arthur Evans (as he was now titled) paid his last visit to the site with which his name remains inextricably linked in 1935, when he attended the festivities surrounding the unveiling of his **bronze bust** in the palace grounds. He died six years later, in 1941.

CONTEMPORARIES AND SUCCESSORS

Although Evans stole the headlines for forty years, much important work was meanwhile being carried out elsewhere. Above all, Federico Halbherr was excavating **Festós** and later **Ayía Triádha**. In the same year that Evans began digging at Knossós, 1900, Halbherr started work on the beautifully situated palace at Festós. He soon acquired legendary status among the country people, thanks to his custom of riding around on a coal-black Arab mare. The bulk of the palace – including a dramatic **staircase** – was laid bare in three seasons of work. Although some restoration was done on the site, it was nothing resembling Evans's efforts at Knossós – in fact Halbherr and his colleagues pursued a far more **rigorously scientific excavation**: the first carried out on Crete. The Italian School has continued its work at Festós, Ayía Triádha and Górtys throughout the century.

In the east **British teams** worked at **Zakrós** (where Hogarth narrowly failed to uncover the

palace) and the Minoan settlements at **Paleókastro** and **Présos**. **John Pendlebury** also made a great impression in this period. A man with great affection both for Crete and the Cretans, he covered vast tracts of the island on foot in his search for evidence of ancient sites. He found countless numbers of these and made many friends along the way. Besides his work at Knossós he also excavated the late Minoan refuge at **Karfí** above the Lasíthi plateau. Pendlebury was killed in the early years of World War II, fighting alongside the Cretans during the German attack on Iráklion in 1941. Work by the British School has continued at Knossós as well as more remote sites such as the Minoan settlements at **Mírtos Pírgos** and **Mírtos Foúrnou Korifí**.

The **Americans** were also active in eastern Crete from the earliest days of exploration. A woman – in a field dominated by men – staked out her claim at **Gourniá** on the Gulf of Mirabéllo. **Harriet Boyd** (later Mrs Boyd-Hawes), a young classics scholar from Massachusetts, visited Athens in 1900 and was gripped by the excitement surrounding the archeological excavations then getting under way. She went to Crete, received the almost obligatory encouragement from Evans, and the following year set off by donkey for the east with her foreman, the Zorba-like Aristides, and his mother, her constant companions. After a number of false starts she alighted on Gourniá and to her own, and the world's, surprise there uncovered the **workers' village**. The telegram she sent to the American Exploration Society, after three days' digging, says it all: "Discovered Gourniá Mycenaean site, streets, houses, pottery, bronzes, stone jars". It was, of course, a Minoan site, but the archeologists were still feeling their way back into a much more ancient past than anyone then realized.

Another skilled American archeologist working in the east was **Richard Seager**. In the early 1900s he excavated the important early Minoan settlement at **Vasilikí**, with its famous pottery, before moving on to the islands of **Psíra** and then **Móhlos** where substantial settlements were found. Seager was a good friend of Evans, who attended the funeral following Seager's sudden death at Iráklion in 1925. "He was the most English American I have ever known" was Evans's quintessential epitaph. The North American contribution (now a joint venture with Greek scholars) continues at Móhlos as well as at **Kómmos**, where Joseph Shaw is excavating an impressive Minoan port to the north of Mátala.

The **French** have also contributed some excellent work at **Mália**. After initial investigations by Joseph Hatzidhakis and during the years of World War I from 1915 on, the French School at Athens were awarded the site in 1922. Having excavated the **Minoan palace** they are now at work on unearthing the extensive settlement which surrounded it.

RECENT DEVELOPMENTS: ZAKRÓS

The discovery of ancient Crete has continued steadily throughout this century – barring wartime interruptions – if not always as spectacularly as it began. The outstanding exception was **Nikolaos Platon's** excavation at **Zakrós** which, from 1962 onwards, finally revealed the palace long suspected to have been there. Sixty years earlier Hogarth had missed the palace by a few yards, and in one of his treks around eastern Crete in 1938 the voracious Pendlebury, accompanied by his archeologist wife Hilda, had combed the area. "We must have been sitting on the very site – and we saw nothing" said Hilda Pendlebury later. Fittingly, one of Crete's greatest archeological prizes of all fell to a Cretan.

Prior to Hogarth and Pendlebury, Zakrós had also been visited by Captain Spratt in 1852, as well as Halbherr, and Evans himself. **Hogarth** did expose parts of the surrounding settlement, with houses containing rich pottery, clay seals and bronze tools. The site then lay dormant until after World War II. Nikolaos Platon became convinced that because of the submerged but excellent harbour – in a prime position for trade with the Near East – there had to be a palace here. With funds from the Greek Archeological Society and two wealthy

American backers, he started work in 1962 where Hogarth had left off. The **unlooted palace**, never reoccupied after its destruction by fire around 1450 BC, was now revealed, together with a rich yield of artefacts, including over three thousand vases. Platon continued to supervise the excavations at Zakrós until his death in 1992, and work on uncovering the town surrounding the palace is still in progress.

In the recent excavations, Greek and Cretan archeologists have finally been able to play a more equal role than in the early days, when foreign archeological teams often treated them with patronizing high-handedness. Some, like Hatzidhakis and Marinatos, were there from the start but unable to compete with the wealthy foreigners in what was very much a private enterprise affair. Now, with mainly state funding, Greek archeologists such as **Yannis and Efi Sakellarakis** (at Arhánes, Anemóspilia and the Idean Cave), **Davaras** (Móhlos, Psíra and many more), **Alexiou** (Leben), **Zois** (Vasilikí), **Tzedakis** (Arméni), **Papadakis** (Koufonísi), **Karetsou** (Mount Yioúhtas), **Kanta** (Monastiráki) and **Tsipopoulou** (Petrás) are contributing greatly to the island's archeological discoveries. These continue to be added to as each season passes and, although it is unlikely that another Knossós will come to light, there are indications – such as those in the work continuing at **Haniá** – that many more sites, particularly in the west, lie awaiting the spade.

A once neglected area of Cretan archeology – the post-Bronze Age, Dorian and Roman – is also now being given more attention than ever before at sites across the island. These Minoan and post-Minoan sites today stand as a tribute not only to the dedicated archeologists who discovered and exposed them, but also to the work of the nameless thousands of Cretans who laboured with spade, trowel and barrow to uncover the past of their illustrious island ancestors.

CRETE IN MYTH

Crete is intimately associated with much of ancient Greek mythology, and in particular with Zeus, who was not only brought up on the island, but according to some ancient Cretans was buried here as well. The Dhiktean Cave (see below), a gash on the face of Mount Dhíkti which soars above the Lasíthi plateau, has most claims to be the birthplace of the greatest god in the Greek pantheon and symbolizes the potent influence of Minoan Crete on the land to the north.

THE BIRTH OF ZEUS

According to the earliest accounts of the myth **Zeus** was the third generation of rulers of the gods. The original ruler, Uranus, was overthrown by his youngest son Kronos. In order to prevent such a fate overtaking him, too, Kronos ate his first five children at birth. When she was bearing the sixth, his wife, Rhea, took refuge in a Cretan cavern (a site much argued over, but most commonly assigned to the Dhiktean Cave, p.131). Here Zeus was born, and in his place Rhea presented Kronos with a rock wrapped in blankets, which he duly devoured. Zeus was brought up secretly in the cave, his cries drowned by the **Kouretes**, who kept up a noisy dance with continuous clashing of shields and spears outside. The Kouretes, believed by Cretans to be the sons of the Earth Mother, were especially revered on the island as the inventors of beekeeping and honey as well as the hunting bow, and an inscription found at Palékastro suggests that they may well have a Minoan origin. The baby fed on milk from a mountain goat-nymph, Amalthea, one of whose horns he later made into a miraculous gift which a wish would fill with whatever was desired (hence the horn of plenty).

Having grown to manhood on Crete, Zeus declared war on Kronos and the Titans, a struggle which lasted ten years. Eventually, however, Zeus emerged as supreme ruler of the gods on Mount Olympus, and Kronos was banished to the Underworld. This myth has a precedent in Hittite texts of the second millenium BC who themselves had taken it over from the earlier Hurrians, a people who had

settled in Syria and northern Mesopotamia. The Minoans passed it on to the Greeks.

THE ORIGIN OF THE CRETANS

The sexual prowess of Zeus led him into a bewildering number of affairs, one of which led to his best-known return to the island of his birth – with Europa – and the **founding of the Cretan race. Europa** was a princess, the daughter of King Phoenix (after whom Phoenicia was named), and Zeus lusted after her mightily. Approaching the shore of Phoenicia, Zeus saw her gathering flowers, and came to her in the guise of a white bull. Fascinated by the creature's docility Europa climbed onto its back, at which he leapt into the sea and carried her off across the sea to Crete. They landed at Mátala, travelled to Górtys (where one version has it Zeus ravished her beneath a plane tree which has never lost its leaves since) and were married at the Dhiktean Cave. One of the presents of Zeus to his bride was **Talos**, a bronze giant who strode round the island hurling boulders at approaching strangers. Jason and the Argonauts were greeted by a hail of stones from Talos when they approached Crete: aided by their companion, the sorceress Medea, they brought about the giant's fall by piercing a vein on his ankle – his single vulnerable spot – thus allowing the *ichor*, a divine fluid which served as blood, to drain from his body.

MINOS AND THE MINOTAUR

The Zeus of the Europa tale, taking the form of a **bull**, is almost certainly mixed up with earlier, native Cretan gods. The sun god of Crete also took the form of a bull, and the animal is a recurrent motif in the island's mythology. In the story of Minos, a bull once again has a prominent role. Europa bore Zeus three sons – Minos, Rhadamanthys and Sarpedon – before eventually being deserted. Later she married the king of Crete, Asterios, who adopted her children. Upon reaching manhood the three brothers quarrelled for the love of a beautiful boy named Miletos – a reflection of the mores and customs of the time. When Miletos chose Sarpedon an enraged Minos drove him from the island. However, before boarding a ship to Asia Minor, Miletos killed King Asterios. Legend associates both Miletos and Sarpedon – who joined him in

Asia Minor – with the founding of Miletus (see p.126), later an important city in Greek and Roman times. With Sarpedon removed **Minos** claimed the throne and settled upon Rhadamanthys a third of Asterios' dominions. Rhadamanthys became renowned as a law-maker, appears in some tales as ruler at Festós, and every ninth year visited Zeus's cave on Mount Dhíkti to bring back a new set of laws. So great was Rhadamanthys' fame as a lawgiver that Homer tells of how Zeus appointed him one of the three judges of the dead along with Minos and Aeachus.

Minos, meanwhile, was another ruler driven by lustful passions. He liaised with a succession of lovers including the Minoan goddess **Britomartis**, whom he chased relentlessly around the island for nine months until she threw herself into the sea off the end of the Rodhópou peninsula to escape his attentions. Rescued from drowning by the net of a fisherman, she became known as Diktynna ("of the net"), and a great temple to her was erected on the site (p.246). Minos's wife and queen, Pasiphae, incensed by her rakish husband's infidelities, put a spell on the king: whenever he lay with another woman he discharged not seed but a swarm of poisonous serpents, scorpions and insects which devoured the woman's vitals. News of his affliction (which bears a striking resemblance to venereal disease) apparently got around and one of his bedmates Prokris, daughter of the Athenian king Erechtheus, insisted that he should take a prophylactic draught before their tryst which apparently prevented her being invaded by serpents and scorpions.

Earlier, when he had gained the throne of his father, Minos prayed to Poseidon (or perhaps his father Zeus) to send a bull from the sea which he could offer as a sacrifice, thus signifying the god's recognition of the justice of his claim to the throne. When the radiant bull emerged from the sea Minos was so taken by its beauty that he determined to keep it, sacrificing in its place another from his herds. Punishment for such hubris was inevitable, and in this case the gods chose to inflame Minos's wife, Pasiphae (a moon goddess in her own right – again the bull symbolizes the sun), with intense desire for the animal. She had the brilliant inventor and craftsman **Daedalus** construct her an artificial cow, in which she hid and induced the bull to couple

with her: the result was the **Minotaur**, a beast half man and half bull (probably human with a bull's head). To hide his shame, Minos had Daedalus construct the labyrinth in which to imprison the monster.

THESEUS AND ARIADNE

Meanwhile Minos had waged war on Athens after Androgeous, one of his sons by Pasiphae, had gone off to that city and won every event in the Panathenaic games, only to be slain on the orders of the outraged Athenian king, Aegeus. Part of the settlement demanded by the victorious Minos was that an annual tribute of seven young men and women be provided as sport or sacrifice for the Minotaur. The third time the tribute was due, **Theseus**, the son of King Aegeus, resolved to end the slaughter and himself went as one of the victims. In Crete he met Minos's daughter **Ariadne**, who fell in love with him and resolved to help him in his task. At the instigation of the sympathetic Daedalus, she provided Theseus with a ball of thread which he could unwind and, if he succeeded in killing the Minotaur, follow to find his way out of the maze.

At first everything went to plan, and Theseus killed the beast and escaped from the island with Ariadne and the others. On the way home, though, things were less successful. Ariadne was abandoned on a beach in Náxos, to be later found by the god Dionysius and carried off to Olympus, and approaching Athens Theseus forgot to change his black sails for white – a pre-arranged signal that the mission had succeeded. Thinking his son dead, King Aegeus threw himself into the sea and drowned.

Back on Crete, Minos imprisoned Daedalus in his own labyrinth, furious at Ariadne's desertion and his part in it, and at the failure of the maze. Locked up with Daedalus was his son, Ikarus. They escaped by making wings of feathers – from birds devoured by the Minotaur – held together with wax. Daedalos finally reached Sicily and the protection of King Kokalos: Ikaros, though, flew too close to the sun, the wax melted and he plunged to his death in the sea. Still set on revenge, Minos tracked Daedalus down by setting a puzzle so fiendishly difficult that only he could have solved it: a large reward was promised to the first person who could pass a thread through a triton shell. When Minos eventually arrived in

Sicily he posed the problem to Kokalos who said it would be easy. He then consulted secretly with Daedalus who drilled the shell at its point and tied a thread to the leg of an ant which was sent into the shell. When the insect emerged through the hole, Kokalos took the shell to show Minos. Now certain that Daedalus was hidden in the palace, Minos demanded that Kokalos hand him over. Kokalos appeared to agree to the request and offered Minos hospitality in the palace. There Minos met an undignified end when he was scalded to death in his bath by the daughters of the king, urged on by Daedalus.

The postscript to all this concerns **Zeus's death**. According to the Cretans, and reflecting the older Minoan idea of a fertility god who annually died and was reborn, Zeus was buried beneath Mount Yioúhtas near Knossós, in whose outline his recumbent profile can still be seen from the palace site. It was a purely local claim, however, and clashed with the northern Greek idea of Zeus as an immortal and all-powerful sky-god. The northern Greeks regarded the islander's belief in a dying Zeus as utter blasphemy and their contempt for the Cretan heresy gave rise to the phrase "all Cretans are liars."

WILDLIFE

Although the south coast of Crete is closer to Libya than it is to Athens, the island's wildlife owes much more to mainland Greece than it does to Africa. This is because Crete lies at the end of the long range of drowned limestone mountains which make up most of the Balkan peninsula: the range peters out in Libya and Egypt, and you need to go a long way south into the Sahara before you again find mountains as high as the Cretan ones. Crete, then, has typically northern Mediterranean fauna and flora.

Islands tend to be short on wildlife because of their isolation from the main bulk of species on the mainland. Not so Crete – it's big in all three dimensions, and provides the full range of Mediterranean habitats. In fact, there are over two thousand species of **plants** in Crete, nearly a third of the Greek flora, and about as many as in the whole of Britain; richer partly because it went relatively unscathed through the Ice Ages, and partly because botanical variety tends to increase the nearer you go to the equator. With the wealth of plant life come far more **insects** than you get further north. The survival of Cretan wildlife in all its richness and diversity has been facilitated by the fact that agriculture remains fairly "undeveloped". Much of the land is steep and rocky with only a thin capping of soil, and you'll see modern intensive agriculture only on the lowland plains – although the pressures are mounting, in the form of widespread use of chemicals, increased water abstraction and tourist development. You won't find many birds or wild flowers among the hectares of plytunnels around Timbáki, but you will in the mountains where such methods remain uneconomic.

The only feature really lacking, as elsewhere in Greece, is **trees**. The Minoan civilization was a seafaring one, so as early as the Bronze Age there was a high demand for timber for shipbuilding. Some of the lower hills were perhaps cut down four thousand years ago, a deforestation process completed by the Venetians. Today, native forests exist only in remote uplands and gorges.

Crete's chief drawback, at least if you hope to combine nature with the rest of the island's sights and life, is the pattern of its **climate**. Because it's so far south, the summers are long and dry, and that period equates to our northern winters, when many plants shut down or die, with a corresponding decline in activity from all other wildlife. Trying to see wild flowers or birds in lowland Crete in August is a bit like going out for a nature ramble in Britain in January. For flowers, the best time to go is March: the season continues through to late June in the mountains, while around the coasts many plants keep flowering right through the winter.

MAJOR HABITATS

Rarely in Europe do you find such a wide range of habitats so tightly packed, or real "wilderness" areas so close to modern towns and resorts, as in Crete. Broadly speaking, you can divide the island into four major **habitats** : the coast; cultivated land; low hillsides less than 1000m; and mountains above 1000m. Crete is the only Greek island which is mountainous enough to have all four of these habitats.

Along **the coast** sandy beaches and low rocky cliffs are the norm. Marshy river deltas or estuaries are rare (simply because Crete is a dry country and there aren't too many rivers) but where you can find them, these wetland habitats are among the best places to look for birds.

Cultivated land is very variable in its wildlife interest. Huge wheatfields, or huge olive groves for that matter, have little to offer, but where the pattern is smaller in scale and more varied, it can be very good. This is especially true of the small market gardens – *perivólio* – often found on the edge of towns and villages, which are particularly good for small birds. Small hayfields can be a colourful mass of annual flowers, and attendant insects, in spring and early summer.

Low hillsides to 1000m include much of Crete. Scrubby hillsides, loosely grazed by goats and sometimes sheep, are the most typical Mediterranean habitat, extremely rich in flowers, insects and reptiles. Botanically, they divide into two distinct types: the first is *phrígana*, the Greek word for the French *garigue*, and consists of scattered scrubby bushes, always on limestone, especially rich in aromatic herbs and wild flowers. You can often find *phrígana* by looking for beehives: Cretan beekeepers know where to find the thyme and rosemary that gives the local honey its wonderful flavour. The other hillside habitat is *maquis*, a dense, very prickly scrub with scattered trees. Of these two hillside habitats, *phrígana* is better for flowers, *maquis* for birds.

Mountains over 1000m are surprisingly common: three separate ranges go over 2000m, and they are responsible for much of the climate, creating rain and retaining it as snow for a large part of the year. The small upland plateaux amongst the mountains – Omalós or Lasíthi most famously – are a very special feature, with their own distinctive flora and fauna. Although the Cretan mountains don't, by and large, have the exciting mammals of the mainland, they are very good for large and spectacular birds of prey.

FLOWERS

What you will see, obviously, depends on where and when you go. The best time is **spring**, which generally starts in mid-February in the southeast corner of the island, is at its peak during March over most of the lowlands (but continues well into April), and in the mountains comes later, starting in late April and going on through to June. In **early summer**, the spring anemones, orchids and rockroses are replaced by plants like brooms and chrysanthemums; this ranges from mid-April in southern Crete to late July in the high mountains. These timings vary from year to year, too, exceptionally by as much as a month – in early April 1986 it was too hot to lie on the beach at Yeoryióupoli at midday, but at the same time in

1987 there was snow on the beach at Réthimnon, just 30km away.

Things are pretty much burnt out over all the lowlands from July through to the end of September, though there are still some flowers in the mountains. Once the hot summer is over, blooming starts all over again. Some of the **autumn** flowering species, such as cyclamens and autumn crocus, flower from October in the mountains into December in the south. And by then you might as well stay on for the first of the spring bulbs in January.

Year round, the best insurance policy is to be prepared to move up and down the hills until you find flowers – from the beginning of March to the end of June you are almost guaranteed to find classic displays of flowers somewhere on the island, and you'll see the less spectacular but still worthwhile displays of autumn flowering species from October to early December. If you have to go in July, August or September, then be prepared to see a restricted range, and also to go high up the mountains.

The four habitats all have their own flowers, though some, of course, overlap.

On **the coast** you might find the spectacular **yellow horned poppy** growing on shingled banks, and **sea stocks** and **Virginia stocks** growing amongst the rocks behind the beach. A small pink **campion**, *Silene colorata*, is often colourfully present. Sand dunes are rare but sometimes there is a flat grazed area behind the beach; these are often good for **orchids**. **Tamarisk trees** often grow down to the shore, and there are frequent groves of Europe's largest grass, the **giant reed**, which can reach 4m high. In the autumn, look for the very large white flowers of the **sea daffodil**, as well as **autumn crocuses** on the banks behind the shore. The **sea squill** also blooms in autumn, with very tall spikes of white flowers rising from huge bulbs.

On **cultivated land** avoid large fields and plantations, but look for small hay meadows. These are often brilliant with annual "weeds" in late spring – various **crysanthemum** species, **wild gladiolus**, **blue and purple vetches**, and in general a mass of colour such as you rarely see in northern Europe. This is partly because herbicides are used less, but mostly because the hot summers force plants into flowering at the same time.

The trees and shrubs on **low hillsides** are varied and beautiful, with colourful brooms flowering in early summer, preceded by bushy **rockroses** – *Cistaceae* – which are a mass of pink or white flowers in spring. Dotted amongst the shrubs is the occasional tree; the **Judas tree** flowers on bare wood in spring, making a blaze of pink against green hillsides which stands out for miles. Lower than the shrubs are the **aromatic herbs** – sage, rosemary, thyme and lavender – with perhaps some spiny species of **Euphorbia**. My favourite of these is *Euphorbia acanthothamnos*, a rock-hugging species which forms low humps with small green leaves and delicate golden flowers. Because Crete is dry and hot for much of the year, you also get a high proportion of **xerophytes** – plants that are adapted to drought by having fleshy leaves and thick skins.

Below the herbs is the ground layer; peer around the edges and between the shrubs and you'll find a wealth of **orchids, anemones, grape hyacinths, irises**, and perhaps **fritillaries** if you are lucky. The orchids are extraordinary; some kinds – the *Ophrys* species – have especially fascinating and unusual flowers. Each *Ophrys* species is pollinated by a particular insect, which they attract by sight and smell: sight by having a flower which imitates the female insect and so deludes the male into "mating" with it; smell by imitating the particular sex pheromone which the insect uses. They're much smaller and altogether more dignified than the big blowsy tropical orchids you see in florists' stores. But beware of orchids – they are addictive, and you can easily become an orchid freak and spend your entire holiday face down on a hillside, to the extreme boredom of your non-botanical friends!

The **irises** are appealing, too; one of them, a small blue species called *Iris sisyrinchium*, only flowers in the afternoon, and you can actually sit and watch them open at around midday. Once spring is over, these plants give way to the early summer flowering of the brooms and aromatic herbs, as well as a final fling from the annuals which sense the coming of the heat and their own death. When the heat of the summer is over, the autumn bulbs appear, with species of **crocus** and their relatives, the **colchicums** and the **sternbergias**, and finally the **autumn cyclamens** through into early December.

Mountains are good to visit later in the year. The rocky mountain gorges are the home of many familiar garden rock plants, such as the **aubretias, saxifrages** and **alyssums**, as well as **dwarf bellflowers** and **anemones**. Look for dwarf **tulips** in fields on the upland plateaux in spring. The mountains are also the place to see the remaining Greek native **pine forests**, and in the woodland glades you will find **gentians, cyclamens** and **violets**. Above 1500m or so the forests begin to thin out, and in these upland meadows glorious **crocuses** flower almost before the snow has melted in spring – a very fine form of *Crocus seiberi* is a particularly early one. Autumn flowering species of crocus and cyclamen should reward a visit later in the year.

BIRDS

There are less speciality **bird species** in Crete than there are flowers, because birds can move around. However, Greece has a good range of the resident Mediterranean species, plus one or two very rare ones such as the **Ruppell's Warbler** or the **Lammergeier vulture**, which have their European breeding strongholds in Greece. The great thing about birdwatching in Crete is that, if you pick your time right, you can see both resident and migratory species. Crete is on one of the main flypast routes for species that have wintered in East Africa, but breed in northern Europe. They migrate every spring up the Nile valley, and then move across the eastern Med, often in huge numbers. This happens from mid-March to mid-May, depending on the species, the weather, and where you are. The return migration in autumn is less spectacular because it is less concentrated, but still worth watching out for.

One drawback is that until recently the "sport" of shooting songbirds was common, and although things have improved, the birds remain understandably cautious. Some are still caught for the cagebird trade, as you will realize from looking at the goldfinches and others hung in cages from the front of houses and apartments. Birds of prey get a rough deal, too, as witness the dusty cases of badly stuffed eagles in many tavernas and *kafenia*.

A general point about watching birds is that they're active at a pretty antisocial time – just after dawn is the peak activity time for most small birds. A walk before breakfast can produce heaps of birds, yet you can walk the same area a few hours later and see almost nothing. Exceptions to this are water birds and wading birds, which are often visible all day, and big birds of prey, which frequently use the rising thermals of early evening to soar and gain height.

On the **outskirts of towns** and in the **fields** there are some colourful residents. Small predatory birds such as **woodchat shrikes**, **kestrels** and migrating **red-footed falcons** can be seen perched on telegraph wires. The dramatic pink, black and white **hoopoe** and the striking yellow and black **golden oriole** are sometimes to be found in woodland and olive groves, and **Scops owls** (Europe's smallest owl) can often be heard calling around towns at night. They monotonously repeat a single "poo", sometimes in mournful vocal duets.

Look closely at the **swifts** and **swallows**, and you will find a few species not found in northern Europe: **crag martins** replace house martins in the **mountain gorges**, for example, and you may see the large **alpine swift**, which has a white belly. The **Sardinian warbler** dominates the rough scrubby **hillsides** – the male with a glossy black cap and an obvious red eye. These hillsides are also the home of the **chukar**, a species of partridge similar to the red-legged partridge found in Britain.

Wetlands and coastal lagoons are excellent for bird spotting, especially at spring and autumn migration, although this habitat is hard to find. There's a wide variety of **herons** and **egrets**, as well as smaller waders such as the **avocet** and the **black-winged stilt**, which has ridiculously long pink legs. **Marsh harriers** are common too, drifting over the reedbeds on characteristic raised wings. Scrubby woodland around coastal wetlands is a good place to see migrating smaller birds such as **warblers**, **wagtails** and the like. They usually migrate up the coast, navigating by the stars; a thick mist or heavy cloud will force them to land, and you can sometimes see spectacular "falls" of migrants.

The **mountains** hold some of the most exciting birds in Crete. Smaller birds like **blue rock thrush** and **alpine chough** are pretty common, and there is a good chance of seeing large and dramatic birds of prey. The **buzzards** and smaller **eagles** are confusingly similar, but

there are also **golden eagles** and **vultures**. One very rare species of vulture, the **Lammergeier**, is more common in Crete than anywhere else in Europe and you may be lucky and see it soaring above the Lasíthi or Omalós plateaux. It's a huge bird, with a wingspan of nearly 3m, and with narrower wings and a longer wedge-shaped tail than the other vulture you are likely to see, the **Griffon vulture**.

MAMMALS

Cretan mammals are elusive, generally nocturnal, and very hard to see. Islands tend to have less species than the mainland, because mammals can't swim or fly to get there, and in this Crete is no exception, with about half the species that you could expect to see on mainland Greece. Even such common animals as red squirrel and fox have never made it across the water, nor will you find large exciting mammals like wolves or lynxes in the mountains, as you might (although very rarely) on the mainland.

However, there are some compensations. Islands often have their own endemic species, and the one in Crete is the **Cretan spiny mouse**, which is found nowhere else. So if you happen to be on a rocky hillside at dusk and you see a largish mouse with very big ears and a spiny back fossicking around – then you might have seen it! The other compensation in Crete is the ancestral **wild goat** or *Kri-Kri*, a small population still exists in the White Mountains around the Samarian gorge, and also on some offshore islands – but you'll be very lucky if you see one outside the zoos. Apart from those, Crete has quite a few **bat** species, as well as **weasels**, **badgers**, **hares** and **beech martens**.

REPTILES AND AMPHIBIANS

The hot, rocky terrain of Crete suits reptiles well, with plenty of sun to bask in and plenty of rocks to hide under, but the island's isolation has severely restricted the number of species occurring: less than a third of those that are found on the mainland. Identification is therefore rather easy. If you sit and watch a dry stone wall almost anywhere you're bound to see the small local wall lizard, **Erhard's wall lizard**. A rustle in the rocks by the side of the road might be an **ocellated skink** – a bit like a lizard, but with a thicker body and a stubbier neck. In the bushes of the *maquis* and *phrígana* you may see the **Balkan green lizard**, a truly splendid bright green animal up to 50cm long, most of which is tail; usually seen as it runs like the clappers on its hind legs from one bush to another!

At night, **geckoes** replace the lizards. Geckoes are small (less than 10cm); have big eyes and round adhesive pads on their toes which enable them to walk upside down on the ceiling. Sometimes they come into houses – in which case welcome them, for they will keep down the mosquitos and other biting insects. Crete has three out of four European species. The island is also one of only a handful of places where the **chameleon** occurs in Europe, although it is nowhere common. It lives in bushes and low trees, and hunts by day; colour is greenish but variable, for obvious reasons.

Tortoises, sadly, don't occur in Crete, but the stripe-necked **terrapin** does. Look out for these in any freshwater habitat – Lake Kóurnas, for example, or even in the cistern at the Zákros palace. There are also **sea turtles** in the Med: you might be lucky and see one while you're swimming or on a boat, since they sometimes bask on the surface of the water. The one you're most likely to see is the **loggerhead turtle**, which can grow up to 1m long. Crete has important breeding populations on beaches to the west of Haniá, around Mátala and the largest (over 350 nests) at Réthimnon, but tourism and the development associated with it are threatening their future. Each year, many turtles are injured by motorboats, their nests are destroyed by bikes ridden on the beaches, and the newly hatched young die entangled in deckchairs and umbrellas left out at night on the sand. The turtles are easily frightened by noise and lights, too, which makes them uneasy cohabitants with freelance campers and discos.

The Greek government has passed laws designed to protect the loggerheads and the Sea Turtle Protection Society of Greece now operates an ambitious conservation programme but, in addition to the thoughtlessness of visitors, local economic interests tend to prefer a beach full of bodies to a sea full of turtles.

The final group of reptiles are the snakes, represented by four species, only one of which is poisonous – the **cat snake**: even this is back fanged and therefore extremely unlikely to be able to bite anything as big as a human. So you can relax a bit when strolling round the hillsides – though most snakes are very timid and easily frightened anyway. One species worth looking out for is the beautiful **leopard snake**, which is grey with red blotches edged in black. It's fond of basking on the sides of roads and paths.

Only three species of amphibian occur in Crete. The **green toad** is smaller than the common toad, with an obvious marbled green and grey back. The **marsh frog** is a large frog, greenish but variable in colour, and very noisy in spring. And **tree frogs** are small, live in trees, and call very loudly at night. They have a stripe down the flank, and vary in colour from bright green to golden brown, depending on where they are sitting – they can change colour like a chameleon.

INSECTS

Insects are a much-neglected group of animals, which is a shame because many of them are beautiful, most lead fascinating lives, and they are numerous and easy to observe. You need to adjust your eyes to their scale to see them best: sit down for half an hour in the countryside by a bit of grazed turf, a patch of long grass, or a shrubby bush, and think small. You'll be surprised at the variety of shapes and colours of insects that will slowly come into focus.

There are around a million different species of insects in the world, and even in Crete there are probably a few hundred which have yet to be scientifically described or labelled. About a third of all insect species are **beetles**, and these are very obvious wherever you go. You might see one of the **dung beetles** rolling a ball of dung along a path like the mythological Sisyphus, and I watched a **rhinoceros-horned beetle** digging a hole in a Cretan sand dune for hours – every time the hole was complete it collapsed, and the beetle had to start all over again.

If you have time to look closely at bushes and small trees, you might be rewarded with a **stick insect** or a **praying mantis**, creatures that are rarely seen because of their excellent camouflage.

The **grasshopper** and **cricket** family are well represented, and most patches of grass will hold a few. Grasshoppers produce their chirping noise by rubbing a wing against a leg, but crickets do it by rubbing both wings

318/C O N T E X T S

together. **Cicadas**, which most people think of as a night-calling grasshopper, aren't actually related at all – they're more of a large leaf hopper. Their continuous whirring call is one of the characteristic sounds of the Mediterranean night, and is produced by the rapid vibration of two cavities, called tymbals, on either side of the body.

Perhaps the most obvious insects are the **butterflies**, because they're large, brightly coloured, and fly by day. Any time from spring through most of summer is good for butterflies, and there's a second flight of adults of many species in the autumn. Dramatic varieties in Crete include two species of **swallowtail**, easily told by their large size, yellow and black colouring, and long spurs at the back of the hind wings. **Cleopatras** are large, brilliant yellow butterflies, related to the brimstone of northern Europe, but bigger and more colourful. Look out for **green hairstreaks** – a small green jewel of a butterfly that is particularly attracted to the flowers of the asphodel, a widespread plant of overgrazed pastures and hillsides. One final species typical of Crete is the **southern festoon** – an unusual butterfly with tropical colours, covered in yellow, red and black zigzags. It flies in the spring, its caterpillars feeding on *Aristolochia* (birthwort) plants.

SITES

You don't need to go that far to see Cretan wildlife – even in Iráklion, patches of wasteland hold interesting and colourful flowers, and nearby Knossós is good for flowers, insects and reptiles. In general, though, people and wildlife don't go together too well, so it's best to get away from the towns and into the villages.

The places described in the following pages are a very personal selection. I've mostly been to them in spring; but in general, a good site is a good site at any time of the year, except in high summer when everything is burnt out anyway. It's also usually true that a good flower site will yield plenty of other wildlife, and vice versa: a wide variety of plants leads to a wide variety of insects, which in turn implies that birds and reptiles will be numerous. So you can often use a blaze of plants as an indicator for a spot that would be worth exploring.

One possible exception to this is birds. Birds are mobile and fickle, often choosing to congregate in unprepossessing places such as wind-

swept estuaries or smelly sewage farms. Birds adapt well to small-scale agriculture, too, even though the native plants may have been outcompeted by olives, artichokes or melons.

Any information on alternative or better sites would be more than welcome.

LASÍTHI

The **eastern end** of Crete is the driest part, and also the part where spring comes first. So it would be good to base yourself here if you were planning a trip **early in the year**, say February. The extreme eastern coast is dry and rocky, although Vái boasts a much-photographed grove of the Cretan date palm – one of only two native European palm species. Further west, the scenery is dominated by the Dhíkti mountains and the big bay of Áyios Nikólaos: even close to the development here, some good sites for flowers and birds survive.

The nearest of these is **Láto**, overlooking plains of olives and fruit trees that run down to the sea. It's a mass of colour with flowers in the spring, and, in common with other ancient sites, its old walls and ruins are a perfect habitat for lizards. **Mália**, similarly, has good flowers in spring and early summer, and the added advantage of being close to seacliffs where you can find many of the typical Mediterranean seashore flowers. Between the ancient site and the shore are the remains of a marsh, which is likely to hold interesting birds including herons, harriers and migrating small warblers. **Gourniá** is also worth a trip for its flowers: they're particularly good at all of these sites because goats are excluded. Look for anemones in the spring. Although there's only one spring species, *Anemone coronaria*, it comes in a bewildering range of colours from white to purple and scarlet. An asiatic buttercup species which grows round here (*Ranunculus asiaticus*, a common plant over much of Crete) is quite unlike the buttercups of northern Europe, being much larger and with colours including white, pink and yellow. Around the walls of Gourniá you'll also find a large yellow and white daisy, *Chrysanthemum coronarium*, a species which is attractive to butterflies.

Just north of Áyios Nikólaos is the island of **Spinalónga**, and nearby, the disused saltpans at **Eloúnda**. The island is good for flowers, and the saltpans are always worth checking out for birds, especially during spring and autumn migration time.

Later in the year, the uplands of **Mount Dhíkti** and the **Lasíthi plateau** come into their own. The plateau is at 850m, so its spring flowers come later than those in the lowlands – April or early May would be a good time, with the summer flowers going on into June. The plateau itself is well cultivated, but the areas round the edge are rich in flowers including many orchids. Try exploring a bit off the well-worn track from Psihró to the Dhiktean Cave. Here you may find two varieties in particular: *Ophrys tenthredinifera*, one of the largest and most dramatic of the insect-imitating orchids, with beautiful pink sepals and a brown lower lip fringed with pale yellow; and the butterfly orchid *Orchis papilionacea*, which has a compact spike of pink florets, each with a large lip spotted and streaked with darker pink. Keep your eyes on the skies, too, since you are close to the mountains: sightings of eagles and vultures, including Lammergeiers, are always possible.

Mount Dhíkti goes up to over 2000m, and boasts most of the dramatic flowers of the Cretan mountains. Look for early flowering crocus species on the edge of the melting snowfields in April and May, and maybe you'll find cyclamens and paeonies under the mountain woodland as well. Rocky gullies amongst the mountains are rich in specially adapted plants called chasmophytes, including endemic Cretan species.

IRÁKLION

Although Iráklion is the only one of the four Cretan provinces that doesn't have a major mountain range, it includes the foothills of both the Dhíkti range to the east and the Psilorítis massif in the west.

The ancient Minoan site of **Festós** is an excellent start. The ruins are only average for wildlife, but the hills around are excellent for flowers, insects, and reptiles, and the river running through Ayía Triádha is always worth checking out for birds. The site of Festós itself is also a good place to look for bird migration; since it's high up, you stand a good chance of seeing migrating birds of prey coming over the plain and up into the hills.

If you walk from the car park heading north, you find yourself on a lovely hillside. There are scrubby bushes of rockroses – *Cistus* species – and round these a wonderful display of anemones, irises, orchids and the whole panoply of Cretan spring flowers. *Anemone heldreichii*, a delicate blue and white variety, is one of Crete's 130 or so endemic species. Another plant with a very restricted distribution is *Ophrys cretica*, one of the insect-imitating orchids with distinctive white markings on its maroon lip. In spring, *Orchis italica* is the most obvious orchid – tall shaggy spikes of small pink florets, each looking like a small man with a cap. I say "man" advisedly, as you will realize if you look closely at the plant! One final flower to look out for is familiar as an annual garden flower, love-in-a-mist *Nigella arvensis*. With blooms varying from deep blue to pale pink, it's best known for its extraordinary inflated fruit, surrounded by a crown of deeply dissected bracts.

There are butterflies here too, attracted by the nectar. Scarce swallowtail was much in evidence when I was there, and many others. Keep your eyes open, too, for Balkan green lizards in the bushes. Further on towards Ayía Triádha the river holds passage migrants including herons, terns and sandpipers – and the bushes are often full of migrating passerines, hotfoot, from Africa. As always, a careful scrutiny of bushes and grasses will produce a horde of beetles, spiders and other invertebrates – with a chance of a praying mantis to brighten things up.

RÉTHIMNON

The two areas selected in this province are both on the south coast. That doesn't mean that you should ignore the rest: three other extremely promising sites are the Nídha plateau above Anóyia, the foothills of Mount Kédhros, above Spíli, and the Amári valley.

Ayía Galíni, for all its summer crowds, is a great spot in spring, with some excellent walks on the headlands and hills roundabout, small scale hayfields and olive groves, and a river bed with some marshy areas. In other words, a really good range of the typical Cretan lowland habitats, and all within easy walking distance.

The river flows into the east of the village. On the far side is a range of hills, worth exploring for spring flowers, and the caves and cliffs overlooking the river have breeding colonies of lesser kestrels and Alpine swifts. The small reedbeds and marshy areas around the river have warblers and nightingales, too, and there are hoopoes in the olive groves.

A series of tracks lead away to the north and along the cliffs to the west. Any of these go through typical *phrígana* habitat, in which are scattered small meadows with wild gladioli and tassel hyacinths. The latter species is related to the grape hyacinth which is often used in boring clumps by British gardeners, but is far more attractive growing wild. Look for Jerusalem sage *Phlomis fruticosa*, a downy shrub whose golden flowers are attractive to bees. Another plant that grows around here (and many other places in Crete) is the unmistakable giant fennel, a huge plant over 2m tall. Its scientific name is *Ferula communis*, which implies to me that it was once used as a walking stick, and, seeing the size of the stems, you can see why. There are orchids growing on the hillsides, including a Cretan speciality that rejoices in the name of *Ophrys fuciflora maxima*; a large orchid, it has a "face" on its lower lip that looks exactly like a Minoan bull. But maybe I have an overactive imagination.

Further along the coast to the west, **Moní Préveli** has a similar range of habitats and less people. Again, there is a river valley that repays exploration for migratory birds, open hillsides with all the flowers and aromatic herbs, and some rugged coastal scenery. If you see a small scrub warbler around here with a black cap and throat, a red eye, and a white "moustache" then you may have seen Ruppell's warbler, probably the rarest warbler in Europe. The whole coastline from Préveli to Ayía Rouméli, some 75km to the west, is wild and rugged, punctuated by gorges, and a good place to look for large eagles and vultures.

HANIÁ

The western end of Crete contains some of the wildest and least developed scenery in the whole of the Med. I've chosen Yeoryióupolis on the north coast and the famous Samarian gorge to describe in detail — but there are lots of other opportunities.

Yeoryióupolis has a wide range of habitats within easy reach — a marsh, a river with reedbeds, dry hillsides along the coast to the north, Crete's only freshwater lake — and an excellent beach as well. Between the main road and the sea are low sand dunes, often a good place for colourful flowers like Virginia

stocks, sea stocks, and the yellow horned poppy. Close to the east of the village is a marshy area, with birds like reed (and other) warblers, and marsh harriers floating overhead. There's a very pleasant walk along the River Almirós, branching up through olive groves and scrubby slopes to the hilltop village above. Here you'll find numerous small birds, attracted by unusually dense and lush woodland. Inland a bit is the small lake at **Koúrnas**; a solitary Squacco heron was the only bird I saw when I was there, but a paddle round the lake revealed loads of stripe-necked terrapins poking their heads out of the water.

The **Samarian gorge** is rightly famous for wildlife as well as scenery, but remember that you'll find very similar flora and fauna at Imbrós and the other less-known ravines. The best flowers and other wildlife all come in the higher reaches, where you have the marvellous combination of rocky cliffs coming down into upland woods.

Still better, if you have time, is to take more than a day over this trip and spend some time on the **Omalós plateau** before heading down. This is especially rewarding later in the year, when the plateau and the slopes around it will have spring and summer flowers long after all is burnt out on the coast. The plateau is renowned for its mountain flowers, including the very variable *Tulipa saxatilis*, a small pink or purple tulip endemic to Crete. Other endemic species found here include Cretan dittany *Origanum dictamnus*, a low shrub with furry rounded leaves and pink flowers, regarded by locals as a medical panacea (you may be offered it as a tea) and *Daphne sericea*, an evergreen shrub, with very unusual two-tone flowers of pink and yellow. There are also rare birds and mammals — watch the sky for golden eagles, Griffon vultures, Lammergeiers and falcons, and the distant cliffs and surrounding mountains for wild goats.

The start of the gorge takes you down the wooden staircase through light woodland. There are rock thrushes on the cliffs — the male has a striking orange breast, blue head and white rump. Rock plants like *Aubretia* grow on the cliffs, along with *Linum arboreum*, a low perennial flax with brilliant yellow flowers. Two endemic cliff plants to watch for are the Cretan rock lettuce *Petromarula pinnata*, which looks nothing like a lettuce and isn't even related, with long spikes of deep blue flowers, and *Ebenus cretica*, a bushy pea with grey foliage and pink flowers.

Under the trees at the sides of the paths are orchids, including the handsome yellow *Orchis provincialis*, with a tight flowerhead of spiked yellow florets. Cyclamens and anemones grow here, and you may find a fritillary *Fritillaria messanensis*, with a drooping purple and green bell-shaped flower. Perhaps the most stunning flower is a white paeony with huge, yellow-centred flowers: called *Paeoni clusii*, it

grows in profusion around a ruined chapel about 3km down the gorge. There are more lovely flower meadows round the village of Samariá, about halfway down, but as you drop lower the cliffs tower above you until it is hard to see anything else, and once you are through the famous Iron gates at the end, the walk is less interesting in every sense. Around the base of the cliffs at the bottom of the gorge are colonies of crag martins — a drab-looking bird, but a dramatic flier.

Pete Raine

BOOKS

Where separate editions exist in the UK and USA, publishers are detailed below in the form "British publisher/American publisher", unless the publisher is the same in both countries. Where books are published in one country only, this follows the publisher's name. O/p signifies an out-of-print – but still highly recommended – book. University Press is abbreviated as UP.

Many of the more popular titles below are widely available in Crete, but local editions tend to be shabby, and imported ones expensive. The more specialist titles might be more easily found at a dedicated travel **bookstore** (some are included under *Map Outlets* on p.30) or a Greek-interest bookshop: in London try the *Hellenic Book Service* (91 Fortess Rd, London NW5 1AG; ☎0171/267 9499) or *Zeno's Greek Bookshop* (6 Denmark St, London WC2H 8LP; ☎0171/836 2522).

ARCHEOLOGY AND ANCIENT HISTORY

There is a vast body of literature on ancient Crete, especially on the Minoans, but a lot of it is very heavy going. Below are some of the more widely available, accessible and useful books. Other names to look out for include **Nikolaos Platon** and **Stylianos Alexiou**, whose books you may find available in local translations. There are also local guide booklets on all the major museums and sites, often with nice pictures, but usually very poor text.

Gerald Cadogan *Palaces of Minoan Crete* (Routledge). Complete guide to all the major sites, with much more history and general information than the name implies.

John Chadwick *Linear B and related scripts* (British Museum Publications/University of California Press). A short version of the decipherment of Linear B by one of those closely responsible – the author of other heavy tomes.

Leonard Cottrell *The Bull of Minos* (Bell & Hyman, o/p/Aeonian Press/Efstathiadis, Athens). Breathless and somewhat dated account of the discoveries of Schliemann and Evans; easy reading.

Costis Davaras *Guide to Cretan Antiquities* (Noyes Press/Eptalofolos, Athens). A fascinating guide by the distinguished archeologist and director of the Áyios Nikólaos museum to the antiquities of Crete (ancient through to the Turkish era). Cross-referenced in dictionary form it has authoritative articles on all the major sites as well as subjects as diverse as Minoan razors and toilet articles, the disappearance of Cretan forests and the career of Venizélos.

Arthur Evans *The Palace of Minos* (o/p). The seminal work, still worth a look if you can find it in a library.

Reynold Higgins *Minoan and Mycenaean Art* (Thames & Hudson/OUP, o/p). Solid introduction to the subject with plenty of illustrations.

J. D. S. Pendlebury *The Archaeology of Crete* (Methuen, o/p/Norton, o/p). Still the most comprehensive handbook, detailing virtually every archeological site on the island. His *Handbook to the Palace of Minos* is still an excellent guide to the Knossós site by someone who – as curator after Evans's retirement – knew it inside out. A local edition has been reprinted in Crete.

Nikos Psilakis *Monasteries and Byzantine Memories of Crete* (locally published). Self-explanatory title: readable and well-illustrated.

Ian F. Sanders *Roman Crete* (Aris & Phillips, UK). Very dry, and hard to come by, but a total record of all Roman remains on Crete.

Peter Warren *The Aegean Civilizations* (Phaidon, o/p/Peter Bedrick, o/p). Illustrated introduction by one of the leading modern experts, a coffee-table book, but informative and easy on the eye. Warren's other publications tend to be technical.

R. F. Willetts *The Civilization of Ancient Crete* (Batsford, o/p/Hakkert), *Cretan Cults and Festivals* (Greenwood Press), *Aristocratic*

Society in Ancient Crete (RKP/Greenwood Press). Rather heavy, scholarly accounts of the social structure of ancient Crete. His *Everyday Life in Ancient Crete* (Batsford/Hakkert) is a more accessible read for the layman.

H. G. Wunderlich *The Secret of Crete* (Efstadhiadis, Athens – widely sold on Crete). The secret is that the palaces were really elaborate tombs or necropoli. Sensationalist nonsense.

TRAVEL AND GENERAL

By contast with the proliferation of ancient history, there is no book in English devoted to modern Cretan history: good general accounts are included in Hopkins's and Smith's books on the island, otherwise you're forced to wade through Greek or Ottoman history, selecting the relevant portions.

Robin Bryant *Crete* (Faber & Faber, UK). Thematic interweaving of the author's observations during his stay on Crete with aspects of the island's history, folklore and festivals, immediately prior to the arrival of package tourism.

Richard Clogg *A Concise History of Greece* (Cambridge UP). More rigorously historical account of Greek history from its emergence from Ottoman rule to the present day, covering the wider aspects of Crete's struggle for independence and union with Greece.

David MacNeill Doren *Winds of Crete* (John Murray UK, o/p; Efstathiadis, Athens). An American and his Swedish wife find enlightenment on Crete – between times, quite an amusing and well-observed travelogue documenting many of the island's customs and curiosities in addition to some hair-raising brushes with Cretan physicians.

Adam Hopkins *Crete, its Past, Present and People* (Faber & Faber). Excellent general introduction to Cretan history and society. Recommended.

Edward Lear *The Cretan Journal* (Denise Harvey, Athens). Diary of Lear's trip to Crete in 1864, illustrated with his sketches and watercolours. He didn't enjoy himself much.

Henry Miller *The Colossus of Maroussi* (Minerva/New Directions). Miller's idiosyncratic account of his travels in Greece on the eve of World War II includes a trip to Crete

where diarrhoea, biting flies and Festós palace all get bit-parts in the epic.

John Julius Norwich *Byzantium: the Early Centuries* and *Byzantium: the Apogee* (both Penguin/Knopf). The first two volumes of Norwich's history of the Byzantine Empire are terrific narrative accounts, and much can be gleaned from them about Crete in this period.

Robert Pashley *Travels in Crete* (John Murray, o/p). The original nineteenth-century British traveller, full of interesting anecdotes and outrageous attitude. Try the library.

James Pettifer *The Greeks: the Land and People since the War* (Penguin, UK). Excellent introduction to contemporary Greece – and its recent past. Pettifer roams the country and charts the state of the nation's politics, food, family life, religion, tourism and all points in between. Only passing reference to Crete, however.

Dilys Powell *The Villa Ariadne* (Hodder & Stoughton, UK/Efstadhiadis, Athens). The story of the British in Crete, from Arthur Evans to Paddy Leigh Fermor, through the villa at Knossós which saw all of them. Good at bringing the excitement of the early archeological work to life, but rather cloying in style.

Pandelis Prevelakis *Tale of a Town* (Doric Publications, Athens). English translation of a native's description of life in Réthimnon.

J. E. Hilary Skinner *Roughing it in Crete* (1868, o/p). Great title for account of another Englishman's adventures, this time with a band of rebels. Interesting on the less glamorous side of the independence struggle, since he spent the whole time searching for food or dodging Turkish patrols.

Michael Llewellyn Smith *The Great Island* (Allen Lane, UK, o/p). Covers much of the same as Hopkins's book, but with more emphasis on folk traditions, and a lengthy analysis of Cretan song.

Capt. T. A. B. Spratt *Travels and Researches in Crete* (Hakkert, US). Another nineteenth-century Briton who caught the Cretan bug whilst surveying the island's coastline, and left behind this account of its natural history, geology and archeology.

Christopher Thorne *Between the Seas* (Sinclair Stevenson). The account of a walk along the length of the island with observations on Cretan country life, past and present.

Jackson Webb *The Last Lemon Grove* (Weidenfeld, UK, o/p). Published in 1977, an account of an American living in the then-remote village of Paleohóra. Wonderfully atmospheric.

FICTION

Níkos Kazantzakís *Zorba the Greek, Freedom and Death* (published in the US as *Captain Mihalis*), *Report to Greco* (all Faber & Faber/ Touchstone; local editions available in Crete). Something by the great Cretan novelist and man of letters is essential reading. Forget the film, *Zorba the Greek* is a wonderful read on Crete which provides the backdrop to the adventures of one of the most irresistable characters of modern fiction. *Freedom and Death* is if anything even better, or try *Report to Greco.*

Ioannis Kondylakis *Patouchas* (Efstathiadis, Athens). The story of a Cretan shepherd on a journey of self-discovery is a wonderfully observed and humorous fictional sketch of Turkish Crete in the last century by a little known Cretan author. Widely available on the island.

Vitzentzos Kornaros *Erotokritos* (tr. Theodore Stefanides; Merlin Press). Beautifully produced English translation of the massive sixteenth-century Cretan epic poem.

Mary Renault *The King Must Die* (Sceptre o/ p/Vintage); *The Bull from the Sea* (Penguin/ Vintage). Stirring accounts of the Theseus legend and Minoan Crete for those who like their history in fictionalized form.

WORLD WAR II

Antony Beevor *Crete: The Battle and the Resistance* (Penguin/Westview Press). Relatively short study of the Battle of Crete, with insights into the characters involved. Beevor looks at recent evidence to conclude that defeat was at least in part due to the need to conceal Allied intelligence successes.

Alan Clark *The Fall of Crete* (NEL, UK/terrible Efstadhiadis edition widely sold on Crete). Racy and sensational – but very readable – military history. Detailed on the battles, and more critical of the command than you might expect from a former British cabinet minister.

W. Stanley Moss *Ill Met by Moonlight* (Buchan & Enright). An account of the capture

of General Kreipe by one of the participants, largely taken from his diaries of the time. Good *Boys' Own* adventure stuff. Moss also translated **Baron von der Heydte**'s *Daedalus returned* (o/p) which gives something of the other side of the story.

George Panayiotakis *The Battle of Crete* (local edition). Pictorial history of the battle and its aftermath using contemporary photos. Available from major bookshops on the island.

George Psychoundákis *The Cretan Runner* (John Murray/Translantic Arts, o/p). Account of the invasion and resistance by a Cretan participant; Psychoundákis was a guide and message-runner for all the leading English-speaking protagonists. Great.

Tony Simpson *The Battle for Crete, 1941* (o/p). A very different way of looking at the subject, putting the campaign into an international context and relying heavily on oral history for details of the combat. Uncompromisingly critical of the command, and far more interesting than straight military history.

I. McD. G. Stewart *Struggle for Crete: a story of lost opportunity* (Oxford UP, o/p). Authoritative detail on the battle from someone who was there. Rather dry, military historian's approach.

Evelyn Waugh *Officers and Gentlemen, Diaries* (both Penguin/Little, Brown). Both include accounts of the battle, and particularly of the horrors of the flight and evacuation.

WILDLIFE

Michael Chinerey *Collins Guide to the Insects of Britain and Western Europe* (Collins, UK). This doesn't specifically include Greece (there's no comprehensive guide to Greek insects) but it gives a good general background and identification to the main families of insects that you're likely to see.

Stephanie Coghlan *Birdwatching in Crete* (Snails Pace Publishing). Slim booklet detailing the best birdwatching sites and what you may see there, with checklists. No pictures for identification, though, so you'll need a guide too.

Anthony Huxley and Taylor *Flowers of Greece* (Hogarth Press). The best book for identifying flowers in Crete.

Christopher Perrins *New Generations Guide to Birds of Britain and Europe* (HarperCollins/

University of Texas Press). An alternative look at bird ecology as well as pure identification.

Peterson, Mountfort and Hollom *Field Guide to the Birds of Britain and Europe* (Collins/Houghton Mifflin). There's no complete guide to Cretan birds; this is probably the best general tome – ageing but excellent.

Paul Whalley *The Mitchell Beazley Pocket Guide to Butterflies* (Mitchell Beazley/published in the US as *Butterflies* by Transatlantic Arts). A useful identification guide.

HIKING GUIDES

Bruce and Naomi Caughey *Crete off the Beaten Track* (Cicerone Press, UK). Details a large number of walks throughout the island; available in many bookstores in major towns.

Marc Dubin *Trekking in Greece* (Lonely Planet). An excellent walkers' guide, expanding on the hikes covered in this book and adding others. Includes day-hikes and longer treks, plus extensive preparatory and background information.

Jonnie Godfrey and Elizabeth Karslake *Landscapes of Eastern/Western Crete* (Sunflower, UK). Full of hiking and touring suggestions which make a useful adjunct to this guide.

FOOD AND DRINK

Miles Lambert-Gócs *The Wines of Greece* (Faber & Faber). Comprehensive survey of the emerging wines of Greece with plenty of fascinating historical detail; a chapter is devoted to Cretan wines.

George Sfikas *Fishes of Greece* (Efstathiadis, Athens). Pictorial guide to all the fish you're likely to encounter in the island's tavernas. Widely available in Crete.

Sofia Souli *The Greek Cookery Book* (Toubi's, Athens). One of the best books to start you cooking Greek food when you get back home. Everything from *tzatzíki* to *kataifi*, including a few Cretan specialities. Profusely illustrated and widely available on the island.

LANGUAGE

So many Cretans have been compelled by poverty and other circumstances to work abroad, especially in the English-speaking world, that you'll find someone who speaks some English in almost any village. Add to that the thousands attending language schools or working in the tourist industry – English is the lingua franca of the north coast – and it's easy to see how so many visitors come back having learnt only half a dozen restaurant words between them. You can certainly get by this way, even in quite out of the way places, but it isn't very satisfying.

Greek is not an easy language for English-speakers, but it is a beautiful one and even a brief acquaintance will give you some idea of the debt western European languages owe to it. More important than that, the willingness and ability to say even a few words will transform your status from that of dumb *tourístas* to the honourable one of *ksénos*, a word which can mean stranger, traveller and guest all rolled into one.

On top of the usual difficulties of learning a new language, Greek presents the added problem of an entirely separate **alphabet**. Despite initial appearances, this is in practice fairly easily mastered; a skill that will help enormously if you are going to get around independently (see the *Alphabet and transliteration* section opposite). In addition, certain combinations of letters have unexpected results. This book's transliteration system should help you make intelligible noises but you have to remember that the correct **stress** (marked in the book with a ´) is absolutely crucial. With the right sounds but the wrong stress people will either fail to understand you, or else understand something quite different from what you intended.

Greek **grammar** is more complicated still: nouns are divided into three genders, all with different case endings in the singular and in the plural, and all adjectives and articles have to agree with these in gender, number and

LANGUAGE-LEARNING MATERIALS

TEACH-YOURSELF GREEK COURSES

Breakthrough Greece (Pan Macmillan; book and 2 cassettes). Excellent, basic teach-yourself course – completely outclasses the competition.

Greek Language and People (BBC Publications, UK; book and cassette available). More limited in scope but good for acquiring the essentials, and the confidence to try them.

Anne Farmakides A Manual of Modern Greek (Yale/McGill; 3 vols). If you have the discipline and motivation, this is one of the best for learning proper, grammatical Greek; indeed, mastery of just the first volume will get you a long way.

PHRASEBOOKS

The Rough Guide to Greek (Rough Guides). Practical and easy-to-use, the *Rough Guide*

phrase-books allow you to speak the way you would in on your own language. Feature boxes fill you in on dos and don'ts and cultural know-how.

DICTIONARIES

The Oxford Dictionary of Modern Greek (Oxford UP). A bit bulky but generally considered the best Greek–English, English–Greek dictionary.

Collins Pocket Greek Dictionary (Harper Collins). Very nearly as complete as the Oxford and probably better value for the money.

Oxford Learner's Dictionary (Oxford UP). If you're planning a prolonged stay, this pricey two-volume set is unbeatable for usage and vocabulary. There's also a more portable one-volume *Learner's Pocket Dictionary*.

case. (All adjectives are arbitrarily cited in the neuter form in the following lists.) Verbs are even worse. To begin with at least, the best thing is simply to say what you know the way you know it, and never mind the niceties. "Eat meat hungry" should get a result, however grammatically incorrect. If you worry about your mistakes, you'll never say anything.

THE GREEK ALPHABET: TRANSLITERATION

Set out below is the Greek alphabet, the system of transliteration used in this book, and a brief aid to pronunciation.

Greek	Transliteration	Pronounced
Α, α	a	a as in father
Β, β	v	v as in vet
Γ, γ	y/g	y as in yes when before an e or i; when before consonants or a, o or ou it's a breathy, throaty g as in gap.
Δ, δ	dh	th as in then
Ε, ε	e	e as in get
Ζ, ζ	z	z sound
Η, η	i	ee sound as in feet
Θ, θ	th	th as in theme
Ι, ι	i	i as in bit
Κ, κ	k	k sound
Λ, λ	l	l sound
Μ, μ	m	m sound
Ν, ν	n	n sound
Ξ, ξ	ks	ks sound
Ο, ο	o	o as in toad
Π, π	p	p sound
Ρ, ϱ	r	rolled r sound
Σ, σ, ς	s	s sound
Τ, τ	t	t sound
Χ, υ	i	ee, indistinguishable from η
Φ, φ	f	f sound
Χ, χ	h	harsh h sound, like ch in loch
Ψ, ψ	ps	ps as in lips
Ω, ω	o	o as in toad, indistinguishable from o

Combinations and dipthongs

ΑΙ, αι	e	e as in get
ΑΥ, αυ	av/af	av or af depending on following consonant
ΕΙ, ει	i	ee, exactly like η
ΟΙ, οι	i	ee, identical again
ΕΥ, ευ	ev/ef	ev or ef, depending on following consonant
ΟΥ, ου	ou	ou as in tourist
ΓΓ, γγ	ng	ng as in angie
ΓΚ, γκ	g/ng	g as in goat at the beginning of a word; ng in the middle
ΜΠ, μπ	b	b at the beginning of a word; mb in the middle
ΝΤ, ντ	d/nd	d at the beginning of a word; nd in the middle
ΤΣ, τσ	ts	ts as in hits
ΣΙ, σι	sh	sh as in shame
ΤΖ, τζ	ts	j as in jam

Note: An umlaut on a letter indicates that the two vowels are pronounced separately, for example Αόös is Ah-oh-s, rather than A-ooos.

GREEK WORDS AND PHRASES

Essentials

Yes	*Néh*	Yesterday	*Khthés*	Big	*Megálo*
Certainly	*Málista*	Now	*Tóra*	Small	*Mikró*
No	*Óhi*	Later	*Argótera*	More	*Perisótero*
Please	*Parakaló*	Open	*Aniktó*	Less	*Ligótero*
Okay, agreed	*Endáksi*	Closed	*Klistó*	A little	*Lígo*
Thank you	*Efharistó (polí)*	Day	*Méra*	A lot	*Polí*
(very much)		Night	*Níkhta*	Cheap	*Ftinó*
I (don't)	*(Dhen) Katalavéno*	In the morning	*To proí*	Expensive	*Akrivó*
understand		In the afternoon	*To apóyevma*	Hot	*Zestó*
Excuse me, do	*Parakaló, mípos*	In the evening	*To vrádhi*	Cold	*Krío*
you speak	*miláteh angliká?*	Here	*Edhó*	With	*Mazí*
English?		There	*Ekí*	Without	*Horís*
Sorry/excuse	*Signómi*	This one	*Aftó*	Quickly	*Grígora*
me		That one	*Ekíno*	Slowly	*Sigá*
Today	*Símera*	Good	*Kaló*	Mr/Mrs	*Kírios/Kiría*
Tomorrow	*Ávrio*	Bad	*Kakó*	Miss	*Dhespinís*

Other Needs

To eat/drink	*Trógo/Píno*	Stamps	*Gramatósima*	Toilet	*Toualéta*
Bakery	*Foúrnos, psomádhiko*	Petrol station	*Venzinádhiko*	Police	*Astinomía*
Pharmacy	*Farmakío*	Bank	*Trápeza*	Doctor	*Iatrós*
Post office	*Tahidhromío*	Money	*Leftá/Hrímata*	Hospital	*Nosokomío*

Requests and Questions

To ask a question, it's simplest to start with *parakaló*, then name the thing you want in an interrogative tone.

Where is the bakery?	*Parakaló, o foúrnos?*	How many?	*Póssi or pósses?*
Can you show me the road to . . . ?	*Parakaló, o dhrómos ya . . ?*	How much?	*Póso?*
		When?	*Póteh?*
We'd like a room for two	*Parakaló, éna dhomátio ya dhío átoma?*	Why?	*Yatí?*
		At what time . . . ?	*Ti óra . . . ?*
May I have a kilo of oranges?	*Parakaló, éna kiló portokália?*	What is/Which is . . . ?	*Ti íneh/pió íneh..?*
		How much (does it cost)?	*Póso káni?*
Where?	*Pou?*	What time does it open?	*Tí óra aníyi?*
How?	*Pos?*	What time does it close?	*Tí óra klíni?*

Talking to People

Greek makes the distinction between the informal (*esí*) and formal (*esís*) second person, as French does with *tu* and *vous*. Young people, older people and country people nearly always use *esí* even with total strangers. In any event, no one will be too bothered if you get it wrong. By far the most common greeting, on meeting and parting, is *yá sou/yá sas* – literally "health to you".

Hello	*Hérete*	My name is . . .	*Meh léneh . . .*
Good morning	*Kalí méra*	Speak slower, please	*Parakaló, miláte pió sigá*
Good evening	*Kalí spéra*	How do you say it in Greek?	*Pos léyeteh sta Eliniká?*
Good night	*Kalí níkhta*		
Goodbye	*Adhío*	I don't know	*Dhen kséro*
How are you?	*Ti kánis/Ti káneteh?*	See you tomorrow	*Tha se dho ávrio*
I'm fine	*Kalá ímeh*	See you soon	*Kalí andhámosi*
And you?	*Keh esís?*	Let's go	*Pámeh*
What's your name?	*Pos se léneh?*	Please help me	*Parakaló, na me voithísteh*

Greek's Greek

There are numerous words and phrases which you will hear constantly, even if you rarely have the chance to use them. These are a few of the most common.

Éla!	Come (literally) but also Speak to me! You don't say! etc.	*Po-po-po!*	Expression of dismay or concern, like French "O la la!"
Orísteh?	What can I do for you?	*Pedhí mou*	My boy/girl, sonny, friend, etc.
Bros!	Standard phone response	*Maláka(s)*	Literally "wanker", but often used (don't try it!) as an infor-
Ti néa?	What's new?		mal address.
Ti yíneteh?	What's going on (here)?		
Étsi k'étsi	So-so	*Sigá sigá*	Take your time, slow down
Ópa!	Whoops! Watch it!	*Kaló taxídhi*	Bon voyage

Accommodation

Hotel	*Ksenodhohío*	Cold water	*krío neró*
A room . . .	*Éna dhomátio . . .*	Can I see it?	*Boró na to dho?*
for one/two/three people	*ya éna/dhío/tría átoma*	Can we camp here?	*Boróume na váloumeh ti*
for one/two/three nights	*ya mía/dhío/trís vradhiés*		*skiní edhó?*
with a double bed	*meh megálo kreváti*	Campsite	*Kamping/Kataskínosi*
with a shower	*meh doús*	Tent	*Skiní*
hot water	*zestó neró*	Youth hostel	*Ksenodhohío neótitos*

On the Move

Aeroplane	*Aeropláno*	Where are you going?	*Pou pas?*
Bus	*Leoforío*	I'm going to . . .	*Páo sto . . .*
Car	*Aftokínito*	I want to get off at . . .	*Thélo na katévo sto . . .*
Motorbike, moped	*Mihanáki, papáki*	The road to . . .	*O dhrómos ya . . .*
Taxi	*Taksí*	Near	*Kondá*
Ship	*Plío/Vapóri/Karávi*	Far	*Makriá*
Bicycle	*Podhílato*	Left	*Aristerá*
Hitching	*Otostóp*	Right	*Dheksiá*
On foot	*Meh ta pódhia*	Straight ahead	*Katefthía*
Trail	*Monopáti*	A ticket to . . .	*Éna isistírio ya . . .*
Bus station	*Praktorío leoforíon*	A return ticket	*Éna isistírio me epistrofí*
Bus stop	*Stási*	Beach	*Paralía*
Harbour	*Limáni*	Cave	*Spiliá*
What time does it leave?	*Ti óra févyi?*	Centre (of town)	*Kéndro*
What time does it arrive?	*Ti óra ftháni?*	Church	*Eklissía*
How many kilometres?	*Pósa hiliómetra?*	Sea	*Thálassa*
How many hours?	*Pósses óres?*	Village	*Horió*

Numbers

1	*énos éna/mía*	12	*dhódheka*	90	*enenínda*
2	*dhío*	13	*dhekatrís*	100	*ekató*
3	*trís/tría*	14	*dhekatésseres*	150	*ekatón penínda*
4	*tésseres/téssera*	20	*íkosi*	200	*dhiakóssies/ia*
5	*pénde*	21	*íkosi éna*	500	*pendakóssies/ia*
6	*éksi*	30	*triánda*	1000	*hílies/ia*
7	*eftá*	40	*saránda*	2000	*dhío hiliádhes*
8	*okhtó*	50	*penínda*	1,000,000	*éna ekatomírio*
9	*enyá*	60	*eksínda*	first	*próto*
10	*dhéka*	70	*evdhomínda*	second	*dhéftero*
11	*éndheka*	80	*ogdhónda*	third	*tríto*

The time and days of the week

Sunday	*Kiriakí*	Saturday	*Sávato*	Five past seven	*Eftá keh pénde*
Monday	*Dheftéra*	What time is it?	*Ti óra íneh?*	Half past eleven	*Éndheka keh misí*
Tuesday	*Tríti*	One/two/three	*Mía/dhío/trís*	Half-hour	*Misí óra*
Wednesday	*Tetárti*	o'clock	*óra/óres*	Quarter-hour	*Éna tétarto*
Thursday	*Pémpti*	Twenty to four	*Tésseres pará*		
Friday	*Paraskeví*		*íkosi*		

GREEK TERMS AND ACRONYMS: A GLOSSARY

ACROPOLIS Ancient, fortified hilltop.

AGORA Market and meeting place of an ancient city.

AMPHORA Tall, narrow-necked jar for oil or wine.

ÁNO Upper; as in upper town or village – Áno Zákros.

APSE Curved recess at the altar end of a church.

ARCHAIC PERIOD Late Iron Age from around 750 BC to the start of the Classical period in the fifth century BC.

ARSENALI Arsenals – a term used rather loosely for many Venetian defensive and harbour works.

ATRIUM Central altar-court of a Roman house.

ÁYIOS/AYÍA/ÁYII Saint or holy (m/f/pl), common place name prefix (abbrev. Ag. or Ay.): Áyios Nikólaos, St. Nicholas; Ayía Triádha, Holy Trinity.

BASILICA Colonnaded "hall-type" church.

BYZANTINE EMPIRE Created by the division of the Roman Empire in 395 AD, this was the eastern half, ruled from Byzantium or Constantinople (modern Istanbul). On Crete Byzantine churches of the fifth to the twelfth century are almost commonplace, and Byzantine art flourished again after the fall of Constantinople in 1453, under Venetian rule, when many artists and scholars fled to the island.

CENTRAL COURT Paved area at the heart of a Minoan palace.

CLASSICAL PERIOD Essentially from the end of the Persian Wars in the fifth century BC to the unification of Greece under Philip II of Macedon (338 BC).

DHIMARHÍO Town hall (modern usage).

DHOMÁTIA Rooms for rent in private houses.

DORIAN Civilization which around 1100 BC overran the Mycenaeans from the north and became their successors throughout much of southern Greece, including Crete.

EPARHÍA Greek Orthodox diocese, also the smallest subdivision of a modern province.

ETEO-CRETAN Literally true Cretan, the Eteo-Cretans are believed to have been remnants of the Minoan people who kept a degree of their language and culture alive in isolated centres in eastern Crete as late as the third century BC.

GEOMETRIC PERIOD Post-Mycenaean Iron Age named for the style of its pottery: beginnings are in the early eleventh century BC with the arrival of Dorian peoples – by the eighth, with the development of representational styles, it becomes known as the Archaic period.

HELLENISTIC PERIOD The last and most unified Greek Empire, created by Philip II and Alexander the Great in the fourth century BC, finally collapsing with the fall of Corinth to the Romans in 146 BC.

HÓRA Main town of a region; literally it means "the place".

IKONOSTÁSI Screen between the nave of a church and the altar, often covered in icons.

JANISSARY Member of the Turkish Imperial Guard: in Crete under the Turks a much-feared mercenary force, often forcibly recruited from the local population.

KAFENIO Coffeehouse/café: in a small village the centre of communal life and probably the bus stop, too.

KAÍKI A caique, or medium-sized boat, traditionally wooden. Now used for just about any coast-hopping or excursion boat.

KÁMBOS Fertile agricultural plateau, usually near a river mouth.

KAPETÁNIOS Widely used term of honour for a man of local power – originally for guerrilla leaders who earned the title through acts of particular bravado.

KÁSTRO Medieval castle or any fortified hill.

KÁTO Lower; as in Káto Zákros.

KERNOS Ancient cult vessel or altar with a number of receptacles for offerings.

KRATER Large, two-handled wine bowl.

LARNAKES Minoan clay coffins.

LUSTRAL BASIN A small sunken chamber in Minoan palaces reached by steps: perhaps actually some kind of bath but more likely for purely ritual purification.

MEGARON Principal hall of a Mycenaean palace.

MELTÉMI North wind that blows across the Aegean in summer and can be vicious in Crete. Its force is gauged by what it knocks over – "tableweather", "chairweather" etc.

MINOAN Crete's great Bronze Age civilization which dominated the Aegean from about 2500 to 1400 BC.

MONÍ Monastery or convent.

MYCENAEAN Mainland civilization centred on Mycenae c.1700–1100 BC: some claim they were responsible for the destruction of the Minoans, and certainly Mycenaean influence pervaded Crete in the late and post-Minoan periods.

NEOLITHIC The earliest era of settlement in Crete, characterized by the use of stone tools and weapons together with basic agriculture.

NÉOS, NÉA, NÉO New

NOMÓS Modern Greek province: Crete is divided into four.

ODEION Small amphitheatre used for performances or meetings.

PALEÓS, PALEÁ, PALEÓ Old.

PALLIKÁRI Literally "brave man": in Crete a guerrilla fighter, particularly in the struggle for independence from the Turks, also a general term for a tough young man.

PANAYÍA The Virgin Mary.

PANIYÍRI Festival or feast – the local celebration of a holy day.

PANTOKRATOR Literally "The Almighty", a stern figure of God the Father frescoed or in mosaic on the dome of many Byzantine churches.

PARALÍA Seafront promenade.

PEAK SANCTUARY Mountain-top shrine, often in or associated with a cave, sometimes in continuous use from Neolithic through to Roman times.

PERÍPTERO Street kiosk.

PERISTYLE Colonnade or area surrounded by colonnade, used especially in Minoan halls or courtyards.

PÍTHOS (pl. PÍTHOI) Large ceramic jar for storing oil, grain etc very common in the Minoan

palaces and used in almost identical form in modern Cretan homes.

PLATÍA Square or plaza. KENTRIKÍ PLATÍA is the main square.

PROPILEA Portico or entrance to an ancient building.

RHYTON Vessel, often horn-shaped, for pouring libations or offerings.

STELE Upright stone slab or column, usually inscribed.

STOA Colonnaded walkway in Classical era marketplace.

THEATRAL AREA Open area found in most of the Minoan palaces with seat-like steps around. May have been a type of theatre or ritual area, but not conclusively proved.

THÓLOS Conical or beehive-shaped building, especially a Mycenaean tomb.

ACRONYMS

ANEK *Anonimí Navtikí Evería krítis* (Shipping Co of Crete, Ltd), which runs most ferries between Pireás and Crete, plus many to Italy.

EA Greek Left (*Ellenikí Aristerá*), formerly the Greek Euro-communist Party (*KKE-Esoterikoú*).

EAM National Liberation Front, the political force behind ELAS.

ELAS Popular Liberation Army, the main resistance group during World War II and the basis of the communist army in the civil war.

EK Fascist party (*Ethnikó Kómma*), consisting mostly of adherents to the imprisoned junta colonel, Papadopoulos.

ELTA The postal service.

EOS Greek Mountaineering Federation, based in Athens.

EOT *Ellinikós Organismós Tourismoú*, the National Tourist Organization.

KKE Communist Party, unreconstructed.

KTEL National syndicate of bus companies. The term is also used to refer to bus stations.

ND Conservative (*Néa Dhimokratía*) party.

OSE Railway corporation.

OTE Telephone company.

PASOK Socialist party (Pan-Hellenic Socialist Movement).

SEO Greek Mountaineering Club, based in Thessaloníki.

INDEX

Accommodation 34
Afráta 246
Ahládha 87
Ahládia 149
Akrotíri 232
Alíkambos 238
Alikianós 279
Almirídha 237
Almirós, Gulf of 189
Alphabet, Greek 327
Amári 200
Amári Valley 199
Ámbelos 284
Amirás 121
Amnísos 76
Amoudhári 263
Amoudhári Beach 77
Amoúdhi 208
Anemospília 85
Ánidhri 277
Anisaráki 274
Áno Viánnos 120
Áno Zákros 159
Anópoli 260
Anóyia 193
Apartments 36
Áptera 235
Arádhena gorge 261
Archéa Eleútherna 192
**Archeological Museum,
    Iráklion** 65
Archeology, Minoan 304
Argiróupolis 189
Arhánes 84
Ariadne 311
Arkádhi, Monastery 187, 297
Arméni 197
Arolíthos 88
Árvi 121
Asigonía 189
Askífou, Plateau of 262
Aspró 237
Athens 16, 19
Axós 193
Ayía Fotiá (Ierápetra) 168
Ayía Fotiá (Sitía) 156
Ayía Galíni 202
Ayía Iríni 279
Ayía Marína 243
Ayía Pelayía 86
Ayía Rouméli 255
Ayía Sofía Cave 271
Ayía Triádha 111

Ayía Varvára 103
Áyii Apóstoli 227
Áyii Dhéka 104
Áyii Theódori 244
Áyios Ioánnis 261
Áyios Konstantínos 130
Áyios Nikólaos 132–137
Áyios Pándes 137
Áyios Pávlos 204
Áyios Yióryios (Ay. Nik.) 131
Áyios Yióryios (Réthimnon) 204
Azoyirés 278

Balí 190
Banks 26
Battle of Crete 243, 262, 278, 298
Beer 41
Bibliography 322
Birds 315
Buses on Crete 31
Buses, from Britain 6
Butterfly Gorge 167
Byzantine Crete 294

Camping 36
Cape Voúxa 270
Car hire 31
Children 49
Chronology 302
Consulates, foreign 22
Contraceptives 49
Costs 25
Credit cards 26
Currency 25
Customs 22
Cycling 33

Daedalus 311
Damnóni 208
de Jong, Piet 307
Dhamásta 191
Dhaskaloyiánnis 225, 260, 297
Dhiktean Cave 131, 310
Dhrápano Peninsula 237
Diktynna 246
Directory 49
Disabled Travellers 20
Dorian Crete 293
Drink 38
Dríros 127
Driving 31
Driving, from Britain 6

Easter 45
Eileíthyia, Cave 77
Elafonísi 273
Eleútherna 192
Élos 271
Eloúnda 138

Embassies, Greek 22
Emergency number 42
Episkopí (Ay. Nik.) 146
Episkopí (Réthimnon) 189
Etiá 164
Evans, Arthur 77, 304
Éxo Moulianá 148

Falásarna 269
Férma 168
Ferries, from Athens 18
Ferries, from other islands 19
Ferries, Italy–Greece 7
Ferries, local 34
Festivals 45
Festós 108–111
Film 49
Fínix 258
Fires 168
Flights, domestic 15
Flights, from Australia 14
Flights, from Britain 3
Flights, from Ireland 8
Flights, from New Zealand 15
Flights, from North America 9
Flória 274
Flowers 314
Fódhele 87
Food 37
Fourfourás 201
Fournés 242
Fourní (Ay. Nik.)128
Foúrni (Iráklion) 84
Fournoú Korifí 174
Frangokástello 265

Gaidhouronísi 172
Galatás 243
Garázo 193
Gavalohóri 238
Gavdhopoúlo 282
Gávdhos 282
Gay Crete 49
Gazí 88
Georgioupolis, see Yeoryióupolis
Getting Around 31
Getting There, from Britain 3
Getting There, from Greece 15
Getting There, from Ireland 8
*Getting There, from North
    America* 9
Glossary 331
Golden Beach 227
Górtys 104
Goúdhouras 166
Goúrnes 91
Gourniá 143
Goúves 91
Gra Ligiá 173

Gramvoúsa 270
Halbherr, Federico 304, 308
Hamézi 149
Handhrás 164
Háni Kokkíni 90
HANIÁ 213–232
  Accommodation 220
  Airport 220
  Archeological Museum 224
  Arrival 217
  Bars 229
  Beaches 226
  Bus station 220
  Buses, local 220
  Cafés 229
  Campsites 222
  Cathedral 225
  Ferries 217
  Food 227
  Harbour 223
  Historical Museum 226
  History 213
  Hotels 221
  Kastélli 223
  Kydonia 216
  Listings 231
  Map 218
  Market 225
  Music 231
  Naval Museum 224
  New town 226
  Nightlife 230
  Orientation 217
  Public gardens 226
  Restaurants 228
  Rooms 221
  Sóudha 217
  Spiantza 225
  Tourist offices 220
  Youth Hostel 222
Harassment 43
Health 27
Heraklion, see Iráklion
Hersónisos 91
Hiking 33
History 289–332
Hitching 33
Hondrós 120
Hóra Sfakíon 264
Hotels 34
Hrissí Aktí 227
Hrissoskalítissa 273

Idean Cave 195
Ierápetra 169–172
Ímbros 263
Independence 297
Information 28
Injections 27
Insects 317
Insurance 23

IRÁKLION 56–75
  Accommodation 60
  Airport 57
  Archeological Museum 65
  Arrival 57
  Ayía Ekateríni 64
  Áyios Títos 63
  Bars 73
  Beaches 75
  Bus stations 57
  Cafés 72
  Campsites 61
  Cathedral 64
  Discos 74
  Ferries 57
  Food 71
  Fortress 62
  Historical Museum 63
  Hotels 61
  Listings 74
  Loggia 64
  Map 58
  Market 64
  Museum of Religious Art 64
  Nightlife 73
  Orientation 57
  Platía Eleftherías 65
  Platía Venizélou 64
  Public gardens 65
  Restaurants 72
  Rooms 61
  San Marco 64
  Tourist office 60
  Walls 62
  Youth Hostels 61
Ístro 142
Ítanos 157
Izzedin 235

Kakodhíki 274
Kalamáfka 173
Kalamáki (Iráklion)116
Kalamáki (Haniá) 227
Kalathás 233
Kalí Liménes 119
Kalíves 237
Kaliviani 270
Kallergi Hut 250
Kaló Hório 142
Kamáres 196
Kamáres cave 305
Kámbos 272
Kandanoleon Revolt 242
Kándanos 274
Karabé 282
Karfí 129
Karínes 198
Kastélli Kisámou 267
Kastélli Pedhiádhos 99
Kastrí 282
Káto Stalós 244

Káto Zákros 159
Kavousi 147
Kazantzakís, Nikos 62, 324, 83
Kefáli 272
Kerá 101
Keratókambos 120
Khania, see Haniá
Kiriakosélia 236
Knossós 77–82, 291, 305
Kókkinos Pírgos 113
Kolimbári 245
Kómmos 116
Kórfos 284
Kotsifóu Gorge 205
Kournás 241
Kourtaliótiko Gorge 205
Koustoyérako 279
Koutsonári 168
Koutsoumátados 271
Koutsourás 167
Krási 101
Kriós 277
Kritsá 141
Kserókambos 164
Kydonia 216, 293

Lake Kournás 240
Lákki 249
Lambiní 198
Language 326
Lasíthi Plateau 100, 128–132
Lató 140
Lefká Óri 247
Lefkóyia 208
Léndas 118
Líkkos 259
Límin Hersonísou 91
Linear A 292
Linear B 292, 305
Lissós 281
Lithínes 166
Loutró 256
Lyttos 99

Mail 41
Makriyialós 167
Máleme 244
Máles 173
Mália 94
Mália, Minoan Palace 96
Mammals 316
Maps 28
Márathos 88
Margarítes 191
Mármara Beach 259
Mátala 114
Máza 278
Medical care 27
Megála Horáfia 236

Melidhóni 193
Menu reader 39
Méronas 202
Mesklá 242
Messará Plain 104–113, 119
Mílatos 126
Minoan Crete 289–293
Minoans 306
Minos 291, 311
Minotaur 311
Mirabéllo, Gulf of 137
Míres 107
Miriokéfala 190
Mirsíni 149
Mírthios 205
Mirtía 83
Mírtos 174
Mitzotakis, Kostas 299
Modern Crete 299
Móhlos 147
Mohós 101
Money 25
Moní 279
Moní Arkádhi 187, 297
Moní Ayía Triádha 233
Moní Faneroméni (Gourniá) 142
Moní Faneroméni (Sitía) 149
Moní Goniá 245
Moní Gouvernétou 234
Moní Kápsa 166
Moní Katholikó 234
Moní Koudoumá 120
Moní Préveli 209
Moní Tóplou 156
Moní Vrondísi 103
Motorbike hire 33
Mount Dhíkti 131, 310
Mount Gíngilos 250
Mount Ida 194, 201
Mount Karfí 101
Mount Kédhros 201
Mount Páhnes 250
Mount Yioúhtas 82, 85
Mourí 241
Mourniés 242
Music 45
Mycenaeans 292
Mythology 310

NATO 300
Néa Mírtos 173
Neápoli 127
Newspapers 42
Nídha Plateau 196
Nirou Hani 90
Níthavris 201

Oasis Beach 227
Oloús 137

Omalós 249
Opening hours 44
Package holidays, from Britain 5
Pahiá Ámmos 145
Palékastro 158
Paleohóra 275
Palm Beach 209
Panayía Gouverniótissa 100
Panayía Kardhiótissa 101
Panayía Kirá 139
Pánormos 190
Papandreou, Andreas 300
Paraspóri 149
Pashley, Robert 304
Pedhiádha, the 99
Pendlebury, John 308
Pérama 192
Pervólia 272
Petrokefáli 119
Phones 41
Phrases 328
Pilalímata 166
Pínes 128
Pireás 16, 18
Pírgos 173
Piskokéfalo 166
Pitsídhia 116
Pláka 139
Plakiás 206
Plataniás 244
Plátanos (Kastélli) 269
Plátanos (Sitía) 147
Platía Perámata 118
Pláton, Nikólaos 160, 309
Plemenianá 274
Police 43
Polyrínia 268
Pómbia 119
Post 41
Présos 165
Préveli, Monastery 209
Prinés 192
Prodhrómi 277
Psihró 131
Psilorítis 194, 201
Psíra 148
Public holidays 44

Reptiles 316
Resistance movement 299
Restaurants 37
RÉTHIMNON 176–187
  Accommodation 177
  Archeological Museum 183
  Arrival 177
  Bars 186
  Beach 184
  Bus stations 177
  Campsites 182
  Ferry 177

Food 184
Fortress 182
Harbour 182
Historical Museum 183
Hotels 180
Listings 186
Map 178
Mosques 184
Nightlife 185
Public gardens 184
Restaurants 185
Rimondi Fountain 184
Rooms 180
Tourist office 177
Wine Festival 184
Youth Hostels 181
Rodhákino 210
Rodhiá 88
Rodhópou Peninsula 246
Roman Crete 294
Rooms 34

Samariá 253
Samarian Gorge 250
Samonás 236
Sarakiníkos 282
Schliemann, Heinrich 304
Selinári, Gorge 126
Sélinos 274
Sellía 210
Sfakiá 248
Sfinári 273
Síses 191
Sísi 126
Sitía 150–155
Skiing 49
Skinés 279
Skotinó Cave 91
Soúdha 217
Soúdha Bay 234
Sóurva 242
Sóuyia 280
Spíli 197
Spinalónga 138
Sport 49
Spratt, Capt. 304
Stalídha 94
Stavrós 233
Stílos 236
Sweetwater Beach 258

Tarra 256
Tavernas 37
Tavronítis 245
Taxis 31
Teménia 278
Thériso 241
Theseus 311
Thólos 147
Thrapsanó 100

Thrónos 199
Tílissos 89
Timbáki 113
Time 49
Toilets 49
Tóplou, Monastery 156
Topólia 271
Tourist offices 29
Tours 31
Trains, from Britain 6
Trápeza Cave 129
Tripití 284
Tsouderos, Emanuel 298
Tsoútsouros 120
Turkish Crete 296
Tzermiádho 129

Union with Greece 297

Vái 157
Vámos 238

Vasilikí 145
Váthi 272
Vathípetro 86
Vatsianá 284
Vegetarians 38
Venetian Crete 295
Venizélos, Eleftheríos 232, 241, 297
Villa Ariadne 307
Villas 36
Visas 22
Voilá 164
Vóri 113
Vorízia 196
Voukoliés 274
Voulgháro 271
Voúxa, cape 270
Vrísses 238

Wace, Alan 307
Walking 33
War cemetery, Allied 235

War cemetery, German 244
White Mountains 247
Wildlife 313
Wine 40
Work 47

Xilóskalon 252

Yeoryióupolis 239
Yerakári 201
Yeráni (Haniá) 244
Yeráni (Réthimnon) 189
Yialós 277
Youth Hostels 35

Zákros 159
Zákros, Minoan Palace 160, 309
Zarós 103
Zeus 131, 310
Zíros 164
Zóu 166

HELP US UPDATE

We've gone to a lot of effort to ensure that this third edition of *The Rough Guide to Crete* is accurate and up-to-date. But things change fast – new bars and tavernas appear and disappear, restaurants and rooms raise prices or lower standards, sites and museums change their opening hours, extra buses are laid on. . . . If you feel we've got it wrong or left something out, we'd like to know – any suggestions, comments or corrections would be much appreciated, in fact. If you can remember the address, the price, the time, the phone number, so much the better.

We'll credit all contributions, and send a copy of the next edition (or any other Rough Guide if you prefer) for the best letters. Please mark all letters "Rough Guide to Crete Update" and send to :

Rough Guides, 1 Mercer Street, London WC2H 9QJ
or, Rough Guides, 3rd floor 375 Hudson Street, New York NY10014.

THANKS

Thanks to all those readers who took the time and trouble to note our omissions, correct our errors and update our facts. On this edition, in no particular order, to:

John Ladbrook, Michael O'Hare, Sally Manders, Christine Bailey, Mark Pearson, Peter Macleod, Claude Geerts, Christine Hall, Sue Taylor, Sakari Puhakka, J.M. Winder, Kelly Hunt, Julian Corbluth, Peter Peck, John Stockwell, Kingsley Jones, Martin J. Hodson, Kenneth Prust, Anne-Marie Sharman, Leslie Whitehouse, Helen Bunce, Richard Blakeway-Philips, Eric Birch, Julie Watson, V. French, D. Priestley, Jeff Aronson, Debbie Sweet, Renée Harris, Chris & Karen Sharwood-Smith, Justin Quinnell, Andrew Tiller, Ken Wood, Yvonne M. Sketchley, Cameron Watt, Jeff Richards, Donald Macgregor, Paul Sutton, W.H. Lannagan, Angela Mugridge, Alan Giles, Mike & Jean Earl, Nick Humphries, David Buscall, Alistair Cant, Ben Kingsley, Maureen Millington-Brodie, Julie Withey, Bill Todd, J. Isted, Jerry Kimsley, H.W.J Theunissen, Tom Savage, Rupert Price, Sue Corfield, David Fry, Sara George, Alan Butler, Sheila & John Packman, Brian Greening, Jerry Kinsley, V.L. Scranage, Tim Darach & Rebecca Reeves, Florence Vuillet, Rosemary Clemence, Elizabeth Raymont, J.R. Auld, Frances Haynes, Peter Dunkley, and many others whose names we couldn't make out or we've simply missed.

From past editions Gareth Bridge, Terence Brace, Carola Scupham, Heather Gourlay & Christine Bell, Eleanor Healey, Joan & Jim Barkley, Cryss Healey, Francesca Melandri, M.J. Frost, Tony Walsh, Elspeth Barker, Caroline & David Watson, Fergus King, Tracy Austin, Freya & Paul Steele, Ken Kimber, Jeremy Pearce, Sarah Chambers, John Bunt, Margaret Stewardson, Wendy Jarvis, Beverly Myers, Sue Manning, Bert Broeckart, Malcolm Clifton, Miss P.A. Womersley, Della Reader, Philip Springthorpe, P.J. McCarthy, Mrs P. Rischmiller, Mrs J. Merz, Christine Hall, David Poyser, Dave Kail, Jan Brookes, Jane Pickering, Pauline Carroll, Maureen Eastany, Jem Eastwell, Philomena Searson, Robin Wilkinson, John Mansley, K. Mitchell, Maxine Gandy, Hilary Roberts, Keith Plant, R. Fletcher, Kay Davies, Michael and Catherine Gaum, Mrs B. Massey, Bill Badham, Denise Walden, Ms S. Graham, Tony Samuel, Elizabeth Adlam and Karl Keyte.

You are
A STUDENT

You **travel**
THE WORLD

You **want** TO SAVE MONEY

Here's
how

The International
Student Identity Card

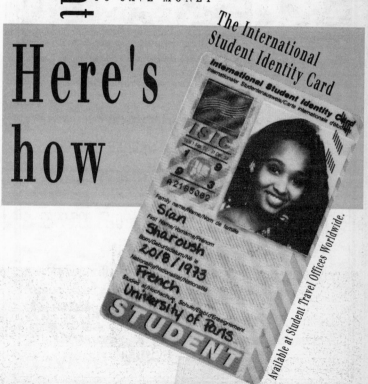

Available at Student Travel Offices Worldwide.

Entitles you to discounts and special services worldwide.